The Mainstreamed Library
ISSUES, IDEAS, INNOVATIONS

The Mainstreamed Library
ISSUES, IDEAS, INNOVATIONS

Edited by
Barbara H. Baskin and Karen H. Harris

Chicago
American Library Association
1982

Library of Congress Cataloging in Publication Data

Main entry under title:

The Mainstreamed library.

   Includes bibliographies and index.
   1. Libraries and the handicapped. I. Baskin,
Barbara Holland, 1929–   II. Harris, Karen H.,
1934–
Z711.92.H3M27 1982   027.6′63   82-16463
ISBN 0-8389-0359-2

Copyright © 1982 by the American Library Association.
All rights reserved except those which may
be granted by Sections 107 and 108 of the
Copyright Revision Act of 1976.

Printed in the United States of America.

Contents

Preface   vii

Introduction   xi

1. The Physical Environment   1

    Design Criteria for Educational Facilities for Special Education Services   4
        Allen C. Abend

    Disabled Libraries: An Examination of Physical and Attitudinal Barriers to Handicapped Library Users   11
        Robert T. Begg

    Sensory Wall Brings Learning   23
        Geraldine M. Matthews

    Users Come First in Design   25
        Philip M. Bennett

    Hidden Barriers   31
        Suzanne Stephens

2. Materials Selection   35

    Selecting Materials for the Disabled Child   40
        Karen Harris and Barbara Baskin

    Selecting and Developing Educational Materials: An Inquiry Model   44
        Sandra B. Cohen, Paul A. Alberto, and Ann Troutman

    Adapting Reading Materials for Hearing-Impaired Children with Low Reading Achievement   50
        David W. Holmes

    Library Services to the Mentally Retarded   55
        Anne-Marie Forer and Mary Zajac

    Selection of Books for Disabled Readers   64
        Marilyn Thypin

    Remediation and Reinforcement: Books for Children with Visual Perceptual Impairments   68
        Mary M. Banbury

Beyond the Alphabet: From Competent Reader to Avid Reader 72
    Margaret B. Rawson
Book Selection for Young Gifted Readers 80
    Barbara H. Baskin and Karen H. Harris

3. Technology 87

An Overview of Progress in Utilization of Educational Technology for Educating the Hearing Impaired 91
    George Propp
Development of a High School TTY Program 97
    Sherry Driver, Terrence Easterwood, and John Schaub
Technology and the Visual Processing of Verbal Information by Deaf People 100
    E. Ross Stuckless
The Optacon Reading System 106
    James C. Bliss and Mary W. Moore
Experimental Provision of Closed Circuit Television at a Danish Public Library 119
    Bodil Pors
A Second-Generation Interactive Classroom Television System for the Partially Sighted 122
    S. M. Genensky, H. E. Petersen, R. W. Clewett, and R. I. Yoshimura
The Kurzweil Reading Machine 126
    Ruth-Carol Cushman

4. Software 129

Traditional Nursery Rhymes and Games: Language Learning Experiences for Preschool Blind Children 134
    Joan W. Blos
Books for Children Who Cannot See the Printed Page 139
    Margaret Bush
Remediating with Comic Strips 142
    Phyllis N. Hallenbeck
Orientation Maps for Visually Impaired Persons 146
    Billie Louise Bentzen
Resources for Creating Tactual Graphics 152
    J. M. Gill and L. L. Clark
Tape Recording Educational Materials for Secondary Handicapped Students 155
    Donald D. Deshler and Steven Graham
Microfiche as a Reading Aid for Partially Sighted Students 159
    Torsten Andersson
Computer-Based Instruction for Hearing-Impaired Children in the Classroom 162
    Sharon Dugdale and Patty Vogel
Television Programs as Socializing Agents for Mentally Retarded Children 173
    Stanley J. Baran
Using Programs for Emotionally Disturbed Children in Mainstreamed or Special Class Settings 178
    Maurice J. Elias

5. Program 187

The Banquet Is Ours 192
    Aaron Kramer
The Visually Impaired Reader in the Academic Library 202
    Jean A. Major
Some Immodest Proposals for Improving Library Services to the Blind: Reflections of a Handicapped Library User 207
    Hanan C. Selvin
Media Services for Gifted Students: An Overview 214
    Janice Smith
The Institutionalized Child's Need for Library Service 222
    Geraldine M. Matthews
Library Service to Institutionalized and Disabled Adults 231
    Linda Lucas
Helping Hearing-Impaired Students 237
    Mary Jane Metcalf
Into the Mainstream: Using Books to Develop Social Skills in Perceptually Impaired Children 241
    Paul J. Gerber and Karen Harris
The Library/Media Center for the Secondary Student with Specific Learning Disabilities—Hazard or Haven? 245
    Sidney G. Becker
Coping with the Disruptive 251
    Pat Dain
Serving the Unserved 252
    Betty Carter
An Autistic Child and Books 257
    Mollie Marcus Wallick

6. Outreach 265

Bridging an Information Gap: A Brooklyn Public Library Kit for the Parents of Children with Special Needs 269
    Marguerite A. Dodson
The Librarian as an Advocate for the Patron with Special Needs 271
    Barbara H. Baskin and Ronne Cosel
Welcome in the Parent 274
    Roger Kroth and Gweneth Blacklock Brown
The Educational Resources Information Center 280
    Robert E. Chesley
Exceptional Child Education Resources: A One-of-a-Kind Data Base 286
    Donald K. Erickson

Index 291

Preface

Our purpose in compiling this book is to provide a guide to school, public, academic, institutional, and special librarians seeking to develop a full range of services for patrons with exceptional needs. The initial stages of our search took us to current library journals where we were gratified to find increases in the quality and quantity of articles addressed to the myriad needs of handicapped patrons.

In addition to searching contemporary library literature for examples of useful ideas or exemplary practices, we looked at materials addressed to teachers, counselors, therapists, architects, and other professionals who work with and provide services to disabled persons. Although techniques, materials, approaches, and insights found in their journals often have direct and equally appropriate application in library media centers, and many articles are cross-disciplinary, librarians are routinely excluded from the audience these essays address. Their periodicals rarely mention libraries—a failing mirrored in their text- and trade books where both index and narrative are typically free of citations or discussions of the role of libraries. Yet common concerns abound. The removal of architectural barriers and improved accessibility are important in hospitals, schools, government offices—and libraries. Improved media equipment offers benefits to students in classrooms—and in the school library. Software with adapted content or format can be used by teachers, counselors, individuals—or librarians—to attenuate the impact of impairment. Unfortunately, those in other professions rarely perceive the scope and extent of the contribution that librarians can make: the latters' expertise and specialized skills remain a largely untapped resource. This situation greatly diminishes the continuity and quality of service available to those with special needs. Where articles from non-library sources have been included and their themes are analogous to, but not precisely directed at, the solution of library problems, readers will have to draw parallels and apply the theories and practices proposed in other fields to the specifics of their own domain.

Some of the innovative programs developed and in current use, but never before reported in the literature, came to our attention. In these instances we solicited original manuscripts so that these practitioners' original approaches, ingenious and effective responses to challenging situations, could be shared with our readers.

We deliberately searched out contributions which provided, directly or inferentially, a theoretical basis for the procedures, techniques, and selection of materials recommended for use with exceptional patrons. Without some understanding of the assumptions, philosophy, and principles upon which behavior is based, one is locked into existing practices. In a society in which change seems the only constant, it is essential to take note of, and repeatedly assess, the criteria upon which recommendations are made. If one understands why something works, changes can be accommodated in the knowledge that the resultant adaptations are founded on a reasoned response rather than intuition or wishful thinking.

On the other hand, we were also interested in pragmatic solutions to immediate and urgent problems. We felt that librarians needed detailed descriptions of programs which could be readily implemented, with procedures adaptable to the particular demands of a variety of situations. We favored the inclusion of articles which were specific rather than general, that precisely defined an area of concern, identified variables that were the focus of interest, and proposed concrete remedies. The challenges posed by mainstreaming are with us today and require both prompt responses as well as thoughtful plans for the future.

In the population whose problems we are addressing, we have included those individuals who must have significant adaptations in the physical environment, in the format or content of materials, or in the delivery of service in order to maximize their ability to function. Specifically, this volume focuses on children and adults who have special needs because of intellectual, visual, auditory, orthopedic, neurological or specific learning disabilities, emotional dysfunction, or giftedness. This last category has been deliberately included since it has been repeatedly demonstrated that traditional procedures are unresponsive to the intellectual requirements of this group. The disparity between the potential and the performance of many cognitively gifted youngsters underscores the necessity for libraries to assess their practices vis à vis this group.

We were particularly eager to include works about individuals whose impairments were so severe or so extensive that they have historically been excluded as candidates for library service: the challenge of responding to such persons was particularly taxing since models were nonexistent and success demanded ingenuity, flexibility, and commitment. Those most outside the mainstream may be the very ones in most urgent need of normalizing experiences. Their achievements reveal in a dramatic way how performance can be improved by raised expectations and increased opportunities. Observations of the means by which these people were served can have profound and immediate implications for revising our presumptions concerning the competencies of less severely affected individuals.

After careful consideration, we decided to organize this work on the basis of components of library function rather than by type of library addressed or category of exceptionality. There are more commonalities than differences among kinds of libraries: accessibility, selection and acquisition, provision of service and the like are problems of all libraries. The removal of architectural barriers and their replacement by a hospitable, supportive environment is equally essential whether the locale is a university, nursery school, or prison library. In sum, libraries are in the business of managing the flow of information in an efficient, organized manner. Their role is to channel information from its various sources to its potential patrons regardless of the particular problems of the users. It is for this reason that the organization of this book focuses on problems and solutions and not the settings in which activity takes place.

We rejected grouping readings by disability. Such an organization would tend to emphasize deficits in users rather than abilities, labels rather than the means to elevate levels of functioning. Although it is often necessary to apply a descriptor such as "blind" or "physically impaired," it is easy to become locked into a perception of someone so described that would override other more important or positive behavioral aspects. Among the members of those groups are individuals with a tremendous range of abilities and needs. Moreover, there is a tendency to think in terms of those most impaired as the norm for that group and expect considerably less than is appropriate. Even more important, though, is the fact that different etiologies often result in similar behaviors by the individuals sustaining them. Often remediation or amelioration is not disability-specific; similar techniques and materials may be indicated no matter what caused the patron's inability to use standard materials. Our hope in arranging the readings in this volume by function rather than by group served was to bring together reports of what had been done for many populations enabling readers to judge what applications could be extrapolated to their own patrons' needs. Further, it is essential to note that in some instances adaptations made for one population may be contraindicated for another and that especially in mainstreamed settings, the requirements of one group cannot be satisfied at the expense of others. It is also essential to look beyond the needs of the groups presently being served to see what implications proposed remedies might have for patrons who will be entering our libraries and media centers in the future.

We are indebted to our contributors for sharing the results of their labors. We have all built on the work of library pioneers who identified and worked at responding to the needs of exceptional patrons long before there was precedence for doing so, or sufficient guidance from the literature and before it was fashionable or fundable. We wish specifically to thank the librarians at C. W. Post Library for the excellence of their collection and their invaluable help in assisting our own endeavor.

Introduction

It has taken almost 200 years for the concept of equity to deliberately and specifically expand to include the disabled in the United States. The movement known as mainstreaming comprises the most recent chapter in the unfolding history of American democracy. The continuing, erratic, but inexorable extension of the definition of those entitled to the benefits of full citizenship has at last been stretched to encompass these citizens.

Changes in the social order generate dislocations in institutions which are consequently forced to reassess their roles and operations. This state of flux inevitably causes confusion as agencies struggle to adjust to new and often unfamiliar demands while simultaneously attempting to maintain their equilibrium. Like other major public institutions, libraries must also respond to mainstreaming while still accommodating local needs and their own special mission. In order to serve populations with exceptional needs whose special requirements have rarely been factored into policy, planning, operations or personnel training, radical adjustments will inevitably be necessary. It is essential then, that those in the field of library science examine the theoretical and practical dilemmas posed by mainstreaming.

This volume is dedicated to the exploration of three fundamental questions: What are the issues libraries must confront to meet the challenges posed by mainstreaming? What changes can libraries make in their policies and practices that will be responsive to the critical and diverse needs of this population? How can libraries modify or broaden traditional services or replace unsuitable methods with appropriate alternatives?

Mainstreaming is in its infancy. When one considers that the first book entirely devoted to the issue of library response to exceptional persons and the whole spectrum of their special needs was published by the American Library Association as recently as 1976, it is evident that definitions and standards for minimal and optimal practice are just emerging. It is a sign of vitality that the search for answers is gathering momentum. However, the profession can neither wait to act on these initial findings nor be content to accept them as definitive.

The decade of the 1970s brought revolutionary changes in the opportunities available to disabled persons in America, opportunities defined primarily by two major pieces of federal legislation. The Vocational Rehabilitation Act of 1973 mandates accessibility of buildings constructed with federal funds, requires that federal contractors establish affirmative action programs for hiring impaired workers, and proscribes discrimination against otherwise qualified applicants in all programs receiving federal assistance. Given the ubiquitousness of governmental involvement in the economy, the numbers of people affected are enormous.

The Education for All Handicapped Children Act of 1975 has potentially even more far-reaching implications. The law states that all disabled children have a right to a publicly financed education and their instruction is to take place in the "least restrictive environment." The resultant movement of such youngsters from isolated settings into public schools made increased contact between formerly segregated students and those in regular classrooms inevitable. The newcomers were then able to participate in activities to which they had had restricted access. While such contacts offered opportunities for restructuring perceptions and correcting misunderstandings, they also created arenas for potential conflict.

Movement into the mainstream is not without hazards. Part of the task of professionals is to provide those with impairments with the skills and resources essential to survival in their new environment. The complementary aspect of this goal is to make the mainstream as hospitable as possible.

Physicians, therapists, counselors, educators, librarians, bioengineers, technicians, and others who work with disabled persons have seen radical alterations in their professional responsibility as a result of these legislative and related judicial actions. The impaired child grows up, matures, needs housing, employment, recreational opportunities, and entry into every aspect of community life. It becomes clear that a multidisciplinary approach is needed: responding to any one aspect in isolation, e.g., education, while ignoring others, is wasteful and counterproductive. Lives cannot be segmented into autonomous components; change in one dimension inevitably necessitates adaptations in other areas. As a consequence, increased attention is now being given to connections between disciplines and to extending the definition of "service" from a single focus to the needs of the whole person.

In-service and preservice preparation for an increasing number of occupations includes a new examination of responsibility and programming for individuals with impairments. Recognizing this exigency, more and more states now require some course work in special education for all teachers. Health care, social work, and library science are among the professions offering special courses, institutes, and conferences on disability.

Although some evidence is available that professional consciousness has been raised, alterations in the social environment are more diffuse, fragmentary, and haphazard, hence more difficult to assess. Society is contaminated with negative attitudes toward disability. Fears learned in childhood and ingrained but erroneous beliefs persist, frustrating the integration process. However, there are some countervailing forces at work. Popular media have begun to explore problems and achievements of the disabled in society. Among the false, maudlin, and distorting films, plays, books, and television shows are instances of honest, forthright, accurate and informative presentations. Current interest is such that scarcely a single dramatic television series has avoided including at least one episode which revolves around a disabled character. Captioned television shows are now a commonplace. Telethons, where disabled tots are paraded as objects of charity, are sharing the channels with features such as the Special Olympics in which the emphasis is on achievement, not limitations. Many celebrities speak openly about members of their families who have disabilities. Advocacy groups are fighting for and achieving greater visibility and, in the process, making substantive gains in reformulating images. Even in the juvenile publishing field, in both fiction and basal readers, quantitative, if not always qualitative, growth is apparent. These events provide antidotes to public indifference to and ignorance of exceptionality.

The most dramatic transformation has taken place within the community of the disabled themselves. They have become more militant, more aggressive in seeking political and social power, and more assertive in demanding improvements in all aspects of their lives. Their own raised consciousness has fueled the activist movement in which they are taking more initiative in pressuring for reform. Moreover, many individuals are displaying more candor about the realities of their impairments. Rather than denying the necessity of special accommodations or adaptations, many talk openly and matter-of-factly about the problems that attend their impairments. As a result, the secrecy surrounding disability is dissolving as the topic becomes more frequently mentioned in public forums. These changes have readied the community for the opening phase of the assimilation to come.

As a key agency of the community, the library can play a significant role in this integration function. Libraries interface with most aspects of the mainstreaming process: they are influenced directly and indirectly by mainstream related legislation; they house resources for a wide spectrum of professionals serving this population; they play a constructive role in shaping and transforming social attitudes; and, they provide particular benefits to exceptional persons.

Developing the specific knowledge, competency, and sensitivity for responsive action begins in professional training programs. Some library schools have been revising their curricula to include courses that give prominence to the implications of disability. Others have changed syllabi, adding components that feature specific adaptations. For example, instructional modules that focus on library design now incorporate federal guidelines on accessibility. Classes in material selection stipulate particular criteria for serving special needs populations where these differ from those applicable to ordinary library users. More sophisticated media courses enumerate and evaluate developments in technology that have implications for those sustaining interfering impairments.

Symposia, institutes, and workshops on this subject are now standard in library schools. State and national professional conferences routinely schedule relevant presentations. Heavy stress on in-service education will undoubtedly continue as a major focus for some time, since information is growing at such a rapid rate that a constant upgrading of skills will be a requisite for the up-to-date librarian. Journals and published books will continue to fulfill a critical function in distilling and disseminating data. However, at the moment, this discipline is so new that the breadth and depth of field has yet to develop: general all-purpose articles and personal experience reports still tend to dominate much of the periodical literature. Research remains scanty and has concentrated on certain areas more than others: data collection, analysis, and reporting to concerned professionals are still in their infancy.

Although there is intense pressure to solve problems immediately in order to comply with the intent and specific provisions of the law, it is even more imperative for libraries to explore the considerations underlying its philosophical thrust. If this reflective approach is not taken, the profession will be locked into perpetually functioning on an ad hoc basis rather than on one derived from carefully thought out, rationally, and humanistically arrived-at positions. Core issues are:

(a) What should be the extent of the library's commitment to mainstreaming?
(b) Who will share the responsibility for formulating policy, establishing criteria, planning, decision making, and assessing results?
(c) How will priorities be set?
(d) How will the library resolve competing or conflicting demands on human and material resources?
(e) How will the library articulate with other agencies and individuals devoted to the same or similar goals?
(f) How can the effectiveness of the library be measured as it seeks to achieve its mainstreaming goals?

The implementation of service cannot be held in abeyance while a comprehensive policy is hammered out. An examination of accounts of some of those in the vanguard of providing service will yield information that can be synthesized to solve problems in similar or analogous contexts. Those early pragmatists supplied models that newcomers can analyze and reformulate as they begin to initiate their own agendas for action. Legal pressures are a spur to prompt response, but there is another compelling inducement to act without delay: disabled individuals are knocking at the library door—right now.

Reliance on traditional practices will prove inadequate when addressing such pressing, everyday problems as:

(a) What skills can patrons be helped to develop to facilitate their entry into the mainstream?
(b) How can blind users be oriented to the physical layout of the library so they can function in it independently?
(c) What safety provisions are essential for people with profound hearing loss?
(d) How can programs be adapted so as to be meaningful for developmentally disabled adolescents or adults?
(e) What reading guidance approach will be most productive for a seven-year-old reading at the high-school level?

In pondering the best means to answer these questions, the librarian is confronted with many perplexing situations. Moreover, discontinuities and limitations in the quality and range of options available complicate library response. Librarians seeking precedents from other outreach programs will find few applicable parallels.

Patrons should always be thought of in personal terms, but some generalizations can be made despite the diversity and variety of this clientele:

1. There is a high correlation between the degree of exceptionality and the extent of accommodation necessitated. That is, a reader having diminished vision may be adequately served by large print materials and some color cues or modest interior design adaptations. However, a totally blind student may require the Talking Book Program, special orientation assistance, access to a Braillewriter or the Kurzweil, as well as heavy library personnel utilization.
2. When a user has multiple handicapping conditions, the difficulties are compounded and the time required to respond to the array of needs may be radically increased.
3. Age may not be as critical a variable in selecting resources; other considerations may override conventional chronological associations.
4. Programmatic actions by the staff might not necessarily be disability specific. Software or hardware designed for one audience could be an equally invaluable tool for another. For example, in addition to the obvious categories of participants, an individual with learning disabilities, under certain specified circumstances, may be eligible for, and could benefit from, some of the services available from the National Library for the Blind and Physically Handicapped.

Although heterogeneity characterizes any population, the range and multiplicity of characteristics exhibited by these individuals is unequalled. Librarians and media specialists will need to resist succumbing to the relief they may feel that they have "solved" a particular problem by providing a resource to a disabled person. For instance, a highly recommended tool for the blind is the Optacon which translates a visual medium into a tactual one. However, some visually impaired persons have difficulty "reading" tactile messages. If neither this medium nor braille is a usable alternative for them, they may have to rely entirely on auditory channels. Changing levels of skills and other circumstances may affect user comfort and satisfaction levels. As with everyone else, idiosyncratic and entirely personal preferences are also salient considerations. Confirmation of the validity, efficacy, and suitability of service must be made repeatedly.

Serving this population well demands that some staff members have special competence in nontraditional, technical, or other areas. Users with communication disorders will be greatly aided by encountering an employee with expertise in sign language, knowledge about the functioning of a telephone teletype unit or the ability to decode a communication board. In certain circumstances, patrons may be unwilling or even unable to signal that they need help. Even though these situations seem minor to the staff, they may be extremely embarrassing to the patron, e.g., an adolescent unable to use a simple reference tool because of a specific learning disability. The staff should have the knowledge and sensitivity to respond quickly and appropriately in ways designed to preserve the privacy and self-respect of the library user.

The delivery of service may depend heavily on a library's location, for people sustaining impairments are restricted to an inordinate degree by geography. Individuals who are disabled are not concentrated in enclaves but are dispersed throughout the country with the numbers in any single community being small. In those few settings in which relatively high density of persons with similar impairments occur, e.g., residential institutions, special schools or hospitals for long-term care patients, heavy investment in library staff or resources is a rarity. Whether patrons live in urban, suburban, or rural areas may govern the nature and scope of service available to them. Remote locations with inadequate or no transportation facilities will severely inhibit library usage. Where geographical barriers combine with past patterns of minimal support—modest collections, gross underfunding, abbreviated hours, nonprofessional staff—library services have not developed adequately for any segment of the population, much less for patrons with exceptionalities. Heroic measures will be required to ensure satisfactory treatment of citizens doubly penalized by inaccessibility and neglect.

A perpetual problem of libraries is underfunding. Fiscal constraints drastically limit the ability of libraries to fulfill their mission. These institutions are caught in an economic squeeze: inflation has ravaged their budgets; they have had a long history of insufficient support; and they are extremely vulnerable to cost-cutting pressures. At the same time, clientele and community outreach efforts have increased, thus putting additional strain on already depleted resources.

Although the fiscal picture appears grim, there are some counterbalancing forces that may diminish budgetary stress. Agencies specifically serving disabled and gifted populations are eligible for earmarked grants and support monies from private as well as public sources. Technology yields the most obvious and imminent prospect for extending services and reducing costs. Interlibrary cooperation allows for the sharing of expenses of high cost/low utilization materials. Moreover, consultation with disabled individuals or their knowledgeable advocates prior to architectural or design modification may not only result in considerable economies, but can make the difference between simple accessibility and total utilization of the physical plant.

It is clear that librarians must carefully examine issues and judiciously evaluate how readily procedures developed elsewhere can be translated into their settings and then move expeditiously to incorporate new ideas into their programs. This book of readings is offered in the hope that librarians will find herein both ideas for contemplation and practical guidance. Articles have been grouped into categories that identify the major areas where accommodations must be made for this target population. These core components are: environmental adaptations, materials selection, hardware utilization, software utilization, program, and outreach services.

Although some procedures derive from disability segregated situations, all overtly or inferentially address the need to alter the milieu, upgrade skills or compensate for deficits so that all people who seek it can find their place in the mainstream. Mainstreaming, like democracy, is an ideal as well as an idea. Both require constant vigilance to ensure that the laws protecting them be obeyed and the spirit animating them be kept alive. Libraries have a crucial role to play in these vital tasks.

1
The Physical Environment

The first priority of a mainstreamed library is a barrier-free physical plant. Potential users must be able to approach the library and enter it with ease. Once inside, they need to have access to all public facilities and be able to function in them with maximum independence. Otherwise, no matter how extensive the collection, how well designed the program, or how knowledgeable the staff, patrons with special needs will be unable to take advantage of these components and will effectively be denied full library service. Accessibility is, however, only a minimum requirement. Just as the environment can serve to restrict, even prohibit usage, so can it function to enable, facilitate or encourage utilization. Size, layout, adapted furnishings, accoustical and lighting modifications, and special safety provisions are basic, essential factors. Factors such as an inviting ambiance and deliberate use of color and design features to encourage utilization go beyond minimum standards.

Of all the factors essential to successful mainstreaming, architectural aspects have received the most attention. Since federal law is very specific in this regard and since structural components serve a very obvious gatekeeping function, such attention is not surprising. Further, a great many of the salient aspects of the physical plant can be quantified precisely so that minimum standards can be specified, measured, and enforced. First steps have already been taken to ensure access to all. It is essential now to move beyond these critical beginnings to modify other features of the physical plant, many of which are less visible, less measurable, but nonetheless vital.

Individuals with orthopedic impairments, particularly those confined to wheelchairs, have received the lion's share of attention in the planning and implementation of architectural modifications. Persons with other mobility problems must also be considered as structural, furnishing, and design changes are contemplated. These patrons may include, for example, individuals dependent on crutches or walkers whose impairments necessitate particular consideration in the design and construction of walkways and floor surfaces.

Library users displaying a wide range of other disabilities may demand special attention as well. Blind and limited vision, hearing-impaired and learning-disabled individuals all must have their special adaptations considered in construction and remodeling plans. Although some of the needs of these populations are more subtle, they are equally critical for the full functioning of these individuals in the library or media center.

The intangible aspects of the physical plant cannot be quantified. Sensitivity to their significance, however, can make the difference between a minimally and an optimally accessible structure. The special message the environment communicates reveals who is welcomed and valued and who is excluded or merely tolerated. Additionally, attention must be paid to support systems within the physical plant but usually not of direct interest to librarians. Without such amenities as accessible water fountains, lavatories, storage facilities, and telephones, utilization of library resources may be drastically curtailed for certain patrons. Those adaptations which make the same facilities available through the same means for all patrons are preferable to separate, specifically designed accommodations: the environment wherever possible should encourage integrated usage. The building site, the edifice, the furnishings, and the individuals using them can be conceptualized as an ecological entity. Inevitably, alterations made in one aspect will affect others; thus, the totality of the project should be thought of as changes are planned.

Barrier-free design has implications beyond making institutions accessible to handicapped persons with impairments. The typical edifice is designed for an adult male of average height, agility, reaction time, stamina, visual and auditory acuity. Obviously, much of the population is unsuited to some degree for optimum functioning in these structures. Recommendations directed toward efficient use of library facilities by those with disabilities will have important ramifications for the general population as well. Improved lighting, more responsive acoustical design, easier access, nonskid surfaces, a hospitable ambiance, and the like, will undoubtedly be welcomed by all patrons.

All articles in this section, although in some instances of a general nature or directed toward facilities primarily serving other purposes, have direct applicability to library media centers.

Abend reports on his state's attempt to develop performance-based architectural and design standards for educational structures. The results of a survey of adapted facilities yielded some guidelines relating to general building construction criteria, environmental variables, and the need to accommodate a variety of instructional functions. The author ties the characteristics of users and the nature of activities in which they will engage to the adaptations recommended and explains the rationale that underlies his proposed standards.

From his perspective as a law librarian, Begg provides what may be the definitive article for libraries on the implications of the Rehabilitation Act of 1973. He interprets how the specific language of the statute applies to this setting and outlines both the legal and professional responsibility to achieve a barrier-free environment. The author compares the differences between adaptations in new construction and in standing structures needing rehabilitation and looks at such problems as distance between stacks, height of shelves, storage of media, and ease of carrel accessibility. Problems of cost are not ignored and approaches that resulted in important economies are offered as models of imaginative problem-solving. Begg concludes that attitudinal barriers are critical and more resistant than architectural ones and proposes some avenues by which these too can be dismantled.

In a very brief article, Matthews reports on a wall designed to provide an extra measure of stimulation in an institutional library. Suggestions solicited from colleagues in related specialties produced a wealth of ideas for materials that concerned promoting growth in sensory discrimination abilities. This singular device of a sensory wall could readily be translated into school or public library settings, and it suggests other devices.

Venturing into the more subtle aspects of environmental design, Bennett has explored areas rarely touched upon by writers on this topic. He has tried to synthesize certain engineering principles and selected physiological aspects of the learner and then hypothesized how these might affect library usage. Many of his suggestions have direct application to those with modest disabilities; other recommendations directly address conditions that could prevent the library environment from inadvertently generating situations that could potentially result in handicapping patrons. Bennett has posited positions that some may challenge, but he has forthrightly described the necessity for a full examination of often overlooked elements in library habilitation and has provided a defensible rationale for his position.

Those who think of architecture solely in terms of its visible, physical aspects will be startled by some of Stephens's contentions. She delves into the subjective aspects of building design for the disabled, probing into the meaning of specific structural and design choices. Stephens makes a particularly strong case against the use of certain materials and decorating practices that are demeaning and encourage passivity, dependency, and infantile response. Above all, she emphasizes the need for sensitivity to the humane and humanizing dimension of the physical/psychological environment, an approach she considers crucial in the creation of an attractive and supportive setting.

Design Criteria for Educational Facilities for Special Education Services

ALLEN C. ABEND

The courts and state and federal legislatures have mandated the right to a free public education suitable to the needs of all handicapped children. The educational rights of the handicapped are outlined primarily in two federal laws: P.L. 94-142 and Section 504 of the Vocational Rehabilitation Act of 1973. There are three basic concepts expressed in these enactments.

1. Zero Reject

    The Concept of Zero Reject is reflected in the P.L. 94-142 stipulation that all handicapped children, including the most severely handicapped, will be provided with a free, appropriate public education. The phrases "all handicapped children" and "including the most severely handicapped" have far-reaching implications which alter traditional views related to populations which utilize public school facilities.

    It is mandatory for all states and local education systems to provide, at a minimum, educational programs for handicapped students at age three.

    The extension of age level responsibility extends at higher age levels as well. Programs and services must be provided through age 21 for all handicapped students unless this requirement is inconsistent with state law practice or court order.

2. Appropriate Education

    The Concept of Appropriate Education is embodied in the P.L. 94-142 requirement that all handicapped children have the advantage of an "individualized education program." The individualized education program must include specific statements agreed upon by a number of interested parties, including parents, related to items such as:
    a. levels of performance,
    b. goals,
    c. educational services to be provided, and
    d. extent to which the student will be participating in regular educational programs.

    There is the necessity for in-depth and ongoing individual assessments. The individual education program is updated yearly and is drawn up by a team of persons with interest and/or knowledge of each student's development potential.

3. Least Restrictive Alternative

    The concept of least restrictive alternative means that, among all alternatives for placement, handicapped children should be placed where they can obtain the best education at the least distance from mainstream society. Each state has to establish (a) procedural safeguards; and (b) procedures to assure that, to the maximum extent appropriate, handicapped children are educated with children who are not handicapped. Also, it should be assured that special classes, separate schooling, or other removal of handicapped children from the regular educational environment occurs only when the nature or severity of the handicap is such that education in regular classes with the use of supplementary aides and services cannot be achieved satisfactorily. When a child is not initially placed in the public school system, the goal should be his eventual integration into an appropriate public school.

Adapted from "Design Criteria for Educational Facilities for Special Education Services," by Allen C. Abend, *Journal of Research and Development in Education* 1979, 12 (4): 23–35. By permission of the *Journal*.

A Problem

The mandate expressed by these three concepts is having and will continue to have an enormous impact on educational programs and school facilities. Large numbers of children with mental, physical, learning, emotional, and multiple handicaps are, and will continue to be, served in public school settings for the first time. The law requires that the environment be designed or modified to meet their needs.

The problems in implementing this mandate are twofold. First, most existing schools do not provide an environment which readily supports the specific educational programs and services required for the handicapped. Second, there now exists insufficient design criteria as a guide for renovating existing facilities or for constructing new facilities.

Placing the Standards for Barrier-Free Architecture in Perspective

The only research-based design criteria available and generally accepted are the ANSI Standards (A 117.1). The ANSI Standard deals with removing basic architectural barriers and focuses on such topics as ingress, egress, parking, lavatories, telephones, drinking fountains, and circulation within a building. Although these elements are extremely important, they represent only a small portion of design variables. The full range of criteria for space, space relationships between activities, acoustics, lighting, climate, furniture, equipment, utilities, storage, and display are equally important. The building that is designed or modified to meet the ANSI Standard only touches the "tip of the iceberg" in realizing a facility that is functional for handicapped individuals. In addition, the ANSI Standard was based primarily on research done with adults with physical disabilities. In designing a building, other age groups and handicaps must also be considered.

It is also important to understand that the ANSI Standard focuses on criteria that, for the most part, are necessary only for handicapped individuals. This characteristic of the ANSI Standard could lead people to conclude wrongly that all design criteria for the handicapped are unique and applicable only to handicapped individuals. In fact, most design criteria for the handicapped are equally applicable to the nonhandicapped person. The only difference is the degree to which one can deviate from the criteria. While the average individual can usually adapt to compromises, the handicapped person may be more dependent upon strict adherence to careful environmental design. Therefore, the design characteristics which may be desirable for the average person may be essential for the handicapped individual.

General Building Design Criteria
Space and Spatial Relationships:

1. The building design should strive for compactness.
   a. The time spent getting from one location to another may be significantly increased with some handicapped populations. Although traveling through the school can be a learning activity in itself, circulating should not take an exorbitant amount of time away from basic learning activities.
   b. Compactness will aid the visually impaired student in striving for independence in moving about the building.
   c. Excess distances may contribute to creating islands within a school. Communication between staff and students is extremely important for the integration of staff, students, and activities. Proximity is a factor in obtaining this goal.
2. The building should give a student a clear sense of moving in time and space.
   a. Homogeneity, sameness, and repetition in design elements can cause problems for any user of a building but particularly the handicapped. These characteristics can convey a lack of direction and movement and, therefore, create a kind of disorientation. For example, walking down a long corridor with repetitive and evenly spaced light fixtures, doors, floor pattern, and wall materials can minimize any sense of direction or movement. Another example is a school which is made up of a series of circular buildings and circular corridors which can be found to be confusing and problematic for supervising students.
3. The building should facilitate coordination and cooperation among administrators, staff, and volunteers.
   a. Coordination and cooperation is critical to a successful program. The ab-

sence of coordination and cooperation is often the major obstacle to the integration of regular and special education services.
  b. Having a single administrative leader for the school is found to be far superior to having a principal for the regular school and a separate principal for special education programs. It follows that a central administrative office for all programs of the school is most desirable.
  c. All special education services should not be clustered into a single location within a building or adjacent to a building. Clustering of this kind does not promote the integration of special and regular education students, teachers, and services. Although some special education services must practically be located adjacent or in proximity to each other, special education services (particularly classroom areas) should be physically integrated throughout the school as much as possible.
     i. Derogatory labeling of some students by their peers is a problem in any school setting. Labeling is encouraged when special education services are placed in a wing, in an adjacent building, or other isolated locations. This may also be true when a student must frequently leave a regular classroom to receive special services.
     ii. Regular education staff can form negative attitudes toward special education staff. This can often be attributed to lack of interaction with and knowledge about special education staff and services. The problem can be minimized by: (a) integrating regular education and special education services, and (b) providing lounges, dining, and similar facilities which encourage interaction between professionals.
4. When possible, it is preferable to provide one location or as few as possible for staff activities such as lounging, dining, and teacher planning.
  a. Arbitrary separation of staff by grade level, special versus regular education, or training, i.e., speech therapist vs. classroom teacher, may inhibit professional interaction and help to create unwanted attitudes or territoriality.
5. All instructional areas should be located to avoid the intrusion from outside noises from service delivery, playfields, and roadways.
  a. Distracting noises can be a significant factor in distracting a student from a specific task and encouraging disruptive behavior.
6. Specific service areas should be located in proximity to each other to allow for the sharing of space and equipment, coordination between staff, and to aid staff members providing services to more than one program.
7. Space(s) should be provided for *all* staff involved in the educational program to store personal items, relax, socialize, meet, and discuss.
  a. A space for staff which accommodates these activities is critical to maintaining a high level of staff effectiveness in the classroom. Special education staff have an unusual number of demands placed on them primarily due to:
     i. the highly individualized nature of the program, often including health and hygiene activities;
     ii. the cooperation and coordination required between staff members;
     iii. frequent observation by visitors, student teachers, and parents; and
     iv. frequent parent contact for conferences and/or training.

Design Criteria by Environmental Variable
1. Furniture should be free of protrusions which can create an obvious safety hazard to the user.
  a. The legs of a chair, for example, should not protrude beyond the outermost vertical plane of the chair.
2. Furniture should be curvilinear and resilient.
  a. These features (curvilinearity and resiliency) are compatible with the human body.
  b. This design approach will maximize comfort and minimize injury.
  c. Furniture should not have edges which are sharp or composed of

hard material. Edges should be rounded and composed of or covered with a resilient material.
3. Furniture should be viewed as objects which potentially give support to people.
   a. Furniture should be sufficiently stable to offer support to the user and the occasional passerby.
   b. A chair should support the user; and, in addition, the chairback should be of a height, strength, and shape which would encourage its use as a railing.
4. Elements in a design of a piece of furniture should be easily distinguishable (the arms, legs, back, and seat of a chair), between objects (a table and a chair), or between an object and its background (a chair and the wall it is placed next to). Objects intended to give support should be easily perceived. For example, the arms of a chair should be distinguishable from other elements of that chair and easily identified against the background surfaces of the wall and floor.
   a. The handicapped individual, in many cases, has difficulty interpreting the physical environment because of a physical, emotional, or visual problem.
   b. Environmental clarity which prevents confusion and injury can be achieved by a variety of techniques such as: (1) the use of color and/or texture to create contrast, and (2) the allowance of spaces between important elements of an object, such as the arm and seat of a chair.
5. Furniture should be safe and provide a feeling of security.
   a. Objects and materials should not appear to be something other than what they are. Materials, for example, which indicate strength or hardness should in fact be strong and dense. Materials which simulate wood, metal, cloth, etc., should be avoided. Storage cabinets should not have fake drawers and hardware.
   b. The repetition of furniture layouts should be avoided where it will contribute to the confusion of the building user. An individual's sense of the space-time relationship (the feeling of moving through time and space simultaneously) can be distorted by environments which have identical, repetitive elements in space. Furnishings can be useful in providing a sequential experience in the environment by introducing variation in color, texture, form, and space definition.
   c. Finishes with high reflectance should be avoided. High reflectance may create confusion.
   d. The design of furniture should maintain structural integrity and should appear secure and stable to the user. For example, objects should not appear to defy gravity.
6. Seating should be functional and comfortable.
   a. Extremely hard seats can compress the flesh excessively.
   b. Excessive padding can increase pressure around the peripheral edges of the body and increases the difficulty of sitting down and rising up.
   c. Seats should afford sufficient friction to avoid slipping.
7. Furnishings should have nonglare surfaces.
   a. Nonglare surfaces reduce eye fatigue and distractions.
   b. Matte finishes should be specified.
8. Furniture should be resistant to staining, scratching, and chipping.
   a. Toileting accidents may occur frequently with some handicapped populations.
   b. The use of such items as wheelchairs, braces, walkers, canes, carts, cycles, and roller boards increase the opportunity for damage to furniture.

Design Criteria by
Special Education Service
   The General Instructional Area
(What follows is only a small portion of the criteria developed for this service)
1. Definition.
   Preschool, elementary, and secondary: The general instructional area refers to one or more spaces in which handicapped students usually spend the majority of the day. These spaces may serve only handicapped students or be an arena for integration of handicapped and nonhandicapped students.
2. General guidelines.

The two basic factors which determine the requirements for a space are people and activities. In regular education programs, these two factors vary to a limited degree. In special education programs, these two factors vary considerably. Some of the characteristics of the people and activities which make special education so variable are discussed below:

Age of students

Handicapped students are usually grouped by ability rather than strictly by chronological age. Therefore, it is not uncommon to find students in a single class whose ages may range between 3 and 7 years. This range may be greater with groups of more severely handicapped students.

Grouping of students

Based on the individualized educational program developed to meet each student's needs, individual and small group activities are the predominant method of grouping for instruction.

Staffing

The diversified instructional program requires a greater number and type of professionals, paraprofessionals, and volunteers. The general instructional area often has to accommodate at least two adults at any point in time. With some student populations, the number of staff may be significantly greater than two.

The nature of activities

There are many diverse activities which occur in the general instruction area. Three or more activities frequently take place simultaneously. In some situations, each student may be engaged in a different activity at the same point in time. The nature of these activities can be quite different and they often have varied environmental requirements. Examples of simultaneous activities include:
a. A small group viewing a film and two students involved in gross motor activities.
b. Five students reading and one student typing.
c. Two students sawing and glueing wood and eight students working on math problems in a group with a teacher.
d. One student receiving training in toileting skills, two students reading, one student practicing balancing skills, and five students painting.
e. One student separated from the group requiring socialization skills and eight students reading.

As the above factors involving people and activities became more diverse so must the environment. Choices in the environment should be available and usually be under the control of the teacher. Singular solutions to each environmental variable are not sufficient. For example, one type of flooring, lighting, or space will not adequately support programs in the general instructional area.

3. Spatial relationships.
   a. Direct, barrier-free access to the outdoors should be provided from the basic instructional area.
      i. Mobility and behavior characteristics of some students preclude their traveling to and utilizing general play areas. An adjacent and sometimes enclosed play area is a requirement of the basic instructional area. This necessity relates primarily to the younger (preschool and elementary) and/or more severely and profoundly handicapped student populations. This requirement should be considered for the orthopedically handicapped, multiply handicapped, and emotionally disturbed.
      ii. Safe and efficient egress during a fire situation and other emergencies must be provided.
      iii. Minimizing the travel time to outdoor play areas is an important factor.
      iv. Direct access to the outdoors facilitates the movement of play equipment such as bicycles, wagons, climbers, and balls.
      v. Direct access can allow outdoor and indoor activities to occur simultaneously with proper visual supervision.
      vi. Direct access provides outdoor activities with convenient access to lavatories located adjacent to the classroom. This is especially important for students with limited toilet control or skills.
   b. Particular attention should be given to providing convenient access to the bus loading/unloading and par-

ent drop-off areas for the following populations:
   i. preschool students
   ii. orthopedically handicapped
c. Access to bus loading/unloading and parking areas should be convenient to the students involved in work/study programs, and/or frequent field trips. This can particularly be applicable to programs for the mentally retarded.
d. Classrooms used for mainstreaming and self-containment should be physically integrated throughout the school.
   i. The nonhandicapped students' awareness and understanding of the handicapped is increased.
   ii. Derogatory labeling of students by their peers is reduced.
   iii. Communication for cooperation and understanding among staff members is improved.
   iv. Travel distances to and from classrooms is reduced, which can decrease behavior problems enroute.
   v. Opportunities for mainstreaming (integrating the same age groups) is improved.
e. There should be options for providing services within or adjacent to the basic classroom.
   i. This may be advantageous to: (a) maintain the teacher's awareness and involvement in supportive services, i.e., speech or physical therapy, and, therefore, encouraging program continuity; and (b) heighten the awareness of nonhandicapped students and aid in avoiding the stigma of a handicapped student being labeled different or strange by his/her peers.
   ii. An adjacent teacher/student workroom for individual and small group activities, such as auditory testing, speech therapy, physical therapy, one-to-one instruction, typing, viewing audiovisual materials, and behavior modification is desirable for most and required by some student populations.
      (a) This room should be acoustically isolated from the classroom but provide for visual supervision from the classroom.
      (b) The sharing of an adjacent room between classrooms should be considered to maximize the utilization of this space. The frequency of use by one classroom may make sharing impractical.
f. Storage must be adjacent to the classroom.
   i. This facilitates quick access to materials and equipment.
   ii. The necessity of a teacher or aide having to leave the room to retrieve a stored item is eliminated.
   iii. Shared storage between classrooms should be considered, especially when specialized equipment can be shared.
4. Surfaces.
Floor, ceiling, and wall material must be suitable for programmatic and individual student needs.
Floors
a. A single floor surface material cannot adequately facilitate all programmatic requirements. A minimum of two floor surface materials are recommended: a dense, resilient material resistant to damage by toileting accidents and spillage of food, paint, and water; and a comfortable, warm material capable of facilitating activities directly on the floor such as reading, rolling, tumbling, and mobility training.
b. A change in floor surface gives students (specifically visually impaired students) a sense of their location in the room.
c. A change in floor surface affords the instructional opportunity for students to learn to negotiate or maintain these surfaces.
d. Generally, the larger percentage of floor surface should be the warm, comfortable material (65–75 percent) with the remainder the dense, resilient material.
e. A combination of carpet and vinyl asbestos tile is a functional solution.
f. The exact percentage of each material required must be related to the specific student population and related services. Many factors affect the area of each floor surface material required. A greater percentage of

a comfortable, warm material should be considered when:
  i. A high frequency of activities occurs directly on the floor. This seems to be prevalent with younger and more severely handicapped students.
  ii. The control of general sources of sound is desirable specifically from students who are prone to seizures, disruptive behavior, or hyperactivity.
  iii. Physical therapy, occupational therapy, or similar activities occur frequently in the classroom.

A greater percentage of a dense, resilient material should be considered when:
  i. Student behavior is a significant factor in the damage of surface materials.
  ii. A high frequency use and/or large groupings are required for art and similar activities.

g. Portable floor surfaces such as rugs and mats can offer options for special activities. The use of area rugs may, however, be inappropriate for populations in wheelchairs or having mobility problems.

h. An area with a wood floor is recommended for preschool and elementary level hearing impaired students to accentuate rhythm for such activities as music, dance, and auditory training.

i. Dense, nonresilient materials such as terrazzo and ceramic tile are not acceptable in classroom areas. These surfaces can be slippery and/or cold or present serious hazards to students prone to falling due to poor balance, assistive devices, etc.

j. Toilet room floor surfaces adjacent to the classrooms should be nonslip and easily cleaned and maintained.

Ceilings
a. The ceiling should have the capability for displaying instructional materials, student work, and other objects.
b. A ceiling with acoustical absorption qualities should be considered as an alternative means of control of general sources of sound and specifically sounds from students prone to seizures, disruptive behavior, or hyperactivity.
c. A standard acoustical tile ceiling is generally viewed as functional.
d. The structure in or above the ceiling may be required to support equipment and/or students in programs serving the orthopedically handicapped and multiply handicapped. The equipment may include hammocks, swings, and ropes.
e. Ceilings which are easily reached and damaged by students should be avoided with certain student populations such as the socially/emotionally disturbed. These students occasionally will throw objects, remove portions of the ceiling, or use the area above a ceiling to hide objects and materials.

Walls
a. Wall surfaces should function as display surfaces to the maximum extent possible.
b. Walls which function as a display surface in their entirety are preferable to providing display boards (tack or chalk) mounted on walls.
c. Plaster, concrete block, and other nondisplay surfaces are acceptable only when sufficient tack or chalk board is provided.
d. Gypsum board can create a warmer, homelike atmosphere but is prone to damage by certain populations such as the emotionally disturbed and some orthopedically handicapped students.
e. Walls which easily transmit airborne and impact sound are unacceptable.
f. Movable walls can cause significant acoustical problems between spaces and often limit the amount of chalkboard, tackboard, and electrical outlets which can be provided.
g. A change in wall texture can give students (especially the visually impaired student) a sense of their location in a room.
h. Wood is an acceptable material if:
  i. it does not splinter.
  ii. it avoids vertical lines since this can cause distractions for students with visual tracking and/or focusing problems, and,
  iii. the population being served does not include students who

      may damage the wall surface because of behavior or the use of assistive and adaptive devices.
i. Variation in wall surfaces can be an instructional tool by heightening students' awareness of materials and providing opportunities for cleaning, repairing, and maintaining surfaces.

Summary

The mandate for equal educational opportunity for handicapped children is an opportunity for all children. Traditionally, the programs and services for the handicapped have represented the best in educational methods and techniques. Special education is synonymous with (1) early and continuous intervention, (2) individualized educational programs, (3) parent involvement, (4) in-service training, (5) differentiated staffing, and (6) interagency cooperation.

These six concepts are appropriate for all children. Mandating these concepts for the handicapped and integrating handicapped children into the public school setting will have the residual effect of improving programs for the nonhandicapped children as well. The implementation of P.L. 94–142 and Section 504 of the Vocational Rehabilitation Act of 1973 can only prove to be a bill of rights for all children.

Disabled Libraries: An Examination of Physical and Attitudinal Barriers to Handicapped Library Users

ROBERT T. BEGG

The 36 million physically and mentally disabled or handicapped persons in the United States constitute our largest and most heterogeneous minority.[1] Their problems should be of interest to us all since, potentially, anyone can become disabled; yet throughout history the handicapped have been subjected to various forms of discrimination and to a number of environmental and social barriers whenever they have attempted to lead active lives. Within the last decade, this plight of the handicapped has been recognized as a national concern and steps have been taken at all levels of government to alleviate the barriers to their full participation in our society.

Section 504 of the Rehabilitation Act of 1973[2] is a landmark in that it represents the first federal civil rights legislation fashioned to protect the rights of the handicapped and to end discrimination on the basis of handicap.[3] The act provides that "[n]o otherwise qualified handicapped individual . . . shall, solely by reason of his handicap, be excluded from participation in, be denied the benefits of, or be subjected to discrimination under any program or activity receiving Federal financial assistance."[4] This is a mandate to end discrimination and to bring the handicapped into the mainstream of American life.[5]

This mandate represents a challenge to all elements of society which provide or should be providing service to the handicapped. Libraries are no exception. It is imperative that librarians take the steps necessary to make their libraries and services accessible to handicapped library patrons and employees. Barriers in the library environment need to be identified and action must be taken to eliminate or counter them if possible. The elimination of barriers can be a simple process requir-

---

"Disabled Libraries: An Examination of Physical and Attitudinal Barriers to Handicapped Library Users," by Robert T. Begg, *Law Library Journal* 1979, 72: 513–25. Reprinted by permission of the *Journal*.

ing only common sense and a sensitivity to the problem; however, there are frequently complex political, social and economic ramifications which must be considered.[6] Librarians must be aware of these ramifications as well as the legal, professional, and practical aspects of providing access to collections and services for a large and growing segment of the population.

Laws, Regulations, Standards

The Rehabilitation Act of 1973 defines the term "handicapped individual" as ". . . any person who (A) has a physical or mental impairment which substantially limits one or more of such person's major life activities, (B) has a record of such impairment or (C) is regarded as having such an impairment."[7] The terminology of this definition has been expanded upon in regulations promulgated by the Department of Health, Education, and Welfare.[8]

This definition is quite broad and is applicable to a far greater range of persons than one might traditionally have considered to be handicapped. Both physically and mentally disabled persons are included as well as those who have a history of an impairment or are just regarded as having an impairment by others even if they do not actually have it. Included are such disorders as drug addiction, alcoholism, heart disease, cancer, epilepsy and speech or hearing defects. Librarians must be aware of and sensitive to the needs of those individuals who are handicapped within the meaning of the above definition, for failure to provide access or to adjust programs with respect to them may place the library or its parent institution in violation of state, federal or local laws and regulations.

While there is a significant body of federal legislation dealing with the handicapped,[9] libraries are not singled out in this legislation for special treatment or concern but much of the legislation is still applicable to libraries directly or through a parent institution. Because of the great variety of types of libraries, it is possible that more than one of these federal acts could be applicable to a particular library.[10] Clearly, any library housed or operated by the federal government is subject to the equal access legislation.[11] In fact, libraries which have any program or activity receiving federal financial assistance are subject to the provisions of the Rehabilitation Act of 1973.[12] This therefore includes most libraries associated with primary or secondary schools, colleges or universities, hospitals, social service agencies, or any other libraries or parent institutions which have received funds through the Department of Health, Education, and Welfare.[13]

The Rehabilitation Act prohibits discrimination on the basis of handicap in programs and activities[14] and in employment.[15] As employers, libraries must make reasonable accommodation to the handicaps of present employees and job applicants unless the accommodation would result in undue hardship to the employer. As providers of services, libraries are required to make programs operated in existing facilities accessible to handicapped persons, to ensure that new facilities are constructed so as to be readily accessible and to operate library programs in a nondiscriminatory manner. Note that the key is *program accessibility*, not necessarily building accessibility. The regulations were carefully drawn to indicate this distinction.[16]

The regulations make it clear that a covered library may not deny a qualified handicapped person the opportunity to participate in or benefit from library services, or provide unequal services, or ineffective services.[17] Different or separate aid, benefits or services to handicapped persons are acceptable, but only if necessary to provide services or programs as effectively as those provided to others.[18] While services are required to be equally effective, they need not always result in an identical level of achievement for both the handicapped and the nonhandicapped, but they must allow for equal opportunity in the most integrated setting appropriate.[19] Such services must be made accessible even if no impaired persons are known to live in the library's service area at the time.[20]

Equal opportunity in the areas of library services, programs, and employment may be meaningless or even impossible if library physical facilities are inaccessible to or unusable by handicapped persons. Since discrimination in programs resulting from inaccessible facilities is prohibited,[21] librarians must be concerned with program accessibility in existing facilities and when planning for new construction or alterations.

The demands for compliance made upon existing facilities are less stringent than those for new facilities or alterations. In existing facilities, programs or activities may be viewed in their entirety to determine if they are accessible and it is not required that every part of the library be accessible to and usable by the handicapped.[22] Structural changes need not be made in existing buildings where alternative methods are available to meet the program accessibility requirements.[23] For example, if services can be provided in a more accessible part of the library, or if home delivery of material is possible, or if materials and services can be provided at an alternative accessible site, such as in a bookmobile, or if clerical or volunteer aid can be provided to reach books on high shelves, then structural changes may not be needed.[24] In providing these alternatives, however, priority must be given to the most integrated setting appropriate.[25]

The standards for new construction of or major alterations to a library are more stringent than for existing structures. New construction[26] must be designed and constructed so that it is readily accessible to and usable by handicapped persons.[27] Alterations to an existing library which affect the usability of that facility must be made to provide accessibility to the *greatest extent feasible*.[28] The federal regulations have adopted by reference the American National Standards Institute [ANSI] accessibility standards.[29] Design, construction, or alteration of libraries in conformance with these standards constitutes compliance with all accessibility requirements for new construction.[30]

The American National Standard Specifications for Making Buildings and Facilities Accessible to, and Usable by, the Physically Handicapped[31] are "intended to make all buildings and facilities used by the public accessible to, and functional for, the physically handicapped."[32] These standards identify, define, and describe in great detail the criteria and specifications necessary to improve the physical environment for handicapped persons. In addition, such general information as specifications for wheelchairs and the space needed to function in a wheelchair or on crutches, plus data on site development are provided.[33] It should be noted that the standards are expressed in minimally acceptable terms and should therefore not always be the maximum provided.[34]

State and local governments have also recognized the need to eliminate barriers to accessibility. All of the states now have laws dealing with architectural barriers to the handicapped.[35] Many of these states have incorporated the American National Standards Institute accessibility standards into state laws, while a few states have incorporated them into their state building codes and yet other states have adopted their own standards.[36] Local building codes and municipal ordinances may also have significance with respect to planning for accessibility, so it is imperative that librarians familiarize themselves with the laws and regulations of local as well as their particular state governments. A number of informative sources are available at the state and local level to provide guidance through this myriad of legislation and regulations.[37] The sources often provide other useful information such as addresses of agencies and bibliographies.

Professional Responsibility

Beyond the legal duty to provide access to programs, services, and facilities, there exists a professional responsibility to meet the needs of the handicapped library patron in a nondiscriminatory fashion. Surprisingly, the Library Bill of Rights[38] does not specifically recognize this responsibility. Article 5 states that "[T]he rights of an individual to the use of a library should not be denied or abridged because of his age, race, religion, national origins, or social or political views." Nowhere is discrimination based upon handicap mentioned, nor is it mentioned in the new draft of the Library Bill of Rights dated January 11, 1979.[39] Nevertheless, it seems clear that librarians are obligated professionally to meet the demands of library patrons having a reasonable need for their services or resources, including the handicapped.[39a]

It is altogether too easy for a librarian to underestimate these needs by assuming that there is no demand for library services by the handicapped or that there are not a significant number of handicapped people in the community to make the effort worthwhile. The reason may be that because of encounters with various types of barriers, these potential library patrons are unable to demand services or make use of or even get to the library proper. They are invisible patrons who both need and want library service but cannot obtain it. Their needs may go unanswered because the librarian has failed to perceive the need, or the extent of the need, since the observable number of disabled is usually lower than the actual number. When accessibility is guaranteed these invisible patrons will reappear. Eliminating these barriers constitutes a professional responsibility.

Once you have recognized, as a librarian,

your legal and professional responsibilities to handicapped patrons, it is necessary to identify the problem areas within your library environment which might restrict access to collections, programs or services. These barriers can be physical or attitudinal. The following discussion will identify some of the more frequently encountered barriers to library access and suggest some possible solutions.

Physical Barriers

Architects and engineers have generally designed and constructed buildings based upon the capabilities of an average or normal person. This person has the health, strength, mobility and capabilities of the average size, right-handed, thirty-year-old male.[40] Obviously, the great majority of our population does not meet this norm and must adapt to utilize an environment based upon it.[41] One of the problems inherent in this design concept is that barriers resulting from use of the norm tend to be invisible to those who fit the norm.[42] If you fit or are relatively close to the norm, you may not be aware that a door is difficult to open or that a telephone is too high to reach. Therefore, it takes a conscious effort by the librarian to identify these transparent barriers because they will not seriously impede nonhandicapped library staff or a majority of library patrons, but they can represent insurmountable barriers to the disabled.

It should be noted in this context that an interesting side effect or fringe benefit often occurs when barriers to accessibility are removed. Not only do the disabled or handicapped benefit but other nondisabled segments of our society are provided with a more accessible and usable environment.[43] Easier access to the library for the disabled means easier access for the aged, children, or pregnant women. Curb cuts in sidewalks surrounding the library eliminate not only barriers to wheelchairs, but also barriers to bicycles and baby carriages. Virtually any step taken in the library to enhance accessibility for the handicapped will benefit some other portion of the library's patron base.

To determine the usability and accessibility of a library, it can be helpful to adopt a systems approach.[44] The systems analysis should determine if there is a barrier-free continuous route of travel into and throughout the library with ready access to services, equipment, and resources along that route.[45] Accessibility problems can begin for the disabled in the parking lot and barriers can stall their progress at any point within the library. Therefore, it is necessary to have an overall view of potential problems. Each component of the library environment should also meet the criteria of being accessible, functional, safe, and convenient within the framework of the overall system.[46] A barrier-free library system requires access to the building and library proper, to the collection once in the library, to files, cabinets, and equipment, and to miscellaneous incidental facilities needed for the comfort and convenience of any library patron.

Access to the building begins in the parking lot. Appropriately marked, parking spaces[47] should be reserved for the handicapped as near as possible to an accessible building entrance.[48] A level area adjacent to the reserved parking space at least four feet wide must be provided to allow the disabled maneuvering room to get into the vehicle.[49] There should be no barriers between the parking area and the building entrance and if possible, persons using braces or crutches or in wheelchairs should not be compelled to travel behind parked cars.[50]

The most frequently encountered barriers between the parking area and the entrance are curbs, steps, or abrupt grade changes. An eight-inch curb is an insurmountable obstacle to a person in a wheelchair, but curb cuts or curb ramps can easily solve this problem. These cuts should be adequately marked, unobstructed, and have a nonslip surface.[51] Exterior steps constitute a problem which is usually solved by the installation of ramps. Ramps should be constructed with a nonslip surface and have a slope with no greater than a one foot rise in elevation for each twelve feet of length.[52] They should also have adequate width and be equipped with handrails.[53] There should be level areas at the top and bottom, at 30-foot intervals and at turns.[54] Abrupt grade changes can be dealt with by ramps or by regrading the landscape to an acceptable slope. Regrading is often more suitable, more esthetically pleasing and less expensive than a ramp.[55]

The next barrier to accessibility is usually the building entrance. At least one primary entrance to the building must be accessible to persons in wheelchairs.[56] This entrance must, of course, be a part of the barrier-free continuous route of travel which is necessary for an accessible library. It is helpful to post at the entrance a map indicating the barrier-free route of travel through the building and library. Posting the map at wheelchair eye level is helpful, while a raised, tactile map is usable by blind patrons.[57]

All doorways must have at least a 32-inch minimum opening[58] with the thresholds as flush with the floors as is possible.[59] A handicapped person should be able to operate the door using a single effort with one hand and with the strength or pressure which can reasonably be expected from a disabled person.[60] If the door seems heavy or awkward to you, there is clearly a problem. Lever or push-type handles are much easier for many handicapped persons, or even persons with a load of books, to use than are door knobs.[61] Unquestionably, automatically activated self-opening doors are the best type available for unrestricted access. Revolving doors or turnstiles constitute obviously impenetrable barriers to some handicapped patrons but are frequently found in libraries.[62] Narrow areas created by automatic book detection and other security systems can also be potential barriers at exit points.

Once inside the library, a barrier-free route of travel should exist to all pertinent segments of the collection or to areas where programs or services are offered. Changes in level are accommodated by elevators or stairs. Elevators are an absolute necessity for those completely confined to a wheelchair, but the elevator compartment must be large enough for both the wheelchair and an attendant and all controls must be at a reachable height.[63] It is also helpful to provide raised or indented markings adjacent to call buttons and floor buttons for persons with visual problems. Braille may be used as an additional aid but not to replace tactile lettering.[64] Stairs should be constructed in a manner which would reduce tripping hazards and they should have easily graspable handrails on both sides.[65]

Consideration must also be given to library floors. Floors must be level and have a non-slip surface.[66] Carpeting or mats should be firmly secured and excessively thick carpeting should be avoided since it creates problems for those in wheelchairs.[67] An effort should be made to insure sufficient color differentiation between floors and walls so that the visually impaired with space perception difficulties can distinguish between them.[68]

Collection Access and Utility

Even if a barrier-free route of travel exists into and through the library, the typical library[69] will still represent a challenge to the handicapped. A person using a walking aid, accompanied by a guide dog, or in a wheelchair requires more space in which to maneuver than an able-bodied man or woman.[70] These patrons also have, in many instances, a reduced area of reach which must be taken into consideration when examining materials accessibility.[71] The greatest challenges are accessibility of stacks, adequate seating and work areas, and access to files, cabinets and machinery.

Book stacks are the predominant physical feature in most libraries since they represent the most common form of book storage but also in most instances they constitute a very formidable barrier. They can inhibit the handicapped if the ranges are too close together or if the stack is too high to reach. The standard width for an open access stack is 36 inches between the stacks.[72] This is the ideal since it allows for adequate lighting of bottom shelves, easy viewing of titles on lower shelves, room for booktrucks and room to pass another person without great difficulty.[73] Such standard 36-inch stack spacings also allow for reasonable one-way access by a patron in a wheelchair or using a walking aid. In reality, many libraries do not use standard widths in order to place more stacks in a given area. Nevertheless, there are minimum widths that must be observed. A person in a wheelchair needs a minimum of 32 inches[74] while a six-foot-tall man on crutches needs a minimum of 32.5 inches between stacks.[75] It should be noted that the width requirement includes the size of the wheelchair plus room for the person's arms and maneuvering room, yet 32 inches would still be a tighter fit than is desirable.

Attention must also be given to the need for turning space for patrons in wheelchairs.[76] Dead-end, one-way aisles between stacks can create problems if there is not adequate width for a turn. Stacks open at both ends are less likely to create problems if there is adequate turning space beyond the stacks. Main aisles in the library should provide sufficient space for two-way traffic. Two-way wheelchair traffic requires at least 60 inches while 48 inches is needed for a wheelchair and a walking person to pass.[77]

A second major accessibility problem with library shelving is its height. A patron in a wheelchair just cannot reach as far or as high as a standing person, nor can he or she climb a ladder or a step stool. An adult in a wheelchair has a vertical reach of from 54 to 78 inches[78] but the average diagonal reach to the shelf is only 48 inches from the floor.[79] This means that for all practical purposes, any shelves beyond the first four shelves in the stacks are inaccessible to patrons in wheelchairs. Many of these patrons would be limited to reach to just the bottom three shelves.

In an ideal world, a librarian might hope that all stacks would be only three shelves high and that there be at least 36 inches between them but in this world, given the reality of economics and politics, this is not feasible for most libraries. Alternative solutions suggest themselves, such as providing library personnel to reach those high books, or in installing computerized databases, or materials in microforms to mitigate the need to be in the stacks in the first place.

In the modern library, resources are available in a variety of formats which one might assume to be accessible but which in reality are not. Microforms, audio cassettes, computerized data bases, and videotapes are some examples of materials which would on the surface appear to be readily accessible to the handicapped but in some instances may not live up to their promise. The features common to these materials are their need for equipment to utilize them and the need to store these materials in some form of cabinet or shelving.

Any library equipment must itself be physically available and convenient for the handicapped. Tables or carrels must be high enough so that a person in a wheelchair can work easily with the equipment. The working reach at a table for a person in a wheelchair is in the range of 28.5 to 33.2 inches,[80] therefore the equipment and all control devices should be located near the lower end of that range if possible. Control devices should be as simple to use as possible for those having difficulty with manual dexterity. Obviously, simplified control mechanisms would benefit all library patrons not just the handicapped. When examining the equipment station, one should be aware that a permanent chair located there can represent a barrier. If possible, try to leave at least one station without a chair so that it will be more accessible to those patrons in wheelchairs.

Storage cabinets for microforms or cassettes can also create obstacles. Most such cabinets are designed with the average, standing adult in mind. It is virtually impossible for a patron in a wheelchair to see or reach the contents in the top shelves of microform cabinets. The same problem is evident when the handicapped attempt to use vertical files, and to a lesser extent, the card catalog. The card catalog's saving grace is that the drawers can usually be pulled all the way out for easier usage. Use of three-drawer filing cabinets or shorter microform cabinets can solve these problems but this admittedly can result in an underutilization of floor space.

Support equipment and facilities within the library should also be assessed to determine their accessibility. Such equipment as pencil sharpeners, photocopiers, newspaper or magazine racks and typewriters must be placed within usable reach. Electric pencil sharpeners and typewriters are easier for the handicapped and other patrons to utilize and so they should be favored over the less expensive manual alternatives.

Adequate general seating and work areas must also be provided for effective library usage and for efficient work by handicapped employees. Some tables or carrels should be high enough to allow the armrest of a wheelchair to fit underneath. The height of the armrest from the floor is usually 29 inches.[81] Chairs should not be placed at these work areas for convenience sake. Work areas, if designed to be flexible and functional, can be utilized by both disabled and nondisabled employees and patrons. Certain design features to accommodate the handicapped are often unnoticeable but very helpful. Cabinets and drawers with recessed handles have no protrusions to obstruct wheelchairs. Partitions without feet are less likely to trip a person on crutches or one with visual problems. Adjustable work surfaces provide flexibility for all library patrons or employees. If edges and corners are rounded or beveled, there is less likely to be injury in those accidental confrontations between man and table or desk.[82] Such design considerations cost little but make for a much safer and usable environment for the disabled.

Convenience and Support Facilities

The disabled have the same bodily needs as any other library users; therefore, it is imperative that support facilities be available and readily accessible. A restroom for each sex should be provided along the barrier-free route of travel on each floor if feasible. These rooms should be equipped for use by the handicapped.[83] Consideration should be given to design of the toilet stall and to the location and usability of mirrors, shelves and dispensers.[84] Water fountains or dispensers should have up-front spouts and controls and be hand operated or hand- and foot-operated.[85] The fountains should be low enough for a person in a wheelchair to use but if this is not possible, then a paper cup dispenser should be installed.[86]

Telephones should be installed so that the coin slot, dial, and handset are reachable by a person in a wheelchair.[87] Volume controls on headsets are helpful for persons with certain hearing disabilities.[88] Some telephones could be provided with braille numerals and instructions for the blind, while push button dials are easier to use for persons with manual dexterity problems.[89] When equipment such as water fountains or telephones are found in a bank or series, it is usually permissible to modify only a set number of them depending upon your handicapped patron base.

A variety of other controls and devices must also be accessible to work on or utilize the library environment. An effort should be made to eliminate barriers to such essential devices as light switches, heat or ventilation control, windows, draperies, vending machines, and fire alarms and extinguishers.[90] These devices must be accessible, low enough to reach and reasonably easy to operate. Any warning signals or alarms should be both audible and visual so as to alert both those with hearing problems and the blind.[91]

Communication of information to handicapped library patrons is essential if they are to fully enjoy the resources and services of the library. It was noted previously that a map indicating a barrier-free route of travel through the library can be posted near the entrance to provide guidance in their use of the facility. This map can also indicate other pertinent information such as locations of restrooms, offices, parts of the collection, and services.

There should also be appropriate signs to enable patrons to determine their location and to identify significant resources and services or to provide instruction in the use of equipment. The message to be imparted must be clear and uncluttered. It is important that the signs be located where they can be easily seen by patrons in wheelchairs. It is helpful to have large letters which contrast sharply with the background so that they are legible to persons with visual problems.[92] For blind library users, it is necessary to have signs with raised or indented letters. Braille alone is not adequate since less than ten percent of the blind are able to read braille.[93] Identification of specific rooms or offices should be by raised or recessed figures on the wall to the right or left of the door at approximately five feet from the floor.[94] It should be apparent that well marked facilities will be advantageous to all library users.

Costs

The preceding analysis indicated some of the steps that could be taken to make library facilities and services more accessible and usable for the handicapped. Underlying any decision to make such changes or to incorporate these features in a new building is the element of cost.

Designing accessibility into a new facility is a relatively inexpensive proposition when viewed against the total cost of the project. Some estimates place the cost of accessibility at as little as one cent per square foot[95] while other estimates place the cost at from one tenth to one percent of total construction costs.[96] These costs are a one-time expenditure, yet once the library is made accessible it can serve disabled patrons through its useful life without additional expense.[97] Remember that federal regulations mandate that new construction be readily accessible and usable by the handicapped.[98]

Some alterations and modifications to existing buildings for the purpose of eliminating physical barriers or for enhancing usability can be very expensive. It can cost up to $15,000 to make a restroom accessible and as much as $25,000 to replace a revolving door with an accessible one.[99] Ramps can cost several thousand dollars to have installed and even minor changes have some cost attached. Nevertheless, a librarian cannot allow himself or herself to be intimidated by the design criteria for accessibility because there are often alternative ways to make the library and its collection accessible which are less expensive than traditional methods but still work equally well.[100] The program accessibility regulations were intentionally drawn with enough flexibility to permit librarians and others to devise ways to make their programs accessible without the necessity of extremely expensive or impractical physical changes in the facility.[101]

If some imagination is applied along with common sense to a problem of accessibility or usability, then a solution can frequently be found at a greatly reduced cost. Some examples may better illustrate this point. A firm in California recognizing that its water fountains could not be used by persons in wheelchairs, solved the problem by spending $40,000 to lower all drinking fountains whereas the installation of paper cup dispensers could have solved the problem for about one dollar per fountain.[102] An alternative to the concrete ramp in some instances is the regrading of the approach to the building which is often less expensive and more pleasing in appearance.[103] Alternative construction materials can also save money, such as in the substitution of a wooden ramp in place of a concrete or brick one. Signs and maps which would be very expensive if done by professionals can often be drawn at lower cost and with more flair if done by a creative library staff member. If new concrete work is needed around the building, it is often no more expensive to specify curb cuts at the time of the concrete pouring since costs are usually calculated on a straight square footage basis.[104] When new equipment is being contemplated for library use, keep the handicapped in mind, for equipment more suitable to their needs may be available at approximately the same price.

An additional solution to the cost problem is the development of outside sources of aid or funding.[105] A number of federally funded programs could conceivably be tapped for aid in architectual barrier removal[106] and in addition, the Department of Health, Education, and Welfare has stated that they are ready "at all times to provide technical assistance . . . in meeting program accessibility responsibilities" and for that purpose they have established a special technical assistance unit.[107] Certain private libraries or their parent institutions could possibly take advantage of the federal or state income tax deduction for barrier removal of up to $25,000.[108] Funding might also be available from state or local governments which could possibly funnel federal general revenue sharing funds into your program. Playing the grantsmanship game can also be effective in this area. Private foundations or locally based civic and service organizations can be a lucrative source of funds for barrier removal or for purchasing special equipment.[109]

Attitudinal Barriers

Perhaps even greater than the physical barriers to access are the attitudinal barriers which have been erected within our society and institutions. These attitudinal barriers are no less real than physical barriers but it takes a greater effort to identify them because they "are more subtle and implicit."[110] It is critically important to remove attitudinal barriers because attitudes influence and underlie all our actions,[111] yet their removal is difficult. These attitudes are bound up with the day-to-day appearance and functioning of a particular service or activity and they have usually been in existence for a long time and are reinforced by the environment.[112] Attitudinal barriers in the library may be created by the library staff, by the disabled patrons themselves, or by a reaction to the physical environment of the library. The interaction between handicapped patrons and the staff or the environment indicates to the handicapped the value which is placed upon them which in turn reflects upon how they value themselves.[113]

The physical environment of the library communicates a message to its users and in many instances the message sent to the disabled is that they are incompetent or inferior.[114] Take for instance the library entrance with monumental stairs which the architect felt would inspire a sense of awe or respect within the library user. Rather than the appropriate positive response, a library user in a wheelchair may have a negative psychological reaction because of his inability to reach his destination.[115] Frustration, anger, helplessness, or a feeling of rejection may be the net result. Such reactions can be generated by any barrier which prevents a disabled person from leading a relatively normal active life.

Consideration must also be given to the reaction to alternative methods of service or access. If the only barrier-free route of access to your library is through a service entrance off the loading dock, there is a not too subtle message of inferiority transmitted.[116] The message is that the disabled are not good enough to utilize the front door but must instead use the servant's entrance. This can be a humiliating experience for the disabled patron.

The attitudes of the library staff toward disabled patrons are critically important because they can possibly offset the negative message of the environment or they can create negative vibrations of their own. Negative attitudes toward the handicapped are usually a result of fear and uncertainty. These reactions are generated by the perception that the disabled are different and the more different a person is perceived to be, the more negative the attitudes toward him are.[117] It is difficult for others to understand the experience of the handicapped or perhaps there is a fear of this understanding.[118] This fear makes us uncomfortable, therefore resulting in a response to the handicapped which may be different from the response to a nonhandicapped library patron.

Fears and uncertainties of the staff can be overcome by providing information concerning disabilities which makes them understandable. Once the staff is aware of the nature of various disabilities and of what they should or should not do when they are servicing the disabled, they will feel more comfortable and project a more positive attitude.[119] It is important that the staff develop a sensitivity to the needs of the handicapped but not a condescending attitude. Disabled adults are not children or holy innocents or objects of pity, but rather library users who deserve to be treated with respect and to be given the opportunity to succeed without always having a self-righteous or patronizing librarian offering to help.[120] The staff must remember that each disabled patron is an individual with his own character, problems, needs, and ambitions. A reasonable approach to library service for the handicapped therefore requires a balancing of sensitivity, common sense and respect.

Each librarian should ask what messages are transmitted by their library to the handicapped. Does the library or staff emit a subliminal message of welcome or exclusion, of first or second class citizenship? As with physical barriers, it is first necessary to recognize the existence of these attitudinal barriers before steps can be taken to eliminate them.

There are several ways in which problems can be identified and the sensitivity of the staff toward handicapped patrons can be enhanced. Role playing or role reversal is a very effective technique for creating empathy. Set up a wheelchair tour of your library starting in the parking lot. Allowing a person to experience limited mobility can produce more results or unexpected insights than merely talking about it. Similarly, a blindfolded tour of the library can suggest problems encountered by the visually impaired.[121] Such tours would be of value if offered in a library school course, in continuing education classes, or as part of an in-house orientation or training program.[122]

A second approach is to seek out advice and comments from the handicapped library patrons themselves. They are obviously more sensitive to attitudes of the staff and to physical barriers than anyone else could possibly be.[123] This client feedback can often identify problems invisible to the library staff and suggest better and sometimes less expensive alternative procedures, services or equipment. The disabled can also help in determining priorities as to which actions need immediate attention and they should always be included in any long-range planning activities.[124]

There are also a variety of other sources knowledgeable in the needs of the disabled which are pleased to provide aid and information at the national or local level. Agencies such as the Easter Seal Society or the American Council of the Blind have a high level of expertise and are a rich source of literature on the subject of the handicapped.[125] Equally helpful would be your state's governor's committee on the handicapped or the state department of rehabilitation or their equivalents and be sure not to disregard local organizations or voluntary groups which serve the handicapped.[126]

Finally, an obvious source of information for any librarian would be a literature search to identify useful publications dealing with specific disabilities, barriers, programs, laws and sources of aid. The literature is quite extensive. There are several periodicals devoted strictly to the handicapped[127] and also some bibliographies.[128] The federal and state governments have published extensive materials as have various agencies which service the handicapped. There are also looseleaf reporting services which provide broad coverage on particular areas of the law of the handicapped.[129]

Conclusion

It is the goal of the handicapped in the United States to be brought into the mainstream of our society. To achieve this goal, handicapped citizens and their advocates have successfully lobbied for legislation at all levels of government.[130] The laws now exist but they are only symbolic unless a good faith effort is made by individuals to strive toward the goal of equal access and services. The alternative to voluntary compliance may well be a lawsuit or administrative action. Plans now call for coalitions of organizations for the handicapped to support teams of attorneys to bring actions in support of these demands.[131] Will your library be one of the institutions targeted? Are you meeting your professional responsibilities to all patrons? These questions can be answered by a self-evaluation or study which should lead to a plan of action for your library. Many larger libraries or their parent institutions already have such documents but they may be unheeded or tucked away in a file cabinet. Now is the time to act; take the time to develop a plan of action or dust off the one you have and then implement it. The cost of your inaction in human terms may be inordinately high.

Notes

1. Estimates of the number of handicapped persons vary from 7.2 million to 50 million, with 36 million being the most frequently utilized estimate. This diversity results from the large number of definitions of handicapped which have been used. See *U.S. Dept. of Health, Education, and Welfare, The White House Conference on Handicapped Individuals: Summary Final Report* 3 (1978); J. P. Northrup, *Old Age, Handicapped and Vietnam-Era Antidiscrimination Legislation* 70–74 (1977). For purposes of this article, the terms *disabled* and *handicapped* will be used interchangeably although the author recognizes that there is a distinction. A disabled person is one with an impairment which interferes with a bodily function or activity for six months or longer. "When disability, in interaction with a specific set of environmental conditions, makes an individual unable to perform certain activities, we say that he or she is handicapped." F. Bowe, *Handicapping America*, 16 (1978).
2. 29 U.S.C. § 794 (1976).
3. 42 Fed. Reg. 22,676 (1977).
4. 29 U.S.C. § 794 (1976).
5. 42 Fed. Reg. 22,676 (1977).
6. Bednar, "Preface," in *Barrier-Free Environments*, ix (M. Bednar, ed., 1977).
7. 29 U.S.C. § 706(6) (1976). Since the employment of the handicapped is beyond the scope of this article, portions of the definition dealing with employment have been deleted.
8. 45 C.F.R. § 84.3(j)(2) (1978). (i) "Physical or mental impairment" means (A) any physiological disorder or condition, cosmetic disfigurement, or anatomical loss affecting one or more of the following body systems: neurological; musculoskeletal; special organs; respiratory, including speech organs; cardiovascular; reproductive, digestive, genito-urinary; hemic and lymphatic; skin; and endocrine; or (B) any mental or psychological disorder, such as mental retardation, organic brain syndrome, emotional or mental illness, and specific learning disabilities. (ii) "Major life activities" means functions such as caring for one's self, performing manual tasks, walking, seeing, hearing, speaking, breathing, learning, and working. (iii) "Has a record of such an impairment" means has a history of, or has been misclassified as having, a mental or physical impairment that substantially limits one or more major life activities. (iv) "Is regarded as having an impairment" means (A) has a physical or mental impairment that does not substantially limit major life activities but that is treated by a recipient as constituting such a limitation; (B) has a physical or mental impairment that substantially limits major life activities only as a result of the attitudes of others toward such impairment; or (C) has none of the impairments defined in paragraph (j)(2)(i) of this section but is treated by a recipient as having such an impairment.
9. There are more than 100 different programs for the handicapped in the federal government. Speech by President Jimmy Carter (May 23, 1977) printed at 2 *U.S. Dept. of Health, Education, and Welfare, White House Conference on Handicapped Individuals; Final Report*, Part A, 100 (1978); see "Some Federal Statutes Which Mandate Accessibility," 3 *Amicus* 41 (1978).
10. Education for All Handicapped Children Act of 1975, 20 U.S.C. § 1412(5) (1976), for example, would appear to be applicable to elementary and secondary public school libraries under the notion of related services offered in the least restrictive environment consistent with the needs of handicapped students. See generally *U.S. Dept. of Health, Education, and Welfare, A Summary of Selected Legislation Relating to the Handicapped: 1975–76* (1977).
11. Architectual Barriers Act of 1968, 42 U.S.C. §§ 4151–4157(1976).
12. 29 U.S.C. § 794 (1976). Federal financial assistance is defined at 45 C.F.R. § 84.3(h) (1978).
13. 45 C.F.R. § 84.2 (1978).
14. 29 U.S.C. § 794 (1976).
15. 29 U.S.C. § 793 (1976).
16. 43 Fed. Reg. 36,034 (1978). Policy interpretation number 3 deals specifically with libraries.
17. 45 C.F.R. § 84.4(b)(1)(i)–(iii) (1978).
18. 45 C.F.R. § 84.4(b)(1)(iv) (1978).
19. 45 C.F.R. § 84.4(b)(2) (1978).
20. 43 Fed. Reg. 36,034 (1978).
21. 45 C.F.R. § 84.21 (1978).
22. 45 C.F.R. § 84.22(a) (1978).
23. 45 C.F.R. § 84.22(b) (1978).
24. 43 Fed. Reg. 36,034 (1978).
25. 45 C.F.R. § 84.22(b) (1978).
26. All buildings for which site clearance was begun after June 3, 1977 would be subject to the standards. U.S. Dept. of Health, Education, and Welfare § 504 *Fact Sheet* 2 (1978).
27. 45 C.F.R. § 84.23(a) (1978).
28. 45 C.F.R. § 84.23(b) (1978).
29. 45 C.F.R. § 84.23(c) (1978).
30. 45 C.F.R. § 84.23(c) (1978).
31. ANSI A 117.1-1961 (R 1971). (Hereinafter, each standard will be referred to as ANSI and its number.)
32. ANSI 1.2, supra note 31.

33. ANSI 3, 4, 5, supra note 31.

34. Steinfeld, "Developing Standards for Accessibility" in Bednar, *Barrier-Free Environments*, 84.

35. Schalter, "Removing the Hidden Barriers to Accessibility," 3 *Amicus* 43 (1978); Ala. Code § 21-4-3 (1975); Alaska Stat. § 35.10.015 (1977); Ariz. Rev. Stat. Ann. § 34-403 (Supp. 1978); Ark. Stat. Ann. § 14-627 (1968); Cal. Govt. Code § 4450 (West Supp. 1978); Colo. Rev. Stat. § 9-5-102 (Supp. 1978); Conn. Gen. Stat. § 19-395a (Supp. 1979); Del. Code Ann. tit. 29, § 6917 (1974); Fla. Stat. § 553.46 (Supp. 1979); Ga. Code § 91-1105 (Supp. 1978); Haw. Rev. Stat. § 103-50 (1976); Idaho Code § 39-3203 (1977); Ill. Rev. Stat. ch. 111, § 13 (1975); Ind. Code Ann. § 16-7-5-2 (Burns 1975); Iowa Code § 104A.2 (1974); Kan. Stat. Ann. § 58-1301 (1976); Ky. Rev. Stat. § 227.305 (1977); La. Rev. Stat. Ann. § 49.148 (West Supp. 1979); Me. Rev. Stat. Ann. tit. 25, § 2701 (1978); Md. Ann. Code art. 78A, § 51 (1974); Mass. Gen. Laws Ann. ch. 22, § 13A (Supp. 1979); Mich. Comp. Laws Ann. § 125,1351 (1976); Minn. Stat. Ann. § 16-85 (West Supp. 1978); Miss. Code Ann. § 43-6-3 (Supp. 1978); Mo. Rev. Stat. § 8.610 (Supp. 1979); Mont. Rev. Codes Ann. § 64-301 (1977); Neb. Rev. Stat. § 72-1101 (1971); Nev. Rev. Stat. § 338.180 (1975); N.H. Rev. Ann. § 275-C:14 (Supp. 1977); N.J. Stat. Ann. § 52:32-4 (West Supp. 1978); N.M. Stat. Ann. § 60-13-44D (1978); N.Y. Pub. Bldgs. Law § 50 (McKinney's Supp. 1978); N.C. Gen. Stat. § 168-2 (Supp. 1977); N.D. Cent. Code § 48-02-19 (1978); Ohio Rev. Code Ann. § 3781.111 (Page's Supp. 1978); Okla. Stat. Ann. tit. 61, § 11 (West Supp. 1976); Or. Rev. Stat. § 447.220 (1975); Pa. Stat. Ann. tit. 71, § 1455.1 (Purdon Supp. 1978); R.I. Gen. Laws § 37-17-1 (1978); S.C. Code § 43-33-20 (1977); S.D. Compiled Laws Ann. § 5-14-12 (1974); Tenn. Code Ann. § 53-2547 (1977); Tex. Rev. Civ. Stat. Ann. art. 678g (Vernon's Supp. 1978); Utah Code Ann. § 26-27-1 (1976); Vt. Stat. Ann. tit. 18 § 1322 (Supp. 1978); Va. Code § 2.1-514 (Supp. 1978); Wash. Rev. Code § 70.92.010 (1975); W.Va. Code § 18-10F-1 (1977); Wis. Stat. Ann. § 101.13 (West Supp. 1978); Wyo. Stat. § 35-13-101 (1978).

36. Winslow, "Access to the Environment" in Bednar, *Barrier-Free Environments*, 102; see 2 *U.S. Dept. of Health, Education, and Welfare, White House Conference on Handicapped Individuals, Final Report*, Part C, 89-90 (1978).

37. See, e.g., Dept. of Rehabilitation State of California, *Digest of State Laws Relating to the Disabled* (1975); *Rights of the Physically Handicapped* (M. Joyce, ed., 1976) (This volume covers Iowa, Minnesota, North Dakota, South Dakota, Wisconsin, and federal legislation); C. Des Jardins and R. Hull, *Rights Handbook for Handicapped Children and Adults* (1976), (Illinois and Federal); Easter Seal Society of Oakland County, *Rights and Information for Persons with Handicaps in Michigan* (1976); Ohio Easter Seal Society for Crippled Children and Adults, Inc., *Rights Handbook for Ohio's Physically Handicapped* (1975); Easter Seal Society for Crippled Children and Adults of Massachusetts, Inc., *Rights Handbook for Physically Handicapped Children* (1974).

38. Adopted June 18, 1948. Amended Feb. 2, 1961, and June 27, 1967 by the American Library Association Council.

39. 104 *Library Journal* 566 (1979). It might also be noted that no mention of discrimination based upon handicap is made in the American Association of Law Libraries Code of Ethics.

39a. "The Library of Congress has awarded a contract to ALA to formulate standards for library services to blind and physically handicapped individuals. . . . The standards will take into account administration, staffing, resource development, services and activities, public relations and physical facilities of all kinds of libraries." These standards are expected to appear sometime in 1979. "Standards for Library Services to Blind and Physically Handicapped Planned," 71 *Law Library Journal* 367 (1978). These standards should provide some professional guidance in this area.

40. Bowe, *Handicapping America*, 74; Bednar, "Introduction: On Barriers," in *Barrier-Free Environments*, 1-2.

41. It has been suggested that up to 160 million of our population do not meet this norm. Jeffers, "Barrier-Free Design: A Legislative Response" in Bednar, *Barrier-Free Environments*, 45.

42. Bednar, "Introduction," 2.

43. Bowe, *Handicapping America*, 97; Bednar, "Introduction," 3.

44. *National Center for a Barrier Free Environment, Opening Doors* 18 (1978) (hereinafter cited as *Opening Doors*).

45. The very serious problem of public and other forms of transportation for the handicapped to the library is recognized here but it is a potentially huge area of discussion beyond the scope of this article, therefore the systems analysis will begin in the parking area of the library.

46. Jeffers, "Barrier-Free Design," 44-45.

47. The International Symbol of Access is a sign with the symbol of a person in a wheelchair on a blue background. The number of spaces reserved would depend upon the number of handicapped patrons utilizing your library. See ANSI 4.3.5.; ANSI 2.13, supra note 31.

48. *Opening Doors*, supra note 44, at 18; ANSI 4.3.1, supra note 31.

49. ANSI 4.3.2, supra note 31. "In existing lots, two regular parking spaces may be combined for two handicapped spaces with a common access aisle." *Opening Doors*, supra note 44, at 18.

50. ANSI 4.3.4, supra note 31. A diagram of a model parking area is set out at *Opening Doors*, supra note 44, at 19.

51. *Opening Doors*, supra note 44, at 19. Recessed ramps (cuts) are preferred to those which project into the roadway or parking area.

52. ANSI 5.1.3, 5.1.1, supra note 31.

53. ANSI 5.1.2, supra note 31. "Ramps should

be wide enough to allow use by ambulatory and nonambulatory people, as well as service deliveries, at the same time. Therefore most ramps should be a minimum of 4'4" and preferably 6'0" clear width to allow for two way traffic of varying types. If only sufficient space can be provided for a one way ramp, it should be a minimum of 2'8" clear width and perferably 3'0" wide. Winslow, "Access," 96.

54. ANSI 5.1.4, 5.1.5, 5.1.6, 5.1.7, supra note 31; *Opening Doors*, supra note 44, at 20 has illustrations.

55. *Opening Doors*, supra note 44, at 21.

56. ANSI 5.2.1, 5.2.2, supra note 31. An accessible entrance must be at the level which allows access to the elevators.

57. "Barrier Free," 8 *American Libraries* 303 (1977).

58. ANSI 5.3.1, supra note 31. "Where there are a series of swinging doors, a space of about 6'6" should be provided between each to prevent people from getting trapped." Winslow, "Access," 102. "If there are double doors, each single leaf must provide 32 inches clear width." *Opening Doors*, supra note 44, at 21.

59. ANSI 5.3.3, supra note 31.

60. Winslow, "Access," 102; *Opening Doors*, supra note 44, at 21.

61. *Opening Doors*, supra note 44, at 21.

62. See *Opening Doors*, supra note 44, at 21.

63. ANSI 5.9, supra note 31. Reachable height would be 48 inches from the floor. *Opening Doors*, supra note 44, at 23.

64. *Opening Doors*, supra note 44, at 24.

65. Ibid.; for more detail see ANSI 5.4, supra note 31.

66. ANSI 5.5.1, supra note 31.

67. *Opening Doors*, supra 44, at 22.

68. See "Barrier Free," 8 *American Libraries* 303 (1977).

69. Obviously, there is no such thing as the typical or average library. The typical library is used here in the sense that it is one not specifically designated to serve the blind or handicapped as, for example, the Library of Congress Division for the Blind and Physically Handicapped or the Alabama Regional Library for the Blind or Physically Handicapped. See "Barrier Free," 8 *American Libraries* 303, 304 (1977); Casey, "Library Service to the Handicapped and Institutionalized," 20 *Library Trends* 350 (1971).

70. There are very informative diagrams and drawings which depict the spatial requirements needed by persons in wheelchairs and those using other types of mobility aids in 4 Report No. 6, at 3 (1978); 4 Report No. 5, at 3 (1978); see ANSI 3.2, 3.4, supra note 31.

71. ANSI 3.3, supra note 31; 4 Report No. 6, at 3 (1978) has an excellent illustration of this.

72. Metcalf, "Book Stack Selection for the Library" in American Library Association, *Library Furniture and Equipment* 15, at 21 (1963).

73. Ibid.

74. 4 Report No. 5, at 3 (1978).

75. 4 Report No. 6, at 3 (1978).

76. ANSI 3.2, supra note 31, provides turning space requirements for a wheelchair.

77. ANSI 3.2.2, supra note 31.

78. ANSI 3.3.1, supra note 31.

79. ANSI 3.3.4, supra note 31.

80. ANSI 3.3.2, supra note 31.

81. ANSI 3.1(4), supra note 31.

82. Campbell. "HEW Furniture Systems," 2 *Disabled USA* 14, 15 (1979).

83. ANSI 5.6, supra note 31; *Opening Doors*, supra note 44, at 25–26.

84. Some mirrors, shelves and dispensers should be located no higher than 40 inches from the floor. ANSI 5.6.4, supra note 31.

85. ANSI 5.7, supra note 31.

86. The paper cup dispenser should be no higher than 40 inches, while 30 inches is the recommended height for a low fountain. *Opening Doors*, supra note 44, at 26.

87. ANSI 5.8.1, supra note 31.

88. ANSI 5.8.2, supra note 31.

89. Winslow, "Access," 100.

90. ANSI 5.10, supra note 31.

91. ANSI 5.12, supra note 31.

92. *Opening Doors*, supra note 44, at 27.

93. Winslow, "Access," 101.

94. ANSI 5.11, supra note 31.

95. Bowe, *Handicapping America*, 96.

96. See, e.g., Osman, "Barrier Free Architecture: Yesterday's Special Design Becomes Tomorrow's Standard," 63 *A.I.A. Journal* 40, 41 (1975); Schalter, "Removing the Hidden Barriers," 43, 45; "Interview with William Ripley: Barrier Free Design Specialist Discusses His Work," 3 *Amicus* 26, 28 (1978); Winslow, "Access," 104.

97. Bowe, *Handicapping America*, 97.

98. 45 C.F.R. § 84.23(a) (1978).

99. Bowe, *Handicapping America*, 96.

100. *Opening Doors*, supra note 44, at 16.

101. 43 Fed. Reg. 36,034 (1978).

102. "Helping the Handicapped without Crippling Institutions," *Time*, Dec. 5, 1977, at 34.

103. *Opening Doors*, supra note 44, at 16.

104. Milner, "Accessibility as a Matter of Course for Every Remodeling Project," 24 *Building Operating Management*, no. 9 (1977).

105. See generally 2 *U.S. Dept. of Health, Education, and Welfare, White House Conference on Handicapped Individuals: Final Report*, Part C, 91-92 (1978).

106. See *U.S. Dept. of Health, Education, and Welfare, Federal Assistance for Programs Serving the Handicapped* (1977); *Opening Doors*, supra note 44, at 12–13. The Architectural and Transportation Barriers Compliance Board, 330 C Street SW, Washington, D.C. 20201 will send at no charge the *Funding Guide for Removal of Architectural Barriers*.

107. 43 Fed. Reg. 36,035 (1978).

108. I.R.C. § 190. For state tax deductions see, e.g., Fla. Stat. § 193.623 (Supp. 1976); N.H. Rev. Stat. Ann. § 72.37-a (Supp. 1977); N.C. Gen. Stat. § 105–151.1 (Supp. 1977); Or Rev. Stat. §§ 316.066 & 316.067(h) (1977).

109. See *Opening Doors*, supra note 44, at 13; U.S. Dept. of Health, Education, and Welfare, *Federal Assistance for Programs Serving the Handicapped*, Appendix II, 311 (1977) for information on funding, fund raising and related resources.
110. Bednar, "Introduction," 2.
111. Bowe, *Handicapping America*, 24.
112. See U.S. Dept. of Health, Education, and Welfare, *The White House Conference on Handicapped Individuals: Summary Final Report* 34 (1978); Schalter, "Removing the Hidden Barriers," 43–45; Bednar, "Introduction," 2.
113. See Steinfeld, Duncan, and Cardell, "Toward a Responsive Environment: The Psychosocial Effects of Inaccessibility" in Bednar, *Barrier-Free Environments*, 8.
114. Ibid. at 9; see also Mays, "Attitudes toward the Handicapped: The Promise," in *Library Services for the Adult Handicapped* (L. Whalen and J. Miller, eds., 1978).
115. See Steinfeld, Duncan, and Cardell, "Toward a Responsive Environment," 9-10.
116. Winslow, "Access," 102.
117. Bowe, *Handicapping America*, 121.
118. Ibid., at ix.
119. Ibid., at 119.
120. Olshansky, "The Albert Schweitzer Syndrome," 2 *Disabled USA* 2 (1978).
121. Bowe, *Handicapping America*, 131–132.
122. U.S. Dept. of Health, Education, and Welfare, *The White House Conference on Handicapped Individuals: Summary Final Report* 38–39 (1978); Van Hoven, "Pioneering N.J. Program Aids Troubled Patrons," 104 *Library Journal* 789 (1979).
123. 2 U.S. Dept. of Health, Education, and Welfare, *The White House Conference on Handicapped Individuals: Final Report*, Part C, 65–70 (1978).
124. *Opening Doors*, supra note 44, at 14.
125. Ibid., 14–15. These pages contain a list, including addresses, of many of these agencies.
126. Ibid., at 16.
127. See, e.g., *Disabled USA*; *Amicus*; *In the Mainstream*; *Rehabilitation Literature*.
128. See, e.g., U.S. Dept. of Health, Education, and Welfare, *Selected Federal Publications Concerning the Handicapped* (1978); Architectural and Transportation Barriers Compliance Board, *Resource Guide to Literature on Barrier-Free Environments with Selected Annotations* (1977).
129. See, e.g., *Handicapped Requirements Handbook* (Fed. Prog. Advisory Serv.), 1978. This service includes a self-evaluation and checklist plus a bibliography; *Education for the Handicapped Law Report* (CCR) 1978.
130. See 2 U.S. Dept. of Health, Education, and Welfare, *The White House Conference on Handicapped Individuals: Final Report*, Part C, 91 (1978).
131. Bowe, *Handicapping America*, 191; Research and Training Center in Mental Retardation, Texas Tech Univ., *Advocacy Systems for the Developmentally Disabled* (G. Bensburg and C. Rude, eds., 1976).

Sensory Wall Brings Learning

GERALDINE M. MATTHEWS

One of the most complicated developmental achievements any child must master is sensory integration. During the critical early years of maturation a great deal of a child's time is spent exploring personal space through the process of feeling and touching, becoming aware of and attending to sound, identifying various odors, making visual judgments and experiencing tastes. In addition to these separate sensory explorations, an overall integrative growth process is ongoing within the child. In this second stage, sounds and visual images are generalized, sensations are gradually being associated with one another and perceptual motor skills become more refined and precise as the child increasingly examines expanding horizons.

For the mentally retarded child these processes are not easily accomplished. They must be patiently and imaginatively taught. And even when the concepts and cause-effect relationships are mastered, it is frequently necessary also to teach generalization in order to make the usable insights dependable and of practical value.

One means that provides the residents at

"Sensory Wall Brings Learning," by Geraldine M. Matthews, *Wisconsin Library Bulletin* 1978 (July–August): 181–82. Reprinted by permission of the *Wisconsin Library Bulletin*.

Central Wisconsin Center for the Developmentally Disabled such sensory experiences is a sensory wall designed for the residents' library. The materials for the wall, which is seven by sixteen feet, were purchased with Library Services and Construction Act Title I funds. The selection of experiences was the result of professional input from a team of specialists representing a variety of disciplines. While visually attractive, the wall is designed to teach all of the children, including a visually and auditorily impaired group, sensory discrimination skills.

From a distance, the wall appears to be a textured mural, and child and adult alike are drawn to it. The recessed tube lighting follows the design cut from carpeting, and the entire area features the yellow, green, orange, and gold colors in the room. Attracted by the design and unusual lighting, almost everyone's first impulse is to touch the various textures of carpeting and feel the cool tubing of the lights. After this initial experience, it is virtually impossible not to start exploring the activities built into the wall itself. The basic need to explore, especially at this sensory input stage, is apparently so strong that a handicapping condition has nothing to do with the instinct to try out the sensory experiences. However, for the residents at Central Wisconsin Center the wall features a combination of items designed to produce basic stimuli in a manner that will not be overwhelming or frightening.

Among the items selected for the wall are large metal mirrors, brushes fastened with the bristles facing out, a bellows, kinetic lights of various colors that are turned on with a knob, a door bell, music box, door knocker, a large linked chain, an electric drier for warm air, a pillow, buzzers, doors that open with latches, door knobs that turn, and slide systems. While these and other items are fastened securely, they can and will be changed as the needs of the residents change or as new ideas are contributed by visitors and staff.

The overall purpose of the sensory wall is to help enhance perceptual, motor, and sensory skills. This goal is appropriate and interesting to all children whether they have major sensory/cognitive deficits or not. In fact, the experiences such a wall provides are valuable, with suitable adaptations, for any child.

If the idea is to be carried out in a community school or public library situation, the wall idea should include simple stimuli for young children and more complex processes for the older child. Examples of such fairly complex tasks would include sandpaper matching, coin identification, or shape matching by reaching into a "hole" or blind area. Older children might enjoy the challenge of an electric maze that buzzes when a stylus touches the side of the path or a sound selection system. As long as the activities on the wall serve to improve sensory, motor or perceptual skills, the actual design can be highly flexible.

Pearl S. Buck and G. T. Zarfoss wrote about the mentally retarded in *The Gifts They Bring* (Day, 1965). Their message was that handicapped individuals, through an intense study of their condition by researchers, contribute to the body of knowledge that permits a clearer understanding of general human physiological and psychological functioning. The relationship of the role of the library programs in Wisconsin developmental disability residential facilities to the responsibilities of general school and public libraries of the state constitutes a parallel situation. Because the job of the facility library staff is to understand the needs of individuals when those needs are extraordinary, the principles, innovations and programs developed in the facilities contribute directly to helping the individuals working in libraries in the community plan services for their general and special publics. The organization of the concepts that went into the development of the sensory wall is just one example of the contributions the developmentally disabled have made to unimpaired fellow citizens.

Further information on the design construction and cost of a sensory wall is available free of charge. For carpentry and electrical instructions write or call: Library Information Center, Central Wisconsin Center for the Developmentally Disabled, 317 Knutson Drive, Madison 53704.

Users Come First in Design

PHILIP M. BENNETT

Physiological Considerations

The structuring of any environment is dependent on information obtained by identifying user needs and program requirements. However, before user needs can be considered, we must go back even further. We must consider the human body's response to the environment.

The environments of sound, space, light, and heat must be constructed to fit not only the uses for which the facility is being designed, but also the human form, the human physiology, and the human sensory receptors which carry the effects of the environment into the operations of the brain.

When the design is to facilitate communications and learning, then it should stimulate the types of human behavior needed to carry out the learning task. Energy sources and intensities must be adjusted to this end. Patterns of form, depth, contrast, color, sound, and heat must provide the most conducive environment. For any specific task, there are specific patterns most appropriate. Movement within these patterns, furthermore, must be guided into the spatial channels that will stimulate all the human senses for optimum learning and understanding.

If brightnesses are uncontrolled, noise levels are unacceptable, or if the environment is in some other way maladjusted to the human system, then learning will be restricted. The age group of users, for example, can be a critical consideration. If libraries for primary school children were furnished with tables and desks inappropriate to their body dimensions and growth patterns, the effect on their learning, and even their health, would be negative.

The following subjects will identify some of the conditions which are critical to understanding how a child or adult interprets the environment in which he or she is working.

Visual Response to the Environment

Through the eye, the brain responds to the distribution, quality, and color of light. Studies reveal, for example, that different behavior patterns result from exposure to different colors. Light which lacks certain bands of the spectrum can affect visual accommodation—how the eyes focus, adjust for distance, adjust for color, and so forth. Control of light is a principal function in library planning. The dominating influences on visual acuity are (1) the time required to see an object, (2) the amount of illumination present, (3) brightness contrast, (4) brightness ratios, (5) movement of objects or the viewer, and (6) glare.

Surfaces should be evenly illuminated. As for the light reflected surface, contrast between the visual task and the immediate surrounding surface should not exceed 3:1. Contrast between the task and the surrounding room should be larger, but no more than 7:1. With too large a contrast the eye will be distracted, tending to fix on the border between bright and dim.

Body posture must be considered in selection of furniture and structuring of surfaces (see fig. 1). The best working surface for reading and writing is 20 degrees off the horizontal, a plane perpendicular to the line of sight and allowing material to be viewed without distortion. Take a paper and hold it at an angle comfortable for reading, with the page perpendicular to the line of sight, and you will see that the page is at 20 degrees. Force a child to work on a horizontal surface and you force him to distort his body and his visual accommodation.

Fixed-position seating also causes stress through postural changes which in time can actually damage vision. According to environmental studies, poor lighting and seating can be blamed for the average child's considerable increase in physical disabilities during his school years. Approximately 18–20 percent of students were found to enter

---

"Users Come First in Design," by Philip M. Bennett, *Wisconsin Library Bulletin* 1978 (March–April): 51–58. Reprinted by permission of the *Wisconsin Library Bulletin*.

26 The Physical Environment

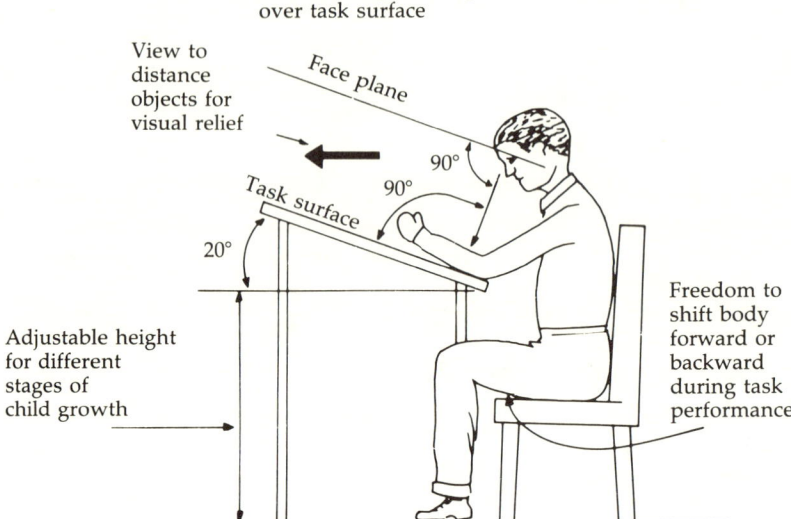

Fig. 1. Reading task support

first grade with certain disabilities. By sixth grade this number had grown. Astigmatism is one of these disabilities. . . .

A working environment should offer both near and far vision. To offset visual fatigue and blur, the user must be able to look up from a near two-dimensional task to a more distant view that will relieve the eyes. For a task an arm's length away, the compensating far view should be at least three meters. For tough visual tasks of extended duration, the visual escape should be at least six meters.

Chromatic aberration of vision occurs because the lens of the eye has different focal lengths for different colors. To focus colors of long wavelength ("warm colors," such as red) on the retina, the lens must tense up. For colors of short wavelength ("cool colors," such as blue) it must relax. Warm colors thus seem nearer than they actually are, which stimulates greater alertness and attention. Reactions are quicker and muscle tone and blood pressure are higher. Cool colors seem more distant and are relaxing. Cool colors are more easily focused by the nearsighted eye (see fig. 2), warm colors by the farsighted eye (see fig. 3). Children below about six years of age tend to be farsighted, and work better among warm colors.

Viewed from 20 feet away, red and blue require a difference in focus equivalent to two and one-half feet. To view magenta, a mixture of red and blue, the eye must alternate its focus rapidly. Magenta, therefore, appears to vibrate, and has a stimulating effect. However, in this case oscillation is much too extreme and can fatigue the eye. It should not be used in the immediate task area.

Pure colors provide no such stimulating vibration, but fatigue the eye by requiring it to stay on one level of accommodation. Blue and yellow fatigue the eye more than red because they cover more of the retina. Pure colors that are highly reflective—bright colors—are especially taxing, and since they attract the eye, can interfere with work if used within the visual field of the task. Before using bright or pure colors, the following should be evaluated: (1) the frequency with which the surface is viewed, (2) the percentage of time in which it is viewed, (3) location of the surface relative to the work area.

Mixtures of color pastels, or desaturated colors, are desirable for work areas because they are less distracting and contain many wavelengths; they are quiet but stimulating on many levels. IQ (intelligence) tests have shown that people think less logically in bright color surroundings. Pastel mixtures have another effect; their many wavelengths provide more information for depth perception.

Dark pure colors should be avoided because they shrink space and foster an aura of monotony. White should be limited in the near task environment, otherwise people

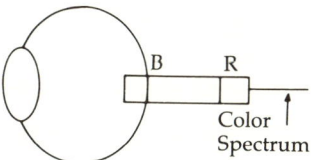

Fig. 2. Color vision considerations, nearsighted person. For a nearsighted person, the blue of color spectrum falls near point of focus thus reducing the required amount of accommodation needed to focus distant objects sharply on the retina. As a result, a nearsighted person will prefer cool colors because they require less accommodation in focusing.

must strain to keep their focus and may grow nearsighted. As stated previously, high brightness contrast, especially between black and white, should be avoided in critical task areas.

Two types of color surroundings should be developed in the library: the immediate task surroundings and the overall library surroundings. Immediately around the task, colors should be slightly warm or in the middle of the spectrum. In the general surroundings, colors should be slightly cool. The immediate task area thus draws attention and stimulates thought processes, while the surroundings are minimally distractive. Cool colors are particularly needed as background relief in library areas where windows are not placed to provide external vistas and good natural lighting.

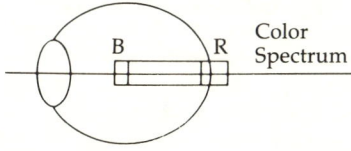

Fig. 3. Farsighted persons. For a farsighted person, the red of color spectrum falls near point of focus thus reducing the required amount of accommodation needed to focus near objects sharply on the retina. As a result, a farsighted person will prefer warm colors because they require less accommodation in focusing.

Lighting should also supply wavelengths in appropriate color temperatures when combined with surface colors. When the radiant energy emerging from light sources and reflecting from surrounding surfaces is long in wavelength, the environment is said to be of low color temperature. Such an environment makes it possible to view near objects with greater ease. Activity within 16 inches of the task, such as in study carrels, should have light at 2850 degrees Kelvin color temperature, light in the moderately warm range where accommodation is induced in the eye and better color judgments and a wider range of color recognition are possible. This temperature can be supplied by an incandescent bulb surrounded by the proper surface colors.

When the radiant energy from light sources and surface colors is in the short wavelength range, the color temperature will be high, and make it easier for the eye to view infinity. The general surroundings should have a higher color temperature, of about 3200 degrees, which can be supplied by flurorescent lighting throughout the general task area (see fig. 4).

A balanced light environment, then, would have fluorescent lighting for general surroundings and incandescent lighting for immediate task areas. This combination would develop an environmental surrounding that could support both reading and eye relaxation during task performance.

Thermal Response to the Environment

The body must maintain a heat balance in order to optimize learning and task performance. Research has shown that people work better in a supportive thermal environment. Thermal design criteria include: (1) orientation of space, (2) dimensions of space, (3) lighting, natural and artificial, (4) materials, (5) colors.

Heat departs the body through radiation, evaporation, and conduction. Radiation accounts for 60 percent of the body's heat loss, evaporation 22 percent, conduction to the air 12 percent and conduction to materials 3 percent. When the surroundings are cooler than body temperature there will be a net flow of heat out of the body. Since the body produces heat, some level of heat loss is desirable to keep equilibrium. Temperature gradients between surroundings and the body must be appropriate to the heat flows required. If surrounding walls and floors are too hot, radiant heat flow into the body will be too great.

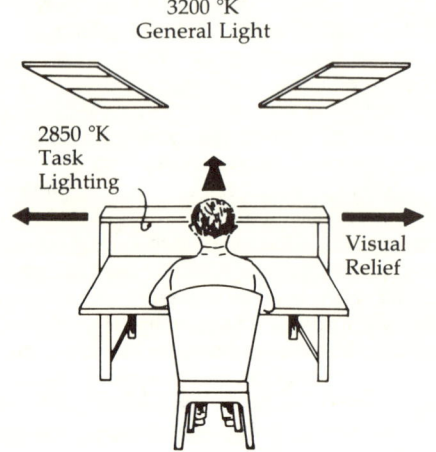

Fig. 4. Lighting placement and color temperature. 15 times more light is available with luminaires placed parallel to the line of sight, and the occurrence of veiling reflections is greatly reduced.

Through radiant heat loss the body will feel cold when surrounded by walls and floors that are too cold, and feel colder in a north-facing room than in one facing south.

The human body is generally more heat sensitive in the upper half. Therefore, complete thermal uniformity in a room is not desirable. The air at the shoulders should be three or four degrees warmer than at the feet. A heated floor can make users feel sleepy.

Age and sex are important. Adults usually require higher temperatures than children. Where teachers are comfortable, the children may be too hot. . . .

For sedentary activities in the library, ideal temperature is between 68 and 72 degrees, shifting upward in summer and down in winter. The value of air conditioning is in reducing fatigue and tension, making the user more agreeable and stimulating concentration. Air conditioning also controls humidity, this control being an important function. The body responds to higher humidity as though it were a temperature increase. . . . Humidity of about 50 percent reduces electrostatic charge in carpets.

The effects of high temperature are magnified when the air is bad. Breathing low quality air, a child lacks interest, experiences stress and is restless in his work. Adequate circulation insures good air in the library by diluting odors, removing dust, pollens, and airborne particles, controlling the amount of harmful bacteria, maintaining sufficient air movement, limiting carbon dioxide buildup, and supplying oxygen.

Auditory Response to the Environment

We live in an environment of many different sounds. Even the movement of air molecules produces sound. Only the louder sounds do we detect over the background. If a sound is unwanted, it is considered noise.

The library must be designed to control sound distribution and noise levels in a manner that will optimize environmental conditions for each task. Loud noise interferes with concentration, even to the point of disrupting visual concentration, yet complete quiet can be equally distracting and can create a sense of fear. To insure a desirable level of background sound, each library task must be analyzed before structuring its surroundings. Certain areas will have to be open to direct communication; others will have to allow only the low background sound needed for concentration.

Research shows that 30 decibels of white sound (a mixture of all frequencies) is an optimum background for study. It should, however, be nondirectional.

Our hearing is binaural—the brain has a different input from each ear. Unbalanced background sound is a distraction. The body tends to align itself to the center of the most meaningful information, and if it cannot, there will be a resulting loss of concentration. Library design should allow freedom to realign the body so that aural, visual and thermal stimuli are most uniformly distributed to the body's receptors.

Noise problems can be broken into three parts: (1) source, (2) receiver, and (3) path. The human voice is a directional energy source. Its path should be analyzed and planned for. Areas requiring the most silence can be identified and isolated from sound generating areas. Isolation can be achieved by increasing distance from the source and by use of sound-absorbing materials.

Six design considerations should be favored in sound control: (1) sound travels through any elastic medium (one in which molecules move freely, like gas, fluid metal, wood, etc.); (2) it travels more readily through light, porous materials; (3) sound absorbent materials can reduce noise within a room but do not keep it from passing through walls, floor or ceiling; (4) sound passes through even very tiny openings; (5) most building materials, especially hard and dense ones, transmit vibrations readily; (6) sound control properties of a construction depend on (a) its mass and (b) whether it is limp or elastic. The library will be noisy, for example, if machinery or structural elements with hard, reflective surfaces are left exposed.

To control sound and noise in the library, the designer must analyze the proper size and configurations of task and activity areas, determining appropriate materials and organizing screens, barriers, walls and rooms for optimum effect.

The task analyses must determine whether there is a need for special quiet areas or speech areas, pockets of private or personal space. Intense reading research demands a high degree of separation, visually as well as acoustically, from activities which produce more sound or require significant movement. For lectures or group discussions an enclosed space is recommended. Surfaces in activity areas must be oriented to reflect or absorb sound according to the learning activity.

Room size is important. Smaller rooms make for easier control. It is critical that room finishes be acoustically absorbent to suppress reverberation. Walls and ceilings are most important; floors and ceilings also cause problems. Walls influence sound by their position, shape and composition. Wall arrangements that tend to focus sound into task areas should be avoided. The heavier and more airtight the wall, the more formidable a barrier it is to sound transmission. Whether walls should be full height, or leave a space below the ceiling, depends on the isolation required.

Tactile Response to the Environment

Once something is discovered by sight or sound, the next reaction is to touch it. Tactile mechanisms enhance the ability to understand forms, space and textures, providing an added dimension through which we can understand the environment.

Sensory inputs to the brain vary from individual to individual. Some perceive the environment primarily through vision while others rely more on kinesthetic, auditory, and tactile responses. Most people perceive the environment through a healthy combination of these inputs. In other words, the environment must contain many different sensory elements to provide all individuals with exciting and new information. A child that is exposed to such variety will be a much better educated individual. A child deprived of such variety will be less well educated and less well developed in his ability to experience new forms.

Physiological Stimuli as Library Learning Tools

In the design and planning of the library environment, we must try to understand how to make the facility as supportive as possible of early growth and development. Here are a few guidelines.

1. Graphic or sculptural displays of key points in stories and texts develop a child's interest. 2. Scientific processes can be demonstrated with instruments or objects that can be touched or examined, smelled, or listened to. 3. Visual and tactile displays of modern technology—perhaps cross-section samples of large power cables with a discussion of the tremendous energy they convey—stimulate learning and keep the child up to date. 4. Display of projects from the art department can be tied in with ideas being studied in the classroom. 5. Living displays such as aquariums, terrariums, and house plants, can make for stimulating visual environment. Plant life, full of interesting shadows and textures, changes each day; fish or hamsters move and react to their surroundings. All living things have to be cared for to some extent, requiring physical involvement on many levels. 6. Geography studies should be stimulated by raised maps, overlays, different colored acetates, and other graphic aids. 7. Hobby display centers may be helpful. Properly presented, the hobby experience of one child can be stimulating to another.

Interesting activity areas—science, geography, biology, hobbies, etc.—should be developed through a mutually reinforcing association of physiological stimuli and related literature. Maps of and displays about or from Russia stimulate the child to read about Russia, just as reading about Russia stimulates greater interest in and appreciation of the maps and displays.

The creative librarian, through close observation, can stimulate and develop many modes of physiological response to the world. The child will respond with greater interest, and come back for further exploration into the areas where his interest has been ignited.

Psychological and Sociological Considerations in Design

Human beings are more alike physiologically than psychologically. The library environment should be structured to satisfy physiological needs above all, but secondary consideration should be given to psychological flexibility to accommodate sociological and psychological differences, and allow users to alter activity patterns at whim. Children and adults must be able to achieve rapport with their surroundings and seek out those elements they require.

Children tend to accept elements, forms, and information with which they have become familiar or which they have experienced in the past. The library should make use of this fact to gain the child's acceptance for the new elements that spark investigation, inquiry, and exploration.

Through the observation of children we can begin to understand better the special needs for personal as well as social space. Personal space is the space immediately surrounding the individual, an intrusion into which causes stress and behavioral changes. Studies show that personal space needs can be quite disparate for different cultures. Some mental tasks require specific levels of concentration and spatial privacy. If these features are not provided for, the child will prefer not to participate in certain types of activities. In some cases screens must be set up to achieve spatial and visual separation.

Cultural differences also affect color preference. For a particular culture, research suggests, certain colors should not be used or should be used sparingly so as not to arouse negative attitudes or emotions.

Obviously, behavior and individual performance can vary greatly in the library and educational environment. We must be careful not to prejudge a situation before studying it. Child behavior in an educational setting might be shaped by: (1) past experiences, (2) attitudinal conditioning, (3) family environments, (4) individual preferences, (5) cultural backgrounds, (6) community attitudes, (7) geographic impact. In certain communities and under certain conditions some or all of these forces may show up in the child's behavior and performance. Therefore, leaders in the educational environment must be on the alert to make appropriate minor adjustments, changing direction in programming or environment to elicit a positive response. This is where flexibility in design of the education environment will help. Through an effective observation and analysis program, the librarian can develop a monitoring system which will help maintain a creative and stimulating learning environment.

Hidden Barriers

SUZANNE STEPHENS

"Barrier-free" architecture is not merely a matter of ramps, curb cuts, and handrails. Its success will depend on how it performs on the mental level as much as the mobile level. With this group of users, perception and reception of a building's formal properties will tend to be judged on more subjective or emotional grounds than allowed those who can take their physical functioning for granted.

The messages a building conveys to its users involve more than a clarification of purpose or ease of access; they implicitly convey a society's attitude toward the handicapped and how the handicapped should in turn view themselves. It should come as little surprise to architects then that current theoretical approaches to architecture, such as analyzing the building as a system of signs, bears a strong relationship to barrier-free design. These approaches implicitly recognize that architecture communicates on more than a functional level; the nature of that communication becomes meaningful due to the social, psychological, and physiological factors affecting individual perception.

It is well known in the field of psychology that a person's self-image depends greatly on interaction with others and with the environment. As Edward Steinfeld, James Duncan, and Paul Cardell point out in *Barrier-Free Environments* (Dowden, Hutchinson and Ross, Inc., 1977, Michael Bednar, ed.) design, space management, social organization, and interaction are all factors that will impinge subtly and not so subtly on the development of a strong sense of worth.

Necessary to a handicapped person's self-image is the ability to manipulate the environment, not just orient oneself to it. Because of the frustration the disabled commonly encounter in their attempts to explore the world, they may not try to adapt. Their sense of dependency increases; self-worth diminishes.

"Hidden Barriers," by Suzanne Stephens. Reprinted from the April 1978 issue of *Progressive Architecture*, copyright 1978, Reinhold Publishing.

Researching the Variables

The research in the area of social and psychological aspects of barrier-free design has concentrated on the mentally handicapped and emotionally disturbed. Here the problems of perceiving the environment are the most acute; here the perceptions of a confusing setting are brought into sharpest relief. The lessons gleaned from work in this area, however, not only inform the design efforts of architects creating environments for the mentally retarded and emotionally disturbed, but the physically disabled, elderly—and the rest of us.

As architects working within this field are aware, the philosophy of "normalization" underlies current practices in therapy for the mentally retarded. The design attitude behind normalization shares certain characteristics with the more general architectural attitudes behind "post-modernism." While normalization relates to a whole system of therapeutic services, in design terms it seeks to overcome the alienating effects of the institutional environment much the same way that "post-modern" architectural principles seek to overcome the dehumanizing effects of modern architecture. In many cases they are synonymous. In terms of general goals, normalization encourages a "deviant" person to feel normal, to provoke an according shift in behavioral responses. Architecture, mirror of social and psychologically based attitudes and values, becomes one instrument for effecting this change in self-perception.

According to psychologist Wolf Wolfensberger in *Barrier-Free Environments*, for example, environments that are indestructible, with heavy-duty immovable furniture, high ceilings, recessed damageproof light fixtures and wired glass are subliminal signs that the user is regarded as somewhat subhuman, a person with an animal mentality who needs supervision, not aesthetics. On a different tack, a clinical atmosphere of a service facility for the handicapped may reinforce the notion that they are diseased. As Wolfensberger observes, the ambiance and arrangement of services in the "clinic" type atmosphere seem to reassure one that a cure is being pursued at the same time suggesting that no cure is possible.

Similarly, handicapped people have long been viewed as objects of ridicule, and, in fact, the deformed and retarded were used to amuse the court during medieval times. Thus when service facilities for the handicapped incorporate clown, circus, and jester motifs into their decor, a sort of cultural atavism seems implicit in these efforts.

Environments may also be designed to be overladen with paternalistic signs, experts in this area commonly agree. Ramps at every turn and overemphatic graphics are only some of the elements that scream "this is a safe environment for the handicapped," reminds architect Clark Neuringer. This kind of architectural treatment, he maintains, further removes the handicapped physically and psychologically from the mainstream of interaction.

More pernicious perhaps is designing for the disabled as if they were children. Here Wolfensberger objects to environments for the retarded in which decorative motifs constantly reinforce this notion through overuse of pastel or bright colors, childlike drawings and murals, or holiday ornaments left up all year-round.

Thresholds of Awareness

Of the several defining features of buildings used by the handicapped, location is one of the most prevalent modes of communicating an attitude of society or the institution toward the disabled. Often, service facilities for "devalued" people, Wolfensberger observes, are placed near other devalued environments, such as cemeteries, garbage dumps, railroad tracks. Sometimes the isolation of the facility on a hill, in a rural area or on top of a high-rise, serves to underscore the association of the disabled with say, a colony of lepers.

The exterior design of the facility provides yet another level of subconsciously read associations—the building that looks like a warehouse is a too obvious case in point. "Recycled" buildings still giving off signs of their previous functions—signs that may conflict with or create ambiguities with the present role of the buildings—represent more subtle examples of this phenomenon. This kind of effect can be psychologically discouraging as well as disorienting to someone who needs to be able to read the environmental cues well.

The building should be psychologically as well as physically accessible for those who must expend a lot of their time and energy approaching the facility. General opinion often holds that accessibility for those entering and using the building can be reinforced and encouraged through an ordering of architectural elements that is identifiable and familiar—that triggers associations with other buildings for similar purposes. Ambiguity has little place. But this conclusion does not mean that the building need resort to an abundance of graphic signs to tell visitors how to enter and where to go once inside, or that the architecture has to be flatfootedly unimaginative or aggressive in its design.

Wolfensberger warns against crude gestures toward ease of access, citing the example of a home converted into a service facility. While it blends with the surrounding residential neighborhood, an ugly, obtrusive ramp slammed against the side of the building or the fire alarm appended to the front announces that something "not normal" is occurring there.

The Signs of Internal Space

The interior domain is generally viewed as most critical in conveying psychological messages to its users on a number of symbolic levels that can help or hinder them in developing and sustaining social identities. Wolfensberger feels particularly strongly that the interior design of the building in which handicapped people will be the prime users should be "culturally appropriate" as well as "age appropriate." A vocational center designed as a typical industrial environment may be appropriate in a general sense. But it may be *too* realistic for occupants who seek to bolster individual identities in a setting that reinforces the notion they are but cogs in a machine. Expression of purpose is one thing; expression of the user's role within that scheme of things adds another dimension.

Homelike settings have been advocated by psychiatrists for the treatment of the mentally retarded where lamps, chairs, carpeting, and plants in small-scale spaces would replace settings with hard surfaces, somber color schemes, industrial blinds, heavy-duty furnishings, long anonymous corridors, dormitory-style living spaces, and so on. But it does matter how it is done. A homelike setting that looks like a child's nursery, Wolfensberger might add, communicates an attitude towards its users that can be debilitating to the fragilely formed sense of self.

Built-in furnishings provide another case in point. A number of experts argue that built-in furnishings are not flexible, personally adaptable or conventionally "homelike." But again it's not so much what you do, but the way that you do it. Built-in furnishings need not be off-limits but they should allow for individual expression and privacy.

In sum, what Wolfensberger and others are promoting is the understanding of the ways a building is read by its users in terms of *their own experience*. The architect legitimately views the building from his or her own vantage point (including where it stands in relation to other architectural oeuvres). The client who commissions the building may see it from his or hers—how the building expresses the program, aids in the distribution of services, allows ease of maintenance. Meanwhile the disabled user may perceive the same building as incomprehensible in terms of its implied functions, intimidating in terms of his or her lack of familiarity with its formal devices, or alienating because of its size or institutional easy-to-clean surfaces. *Or* he or she may subconsciously register the building as condescending because its design elements overstate the solution to the problems they address; cloying because the architectural motifs are aimed at a group with which he or she does not want to be associated, or even banal, because the gestalt is too readily available to permit the adventure of individual adaptation.

Becoming What You Behold

Most of us think ourselves immune to handicaps. Yet most of us someday will be elderly—if we live so long. And the problem is, we may. Advances in medicine are making it possible for more of us to live longer with and without severe handicaps. Gerontologist Leon Pastalan speculates that by 2000, 30 million Americans will be over 65; right now the figure is 22 million, or one in every ten.

But just because we live longer doesn't mean we'll be out jogging every morning, turning out architecture in the afternoon, or writing treatises by night. If a good many of us aren't rolling around in wheelchairs, tottering about on canes and crutches, trying to remember what day it is (though we can't forget all the things we did on a day way back in '78), if we can avoid all that, we will still probably be afflicted by one thing very common to the elderly: loss of sensory perception. The physiological obstacles to perceiving the environment will greatly influence our social and psychological experience of it.

Because of sensory impairment and the loss of visual, tactile, aural levels of perception, the environment will be increasingly confusing and frustrating. Needless to say, the long corridor seems to extend to infinity for someone who can't see the end, or has trouble distinguishing the door to his or her destination. Pastalan, who is Director of Research for the Institute of Gerontology at the University of Michigan, finds age-related changes that occur to the human eye (important since 85 percent of the environmental information is visual) affect both acuity and opacity of the lens.

The visual acuity of the eye of course influences how we perceive objects at a distance. The opacity of the lens, however, determines the way light is transmitted, affecting perception of colors and textures. For example, Pastalan finds that the elderly see colors almost 20 percent less keenly than those with normal vision; particularly in the cold end of the spectrum. Colors too often blend, and closely related textures can't be differentiated.

Glare is a major visual difficulty with the elderly. But Pastalan warns against the common tendency to confuse glare with light level. The light level must be increased as the elderly get older and glare reduced. If a south-facing room is filled with natural light bouncing off shiny white surfaces, the glare of course will be intense, drawing the shades, however, will not solve the problem of needed light. Pastalan argues for balanced lighting between the natural and the artificial, the direct and indirect. Fluorescent lighting may in many cases be inappropriate for a homelike setting, but in a clothing store, for example, it does help in distinguishing blues and greens.

Aural considerations, of course, must not be forgotten. Again Pastalan points out, sound is not the problem—noise is. The elderly, in particular, have trouble distinguishing meaningful sounds. The background hum of heating and ventilating and air-conditioning systems, easy for younger people to adapt to, along with television noises, children yelling, etc., need to be modified for the elderly who cannot differentiate between meaningful sounds. On the other hand, living in a world of silence would be psychologically harmful. (Sounds and textures assume different and even greater significance for the blind, a topic which there is not sufficient space to discuss fully here.)

To try to aid designers in understanding how the elderly perceive the environment through their senses, Pastalan has developed an "empathic model." Using already collected data on the opacity of the lens, the increased rigidity of the middle ear, diminished tactile and olfactory sensitivity, he has been able to simulate the experience through the use of mechanical appliances. The basic simulation is restricted to normal sensory losses for people about in their late seventies.

But the ramifications are immense. Pastalan finds that an environment should make use of redundant cuing to compensate for lessened sensory perception—through aural, visual, and tactile stimuli that are all associated with a particular setting. Spaces also need to be organized with a certain amount of predictability. Again ambiguity has little place in the world of the elderly. As Pastalan adds "the usual subtle and complex architectural statements are not only largely unappreciated but are dysfunctional as well." For example, he explains, the elderly tend to bump into walls that are, say, light green in a room with blue-green carpeting owning to faulty perception of depth, colors, textures, and even contours.

This kind of research briefly discussed in these pages obviously presents a challenge to architects already designing for the disabled. No doubt that challenge will grow as the population of the handicapped and elderly increases. Yet as gerontologist M. Powell Lawton wrote in a recent issue of *Journal of Architectural Education* "the goal of environment design is to create situations that are modestly demanding on an individual without being excessively demanding." This goal, which affects old, young, physically impaired, and physically active people suggests that *balance* is the key word. The environment still must be challenging enough to be interesting, to engage the attention and participation of the occupant in adapting to it, trying to manipulate it, interacting with it. But it shouldn't be too disorienting, too aggressive, too demanding. The trick is to determine where to draw the line, how to design an environment in which there are no hidden barriers to its appreciation, but hidden delights, hidden richness, hidden (and healthy) meanings.

2
Materials Selection

The collection is the heart of the library. It determines what information can be transmitted, who will have access to it, and how communication will take place. There is no more critical function than that performed by the selector who chooses materials to meet both the immediate and anticipated needs of a particular clientele who need data presented in an array of formats.

Expanding collections to make them accessible and responsive to the needs of exceptional patrons does not, indeed *must* not, change the character or the mandate of the library. Selection of materials for this group does, however, require examining potential purchases using different criteria and seeking advice and guidance from nontraditional resources.

In choosing materials for the library collection, consideration is routinely given to content, format, and structural elements. When planning for patrons with special needs, these elements are still critical, but the various components may have to be given differing weights or judged by different standards.

When the content is evaluated, the substance of the message and the manner, style, and complexity of the delivery must all be considered. Occasionally, some traditionally desirable values may have to be jettisoned in the selection process. For example, most young readers require a strong correlation between the level of their maturation and the difficulty of their books. Youngsters with language deficiencies, however, may be attracted to subjects similar to those of their chronological age peers, but these readers may need to have that information expressed in simpler terms. Highly able youth, on the other hand, may be chronologically on a par with their classmates, but capable of assimilating sophisticated, complex data with ease and pleasure. The relationship of age and difficulty of materials is reversed for these two groups but, without accommodation to their vastly differing needs, neither will find satisfaction in their attempts to use the collection.

Those children for whom the schools have designated an Instructional Educational Plan (IEP) will have precisely prescribed academic goals set down in writing. Their programs will require them to obtain and integrate specified information, develop and practice skills, and synthesize and apply what they have learned.

Materials that will permit and promote achievement of these objectives and that will, moreover, add pleasure to the learning process must be available in school and public libraries.

The most obvious format concerns relate to the channels through which information is best communicated; therefore, the provision of comprehensive basic holdings in a wide variety of media is critical. Further, within each medium, other considerations must be made. In choosing trade books for readers with vision disorders, print size and style, amount of leading, paper color and finish, and the presence of well-delineated images in illustrations are all salient factors. When selecting audiotapes, records, or other media with sound components, the presence of background music or multiple sound effects may interfere with comprehension. Tone, balance, clarity, and pacing are all elements that should be assessed because, individually or in combination, they could reduce or negate utility for listeners with sensory deficits.

Some patrons with motor or neurological impairments will experience difficulty using materials that only require an ordinary amount of dexterity. When software is selected, products embodying the most fully automated mode may be essential. Since independence is almost always a prime goal for these individuals, this factor should never be overlooked. For others, purely idiosyncratic preferences or the availability of certain hardware may make one mode preferable to another.

Sturdy, well-made products are critical attributes in evaluating potential purchases. Fragile, poorly bound books or badly constructed or packaged media may not survive the hard use that can be anticipated from some borrowers. Conversely, in some situations, generally less durable materials might actually be preferred. For example, the lighter weight of paperbacks and their easier portability make them the medium of choice under certain circumstances. Increased production costs have caused some publishers to economize in ways that preclude or severely reduce the utility of their materials for users with impairments. Some new books currently on the market are printed on paper so transparent that images bleed through from the reverse side. Although this may be a mere annoyance to some readers, to others with reduced visual acuity or perceptual disorders, such books will be totally useless. Blind persons hoping to have access to those titles through the Kurzweil machine will be frustrated since such visual interference may sabotage the ability of the equipment to interpret the print symbols.

Librarians looking at salient features may find numerous items already on their shelves which satisfy the necessary criteria. Many suitable new purchases can readily be made from standard trade catalogs. Some patrons, however, need materials that are expressly designed for persons with their impairments. If this user population is numerically small and the necessary types of materials are disability-specific, the library's ability to supply adequate materials may be limited. It will then be necessary to identify agencies providing resources with which to augment the basic, in-house collection.

In some instances, there is a dearth of materials from which to choose. The needs of exceptional children for curriculum materials have not yet been adequately fulfilled by publishers although this lack is slowly being redressed. However, their equally essential need for supplemental and recreational resources continues to be ignored. With the advent of mainstreaming, it has become essential to include all children in every phase of school activities and the scarcity of appropriate library fare further exacerbates the selection process.

Two categories of exceptional users require particular comment: learning-disabled and gifted youth. As recently as when *The Special Child in the Library* (American Library Association, 1976) was published, few researchers or writers had addressed the role of the library media center in the education of children with learning disabilities. The entire field is undergoing radical changes including scrutiny of the roles of all support agencies, personnel, and services within the schools. This increased attention is especially fortuitous because youngsters with specific learning disabilities are prime candidates for successful mainstreaming, and the library can play a key part in facilitating their integration into regular settings.

At first glance, it would appear that selecting materials for intellectually able youngsters should not present any noteworthy problems. They are typically avid, accomplished, and self-motivated readers. Their only problem may seem to be a quantitative one: having access to enough books to satisfy their voracious appetite for reading. Too often though, these youngsters are restricted to printed matter that is insufficiently challenging or left to wander undirected through adult fare, much of which is developmentally unsuitable or so dependent on prior learning as to be potentially frustrating. Although these children are frequently the most enthusiastic library users, little attention has been devoted to investigating the materials that are most responsive to learning style and interests common to members of that group.

Standard selection aids have proven inadequate in building a collection that provides services to patrons with exceptionalities. Critical features of materials for these users are generally not noted in professional library journals and overlooked in standard selection guides. Library media specialists may have to consult reviews in special education and rehabilitation publications as well as seek suggestions from teachers, counselors, therapists, and other professionals with expertise in these fields. Additionally, it may be extremely productive to solicit recommendations directly from exceptional patrons.

To build and maintain a collection is a continuous challenge. When a relatively small segment of the population has specialized, often highly technical needs, the pressures on librarians and media specialists to make wise decisions is considerable. To aid in this task, this section includes not only suggestions for individual titles, but also discussions of the theoretical bases for these recommendations. Once a rationale is understood, principles can then be applied to a constantly changing market.

Harris and Baskin survey the major categories of disabilities and suggest guidelines for choosing suitable books and products for children who sustain particular impairments. The principles which underlie their approach are: working through strengths, circumventing deficiencies, responding to developmental, academic, and social needs, and including materials for pure pleasure. These authors underscore the necessity of having fiction and nonfiction books on impairment to inform and shape positive attitudes in nonhandicapped readers.

Although the article by Cohen, Alberto, and Troutman is specifically directed to the classroom teacher, librarians actively involved in implementing the academic goals of exceptional youth can use a similar approach to the selection of supplementary and recreational materials. The authors' articulation of relevant standards for materials and their excellently designed Instructional Material Evaluation Form can provide direction, not only for purchasing and producing materials, but for program planning and individual reading guidance as well.

Holmes examines the reading problems of severely hearing-impaired children and comes up with tools to aid in amelioration. He cites the critical problem of language deficiency and prescribes the use of literature as a remedial tool. Holmes has found that traditional basal reading programs have serious limitations. He contends that contact with high quality and substantive reading will inevitably capture the interests of even the most inexperienced, inexpert readers, spurring them on to further involvement. Particularly for those youth whose hearing deficits preclude ordinary knowledge of language structure, literary masterpieces have such magnetic appeal that they override the child's inadequacies. Holmes's experiments, which substituted adapted classics for traditional instructional materials, produced improved performance and had the additional advantage of introducing hearing-impaired students to an exciting part of their cultural heritage. He concludes with guidelines for librarians who seek to select or design materials for these youth and points out some media center activities that can directly influence their educational success.

Forer and Zajac describe an innovative public library program specifically designed to provide services to intellectually impaired children and adults. Although all phases of Project L.I.F.E. (Learning Is For Everyone) are briefly reviewed, the implications for selection are especially significant. Making the collection more responsive includes giving special attention to the information needs of intellectually impaired library users. Accordingly, criteria for choosing books, periodicals, media, toys, puzzles, and games as well as suggestions for the kinds of materials especially useful in programming are delineated. Full service also demands responding to the questions of parents, teachers, and advocates who are directly involved in their lives and often require extensive, varied, changing and not yet clearly defined data in order to function effectively in their relationship with the target population.

Increased interest in the multifaceted needs of learning-disabled youth has focused attention on books which can serve diagnostic, remedial, informational, and pleasure-seeking goals. Three authors analyze different aspects of the reading experience and how these affect selection. Thypin looks at high interest/low reading level books, but her discussion reveals that the concepts underlying their use are far more subtle and complex than the simple appellation would indicate. Readability for any one child involves a cohort of factors that relate both to the inherent qualities in the printed matter and individual traits, abilities, and experiences of the potential reader. These elements are enumerated and their relevance to the provision of appropriate fare articulated.

"Learning disabilities" is an umbrella term used to describe children of average or above average intellectual ability who have disorders in motor coordination, spatial orientation, receptive, inner, or expressive language, visual or auditory perception, or certain specified behaviors. Banbury examines one area—visual perception—in detail, explaining the possible component areas of malfunctioning: visual discrimination, figure-ground, form constancy, memory, sequential memory, or closure. Using a diagnostic-prescriptive approach, she then analyzes over a dozen popular children's books in terms of their potential for improving functioning in specific deficit areas. Banbury notes that the problems of youngsters with learning disabilities can be remedied as well as circumvented and gives practical, precise guidance for choosing materials for this urgent task.

Rawson contends that the mere developing of decoding skills is an insufficient goal for learning-disabled children. She argues they, too, need experiences that will allow them to learn to love and see books as an inexhaustable source of knowledge and enjoyment. Any behavior short of this, she insists, is a deprivation not to be countenanced. Her approach is also primarily literary and she eloquently maintains that access to the wonder and excitement of reading is a motivator of unequalled potency.

Baskin and Harris focus on selecting books to promote cognitive growth in gifted children. They suggest that titles be judged on the basis of qualities inherent in the works themselves and on levels of cognition that the books demand. The characteristics of books that are intellectually challenging are given, and individual titles are considered for their adherence to standards of quality.

In sum, the contributors agree that selection cannot be made arbitrarily or capriciously but must be intimately connected with and based upon the unique strengths and weaknesses of the special population being served. Library professionals must seek out uncommon resources and move beyond the ordinary guides in order to be responsive to the nonstandard, sometimes subtle requirements necessitated by accommodation to disability.

Selecting Materials for the Disabled Child

KAREN HARRIS and BARBARA BASKIN

The first responsibility of any library is to assemble appropriate materials for those who will be using the collection. Selection to meet the needs of handicapped youngsters is guided by the same principles that govern all libraries: choose materials that will satisfy the interests, needs, and abilities of the patrons.

Interests of disabled children are as varied as those of their age mates. They share the enthusiasms and concerns of their generation, and like all other children, each is a unique individual whose imagination may be captured by any topic from aardvarks to zygotes.

Libraries serving children, handicapped or otherwise, must provide books and materials which address informational, developmental, and recreational needs. Youngsters require information to satisfy school assignments and their own curiosity. They should encounter literature which can help them meet the inevitable personal, familial, and social challenges that accompany maturation. And, most of all, they should become convinced that the library is an inexhaustible source of pleasure, relaxation, excitement, and understanding.

It is in the area of abilities that handicapped children most differ from their peers and where they are most apt to need special accommodations. Some youngsters may have physical impairments that make the handling of traditional materials a difficult or even impossible task; others may be limited in their understanding because of intellectual deficits; still others may have problems in receiving or processing information through visual or auditory channels or may find emotional stress severely limits their functioning. With such children, adaptations may have to be made in either the content, presentation, or format of materials if they are to find success and pleasure in their library experiences. For some boys and girls, the content of books and media routinely used by their peers may be too demanding, confusing, or threatening. Other children may be able to deal with intellectually demanding topics, but may have communication disorders which necessitate simplified vocabulary, sentence structure, or the like. Some youngsters may not find print a suitable medium and will have to depend on other formats.

Generalizations are particularly hazardous in this area since the degree of variation among children all carrying the same descriptor will be enormous. The type, extent, and specifics of impairment will determine what accommodations—if any—are appropriate. In addition, each child embodies a unique combination of characteristics and traits which make him or her responsive in special ways. Despite these potential pitfalls, it is possible to specify considerations which children's librarians should keep in mind when ordering materials for young patrons who are disabled. Each major category of impairment will be discussed in sequence. Some children may be multiply handicapped and thus require adaptations in more than one mode. The permutations are infinite and decisions as to the best response to their needs will have to be individually determined.

Physical Handicaps

The interests of physically handicapped children parallel those of their age mates. They need books and media on the same topics but may have to have some specially selected to answer their particular limitations. In recent years, juvenile titles in areas such as cooking, crafts, travel, camping, etc., have appeared which have been especially written for a special needs audience. Additionally, resource books are now available which specify camps, schools, universities, travel services, and the like which provide adapted environments in either special or

---

"Selecting Materials for the Disabled Child," by Karen Harris and Barbara Baskin, *Texas Library Journal* 1980, 56: 193–95. Reprinted by permission of *Texas Library Journal*.

mainstreamed settings. Such volumes should be included in a well-stocked library.

Books which are popular with ablebodied youth in helping them through developmental crises may not be useful for this population. Adolescence is a particularly challenging time for these youngsters and books which are honest and forthright about pubertal and prepubertal problems of disabled youth are essential to have in a collection.

For some few children there is another tragic problem that has not been adequately responded to. Those youngsters who have progressively debilitating terminal disorders are in particular need of help in coming to terms with their prognosis. They need assistance in maximizing their intact abilities and enjoying those pleasures life has to offer for as long as they are able.

Most physically handicapped children will need no other special adaptations in the content of the collection. If the environment is barrier free, they will, for the most part, choose and use the same materials as their peers. Some, however, will need special formats. The Library of Congress has now made talking book services available to anyone who cannot handle standard print. Some children with muscular, skeletal, or neurological disorders or chronic health problems have found hours of pleasure through this resource. Some few children will be able to handle paperback editions more easily than hardbound ones and some may manage the latter with the assistance of mechanical page turners.

Intellectual Impairment

The interests of retarded children generally parallel but are more restricted than those of their peers. These youngsters are often deficient in interpersonal relationships, a problem which may distress them far more than academic failure, and so need books and materials which can promote social skills and which provide good models for them to emulate.

Their most serious deficit, however, is in the area of intellectual functioning. These boys and girls are typically inefficient learners: their language skills are inadequately developed; their attention span is limited; they generally are only able to focus on one topic at a time and cannot deal easily with several ideas simultaneously; they are less able than their age mates to separate the main idea from peripheral or extraneous issues; they often have extensive gaps in their knowledge base; and they deal best with concrete, specific, experience-related ideas rather than abstract, generalized, or theoretical concepts.

As a consequence of their limitations, they need considerable redundancy and reinforcement in their materials if learning is to take place. It is especially imperative that text and pictures in books, sound filmstrips, and other media be compatible and free of discrepancies, that stories are free of sub- or parallel plots or extraneous elements added for "color." Their literature should have a single focus and should develop through a step-by-step logical or chronological progression. These youngsters need materials which are identical in appearance to those used by peers, for they are sensitive to the stigmatizing component in books and other media they perceive as "babyish." They do not need materials which are ambiguous, paradoxical, or open ended since these qualities tend to be confusing and frustrating rather than challenging. Many may benefit from multisensory experiences such as those found in combined media approaches. Reading a book while simultaneously hearing the text read on a tape can be a very effective and pleasurable learning encounter. These boys and girls need materials that are short or that can be segmented into brief, self-contained components. They need materials that address the gaps in basic knowledge of their immediate environment, thus helping them in the often difficult process of acculturation. In addition to the numerous regular trade titles that satisfy these requirements, publishers have added many high interest-low ability works to their lists.

A special mention should be made of the virtues of magazines as a major resource for mentally retarded youth. Many popular magazines contain brief, generously illustrated articles or features written in a style and containing a vocabulary within the reach of the youngsters. In some, captioned pictures carry enough of the message that the import can be gleaned even if the text alone would otherwise be beyond their abilities. Magazines camouflage the discrepancy between intellectually impaired children and their age mates. Periodicals, although directed to the general public, can be successfully used by this population and they have the potential of sparking a lifetime reading habit.

Visual Impairments

Visually impaired children have the same range of interests and abilities as those without this sensory deficit. Because they live in a world in which overwhelming amounts of information are directed through visual channels, they must learn to use efficiently what sight they have or, in some instances, rely on tactile and auditory channels for supplementation or substitution. Format then is the critical variable in choosing materials for blind or low-vision children. With judicious selection, there is no reason why these youngsters should expect reduced access to the literary world.

Many picture books are available in outsize print in 18-point, 20-point, or larger type and contain pictures which are large, clear, and uncluttered with good color contrast. For older children, large print books, now available in covers which make them similar in external appearance to regular books, may mean the difference in their ability to read. Some girls and boys may use portable magnifiers to make images discernible.

For those who depend primarily on other channels, there are two recent tremendously exciting technological breakthroughs. One is the Optacon which can scan standard print and translate the images into a tactile message. The other device, the Kurzweil machine, is not portable, is expensive, but does not require extensive training. This can read any standard print typed copy, computer printouts, books, journals, etc., and convey the source document as an audible message. In other words, the Kurzweil acts as an electronic friend who accepts any printed work and reads it aloud to a blind listener! Talking Books and brailled materials are provided by the Library of Congress and other specialized agencies. These are the most significant resources for patrons who cannot rely on vision for information gathering.

One other category of materials has special significance in promoting mainstreaming goals. Twin Vision books contain both standard print and braille on the same page. These allow blind and sighted children to share a reading experience.

Hearing Impairments

Severe hearing loss at birth or in early childhood places an enormous learning burden on youngsters. Even with early intervention, most of these children experience communication difficulties that impede language development, and this generally results in reading levels below what their intellectual abilities would otherwise have allowed. Because the process of vocabulary acquisition is so arduous, and because the subtleties involved in more complex grammatical constructions are so elusive, high interest-low ability books, developed for other populations, are useful for these children too.

Learning Disabilities

The term "learning disabilities" covers such a range and diversity of impairments that it is difficult to make generalizations about children so described. The expression encompasses anyone who has serious difficulties in receiving, interpreting, or expressing data transmitted through the senses. These children usually have average or above average intelligence and are not primarily bothered by visual or auditory acuity, so neither classes for retarded children nor glasses or hearing aids address their basic problem. These children are often hyperactive, distractable, have short attention spans, and cannot separate peripheral from core messages. They are aware of and understand their peer culture, but are often excluded because of poor social skills and behavior which others perceive as annoying or inappropriate. Too often a poor self-concept caused by social or academic failure exacerbates their situation.

Although some children with learning disabilities will read with facility, many will require adaptations in either form or content or both. Often social ostracism is seen as a far greater problem than academic failure. Stories which can sensitize them to and help them interpret the social behavior of others are of particular importance. Since these youngsters typically have trouble in all aspects of organization, books need to be chosen which have a single unified theme without subplots, extraneous characters, or other distracting elements. Text and illustrations should be mutually supportive with the latter depicting major characters and the central concerns of the work. In stories, straightforward, chronological narratives that maintain a consistent point of view are best. Pictures should be clear, well outlined, uncluttered, with contrasting colors defining spaces and have ample leading. For some children auditory channels may need to be completely bypassed; for others, visual channels are too inefficient and these boys and girls may do best with audio materials.

Emotional Dysfunction

Children who have emotional disorders exhibit the same range of intellectual ability as their nonimpaired peers. Their problems interfere with their functioning though, and consequently they too may experience serious academic deficits. These boys and girls often have difficulty attending to task, are distractable, and may have poor attention spans. Like anyone else, they have a high need for success, although in their case this may be much exaggerated. Books which may be too challenging should be avoided initially; in new situations these youngsters may want materials below their abilities so they can be confident that they will avoid failure. Books on threatening topics should be avoided: the enthusiasm for so-called relevance in children's literature has resulted in publication of numerous works on child abuse, desertion, substance abuse, gang violence, etc.—all of which are likely to be inappropriate for emotionally dysfunctional youth. In terms of content, it is particularly important that materials which illustrate models of acceptable interpersonal behavior be chosen, and those which reinforce societal values be provided for these patrons.

Children who have experienced failure with print materials may be more comfortable with other media. Two cautions should be observed: the range or focus of phobias is infinite and if a child engages in avoidance behavior, his or her resistance should be respected; for some children simultaneous audio and visual input creates sensory overload. For the latter, they can look or listen, but may be uncomfortable with such materials as sound filmstrips.

Mainstreaming

In addition to selecting books and other materials for disabled library users, it is imperative that a collection contain works *about* impairments and impaired persons for the enlightenment of nonhandicapped patrons. No matter how much support and guidance handicapped children have, if their peers are hostile and rejecting, then mainstreaming will be a sham. Children have many erroneous ideas about people who have disabilities. These are often based on inaccurate information, superstitions, and faulty perceptions. To help correct these distortions, children need books which honestly and forthrightly, without exaggeration or misrepresentation, depict people with impairments. Not all titles are accurate, constructive, or empathic: many distort, minimize, or falsely inflate qualities of disabled persons, treat them with pity or condescension, or emphasize helplessness and dependence, thus setting them apart from the rest of humanity. Fortunately, in recent years, a great number of first-rate titles have appeared which can meet stringent standards of accuracy, quality of information, and literary excellence.

Children with special needs must have the skills and competencies that allow them to function outside the sheltered, segregated environment in which they have been confined for years. On the other hand, the members of the larger community must be readied to receive those once excluded. Libraries have a critical role to play in answering the needs of both these populations if mainstreaming is to become a viable social reality.

Selecting and Developing Educational Materials: An Inquiry Model

SANDRA B. COHEN, PAUL A. ALBERTO, and ANN TROUTMAN

Teachers whose names have been placed on mailing lists for catalogs and advertising from educational companies are well aware of the vast proliferation of commercial materials purporting to be useful for student instruction. There has also been an increasing number of workshops available to aid in the production of teacher-made instructional aids. In the past, teachers had to make do with textbooks, chalk, and construction paper. Today's teacher is faced with the difficult task of spending limited funds wisely to acquire or manufacture the best available materials for the instructional program.

Today's special educator needs to choose educational materials that have direct application to the short-term objectives and annual goals specified in the individualized education program (IEP). The development or selection of a material should relate to its function as an instructional facilitator closely associated with the prescribed methodology for remediation.

With this goal in mind, the haphazard selection of materials based on factors such as visual appeal, convincing advertising, or hearsay is self-defeating. The teacher should approach the selection of materials with the intention of acquiring the best possible teaching aids to facilitate the attainment of specific goals. The purpose of this article is to provide a teacher with guidelines for appropriate selection or development of materials.

Inquiry Model

Figure 1 represents the Inquiry Model of Material Development and Selection. The model is based upon three interrelated components: (1) *input* is composed of curriculum and assessment information. (2) *intervention* represents educational procedures and materials, and (3) *output* signifies the learning achievement. The material, along with the associated methods, functions as an instructional facilitator by linking input information to output responses. The intent of the material should be to increase the child's performance to the criterion level of the instructional objective. The material can best achieve its purpose when all inquiries—*who, why, what* and *how*—are answered.

Selection Guidelines

Four questions—who? why? what? and how?—provide the guidelines for materials selection and development. Each of these basic inquiries relates directly to the following pedagogic concepts:

1. *Who*? refers to the target population.
2. *Why*? refers to the purpose of the material(s).
3. *What*? refers to structure, format, methodology, construction, function, and quantity.
4. *How*? refers to process, management, feedback, response mode(s), generalization, adaptation, and sequencing.

Who? The Target Population

The first component of the model concerns the "who"—the target population. Before developing or purchasing a material, the population must be defined or identified. In specifying the target population, the teacher should first decide if the material is to be used for individual or group purposes.

"Selecting and Developing Educational Materials: An Inquiry Model," by Sandra B. Cohen, Paul A. Alberto, and Ann Troutman, *Teaching Exceptional Children* 1979, 12: 7–11. Copyright 1979 by The Council for Exceptional Children. Reprinted with permission.

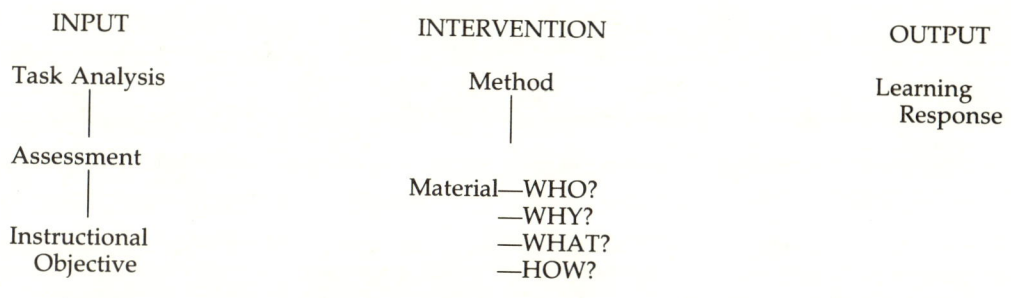

Fig. 1. Inquiry Model of Material Development

Individual Materials

Is the material intended for one child's needs or will several children use it at different times? If the material will be used repeatedly, it should be nonconsumable and contain enough of each element for each child assigned to the task. The teacher should consider if any of the elements can be reproduced or duplicated.

If a number of children will be using the materials on an individual basis, they should incorporate a variety of developmental tasks which are sequenced from simple to more complex skills and two or more learning modalities to provide success across different children. The materials should be well constructed, durable, and attractive to provide maximum flexibility. The time spent creating the material will save reproduction at a later date.

When choosing or developing a material, both the common and individual needs of the students should be considered. A teacher cannot assume that, because two children are learning addition facts, they learn at the same rate, through the same modality, with the same reinforcement system, or that their present performances are equivalent.

A material intended for use by only one child can be narrower in scope. Design of the material reflects the particular target student's learning needs and style. It is a prescribed material which is determined by the diagnosis and specified remedial needs of a single child. As such, the actual material may encompass a range of developmental tasks, durable and reusable components, and alternative learning avenues. In many cases the material may serve a "one shot" purpose to be used and completed in one activity session.

Group Materials

The alternative to individual materials is a product intended for group use. The following should be considered when developing a group material:

1. *Instruction.* Is the material teacher directed or student directed?
2. *Numbers.* How many children can participate at one time?
3. *Interaction.* How does the group function around the material?
4. *Prerequisite and requisite skills.* What range of abilities does the material encompass?

The first thing to consider is whether the material is to be student directed or teacher directed. Student-directed materials provide such things as answer keys for peer or self-correction and allow the group to proceed with the material independent of the instructor. A teacher-directed material requires teacher instruction, guidance, and verification of correct responses.

The responses to the second and third questions are situation specific and will reflect the best judgment of the teacher. After evaluating group needs and class struture the teacher should decide how many children can comfortably interact at one time with the material. For example, an open classroom versus a traditional classroom will affect the type and size of group activity. Space and noise level should also be considered.

The fourth question requires careful consideration by the teacher. During the planning stage, it must be decided whether the material is both chronologically and developmentally appropriate for the intended student audience. It should be attractive and motivating to the age and abilities of the target group. The material should be organized to provide a challenge without causing unnecessary frustration. For expanded use, a material that ranges across the developmental continuum from concrete to abstract elements will have the greatest potential. Learning kits, such as the Peabody Language Development and Beginning Kits, successfully cover a range of learning needs and allow for successful heterogenous grouping. Such materials facilitate children learning from other children.

Why? The Purpose of the Material

The teacher needs to make several decisions related to the reasons for choosing or developing a particular material:

1. Is this an appropriate concept or skill for this particular child at this particular time?
2. Will any materials be necessary or helpful in reaching long- and short-term goals?
3. Are the materials flexible enough to adapt to a child's individual pace?
4. Will the material help the child meet short-term or annual goals?

The first decision concerns the rationale for teaching a specific concept or skill. This decision is made during the development of the child's individualized education program (IEP).

The long- and short-term goals for the child will be stated in the IEP. The teacher needs to determine if any materials will be necessary to help the child reach these goals. The teacher should adopt the attitude that the usefulness of a material must be proved. This will prevent a tendency to expose children to a program with the justification that, although it may not facilitate learning, it "couldn't hurt." The failure to do harm is not a sufficient justification for the use of any program with any child.

The material chosen should enable the child to reach the specified goal more quickly, more efficiently, and with a higher degree of motivation. A material that requires a child to work at a predetermined pace (e.g., six problems, two worksheets, or one activity per day) may set limitations on his or her learning. A task or concept must be broken down into steps only small enough to maximize learning for the individual child. An inflexible program may hinder the child's progress. If the steps are too large for the child, they may prevent efficient learning. A material that can be adapted by the teacher for an individual child is to be preferred. Different materials can be chosen to facilitate new learning, provide practice, or ensure overlearning of skills or concepts. Materials that can be adapted for several purposes are more economical than those whose usefulness is limited to a single purpose.

A teacher who chooses a material to help a child meet long-term or annual goals assumes that the components will enable the child to meet specific short-term objectives leading up to the long-term goal. This assumption should always be confirmed by careful examination of the material. A child may require supplementary materials to reach the goal. A teacher may choose to acquire specific materials to meet each short-term goal. Thus, a child may use a variety of programs while working toward an annual goal. The choice of a material should reflect its usefulness in promoting the child's acquisition of instructional competencies. The choice of materials should be stated and justified on each child's IEP.

What? The Structure of the Material

The third component—"what"—concerns the production of educational materials. When selecting or developing a material, three elements should be considered: (1) format, (2) methodology, and (3) construction. The success of an educational material will depend on the teacher's understanding of the interaction of these three elements.

Format

The term *educational material* is applied to a wide range of activities and tasks. Formats for these materials include games, worksheets, manipulatives, and media.

Games Thiagarajan defined a game as encompassing three essential characteristics:

control, conflict and closure. An instructional game allows the players to learn or practice a skill with deliberation toward a specific objective.

Worksheets Whereas a game is likely to be group-oriented, a worksheet is an individual activity and tends to fulfill a drill function. It allows the child to rehearse a pre-learned skill (e.g., initial consonants) with minimal materials and time. Worksheets should be created with thought given to spacing, number of stimuli, and response level.

Manipulatives Manipulatives are another form of educational material. They include a variety of elements that must be arranged by the child in a demonstration of learning. Cuisenaire Rods are a primary example of a manipulative material.

Media The last format, media, may or may not include elements of the first three formats. Media include technical and visual elements, such as tapes, cassettes, slides, and filmstrips. They provide instruction through a combination of educational hardware and software.

Methodology

Consideration must be given to whether or not the material is appropriate to the prescribed *method* of goal attainment. This structural element aligns the teaching mode of the material to the learning style of the child(ren). Planning at this level involves such decisions as: Should the material provide inductive or deductive learning processes? or What is the functional interaction of the material, the participants, and the environment? Field testing a material often uncovers additional functions, both positive and negative, that may alter attainment of the goal and that should be assessed before final production.

Construction

Construction is the most obvious subcomponent of the "what" question. The ultimate construction of the product requires consideration of the following questions:

Quantity
1. How many children is the material designed for?
2. How many dimensions (pieces) are included in the material?
3. Can the material elements be easily reproduced?
4. Can the commercial material be reproduced under copyright laws?

Composition
1. Is the material attractive and motivating?
2. Is the material self-correcting? (Are answer keys provided?)
3. Are all parts of the material self-contained? (Does a child have to bring markers or paper to the task?)
4. Is the material durable? Will it last?
5. What is the stimulus intensity? (Will one element distract from another? Is there novelty?)
6. Is the material or any part of it consumable?

Component Interaction

In addition to answering these questions, a teacher should also consider the interactive effect of format, methodology and construction to resolve the "what" question. In essence, the combination of these subcomponents results in the production of the physical material. However, the concern for the structural (what) component, independent of the other three (who, why, and how) components, can only produce a material with chance application to educational programming.

Neither the purchase nor the manufacture of any material, however attractive or expensive, will guarantee the attainment of instructional goals. It is the teacher's job to design programs that may or may not be improved by the use of a given material. At worst, a product may actually interfere with learning; at best, the use of such instructional aids will complement the teacher's efforts. The purpose of the material is not to teach but to facilitate; teaching remains the responsibility of the teacher.

How? The Use of the Material

Several considerations will determine the way a material will be used in the classroom.

1. Will the material require teacher direction or is it designed to be an independent student activity?
2. How will feedback be provided? Is the material self-correcting or will it be checked by the teacher or a peer?
3. What is the response mode of the material?

Management

The teacher decides if the material is teacher-directed or student-directed. If the student or group of students is expected to work independently, instructions for the material should be self-explanatory or familiar enough so that the teacher's presence is not necessary.

Feedback

Whether a material is teacher-directed or self-directed, provision must be made for feedback. The frequency of feedback should be determined according to the needs of the individual and his or her stage of learning (i.e., acquisition, retention, or maintenance). The acquisition stage requires more feedback than the retention and maintenance stages. A material may provide for evaluation after every response (as in programmed texts) or after a series of responses, according to its teaching objective.

An important consideration is the method of providing feedback. A material may be self-checking so the student evaluates his or her own responses. A teacher can adapt materials for self-checking by providing answer sheets, transparent overlays, or coded question-answer pieces. Some materials provide for feedback through manuals to be used by peer tutors or evaluators. It is important to choose peers who have reached a high enough skill level to correctly evaluate responses and provide appropriate feedback.

The most common method of feedback is teacher or paraprofessional evaluation. The advantages of this method are increased accuracy and direct teacher-student interaction. A disadvantage is that it requires increased teacher time. Periodic teacher evaluation is necessary to ensure that goals are met. However, with the increasing demand for individualized programs, use of self- and peer evaluation is highly desirable.

Response Mode

Response mode—oral, written, or other—may be specified by the material or be elected by the teacher or student. The following should be considered when choosing the response mode:

1. What are the needs and abilities of the student?
2. Will oral responses disturb other students in the classroom?
3. Is a permanent (i.e., written) product needed for record keeping?
4. Does the response mode motivate the student? Is there enough variety within and between tasks? Is there opportunity for oral or novel responses (coloring, marking, building, cutting, etc.)?
5. Does the material contain multiple formats and rsponse modes that will lead to student generalization of the learned skill or concept?
6. Does the material provide for fading to more typical or mature response modes?

Variety is an important aspect of material selection or development. A student may tire of or become bored with one response mode. Students should not become dependent on a specific material because skill acquisition may be hindered. A program that provides multiple formats and response modes is more likely to lead to the acquisition of generalizable skills. In determining the appropriateness of a material, the time of its use and the interaction of the material with other materials and intervention strategies are important considerations.

Field Testing a Material

Field testing a material is the final step in the development or selection process. Once the material has been used by the student(s), the teacher may assess its ability to facilitate achievement of the desired learning outcomes. The Instructional Material Evaluation Form (see fig. 2) can be used as a guide for making adaptations to any material selected or developed according to the four components—who, why, what, and how.

Success of Materials

The teacher and teaching materials cannot be separated. A material can be successful as an instructional aid only when its selection and application are based on analysis of its structural components. By asking relevant questions the teacher provides students with a material that is systematically designed to increase learning opportunities. Attention to sound pedagogic principles when selecting or developing a material will eliminate wasteful spending, unnecessary production, and irrelevant use of instructional time.

Material Name _____
Objective(s) _____
_____

Input modality   V A K T
                                _____
Output modality V A K T
                                _____
_____

Scale:
        1 — — 2 — — 3 - - - — NA
   Inappro- Effec- Best material   Not
   priate   tive   for purpose   applicable
_____

WHO—THE TARGET POPULATION
The material is designed:

1. To be used by one child
   at a time.   1 2 3 NA
2. For group use.   1 2 3 NA
3. To accommodate different
   learning levels.   1 2 3 NA
4. To allow for different
   learning styles.   1 2 3 NA
5. Appropriately for the
   child(ren)'s age
   and ability level.   1 2 3 NA

   Comments _____
   _____
   _____
   _____
   _____
   _____

WHY—THE PURPOSE OF THE MATERIAL
The material:

1. Effectively meets the
   stated objective.   1 2 3 NA
2. Provides new learning
   skills.   1 2 3 NA
3. Provides sufficient
   practice.   1 2 3 NA
4. Provides motivation
   for learning.   1 2 3 NA

   Comments _____
   _____
   _____
   _____

WHAT—THE STRUCTURE OF THE MATERIAL
The material:

1. Uses a format appropriate
   to the stated objective.   1 2 3 NA
2. Matches the teaching
   style to the child's
   learning style.   1 2 3 NA
3. Includes directions.   1 2 3 NA
4. Is attractive and invites
   learning.   1 2 3 NA
5. Is a self-contained learning
   tool (no additional
   pieces are needed).   1 2 3 NA

   Comments _____
   _____
   _____
   _____
   _____
   _____
   _____
   _____
   _____

HOW—THE USE OF THE MATERIAL
This material:

1. Is appropriate without
   teacher assistance.   1 2 3 NA
2. Provides sufficient
   corrective feedback.   1 2 3 NA
3. Allows for active learner
   participation through
   an appropriate response
   mode.   1 2 3 NA
4. Structures learning in small
   units of achievement.   1 2 3 NA
5. Provides opportunity for
   generalization of
   knowledge.   1 2 3 NA

   Comments _____
   _____
   _____
   _____
   _____
   _____

Fig. 2. Instructional Material Evaluation Form

Additional Reading

Kohfeldt, J. "Blueprints for construction: Teacher-Made or Teacher-Adapted Materials." *Focus on Exceptional Children* 8 (1976): 1–14.

Thiagarajan, S. "Designing Instructional Games for Handicapped Learners." *Focus on Exceptional Children* 7 (1976): 1–11.

Adapting Reading Materials for Hearing-Impaired Children with Low Reading Achievement

DAVID W. HOLMES

Research dealing with reading achievement has demonstrated a discrepancy between the mean reading scores of hearing and hearing-impaired children. Such disparity has demonstrated hearing-impaired children to be from two-to-eight years behind the hearing child in reading skills, depending upon the age and type of comparison being made.[1] In general, the reading achievement scores of hearing-impaired students in the United States are far below the scores of their hearing peers.

One major obstacle for the hearing-impaired child in learning to read is his difficulty in mastering phonological coding rules. Conrad addresses this as the primary difficulty hearing-impaired children face in learning to read.[2] Others have also recognized this as a problem in the reading process.[3]

Basal reading systems are the most extensively used reading approach in schools for the hearing impaired. Most basal reading systems consist of a series of graded materials designed to provide a sequential program in the development of basal reading skills by providing a controlled vocabulary.

Basal readers for hearing-impaired children have been criticized for various reasons. That is, while vocabulary has been controlled, the complexity of syntax has not.[4] Even though a trend away from white middle-class stereotypes to characters from different ethnic and environmental backgrounds is evident, folk and fairy tales are still common within primary basal reading materials.[5] Others have been critical of the lack of motivational reading materials for children with low reading abilities.[6]

Several writers have proposed the use of literature in school reading programs.[7] They suggest that students will not succeed if their primary task becomes one of laborious dissection and analysis of each passage within the story. Therefore, the use of adapted "classics" should maintain a level of high interest and readability (if adapted to an appropriate reading level).

Anken and Holmes attempted to validate the hypothesis that hearing-impaired children provided with high interest adapted reading materials would demonstrate higher reading achievement abilities than hearing-impaired children using a basal reading program.[8]

Eleven classics were adapted and presented to the experimental group in the following order:

1. *Daniel Boone*
2. *Ulysses and the Cyclops* by Homer
3. *Legend of Sleepy Hollow* by Washington Irving
4. *Jumping Frog* by Mark Twain
5. *Thomas Gallaudet, A Deaf Educator*
6. *Christmas Carol* by Charles Dickens
7. *Treasure Island* by Robert Louis Stevenson
8. *Adventures of Tom Sawyer* by Mark Twain

9. *Adventures of Huckleberry Finn* by Mark Twain
10. *Rip Van Winkle* by Washington Irving
11. *Moby Dick* by Herman Melville

Anken and Holmes found that their experimental group using adapted classics as reading material gained .95 years in word meaning and .68 years in paragraph meaning. This is quite remarkable when one considers that the same group of children using a basal reading program the previous year showed a deterioration of −.14 years in word meaning and only .07 years gain in paragraph meaning. A matched control group using a basal reading program also demonstrated a loss of −.13 years in word meaning and a modest gain of .23 years in paragraph meaning.

One reason for the success of the adapted classics may have been the use of simpler syntactic structures in them. Anken and Holmes attempted to control for the introduction of vocabulary and syntactic structures.[9] The initial adapted classics selections were written employing the syntactic structures and vocabulary words the hearing-impaired students had used in their own compositional work. New vocabulary words were gradually introduced and frequently repeated; simple syntactic structures were used in the initial reading selections and progressed to more complex structures in the later selections. However, the vocabulary and type of syntactic structure incorporated were not experimentally controlled, but only empirically introduced. Thus, it was not known what sentence structures were used and whether there actually existed differences in syntactic form between the early and later adapted classic selections and between the basal readers.

In a later study, Layton, Schmucker, and Holmes attempted to determine: (1) whether the adapted classics used by Anken and Holmes contained different and fewer sentence types than did the basal reader; (2) whether the adapted classics and basal readers contained simpler syntactic structures in the initial selections and progressed to more complex structures in the later; and (3) whether the adapted classics and basal reader controlled for the introduction of vocabulary.[10]

The purpose of their study was to examine the vocabulary and syntactic structures found in the adapted classics and to compare these to the vocabulary and syntactic structures found in the basal reader, *City Sidewalks*.[11] The results indicated that the adapted classics and the basal readers contained the same variety of sentence types. Also, the early and advanced selections contained the same variety of sentences for both the adapted classics and the basal reader. However, there was a significant difference in the *frequency* of specific sentence types between and within the reading program.

No significant differences were found between or within the two reading series on kernel sentence type II (intransitive or "be" verb forms). This may have resulted because so few sentences were of the "be" form—only an average of six to eleven were found in the various readers.

Significant differences were found for kernel sentence type I (transitive verbs) and type II (intransitive verbs). The basal stories contained significantly more intransitive and transitive verb sentences than did the adapted classics. However, when the early and advanced categories were compared within each series, the frequency of intransitive/transitive verbs was the same.

When Anken and Holmes adapted the classical stories, they used sentences with fewer intransitive and transitive verbs than did the basal readers.[12] This indicated a less complex level of syntax for the adapted classics. However, they did not use fewer intransitive/transitive verbs in the earlier stories than in the advanced stories. Thus, the level of difficulty for intransitive/transitive verbs did not differ within the adapted classics series.

The results of their study also indicated no qualitative differences between the adapted classics and the basal reader on transformational types. That is, those transformational types found in the adapted classics were also found in the basal reader, and vice versa. The data analysis did, however, indicate a statistically significant difference in the frequency of transformations used between the two reading series. In other words, there were quantitative differences between the reading series, but there were no qualitative differences.

The statistical results also indicated that within each reading series, no differences were noted for frequency of transformation. The exception to this was Grammar II (more complex transformations) in the adapted classics, where fewer transformations occurred in the earlier adapted stories than in the advanced adapted stories.

They also found that the sentences in the adapted classics were significantly shorter than those in the basal reader. However, no differences were noted within either reading series.

The results of their study indicated that the basal reader controlled for the introduction of vocabulary, but the Anken and Holmes adapted classics did not. When the data were analyzed for number of different types of words between and within the reading programs, no differences were found. There were as many different words used in the early adapted classics as in the advanced classics and in the early basal stories as in the advanced basal stories. However, there were significantly more total words used in the basals than in the adapted classics, the effect being that the same words were used more frequently in the basal stories than in the adapted classics. Stated differently, new words were introduced more slowly in the basal reader than in the adapted classics.

The results of the Layton, Schmucker, and Holmes study[13] substantiated several previous studies in that basal reading systems introduce complex syntactic structures in a random manner.[14] The frequency of transformations was the same between the early and advanced basal selections. In other words, the level of difficulty was the same for both the early and the advanced selections; progression from the least to the more difficult sentence patterns was not found in the basal reading program.

In contrast, Anken and Holmes's adapted classics controlled for the introduction of syntactic structures more effectively than the basal reader. Although no progression of difficulty was found within the classics for sentence types, the classics were found to contain fewer transitive and intransitive verbs (kernel sentence types I and II) and significantly fewer transformations than the basal reader. Therefore, a less complex level of syntax was found in the classics.

In addition, a progression for level of difficulty was noted for Grammar II transformations in the beginning classics as compared to the advanced classics, indicating that these structures were gradually introduced.

The results substantiate Anken and Holmes's hypothesis that the adapted classics were written with simpler syntactic structures than the basal reader.[15] Also simpler syntactic structures were used initially, and progressed to more complex structures in the later adapted classics. However, the results did indicate the researchers controlled for the introduction of vocabulary in the adapted classics less effectively than in the basal readers.

The use of adapted classics in a reading program designed specifically for hearing-impaired students did result in significantly higher reading achievement gains in word meaning and paragraph meaning as compared to other reading programs using basal reading systems. After eight months with an adapted classics reading program, Anken and Holmes's students reacted more positively to reading. As Shrayer suggested, a positive reading interest among so-called poor readers should enable them to increase their level of comprehension.[16] The high gain in reading achievement scores among the experimental group during the academic year would tend to confirm Shrayer's conclusions. In contrast, Shrayer suggested that low interest reading materials would result in a negatively cumulative effect on low ability students. The low reading gains achieved by the basal reader classes may indicate that the materials were inadequate to create a positive reading interest.

Schotanus's findings suggested that students enjoyed reading easier materials. His study found that students who reacted unfavorably toward reading consistently chose easier reading material.[17] Thus, the experimental group's positive interest in adapted classics may have been a response to easier material. This easier material was the result of adapting classics to reflect the low linguistic competence of the experimental group. Fleming's findings indicated that a significant positive relationship existed between a student's level of comprehension and the level of material that he chose to read.[18] As Fleming's findings may suggest, the experimental group's high gains in paragraph meaning scores (comprehension) may have been the result of reading easier materials.

The results of Anken and Holmes suggest that an adapted classics reading program had a positive impact upon the reading achievement gains among thirteen-year-old hearing-impaired students.[19] A partial reason for the success of adapted classics may be its content. The content of adapted classics was at a higher interest level than those stories found in the basal reading system. The content of a second-grade basal reading book was inappropriate to generate a positive reading attitude among thirteen-year-old hearing-impaired students. Thus the introduction of an adapted classics reading program was enthusiastically received by the experimental group. The content of the adapted classics was derived from some of the world's finest literary works. Stories such as *The Adventures of Huckleberry Finn*, *Treasure Island*, and *The Legend of Sleepy Hollow* have served through the years to awaken curiosity and interest within all children. Likewise, for the young hearing-impaired reader, Huckleberry Finn and Tom Sawyer become more than mere fictional characters in a book. These two characters, as well as others, represented real people with human characteristics. The young hearing-impaired reader could identify with Tom and Huck and relate to the many exploits that they encountered during their young lives along the Mississippi River. In addition, the young hearing-impaired reader could easily identify with young Jim Hawkins and relate to his experiences in *Treasure Island*, as well as those of Ishmael in *Moby Dick*, and many other characters found in adapted classics.

In many reading programs for the hearing impaired, basal reading systems are extensively used. Yet the basal reading systems were developed specifically for hearing students. Most basal reading systems assume that the child has an adequate mastery of phonological rules and syntactical structures. For the young hearing-impaired student, this assumption is incorrect. The hearing-impaired child's ability to perceive and comprehend speech sounds is severely limited. The auditory feedback that he so desperately needs to improve and expand his speech utterances is often inadequate even with the use of auditory amplification. Thus the hearing-impaired child's inability to develop and master phonological coding rules prevents him from developing language as quickly as hearing children.

Basal reading systems tend to introduce complex syntactical structures in a random manner. Efforts to repeat specific forms of syntactical structures within a successive series of basal readers are not consistent. The hearing-impaired student is unable to master and comprehend the true meanings that these complex syntactical structures convey. As more complex syntactical structures are introduced into each successive selection of a basal reading system, the hearing-impaired student's level of comprehension begins to decrease rapidly. This decrease in comprehension is a result of his low linguistic competence. The hearing-impaired child remains a word reader. Due to his limited vocabulary, he selects the words that he knows to guess at the total meaning of the syntactical structure. This procedure often leads to repeated failure. Gradually, the frustrated hearing-impaired student perceives the reading process as unrewarding.

The adapted classics reading program controls the introduction of new vocabulary and complex syntactical structures. Simple syntactical structures were used in the initial reading selections. As the adapted classics reading program progressed, more complex syntactical structures were gradually introduced and frequently repeated. The hearing-impaired student's ability to master and comprehend a given reading selection became more dependent upon the meaning conveyed by the particular syntactical structures involved than by the semantic units with which he is familiar.

An adapted reading program could then provide the hearing-impaired student with a sense of enjoyment and success. The adapted classics encouraged the young hearing-impaired readers to read for general meanings rather than going through the laborious process of analysis and dissection characteristic of basal reading systems.

Librarians can play a critical role in encouraging hearing-impaired children to develop recreational reading habits. This can best be accomplished by selecting materials which will hold the readers' interest and yet be written at a level appropriate to their linguistic abilities. Audiovisual materials (films and filmstrips) will often foster added interest and enhance reading materials. An excellent source of visual aids and captioned films can be obtained from: Captioned Films and Telecommunications Branch, USOE-BEH-DMS, 400 Maryland Ave., SW, Donohoe Building, Corridor 4800, Washington, D.C. 20202.

Most of us have read many classics and take for granted their part in our cultural heritage. Hearing-impaired children are inadvertently denied access to the classical literature due to the disparity between the linguistic level of the books and the abilities of the readers. This has the effect of excluding hearing-impaired children from participating in this part of our cultural mainstream. Even though they may not be able to derive enjoyment from such works in their original form, their availability in condensed or adapted form is still valid, even essential!

In preparing or selecting books or other instructional material for hearing-impaired children, the following are suggested:

(1) Materials should correspond to the age level and interest of the hearing-impaired student. Such material serves to create a sense of enjoyment toward reading.
(2) Language samples of hearing-impaired students should be obtained prior to writing or rewriting reading materials. This would also assist librarians in determining the sophistication of their readers.
(3) Vocabulary and syntactical structures familiar to hearing-impaired students should be used initially, with a progression toward new vocabulary and complex syntactic structures in the later selections.
(4) The introduction and repetition of new vocabulary words should be controlled. New words should be gradually introduced and frequently repeated.
(5) Materials such as filmstrips, captioned movies, video tapes, transparencies, and posters should be utilized.
(6) Role-playing and storytelling through total communication are also recommended.
(7) Reading materials should be incorporated into the areas of language development, math, and American history.
(8) Adapted materials should be read for enjoyment.

Librarians usually do not engage in writing and rewriting stories as teachers must do for their hearing-impaired students. However, librarians can perform many necessary and vital functions in promoting an interest in reading for this special population. Hearing-impaired adults and teachers can be recruited to assist in selecting appropriate books. These same individuals can also be enlisted for story telling in sign language. Videotaping these presentations can be a way of preserving them for future use. Playlets can be organized and the children given parts. Puppets, small models, and other manipulative-type characters can be used to make the story more visual and alive. In essence, librarians must use every possible creative and ingenious method they can generate to develop a thirst for reading among hearing-impaired readers.

Notes

1. J. W. Wrightstone, S. M. Aronow, and Sue Moskovitz, "Developing Reading Test Norms for Deaf Children," *American Annals of the Deaf* 108 (1963): 311–16; David Denton, *The North Carolinian* (Morgantown, N.C.: North Carolina School for the Deaf, 1965); Office of Demographic Studies, "Academic Achievement Test Performance of Hearing Impaired Students," *Annual Survey of Hearing Impaired Children and Youth*, Series D, no. 13 (Washington, D.C.: Gallaudet College, 1969); Charles H. Hargis, "The Relationship of Available Instructional Reading Materials to Deficiency in Reading Achievement," *American Annals of the Deaf* 115 (1970): 27–29.
2. R. Conrad, "Speech and Reading," in James F. Kavanagh and Ignatius G. Mattingly, eds., *Language by Ear and by Eye: The Relationships between Speech and Reading* (Cambridge: M.I.T. Pr., 1972), pp. 205–40.
3. Harris B. Savin, "What the Child Knows About Speech When He Starts to Learn to Read," in Kavanagh and Mattingly, eds., *Language by Ear and by Eye*, pp. 319–26; Ronald Schiller, "The Lonely World of Silence," *The Banner*, North Dakota School for the Deaf at Devil's Lake, Nov. 1974, pp. 1–2.
4. Bjorn Karlsen, "A Research Basis for Reading Instructor of Deaf Children," *American Annals of the Deaf* 110 (1965): 535–39; Hargis, "Relationship of Available Instructional Reading Materials."
5. Albert J. Harris, "New Dimensions in Basal Readers," *Reading Teacher* 25 (1972): 310–15.
6. Bessie Pugh, "Utilizing Research in Teaching Reading," *Volta Review* 64 (1962): 379–87; Roma Gans, *Common Sense in Teaching Reading* (New York: Bobbs-Merrill, 1963); Jeanne Chall, *Learning to Read: The Great Debate* (New York: McGraw-Hill, 1967).
7. Sara Lehrman, "What Is a Good Children's Book?" *Reading Teacher* 23 (1969): 9–11; Robert Karlin, *Teaching Reading in High School*, 2nd ed. (New York: Bobbs-Merrill, 1972); William A. Jenkins, "The World of Children's Books and Reading," in Eldonna L. Evertts, ed., *English and Reading in a Changing World* (Urbana, Ill.: National Council of Teachers of English, 1972), pp. 77–92.
8. J. R. Anken and D. W. Holmes, "Use of Adapted 'Classics' in a Reading Program for Deaf Students," *American Annals of the Deaf* 122 (1977): 8–14.
9. Ibid.

10. T. L. Layton, K. J. Schmucker, and D. W. Holmes, "Vocabulary and Syntactic Structures in Adapted 'Classics' Readers for Deaf Children," *American Annals of the Deaf* 124 (1979): 433–43.

11. Anken and Holmes, "Use of Adapted 'Classics'."

12. Ibid.

13. Layton, Schmucker, and Holmes, "Vocabulary and Syntactic Structures."

14. R. G. Strickland, *The Language of Elementary School Children: Its Relationship to the Language of Reading Textbooks and the Quality of Reading of Selected Children* (Bloomington: School of Education, Indiana Univ., 1962); A. N. Anderson, "An Application of a Generative-Transformational Model of Linguistic Description to a First Grade Basal Reader" (M.A. thesis, Univ. of Cincinnati, 1976); S. P. Quigley et al., *Syntactic Structures in the Language of Deaf Children*, Project Report no. 232175 (Washington, D.C.: Dept. of Health, Education, and Welfare, 1976); T. L. Layton and J. M. Weber, "Analysis of Kernel Sentences and Transformations in Four Basal Reading Series: Their Types and Frequencies," unpublished working paper (Chapel Hill: Univ. of North Carolina, 1977).

15. Anken and Holmes, "Use of Adapted 'Classics'."

16. Sidney W. Sharyer, "Some Relationships between Reading Interest and Reading Comprehension" (Paper presented at the International Reading Association Conference, Boston, Mass., 1968).

17. Helen D. Schotanus, *The Relationship between Difficulty of Reading Material and Attitude toward Reading* (Madison: Univ. of Wisconsin, 1967), ED 016 596.

18. James T. Fleming, "Children's Perception of Difficulty in Reading Materials" (Paper presented at the American Educational Research Association Conference, New York City, 1967), ED 017 398.

19. Anken and Holmes, "Use of Adapted 'Classics'."

Library Services to the Mentally Retarded

ANNE-MARIE FORER and MARY ZAJAC

Introduction

The adage "free people, free libraries" expresses the pride which we Americans have in our public libraries and their services. Recently however, many have become aware that our libraries are generally unresponsive to the needs of all Americans. While library services meet the needs of the average resident, appropriate service for the thousands who deviate from the norm is generally lacking. As a result of this realization, libraries across the country are beginning to make concerted efforts to serve these "nonaverage" groups, particularly the handicapped. Pilot projects are being funded so that new concepts of appropriate library services and programs for the handicapped will emerge. L.I.F.E. is such a pilot project concerned with providing library service to the mentally retarded. It is a project of the Altoona Area Public Library, funded by Title I of the Library Services and Construction Act from September 1975 to June 1977.

The purpose of this article is to describe the L.I.F.E. project and to offer suggestions for programming and collection development which we found to be effective and appropriate for our retarded patrons. L.I.F.E. is only a beginning. We hope that others will examine these suggestions, refine them, add to them, create new and better ideas so that library service to all retarded Americans becomes a reality.

"Library Services to the Mentally Retarded," by Anne-Marie Forer and Mary Zajac, ERIC No. ED165728. Reprinted by permission of the Educational Resources Information Center (ERIC). Funded by an L.S.C.A. Title I Grant, State Library of Pennsylvania, U.S. Office of Education.

The Facts About L.I.F.E.

The L.I.F.E. [Learning Is For Everyone] program encompasses three major objectives. The first is to serve mentally retarded persons of all ages and abilities by:

1. Providing a collection of multimedia materials which they can borrow and that are best suited to their special needs,
2. Providing appropriate programs in which they can participate and find enjoyment, and
3. Providing situations in which they can interact comfortably with other regular patrons.

Secondly, L.I.F.E. is meant to serve parents, teachers, and advocates of retarded citizens by:

1. Providing a multimedia collection on all aspects of mental retardation,
2. Providing a parent resource collection of instructional materials which will help them teach specific skills and concepts at home to their retarded children,
3. Providing an information-referral service, and
4. Providing programs in cooperation with the local chapter of the Pennsylvania Association for Retarded Citizens to help parents of retarded children with their many special needs.

Thirdly, L.I.F.E. is meant to serve the general public by:

1. Providing access to information on all aspects of mental retardation including career opportunities in this field, and
2. Providing a forum in which normal children and adults interact with the retarded, and through which their attitudes and misconceptions will hopefully be changed.

L.I.F.E. was started because Blair County in which Altoona is located has a rather large population of retarded citizens which is growing due to the existence of one state hospital and two state schools. This population also includes an increasing number of children who are being diagnosed through the regular public school system. Specifically, over 3,000 people are identified as mentally retarded. That is close to 3 percent of the total population of Blair County. The national average is slightly more than 3 percent. So L.I.F.E. was started to serve a rather numerous group of people who have never been served before.

The primary impetus for initiating the L.I.F.E. library program was the change in the educational and residential situations in the Blair County area, a change which is not only occurring in Altoona but also all over the country. This new philosophy is called mainstreaming. The Education for All Handicapped Children Act mandates that by 1978 states will locate and provide free and appropriate education for all handicapped children. It also indicates that all exceptional children have the right to the fullest and richest life possible which the community can offer. Current opinions suggest that mainstreaming is the best method for implementing the law.

Although there is no clear cut definition for mainstreaming as yet, most educators, social workers, authorities, and other professionals agree that it encompasses the concept of providing specialized, individualized training and help when needed to the handicapped and in the least restrictive setting possible. In the words of one mother who wrote an article for *Exceptional Parent* magazine: "Mainstreaming means giving everyone an equal opportunity to participate in community life. For disabled people, mainstreaming means access to every part of the community—schools, churches, parks, libraries, drive-ins, and taverns."

The initiators of the L.I.F.E. program felt strongly that the majority of retarded people, including the severely and trainably retarded as well as the educably retarded, could profit from the experiences and services which libraries can provide if some special materials and knowledgeable programming are utilized. They also felt that it was the library's lawful obligation to provide service which the retarded who as citizens, as recognized members of the mainstream, have the right to receive.

The L.I.F.E. collection provides materials for a wide range of individuals who vary in abilities and intellectual functioning from profoundly to mildly retarded. It also contains materials for learning disabled children and young adults. The collection includes toys, games, puzzles, high-interest, low-vocabulary books and magazines, records, multimedia books and filmstrip kits, films, and conventional print materials. It was necessary to offer such a wide and unusual variety of materials because such things not only provide enjoyment but also opportunities for learning. For years now educators have recognized that a multisensory approach is probably the most effective method for teaching the retarded and learning disabled. It is only logical that a library collection for these people should include multisensory materials.

The extended L.I.F.E. collection also includes materials for parents, teachers, and advocates as well as the general public. The collection includes most of the professional and lay journals available in the mental health, mental retardation field, the most recent books including those of a general nature, a professional nature, and those written as "how-to's" for parents. Filmstrips and films on mental retardation, on accepting exceptionality, on parenting and training of certain self-help skills, on sexuality and the retarded are available. Copies of the most recent and pertinent state and federal government documents and pamphlets concerning mental retardation are shelved with the L.I.F.E. collection along with pamphlets and booklets published by various service agencies. Specific teaching aids such as lacing boards, double handled scissors, and concept-oriented games are available for parents to borrow. Directories to special schools and services are available but shelved in the regular reference collection rather than with the special L.I.F.E. parent resource collection. Other books of a general nature are intershelved with the regular adult collection also.

Programs for the retarded patrons include story hours, film programs, dramatics and puppetry, arts and crafts, hobby clubs, and special holiday events. Many programs are designed to include average or normal children with the retarded children. School visits are made to the special education classes in the area. Special education classes are also invited to make field trips to the library, and many teachers from schools within walking distance of the library regularly bring their children to the L.I.F.E. Center. A rotating collection of materials from L.I.F.E. is also available in one of the state school facilities in Altoona. This collection and program is handled by a volunteer teacher who works closely with the L.I.F.E. staff.

Programs for parents include film programs and discussion groups. Topics may include housing alternatives for retarded adults, right to education, legislation, parenting, how to teach certain self-help skills utilizing the materials available from the L.I.F.E. collection and so on.

Programs are also prepared for general audiences, especially school-age children and teenagers. These programs are given in an effort to help the regular children accept and understand their retarded peers and to dispel their fears and misconceptions. Several programs for both parents and the general public have been videotaped and televised over local television channels.

The L.I.F.E. Center is a self-contained center. Since many of the materials in the L.I.F.E. collection can be rather distracting when they are used, it was felt best to locate the collection in a room of its own. All children, whether handicapped or not, are encouraged to use the L.I.F.E. Center so that mainstreaming is an actuality. All children seem to enjoy and can profit from the variety of L.I.F.E. materials. It has been found that many of the more retarded adults feel more comfortable in the L.I.F.E. Center than in the regular adult sections of the library.

Those adults who want to use the rest of the library are encouraged to do so and given assistance in finding appropriate materials and in using the facilities.

Although books are cataloged in the traditional way, a simple symbol plus accession number system is used to classify and catalog the toys, games, puzzles, and multimedia kits. For example, a puzzle is PUZ 12 or a toy is TOY 43. It was found that utilizing such a scheme keeps all the same types of things together in a single area making storage and reshelving much more convenient than intershelving the materials would. This organization of the materials also has enabled the staff to divide the center into areas oriented towards adults, children, quiet activities, and play or noisy activities. Since most of the L.I.F.E. patrons request materials by format rather than by subject and tend to browse for topics of interest within a single format, intershelving by subject classification did not seem necessary or advantageous. Strong subject cataloging is emphasized to facilitate the selection of materials by teachers and parents who primarily ask for materials by subject and who know how to use the catalog.

Suggestions for Developing Library Services and Programs for the Retarded

L.I.F.E. represents a maximum investment of effort and money. Effective library service for the retarded does not necessarily require such a large investment. Meaningful service can be provided at little or no additional cost to the library. The only requirements really necessary are energy, adaptability, creativity, understanding, and a committed dedication to the principle of suitable library service for all citizens.

Whether contemplating a comprehensive program such as L.I.F.E. or more limited services, the first step is to identify the retarded population in your community. To determine how many retarded people there are, contact the public schools, rehabilitation agencies, sheltered workshops, United Fund, associations for retarded citizens, and other service agencies. Not only will their information tell you about the size of the retarded population, it will also divide this population by age and by degree of disability. This information will help you decide your service priorities.

Our experience has shown that it is better to approach provision of service on a step-by-step basis starting with one target group such as the trainably retarded school age children, and then expanding slowly to other groups. Concentrating upon a single group will help keep you from becoming overwhelmed and confused. It will enable you to set clearly defined goals which you can successfully attain in a relatively short time span. Success with one group will be so rewarding and reinforcing that you'll be eager and fresh to tackle the next. Also developing service for the next group will be much easier because you will be familiar with some of the pitfalls and problems as well as what works with retarded people.

A second step to consider before beginning to develop a library program is to learn about mental retardation. A general knowledge about etiology, terminology, educational and rehabilitative philosophies, medical treatments, social, psychological and behavioral problems, etc., will be valuable to you as you communicate with parents, teachers, and other professionals who work with the retarded. Also become knowledgeable about legislation concerning the rights of the retarded, especially in the areas of education, housing, employment, vocational training, social services, social security benefits, civil rights, etc. Become familiar with agencies both public and private which can offer help, services, and resources to the retarded and their families. Finally, become acquainted with the specific learning problems, informational needs and interests of the retarded people you plan to serve. Find out from their teachers what kinds of multisensory experiences and multimedia materials are the most appropriate and successful. Armed with this knowledge you can adapt your programs and make informed selections which will help the retarded patron enjoy and profit from the library experience.

Probably the best way to determine what services your library can provide for the retarded is to ask their parents, teachers, other professionals who work with them, and last but not least, the retarded themselves. They are the best authorities on what interests them and what they like to do. The following list offers suggestions for providing needed and appropriate library services to the retarded. It is by no means inclusive.

1. Include retarded children in your regularly scheduled story hours. Generally the activities such as finger play or singing games which are usually included in story hours for young children will be successful for the young retarded child, too. Also plan some special programs for groups of retarded children alone.
2. If your library has a policy of making public school visits, include visiting the special education classrooms with your programs. Generally the retarded have the same interests as their normal peers, so programs for the latter group with some adaptations will suffice for the retarded, too.
3. Invite the special education classes and groups from sheltered workshops and homes to come to the library on field trips. Be prepared with a brief program about the library which includes actually taking a tour. Show them the location of those materials which are of most interest to them. Demonstrate how to ask for and use equipment such as a record player. Teach them only those library skills which they will need to use the materials responsibly. Finally, issue them cards and help them select something to borrow.
4. Arrange programs on mental retardation both for parents specifically and for the general public. Topics may include housing alternatives, educational rights, mainstreaming, vocational education, and general information on retardation. Get community professionals involved. Have debates and discussions as well as films. If you have the capacity, prepare videotaped

programs for use over local television stations. These programs can also be saved and borrowed by interested groups for their own programs.
5. Develop programs on mental retardation for regular school-age children so that they can learn to respond to and accept the child who is different.
6. Provide in-service for your library staff so that they will feel comfortable with the retarded and can thus serve them better.
7. Prepare film programs for retarded adults and present them at sheltered workshops or sheltered care facilities. Remember that it is probably more difficult for the more severely retarded adult to come to the library than it is for you to go to them. If possible, take some materials along which they can borrow and use until your next visit.
8. If there is a residential institution in your service area, contact the librarian and develop ways for your two libraries to cooperate. A visit to the public library can be extremely beneficial and exciting for the institutionalized retardate.
9. Become an advocate for the retarded. Speak out on their behalf. Set an example for the rest of the community by encouraging and supporting mainstreaming of the retarded into community life.
10. Become involved with other service professionals who work with the retarded so that you become a respected and integral part of the total rehabilitative effort. By doing this you will ensure that your information and services will be frequently used.

Tips on Storytelling and Program Planning

Planning story hours for mentally retarded children is not much different from planning for average children, especially in terms of interests and activities. There are some considerations to keep in mind, however.

First consider the level of the children and their ability to comprehend and understand. Then consider their learning problems and the generally shorter attention span. The teacher is the best source of information and feedback on your programs, so it is advisable to communicate with him/her regularly. Routine, repetition, and consistency are necessary, so it is helpful to structure your programs along the same formats, use consistent methods of discipline, and build in repetition for optimum learning. It is also necessary to use positive comments and reinforcers frequently. Retarded children need to be praised often when they are sitting correctly, waiting their turn, paying attention or behaving appropriately. They also learn more through multisensory experiences. So provide a variety of media coupled with activities and songs which focus upon the main theme or concept. In this way the children become involved verbally and experientially with the concept.

Following is a list of points which we found useful in planning story hours or film programs for the retarded. In addition to the planned programs we always allow ample time for browsing and interaction with the materials in the collection. During this time we are able to work with people individually to help them learn to use the materials.

Preschool Programs

1. Storytelling: It is inadvisable to use storybooks as the only visual aid. It is better to tell the story while using puppets, flannel board figures, or drawing pictures as you go along. Actual objects are even better because they are concrete and the children can feel them. Two excellent resources are:

    Tell and Draw Stories by Margaret J. Oldfield (Creative Storytime Pr., Arts and Crafts Unlimited, Box 572, Minneapolis, Minn., 55440).
    Storytelling with the Flannel Board by Paul S. Anderson (T. S. Denison, Minneapolis, Minn. 55437).

2. Films: It is advisable to use films with loose storylines and little or no words. Familiar sounds, music, and bright colors are best. General length: 5–10 minutes.

3. Related Activities:
    Music: Finger plays set to music, action songs.
    Art: Simple activities involving only one or two skills such as coloring pre-cut feathers and gluing them to the body of a turkey. Avoid cutting activities unless you have one-to-one instruction.

Movement: Games involving one or two different movements.

Themes: Animals, make-believe characters, seasonal characters, simple concepts such as colors, counting, etc.

Primary Programs

1. Storytelling: At this level, involvement is greater on the part of the children. Have them take part as much as possible by acting out parts of the story or answering questions or finding things in pictures. Large storybooks can be used, but techniques such as tell and draw still are most successful and should be used in combination with storybooks.
2. Films: Lively animation is best. Elementary vocabulary. Sound filmstrips are generally not successful at this level. General length: 10–15 minutes.
3. Related Activities:

   Music: Simple songs with repeating verses.

   Art: Activities involving primary skills such as cutting, coloring, pasting, folding. Paper bag puppets are an example of a good activity for this level.

   Themes: Fairy tales, animated comedies, familiar experiences such as going to the doctor or zoo, seasons and holidays, animals, situations involving children their age such as making friends, fighting, etc.
4. Special Suggestions for pre-primary and primary groups:

   Seat children in an area where distractions are minimized.

   Provide mats or chairs for each. This helps define their space and lessens excessive movement.

   Start all programs with the same format. This signals the children to quiet down and get ready to attend.

   End all programs by providing something for the children to take home as a reward for good behavior. This also helps them relate their experience at the library to others.

Intermediate Programs

1. Storytelling: They can follow storybook presentations, mature themes, and enjoy plays particularly if they are given a role. They may have some problem speaking the parts, so allow them to act them out while the story is being narrated.
2. Films: Most films can be used with this level. Lively sound filmstrips can also be used at this level. General length: 15–30 minutes.
3. Related Activities:

   Music: Rounds and songs involving several actions.

   Art: Use unusual media for appeal such as styrofoam, pine cones, sponges, etc.

   Movement: Children of this age are very competitive. Team games such as relay races, passing games, etc., are excellent.

   Themes: Adventure and mystery stories, unfamiliar experiences such as living in a different land, mountain climbing, seasons and holidays, cars and motorcycles. Generally the interests of these children will closely resemble the interests of normal children this age.

Young Adult–Adult Groups

1. Discussions: Use actual photographs or objects as an introduction to a film and discussion. Provide background information. Or tell an interesting story which creates interest in the program topic. Ask many questions to discover their interests and present knowledge on the topic and to promote their participation. They can be very passive if you don't stimulate them and get them going.
2. Films: Mature themes, yet simplified plots and vocabulary. General length: 20–40 minutes.
3. Related Activities:

   Music: Folk songs sung with guitar accompaniment or record. Modern rock music often liked.

   Art: Should center around a particular craft with a mature finished product that does not look childish.

   Movement: Modern or square dancing. Games such as darts, table top bowling, etc.

   Themes: Sports, heroes, popular singing stars, comedies, adventures, mysteries and romance, nature seasons and holidays. Also, invite speakers from local community organizations such as forest rangers, museum naturalists, firemen, local radio and television personalities to talk and introduce films. Current events are also popular topics.

Criteria for Material Selection

The most effective service a library can provide for the retarded is access to multimedia materials which have been selected to meet their special needs. Establishing a special collection exclusively for the retarded is not the goal however. The more practical and philosophically sound goal is to include materials for the retarded in the regular collection. Inclusion of special materials is philosophically sound because it encourages mainstreaming. Everyone can select from these things, and the retarded are not singled out. Inclusion is practical since everyone can use and enjoy the materials. The game which is instructive for the retarded child can be equally instructive for the average child. The lacing boards, double-handled scissors, and other specialized materials can be used to teach the older trainable child as well as the preschool child. The books, records, media kits, etc., can be universally used by all. So the cost of selecting materials using the specific criteria developed for the retarded can be justified because more than one type of patron can use it. This cannot always be said of materials selected for the general public. Often, not only are the retarded excluded from their use due to their handicap, but so are other handicapped and low-functioning individuals.

Another consideration for adding special materials to your existing collections, particularly high-interest, low-vocabulary books, is the fact that the special needs of the retarded are often shared by other handicapped groups such as the learning disabled and those with speech and language problems. Poor readers and unmotivated readers who are reading significantly below grade level can profit from many of the same things selected for the retarded as long as these things are not separated from the regular collection. So providing special multimedia materials will help make it possible for libraries to serve many more nonusers.

In general, material selection is based upon the same considerations as program planning, i.e.: age, ability, level of functioning, length of attention span, special learning problems which interfere with reception of visual or auditory information, and other complicating factors such as an additional physical handicap. As mentioned earlier, teachers and therapists are the best sources of advice on what materials are appropriate.

The most important criterion for developing a collection for the retarded is its multimedia nature. Although books should be the heart of the collection, most libraries undoubtedly have many books in their existing collections which are suitable for the retarded. Therefore, we advise spending more at the outset on multimedia materials, especially book and record kits and manipulative materials such as games and educational toys or devices. The retarded individual learns and comprehends more easily if a concept is presented in several different modes so that he/she is required to respond visually, auditorially, and experientially.

Books

Easy or picture books:

1. Pictures should be simple and uncluttered.
2. Pictures should be as realistic as possible. Photographs are preferred.
3. Text should not be very long since the retarded child's attention span may be shorter than average.
4. Color drawings are more effective than black and white.
5. Storyline or plot should be simple. Many young retarded children have difficulty following a storyline. They like to point out and name different things in the pictures. Older retarded children often enjoy hearing the stories in picture books.

Fiction and nonfiction:

1. Reading level should not exceed 5.0. The majority of books should be at and below the 3.5 level of readability.
2. Pictures should be numerous but not babyish.
3. Print should be fairly large and evenly spaced so that an overwhelming amount of text per page is avoided.
4. Books should be quite short and thin. Books of very low readability (3.0 and below) should not exceed 100 pages and include a good number of pictures. The shorter book is more apt to be finished by the retarded reader and therefore, give him a sense of satisfaction and completion.
5. Subjects of interest in the nonfiction area: Cars, racing, motorcycles, horses, dogs, cooking, nature, animals, biographies of sports heroes or movie stars

(biographies of other types of successful and famous people are generally not popular with the retarded). Generally, retarded people have the same interests as their average peers.
6. Subjects of interest in the fiction area: mysteries, ghost stories, romance, adventure, social novels which involve teenagers dealing with personal problems and family conflicts.

Multimedia Book Kits

1. Follow the same criteria for selecting books.
2. If a record or cassette accompanies a book, choose the record version since more patrons have record players at home to use. It is also easier for them to operate a record player than a cassette player.
3. Clear signals or instructions should be given on the recording to indicate when to turn the pages of the book.
4. Be careful of some publishers' packaging. They often include multiple copies of the same title. If we order a title which has multiple copies, we put the extras on the book shelf so that a retarded reader can borrow and read the same title which he/she has learned to read from the record version.

Periodicals

1. High interest easy reading are desirable.
2. Lots of pictures. If the readability level of a magazine is high, but it contains many pictures, it will be used.
3. Areas of interest: beauty and fashion, nature, cars, sports, crafts, and comic books.

Some suggested special titles: *Sesame Street, Electric Company, News for You* (New Readers Press), *National Geographic World, Spidey*, a high-interest, low-vocabulary comic book (Marvel Comics).

Multimedia Filmstrip Kits

1. Captioned (silent) filmstrips should not be purchased since most retarded patrons will have difficulty reading the captions.
2. Color is much more effective than black and white.
3. Cassettes are probably more convenient than records. The program should be repeated on both sides, one side with audible signals and the other with automatic inaudible signals. The automatic signal is most necessary since many retarded patrons may have difficulty following directions for advancing the filmstrip at the proper time.
4. Emphasis should be placed upon selecting nonfiction subjects, especially in the areas of social studies and elementary science. We have found that retarded individuals more easily comprehend and understand difficult concepts which are presented in an audiovisual format than those in a print format.
5. Fables, legends, folktales and other more high level stories that are too difficult in book format are most suitable for selection in the fiction area.

Records

1. Albums are better than 45 rpm discs.
2. Most children's records which are song and/or game type are preferable. More capable children do like to listen to stories on records which have no accompanying pictures. However such stories require higher listening comprehension skills than most retarded children have acquired.
3. Adults prefer music, especially country-western, current popular songs of singers like Tony Orlando, the Carpenters, Neil Diamond, etc.

    "Oldies but goodies" are moderately popular. Classical and hard rock are not recommended.
4. Special education records should be carefully selected. Some are too instruction oriented, and without a teacher to provide direction, these do not make good records for the children to listen to alone. Parents and teachers, on the other hand, can make great use of this media.

Toys

1. No sharp edges.
2. Made with non-toxic paints and dyes.
3. Sturdy construction with few moving parts.
4. Few accompanying pieces or parts. They get lost too easily.
5. Large parts or pieces which cannot be swallowed easily.
6. Washable.
7. Educational, i.e.: Teach a concept or encourage development of coordination or language.

8. Puppets can be included, but ordinary dolls and stuffed animals should be avoided. Children usually have these at home.
9. Included in this category are teaching devices such as lacing boards, double-handled scissors, etc. Although they require some direction, we found that the children like to practice with these things unassisted.

Puzzles

Primary puzzles:

1. Knobbed, wooden puzzles with pieces which fit into a contained space are the best for young educable and older trainable children.
2. Wooden puzzles should not exceed 10 large pieces.
3. Puzzles with pictures beneath the pieces provide clues so that reassembling the puzzle is easier.
4. Crepe or rubber puzzles are also very good since these materials have more give and make it easier for the child to succeed.

Intermediate puzzles:

1. Heavy pressboard or cardboard pieces should be large with 25–50 per puzzle.
2. Wooden puzzles with more than 10 pieces are good for this level also.
3. Since trainable adults use these puzzles, select those with pictures which are not too childish.

Advanced puzzles:

1. 75–100 pieces are best, although a few retarded patrons may be able to handle a 250–500 piece puzzle.
2. Pictures of lakes, forests and the like which contain many pieces of the same color and few distinguishing marks should be avoided.

Games

1. Should be primarily educational. Colors, numbers, letters, money, time, etc., are concepts which should be emphasized. Following directions and playing fairly are also concepts which are taught through games.
2. Clear and uncomplicated rules and directions.
3. Minimum of playing pieces.
4. Sturdy construction of game boards and spinners.
5. Uncluttered game boards with large spaces to make counting out easier.
6. Playing time short since a retarded child's attention span is usually short.
7. Outdoor type games can be included if they encourage development of large muscle coordination, can be easily carried and conveniently used at home.

Pictures and Posters

1. Pictures should be appealing to the retarded patron. They do not necessarily have to be great art.
2. Modernistic or psychedelic posters are not recommended. Realistic pictures or photographs are more readily understood.
3. Inexpensive.
4. Posters seem to be more popular than art reproductions.
5. 8½" x 11" or larger are recommended.

Librarian-Made Kits

1. Combining materials into a kit should be based upon a specific theme or title.
2. Example kits: record and puppet, puzzle and puppet, record and puzzle, book and puppet, etc.
3. Be sure that all parts of a kit can be contained in a single box or media bag.

General Comments

1. Provide plastic bags or cloth bags for the patrons to carry home games, toys, puzzles, etc. This helps keep things together and will reduce the loss of pieces and parts.
2. If a patron consistently borrows the same type of materials, encourage him/her to try something else. For instance, if he/she always borrows records, encourage taking home a book and record kit. In this way, you will help interests and tastes to grow and develop.
3. Be careful not to make selections for the retarded. There is so little opportunity for them to make their own decisions and voice their interests. This is especially true of the more severely retarded.
4. Set a limit on the number of things that can be borrowed at once. The wide variety of things to pick from may overstimulate the retarded child and he/she may just grab anything. Setting a limit

forces him/her to make thoughtful selections.
5. Enforce your rules concerning borrowing and returning materials. Don't feel sorry for a retarded user who consistently returns things late or in poor condition. They, too, must learn to be responsible and to pay the consequences for breaking the rules. A little latitude may be given however, since failure is so very prevalent for the retarded. The point is to teach them to use things responsibly, to share with others, but to also encourage them to use the library and to feel welcome and successful there.

Selection of Books for Disabled Readers

MARILYN THYPIN

Although certain disabled readers may be categorized educationally as "learning disabled," educable mentally retarded" or "dyslexic," the overriding characteristic is their inability to read at the level expected of students their chronological age. This delay in acquisition of reading skills may be more than three years. Disabled readers exhibit moderate to severe deficiencies in reading skills such that standard juvenile printed materials do not provide effective instrumentalities for the development of their reading abilities.

High interest/low reading level books have been created to service the instructional needs of disabled readers. This type of printed material involves more mature content than juvenile material, while retaining a low level of demands in reading skills.

Traditionally all types of printed material have been evaluated by "standard" readability formulas all of which involve the difficulty of the vocabulary and the sentence length.[1] Created primarily for the evaluation of primary material, these formulas provide a fairly adequate measurement of the difficulty of such printed material.

Readability formulas can be criticized on several grounds: (1) the formulas generally ignore the concept load, organization of the ideas, and the format of the printed material; (2) measurements of readability of the same material yield different results depending on the formula used;[2] (3) the formulas do not consider the interests, background, cognitive skills, and language competence of the target reader; (4) the formulas may be inaccurate when used in conjunction with target readers or printed material dissimilar to that used in computing the formulas.[3]

For the evaluation of high interest/low reading level books, the readability formulas may be criticized for their heavy reliance on the use of existing graded word lists. These graded word lists were developed by the authors of the readability formulas from primary reading material. The original grading of words in basal reading material was executed according to the sequential development of reading skills as well as the vocabulary requirements for enhancing the content of such material. Although the sequential development of reading skills should be considered in grading words for high interest/low reading level books, the more mature content in such books may require the grading of certain words at a lower level than their grading in the existing word lists. Therefore, primary graded word lists may be an inappropriate factor in the evaluation of high interest/low reading level books.

For example, although the decoding of words such as "surprise" and "restaurant" requires more advanced reading skills than those learned at first-grade level, "surprise" is generally graded at the first-grade reading level, while "restaurant" is considered to be at a higher reading grade (fifth grade). Although the word "surprise" has been deemed necessary to enhance the content of material at the first-grade level, the word "restaurant" may be considered necessary for increasing the interest level in high interest/low reading level books at a low reading level. Therefore, the evaluation of vocabulary in high interest/low reading level material should include considerations of the demands of the content in such material.

The selection of high interest/low reading level books should not depend on readability formulas as the sole criterion. Instead, the interaction between the target reader and the proposed printed material should be considered in terms of interest level and syntactic, semantic, and cognitive structures. The essential factors to bear in mind when selecting a high interest/low reading level book for a target reader center around the following concepts:

(1) *The content should be appropriate and relevant to the interests and/or informational needs of the target reader.* Interest level affects the reader's motivation to read which in turn influences the development of reading skills. Generally, a low interest level has a negative effect on motivation, and subsequently on the acquisition of reading skills. Since disabled readers have experienced so much failure, a low interest level in printed material affects their comprehension more than that of high ability readers.[4] High interest/low reading level books have been created to motivate disabled readers through a more mature interest level. Moreover, they are most effective when the topic is of interest to the target reader.

The variety of high interest/low reading level books is no longer limited to stories about cowboys (*Cowboy Sam*) and how-to books written for the retarded. Commercially produced high interest/low reading level books involve fiction on mature themes such as *Run for Your Life*, biographies such as *Women Who Win*, and direct instructional material related to a multitude of content areas.[5] This extension is particularly important because disabled readers frequently demonstrate less flexibility in reading interests than high ability readers.

The selection of high interest/low reading level books for adolescent/adult disabled readers should also consider the informational needs of such readers. The informational needs may be categorized as consumer economics, occupational knowledge, health, community resources, and legal knowledge.[6] These areas of information have been deemed necessary for survival in today's society. Because of the inefficient reading skills of disabled readers, books, magazines, or governmental pamphlets can not provide such information to them. But high interest/low reading level books may convey such information at a low reading level in a fictionalized form, *Pacemaker Vocational Readers, Consumer Education I and II*, or in an expository form, Be Informed Series.[7] The selection of such informational high interest/low reading level books may inform disabled readers about relevant areas of knowledge. In addition, they may motivate them to learn to read by indicating that reading may provide information to improve their lives.

(2) *The level of content difficulty should be differentiated from the level of reading difficulty.* Intuitively, the judgments of the content level influence estimations of readability. However, high interest/low reading level books are a method of presenting material that is more mature in its content than juvenile books, but they maintain the same low reading level as juvenile books. The following sentences may serve as examples that negate the seemingly logical assumption of a direct association between content and reading levels:

The question is to be or not to be.
   Reading level—first grade
   Content level—high school

Homo sapiens are omnivorous bipeds cohabiting among the stalagmites.
   Reading level—high school
   Content level—fourth grade

As seen in these sentences, the content level of printed material does not depend on the level of readability. Rather, the content level is related to the difficulty to the concepts and the interest level in the text.

The evaluation of the content level of printed material should also involve the concept load. Primary material generally presents simple concepts in such a way that the number of ideas in the text is limited. More advanced reading level material involves more difficult concepts presented in a more compact fashion. In high interest/low reading level books, complex concepts are explained in the simplest fashion possible. Explanations may involve several sentences rather than a single sentence. Each component of the concepts may have to be explained. Moreover, complex concepts are reiterated in various simple ways so as to decrease the conceptual load of the printed material.

High interest/low reading level books may be judged too easy or too difficult for the target reader because the content and readability levels may be confused in the following ways. First, the content level of a high interest/low reading level book may appear too difficult because of the selector's familiarity with the typical content of primary material and unfamiliarity with high interest/low reading level books. Second, the content may appear too easy because of the print size and/or liberal use of pictures in the text.

A superficial review of either the appearance or content may be insufficient to assess the readability of a book for a target reader. The content level is not directly related to the readability of the text. Rather the evaluation of the content level should consider the complexity of the concepts, the vocabulary employed in the presentation, and the conceptual load.

(3) *The concepts and the cognitive skills required in the comprehension of the text should be within the grasp of the intellectual capacity of the target reader.* Comprehension of printed material depends partly on the interaction between the cognitive demands presented by the text and the reader's general knowledge and cognitive skills. The cognitive demands of the text involve the complexity of the concepts, the concept load, the organization of the concepts, and the types of cognitive skills required for comprehension. The interaction of these variables and the target reader's intellectual capacity must be considered in the selection of a high interest/low reading level book for a particular target disabled reader. For example, in selecting printed material for disabled readers who demonstrate a low level of cognitive development (i.e., inadequate for their chronological age), the conceptual demands of the text should be at or only slightly above their cognitive capacity. On the other hand, in selecting printed material for disabled readers who demonstrate an adequate level of cognitive development, it is possible to select material at a considerably higher conceptual level than their depressed reading level.

In another vein, the acquisition of reading skills may directly affect the development of cognitive skills. Because primary material is prepared for normal developmental readers, the cognitive demands in primary reading material are at a level similar to the readability level. Disabled readers exposed only to basal readers are not exposed to concepts at an appropriate level; nor are they required to employ higher level cognitive skills in the comprehension of the text. High interest/low reading level books are designed to incorporate these elements into the text so that disabled readers may acquire skills to function at a higher conceptual level. For example, the comprehension of high interest/low reading level books may include understanding complex concepts, analyzing adult situations, and making sophisticated judgments. Accordingly, exposure to more mature printed material may enlarge the disabled readers' oral and reading vocabularies, their general knowledge, their cognitive skills, and their functioning in reading. Consequently, their general functioning in nonreading tasks may become more effective.

(4) *Most of the vocabulary in the text should be part of the oral language of the target readers and/or within the grasp of their decoding skills.* Reading comprehension is related to the decoding skills of the readers and their knowledge of the meaning of the separate lexical items. The phonetic structure of the vocabulary in the text should be examined in relation to the word analysis skills of the target readers. Decoding multisyllabic words, for example, may be beyond the decoding skills of the target readers. Similarly, the target readers may only know the sound/symbol correspondence for certain dipthongs and digraphs. A text containing a large number of words that are beyond the phonetic skills of disabled readers may impede their comprehension of the text.

On the other hand, some words containing complex phonetic structures have been graded at a low reading level in the existing word lists due to the necessity for such words for the composition of primary material. Some phonetically complex words which have not been graded at a low level in the primary word lists may be needed to convey the mature content in high interest/low reading level books. High interest/low reading level books should include such words repeatedly so that the target reader learns to read them by sight. Similarly, since disabled readers have had more experiences than their primary reading level counterparts, they may be able to read by sight some phonetically complex words such as "restaurant" and "hamburger" due to everyday exposure to such words.

Knowledge of the usual meaning of a lexical item may not guarantee the comprehension of the word in a given context. The following sentences demonstrate that the word "run" may be familiar to the target disabled reader in one context but quite unfamiliar in a different context.

> The gray dogs run along the trails in the woods.
> The press run continued all night at the factory.

It is easy to see that a word may be part of one's oral vocabulary in one context and unknown in another context.

Since disabled readers tend to have an inflexible understanding of the word meanings, multiple meaning words such as "run" may hinder oral language comprehension. In turn, they impose greater difficulties in the comprehension of written language. For example, in the second example, the reader may assume that the word "press" is a noun which would be followed by a verb, and may be confused by the transformation of the noun "press" into an adjective.

It should be remembered that existing graded word lists do not consider the multiple meanings of the words, or the experiential background of disabled readers. Their use, therefore, does not assure that the vocabulary load of the text is appropriate to the oral language of the target reader. The reader's knowledge of vocabulary may be dissimilar to the considerations involved in compiling the graded word lists.

(5) *The sentence patterns in the text should approximate the syntactic competence of the target reader.* The syntactic competence of the target reader has a significant effect on comprehension of the text. If the target reader's oral language does not include specific syntactic patterns, e.g., dependent clauses, embedded phrases or clauses, passive sentences, and changes from normal word order, such syntactic patterns in the text may hamper comprehension. For disabled readers who demonstrate a limited knowledge of embedded clause, for example, the sentence "The house that Jack built is on Main Street" will be more difficult to decode and comprehend than "Jack built the house on Main Street." Therefore, the target readers' knowledge of syntactic patterns should be considered in the selection of printed material for them.

High interest/low reading level books may include some syntactic structures that are unfamiliar to the target reader. A particular unfamiliar structure should be repeatedly used within the same text so that explanations of its first occurrence increase the target reader's knowledge of syntax and improve the subsequent reading of such structures. The selection of high interest/low reading level books for target readers should involve consideration of the syntactic load of the text, the syntactic competence of the target readers and their facility in learning new syntactic patterns.

Knowledge of syntactic patterns should be separated from knowledge of surface grammatical structures. The former involves grammatical transformations which affect the meaning of the sentence; the latter involves slight variations in the surface structure of the sentence. The speaker of black English who slightly varies the reading of "I am home" to "I be home" has essentially decoded and comprehended the text. On the other hand, passive sentences can seriously disturb the decoding and comprehension of disabled readers whose oral language does not include such a pattern. For example, the sentence "John was hit by Mary" may be erroneously understood as "John hit Mary." This error confuses the reader's comprehension of the paragraph story. The sentence "The tree was hit by the car" may confuse the disabled readers to a greater extent. Because they attempt to read the sentence as an active sentence, they can not attain any logical meaning from the sentence.

Although most readability formulas rely on sentence length as a measurement of difficulty, syntactic complexity has begun to be considered as an important component of readability. Short sentences may not necessarily be syntactically simple due to their inclusion of implied clauses. One readability formula assigns numerical values to the syntactic complexity of the text.[8] Similarly, this formula may be used as a guideline for the assessment of the target reader's oral comprehension and expression of syntactic patterns. By this method, the syntactic competence of the target reader may be matched to the syntactic patterns of the text. Attention to this factor will aid in maximizing the effectiveness of high interest/low reading level books.

(6) *The text should be appealing and interesting in appearance.* High interest/low reading level books should have an age-appropriate format. This suggestion does not prohibit the use of pictures and other aids, but rather implies that the quality of such aids and the text in general should be mature in tone.

In conclusion, readability formulas can only provide a gross estimation of the appropriateness of high interest/low reading level books for target disabled readers. Disabled readers vary greatly in terms of their interests, their knowledge of concepts and content areas, and their linguistic competency. These characteristics in the target reader should be considered carefully in conjunction with the characteristics of the text, so that the reading of a high interest/low reading level book will be most beneficial to the target reader.

Notes

1. E. Dale and J. Chall, "A Formula for Predicting Readability," *Educational Research Bulletin* 27 (1948): 11–20, 37–54; E. Fry, "A Readability Formula That Saves Time," *Journal of Reading* 11 (1968): 512–16, 575–78; A. Harris and E. Sipay, *How to Increase Reading Ability* (New York: McKay, 1975); G. H. McLaughlin, "Smog Grading—A New Readability Formula," *Journal of Reading* 12 (1969): 639–46; G. Spache, *Good Reading for Poor Readers* (Champaign, Ill: Garrard, 1968).
2. E. Jongsma, "The Difficulty of Children's Books: Librarians' Judgments versus Formula Estimates," *Journal of Reading* 49 (1972): 20–25.
3. D. Hittleman, "Readability, Readability Formulas and Cloze: Selecting Instructional Materials," *Journal of Reading* 22 (1978): 117–22.
4. S. W. Schnayer, "Some Relations between Reading Interests and Reading Comprehension" (Ph. D. diss., Univ. of California at Berkeley, 1967).
5. K. Platt, *Run for Your Life* (New York: Watts, 1977); L. Jacobs, *Women Who Win* (St. Paul, Minn.: EMC Corp., 1974).
6. Adult Performance Level Project, *Adult Functional Competency: Final Report* (Austin, Tex.: Univ. of Texas, 1977).
7. L. Glasner and M. Thypin, *Pacemaker Vocational Readers* (Belmont, Calif.: Fearon, 1976); idem, *Consumer Education I and II* (St. Paul, Minn.: EMC Corp., 1980); Be Informed Series (Syracuse, N.Y.: Laubach Literary International, 1975).
8. M. Botel, J. Dawkins, and A. Granowitz, "A Syntactic Complexity Formula," in W. M. McGinite, ed., *Assessment Problems in Reading* (Newark, Del.: International Reading Assn., 1973), pp. 77–95.

Remediation and Reinforcement: Books for Children with Visual Perceptual Impairments

MARY M. BANBURY

Learning Disabilities

In 1968, Congress, upon recommendation of the National Advisory Committee on Handicapped Children, accepted the term *learning disability* to describe a specific category of handicapped children. It was agreed that the term incorporated conditions that previously had been described by such terms as *minimal brain damage, minimal brain dysfunction, minimal cerebral dysfunction, dyslexia, dysgraphia, dyscalculia, perceptually handicapped, neurologically handicapped, educationally handicapped, attention disorders, psychoneurological disorders,* and *language disorders.* There was no agreement, however, as to the exact prevalence of learning-disabled children, the exact cause of the problem, or the exact definition of the term.

There are experts in the field of learning disabilities who estimate that there are at least two million learning-disabled children in American schools; other authorities suggest that the number may reach as high as eight million. Percentage estimates range from 1 to 30 percent of the population. Not surprisingly, prevalence figures vary depending upon which definition and criteria for selection are used.

There are specialists in the field of learning disabilities who attribute the cause of the condition to prenatal or perinatal problems;

"Remediation and Reinforcement: Books for Children with Visual Perceptual Impairments," by Mary M. Banbury, *Top of the News* 1980, 37: 41–46.

others attribute the cause to such diverse factors as heredity, high fever, head injuries, malnutrition, pollution, or food additives. Etiological theories vary depending upon the perspective of the specialty group.

There are professionals in the field who define this exceptionality as a maturational or developmental imbalance, a neurological or organic impairment, a discrepancy between expected potential and actual performance; other professionals define the disability by exclusion, by stating that it is a condition not caused by mental retardation, emotional disturbance, environmental disadvantage, or sensory impairment. The definitions vary depending upon the point of view of the professional.

Although the experts do not concur on prevalence, the specialists do not agree on causes, and the professionals do not absolutely accept one definition, there are several generalizations that, for educational purposes, can be made:

1. There are a significant number of learning-disabled children in the schools.
2. Educators should focus on the symptoms and the learning characteristics of children rather than on causes.
3. Learning-disabled children, who are intellectually capable of learning and who have had the opportunity to learn, do not perform in expected ways or achieve at expected levels.

Learning disabilities vary from child to child according to the severity of the condition and the type of disorder that is exhibited. A learning disability could mildly, moderately, or severely affect one, several, or many of the following areas of learning: large or small motor coordination, spatial orientation, receptive language (listening), inner language (thinking), expressive language (speaking), visual or auditory perception, or behavior. These disorders are most noticeably manifested in the academic areas of reading, writing, spelling, and arithmetic.

Role and Responsibilities of Librarians

Many disciplines have contributed to the study of the diagnosis, prevention, remediation, teaching, and accommodation of the learning-disabled child. Much has been said and written on the roles and responsibilities of individuals in the fields of medicine, optometry, audiology, psychology, speech and language, and education. Little, however, has been said or written about the role and responsibilities of librarians.

Librarians possess special skills needed in the multidisciplinary response to children with learning disabilities; they are vital agents in the delivery of services to these youngsters. Their expertise includes a comprehensive knowledge of reading materials according to subject matter, reading level, and skill development; a thorough understanding of the developmental and sequential process of reading; and an insight into the child as a reader. Librarians can select or assist in the selection of books that will interest the leaning-disabled child, that will match the appropriate ability level, and that will remediate, sustain, or develop specific reading skills.

Visual Impairments

The following analysis of books and guidelines for selection of appropriate remedial and developmental materials focuses on children who have limited strengths or mild impairments in the area of visual perception. Other areas will need other books and other guidelines. If children are dependent on the visual channel, then it is important that their skills in this area be highly developed since they will be compensating for deficiencies or lack of input in other areas. If children are impaired in the visual channel, then it is important that they be helped in overcoming deficiencies in the various components of visual perception.

Visual perception is an umbrella term. This general area encompasses the following abilities:

1. *Visual discrimination*: the ability to distinguish similarities and differences among objects, pictures, or symbols.
2. *Visual figure-ground*: the ability to attend to the salient features of an object, picture, or symbol while disregarding the extraneous visual background.
3. *Visual form constancy*: the ability to identify an object, picture, or symbol although it alters in size, color, or position in space.
4. *Visual memory*: the ability to recall objects, pictures, or symbols that have been visually presented.
5. *Visual sequential memory*: the ability to

recall the correct succession in which objects, pictures, or symbols have been visually presented.
6. *Visual closure*: the ability to recognize an object, picture, or symbol when a partial or incomplete visual stimulus is presented.

Since there is a high degree of interrelation and overlapping among these components of visual perception, it is not possible to select one particular book to remediate or reinforce one particular skill; it is possible to suggest books that, moving along a continuum from the very obvious to the subtle, provide special assistance for visual difficulties and enhance visual strengths. These books, then, can be used sequentially and prescriptively.

Useful Books

One of the simplest and most enticing books is *Snail, Where Are You?* Tomi Ungerer, the author, used the figure of the snail as the chief component in a series of pictures. The identical shape appears in each illustration, but its function changes. The lines of the snail, varying in size, color, and position, are concealed in such forms as a pig's tail, a ram's horns, an owl's eyes, a harp, a party favor, and an umbrella handle. The signature, found in enough forms to maintain interest, is always there. Since the pages are uncluttered and there are few distracting elements, the child will succeed in the search for the elusive snail.

In Ungerer's next book, *One, Two, Where's My Shoe?*, detection of the figure is fractionally more difficult since the shoe changes shape as well as size, color, position, and function. Category is the only constant concept. Concealed pumps, boots, loafers, and slippers are incorporated in such unlikely objects as the face of a dog, the hull of a ship, the gown of a magician, the head of a snake. Clues are everywhere, however, as color and distortion are frequently used to set the shoe off from the rest of the figure. Uncluttered pages assure a challenging yet successful experience.

Two delightful books that can be read to preschoolers contain illustrations that require children to use imagination and experience to visualize internal detail and to recognize partial figures. The first, *It Looked like Spilt Milk*, by Charles E. Shaw, presents simple white figures on a dark blue background. As the text is read, children are actively engaged in guessing the actual identity of the object while visualizing the internal detail of suggested shapes. The second book, Janet and Allan Ahlberg's *Each Peach Pear Plum*, is an I Spy story that challenges children to locate the partially hidden figures of such characters as Mother Hubbard, Cinderella, Jack and Jill, and Robin Hood. The book allows the teacher or librarian to be as directive as the child requires in screening out background stimuli and locating and recognizing partially presented figures.

Tana Hoban's *Circles, Triangles, and Squares* and Bruce McMillan's *The Alphabet Symphony* use photographs to move children into the real world to search for shapes and letters in the environment and in architectural and instrumental designs. Hoban's photographic message is that shapes are everywhere. They can be found in bicycles, bubbles, bridges, trains, trucks, typewriters, houses, hoops, and hats. Regardless of dimension, viewing angle, or situation, the shape is constant. McMillan's camera eye sees letters in the music world. The bass clarinet is in the shape of a *J*; the *E* is embedded in the French horn; the first strand of strings and conductor form a *G*; the crossing of two flutes constitutes an *X*. To assure success in identifying the letters hidden in the symphony, McMillan isolates each one by reproducing it in white outline under each photograph. This serves to clarify perception and to reinforce recognition.

Through the vivid illustrations of José Arguego and Ariane Dewey's *We Hide, You Seek*, children learn that colors, textures, and patterns camouflage animals not only for the enjoyment of the reader but also for the survival of the animal. Fine drawings on the inside and outside covers depict animals who inhabit the bush, desert, swamp, plains, and river or forest areas of East Africa. These animals are engaged in a game of hide-and-seek with a rhino. Children join the game as they seek out animals that blend into the environment and assume such guises as trees, leaves, rocks, rushes, or roots. On one page the animals are hidden; on the next page they stampede out of their hiding places. Children go back and forth from page to page and cover to cover as they detect, compare, contrast, identify, and categorize the animals.

There is a natural movement from the

drawings of *We Hide, You Seek* to the photographs of *Hidden Animals* by Millicent E. Selsam. The game of hide-and-seek, however, is no longer fun for the animals; it is essential. This book (A Science I Can Read Book) stresses the fact that the animals' very lives depend upon their ability to be inconspicuous. Although both story and pictures are simple, children are challenged mentally and visually. The text examines the relationship between predator and prey, explains how natural camouflage evolved, and gives the reader clues as to how the animals merge with their surroundings. The task of separating the figure from the background is more meaningful because of this information and easier because of the clues.

The following three books are designed to reinforce, enhance, and challenge the visual abilities of children. Backgrounds are more complex, figures are less obvious, number of stimuli is increased, and degree of abstraction is heightened.

In *Where Is It? A Hide-and-Seek Puzzle Book* by Demi, children are required to locate the exact duplicate of each object in the black square. Locating that one object among a myriad of similar ones is a challenge. If children are not ready for this task, it is an exercise in frustration rather than a test of discrimination. The puzzles vary in complexity, shifting the invariant properties of the designated object while changing the number of figures from which the object is to be singled out. The search requires skill in visual discrimination, figure-ground, and form constancy.

One Dragon's Dream by Peter Pavey requires children to count from one to ten, thus enumerating all the animals and objects in the dragon's dream. However, when the dragon dreams that "two turkeys teased him" or that a "team of ten turtles towed him home to bed," children not only must count two turkeys or ten turtles, they also must count all the sets of twos and tens that appear on the pages. Since only one set is labeled for each number, children must discover what the other sets are as well as where they are located. This is a demanding task because the pictures are both complex and complicated. Drawings cover the whole page; every section is rich in stimuli. Not only are figures rotated and partially obscured, but also the only property that remains constant is that of category. Children search for sets of such categories as writing utensils, brushes, dogs, insects, and flowers. The items vary in size, color, position, function, shape, and location. Children need to be able to associate visually similar items as well as to discover, discriminate, and provide closure.

Anno's Alphabet: An Adventure in Imagination by Mitsumasa Anno challenges children's perception and perspective. "Flaws" in the paintings of the three-dimensional wooden letters are barely perceptible; however, they are there. Upon careful inspection children will notice that the letters are twisted in the manner of a Möbius strip, or are half-completed, their other half seen through a strategically placed mirror or hinged in unworkable ways. Each letter provides the initial sound for the picture on the following page. Components are subtly transformed, and children sense the visual presentation is not possible. Careful scrutiny and an understanding of visual possibilities lead children to such observations as: a brand of wood cannot be heated to red hot because it would turn to ash; a tube of paint does not grow out of the artist's palate; pen nibs do not have pencil points; a scale cannot rest in its own balancing pan. The border surrounding each letter and picture is a pen-and-ink sketch containing many embedded figures whose names begin with the sounds of each letter. The children will be able to detect the figures, but they will need the glossary to label such flowers, animals, and creatures as *acanthus, knapweed, yew, iguana, quail, vole, dwarf, elf,* and *mermaid.* Intellectually and visually subtle, Anno's book is an adventure and a challenge.

John S. Goodall's book, *The Story of an English Village,* and Jörg Müller's portfolio of pictures, *The Changing City,* require a sense of persistence of images. The first depicts the same view of a medieval English village at intervals of approximately one hundred years; the second shows the same section of a contemporary European city at intervals of approximately three years. Both are beautiful and compelling statements concerning the mutability of the physical and social world. Both are vivid illustrations of spatial and temporal differences, and detailed portraits of progress and decay as well. Caught up in this panorama of life, children visually recall, compare, and contrast images, lifestyles, and social patterns. They perceive the obvious and subtle ways in which architecture, transportation, fashions, and occupations are altered, modified, and revised. These books engage children visually, cognitively, and emotionally.

Conclusion

There are many more challenging and interesting books that remediate and reinforce the visual perceptual skills of all children and, in particular, learning-disabled children. Librarians should select and suggest books that require children to compare and contrast visually, to distinguish and separate the stimuli from the visual background, to identify the visual constant regardless of changing properties, to recall sequentially visual images, and to recognize partial visual stimuli. Librarians should select and suggest books at the children's ability and interest level, utilizing the books to develop cognitive as well as perceptual abilities.

A learning disability is not always an immutable condition. It can be circumvented by working with intact channels, or it can be remediated by working with specific components. Learning-disabled children require the services of many individuals, and librarians play an integral part in the delivery of those services.

Bibliography

Ahlberg, Janet, and Allan Ahlberg. *Each Peach Pear Plum*, New York: Viking, 1978.
Anno, Mitsumasa. *Anno's Alphabet: An Adventure in Imagination.* New York: Crowell, 1974.
Aruego, José, and Ariane Dewey. *We Hide, You Seek*, New York: Greenwillow, 1979.
Demi. *Where Is It? A Hide-and-Seek Puzzle Book.* New York: Doubleday, 1980.
Goodall, John S. *The Story of an English Village.* New York: Atheneum, 1978.
Hoban, Tana. *Circles, Triangles, and Squares.* New York: Macmillan, 1974.
McMillan, Bruce. *The Alphabet Symphony.* New York: Greenwillow, 1977.
Müller, Jörg. *The Changing City.* New York: Atheneum, 1978.
Pavey, Peter, *One Dragon's Dream.* Scarsdale, N.Y.: Bradbury, 1978.
Selsam, Millicent E. *Hidden Animals.* New York: Harper, 1969.
Shaw, Charles E. *It Looked like Spilt Milk.* New York: Harper, 1947.
Ungerer, Tomi. *One, Two, Where's My Shoe?* New York: Harper, 1964.
———. *Snail, Where Are You?* New York: Harper, 1962.

Beyond the Alphabet: From Competent Reader to Avid Reader

MARGARET B. RAWSON

This paper is addressed to those who know, as I do, how vitally important it is for people to become competent readers. We are the convinced. We need not reiterate that it may even be literally a matter of life and death, of school and economic survival, of any sort of employment or vocational success, of staying out of jail or hospital, of driving a car, of protecting oneself against exploitation, of reading a menu or a mail order catalog, or of just having something to do while awaiting one's turn at the dentist's.

But survival is only the first step. If that is all we are working for in life, perhaps it is not worth all the effort that we and our students put into the struggle against tremendous odds. Some people have thought so. However, we do know two things that can make all the difference. First, we now know enough to be able to teach everybody to read at the functional or survival level and beyond. Second, we know that learning how to read is just the beginning of what can be a fascinating good trip in life—a trip that, if you have the competence, you will be free to take

"Beyond the Alphabet: From Competent Reader to Avid Reader," by Margaret B. Rawson. Reprinted with permission from *Bulletin of The Orton Society*, XXIX, 1979.

if you want to. Will you want to? To make reading barely possible is one of the basic jobs of education. To provide the opportunities that will help the young person find out what life is like, what is in it for him or her, is the other aim of education. It is both concurrent and all-embracing. This major job begins with the child's beginnings, takes the rest of his life, and can provide some of his richest experiences.

Education is for understanding, in the largest sense; training is for mastery. Education and mastery work best as partners. For example, take the Orton approach to the education of *dys*lexic children and young people, those with excessive difficulty in mastering language. Here the careful training aspects may take more attention than is needed by the *eu*lexics, those who are naturally gifted in the learning of verbal skills. But the very process is designed to be cognitively oriented and full of its own satisfactions to the growing self. We need to obey Anna Gillingham's admonition, "Teach to the intellect," for it is, happily stronger than the rote memory, and so we lean on it, finding real virtue in necessity.

Let us go on from "Supposing that I *can* read," to "Why should I *want* to?" There are several reasons. If the first response is, "Your sense of duty as a school child," that will not get anyone very far. Says Emerson, "When Duty whispers low, 'Thou must,' the youth replies 'I can!' " But perhaps he says instead, "Oh, damn" or even, "Why should I?"

Another reason to read might be utility—a means to an end. That is a bit more compelling than duty, though perhaps not enthralling. There are many kinds of utility, some of them genuinely ego-supportive and not bad fun. But there must be more to it than this.

Annis Duff, one of the best writers on children's books, takes from Emily Dickinson the phrase, "The Bequest of Wings," and uses it as the title of a book which, metaphorically, says it all.

Bequest of Wings

He ate and drank the precious words
His spirit grew robust;
He knew no more that he was poor,
Nor that his frame was dust.
He danced along the dingy days,
And this bequest of wings
Was but a book. What liberty
A loosened spirit brings.

From *First Series, Life, XXI, A Book*

Another title, this time of a program, *Reading Is FUNdamental*, marries the two, utility and delight, and helps to get the young person *Hooked on Books*, another seminal title and an aim of the first importance.

We can surely agree that we need to be scientific as well as humane. In our context, what does that mean? To describe, explain, and perhaps to predict; to know what works and why. A book edited by Arnold and Virginia Binder and Bernard Rimland, *Modern Therapies*, considers these aspects of therapy and goes on to discuss ways of measuring success. These depend, they say, upon one's goals.

One can judge by rating somewhat subjectively, based on a single instance "How did he come out?" or comparatively "Did he catch up with the others? Do better? Lag behind?" One can use rating scales, still with a considerable complement of subjectivity and sampling limitations (grades, class standing, and the like). One can use the standardized tests, psychological or educational, normative, or criterion-referenced. If appropriate, one may use the more exact measurements of physical growth, strength, or certain kinds of behavioral functioning. As criteria of success, one can use relation to norms, or one can look at intra-individual change and growth toward the more general goals of competence and enthusiasm for living and for continued growth.

To these authors, it seems unlikely that a given therapy will produce beneficent change simultaneously in all of the three dimensions of cognition, emotion, and behavior; but in the Orton-Gillingham framework I have seen this happen so consistently that I think of it as the probable outcome. If it does not all happen, we want to know why and to do something about it ourselves or call for appropriate additional help. We may not always be able to see the process through to the end in our own time with the student, but if we have not attended to all the dimensions as far as we have gone, we have not done our job. If, however, we have kept all three balls in the air as long as we have been at work, life can and often does take it from there, as we find when we encounter our ex-student years later.

Now to focus again on our title, going beyond the alphabet is something for which we are glad to be noted—even notorious. One needs, in fact, to go beyond it in both directions, to pre-reading and post-training, if along with intellectual challenge, the spirit is to be fed and the thirst for life, as found in and through books, is to be developed to the full. Logically, love of spoken language, with its fruits, comes first and provides the matrix for the love of books. Experience with print, in turn, enriches spoken language and thought and extends and enlarges vocabulary and the capacity for living, both vicariously and directly. As Dr. Ralph Sockman has put it, "The larger the island of knowledge, the longer the shoreline of wonder," and we might add, the more will be the "peak[s] in Darien" and the harbors in which to come snugly to anchor. And so any competent reader profits from becoming an avid reader.

Of course what is good education (in the comprehensive sense) for the eulexic is good for dyslexics and vice versa. Everybody, whatever his language-learning aptitudes, rates "the bequest of wings." By the time the dyslexic-type starter gets really underway, the same principles apply to both, though the details and the pace vary with the needs and tastes of the individual. While the child who has learned to read easily may come readily and eagerly to the literary hearthside, the child burnt by failure and a sense of ineptitude may need more inducement and helpful companionship as he learns to enjoy his birthright. He is the one we, as therapists, must find some special ways to approach. That is part of the art and science of the whole of education.

We should repeat, for we must keep it well in mind, that as much training as is needed in the skills of competence is a necessary component of education, just as are understanding and enjoyment, with the functional integration of the two approaches as our aim. Therapy of both kinds begins on day one of our contact with the delayed reader, with diagnosis and explanation, and goes on through the achievement of functional literacy to competence, self-confidence and independent, purposeful school and lifetime learning and enjoyment. There is a scenario, with variations, and there are ways to set the stage and keep the play moving. You know most of the standard ones, and have developed many of your own or, as I have, can do so—devices for enriching vocabulary and engendering enthusiasm, selections of sequences of books that lead to that benign addiction to print, and so on. Most of all, we want to keep the pace right, "as fast as possible but as slow as necessary," as Anna Gillingham said. And we want to see that our students have fun—not as a distraction, but as an integral part of the growing process. Little children seem to have a "set" for going at it this way, and we want to keep that attitude alive in the younger ones who come to us at the prevention stage and to restore the older ones to it according to each one's need.

In its particulars, the scenario is not detailed, but it is broadly outlined before the language learner ever gets to the beginning of reading-as-decoding. The love of books is best caught, rather than taught. It is best if the first exposure comes early, in the nursery, from a person who is a "carrier," who genuinely enjoys children, is enthusiastic about his or her own adult reading, and either already has a taste for children's books or is open to the development of such a taste.

The advice to read to children books that you like, too, needs emphasis on the modifier, "too," to keep things in perspective. Sometimes the absurdity of omitting that little word is obvious, as when the science historian, George Sarton, gave to his little daughter, May, an elegant two-volume English-French, French-English dictionary, which served him long and well, but her only many, many years later. Who is it who plays with Junior's elaborate electric train set? On the other hand, there was five-year-old Holly who named her kitten Hamlet because, said she, "he wears a customary suit of solemn black!" Her actress mother explained, "When I read to her, I read things I like to read," and she read so well that Holly really did like it, too—and for always, and with deepening understanding as she grew up.

For most of us, the options are less spectacular—say to present Marjorie Flack's *Story about Ping* rather than to get entrapped by *Ducky Daddles and Jimmy Joe at Breadcrumb Pond*. You'll have to read whichever one it is three score times and ten. For both adult and child it might better be Wanda Gag's *Gone Is Gone*. Need I say more? And if engines are to be personified, why not share the delight of Hildegard Hoyt Swift's *Little Blacknose*? Forget, if you are allowed to, the banal moralizing of *The Little Engine That Could* and banish the demoralizing falsity of *Tootle*. (If you have escaped that one and wonder at my vehemence, consult David Riesman in *The Lonely Crowd*.) I have just had the fun of introducing a whole new family, parents and children, to Blacknose, and they love him as much as my children did 40 years ago, and as their children did later. If this engaging little pioneer has nourished one's mind, spirit, and literary taste by the auditory route, he may be just the one to guide the eyes into reading a first "real, long book," already familiar, when skill has come to that point.

Now, whether the future bookworm is a natural reader, a preventively nurtured dyslexic, or an older child being rescued from failure, frustration, and refusal to have anything to do with print, let us assume that he is now getting the graphic form of language straight, as it is. He has the alphabet and its clusters of letter-sound relationships "down cold" and, from $a + t = /a/ + /t/ = at$, he has been learning about blending sounds and syllables and longer and longer words. Simultaneously, he has been combining words into sentences and sentences into paragraphs, phrased and read like talking. At first he has met the *Fat Sam* type of sound-controlled vocabulary booklets. He knows these are only a kind of finger-exercise reading—but what is wrong with playing "Three Blind Mice," or practicing throwing spitballs, until you get the hang of things? That is how skills are built, to begin with.

Is this child really a bookworm-to-be? Very often we can make a good clinical guess, but I think it works best if we first assume that he is going to want to be a reader. We can then leave the rest to him, with whatever good press we can give to the activity. I remember Tommy. He looked like a future literature addict to me, so I predicted to his mother that she would someday be saying, "Tommy, get your nose out of that book and go play ball!" "That," said she, "will be the day!" Sure enough, a year or so after our lessons had ended, she called me, chuckling, "Remember what you prophesied? Well, it's just happened and I thought you ought to know."

Someone, regrettably a noted reading teacher (from the *Dick and Jane* school) said, "I believe in nurturing individual differences—everyone has the right not to read." "A half-truth," said I. "How can you choose not to read unless you are able to read?" That stopped her, at least for then, I am happy to report. Of course, for some people like Pooh-Bear, exercise means "falling off the ottoman [without] the energy to clamber back." For some, the access to literature comes via the Saturday morning television, or even "Masterpiece Theater" of the Public Broadcasting Corporation, to which all honor.

There is the true story of Mason, a clinic patient, 14 years old and a complete nonreader, despite the IQ of 110 brought out by the WISC* I was giving him. You may remember the question on the Information subtest, "Who wrote *Romeo and Juliet*?" Said Mason, thinking hard, "I ought to know that. . . ." [How? I wondered.] ". . . I think he lived in olden times . . . and his name had 'spear' in it . . . Allspear? . . . Something like that!" "How did you know?" [As tester, I dared not also teach.] "Oh!" said he, "I saw that play on TV. It was really good!" And he told me about it—well enough to pass a high school test. Was he exercising his right not to read Shakespeare but to watch the tube that night? I might have been, but he had no choice. He could have learned to read and wanted to; but at that time there was no program open to him and so, though he is a successful, skilled workman—a mason—he is still cut off from the world of books.

Supposing the person can read, will he want to? He cannot choose intelligently and freely until he has experienced what may be in it for him—and that part of his teaching, too, had better be extra wise and positive so that it can supplant the negative conditioning of his earlier failure. His hope and his enthusiasm, once aroused, can hardly afford more than a very occasional "dud" or boring book experience. Many things will need to happen concurrently as he moves beyond the alphabet—or elementary skill learning—to being enthusiastically hooked on books and launched on a lifetime of use of printed riches for his own purpose.

He may need continued help in skill development. Eulexics seem to win without much help the needed facility in word decipherment and recognition, a growing vocabulary of understanding, familiarity with complex sentence structure, flexibility of attack suitable to varied texts, and increased speed and power. Dyslexics, however, may need continued help for a long time with one technique or more, or periodic "booster shots" at crisis points in their schooling. Generally, I have found the best promoters of good comprehension, which so many people worry about, to be the degree of interest, felt need, and the quality of educational experience. Given these, only basic general intelligence seems to be the limiting factor.

Sometimes, however, some students need specific supplementary help with specific skills of understanding. Perhaps problems in

---

*Wechsler Intelligence Scale for Children.

mathematics need to be made real, with words translated into facts in sequence; history can be brought to life; science or art forms can be experienced; metaphor as a literary device can be brought to conscious awareness—all beyond what teachers need to do for others in the class who seem to get there mostly by themselves. These are what Weaver, in the pages of this journal last year, referred to as schemata for increasing comprehension. If they are needed, of course they should be brought into play.

Certainly, it is vitally important to make sure that the student meets the books that are right for him at the right time, as Vail made so clear, also in this journal last year. Nothing in this essay is as deserving of bold-face capital letters as this! I have always been glad that I started my teaching career as a limited-budget librarian for the school. With only 50 or 75 dollars a year to spend, I had to borrow and read a couple of thousand children's books so that I could know which few we could afford to buy when they came on the second-hand market. What is more, I knew that we, as churchmousely administrators, could afford very little junk. Neither, was I to learn, could the slow-starting reader afford to spend his limited time on inferior volumes when—and this is important—he could get all the profit and more of lasting satisfaction from the high quality ones. There are those who say, "Let him read all kinds so he will have a basis for discrimination." That is one route, especially if he is a facile reader with a large library available. I'd not stop him, but I believe one can find virtue in necessity, as we had to—a place for critical adult review before offering selection, but not done in a spirit of censorship. Ed's experience is an illustrative example.

Ed's first 12 years, at home and at school, presented him with a nourishing literary diet, controlled by budgetary necessity and parental choice in use of available resources. His junior high school library had no such restrictions. The very first day in 7th grade, its bursting shelves nearly overwhelmed him with joyous excitement. He discovered the Ralph Henry Barbour series-type school stories in which I too, his mother, had reveled at his age. He polished off one the first night. With the second one-night stand, came the heady announcement, "Boy! There are 27 of them and I'm going to read them all!" Two weeks later I asked, "Isn't that third Barbour book due today?" I was mean enough to add, "And what about the other 24?" "Aw," said he, "I've had enough. You read one, you've read them all!" So, in developing literary taste, as in skinning the cat, there are more ways than one. As an adult, Ed is no pedantic snob, but he is a discriminating reader.

When I became a reading teacher—a language therapist, in fact—it stood me in good stead to have used juvenile literature instead of adult who-dunnits for some years of leisure reading. It helps enormously to be able to say, "Here are two or three stories that kept me awake half the night when I read them. They are about [this and this and this] which are up your alley. You might like to consider one of them next. Take your pick." If your youngster has found your previous suggestions rewarding, and you have to see to it that he generally does, he'll feel helped, not manipulated, by this reasonable narrowing of the field. If you have guessed wrong, of course, you have to be genuinely ready to alter course. Some people thrive on *The Wind in the Willows*, but it is not everybody's dish and may, anyway, be better listened to than read to oneself. But *The Phantom Toll Booth* is an almost sure-fire success with its delicious mixture of fantasy and modernity. It is fun with words at Dictionopolis and with the Mathemagician, and all the other ways that Norton Jester, with help from illustrator Jules Pfeiffer, has found to play with character and philosophy and the high adventure of outdoing evil and rescuing princesses. There is something exciting and amusing happening on every page. But you do not *start* here.

In pursuit of the goal of fluent—not merely functional—literacy for the dyslexic and enthusiasm for the hitherto reluctant reader, I generally though not invariably follow some such line as this:

1. First comes the therapy of diagnosis—taking the language differences seriously, trying to understand your pattern and the difference it makes for you and explaining both it and the treatment rationale.

2. Then I make the promise, as a probability prediction, that if we tackle the job this way and take advantage of the scientific approach to language, describing the Orton-Gillingham techniques, it won't be too terribly long before you will be reading real books about things you are interested in. No more of that baby-reader stuff for you! It will go slowly at first, and I'll give you a lot of help with figuring things out for yourself. Then, as your power grows with skill and practice,

you'll do more and more for yourself and do it more easily and faster.

3. Then comes the alphabet chapter—technique, well and thoroughly done. It works: ask those who have used it.

4. As soon as possible, I like to substitute a tried and true sequence of good, so-called trade books for the standard or even the special reading texts. Adult reading aloud is mixed more and more with the student's oral reading in the books we are enjoying together, leading eventually to independent silent reading and an expansion of power and a sense of growth. The student is not asked to read any words which he does not have the skills to figure out on his own. There may be only a few he can do as he begins *Liang and Lo* or *The Outside Cat*, but there will be more by the end of each volume. It is a great morale booster when he realizes what is happening, as you see that he does periodically.

There will be as many of these brief, wide age and interest range books as he needs and wants, followed by those at the level of *Billy and Blaze, High Water in Arkansas, Little Blacknose, Max* (a realistic story of a bear cub and a boy), *Greased Lightning, Honk the Moose, Homer Price, The Enormous Egg, Mr. Popper's Penguins, Farmer Boy, Nuvat the Brave, Call It Courage, Justin Morgan Had a Horse,* and so on through more and more challenging but always interesting pieces of the world of reality, adventure, fantasy, humor, beauty and other joys. There are dozens of winners at every level until at last you are on your own, with only as much help in selection as you want.

5. Concurrent and advanced skill techniques and encoding (spelling and writing) are parallel and cross-connected. Still, however difficult and time-consuming are the writing skills, one should not get so carried away by their obvious importance that reading and its joys are supplanted, or neglected.

Then there is the whole question of what is sometimes called bibliotherapy. From my viewpoint, just becoming a competent reader is perhaps the most important bibliotherapy there is for a dyslexic, potential or confirmed. As the term is usually used, however, it refers to the deliberate choice of books with certain content for the student to read because of the contribution they are likely to make to his mental health, to the solution of his emotional or social problems.

A great many of the best books give us a golden opportunity to do this and I am all for using them. However, we are no longer in the era of Goody Two-Shoes, the laughing stock of even my youth. If bibliotherapy is to work, it must be subtle. Pointing out the moral, or even drawing it out of the reader, will not only adorn the tale, it will probably kill it—and your relationship with the student, too. It is, if anything, worse than studying Shakespeare by dissection or insisting on the mastery and acceptance of Mao's Little Red Book. The discussion of feeling, ethics, and social relations is certainly not taboo and merits frank, sensitive, and respectful handling. But that is a different matter. One has other reasons for offering or choosing a story, and the psychosocial therapy, while it is often intended by the adult, must seem "serendipitous" to the youngster or, very often, enter his world without benefit of conscious identification or acceptance. To achieve this is not so much manipulation as the high art of ministry and a mark of able therapy.

Some of the themes are universal, whether they are personal like fear or broadly philosophical like the age-old struggle between good and evil. There is the need to belong, to be accepted. Who of us has read *The Outside Cat* without identifying with Samuel who desperately wanted to be an inside cat? Samuel labors persistently in his own way to bring this about and, still true to his feline nature and dignity, finds his way to happy acceptance. Certainly, no dyslexic, unwillingly excluded from the most important life of his world, its language, and longing to be a full participant, can fail to identify with Samuel. Kate, in *The Good Master*, and many another in both real and imaginary time and circumstances—notably Madeline L'Engle's older young people—touch this theme, and through it the inner life of their readers.

Or is it the sense of identity, the "who am I and why am I here," that concerns us? Little Blacknose, sometimes puzzled and often triumphant, finds out as he lives through a hundred years or so into the history of science and technology. So do David, in *It's Like This, Cat,* and preteen Margaret in *Are You There, God? It's Me, Margaret,* to contrast divergent settings. It is a universal theme we find everywhere, often in the current rash of problem-oriented novels too explicit and obvious for good literary taste but apparently acceptably helpful to young readers.

Are you beset by fears, amorphous and terrible or specific but perhaps unmentionable? You, too, will welcome with Wagtail

Bess, the therapeutic ministrations of Angus, the irrepressible, sympathetic Scottie dog as he helps her to get over being afraid and to "wag [her] tail and *smile* as an Airedale should." When the tiger who terrifies Liang, Lo and their erstwhile intrepid water buffalo turns out to be a paper structure (you knew he would, from the pictures), you are suffused with a warm glow of amusement, laced with unadmitted relief at the jolly homecoming paraders' acceptance of the destruction of their festival paper beast and their friendly invitation to "come back next year . . . creep into the tailpiece and make it wiggle." From here, all the way through the terrors of the road to the rescue of the Princesses of Sweet Rhyme and Reason, relieved with humor in *The Phantom Toll Booth*, and almost unbearable in the climaxes of *A Wrinkle in Time*, *Narnia*, *The Lord of the Rings* and Alexander's *Taran* books, you learn, if you are ready, to face terror and live in triumph. But here is an area in which great wisdom is called for in the mentor. Some hardy youngsters seem to thrive on such challenges, but it is possible to push matters too far and too fast for a vulnerable child's tolerance. *The Hobbit*, just right for some people at some times, can bring on nightmares, as can so innocent seeming a tale as *Karoo, the Kangaroo*, when wild dogs almost overtake the mother kangaroo, terrifying a too frightened five-year-old imaginative identifier. It is well to read for oneself and re-read with *this* child in mind when one is walking the thin ice of therapeutic prescription.

Or are you a little girl, by turns glorying in and cramped by the chromosomal chance that made you female? *Joan Wanted a Kitty* (beautiful but in first reader vocabulary) or *Caddie Woodlawn* or *Roller Skates* may be your meat—being a girl can be great fun. Or *The Golden Horseshoe* and *Master Skylark*, and later, *As You Like It*, can give you the thrill of delightful, and eventually triumphant masquerade.

Small may not always be beautiful to you, but you can have recourse to Tom Thumb and his tribe, and all those put-upon third sons and daughters who star in the old tales; to *Paddle-to-the-Sea* and other artifacts, toys and animals come alive; to *Stuart Little*; and to that heroic humorist, 6-inch Peter Peabody Pepperell III and his airplane, Gus the Gull, in their exciting *Fabulous Flight* and its hilarious preliminaries.

Dyslexic children don't, praise be, think of themselves as handicapped, but it helps to know such people as the characters in *Little Magic Painter*, David in *Two Children of Tyre*, Mary in the *Little House* series (before the media got hold of the *real* Ingalls). Time was, perhaps still is, when there was a lot of tear-jerking about people's physical and social-economic misfortunes, but it is not hard nowadays to find whole boys, girls, and adults living lives with aspects of wholeness and often super-humanity where once there were but sentimental Lame Prince-Little Matchgirl stereotypes. But don't take them from memory—read them afresh before you introduce them. They may be worse than dated!

One characteristic frequently met among dyslexic readers merits a special look because it may have to do with the special capacity many of them have to think, perceive and solve problems globally, as whole chunks of reality, rather than analytically and verbally. They have a thirst for realism. Perhaps, as the reading of Samuel C. Florman's *The Existential Pleasures of Engineering* suggested to me, it is because some books give our "right-hemisphere-active" youngsters just the kind of vicarious experiences in living they can feel most at home with. They can see and feel themselves making use of the artifacts of Nuvat's Arctic ancestors with him. They can milk cows and train steers with Almanzo in *Farmer Boy*, fight blizzards and grasshoppers and bears with Pa and Ma and Mary and the others in the (real) *Little House* sequence. They practice woodlore and camping with Dickon, as he lives with the Lenape Indians, and they can climb the rigging in Alan Villiers's schoolships.

Florman points to *The Iliad* as a source of aesthetic satisfaction as well as practical interest to the adult engineer, who relishes its exact description of construction details of ships and buildings and other vivid bits of reality. Perhaps it has the same bi-hemispheric appeal to dyslexic boys, such as those to whom George Hayes read it at the Linden Hill School, their natural bent attuned to his Homeric enthusiasm. An imaginative inspiration (and an enabling grant) gave him and his older boys a chance to explore the real Troy, sail the Aegean, play soccer with boys in Rome, and experience the Pillars of Hercules for themselves. It did not, in all likelihood, make epic poets or civil engineers of the boys, but neither they, George, the board member who photographed it all, nor those of us who have seen the film are ever likely to forget the reality of that experience.

I think of Ralph, as bright and as dyslexic as they come at age 8, who became a voracious and independent reader of all the seagoing stories we had by 11, made and more or less mastered his own shop-built sextant at 12, and by 14, had become a knowledgeable authority on naval matters—history, ship design, and marine lore. For him this was an intense but passing phase; he now has a double doctorate and a professorship in medicine and biochemistry—and a son as dyslexic as he was himself. One reads for many purposes—to learn how, to satisfy curiosity, to extend experience, to enjoy life, and sometimes as a precursor to a career. Ralph might have gone on, as did his younger look-alike, temperamentally twin fellow-alumnus who has sailed the waters of Southeast Asia in a small boat and, along with becoming a physicist, has written seagoing sagas himself.

Much, much more could be said about the uses to which one can put reading experience, but this is enough. Let us turn for a moment to the general criteria appropriate for selection of books for our children. Where can you get help in looking? You can ask the voice of experience. There is none better than Dorothy Tower in her letter to her grown-up daughter, "Books and Children" (see Orton Bulletin XXIII). Or, for fuller treatment, there are those standard library references: May Hill Arbuthnot's 1977 edition of Children and Books; Annis Duff's Bequest of Wings; and Constantine Georgiou's Children and Their Literature.

These and many others tell what books are available and what they are about, but they do not tell—because most librarians and their guides do not know—which volumes are for which dyslexic readers. For this there is no substitute for doing it yourself. Some librarians can be very helpful, others moderately so, but they are very much worth consulting, especially school librarians. So are some teachers; but the final judgment rests on your informed and responsive experience and your students. You will build your lists of books, as I have mine, and they will be among your best and quite indispensable teaching tools. Certainly you should not lean heavily on *my* guidance, especially for specifics.

I have told you somewhat autobiographically of just a few of the well-worn volumes I would pull again from my own shelves. In principle, I'll vouch for the choices, but your world and its children and its resources are different. To some extent, that is as it should be, though I find it an impoverishment that many young librarians and modern libraries are unaware of the still viable treasures with publication dates before 1969. This is as true here as it is in professional bibliographies, where only an occasional reference over 15 or 20 years old is cited, and even the products of the 1960s tend to be put in the half-price, stale-bread sales bins. On the other hand, you have undoubtedly noticed that most of the books I have referred to by title and most of the ones I have listed as the larger set I want to take to my desert island school for all-age dyslexics are very much out of date by publishers' standards. Such are the unfortunate facts of publishing life that many of the best books are out of print and not always available in even rather good libraries. Quite a few of them, a knowledgeable author of children's books tells me, would probably not be read spontaneously by most modern children, who really want—are sure they do—more of the here and now, social problem stories, and more science fiction. I agree with them on the merits of sci-fi. I am, in fact, quite a fan and have been since the early days of Heinlein and the rest. Still, I think I could sell almost any of my enthusiasms to the right child at the right time, just as I saw a fine male therapist at a summer camp a few weeks ago enjoying that social satire, Fatapoufs and Thinifers, with a 10-year-old boy in just the way I used to do thirty-odd years ago. The principles are basically timeless. So, what does one look for in a good book?

In the first place, I don't think I could have a valid opinion on books for children unless I kept on reading adult books for my own information, growth, and pleasure. In literature as elsewhere, what do they know of England who only England know? One needs to encourage the open personality and a wide range of taste, at home as well as in the classroom and the clinic. I'll be attracted to a book if it is well-written by adult standards, with clear, felicitous prose (or verse, about which I have not spoken, though not for lack of enthusiasm), well-planned plot and characterization, accurate but well-assimilated and usually unobtrusive background research, clear explanation if its purpose is to give a matrix for further information. I'll be likely to use a book with students, and enjoy it myself, if it has humor and imagination and is alive and paced appropriately for its subject and readers, with the right amount of print on each page and chapter and between the covers. It should, of course, be appropriately printed, bound and illustrated with pictures of artistic worth and essential conformity to the facts of the text, and so arranged as to enhance without being intrusive. Then one can enjoy it aesthetically and physically as well as intellectually. Genuine sensitivity, not sentimentality, is important. It takes the genius of an E. B. White to address with satisfying subtlety, as he does in *Charlotte's Web*, such great moral issues as good and evil, justice and mercy, appreciative acceptance of one's own self and the precious difference of others, the whole business of how to meet the joys and vicissitudes of life, and the growth of real people in real and satisfying ways. But it is this kind of excellence we are looking for in a book for any age or reading ability.

Can books really touch the lives of children? I think Edward Eager knew when he gave his children in *Seven-day Magic* the experience and the words we may well listen to. Here is Barnaby, the prime idea-man among the five quite real, not quite prosaic children who were returning to the library with the book itself as a flying carpet, using the library roof as their heliport. The children were following Barnaby's lead. As the story goes from here:

> They went down a ladder and found themselves in the upper part of the library, where they had never ventured before because only grown-ups were allowed.
> "Think of all those books we haven't read yet," said Abby [the poet].
> "Maybe some of *them* have magic inside, too!" said Fredericka [the youngest].
> "*All* of them, I should think," said Barnaby, "one way or another."

Barnaby already knew, and perhaps said better than any of us, that if man cannot transcend himself and partake of the nature of his growing, innovative kinship with the universal—his full humanity—it will not be for lack of stimulation and liberation provided par excellence in books. Those people, be they few or many, whom we teach to read with skill and enthusiasm and who use their skills to give them touch with their heritage and to feed their minds and spirits, make our game well worth the candle.

Book Selection for Young Gifted Readers

BARBARA H. BASKIN and KAREN H. HARRIS

Gena was brought into the school library at the age of seven by her mother who felt the girl was in urgent need of reading guidance. Gena was very comfortable reading books written at a level of difficulty comparable to those in the high-school curriculum, so few books were beyond her ability. Since she was afraid of airplanes, she began to settle down for a presumably satisfying afternoon of reading. Her mother felt rather strongly that there must be more appropriate fare for a second grader, no matter how precocious, than *Fear of Flying*.

Soon after, Laura arrived at the library. She was six and her test results revealed an eleventh grade reading comprehension level. Her parents were similarly concerned that their daughter's encounters with books were developmentally inappropriate. Laura, like Gena, had another problem common to high ability children—she was a voracious reader. When asked what stories she had enjoyed recently, she replied: "Wednesday, I read *Tom Sawyer* and liked it very much." The

---

"Book Selection for Young Gifted Readers," by Barbara H. Baskin and Karen H. Harris. Reprinted by permission of *Roeper Review*. Copyright 1980, vol. 3, no. 2.

problem of keeping such children supplied with proper fare has not been seriously addressed by either librarians or teachers of gifted children. In the wake of tremendous focus in recent years on children who perform many years below grade level, educators appear unimpressed with the seriousness of the reading problems of children like Laura or Gena. Yet the concern about finding books which are intellectually stimulating, accommodate their limited experience and relate better to their social and emotional growth and interests, is a real one.

Typically, these girls and their intellectual equals of like age are directed to adult books, award winning titles, recommendations of peers, or, most commonly, are forced to rely on their own resources. The dilemma with adult literature is exemplified in Gena's near encounter with Erica Jong. Although there are some titles that are suitable, adult books appropriately deal with adult topics. They involve emotional, societal, economic, personal, and sexual behaviors that are often beyond the child's understanding or coping abilities. Although some stories may be neutral in impact, others are so suffused with violence or threatening situations as to be deeply disturbing to youngsters. Nonfiction works are generally less of a problem, particularly those in technical areas in which a child may already have displayed interest, knowledge or even expertise. Aside from some difficulties in vocabulary, syntax, and occasional incorrect assumptions the authors of nonfiction may have made about the extent of background the reader would bring to the text, there are often few insurmountable problems. Still, books that merely describe may be minimally stimulating, calling for lower levels of cognitive response only; thus they may serve to broaden the child's knowledge base, but they will rarely necessitate analytical or other high level behaviors.

Award winning books are routinely suggested as proper reading for high ability youngsters, with Newbery award winners the favored choice. This prestigious medal is presented annually to the work of an American author recognized by the award committee as having made "the most distinguished contribution to American literature for children" in the preceding year. Emphasis is on literary merit, not on cognitively challenging content, and although there may be some overlap, the two qualities are far from congruent. The committee does not consider foreign authors among its eligible candidates even though within that cohort can be found writers of the most complex and demanding books. In fact, the general level of expected intellectual functioning of youthful readers is higher in several European countries, a situation which becomes obvious when domestic and foreign text and trade books for equivalent grade levels and audiences are compared. The selection of an annual Newbery winner inevitably leads to some lesser quality titles receiving recognition which, had they been published in other years, would not have even become candidates. Within the library profession, the awards are an endless source of controversy and complaint and, when viewed in their entirety, hardly seem to reflect an absolutely unassailable standard of writing for children.

Other major awards such as the Hans Christian Andersen Prize and the Laura Ingalls Wilder Award look at attributes in books which are peripheral to a child's need for intellectual growth. These two honors are given to authors for the totality of their literary contribution, hence necessarily encompass a wide range of works, often of varying quality. Although such challenging competitors as Maria Gripe have been honored, such homey, enjoyable, but intellectually bland writers as Beverly Cleary and Meindert DeJong are more typical of the prizewinners.

There can be little justification for the promotion of Caldecott books as specifically suitable fare for primary level, high ability youngsters. Those books are judged exclusively on perceived artistic merit with no consideration whatsoever of text. The aesthetic judgment of the committee has been severely criticized but, even had their members been unfailingly astute, their indifference to the written content would limit the validity of their selections as being suitable for the particular audience we have identified.

Some educators and librarians have felt that peer choices were most useful. From time to time, gifted children have been questioned about their favorite books and the most popular titles were transferred to a list of recommended reading for their peers. Often these were edited (*The Amityville Horror* was removed from one recent local list), but the results are obviously still less than satisfactory. Expecting youngsters to make more judicious choices than professional educators implies an abdication of responsibility on the part of adults and assumes a level of experience and competence in children that has not proven warranted. High ability youngsters are likely to prefer Judy Blume to Alan Garner just as adults are as apt to prefer Judith Krantz to Flannery O'Connor. While Blume's books are very useful in exploring attitudes and examining developmental crises, they have probably never been accused of being particularly intellectually demanding—nor is that their intent: they serve other purposes. Whether high ability children are left alone or guided by their peers, such book selection procedures leave to chance optimal utilization of a major source for intellectual growth.

Textbooks in methods and materials for the instruction of high ability youth are strangely vague about or indifferent to the value of books. Typically they think of reading as a skill to be mastered rather than a dynamic, emergent behavior which requires planned, careful nurturing. They readily acknowledge that high ability children are early and eager readers, but are almost universally unconcerned about the quality of that experience. Libraries, when recognized at all as part of the instructional plan, are seen as a source of undifferentiated knowledge. A brief nod is sometimes made in the direction of reference books and the card catalog, but it is abundantly clear these are merely pro forma gestures. Considering that gifted children typically cite reading as a favored activity and that books offer one of the least expensive, more individualized, and most pleasurable and efficient channels for intellectual growth, such negligence is astonishing.

Books serve multitudinous purposes. They articulate facets of the children's world, elucidating and confirming observations about their lives. They open vistas beyond a youngster's necessarily limited experiental base, filling lacunae which impair comprehensive consideration of complex issues and impede scholastic success. They provide intense emotional involvement, making learning more memorable: such dramatic presentation of situations can capture a reader's attention and concern in a manner that must ever elude the most carefully designed workbook, filmstrip or transparency. Alternately, books can provide an affect-free objective examination of those topics which benefit from emotional distance. Books allow creative escape—immersion in another world with conflicts far removed from the tedious minutiae of everyday life. Escape is, after all, not only from, it is also to something or somewhere and can be a creative act which prepares a child for coping imaginatively with authentic problems.

Obviously all books are not equally capable of fostering cognitive growth. Identifying suitable titles requires an examination of qualities inherent in the books themselves as well as assessing the kinds of thought processes required to read them successfully. Of the many factors which comprise any book, three are of special significance: language, structure, and content.

Language is the most basic tool for thinking. Until experiences are expressed, they cannot be digested, compared, evaluated or integrated—and even this does not define the limits of language. The formation of new ideas, the generation of unique proposals or solutions, in other words, creative thought is primarily dependent on language. Bronowski (1978) asserts a specific organic, indissoluble tie between language and science: "So I am putting forward the view that the method of science, the objectification of entities, abstract concepts, or artificial concepts like atoms, is in fact a direct continuation of the human process of language, and that it is right to think of science as being simply a highly formalized language."

Since children acquire language primarily through mimetic behavior, it is important to provide them with excellent models. The earliest and most quantitatively significant models will come from the speech of family and community and from popular media. These are generally deficient in important aspects. Most spontaneous speech follows prescribed forms employing a limited, highly redundant vocabulary, favors simple grammatical constructions and only slight variations in tone. Popular media are rarely better as language models and often worse, for by definition they are directed to the widest possible audience which they reach through making their appeals as simple and straightforward as possible. While exceptions occur—they are just that—exceptions.

Literature, on the other hand, is deliberate, studied and carefully structured. Words are used or rejected because of connotations as well as denotation to a much greater extent than is found in spontaneous speech. More elaborate grammatical constructions expressing various degrees of subtlety or making fine, but possibly significant, distinctions are used. Books can utilize language patterns common to other eras or indigenous to other cultures and thus demonstrate meanings unhinted at in everyday conversation. Literary and historic allusions, symbols, imagery and multiple levels of meaning are absent from all but the most sophisticated talk, yet are commonplaces in literature.

Titles selected for their potential in fostering language growth provide young readers with the tools they can use to understand their world. For language is the means through which the intellect records, recalls, organizes, integrates, correlates, accepts or rejects information. As Farb (1973) concluded: "Until language has made sense of experience, that experience is meaningless."

The potential for language growth is obvious in some beginning books for children. These titles are a rich source of humor and word play as well as intellectual content. Even so ostensibly elementary a genre as alphabet books can introduce children to such irresistable and delicious words and phrases as "ghastly garrulous gargoyle" and "quintessential quail" if Leonard Baskin's *Hosie's Alphabet* is employed. Fred Gwynne plays games with language in *The King Who Rained* and *A Chocolate Moose for Dinner* in which the wrong homonym of a pair is deliberately employed. The blue prince is depicted as a royal personage monochromatically garbed, examining the written plans for a partially completed structure. Elsewhere, the narrator's mother is stretched stiffly between two pieces of furniture while the household pets step nimbly across her body in an unusual game of bridge. The extreme literalness of the characters forms the absurd element in *The Twenty-Elephant Restaurant*. When the husband tells his wife the table he has just built is strong enough to support the weight of an elephant, she advertises in the newspaper for pachyderms to test his claim. The irrational logic motivating the characters will also generate amusement in readers attuned to such offbeat fun.

Stories that use figurative language routinely and include historic, mythic, or literary allusions are more taxing than those whose substance remains on the surface and is consequently accessible without much effort. In Merrill's retelling of the classical Taoist legend, *The Superlative Horse*, she describes the sought after creature as "one that raises no dust and leaves no tracks—that mark is evanescent and fleeting, as elusive as air." It becomes clear to the attentive reader that the central issue of the tale transcends the selection of a superior animal and is concerned instead with excellence as an abstraction, applicable to all situations. When Garfield and Blishen retell ancient Greek myths in *The God beneath the Sea* and *The Golden Shadow*, their selection of words and grammatical constructions is so artful that the core mythic meaning is discernible in these superficially familiar tales and the reason for their continuing hold on the hearts of generations of readers becomes obvious: they have endured because they concern persisting essential human behaviors. When Hermes confronts Hephaestus after the latter's many trials he greets him: " 'Come brother;' murmured the god of illusion with his sideways smile. 'Between you and me, eh? It is always between you and me' . . . Their hands were still clasped and for many minutes they remained thus, with their backs to Olympus and their faces toward mankind, the artificer in gold and bronze and the artificer in dreams."

Enchantress from the Stars uses three distinct speech patterns for the narrative, each representing a different viewpoint, level of sophistication and purpose. The language guides readers to see the same events through three different perspectives. The book's language and structure allow the assessment of the respective merits of the competing visions.

Some books examine language directly. In *Rabbit and Pork Rhyming Talk*, lower-class Cockney and Victorian underworld jargon are explored. Some aspects of the subtlety of language are revealed as it is seen functioning both as a device that identifies one as an "insider" and as a deliberately colorful means of linguistic play. *They Discovered a Head in the Box for the Bread* introduces limericks as a particular kind of linguistic game and encourages participation through provision of incomplete examples. The child reader is shown models of this rigidly structured form of language manipulation and thrown on his or her own resourcefulness in formulating proper lines of the correct number of syllables, rhyme, stress, humor and meaning.

Ab to Zogg is a pseudo-glossary of fraudulent science-fiction terms which wryly defies the reader to identify the hidden obscure wit in each entry. The humor is dependent upon the reader's skill in synthesizing a vast, detailed, and specific knowledge of history, mythology, lexicography, geography, science fiction, and the literature of fantasy. Although the audience for this particular title is limited, those youngsters willing to wrestle with this challenge will be rewarded with many hours of delight.

Poetry is, by definition, language compressed, rich and precise, displaying awareness of connotation, image-generating properties, and sonorous effect. Serious works of poetry, then, are inherently sensitizing to language. One of unusual utility is Merriam's *Finding a Poem*, in which the poet shares the evolution of a single example, the search for precise words, phrases, and sequences of images that would transmit the content, attitude, and emotions the poet wished to share with her readers.

The structure of a book determines how the content will be perceived and processed by the alert reader. A simple third person narrated omniscient chronological story with no sub- or parallel plots is the easiest to comprehend. Some authors eschew such uncomplicated construction, even in stories for preschool level readers. *Time to Get Out of the Bath, Shirley*, is a picture book which employs two parallel plots simultaneously. In one, a little girl takes a bath while her mother berates her for her sloppiness, self-absorption and lack of sensitivity to such adult concerns as neatness and avoidance of waste. In the companion story, Shirley disappears down the bathtub drain into a fantasy world filled with royal personages and knights on gallant chargers. The two worlds merge as Shirley, wrapped in her towel, leaves both the tub and her romantic adventure. Both stories proceed on facing pages so youngsters must read them alternately, yet keep the strands separate. It is in the management of the contrapuntal themes that the inherent demands of this "simple" picture story are revealed. For older children, Tate's *Ben and Annie* presents a dramatic story up through the climax, but fails to provide closure. Readers must carry the compelling narrative through to its conclusion, projecting the devastating impact of the climax on the lives of the principal characters. Alan Garner is certainly one of the most demanding authors writing for a juvenile audience. His *The Stone Book* forges an even more demanding collaboration from his readers. In this slim volume, he offers the sparest outline of a family chronicle requiring youngsters to flesh out the narrative with their own imaginative reconstruction. The real nature of the relationship of the central characters is only obliquely hinted at and their sense of purpose and meaning must be educed from the minimal story line.

The structure of nonfiction books is equally critical. Some go far beyond merely effectively presenting information. Instead they show the child reader how to develop the talents necessary for independence in the subject area. *The Many Ways of Seeing* and *Looking at Art* alert the young viewer to those components in a work of art that are essential to its understanding and appreciation. They teach the child what kinds of questions to ask and how to think about what they observe. Books such as *How to Build a Better Mousetrap* are not just recipe books for scientific experiments, they are introductions to the scientific method, to identifying and isolating variables in a situation, to designing questions which can be answered through experimentation and to setting up means for finding solutions. In other words, they place the young reader in the posture assumed by professionals in the field.

The content of books for gifted youngsters should be substantive. Stories which are simplistic are inadequate. If they protray stereotypical characters, plots and resolutions, then child readers are not better off than they are with the pap that pervades television. In nonfiction, if works are distorting, patronizing, and confuse facts and hypotheses, they are totally unacceptable. If they only expand the knowledge base of the reader, they are minimally useful. Every discipline has ways of perceiving and articulating its subject, vital controversies, and questions of immediate concern. Some authors are willing to share these even with very young children. Goldin's *The Shape of Water*, addressed to primary level children, explains the behavior of water as a function of molecular action, an approach usually reserved for an older readership. *Watching the Wild Apes* chronicles the discoveries of three field primatologists. The nature of their difficulties and the excitement of the discoveries of Goodall, Fossey, and Galdikas form the heart of this memorable work which immerses young readers into the real problems of such researchers. Rannuci and Rollins share their passion for geometry in *Curiosities of the Cube* which contains a high level examination of the properties of this form. Concepts often first encountered in college level geometry courses are explored with young readers in the expectation that they will see them as an exemplary source of intellectual pleasure.

Struble explains Einstein's theory of relativity in *The Web of Space-Time*. Although explication is narrative rather than mathematical, the demands on the reader are exacting. Emphasis is on the evolution of scientific understanding of the basic physical laws of the universe, that is, not only on what is known, but how it came to be known. These books, restricted to extraordinarily gifted, intensely interested, and highly motivated youngsters, are of unequalled value to that select group.

When children express the desire for a good book, generally what they want is a story that will engage their attention and emotions, transporting them to a world of excitement, danger and suspense. Fiction can offer an innocuous interlude of escape or can reveal the complexities of human nature, elucidating the dreams and aspirations that goad and inspire. It can explore the dilemmas that confound each new generation, tie them to the past or hypothesize about the mystery of the future. Some novels, obviously directed to a juvenile audience, are as provocative to their readers as the works of Tolstoy, Mann, and Melville are for adults.

The Bear Who Wanted to Be a Bear explores the predicament of a creature trapped by technology into a role that violates his sense of self, conflicts with his biological nature and threatens his very survival. This parable of the modern human condition is delivered through the medium of a picture book. The novels, *The Human Apes* and *Mrs. Frisby and the Rats of NIMH* raise questions concerning the ideal society and the responsibility of the scientific community for the results of their research. *In the Time of the Bells* grapples with the conflict between personal goals and social expectations. These address issues which very bright children (as well as adults) find intriguing.

While qualities inherent in books are of critical importance, they are only half of the reading equation. Reading involves an interaction between the author's words as they appear on the page and the reader's mind as it absorbs and recreates the message. Most juvenile literary works are effectively communicated if the reader is simply able to understand the literal meaning of the text. The levels of intellectual activity usually involved are only cognition, recall, and interpretation. Benjamin Bloom designates these as the most elementary levels of thinking in *Taxonomy of Educational Objectives*. The academic experiences of high ability children should place minimal emphasis on these activities, redirecting a major portion of time to application, analysis, synthesis, and evaluation. Books as a prime instrumentality of intellectual growth should make comparable cognitive demands.

Gallagher cites four principles which should govern instruction for the gifted:

1. Teach to the highest cognitive level possible.
2. Teach gifted children to utilize all their thinking processes.
3. Teach important ideas about all aspects of their life and times.
4. Teach methods by which the gifted children can discover knowledge for themselves.

It is these same principles which should be applied in book selection.

The Night Sky Book necessitates application and analysis. Information is given which the reader must use to solve problems and explain apparently contradictory phenomena. *The Changing City* consists of eight separate sheets which depict the same European city from the identical vantage point at approximately three-year intervals. The transformation of a quaint and charming community into a modern technological nightmare is documented without a word of text other than a phrase specifying the date. The child reader must not only note the physical changes in the environment, but must also infer the resultant impact on societal behavior. The astute observer will see people as part of a fragile ecosystem in which changes in the components necessitate changes in their adaptive responses. Inevitably, the child is confronted with judgments involved with weighing the cost of technological progress in social and personal terms.

The Book of Think invites the readers to consciously examine the thought processes they engage in. Although all levels are explored—at least briefly—emphasis is on divergent thinking and the means by which more inventive, creative nonstandard approaches to problem solving can be maximized. *Solve It!* differs from most puzzle books in that higher levels of cognitive functioning are required to find answers to the enigmas. Rhoda Hoff's *America's Immigrants* assembles commentaries on their experiences by immigrants to this country who have arrived during the last two hundred years. From these diverse, often contradictory accounts, the reader must assemble a cohesive, coherent picture of this phenomenon using selected examples of first-hand source material as the historian or sociologist might.

Literature can be assessed in terms of the level of response it elicits. Some stories require no more than the reader's sustained attention; others ask that they assess competing versions of events, compare responses, define stands and judge moral issues.

Every book is not suitable for every child. Factors such as developmental stage, prior knowledge and interest will cause some children to choose one title, some another. In addition, children sometimes want a book for relaxation, as a relief from the intellectual demands of academic goals, for idiosyncratic research or pursuit of recreational interests. But children also enjoy intellectual stimulation, see it as a desirable, pleasurable activity. Moments of insight and understanding are exciting and profoundly satisfying. Sagan (1979) comments: "We are an intelligent species and the use of our intelligence quite properly gives us pleasure. In this respect the brain is like a muscle. When we think well, we feel good. Understanding is a kind of ecstasy." Books, judiciously chosen, are a limitless source of such delight.

Additional Reading

Baskin, B., and K. Harris, *Books for the Gifted Child*. New York: Bowker, 1980.
Bloom, B. S., ed. *Taxonomy of Educational Objectives. Handbook I: Cognitive Domain*. New York: McKay, 1956.
Bronowski, J. *Magic, Science and Civilization*. New York: Columbia Univ. Pr., 1978.
Gallagher, J. J. *Teaching the Gifted Child*. Boston: Allyn & Bacon, 1975.
Sagan C. *Broca's Brain*. New York: Random, 1979.

Bibliography

Baskin, Leonard. *Hosie's Alphabet*. New York: Knopf, 1972.
Breton, James E., and Lorraine A. Blackburn, eds. *They've Discovered a Head in the Box for the Bread—and Other Laughable Limericks*. New York: Crowell, 1978.
Burningham, John. *Time to Get Out of the Bath, Shirley*. New York: Crowell, 1978.
Burns, Marilyn. *The Book of Think (Or How to Solve a Problem Twice Your Size)*. Boston: Little, 1976.
Carlson, Dale. *The Human Apes*. New York: Atheneum, 1973.
Chase, Alice E. *Looking at Art*. New York: Crowell, 1966.
Engdahl, Sylvia L. *Enchantress from the Stars*. New York: Atheneum, 1978.
Fixx, James F. *Solve It! A Perplexing Profusion of Puzzles*. New York: Doubleday, 1978.
Garfield, Leon, and Edward Blishen. *The God Beneath the Sea*. New York: Pantheon, 1971.
Garner, Alan. *The Stone Book*. New York: Collins, 1976.
Goldin, Augusta. *The Shape of Water*. New York: Doubleday, 1979.
Gripe, Maria. *In the Time of the Bells*. New York: Delacorte, 1965.
Gwynne, Fred. *The King Who Rained*. New York: Windmill, 1970.
Hoban, Russell, *The Twenty-Elephant Restaurant*. New York: Atheneum, 1978.
Hoff, Rhoda. *America's Immigrants: Adventures in Eyewitness History*. New York: Walck, 1967.
Jobb, Jamie. *The Night Sky Book: An Everyday Guide to Every Night*. Boston: Little, 1977.
Kevles, Betty. *Watching the Wild Apes: The Primate Studies of Goodall, Fossey and Galdikas*. New York: Dutton, 1976.
Lawrence, John. *Rabbit and Pork Rhyming Talk*. New York: Crowell, 1975.
Merriam, Eve. *Ab to Zogg—A Lexicon for Science-Fiction and Fantasy Readers*. New York: Atheneum, 1977.
———. *Finding a Poem*. New York: Atheneum, 1970.
Merrill, Jean. *The Superlative Horse*. Reading, Mass.: Addison-Wesley, 1961.
Moore, Janet Gaylord. *The Many Ways of Seeing: An Introduction to the Pleasures of Art*. Cleveland: World, 1968.
Muller, Jorg. *The Changing City*. New York: Atheneum, 1977.
O'Brien, Robert C. *Mrs. Frisby and the Rats of NIMH*. New York: Atheneum, 1971.
Ranucci, Ernest R., and Wilma Rollins. *Curiosities of the Cube*. New York: Crowell, 1977.
Renner, Al G. *How to Build a Better Mousetrap Car—and Other Experimental Science Fun*. New York: Dodd, 1977.
Steiner, Jorg. *The Bear Who Wanted to Be a Bear*. New York: Atheneum, 1976.
Struble, Mitch. *The Web of Space-Time: A Step-by-Step Exploration of Relativity*. Philadelphia: Westminster, 1973.
Tate, Joan. *Ben and Annie*. New York: Doubleday, 1974.

3
Technology

Webster's Third New International Dictionary states that technology means "the application of scientific knowledge of practical purposes in a particular field." For the library user who is disabled, technology often has a more personal definition: it means the difference between exclusion and participation, limited and full functioning, failure and success.

The traditional role of educational technology has been to facilitate or promote learning by delivering instructional messages in the most appropriate format. Every medium has specific advantages and limitations; each is useful in certain kinds of teaching situations and contraindicated in others. For optimal utilization, the particular characteristics of the medium must be considered and the following questions need to be answered:

Would information best be transmitted through audio, visual, tactile, or a combination of channels?
Should learners be active or passive during the instructional process?
Should the information, or segments of it, remain readily accessible for extended study?
What type of projection is preferable?

Additionally, before determining which, if any, equipment should be used, presenters need to take into account physical plant constraints, the size, composition, and particular needs of the audience and the nature of the learning that is expected to take place, i.e., whether it involves identification, acquisition of factual information, understanding of principles, concepts or procedures, development of skills or exploration of feelings and attitudes. Attention to such considerations will result in appropriate, judicious decisions by media specialists.

When using instructional media with special needs patrons, other factors must also be weighed. For some individuals, certain sensory channels may not be practical or may have limited utility as a route for the transmission of information. For example, children who have experienced extensive loss of visual acuity or who have severe visual perceptual deficiencies may have to rely heavily, or even exclusively, on auditory, tactile, or kinesthetic modes of learning. Students dependent on speech reading need to have the presenter in their line of sight and sufficient illumination on the face and hands of all speakers. A darkened room may be unsettling to some learners; simultaneous audio and visual messages may cause sensory overload for others. Library patrons with poor muscle control may need fully automatic equipment when involved in self-instructional tasks. While some technological approaches appear obligatory in compensating for impairment, the individual preferences of the user should also be a determining factor in the ultimate choice.

If, however, these additional considerations are met, most library users with special needs can be adequately served. But others, particularly those with severe sensory impairments, will require more sophisticated hardware if their deficits are to be addressed. Fortunately, the last few years have seen exciting advances in the development and improvement of communication devices, concentrating on certain subsets of this population.

The authors reporting in this section are knowledgeable about the obstacles to information processing that sensory deficits pose and have applied their expertise in exploiting the potential of technology to ameliorate or circumvent the impact of limitations.

Propp chronicles the use of instructional technology in the education of hearing-impaired students. Extensive utilization of media is a fairly recent and widespread phenomenon for this population. The particular contributions made by creative individuals and the role of various agencies in funding research and providing for the distribution of both products and information is described. Although this author applauds the gigantic strides that have been made in hardware development, he is critical of the persisting underutilization of readily available devices with the potential for radically altering the prospects for fuller functioning of deaf children and adults.

The problems of hearing-impaired persons are frequently not limited to inadequacies in receptive communication abilities. Often they have problems in expressive language and in social skills as well. Difficulties in receiving and transmitting emergency information, and in communicating with nonimpaired persons or with individuals at distant locations seriously handicap the lives of those with auditory deficits. Driver, Easterwood, and Schaub report on the use of a telephone typewriter designed for the deaf (TTY) to assist in such situations. Even though the number of sites involved in their study was limited, the advantages of having such units available were immediate and obvious. The placement of TTYs in all kinds of library settings would facilitate both linguistic and social growth among the hearing-impaired population, unquestionably expanding their utilization of the library.

Stuckless's provocative paper suggests a constructive way to approach the learning/communication problems of individuals with auditory impairments. He analyzes the differences between temporal and spatial messages and reports on how these two core attributes affect information processing. He emphasizes that when hearing is the deficit area, vision should be selected as the alternate learning channel: more attention must be paid to the stronger mode to maximize the potency of the learning experience. The author further proposes that since spatial sequencing is so efficient, technology needs to focus more efforts on this form of language presentation, thereby attending not so much to remediation of the auditory domain but capitalizing on the intact visual strengths.

The backbone of the library collection for blind or visually impaired readers has consisted mainly of brailled materials, Talking Books, or large print editions. While these formats will remain fundamental to any basic service to the visually impaired for the forseeable future, certain important technological advances have overcome many of the limitations inherent in these popular forms.

The Optacon, reported on here by Bliss and Moore, is a light portable and versatile device that transforms standard inkprint material into tactile messages. The reading theory underlying its design, the techniques for using and improving fluency with this device, and the special problems and unique virtues of the machine are explained. Although not usable by all blind readers, the potential significance for those capable of mastering its procedures is inestimable: such readers are henceforth not limited by the availability of brailled materials, restricted to the volumes in a single library, or temporarily stalled waiting for books mailed from a depository. Consequently, users of this new technological aid have a much wider array of matter from which to select and need tolerate no delay while standard print is transformed into another format, i.e., braille or Talking Books.

Two articles report on the uses of television with visually impaired persons. The first concerns the employment of a closed circuit system which enables public library patrons to select regular or inverse (white on black) images and to sufficiently enlarge the print on any document to make it legible. The results of Pors's study reveal another productive direction librarians may consider in expanding services to clientele with low vision.

A further use of television involves an interactive arrangement between partially sighted students and their instructor. Although the application described by Genensky and colleagues is classroom specific, the particularly adaptable features—easily constructed split screen images, constant two-way visual contact between users of the system, capability of different displays appearing on each monitor—all have direct implications for library usage.

The Kurzweil Reading Machine takes printed works and transforms them into synthesized speech. Its special features allow for browsing, repetition of words and phrases, spelling of words that are not initially understood, and adjusting tone and reading rate. Cushman reports on the capabilities of this technological breakthrough and its impact on blind readers. Both this device and the Optacon free such library patrons from dependence on others and increase accessibility of printed material, particularly ephemeral or dated matter. Probably more than any other device, the Kurzweil reveals the potential of technology for dramatically reducing the consequences of impairment.

Although the application of technology to the problems of the disabled library user have been empirically demonstrated to be significant in their potential to change the lives of individuals who have been able to take advantage of them, much yet remains to be done. Library and media professionals should be aware of the necessity for matching the medium with the unique requirements of the user and sharing the benefits of these technological advances with those who could profit from them.

An Overview of Progress in Utilization of Educational Technology for Educating the Hearing Impaired

GEORGE PROPP

The history of educational technology predates the invention of the term by a considerable period of time. From a historical perspective, technology applied to education must be seen in reference to the available technology of the society and the times of which we speak. When Moses brought the Ten Commandments from the mountain engraved in stone, there is no question but that it carried a greater impact than if it had been hand lettered on papyrus or whatever alternatives existed. One might say that engraving the Ten Commandments in stone added an appropriate kinesthetic dimension to such a weighty message and it didn't discriminate against the deaf and blind. However, you can be sure that, had the technology been available, Moses would have recorded the voice of God on Memorex audiotape and played it back full volume on a stereo system with appropriate psychedelic lighting. To pursue ancient history a bit longer, we hardly need to point out the massive effect of printing technology in the dissemination of knowledge and God's Commandments. Printing, we might say, has been and still is, the backbone technology of the world's various educational systems.

The dawn of educational technology for hearing impaired is generally regarded to be the year of 1958 when P.L. 85-905 established Captioned Films for the Deaf. In terms of modern communication technology, particularly electronics, this is as good a starting point as any, although there are educators of the deaf who would insist that hearing aid technology has made as great an impact as Captioned Films for the Deaf. We would all agree, however, that learning technology in a general sense was applied to the problems of teaching the deaf long before the 1958 milestone.

The author of this paper obtained his elementary education in a one-room Nebraska school and may be said to have been technologically deprived during his formative years. The first arc projected 16mm educational film he ever saw was around 1930. It was film developed by the Department of Agriculture for use of county agents on the use of electricity on the farm. His introduction to technology for the hearing impaired occurred some years later, and interestingly enough, concerned radio. Harvey T. Christian, a math teacher at the Nebraska School for the Deaf, was one of those people who applied available technology to the unique communication needs of the deaf. In the late thirties, Mr. Christian rigged up some ropes and pulleys on a chalkboard to communicate World Series radio broadcasts to deaf students at school. By manipulating a drawstring he was able to provide a very realistic play-by-play and thus bring radio communication and baseball vocabulary to the deaf. Mr. Christian also designed a cover for a card table with which football games were made highly visible to deaf gridiron fans. If this wasn't communication technology, it is only because we lack agreement on the meaning of the term.

Despite occasional ingenuity such as described above, the pre-1958 level of media utilization in schools for the deaf was rather skimpy. The writer's teaching experience at the Nebraska School for the Deaf may have been more or less typical of many schools during the 1940–58 period. The duplicating machine was unquestionably the major vehicle of educational communication during this era, although there was an annual tendency to run out of paper stock early in November. Other than ditto handouts, the educator of the deaf may have had access to a collection of filmstrips that, most likely, numbered less than 50. The showing of a 16mm film, such as

---

"An Overview of Progress in Utilization of Educational Technology for Educating the Hearing Impaired," by George Propp, *American Annals of the Deaf* 1978, 123: 646–52. Reprinted by permission.

Chronicles of America, was such a momentous occasion that it was usually shown to the entire student body in an assembly program. The earliest filmstrips to appear at the Nebraska School were, for the record, freebies distributed by the National Council of Churches and used for Sunday school instruction. The athletic coach, with access to athletic funds, probably was occasionally able to schedule an athletic demonstration film which was borrowed for a small fee from a nearby university film library. Bulletin boards were usually a form of second life for picture magazines which abounded at that time.

While deaf students in the late forties were being tantalized by occasional exposure to new learning technology, events were transpiring in the New York area that would turn this infrequent utilization into a tide that within a short period of time would revolutionize the education of the deaf. Before going into the details of the coming revolution it is perhaps necessary to digress a bit and try to explain why this particular area of education was such a fertile field for learning technology.

General educators keep asking what's so special about special education? Or what is so unique about the needs of the hearing impaired? The partial answer to this is that education is primarily a process of communication between the learner and his society. Without communication an individual cannot assimilate his or her culture. In a society where the spoken word is dominant, it is most difficult for the hearing-impaired individual to become a fully participating member. Effective communication is a necessary condition for all members of a society. An individual's role hinges, more than anything else, on his ability to communicate, to initiate, propagate, and share ideas, to interpret communication from other persons and the environment. To achieve this objective it is logical that communication technology should be enthusiastically embraced by everyone concerned with the education of the hearing impaired.[1]

Educational technology can free the hearing-impaired student from the limited and sheltered interpretation of the world that heretofore had restricted his learning and his participation. For the handicapped, educational technology vastly enlarges the window through which they view the world. Technology, thus, is the most effective way of overcoming one's sensory deprivation. As important as the basics of reading and writing may be, the illiterate of the future is one who cannot grasp the complexities of the world in which he lives.

To return to the chronology of events that comprise the technological revolution in the education of the deaf, one may establish 1958 as the dawn of educational technology in the education of the deaf. One must recognize that P.L. 85-905 marked the beginning of massive and effective application of communication technology to the needs of the hearing impaired. With the possible exception of better amplification devices, there was very little difference between the classrooms of 1930 and those of 1950. The change from 1958 to the present, on the other hand, has been little short of phenomenal. Legislation in the American system of government, however, doesn't just happen, so it is appropriate to describe the gestation of events that preceded P.L. 85-905.

The idea for Captioned Films for the Deaf was spawned in a doctoral dissertation during the 1946-48 period by Ross Hamilton; a student in the Department of Special Education at Teachers College, Columbia University. Dr. Hamilton was at that time administrative assistant to Dr. Clarence D. O'Connor, Director of the Lexington School for the Deaf in New York City. Hamilton's study involved a technology that appears primitive by today's captioning technology and involved the use of two cameras, one for the movie and one for the captions. Dr. O'Connor became intrigued by the concept and he in turn interested Dr. Edmund B. Boatner, Superintendent of the American School for the Deaf in West Hartford, Connecticut. These people expounded the concept of systematically providing captioned materials for the deaf, and gave their enthusiastic support and direction to subsequent events.

Kundert reports that with some funding from the Junior League of Hartford, Captioned Films for the Deaf, Inc., was organized as a nonprofit corporation under the laws of the state of Connecticut.[2] With technical expertise provided by Jules P. Rakow, a vocational teacher at the American School, the fledgling corporation soon acquired a library of 30 captioned feature films which were rented to schools for the deaf. The demand for films shortly outgrew the resources of Captioned Films for the Deaf, Inc., and alternative sources of funding were sought. The general idea was to provide captioned films for the hearing impaired on the same basis as talking books are provided for the blind. One step led to another and on September 2, 1958, President Eisenhower signed P.L. 85-905, An Act to Provide for a Loan Service of Captioned Films for the Deaf in the Department of Health, Education, and Welfare.

Captioned Films for the Deaf

Initial funding for CFD was an inconsequential $78,000. The purpose essentially was to "provide enriched cultural, educational, and entertainment experiences for hearing-impaired persons."[3] The program became operational in 1959 under the direction of John A. Gough. Negotiations with film producers developed criteria for acquisition of films. Research and experimentation was conducted to determine the most favorable captioning techniques, and three depositories were established for distribution of the films. During this period, films were of an entertainment nature and were distributed largely to deaf clubs and organizations. From the very beginning, the demand for the films exceeded the supply.

P.L. 87-715 in 1962 amended the Captioned Films Act and increased funding to $1,500,000. The amendment added authorization to provide for educational and training films for use with the deaf and to conduct research. This legislation initiated various activities which in a short time led to the condition where captioned films and other innovative educational media became an integral part of classroom instruction for the hearing impaired. The national office at this time extended its effectiveness by an arrangement with the New Mexico Foundation at New Mexico State University in Las Cruces whereby the latter agency served as a facilitator for change by developing awareness and familiarity with new equipment and materials.

Media Services and Captioned Films

In 1965 Congress passed P.L. 89-258 which again expanded the original Captioned Film Act and the 1962 amendments. This law increased funding from $1,500,000 to $3,000,000 for the fiscal years of 1966 and 1967; to $5,000,000 for fiscal years 1968 and 1969; and to $7,000,000 thereafter. With increased funding came revised objectives. Public Law 89-258, for example, also established the National Advisory Council on the Education of the Deaf (NACED). Amendments in 1967 extended similar media services to other handicapping conditions, and further amendments in 1970 established the National Center for Educational Media and Materials for the Handicapped (NCEMMH) at Ohio State University. During this period there was extensive reorganization within HEW. The Bureau of Education for the Handicapped (BEH) was established and Captioned Films for the Deaf became the Media Services and Captioned Films Branch (MSCF) of the Division of Media Services (DMS).

During the 1965–74 period, vastly expanded services were provided for teachers of the deaf. The Educational Media Distribution Center (EMDC), established in 1966, provided distribution and dissemination services for MSCF and related agencies. Some 4,000 classrooms and training centers were provided with basic media equipment consisting of overhead projectors, filmstrip projectors, screens and tables. Over two million discrete items of instructional software, largely transparency masters, filmstrips, transparencies, and other print and nonprint materials, were made available to teachers of the hearing impaired by EMDC and the RMCDs. Included in the free distribution program were nearly 200,000 manuals and curriculum guides.[4]

Over this period of time, 16mm films were being captioned at the rate of 65 titles per year for both entertainment and educational films, a total of 130 titles. Some 65 prints were produced for each captioned educational title. These were distributed through 60 depositories to enhance accessibility. Captioned Films services involves much more than the captioning and distribution process. A mechanism for screening and selecting films for captioning has been established; study guides are developed annually for the new films entered into the educational library; workshops are conducted for writing captions which in the case of Syncapped films involves rewriting the entire sound track; and catalogs are printed and disseminated to all potential users of both educational and entertainment films.[5] Utilization data collected indicates that bookings of theatrical and documentary films to schools, organizations, clubs and eligible agencies exceed 19,000 per month.[6] The educational films are seen by more than 1,500,000 hearing-impaired viewers every year.

From 1966 onward, the four Regional

Media Centers for the Deaf (RMCDs) carried out a significant portion of MSCF functions. The four centers had common objectives of media in-service training for teachers and materials production. Additionally, each had a unique function. The Southwest RMCD concentrated on programmed instruction and instructional design. The Midwest RMCD at the University of Nebraska stressed the utilization and production of 8mm films and related media. The Northeast RMCD at the University of Massachusetts gave its attention to transparencies and overhead projector utilization, while the Southern RMCD at the University of Tennessee focused its attention on educational television. The Midwest RMCD, for example, had a six-week summer media institute for teachers of the deaf which annually involved 30 teachers of the hearing impaired. They also had a one-week institute during the school year for supervising teachers and another for IMC personnel. They also conducted about 10 or 12 short-term workshops (two days as a rule) within an 11-state area.[7] In-service training activities at the other RMCDs was of a similar magnitude. Many of the workshops and institutes were exemplary models of instructional design. The Southwest RMCD sponsored Project Hurdle which featured a van loaded with media equipment which traveled all over the West to impact selected schools with media skills and utilization. Consultation services to schools were also provided.

In addition to in-service activities, the RMCDs made other contributions to the media revolution too numerous to mention. The Northeast RMCD developed several sets of transparencies which were made available to teachers of the hearing impaired. The Midwest Center produced a number of films, multimedia kits, and a set of transparencies. The Southern RMCD experimented with captioned television and provided videotape duplication services. The Southwest Center produced programmed learning materials and guides and manuals for program writing. The Midwest RMCD also conducted an annual Symposium on the Research and Utilization of Educational Media for Teaching the Deaf. The reports from these ten symposia were reprinted in the *American Annals of the Deaf* from 1965 through 1974.

Perhaps the greatest impact of the RMCDs was an activity that never developed much visibility. In-service training projects developed numerous educational products of a useful nature which were taken home and used with hearing-impaired students. The same in-service training functions developed production and utilization skills which undoubtedly led to hundreds and hundreds of items of teacher-produced materials which have enhanced the learning of hearing-impaired children.

An attempt to evaluate the impact of MSCF and RMCD activities was made in a survey conducted by the Midwest RMCD in 1973.[8] A questionnaire mailed to 423 symposium participants yielded a response rate of 71.3 percent. Data obtained indicated that 85 percent had an IMC and that 82.2 percent of them had one or more full time media specialists, compared to 7.9 percent in 1964. Other interesting data were as follows: the average teacher was using an overhead projector for 33.2 percent of instructional time; 73.5 percent of schools were using Project LIFE [Learning Is For Everyone] materials; the average use of captioned films was for 18.5 percent of instructional time; and that educational television was being used on the average of 7.6 percent of instructional time.

The events described above were paralleled by other developments which vastly increased the impact of educational media on the education of the deaf. It is not within the scope of this paper to make an exhaustive listing of all the events and activities that had a direct or indirect bearing on the impact of educational technology on the education of the deaf. We can only highlight some of the related events. One of the enhancing factors was the rapid development of communication technology in America. The overhead projector came on like gangbusters along with commercially available materials to use with it. Developments in educational television, spearheaded by "Sesame Street," were similarly phenomenal. Continuous Project LIFE activity eventually brought innovative hardware and a comprehensive collection of over 400 filmstrips and other materials into classrooms for the deaf.[9] At the same time BEH supported the development of numerous other projects and activities, such as the Programmed Learning Electronic Assembly Program for the Deaf, a doctoral program in educational technology for educators of the deaf at Syracuse University, Career Media at the Technical-Vocational Institute in St. Paul, and many similar activities.[10]

Also conducive to educational technology developments for the hearing impaired were various pieces of legislation that supported educational services for the handicapped. Chief among these was the Elementary and Secondary Education Act of 1965.[11] The various titles and amendments of this act had a significant impact on the education of handicapped children. School administrators who a few years earlier could hardly support the appetite of a ditto machine could now think in terms of installing costly video equipment and building new facilities. A survey conducted by the Southern RMCD involved a questionnaire that was sent to 200 of the larger school programs for the deaf in this country.[12] Of the 180 schools that responded, 142 indicated that they had television receivers/monitors. The number of receivers/monitors added up to about 2,000. Some 123 of the respondents indicated that they had video recorders, and 109 had some sort of production capability. Another 42 of the schools had cable systems and 6 had color production capabilities.

Effective September 1, 1974, the Bureau of Education for the Handicapped established the Learning Resource Center Program to provide regional centers and specialized national offices to assist the handicapped child. This was done largely in response to a mandate for a generic approach to services for the handicapped and for channeling these services through state education agencies. The Learning Resource Center Program consisted of 13 Regional Resource Centers (RRCs), 13 ALRCs, a coordinating office for the RRCs, four Specialized Offices, and the National Center for Educational Media and Materials for the Handicapped. The network's prime purpose was to help states develop delivery of such supportive services to the handicapped as necessary to achieve 1980 educational goals for the handicapped. For this new structure, the Division of Media Services split into two branches—the Learning Resource Branch and Captioned Films and Telecommunications Branch.

Under the new program, services to the hearing impaired previously provided by the RMCDs was to be carried out by state agencies with assistance from the RRCs and ALRCs. The Specialized Office for the Hearing Impaired (SO-2) at the University of Nebraska–Lincoln continued with the development of instructional materials for the hearing impaired, but the major function of the office was to review and abstract materials for entry into the National Instructional Materials Information System (NIMIS). During the three years of operation as a Specialized Office, more than 15,000 items of instructional materials were reviewed and approved items were entered into NIMIS. SO-1 and SO-3 achieved similar objectives for the visually impaired and for other handicapping conditions. This data bank in 1977 was transferred from Ohio State to the National Information Center on Educational Materials (NICEM) in Los Angeles. NIMIS data can presently be retrieved from the Lockheed computer bank in Palo Alto. The NIMIS data base is of incalculable value in prescriptive teaching.

In the meantime, Captioned Films and Telecommunications (CF&T) continued to provide continuity in the form of developing new and innovative approaches to the education of the handicapped. As part of CF&T functions, the captioned films program was continued and expanded to the point where there are now more than 800 films in each of the educational and entertainment libraries. Most of CF&T activities as they pertain to the hearing impaired during the 1974–77 period were in the development of television programming. Most people are aware of the "Captioned ABC News" being broadcast regularly by PBS stations. Deaf citizens now accept "Captioned ABC News" as a fact of life. This activity is being carried out by WGBH in Boston and fed into the PBS network from Washington, D.C. WGBH was involved with open captioning some time before 1974. Julia Child's [program] was captioned experimentally several years earlier. WGBH has captioned other programs, including segments of "Zoom," and has conducted experimentation and evaluation for various captioning techniques. The Caption Center at WGBH has been funded by CF&T.

While open captioning was being developed at WGBH, another series of contracts with PBS in Washington, D.C. has developed closed captioning using the Line 21 feature of video broadcasting. PBS has developed the necessary decoding device, a self-contained or freestanding captioning unit; they have also obtained a favorable ruling from the FCC that Line 21 be reserved exclusively for the hearing impaired; and they have also been improving captioning equipment and training captioners. This closed captioning technology now makes it possible to broadcast captioned programs into the television receivers of the hearing impaired without cluttering up the picture of normal users. As an outgrowth of PBS and WGBH activities a considerable number of PBS stations are regularly telecasting captioned programs for hearing-impaired viewers.

In 1977 the Learning Resource Center Program was phased out, but various activities are being continued. The National Instructional Materials Information System is being refined and after necessary modifications will be known as NIMIS II. Teachers of the deaf can retrieve data on an interim basis from NIMIS by contacting the National Information Center on Special Education Materials (NICSEM). The funding that went into the Learning Resource Center Program has been reallocated. A considerable number of the numerous contracts and grants funded by CF&T are concerned with the needs of the hearing-impaired learner at all ages and grade levels. One of the major projects currently funded by CF&T is the Media Development Project for the Hearing Impaired (MDPHI). This new project at the University of Nebraska–Lincoln, under the direction of Dr. Robert E. Stepp, Jr., has several functions. The major activity involves the adaptation and development of materials for the hearing impaired in areas where extant materials do not meet identified needs. MDPHI also does evaluation and field testing, does search and retrieval, conducts marketing activities, and is renewing the annual Symposium on Research and Utilization of Educational Media for Teaching the Deaf.

It is not within the scope of this paper to deal fully and appropriately with the many current and projected activities in learning technology that will affect the hearing-impaired population. Most of the current activities in learning technology for the hearing impaired will be reported by other presenters at this and future conferences.

The saying goes that the past is but a prelude. The past two decades have seen more change in the education of the deaf than the previous 100 years. Learning technology, to be sure, is making a significant contribution in the amelioration of sensory impairment and is reducing the disparity that exists between the deaf and the normal population. However, in our information rich society, we have not fully managed our technical resources to the point that permits optimal transfer of knowledge to the new generations of handicapped children.[13] A reader of the literature on learning technology may possibly be dismayed between what is and what might have been. Not everyone has embraced the available resources.[14] Thousands of effective items of instructional materials remain unpurchased; hundreds of pieces of useful equipment are gathering dust; countless children are being taught with outmoded methods; however, in the overall sense, education of the deaf has been first and foremost in harnessing the potential of learning technology.

Learning technology will need to be heavily employed to achieve the handicapped individual's rights for full development of his or her educational potential.[15] The current mainstreaming concept for education of the handicapped will require a massive application of the resources that exist as well as the development of technology that lies beyond our present dreams. American ingenuity and determination will, you can be sure, be equal to the new challenges and new dimensions necessary to bring the handicapped into the mainstream of American life.

Notes

1. R. E. Stepp, "Educational Media and Technology for the Hearing Impaired Student" (Occasional paper, 1975).
2. J. Kundert, "Captioned Films for the Deaf" (Unpublished paper, U.S. Office of Education, 1967).
3. R. G. Brill, *The Education of the Deaf* (Washington, D.C.: Gallaudet College Pr., 1974).
4. Ibid.
5. S. J. Parlato, "Those Other Captioned Films . . . Captioned Educational Films," *American Annals of the Deaf* 122 (1977): 33–37.
6. M. J. Norwood, "Captioned Films for the Deaf," *Exceptional Children* 43 (1976): 164–66.
7. R. L. La Gow and R. Kelly, "The Midwest Regional Media Center for the Deaf: Eight Years of Media Service," *American Annals of the Deaf* 119 (1974): 554–64.
8. R. E. Stepp, "Summary," *American Annals of the Deaf* 119 (1974): 612–18.
9. G. Pfau, "Project LIFE a Decade Later: Some Reflections and Projections," *American Annals of the Deaf* 119 (1974): 549–53.
10. L. E. Persselin, "Electronic Assembly Programmed Learning System for the Deaf," *American Annals of the Deaf* 116 (1971): 515–25.
11. Ibid.
12. I. W. Jackson and R. Perkins, "Television for Deaf Listeners: A Utilization Quandary," *American Annals of the Deaf* 119 (1974): 537–48.
13. W. D. Lance, "Technology and Media for Exceptional Learners: Looking Ahead," *Exceptional Children* 44 (1977): 92–97.
14. R. Kelly, "Is Educational Technology an Intruder in the Classroom?" *Education and Training of the Mentally Retarded* 7 (1972): 94–98.
15. F. B. Withrow and C. J. Nygren, *Language*

Materials and Curriculum Management for the Handicapped (Columbus, Ohio: Merrill, 1976), chaps. 7 and 16.

Additional Reading

"Affecting the Human Potential of the Deaf Student: Another Role for Educational Media." *American Annals of the Deaf*, Oct. 1972, complete issue.

"Audiovisual Research and the Education of the Deaf." *American Annals of the Deaf*, Nov. 1965, complete issue.

Braverman, B. B. "Review of Literature in Instructional Television: Implications for Deaf Learners." *American Annals of the Deaf* 122 (1977): 395–402.

"Career Education and Educational Media for the Deaf Student." *American Annals of the Deaf*, Oct. 1973, complete issue.

"Communicative Television for the Deaf Student." *American Annals of the Deaf*, Oct. 1970, complete issue.

"Designing Instructional Facilities for Teaching the Deaf: The Learning Module." *American Annals of the Deaf*, Nov. 1968, complete issue.

"The Educational Media Complex." *American Annals of the Deaf*, Nov. 1967, complete issue.

"Individualizing Instruction for the Deaf Student." *American Annals of the Deaf*, Nov. 1969, complete issue.

"Programmed Learning for the Deaf Student." *American Annals of the Deaf*, Oct. 1971, complete issue.

Propp, G. "Introduction: 1974 Symposium on Research and Utilization of Instructional Media for Teaching the Deaf." *American Annals of the Deaf* 119 (1974): 455–59.

"Systems Approach in Deaf Education." *American Annals of the Deaf*, Nov. 1966, complete issue.

"Update '74: A Decade of Progress." *American Annals of the Deaf*, Oct. 1974, complete issue.

Development of a High School TTY Program

SHERRY DRIVER, TERRENCE EASTERWOOD, and JOHN SCHAUB

The Telephone Teletype for the Deaf (TTY) is fast becoming an important and useful tool for deaf persons, allowing communication with peers and the public, and emergency services via the telephone.

In 1973, the Toledo, Ohio, Public Schools, in conjunction with the Ohio Northwest Telecom and the Telephone Pioneers of America (Ohio Valley Chapter, #80, Toledo Council), implemented a program designed to: (1) develop awareness of the TTY's potential among deaf students; (2) foster its use in emergency, inquiry, and social situations; and (3) improve overall communicative functioning.

The TTYs (Models 15 and 28) which provide a printed tape readout were chosen for use, rather than the newer LED displays, for several reasons. When saved, tape readouts provide a current file for ongoing evaluation of language patterns, spelling corrections, and vocabulary building. Thus, students retain a permanent visual record of their communication for review at a later date, allowing for recognition and correction of errors.

"Development of a High School TTY Program," by Sherry Driver, Terrence Easterwood, and John Schaub, *Volta Review* 1979, 81: 517–20. Reprinted with the permission of the Alexander Graham Bell Association for the Deaf, 3417 Volta Pl., NW, Washington, D.C. 20007.

Early TTY Use

Three TTYs were placed in the hearing-impaired program, one each at the elementary, junior, and senior high-school levels, before the TTY home program was implemented. The senior high hearing-impaired students were oriented to TTY usage: to report emergencies (sheriff's office), to obtain and/or relay vocational information to the local B.V.R. office, and to facilitate social/sport activities with the local deaf club and social interaction with the junior high students. Students at both the junior and senior high schools were assigned to send school-related information (class lists, schedules, school news, etc.) via the TTY. The initial response of hearing-impaired students was that of curiosity and interest, and interest has grown in proportion to the increased availability of TTYs.

Mainstreaming of hearing-impaired students at the high school has been an ongoing process for the past ten years in both academic and nonacademic areas in accordance with the individual student's ability, interest, motivation, and the availability of classes.

Articles have been written about the use of TTYs in the school newspaper. As the hearing-impaired department takes part in school open houses for parents, the TTY has been demonstrated for both hearing-impaired and hearing parents. The response has always been positive.

To maximize students' use of the TTY, the program was expanded in September 1976, adding six TTYs which were placed in the homes of selected high-school students for a one-year period. Some anticipated outcomes of the programs were that:

1. Student use of the TTY would increase in frequency as measured over the one-year period.
2. Student response on a post-project questionnaire would indicate positive attitudes toward TTY use.
3. One or more students would continue using the TTY equipment in their homes after the one-year free use.

The 1976–77 year proved successful in many areas. The six students made an estimated 850 calls, averaging between 2 and 4 calls per week per student. A 30 percent increase in calls made and received was noted from November 1976 to October 1977. In the post-project questionnaire students reported the following: (1) 85 percent of the participants said they used the TTY 2 to 4 times per week; 15 percent used it more than 5 times per week. (2) 66 percent of the students' family members used the TTY "occasionally," while 34 percent used it "often." (3) All the students used the TTY to contact members of the hearing and deaf communities who were not within their student peer group. (4) Most of the calls were for social interaction (there was no need for emergency calls). (5) The students all reported they enjoyed having a TTY in their homes and considered it a beneficial tool for deaf persons. Only one student reported that he would not miss having a TTY. (6) Five participants expressed an interest in acquiring a personal TTY, but only one could afford to do so.

Family TTY Use

One half of the participating students had one or more deaf siblings residing in the same household. These brothers and sisters used the TTY frequently to communicate with their peers owning TTYs. Because these siblings often had different friends than the participating high-school students, the TTY use was expanded to include communication with deaf individuals that would otherwise have been impossible. Hearing family members used the TTY in the following ways:

1. Communication with the students while at school (calls were initiated by both parents and students).
2. Communication with a son or daughter visiting a deaf friend who owned a TTY.
3. Communication with the Ohio Northwest Telecom to report malfunctions in the TTY equipment.

The use of a TTY in this manner allowed parents and students the independent use of a telephone without the usual necessary third party involved when hearing and deaf individuals attempt to communicate via the telephone.

Communication Skills Improved

It is widely believed that TTY use can improve communication skills, but the degree of improvement is difficult to measure. To what extent can the use of the TTY be held accountable if the student demonstrates gains in reading, spelling, vocabulary, and correct sentence patterning while he or she is receiving instruction in these areas at school and at home? Interesting results shown in several areas led the authors to believe the TTY played a definite role in improving these skills.

During the year a sampling of each student's tapes was filed to measure any improvement in expressive and receptive communicative skills. It was determined that student progress reflected gains in the following areas.

Students began building sentences where previously only phrases were used. For example:

1. "Connie Home?" changed to "This is Patty. Is Connie home?"
2. "You want to talk more me?" changed to "Do you want to talk with me?"

Students showed greater skill in punctuation and greater thought separation, eliminating many run-on sentences. For example:

1. "I raked leaves to Bill Knapps for supper I painted the trim" changed to "Yesterday I was cleaning up branches and old leaves. We went to church."
2. "I is mad" changed to "My mother and I were sad."

Correction of sentence patterns also allowed for greater practice in vocabulary building.

Though expressive skills definitely improved, the greatest improvement was apparent in the receptive communication skills. When students began using the TTY, there was no real communication. Each seemed to be typing his or her own thoughts with no regard for the other's response. As the year progressed, these one-sided conversations began to evolve into genuine communication. Students began making the corrections themselves. They asked such questions as "What do you mean?" and "You did not answer me," thus forcing each other to observe and comprehend the printed message. Though some students took many months to acquire this skill, each one learned to communicate via the TTY. At the end of the 1976–77 year, the TTYs were loaned to six different students, a pattern that is now followed each year.

The TTY is a beneficial tool for hearing-impaired high school students. Through a program such as the one described above, awareness and use of the TTY grows, permitting more deaf persons to make it an integral part of their lives. Increased availability and knowledge of the machine also improves chances for its expansion into the areas of business and industry. When the TTY is readily available in quantity and at a reasonable cost, its true impact will be seen on the lives of hearing-impaired persons.

Technology and the Visual Processing of Verbal Information by Deaf People

E. ROSS STUCKLESS

Communication and Technology

I apologize for the wordy title of this presentation. For most purposes, we can consider verbal information as language; and at least for hearing persons the visual processing of language is synonymous with the reading of print and other graphic materials.

So why have I not simply entitled this paper "Reading?" First, to a much greater extent than most hearing people, deaf children and adults read language in forms other than print, i.e., they also read speech, fingerspelling, and the language of signs. Second, reading has always been associated with conventional materials like books, the chalkboard, and notes. Technology has changed much of that. With the advent of captioned films and television, computer-based visual displays of English, the use of the teletypewriter for communication, and the not-too-distant application of automatic translation of speech into print, we are no longer talking about reading in the conventional sense. As a result of these impressive technologies, we are faced not only with the always perplexing questions in teaching deaf children to read, but with new questions like how to display captions and what their content should be. Should telecommunication devices feature a moving electronic display or should there be a hard-copy printout? The list of questions goes on. Most important, we are beginning to ask questions about how to apply this technology most effectively to the communication needs of deaf children and adults.

But I am moving ahead of myself. Let's examine for a few moments the special applications of technology with deaf children and adults. Virtually all that come to mind are designed to aid in communication, either to train communication skills or to facilitate the transmission of information in everyday life. Often both these functions are served. Amplification devices, for example, offer support for training speech and auditory skills, and at the same time serve to facilitate everyday communication. Also there is some speculation well worth pursuing that the captioning of entertainment films, while intended primarily for the pleasure of deaf people, may also be contributing significantly to their reading skills. One might also speculate about whether the frequent use of the TTY by deaf people coincidentally also leads to improved English skills. If so, this technology is of added value.

Beyond the fact that the special applications of technology to deaf people focus on communication, most are aimed primarily at the *reception* rather than the expression of verbal information by deaf persons. The hearing aid again comes to mind, as do the various captioning technologies and most media devices such as the overhead projector. There are of course some exceptions, e.g., speech-processing aids which are designed to facilitate expressive communication, and still others which serve both expressive and receptive functions, e.g., the TTY, and the videophone.[1] Unfortunately, the latter has not proven commercially feasible on a broad scale, with the consequence that deaf people have not yet been able to avail themselves of this promising technology except within such special-purpose institutions as NTID. The coupling of the computer with what we know about learning has given us another powerful two-way communication tool for instructing deaf students.

I would like for the purposes of this paper to focus on the receptive side of communication toward which the bulk of our technological efforts have leaned. Without exception, these technologies stop at the senses. That is to say, they enable a communication signal to reach the eyes or the ears (or in the case of vibro-tactile devices, other sense endings of the skin). Here, as it were, the deaf child or

---

"Technology and the Visual Processing of Verbal Information by Deaf People," by E. Ross Stuckless, *American Annals of the Deaf* 1978, 123: 630–36. Reprinted by permission.

adult must take over. He or she must be able to sense the visual or auditory stimulus, store the impression at a prelinguistic level long enough for the brain to process and give it meaning, store it in memory for later retrieval; and he or she must be able to respond to the information which has been perceived, whether it be verbally or nonverbally, appropriately or inappropriately, overtly or covertly.

No matter how elegant the technology might be, no matter how advanced its engineering, no matter how many human and dollar resources have gone into its design, if it is not adapted to the deaf person's ability to process the signal it presents, it is useless and perhaps even detrimental. How many Americans have plugged an electric razor or hair dryer in perfect working order into an outlet in Europe only to discover that what works here doesn't work here without an adaptor? This experience contains far less real significance, although considerable inconvenience, a point to which some of us can probably attest.

Temporal and Spatial Characteristics of Language

Regardless of how a language is expressed, it has a sequential property. Speech is presented by linking phonemes in an orderly sequence to form words; words in turn follow one another in a prescribed sequence to form sentences.

Similarly, a message which is fingerspelled or signed contains sequential order. In this connection one of the major thrusts in the use of signs for the instruction of deaf children has been toward the use of Signed English and its several variations, and away from ASL. The major rationale underlying this movement is to present, and hopefully reinforce, the basic sequence of English. This, of course, has always been basic to the Rochester Method or Visible English, which incorporate fingerspelling to preserve the sequence of letters which form words, and the patterns of words which constitute English sentences.

Printed and written communication, of course, preserves this same characteristic of sequence. In order to understand how language is processed through either the eye or the ear, we must bear in mind that it has a characteristic of sequence. However, while all these communication modes have a common property of sequence, they differ in a way which has special implications for how they are processed by deaf children and adults.

Speech, fingerspelling, and signing all have a *temporal* property. This is to say that one unit or bit in the message appears and disappears in time to be followed by another. No two units appear simultaneously. Once the unit disappears it cannot be recaptured unless the speaker or fingerspelling repeats the message.

On the other hand, conventional print has a *spatial* property. In printed and written form, words are sequenced over space rather than over time. The reader can pause as long as he or she wishes over a particular word or group of words. We can enter a book at any point and move forward or backward through its pages. We can move up or down in a column of numbers without risk of the disappearance of the words, or numbers, or pictures.

It is true that technology is adding a temporal dimension to print, e.g., captioned television, but I will speak of this later. In the meantime, I suggest that the distinction between the temporally sequenced and the spatially sequenced message has particular implications for deaf people who are dependent on their eyes to process incoming verbal information.

Processing Language through the Ear and the Eye

Communication is generally received through either the eyes or the ears, and sometimes through both simultaneously. If we have audition, we hear spoken messages; if we have vision, we see printed or written messages.

While the eye and the ear have many overlapping functions in enabling the individual to maintain contact with the surrounding environment, each seems to be quite strongly committed to its own functions when it comes to processing verbal information.[2] In my opinion, those of us who work with and on behalf of deaf children, have given altogether too little attention to what the eye does well and what the eye does poorly. I have difficulty understanding why our field has focused so much clinical and scientific attention on the deaf child's ears while virtually ignoring his principal sensory modality for receiving information, his eyes. I am not suggesting that we reduce our efforts in audiology and auditory training but that we begin to attach at least as much attention to the deaf child's vision and its use for processing visual information. Parenthetically, it is likewise curious that educators of the blind have been highly attentive to the blind child's eyes while largely ignoring his hearing.

The normal *ear* and its associated neural network is remarkably well suited to accept *temporal-sequential* information. In attending to speech, the ear absorbs a temporal sequence of sounds which move to a transitional auditory or echoic memory before being processed centrally. Our echoic memory is able to accept and retain the temporal order of sounds for several seconds in prelinguistic form before they must be processed and given meaning.[3] We can store a brief sentence in echoic memory from beginning to end before we give it linguistic meaning. An example is the ability to hear an expression in an unrecognized foreign language and repeat it back virtually intact without attaching meaning. If we are unable to give meaning to this temporal sequence of sounds on its first pass, we often have time to play it back a second time before it decays and leaves our echoic memory. Echoic memory retains not only these sounds but retains them in their original temporal order.

The normal *eye* and its associated neural network is equally well adapted to accept *spatial-sequential* information. Like the ear, the eye has its own prelinguistic depository called iconic memory. Unlike echoic memory, iconic memory has a virtually unlimited capacity for the amount of visual information it can store.

To illustrate this capacity, subjects have been shown up to 1,000 unfamiliar slides in rapid succession. They were then shown the slides again with half the original slides removed and other unfamiliar slides substituted. When asked to indicate which slides they had seen in the first presentation and which slides they had not, they were able correctly to identify these slides with few errors.

Unfortunately, iconic memory, unlike echoic memory, has a very brief life span. Iconic memory is only able to hold visual images in its storage up to one second, and often no more than 200 milliseconds, depending on what precedes and what follows.[4] That is, the mind has one second or less to process the visual information which passes through the eye.

Consequently, unlike the ear, the eye is poorly equipped to receive and retain the order of temporal-sequential information. If a succession of visual stimuli follow one another in rapid temporal order, we have less than one second, and often no more than 1/5 of a second, to pull that information out of iconic memory and to attach meaning. If we cannot, we lose information. Furthermore, unlike echoic memory, the brief duration of iconic memory is such that we have no time to replay the visual image. If it doesn't register on the first pass, it is irretrievable.

To illustrate this point, many of us have had the experience of learning to read fingerspelling. When first learning, we found ourselves vocalizing or subvocalizing each letter of a word as it passed through our eyes. In so doing, we were pulling that letter out of iconic memory and depositing it elsewhere in short-term auditory memory. This enabled us to retain the sequence of the letters long enough to attach meaning to the word. However, we soon learned that when confronted with trying to process fingerspelled information presented to us at the rate of 60 words per minute this became an impossible strategy.[5] So we learned to "chunk" fingerspelled words rather than individual letters for storage. Fortunately, such a strategy is possible to deaf as well as hearing persons.

The very fact that deaf people are able in varying degrees to give meaning to what they see in speech and what they see in fingerspelling, both of which involve visual processing of temporal-sequential information, is a clear indication that temporal-sequential information can be processed through the eye. However, the skill of many deaf people notwithstanding, it is doubtful that the eye can ever process temporal-sequential verbal information at the same level of efficiency as the ear.

Let us now turn to a more positive attribute of the eye. The eye is well equipped to process spatial-sequential verbal information, i.e., print. Conventional print has a static, time-free, spatial attribute which allows the eye to examine its content at the reader's leisure. We can focus on a chunk of printed or written message indefinitely without risk of its disappearance. We can "take a picture" of the message as many times as we wish, "replaying" it again if we cannot give it meaning at first reading. It is popularly believed that when we read, our eyes are constantly in motion, in effect forcing temporal-sequential processing. But this is not so with conventional print. It has been demonstrated across a variety of types of reading materials and across a variety of readers, that only around 6 percent of the time is the eye in motion, while 94 percent of the time is spent by the eye in fixation pauses.[6] During this fixation on space, we are maintaining (or repeating) the same image in iconic memory, taking and retaking the same picture until we have time to give it meaning.

It should again be noted that technology has introduced some temporal elements into print. For example, the captioning of a motion picture film or videotape interposes a temporal dimension on print in that the viewer has just so long to process the particular caption before it disappears and is replaced by another stimulus. Similarly, some teletypewriters in the interest of portability and convenience, have substituted an electronic display for the more conventional hard-copy printout. In the wake of these developments, it is important that we not sacrifice the spatial attributes of print in visual processing. Parenthetically, I am much impressed with the capabilities of the new videodisc technology to restore to the deaf child and adult the ability to control their own reading pace, and to eliminate the temporal restraints which are forced on captioned films and television.

Some Basic Research

I would like now to review some of the more basic research germane to this topic. A little later, I will describe some research which is directly applicable to practices with deaf persons.

Pollard visually presented lists of words to groups of deaf and hearing students.[7] Some words were presented spatially, i.e., the full word appeared intact on a screen, while other words were presented temporally, i.e., each letter appeared and disappeared individually, in sequence. While his findings were mixed, they produced some evidence of better processing of those words which were presented intact in space than of the words in which letters were presented in temporal sequence.

Olson and Furth and Odom and Blanton found that both deaf and hearing subjects performed better on a variety of visual-sequential tasks when the sequences were presented simultaneously in space than when presented in temporal sequence.[8]

Stuckless and Pollard examined the relative ability of deaf students to process fingerspelled sentences, a temporal-sequential activity, and to process printed sentences, a spatial-sequential activity.[9] For this experiment we used three intermediate and secondary-level classes at the Rochester School for the Deaf which, as you know, pioneered the use of fingerspelling, coupled with speech, for the instruction of deaf students. This is commonly known as the Rochester Method. It could be assumed that these students were no strangers to fingerspelling.

These students, totaling 19 subjects, each viewed two lists of sentences matched for their vocabulary difficulty and syntax. Each list contained 59 words. The first list was presented on videotape and showed a competent fingerspeller fingerspelling each sentence at her normal rate. It should be added that she did not use speech so the Rochester Method itself was not being employed. The second list of sentences was displayed in spatial sequence on a cathode ray tube. The total "on" time for each of these printed sentences was the same as the time required to fingerspell its matched sentence. For each list, the student was presented with the individual sentence and instructed to write what he or she had seen.

Of the 19 students, 18 were able to correctly produce more of the words in the 10 sentences presented spatially than in the 10 sentences temporally, i.e., through fingerspelling. Overall, 50 percent of the words in the fingerspelled sentences were correctly reproduced, and 64 percent of the printed words were correctly reproduced, a difference statistically significant well beyond the .01 confidence level.

One of the classes in this study was an academically talented group of seniors. Unlike the other two classes, the students in this class were able to reproduce 99 percent of the words in print, and 92 percent of the fingerspelled words. Why did these students do so well in processing information which was presented temporally? We concluded it was probably because they already possessed English of a high order, and were able to process the fingerspelled letters in "chunks" which they already understood as the words and grammar which constitute English.

It might be conjectured that deaf people, because they are called on more than hearing people to visually process temporal-sequential information, are superior to hearing persons in this regard. While research on this question has produced mixed results, this hypothesis tends not to be supported, and indeed several studies have found the reverse.

Olson and Furth, Withrow, and Pollard have all reported superior performance by hearing subjects over deaf students on several visual temporal-sequential tasks.[10] Withrow speculated from his own research that the superiority of hearing persons may be due to their experience in processing temporal-sequential information through their hearing.

The single exception to this general finding came from the work of Zakia who found that deaf college students were superior to hearing college students in visually processing a temporal sentence of letters to produce meaningful words.[11] It should be noted that Zakia found the opposite for nonsense words. Presumably the ability of the deaf subjects to chunk the letters forming meaningful words was an obstacle in identifying nonsense words. He also observed a relatively high correlation, above .70, in the ability of deaf students to process meaningful words when the printed letters appeared in temporal sequence, and their ability to read fingerspelling. This finding led him to speculate that the superiority of some deaf subjects may be due to their greater experience with the visual processing of temporal information such as produced by fingerspelling.

None of this research, of course, allows us to observe verbal processing directly. The brain itself remains something of a "black box." However, a number of researchers, including Kelly and Tomlinson-Keasey are beginning to study where in the brain deaf people are processing verbal information.[12] For example, they are asking whether signs are processed in a region normally reserved for language or in a region generally associated with the processing of visual images. There is some early suggestion that where deaf people process signs may have bearing on their English literacy.

Research on Receptive Communication of the Deaf

There is a huge volume of literature on the training of various communication skills among deaf children. Until the sixties, however, there was little research on the usefulness of these skills to the deaf child himself. About 15 years ago, researchers became interested in exploring some of the extended effects of communicating in different modes with deaf children, focusing particularly on some of the educationally significant concomitants of manual communication.[13] Similar research focusing on the extended effects of training in oral/aural communication is now beginning to emerge.[14]

More recently, researchers began to investigate different visual modes of presenting verbal information to deaf persons, evaluating each in terms of the deaf person's ability to recall and reproduce this information. Included in these various studies have been fingerspelling, speechreading, signs, and print.[15] All these studies have consistently pointed to print as being more readily processed by deaf persons than these other modes, all of which require temporal-sequential processing.

Norwood's study is particularly notable for its immediate implications. Norwood presented a videotape of a national news broadcast to a large group of deaf adults.[16] Half the group viewed the broadcast with captions, and half the group viewed the broadcast with an interpreter superimposed in a corner of the screen. Each of the two groups was further divided into two subgroups, one of which had attended college, and the other had not. This was done to indirectly vary English literacy.

Recall was much better on the part of those who had viewed the captioned version than on the part of those who had viewed the interpreted version, among both the college-educated and the noncollege-educated subjects. It is notable also that almost all the subjects expressed a preference for captions.

In summary to this point, the results of both basic and applied research on the visual processing of spatial-sequential and temporal-sequential stimuli by deaf and hearing persons, furnish considerable support for the use of print for receptive communication by deaf persons.

Implications for Communication and Technology

It would be both irresponsible and impractical to conclude that we should communicate with deaf children and adults, and deaf people should communicate with one another, exclusively through print, writing, or captions. To take such a position would be to ignore many facts, including the following:

1. We cannot categorically assume the absence of echoic memory among all deaf people, e.g., those with hearing discrimination for speech, and those who have become postlingually deafened.
2. We cannot assume that merely presenting language to deaf people in print, written, or captioned forms, assures that it is processed with meaning. Reading obviously involves more than seeing a word in space.
3. Interpersonal communication is not all verbal. Without debating whether manual communication is verbal or not, we would all agree that the language of signs is a highly functional interactive communication system for many deaf people.
4. At the most practical level, speaking, signing, and fingerspelling are all temporal-sequential activities which unless captured on audiotape or videotape, are literally "real-time" communication events. Print is not. It may be a year or more before a book or an article is published; minimally it requires several hours to caption a live telecast; writing on a chalkboard requires longer than speaking; even communicating a message by TTY takes longer than to communicate by voice.

These are some of the constraints on print in communicating with a deaf person, and indeed they are severe constraints. This is also where the educator must turn for help to his colleagues in technology.

Technology gave us printing and the ability to reproduce multiple copies. Technology gave us things to write upon like paper and the chalkboard, and things to write with like the pen, pencil and chalk. Technology then gave us the overhead projector and transparencies to print and write upon. Technology gave us the typewriter, and then the teletypewriter which not only allows deaf people to communicate from a distance, but which "talks" back to them in print or electronic display. Technology gave deaf people the ability to read in captions what people were saying on film and on television. These technologies have transformed temporal-sequential communication into spatial-sequential communication.

In view of these achievements, what remains for technology to do? For the deaf person who depends heavily on vision for processing verbal information, we need refinements in what is now being done. For example, we need better turn-around time, and ultimately, instantaneous captioning of films and movies.

We need a practical way for a deaf infant to literally see in space the love sounds of a mother and the conversation of a family at the dinner table. We need a system which allows the deaf child to acquire English through seeing, just as the hearing child acquires English through hearing.

Most anthropologists and linguists consider the true language of a people to be the language they speak and hear. Where does this leave the young deaf child who can neither speak nor hear? What will his true language be? I submit to you that for many deaf children it should be, and with the aid of technology it can be, the spatial-sequential language of written and printed English.

Notes

1. J. M. Pickett, "Speech-Processing Aids: Some Research Problems," in R. Frisina, ed., *A Bicentennial Monograph on Hearing Impairment: Trends in the U.S.A.* (Washington, D.C.: A. G. Bell Assn. for the Deaf, 1976), pp. 82–87; P. Bellefleur, "TTY Communication: Its History and Future," in R. Frisina, *Bicentennial Monograph*, pp. 107–12; D. Castle "Telephone and Distance Communication Devices for the Hearing Impaired," *Deaf American*, June 1977, pp. 15–16; E. M. Dickson, *The Video Telephone, A New Era in Telecommunications: A Preliminary Technology Assessment*, National Science Foundation, June 1973.

2. I. J. Hirsch, "Temporal Aspects of Hearing," in D. B. Tower, ed., *Human Communication and Its Disorders* (New York: Raven Pr., 1975).

3. U. Neisser, *Cognitive Psychology* (New York: Appleton, 1967).

4. E. Averbach and A. S. Coriell, "Short-Term Memory in Vision," *Bell System Technical Journal* 40 (1961): 309–28; R. G. Crowder, "Visual Auditory Memory," in J. F. Kavanagh and I. G. Mattingly, eds., *Language by Ear and by Eye* (Cambridge: MIT Pr., 1972).

5. H. Bornstein, *Reading the Manual Alphabet: A Research Program for Developing a Filmed Program for Teaching the Manual Alphabet*, Centennial Series, no. 2 (Washington, D.C.: Gallaudet College, 1965).

6. M. A. Tinker, *Bases for Effective Reading* (Minneapolis: Univ. of Minnesota Pr., 1965).

7. G. W. Pollard, "Information Processing in Two Presentation Modes by Deaf and Hearing Subjects" (Ph.D. diss., Univ. of Illinois, 1977).

8. J. E. Olson and H. G. Furth, "Visual Memory-Span in the Deaf," *American Journal of*

Psychology 79 (1966): 480–84; P. B. Odom and R. L. Blanton, "Rule Learning in Deaf and Hearing Subjects," *American Journal of Psychology* 80 (1967): 391–97.

9. E. R. Stuckless and G. Pollard, "Processing of Fingerspelling and Print by Deaf Students," *American Annals of the Deaf* 122 (1977): 475–79.

10. Olson and Furth, "Visual Memory-Span in the Deaf"; F. G. Withrow, "Immediate Memory Span of Deaf and Normally Hearing Children," *Exceptional Children* 35 (1968): 33–41; Pollard, "Information Processing."

11. R. Zakia, "Fingerspelling and Speechreading as Visual Sequential Processes," Occasional paper 3 (Rochester, N.Y.: National Technical Institute for the Deaf, 1972).

12. R. Kelly and C. Tomlinson-Keasey, "Hemispheric Laterality of Deaf Children for Processing Words and Pictures Visually Presented to the Hemisfields," *American Annals of the Deaf* 122 (1972): 525–33.

13. E. R. Stuckless, "An Interpretive Review of Research on Manual Communication in the Education of Deaf Children: Language Development and Information Transmission," in P. Henderson, ed., *Methods of Communication Currently Used in the Education of Deaf Children* (London: Royal National Institute for the Deaf, 1976).

14. G. Walter and D. Sims, "The Effect of Prolonged Hearing Aid Use on the Communicative Skills of Young Deaf Adults," *American Annals of the Deaf* 123 (1978): 548–54.

15. R. Gates, "The Reception of Verbal Information by Deaf Students through a Television Medium: A Comparison of Speechreading, Manual Communication, and Reading," Proceedings of the Convention of American Instructors of the Deaf, Little Rock, Ark., 1971, pp. 513–22; M. Norwood, "Comparison of an Interpreted and a Captioned Newscast" (Ph.D. diss., Univ. of Maryland, 1976); G. Propp, "An Experimental Study on the Encoding of Verbal Information for Visual Transmission to the Hearing Impaired Learner" (Ph.D. diss., Univ. of Nebraska, 1972); Stuckless and Pollard, "Processing of Fingerspelling."

16. Norwood, "Comparison of an Interpreted and a Captioned Newscast."

The Optacon Reading System

JAMES C. BLISS and MARY W. MOORE

The Optacon does just what is described by its full name: OPtical-to-TActile CONverter. That is, the Optacon converts, or copies, an optical image into a corresponding tactile image, primarily for the purpose of enabling a blind person to read ordinary inkprint documents and books. By producing tactile images of the same patterns a sighted person sees, the Optacon enables a blind person to read by touch. Thus, the interposition of this "optical-to-tactile converter" between the blind person and the printed page opens up the world of print without the necessity of sighted transcription.

"The Optacon Reading System," by James C. Bliss and Mary W. Moore. Reprinted with permission from *Education of the Visually Handicapped*, December 1974, pp. 98–102; March 1975, pp. 15–21; and May 1975, pp. 33–39.

This is the basic concept that Professor John G. Linvill of Stanford University was concerned with in 1962 when he was on sabbatical leave in Switzerland.[1] Because he had a blind daughter, Candy, who attended a neighborhood school without a resource room or itinerant teacher, he knew firsthand the enormous amount of time his wife spent manually performing an optical-to-tactile conversion from inkprint-to-braille with a Perkins Brailler. If only this conversion could be done by the blind person himself using a small machine, not only would there be a great labor saving, but the independence, privacy, and educational opportunity of that person would be greatly enhanced.

Professor Linvill had very early rejected the idea of making a machine that would produce braille. Not that braille was undesired, but the difficulty of endowing a machine with sufficient intelligence to recognize all letters, numbers and symbols in the vast variety of typestyles normally encountered, would be too ambitious an undertaking and would result in too complex a machine to be personally owned and operated.

Reading machines for the blind with tonal outputs have been discussed since the announcement of the Optophone in 1912.[2] The fifty-year history of attempts along this line was well known to Professors Linvill and Bliss. They rejected this approach because reading performance with these tonal systems is inherently low due to the inefficient use these systems make of the auditory sense. Also, they felt that a tonal display of an optical spatial pattern, such as a lettershape, was less natural and more difficult to learn than a tactile spatial display. More complex sound displays, that could produce spoken letters or words, suffer from the same difficulty as a braille system; that is, they require a machine with extensive recognition capability. If the machine did not produce braille or spoken words, but instead merely copied the optical image into tactile form, could these tactile lettershapes be recognized with enough efficiency to be practical? In 1965, Linvill and Bliss initiated a series of experiments to answer this question.

Two-dimensional arrays of lights which are switched on and off to make letters appear to move (as in Times Square, New York City, or on Hollywood marquees) are familiar to us all. It was decided to determine if Candy Linvill could read the same type of display, but with the lights replaced by tactile stimulators. During his sabbatical in 1962, Professor Linvill had observed a high-speed printer in Germany that printed letters with a small array of pins which were made to vibrate axially. Each lettershape was formed by electromechanically driving only certain pins against a ribbon and the page. Professor Linvill had reasoned, if letters could be printed in this way, then perhaps the letters could be "printed" directly on the skin and recognized tactually.

Professor Linvill, an authority in the field of solid-state electronics, conceived the idea of using piezoelectric crystals to drive the pins, a method which has proven to be very efficient and effective. Linvill and Bliss began by designing an array, or screeen, of such tactile stimulators with enough individual display points to reproduce all of the lettershapes. The physical size of the array was appropriate for sensing with a fingertip without finger movement.

In January 1966, Linvill and Bliss reported the success of this crucial experiment. Thirteen-year old Candy Linvill had achieved a reading rate above 30 words per minute after only 45 hours of practice! This result led to their commitment of the next five years to the development of a small portable and convenient machine to perform this function. The machine was named the Optacon and it was first available in manufactured form in 1971.

There are now over 1,000 Optacons in use around the world and Optacon instruction has become a standard part of the education of blind children in many locations. Table 1 lists some of the independent evaluations that have been performed on the Optacon. Instruction in teaching reading using the Optacon is available in some universities and may soon become a part of the curriculum for educators of the visually handicapped. There is every indication that usage of the Optacon will continue to increase, and that there will continue to be evolutionary improvements and requirements in Optacon equipment and instructional techniques.

To describe the Optacon, imagine a case with dimensions of 2x6x8 inches and weighing about four pounds, somewhat similar to a cassette tape recorder. This highly portable case contains the batteries, electronic circuitry, and tactile screen. A pocket-knife-sized camera is connected to this case by a small flexible cord which conducts the electrical signals representing the optical image. The optical image is acquired by the lenses and silicon retina in the camera. With one hand the camera is moved along a line of type on two long rollers built into the base of the camera while the index finger of the other hand senses the tactile images produced by the tactile screen. As Fred Gissoni once remarked, "the Optacon lets your left hand know what your right hand is doing."

Mastery of Optacon reading is at least as difficult as mastery of braille reading, with the added ingredient of a technological device. To use an Optacon effectively, a blind person needs to learn lettershapes, operation of the equipment, the great variety of formats and typestyles found in print, language skills, and manual skill in tracking the camera along the lines of print and from line to line. For many teachers, the responsibility of understanding and dealing with this type of equipment will be a new experience.

How a teacher reacts to equipment can have a great bearing on how his students react. Attitudes toward equipment are changing rapidly, with the children of today

TABLE 1
Independent Evaluations of the Optacon

Authors	Title and Publisher of Report	Date
Tobin, M. J. James, W. R. K. McVeigh, Alison Irving, Rita	"Print Reading by the Blind. An Evaluation of the Optacon and an Investigation of Some Learner Variables and Teaching Methods." Research Center for the Education of the Visually Handicapped. School of Education, Univ. of Birmingham, England.	1973
Marmolin, H. Nilsson, L. G.	"The Optacon Aid, an Evaluation," Report No. 43, 1973. Dept. of Educational Research, School of Education, Uppsala, Sweden.	1973
Bertora, F. Biorci, G. Gambardella, G. Tagbasco, V.	"Nuova Metado di Lettura Tattile." Le Scienze, Edizione Italiana di *Scientific American*, Numbero 66, Febbraco 1974, duno Vil, Volume XII, pp. 34–41.	1974
Goldish, L. H. Taylor, H. E.	"The Optacon: A Valuable Device for Blind Persons." *New Outlook for the Blind*, pp. 49–56.	1974
Weisgerber, R. A.	"Educational Evaluation of the Optacon (Optical-to-Tactile Converter) as a Reading Aid to Blind Elementary and Secondary Students." Final Report under Contract No. OEC-0-72-5780, Bureau of Education for the Handicapped, U.S. Office of Education. American Institutes for Research Report No. 34500-9/74-FR, Palo Alto, Calif.	1974

taking for granted the existence and availability of equipment their grandparents didn't dream was possible. The Optacon is just another tool to be used when appropriate. A teacher needs to be completely comfortable and confident with the Optacon and to project a utilitarian attitude toward it.

To develop this confidence requires both a thorough knowledge of how the equipment functions and hands-on experience in operating the equipment. The Optacon was designed taking many human factors into consideration. Also, the design was based on the concept of a system which could be extended, through accessories, to other applications in which optical-to-tactile conversion would be useful to a blind person. Yet, at the same time, operation of the Optacon is inherently simple.

For example, there are three basic controls on an Optacon, all of which are designed to be adjusted by the blind user without removing his hands from the tactile screen or camera. These controls adjust the intensity of the tactile vibration, the threshold decision level between black and white (which has the effect of varying the stroke width of the letters), and the degree of magnification of the image. However, since the Optacon is a new experience for the beginning student, there is no way he can discern if the Optacon is properly adjusted. The responsibility for ensuring the Optacon is properly adjusted is initially the teacher's, and the teacher must guide the student in his development of independence in this task.

The Optacon has several other features which significantly expand its range of usefulness. First, there is a switch which reverses the mapping between black and white and vibration and no vibration. This feature permits white print on black paper to be read as well as luminous electronic displays such as those found on electronic calculators and other instruments. Second, the camera lens is easily detached from the silicon retina, which is analogous to being able to change the lens on an ordinary camera. This feature permits the Optacon, in conjunction with the appropriate accessory lens, to be used in instances where different optical characteristics are necessary, such as on a typewriter, where a working distance of several inches is needed to permit the typewriter keys to strike the page. The Optacon, used with this typewriter accessory lens, permits a blind typist to correct mistakes, fill out a preprinted form, and to restart after an interruption—all without removing the page from the typewriter. This typing aid could also be important in teaching typing to a blind student by providing immediate tactile feedback analogous to that provided by a braillewriter.

In addition, the Optacon has an input/output connector which adds some functions important in teaching. For a sighted teacher a visual display is an essential accessory. This display is an array of lights arranged in the same row and column format as the tactile stimulators in the tactile screen. The visual display plugs into the input/output connector of an Optacon and enables the instructor to see the same image that is being displayed on the tactile screen. By viewing this image, an experienced teacher can correct the adjustment of the threshold and magnification controls, determine if the camera is correctly aligned to the print, and detect a wide variety of reading problems.

The same monitoring feature is available to a blind teacher when a special repeater cable is plugged into the input/output connectors of two Optacons. With this arrangement, one Optacon camera drives the tactile screens of both Optacons. This feature also permits a teacher to work with two or three students simultaneously.

Another essential teaching device is the tracking aid. This is a simple mechanical aid for keeping the camera properly aligned to the print. A beginning student needs to recognize simultaneously tactile images of lettershapes and make precise camera movements which he coordinates with his sensory input. For many students, especially younger students, the dual tasks of tactile letter recognition and camera tracking are too difficult for a beginning step when full concentration is needed for either task. Since the tracking aid makes proper alignment of the camera to the print easier, the beginning student can devote more attention to the letter recognition task.

Another teaching aid, the automatic page scanner, completely relieves the student from the tracking task. This machine automatically moves an Optacon camera precisely along the lines of print of a page, with rapid preprogrammed movements from the end of one line to the beginning of the next line. The speed of movement along each line is adjustable and there are convenient controls for backing up, fast forward, and line changing.

The effectiveness of a machine such as the automatic page scanner first became apparent in 1965 in the initial experiments on tactile reading of lettershapes. This pacing technique was first recognized as an effective method for building reading speed. Later this type of teaching tool was found to also be helpful for illustrating to the beginning student perfect tracking movements, for relieving the beginning students from the burden of tracking, for diagnosing whether the constraint on a student's reading speed is tracking or tactile perceptions, for shortening the training time, and for a needed diversion in the training program. In the training courses in Palo Alto which have trained over 150 blind students (mostly adults), a significant increase in reading speed at the end of training has been documented since the automatic page scanner was introduced in 1973.

This array of equipment may seem staggering at first. It certainly requires added teacher competency and responsiblity. But with this advancement in reading methods for the blind we will learn more about the cognitive processes involved in reading which will allow future advancements to be made. Most importantly, though, this teaching system, in the hands of a well-trained and enthusiastic teacher, can dramatically stimulate students educationally and provide them with a skill and tool which can be immensely important throughout their lives.

. . . When a visual reader scans a printed page, the eyes move in a series of extremely rapid jerks (called saccades). Between the saccades are periods of comparative rest (fixation pauses) during which the eyes take in the information encompassed in 7 to 10 letterspaces or more. The wide span of vision of a visual reader enables him to read in units of meaning. The tactual reader, however, receives the information contained in single configurations (graphophonic information) serially over time and must integrate this into words and groups of words mentally. For the braille reader, a single cell may contain more information than a single letter in print contains for the Optacon reader because of the braille code system of contractions and short form words. In either case, however, the information transmitted by an outline of the whole word, or by the presence or absence of distinctive letters in the scan of the whole word, is not available at once in a single glance to the tactual reader. The cognitive processes involved with reading with the Optacon probably do not differ from those involved with reading in braille, except in degree. Either mode of reading, however, involves unique cognitive processes which differ from those utilized by the visual reader.

If we can consider the reader being an information-handling channel, having individual perceptual limitations, analysis of the reading process based upon Shannon's communication theory gives direction to a consideration of the cognitive processes involved. Shannon postulated communication as a system which could be represented symbolically in the model shown in figure 1.[3]

In reading with the Optacon, the information source is the author who uses the written word as the transmitter of his message. The signal emitted (tactual letters) is received through the nerve endings of the finger (receiver). The message reaches its destination when it is translated into meaning by the reader. There may be some loss of communication between the author and reader through the translation of a mental message into written words; through limitations in the channel capacity, that is, the limitations of the tactual senses and perceptions; and through limitations of the reader in assigning meaning to received words. Unwanted signals which tend to change the message are called "noise" in the system. Difficult to read type style, poor quality printing, smudges on the paper, poor motor habits, or any part of the message which the receiver lacks the skill to comprehend, create noise in the system.

Information is defined as that which removes or reduces uncertainty. The unit of measurement of information is a "bit" (for binary digit). A bit is the amount of information required to reduce uncertainty by one-half, or the number of yes-no questions which must be asked in order to specify one alternative out of many possible ones. For example, if in a twenty-question type of game, the leader says, "I am thinking of a letter," and the questioner asks, "Is the letter in the first half of the alphabet?" the questioner is asking for one bit of information. It can be seen, then, that a little over four bits (or four yes-no questions) would enable the questioner to guess the leader's letter. A reader begins with a finite uncertainty about the message being transmitted by the author. Letters grouped into words, that is, the orthographic characteristics, contain information which reduces the reader's uncertainty. However, constraints are put upon the order of the letters and words which are defined by the parameters of the syntax of the language, the semantics from context, and the spelling patterns of words in the language. Knowledge of these constraints can contribute information, or reduction of uncertainty to the reader. Whenever the same alternatives can be eliminated in more than one way, or can be eliminated from more than one source, redundancy exists. For example, if the first four words of the message, "Four score and twenty . . ." have been read, the reader, from his knowledge of word order in the language, will anticipate a noun or an adjective, not a verb, to follow. In communication theory terms, his uncertainty or number of alternatives will be reduced. The letters of the word *years* which follow also reduce his uncertainty. The syntax of the language has contributed redundancy. It has been estimated that English is 75 percent redundant.[4] That is, in a string of English letters in text, 75 percent fewer guesses would be needed on the average to guess the next letter in the string than would be needed if the letter string was completely random. Most good readers utilize their prior knowledge of this redundancy in the language to increase speed.

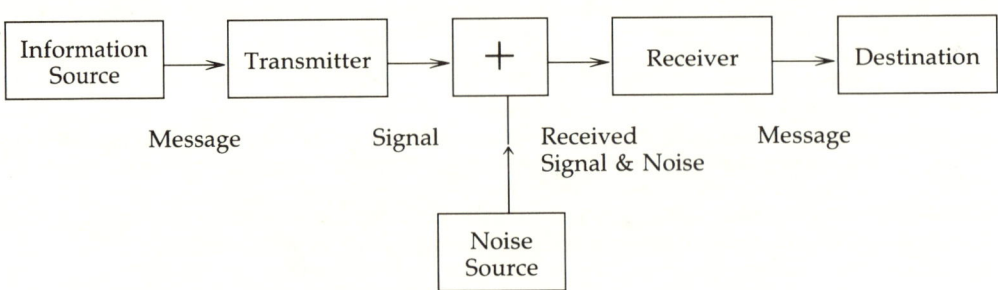

Fig. 1. Model of Information Processing System

Communication theory provides a model for analysis of the information-bearing characteristics of the tactual stimulus, and the skills which must be developed in the reader to enable him to add information to the communication process. Defining information, uncertainty, and redundancy in units which are independent of the type of transmission (written words, spoken words, electronic signals, braille, tactual letters, etc.) has made possible the quantification of situations and the conceptualization of these situations in new and precise ways.

Psychologists have used the mathematical theorems of communication theory to analyze and quantify human absolute judgment capacities, and have measured the effects of increasing complexity of stimuli and of presenting stimuli sequentially, rather than simultaneously, upon the human capacity to process information. It has been demonstrated that there is a finite limit in the number of bits of information which can be humanly processed on a single dimension. Miller extended the experiments on absolute judgment to the quantification of immediate memory by requiring subjects to withhold response until several stimuli were given in succession.[5] He demonstrated that, while bits of information remain constant for the span of absolute judgment, immediate memory is limited, not by the amount of information in the stimuli, but by the number of items presented. He postulated that information is organized, or recoded, into familiar units which he called "chunks," and that immediate memory can extend over approximately seven of these chunks. Humans learn to formulate chunks through extended demonstration and practice.

To analyze reading with the Optacon, then, the meaning in the mind of the writer is transformed into a series of graphemic configurations based upon the constraints of the language. These configurations are presented tactually to the reader in a serial order, and the reader must decode the meaning. The efficient reader selects partial clues and anticipates the message he reads. In communication theory language, the efficient reader depends upon the graphemic configuration to supply a minimum of information, and utilizes his knowledge of the constraints of the language and contextual clues to supply a maximum of the information needed to extract meaning.

Since the information-bearing features of the whole words which are available in a single glance to the visual reader are not available all at once to the tactual reader, the graphemic information is mainly contained in single letter shapes. The reader with the Optacon perceives and processes the information contained in each letter. The parts of the letter which contain the information, which reduce the number of possible alternative letters from 26 to a single letter, are considered the critical features of the letter. For example, consider a reader who encounters a word beginning with a capital letter H. The reader first peceives a vertical line. From all twenty-six letters of the alphabet which initially comprise the reader's uncertainty as to which letter he is about to read, this vertical line narrows the alternatives to the letters: B, D, E, F, H, I, K, L, N, P, and R, or to eleven letters. The single vertical line has given him a little more than one bit of information, since it has reduced his uncertainty by a little more than one-half. Next, the reader encounters a single horizontal line which, in its "horizontalness," reduces the alternatives to E, F, H, or L; in its "singleness," reduces the alternatives to H and L; and in its spatial position in the middle of the vertical line reduces the alternatives to the single letter H. The critical features of H, then, are the vertical line coming first and the single horizontal line in the middle. The final vertical line represents either redundancy to the poor or beginning reader, or noise to the efficient reader. The reader with the Optacon must quickly and efficiently utilize the critical features of the letter to identify each letter and assign to it an unique sound in the language.

In any type style, the critical features of the letters are maintained. Serifs or other embellishments in letters mainly create noise in the system, and the good reader who makes the most flexible use of the Optacon has developed the tactual communication channel capacity to perceive the critical features even if there is a great deal of confusion because of noise. Features and mental images of letter shapes exist in the reader's memory. Associated with each of these feature sets and mental "pictures" is a name or label. For example, the features and mental image of the shape of the letter A are recallable when the name A is mentioned. The good reader selects from his tactual perceptions those critical features which enable him to categorize the perceived shapes into letters previously learned and labeled as A, B, C, etc. To do this, he must understand how the Optacon operates and the capabilities and limitations of the machine. The adjustment of the magnification and threshold controls and a knowledge of the relationship between them enables him to "bring in" or sharpen the stimulus to maximize perception of the critical features. In this fashion, he contributes to the communication process by improving the transmission signal to the extent needed to overcome some of the noise, that is, he increases the information in the transmitter. Some of this information will be lost in the noise, and the good reader also makes his tactual sense more effective as a receiver, and the resulting communication process is more efficient.

Now, consider again our reader, and the letter which follows the capital H. If the reader has some knowledge of spelling patterns in the language, he can supply from this knowledge the information which would eliminate from his possible alternatives the letters: B, C, D, F, G, H, J, K, L, M, N, P, Q, T, V, W, X, Z, and probably R and S. Suppose the letter turns out to be an A. The reader will have anticipated a vowel sound, and he will require less information from the critical features of the letter a because of its serial position following an H. Since he requires less information, he should be able to perceive and categorize the letter more quickly.

If a reader has a good knowledge of the spelling patterns of the language he will suspend judgment as to the sound of *Ha* until he encounters the unit pattern which establishes the short *a* or long *a* sound. When he does so, he chunks or recodes the entire graphemic information into a single sound group and retains it in his memory while he processes the remaining graphemic information in the word. If he is unable to chunk the information into a single sound, then he must retain the individual letters throughout the entire word. Since retention in immediate memory is limited by the number of single units, if the word he wishes to read is very long, he will have forgotten the first letters before he processes the last ones, and will need to retrace the word from the beginning. The good reader with the Optacon has learned to chunk the graphemic information efficiently.

The reader with the Optacon utilizes more than the graphemic information and the information supplied by his knowledge of the spelling patterns of words. He uses his knowledge of the syntax of the language to reduce his uncertainty. His knowledge of the order in which words may appear in the language not only enhances meaning, but provides information to the communication process. For example, the reader anticipates a verb-direct-object order after a subject, or eliminates the probability of a noun-direct-object form following a form of the verb to be. The use of affixes such as those establishing verb tenses, singular, plural and possessive forms of nouns, etc., give information to the knowledgeable reader. Those words such as: *of*, *the*, and *but*, which are function words, signal the function of other words in the sentence and enable the efficient reader to anticipate or reduce uncertainty about what follows. The efficient reader does not read word by word, but chunks words into meaningful phrases to retain more words in his immediate memory to give meaning of a sentence.

Anticipation, or reduction of uncertainty, is enhanced by the reader's utilization of semantic information, that is, information derived from previous experience and vocabulary relating to those concepts which have been developed as a result of previous experience. The reader with the Optacon must process the information in an unfamiliar or unexpected word letter by letter, depending almost wholly on the graphemic information, in the same manner as a beginning reader. The more semantic information the reader has and utilizes, the more efficient becomes his reading. He can anticipate the appropriate word or words which should occur from the context, using the grapho-phonemic information to affirm his expectancies, and thus increase his speed of reading and comprehension.

As a student develops his Optacon reading skill, he learns to make scanning movements with the camera which interact with and assist his cognitive processes that are attempting to determine the author's message from the tactile impressions received from the Optacon. These scanning movements are constrained by limitations on the speed and accuracy of human muscular control. For instance, roughly a quarter of a second may elapse between the occurrence of a stimuli and the resulting arm movement response. Also, it is difficult to position a camera by hand more accurately than a few thousandths of an inch, which may be an appreciable distance compared with the size of printed letter features.

These limitations, together with the small tactile field of view compared with vision, result in major differences between the visual and tactile reading processes.

Consider the beginning Optacon student reading at a rate of five words per minute. At this reading speed, the camera moves only about one-eighth of the way across a letterspace during the quarter second of a human reaction time. Thus, at this relatively slow reading speed, the distance the camera travels along the line of print during a human reaction time is not very significant compared to letterspace dimensions. Thus, the student is able to vary the speed of camera movement to match his cognitive requirements for letter recognition. That is, he can slow down to "see" a particular letter better or speed up if he has already determined what the letter is from previously recognized features and context.

However, as the student's reading speed increases, the camera begins to travel a significant distance in the time required to make a muscular response. At forty words per minute, a complete letterspace will be scanned in a quarter of a second. Thus, it is less possible to tailor camera movements to aid the cognitive letter recognition process. As a result, rapid Optacon readers tend to scan the lines of print at a more uniform rate than slower readers. The rapid readers have developed the mental ability to store the perceived letter features in their immediate memory as they scan the camera at a uniform rate until enough pattern and contextual cues are accumulated for letter and word chunks to be recognized.

This uniform scanning is in marked contrast to the eye scanning movements of visual reading. In visual reading, the number of fixation points along a line of print depends on the familiarity of the text. Common phrases require fewer fixation pauses, or are leaped over by saccadic jumps. The speed of visual reading is in part due to the way the eyes and brain work closely together as a team. The saccadic jumps and fixation pauses group the printed letters and words into chunks of variable length, but of approximately equal information content to the reader.

These efficient eye control movements are possible because of the wide field of view of vision. While the tactile sense also has a spatial aspect, the equivalent "field of view" is much more limited, and experiments indicate this limit is approximately one letterspace.[6] The design of the Optacon is based on this finding, so only an area equivalent to about one letterspace is displayed at a time. Since a letterspace is not a sizable enough chunk to work on for grouping letters into equal information chunks, there is no advantage for tactile reading to consist of saccadic jumps and fixation pauses. Instead, the brain and tactile sense have to work together in a different way in which the Optacon reader scans single letters (instead of groups of letters of equal information) at a fairly constant rate. These letters are accumulated in immediate memory until they can be organized into progressively larger language units, such as syllables, words, and phrases, leading to the attainment of memory. It is interesting to note that, compared to the highest achieved Optacon reading rate (approximately 80 words per minute), visual reading is seven to ten times faster, roughly the same ratio as between the fields of view of the two senses.

This theoretical analysis of the cognitive process involved with reading with the Optacon gives direction to an analysis of teacher competencies which are necessary for successful instruction, as well as curriculum development and material needs.

. . . Some studies have been conducted in an attempt to define the physical and personality variables in children which contribute to success in learning to read. In education, however, success in learning for children depends, to a large degree, upon the competencies of the teachers involved. Teachers who have the opportunity to participate in the development of an entirely new discipline are faced with an exciting challenge. Without the aid, or imposition, of published teaching guidelines, all the personal knowledge, skill and artistry of teachers must be brought to the teaching situation in additional ways. But this is what teachers dream of when they are in training; this is what makes teaching truly rewarding! The teaching of reading print with the Optacon to blind children is just such a new discipline. Experience in the field has been mainly with adults, and the relatively few children who have been learning have been chosen, systematically or unsystematically, because they have already shown excellent reading skills in braille. As more and more schools elect to provide the opportunity for their students to learn to read print with the Optacon, it will be the responsibility, and the privilege, of teachers of blind children to contribute to the development of the methods and materials for instructing the children. If teachers are to be successful, then, they must develop some unique competencies for the task.

The teacher must be completely familiar with the care of the equipment and understand enough of the structure of the Optacon to be able to detect faulty equipment. All equipment should be checked before each teaching session, as faulty equipment can waste much precious teaching time and frustrate the student.

The teacher should also understand the capabilities of the instrument. For example, the machine is equipped with controls that make it possible to read from 6 to 21 point print. The magnification control will convert small print to a larger tactual image. In other words, the tactual image for the blind reader is approximately the same size, regardless of the size of print being read. However, not just the size of the letters are magnified or diminished, but the features, the thickness of each stroke in the letters, are also magnified or diminished. These features can be adjusted by means of the threshhold control for maximum discrimination by the reader. The magnification and threshhold controls are interdependent. Also, poor quality print with uneven strokes, varying amounts of ink, and/or missing features, can often be picked up by adjusting the threshhold control skillfully, thus enabling the photosensors to react appropriately. The teacher should be competent to make the adjustments which will enable the machine to present the ideal tactual image to the student and to instruct the student in making his own independent adjustments while reading. The visual display will be used by the sighted teacher to monitor the student's adjustments. The teacher will also use the visual display to monitor student's tracking in order to correct such errors as "skewing," or slanting of the camera, excessive up and down movements with the camera, frequent backtracking, etc.

Whether the student is a beginning reader or a braille reader learning to read print, the first task of the teacher is to develop in the student the ability to discriminate, recognize, and identify letters. The teacher should be able to describe the letters in terms of their critical features or be able to assist the student in developing insight into those features which enable him to identify the letters. Feature analysis of letters reveal that critical features include not only the presence or absence of geometric shapes, i.e., horizontals, verticals, etc., but the position of these geometric shapes in relation to the line of writing, i.e., ascenders and descenders. Thus, the position of the letter upon the tactile array becomes important. Since this is controlled by the position of the camera upon the printed letter, good tracking skills and the ability to make very fine movements with the camera are necessary. Discrimination and tracking skills are interdependent since it is the discrimination of the letter which provides feedback to the reader to give him direction as to camera movements. On many occasions, particularly when the student is beginning to identify letters, the teacher will choose to separate the two tasks of letter recognition and tracking with the camera, and will need to take over the tracking task for the student. While the sighted teacher, then, need not be competent in tactual letter recognition, he/she must be able to track with the camera skillfully, using the visual display as a guide. The teacher must be able to control the camera for the letters to progress evenly across the tactual display in the proper position for ascenders and descenders to be discriminated by the reader. Since the automatic page scanner, which automatically moves the camera precisely along the lines of print of a page, also completely relieves the student from the tracking task, the teacher should be familiar with the control and manipulation of this teaching aid.

As the student progresses to integration of letters into words, and words into complete ideas in sentences, the teacher should be aware of the skills which must be emphasized for the tactual reader. For example, to increase his memory span as he integrates longer strings of letters into words, the student must learn to chunk the information into longer units than a single letter. The teacher must assist the student to develop effective units of chunking, e.g., common spelling patterns, morphemes, phonic blends, etc.

Reading is a process of selecting partial cues and anticipating the message as it is read. In this process of partial perception of cues, the reader uses three kinds of language information available in the written passage: grapho-phonic information, syntactic information, and semantic information. The teacher should have a knowledge of the sources of redundancy in the language, and be able to teach the student to utilize the redundancy for appropriate anticipation in his reading, and ultimately to increase speed. One approach which has been shown to be effective in increasing speed of reading is to provide concentrated forced-speed practice. The theory behind this strategy is that the student will utilize his already learned language skills and learn through practice to select partial cues in his reading. However, there may be blind children who will not be able to increase their speed of reading by this forced-speed practice. Utilization of a theoretical model such as that proposed by communication theory will help the teacher to diagnose students' difficulties and needs in this area. The teacher who understands that, especially in tactual reading, the amount of information which the reader supplies from his knowledge of syntax and semantics is critical to the speed of reading, can develop instructional materials and strategies for enhancing this process.

Some printed materials are now available, or soon to become available, for teaching reading print with the Optacon. However, we have had so little experience with teaching young children or with teaching children who have not already demonstrated above average reading ability in braille, that teachers in the field may find they will need to develop curriculum, methods and materials for individual children. One systematic method for developing curriculum through the sequential ordering of objectives in a manner which will ensure the child's success at each level is the technique of component analysis [fig. 2].[7] Using this technique, the teacher may order tasks in a sequence which is far more likely to be effective than one which is intuitively constructed.

A component analysis of a stated task begins with the identification of the actual steps involved in performing the task. At this level, the technique resembles a simple task analysis such as is frequently employed with behavior modification procedures to shape behavior and teach motor tasks. These steps are listed horizontally across the page, and are considered to be the components of the terminal task. Each of these steps is then considered in isolation. For each step, the question is asked, "What must the child be able to do, or what must the child know to perform this step?" The skills or knowledge thus identified comprise the second level, listed vertically on the page. Each of these second level skills and knowledges are then considered separately in isolation, and again the question is asked, "What must the child be able to do, or what must the child know in order to perform this step?" Continuing in this fashion, prerequisites at each level are established. The analysis is complete when the level is reached at which the teacher may safely assume the entering student is competent. The tasks are sequenced in levels from the final task to the most fundamental, and the chart is read from the bottom up, that is, from the most fundamental to the final.

When the component analysis is complete, instructional objectives, written in behavioral terms, may be assigned to each step. Arranging the instructional objectives in sequential levels corresponding to the component analysis results in a curriculum guide for instruction. As success at the lower level is demonstrated, the teacher moves to the next level for instruction of the child. With this as a guide, the teacher will be able to individualize instruction for each child, allowing the child to progress through the steps at his own pace. The sequence also serves the teacher as an assessment instrument to establish entry level of each child, and/or as a guide to the construction or selection of appropriate instructional materials. One example of a component analysis of the task, "Read Sentence with Optacon," which was developed by teachers in Special Study Institutes for the Professional Preparation of Teachers of Reading with the Optacon, is included in this article.

The teacher of a child who is encountering a specific problem in learning can use the Component Analysis and the sequence of instructional objectives as a "road map" for diagnosis and remediation. As a simple example, suppose a child consistently reads "pat" for "pot," and "hat" for "hot." The teacher can have the child repeatedly try to identify the letters o and a, or words which contain o or a. However, much time may be lost and the child may become frustrated if this task is too difficult. As a diagnostic technique, the teacher can check through the sequence of instructional objectives, e.g.:

1. Task: Understand concepts: open and closed curves
   Given line of three closed circles and one open circle, the child will verbally identify the open circle.
2. Task: Discriminate critical features of letters
   Given line of three circles open on right and one circle open on left, child will identify the one which is not the same.
3. Task: Discriminate shapes of letters
   Given three o's and one a in line, child will verbally identify the one that is not the same.
4. Task: Recognize letters
   Given stimulus letter o and line of four letters, three a's and one o, child will match letter o with stimulus.
5. Task: Identify letters

116 Technology

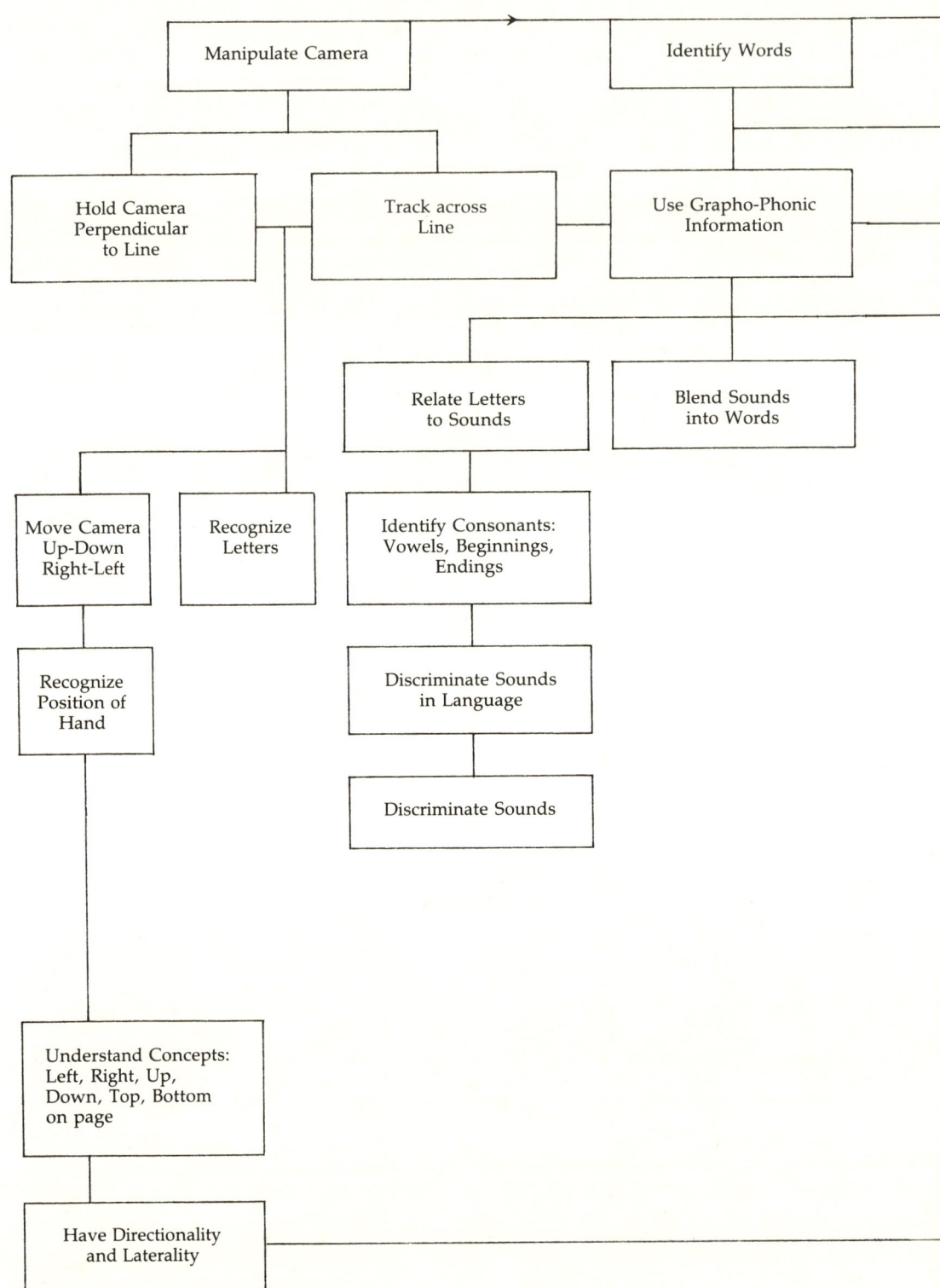

Fig. 2. Component Analysis

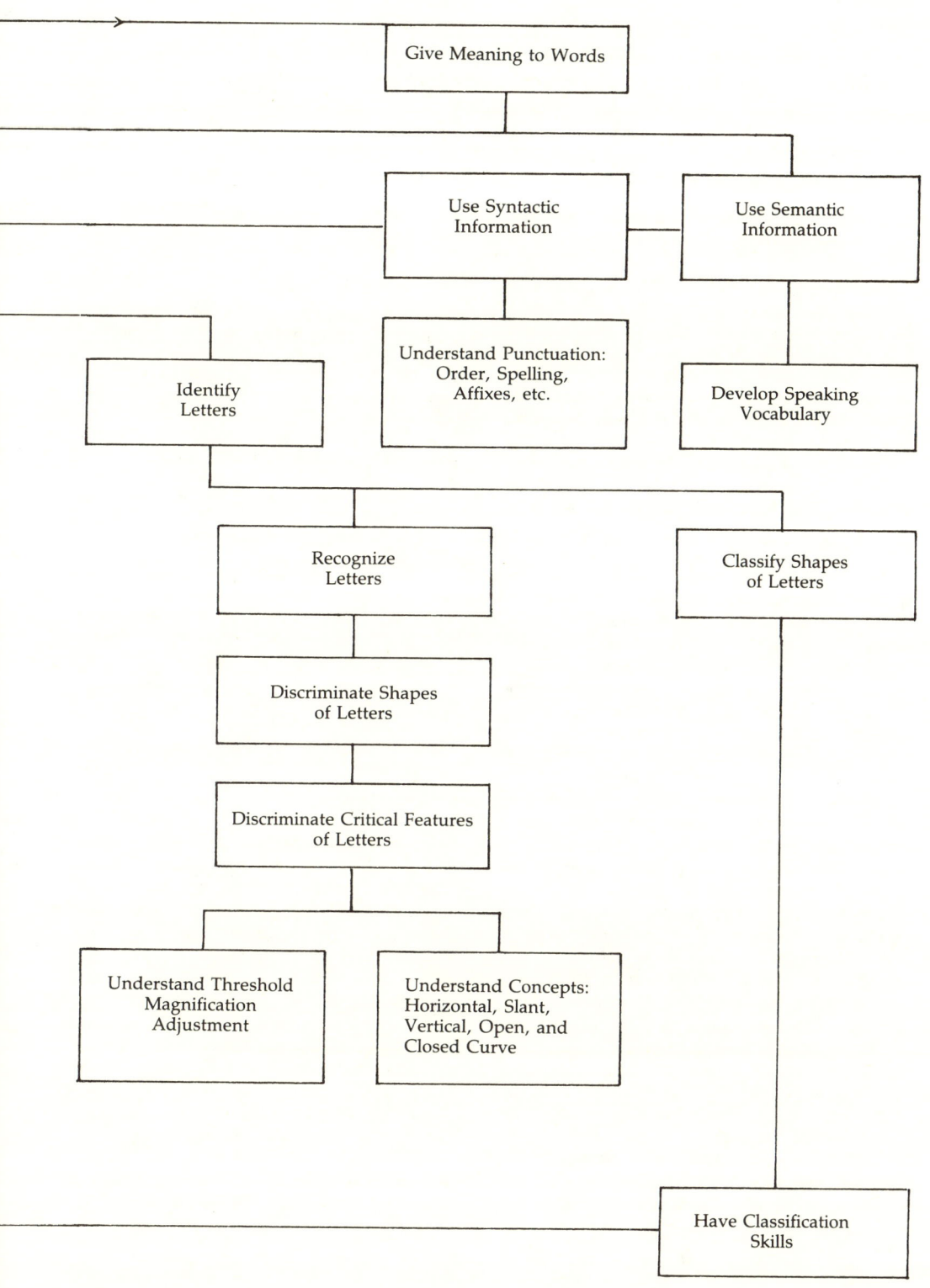

Given series of mixed o's and a's in the line, child will verbally name letters.
6. Task: Understand spelling patterns
Given, orally, letters h-o-t and/or letters h-a-t, child will verbally identify word spelled.
7. Task: Use semantic information
Given sentences "The sun is hot," and "The sun is hat," child will verbally identify which one makes sense.

In this precise fashion, the teacher can identify the source of confusion, which may be tactual discrimination, letter recognition, letter identification, spelling, or semantics (vocabulary), and can work with the child to remediate the specific problem. This technique will prove to be a more efficient teaching strategy than simply providing the child with repeated practice with a's and o's.

Materials from the training manuals which are now available may be used, but it will be necessary to supplement these materials as the student progresses. To select and adapt commercial materials, the teacher should be aware of appropriate criteria for print styles, format, reading levels, and interest levels. Some regular school materials, such as spelling lists, math workbooks, weekly readers, etc., may be used. The learning process culminating in independent practical use of the Optacon for school work requires a long period of several years before its full potential is achieved. The student may require considerable encouragement and help to build his abilities and confidence after the basic skills have been established. The teacher's role will be crucial in helping to maintain the student's motivation.

Finally, the administrative role of the teacher in maintaining a new program such as Optacon training involves not only organization, that is, scheduling of students, record-keeping, maintaining equipment, etc., but involves working closely with administrative personnel and with classroom teachers. The enthusiasm, flexibility and cooperation of the teacher of reading with the Optacon is crucial to the success of an Optacon training program.

Training is important for developing the competencies of the teachers; however, the educational and vocational opportunities opened up to blind children and youth who can read print is so exciting that more and more teachers are seeking this training, and are looking forward to being a part of this new development in the field of education of blind children. With these competent teachers, blind children will be provided with skills and tools which may dramatically effect their whole lives.

Notes

1. J. G. Linvill and J. C. Bliss, "A Direct Translation Reading Aid for the Blind," *Proceedings of the IEEE* 54 (1966): 40–51.
2. E. E. Fournier d'Albe, "The Optophone: An Instrument for Reading by Ear," *Nature* 105 (1920): 295–96.
3. C. E. Shannon and W. Weaver, *The Mathematical Theory of Communication* (Urbana: Univ. of Illinois Pr., 1949).
4. C. Cherry, *On Human Communication* (New York: Technology Pr. and John Wiley, 1957).
5. G. A. Miller, "The Magical Number Seven, Plus or Minus Two: Some Limits on Our Capacity for Processing Information," *Psychological Review* 63 (1956): 81–97.
6. J. C. Taenzer, "An Information Processing Model for Visual and Tactile Reading," *Perception* 1 (1972): 147–60.
7. L. B. Resnick, *Design of an Early Learning Curriculum* (Pittsburgh: Univ. of Pittsburgh, Learning Research and Development Center, 1967).

Bibliography

Attneave, F. *Applications of Information Theory to Psychology: A Summary of Basic Concepts, Methods and Results*. New York: Holt, 1959.

Garner, W. R. "An Informational Analysis of Absolute Judgements of Loudness." *Journal of Experimental Psychology* 46 (1953): 373–80.

Hake, W. H., and W. R. Garner. "The Effect of Presenting Various Numbers of Discrete Steps on Scale Reading Accuracy." *Journal of Experimental Psychology* 42 (1951): 358–66.

Pollack, I. "The Information of Elementary Auditory Displays." *Journal of Acoustical Society of America* 24 (1952): 745–49.

———. "The Information of Elementary Auditory Displays, II." *Journal of Acoustical Society of America* 25 (1953): 765–69.

Experimental Provision of Closed Circuit Television at a Danish Public Library

BODIL PORS

In early 1978, the Frederiksberg Public Library in Copenhagen, Denmark, provided closed-circuit television (CCTV) to visually impaired users in the reference department of the central library for six weeks (January 16 to February 28). The object of this experiment was to determine the extent to which a group of citizens with impaired sight, who until then had no access to the sources of information and reference materials offered by public libraries, could gain access to this material with the help of CCTV. The experiment sought to evaluate the extent to which CCTV should be provided by public libraries. It was not designed to obtain information about visual handicaps and eye diseases.

A librarian was engaged five hours daily specially to instruct participants in the use of CCTV and the library's resources. The television equipment used was a Swedish model called Magnivision. Information about the experiment was distributed widely through periodicals, newspapers, radio, and television as well as eye specialists and teachers.

A total of 106 partially sighted persons took part in the experiment (as shown in table 1, over half were age 60 or older). The majority were well motivated; many came to the library more than once, and many traveled long distances. The demonstrations or tests were observed by 253 relatives of the participants and staff of libraries and other institutions.

The publicity letter sent to the partially sighted included an invitation to bring personal papers with them to the test. Thus several arrived with letters, Christmas cards, income tax returns, and so forth. Those who could use CCTV were invited to state their wishes with regard to reading matter after the librarian had described the materials available in the reference department. The majority expressed a desire to read the daily paper; others wanted to read periodicals, articles in weeklies, local papers, town maps, and the like.

After each trial, the librarian completed a worksheet designed to provide information about the participant's ability to read before the trial, the benefit of reading by CCTV, and the participant's evaluation of CCTV's suitability for library purposes.

Method

Table 2 indicates that the duration of the tests ranged between 15 and 60 minutes. The test times included the time devoted to instruction in the use of CCTV, the duration of the test itself, and the period that individual participants read with CCTV by themselves. The average reading time for persons who came to the reference department more than once was about 50 minutes.

Participants who could read before the experiment were divided into two groups: Group I, those who could read ordinary black print, and Group II, those who could read only headlines or perhaps books in large print. For each group, we assumed that the participants had been tested with the best

---

"Experimental Provision of Closed Circuit Television at a Danish Public Library," by Bodil Pors, *Visual Impairment and Blindness*, March 1980, pp. 102–4. Reprinted by permission of the American Foundation for the Blind.

TABLE 1
Percentage of Participants in Different Age Groups, by Sex

Age	Men (47)	Women (59)	Total (106)
10–19	0%	2%	1%
20–29	2	2	2
30–39	17	7	11
40–49	9	10	9
50–59	4	13	10
60–69	34	13	23
70–79	23	39	32
80–89	11	12	11
90–	0	2	1

TABLE 2
Duration of Tests

Minutes	Participants (106) No.	%
Less than 15	8	7%
15–20	36	34
25–30	22	21
35–40	7	6
45–50	14	13
60	15	14
90	3	3
150	1	1

optical aids available. Group III consisted of those who could not read. (Note that since members of Group III evaluated their own reading abilities, their actual ability is uncertain.)

During a 15-minute test, it was possible to determine whether participants could use CCTV—in other words, whether they could operate the platform and the enlargement and focusing controls. It was also possible to demonstrate other controls, even if a user could not become familiar with them in such a short time. (Tests lasting less than 15 minutes involved persons who proved unable to use CCTV.) One factor that influenced the duration of the tests was time of day. Because afternoon hours were generally preferred, a number of users had to stop reading sooner than they would have wished. Another factor was that persons who were undergoing education or were employed may have used CCTV at the State Institute for the Blind and Partially Sighted and thus may have been familiar with the reading aid beforehand.

Participants who managed to read satisfactorily had the opportunity to read various typographical forms such as those found in newspapers and ordinary books; a number used CCTV for writing. It should be noted that the majority preferred to read inverse video—white text on a black background.

To determine the degree of enlargement each participant required, the height of the letter n was measured on the television screen after each test. This made it possible to determine the letter height needed, independent of the size of the text being used. As illustrated in table 3, most participants used letters ranging in height from 2 to 6 cm (approximately ¾"–3½"). The distance between the participants' eyes and the television screen was not measured. In each case, the degree of enlargement recorded was the one that gave the user the best reading position on the whole.

TABLE 3
Degree of Enlargement Required by Participants

Height of Letter n (in centimeters)	Persons (106) No.	%
1.8 [c. ¾"]	5	5%
2.0	9	8
2.2	4	4
2.5	9	8
3.0	6	6
3.5	7	6
4.0	7	6
4.5	10	9
5.0	9	8
6.0	9	8
7.0	3	3
8.0	1	1
10.0	2	2
12.0	3	3
13.0 [c. 5⅛"]	2	2
15.0 and above	4	4
Could not read	16	15

Results

Table 4 shows the reading ability of each group before the experiment, the number in each group who could read using CCTV, and the number who expressed a willingness to use CCTV in their own libraries. Note that the participants with the poorest sight (Group III) constituted the largest group: 61 out of 106. As one would expect, all participants in Groups I and II were able to read continuous text with CCTV.

Group I. Only 4 of the 13 persons in this group said that they would use CCTV regularly if it were installed permanently in their local libraries. The others did not wish to make use of this aid, on the grounds that their handicap was not yet so marked that CCTV was necessary for reading.

Group II. Sixty-three percent of the participants in this group expressed an interest in reading regularly with CCTV, stating that the equipment provided them with possibilities for reading which they had not had before. Among those who did not wish to use CCTV, some were exposed to books in large print for the first time, found they could read these books with their own optical aids and ceased

TABLE 4
Reading Ability in Groups I, II, and III before and during the Experiment and Willingness to Use CCTV

Reading Ability before Experiment		Number of Participants		Reading Ability Using CCTV			
				Able to Read		Would Use CCTV in Own Libraries	
Group	Reading Ability	No.	%	No.	%	No.	%
I.	Ordinary black print	13	12%	13	100%	4	31%
II.	Headlines or books in large print	32	30	32	100	20	63
III.	Cannot read	61	58	45	74	28	46
Total		106		90		52	

to be interested in the other reading aids offered by the library.

Group III. On the average, the persons in Group III had been unable to read for about six years. It is noteworthy that 74 percent of this group was able to read with CCTV. Moreover, almost two-thirds (63 percent) said they would be interested in using the reading aid if it were placed permanently in their own libraries. Most of the 17 persons who were able to read with CCTV but said they would not use this equipment regularly explained that they were dependent on companions to bring them to the library.

Among the participants who could not use CCTV, the visual acuity of some was so limited that reading was impossible. Others had lost their ability to read, in part as a result of lack of practice; some of them could perhaps benefit from CCTV if their reading skills could be improved with the help of a reading specialist. A few could not manage to move the platform satisfactorily with the text under the camera.

Conclusion

It was heartening that 84 percent of the participants in this experiment could use CCTV satisfactorily and that the majority (58 percent) in this group said they would like to use the aid regularly in their local libraries. The pleasure expressed by individual participants about being able to gain access to everyday information was characteristic throughout the experiment.

Although it would not be reasonable to draw too far-reaching conclusions on the basis of 106 participants, the results were sufficiently positive to justify the recommendation that libraries acquire CCTV. In this way, partially sighted citizens would, in principle, have access to all the information resources of the library. (In January 1979 CCTV became available permanently in the Reference Department of Frederiksberg Public Library.) The ideal place for CCTV equipment is in carrels that are easily accessible to the handicapped. This permits the display of private papers on the screen and provides a quiet atmosphere in which to concentrate on time-consuming reading.

A Second-Generation Interactive Classroom Television System for the Partially Sighted

S. M. GENENSKY, H. E. PETERSEN,
R. W. CLEWETT, and R. I. YOSHIMURA

A second generation multicamera-multimonitor interactive classroom television system, referred to as an interactive classroom TV system (ICTS), was built with funds provided by a contract between the Department of Health, Education, and Welfare's Office of Education and the Rand Corporation. It is now being used by partially sighted children and their teachers in a classroom for the visually impaired in the Killian Elementary School, Rowland Heights, Los Angeles County, California.[1] Evaluation of the class is part of a program to determine the effective use of such systems by partially sighted elementary school children in operating settings. Also included in the program is a first-generation ICTS, in a classroom for visually impaired children in Madison Elementary School, Santa Monica, California. (The first-generation ICTS was built with funds provided by a grant from the Department of Health, Education, and Welfare's Rehabilitation Services Administration; the system is described in Genensky et al. 1974.)[2]

An ICTS permits partially sighted children to be in continuous visual communication with their teacher. It permits them to see their teacher writing on a chalkboard while explaining what he is doing, as do sighted children in a regular classroom. The children do not have to wait to see what the teacher has written on the board *after* he has completed writing and is explaining what he has written. The flexibility and versatility of an ICTS in creating a visual and auditory atmosphere in which a partially sighted child can experience many of the perceptual interactions of fully sighted children, will become apparent in this article.

In what follows, a person will be considered to be partially sighted if the visual acuity in his better eye, even with the help of ordinary corrective lenses, does not exceed 20/70 but is sufficient to permit him to read and write as the literate sighted do or to recognize familiar objects as the illiterate sighted do, with or without the help of an optical or electro-optical aid. (A person whose visual acuity cannot be corrected to better than 20/70 in his better eye, even with ordinary corrective lenses, in general would not be able to read ordinary newspaper column type with or without such lenses.) At least 1.7 million Americans meet the criteria of this definition, and about 339,000 make up over 75 percent of this nation's 450,000 legally blind, supporting the assertion that the vast majority of the legally blind are not blind but are partially sighted.

The New ICTS

The new ICTS consists primarily of eight stations, a master control unit, a room-viewing camera, a room-viewing camera control unit, a videotape recorder, and a color TV monitor/receiver.

Each station consists of the following components: a 17-inch (42 cm) Shibaden VM 172 TV monitor; a down-pointing Shibaden HV 40 CSR TV camera equipped with a 5-to-1 Visualtek VL6 zoom lens; an Art Beam Lite 75 illuminator; and a 16-x-14 inch (41x35 cm) X-Y platform equipped with adjustable margin stops in the X- or line-traversing direction and a variable friction control in the Y- or line-to-line direction.[3] Each station camera is equipped with a switch to change the image originating from the camera from positive to negative. The contrast and brightness of the image on each monitor, as well as the vertical and horizontal hold, are controlled at the

---

"A Second-Generation Interactive Classroom Television System for the Partially Sighted," by S. M. Genensky, H. E. Petersen, R. W. Clewett, and R. I. Yoshimura, *Visual Impairment and Blindness*, February 1978, pp. 41–45. Reprinted by permission of the American Foundation for the Blind.

monitor by knobs conveniently located near the bottom of its front face. Seven stations are used by students and the eighth primarily by the teacher. The eighth station could also be used by students whose vision is good enough to see that station's monitor, which is located on top of the master control unit rather than with the rest of the teacher's station equipment.

At the student stations, the TV monitor rests on its own stand, designed to permit the edge of the X-Y platform, on which the printed or handwritten material lies, to pass below the monitor. The TV monitor can then be brought closer to the TV camera and still accommodate the large books used by young school children. The TV camera and its lens system are attached to a stand designed to allow the camera to be moved up or down easily. It also supports the illuminator and the X-Y platform. The station's power switch is on the front face of a boxlike structure at the right base of the camera stand's vertical support. The station's power line plugs into the rear of the box, keeping the power line receptacles safely out of reach. To the left of the camera stand's vertical support is a box housing the station's speaker, volume control knob, and receptacles for the station's microphone and earphone jacks. The receptacle for the cable that carries signals from the station to the master control unit and vice versa is at the rear of this box.

The monitors used at each station of the system were tested by J. L. Shepherd and Associates, Glendale, California, to determine if there was any X-ray hazard to a person viewing the monitors for long periods of time with eyes very close to the face plates. There was found to be none whatever, even in such close proximity to the user.

In the ICTS student station for use by a right-handed person . . . the illuminator is attached to the left of the camera stand's vertical support and its beam is directed down and to the right. The station's monitor is located to the left of the camera stand. (The station can easily be rearranged for use by a left-handed child.)

The teacher's station differs from the student stations in that its monitor is mounted on top of the housing that contains the master control unit. The housing is located near the desk that supports the station's camera stand. It is also for right-handed use. The room-viewing camera remote control unit is on the teacher's desk directly to the right of the station's X-Y platform.

The X-Y platforms of the new ICTS are 2 inches (5 cm) wider than those of the first ICTS to accommodate the larger books used by young school children.

The Master Control Unit

The master control unit is the nerve center of an ICTS. It controls the source of the image presented on each of the system's TV monitors. By pressing appropriate buttons on the master control unit, the teacher can present material on any of the system's eight station monitors *independently of what is displayed on any other monitor*: The material displayed can consist of any of the following images:

1. A full screen image of what is being transmitted from any of the system's nine cameras or from its videotape recorder.
2. A horizontally split image from any two of these ten sources.
3. A superimposed full screen image from any two of these ten sources.

Experience with the first ICTS indicated a need to simplify two important frequent operations.

1. Simultaneous presentation on all eight station monitors of any single or composite image.
2. Full screen display on each station monitor of what the camera at that station is viewing.

The first operation, the "all" mode, involves pressing at most five buttons, and the second operation, the "self" mode, requires pressing no more than three buttons. The first master control unit design required pressing as many as 24 control panel buttons.

The master control unit is largely responsible for the versatility of the ICTS, which can be better appreciated by an examination of the following examples.

. . . A negative image of a bird results from a station camera viewing the picture of the bird on its X-Y platform, superimposed upon a positive image of the word "bird" viewed by a camera at another station. The image on the monitor screen could have been at either one of these stations or at any other station, because the master control unit permits the image on any one monitor to be duplicated on as many other monitors as desired.

. . . In contrast is a positive image of a bird superimposed on a negative image of the word "bird." This image can be produced . . . by reversing the polarity of the negative image with the contrast reversal switches on the cameras that are viewing the pictures of the bird and the word "bird."

. . . It is possible also to split the above image horizontally; the upper half from a station camera viewing the picture of a bird, on its X-Y platform, the lower half from another station camera viewing the word "bird" on its platform. The first camera transmits a positive picture and the second a negative picture. . . . Only the upper half of the picture sent out by the first camera is displayed on the monitor screen, and only the lower half of what the second camera is transmitting is shown on the screen.

The same composite image . . . may be produced but with both cameras transmitting positive images.

. . . In another example the teacher and a student are standing in front of the classroom saying the word "Oh" that is superimposed on the negative image of a lowercase "o" and an uppercase "O" viewed from the camera at the teacher's station. The teacher is standing on the floor and the student is standing on a chair. During the lesson that accompanied this photograph, another teacher, seated at the teacher's desk, used his station camera and X-Y platform to display a lowercase and uppercase letter pair on all station monitors. He then asked the students to identify the letter they saw on their monitors. One or more identified the letter correctly. He reinforced the correct response by showing on each student monitor teacher and student making the sound associated with the letter, and superimposing the appropriate letter pair on their image. . . . The children not only observe the upper and lower case "O" on their station monitors, but they also see the faces of their classmate and teacher saying the word "Oh!" In addition to the phonics lesson, they see *in detail* the faces of these two people. Without the help of the ICTS, most students would only be able to see the general shape and form of these faces. Through the ICTS, even a simple lesson in phonics becomes not only a visual and auditory experience in the building of written and verbal communication, but also an experience in recognizing faces and expressions.

Teachers and teaching aides frequently go to a student's desk to work directly with the student. It is not the function of the ICTS to replace the important, personal, one-to-one relationship between teacher and student, but rather to supplement and support this relationship. Experience in both classrooms indicated that the ICTS has achieved this objective.

In the last example, a student is learning to play a harmonica by watching his teacher, who seems to be placing his mouth on a sketch of the mouth edge of a harmonica, while inhaling or exhaling at the appropriate times. The image on the student's monitor is a superimposing of two images on the whole screen. One image is of the teacher as seen by the ceiling-mounted, room-viewing camera; and the other is a negative image of a sketch of the mouth edge of a harmonica, located on the teacher's X-Y platform.

The Room-Viewing Camera

The room-viewing camera is a GBC CTC-6000 equipped with a 10 to 1 zoom lens, and hung from the ceiling of the classroom so that it can "see" virtually any part of the room. It is operated by a remote control unit. The classroom is approximately 64 by 32 feet (19.2×9.6 m), roughly half of which is occupied by tables, chairs, and sandboxes, where the children eat lunch and play games, and by open space where they sing, exercise, listen to stories, etc. The ICTS occupies approximately 600 square feet at one end of the room. Because the classroom that houses the ICTS is very large, three receptacles have been provided to permit the remote control unit to control the room-viewing camera. One is at the teacher's desk, another is near a chalkboard, and the third is near the room monitor/receiver.

The Room Monitor/Receiver

The room monitor/receiver of the new ICTS is a KV 1910 19-inch (48 cm) Sony color receiver. Like any other color TV receiver, it is used to display off-the-air color or black-and-white TV programs. It is also used to display color or black-and-white TV programs that are being recorded by the ICTS's videotape recorder and to display in black and white what is being shown on one or more of the ICTS's station monitors.

The room monitor/receiver sometimes is viewed by small groups of students. However, only those students who can see the image on the screen in sufficient detail, at distances that do not interfere with other students grouped around and watching it, can participate successfully in this group activity.
. . .

The room monitor/receiver can be used independently of the rest of the ICTS, including the videotape recorder.

The Videotape Recorder

The new ICTS's videotape recorder is a JVC 6100. It is much more versatile than the videotape recorder in use with our first ICTS. Both videotape recorders can:

1. Record what is displayed on a station monitor and what is being said at or near the station of which that monitor is a part.
2. Play back, on one or more station monitors or on the room monitor/receiver, what was recorded previously on the system's videotape recorder or on another videotape recorder, including both the video and audio portions of the recording.

Both ICTS videotape recorders can record or play back in color or black and white. However, because the first ICTS has no color TV equipment, its videotape recorder cannot record and play back in color. Unlike the first ICTS's videotape recorder, the JVC 6100 can record off the air and is equipped with a timer that permits it to record, completely unattended, at a predesignated time. Further, it can make recordings of off-the-air material regardless of whether the color TV monitor/receiver is turned on or off. Note that having a color TV monitor/receiver as part of the new ICTS makes the capacity to record and play back in color very worthwhile.

With both the first and second ICTSs, the videotape recorder is used to record classroom activities such as a student working by himself, student-to-student interaction, and student-teacher interaction. These videotapes are used by the teachers to analyze student progress and problems, teaching techniques, and participant interactions. The videotape recorder is also used to prepare lessons in whole and in part. For example, it can be used to experiment with visual and auditory learning techniques, many of which would not have been considered possible when working with partially sighted children before the development of ICTSs. Further, the presence of compatible videotape recorders in the two participating classrooms makes it possible for the teachers in these classrooms to share videotaped materials.

Since the fall of 1975, educational and psychological data have been collected and classroom observations made at the Rowland Heights and Santa Monica ICTS sites, and will be continued to the close of the 1977–78 academic year, at which time a Rand report will be written describing the ICTS evaluation and the results of that evaluation. Indications are that the ICTSs are proving to be of value in teaching basic skills to non-mentally retarded partially sighted students. The participating students have developed healthier images of themselves and their parents are pleased with their progress and with what the ICTS classrooms are doing for them. There is no indication that student interest and enthusiasm for the ICTS is beginning to wane, which is not surprising because students soon begin to appreciate the visual link that an ICTS gives them with their teacher, classmates, and classroom. Students and teachers look forward to trying more academic innovation that without an ICTS would be visually impossible.

It is our conjecture that, relative to elementary education involving the acquisition of basic skills, it would be advantageous to place partially sighted students in classrooms of their own and, with the aid of interactive classroom television systems, give thorough instruction in basic skills. It would be beneficial at the same time to instruct them on the use of other visual aids, such as binoculars, monoculars, and telescopic spectacles, which they could use to establish and maintain visual communication with their teachers, classmates, and classroom when they have acquired the basic skills and have moved into regular classes.

We recognize that suggesting special classrooms for partially sighted students, even for only the teaching of basic skills in the early years of elementary education, may be viewed as retrogressive, but, in view of the experience in our ICTS classrooms, currently accepted theories regarding the *early* education of partially sighted children may need reexamination. When the decision was made to move partially sighted children from special classes into integrated classes, practical technological sophistication was not at the level it is today. In light of current practical technology, a modification of that decision might be appropriate. We agree that decisions as to how to educate children should not be made lightly, but we believe that they should be made in the light of current knowledge and with the full realization that the body of knowledge changes with time. A decision that appeared to be right yesterday may not be appropriate today.

Notes

1. S. M. Genensky et al., *A Second Generation Interactive Classroom Television System for the Partially Sighted*, Rand Corporation, R-2138-HEW, June 1977.
2. S. M. Genensky et al., *Interactive Classroom TV System for the Handicapped*, Rand Corporation, R-1537-HEW, June 1974.
3. R. W. Clewett, S. M. Genensky, and H. E. Petersen, *An X-Y Platform for Randsight-Type Instruments*, Rand Corporation, R-831-HEW/RC, Aug. 1971.

Bibliography

Genensky, S. M., H. E. Petersen, R. W. Clewett, and H. L. Moshin. *A Double X-Y Platform for Randsight-Type Instruments*. Rand Corporation, R-1614-HEW, Dec. 1974.

The Kurzweil Reading Machine

RUTH-CAROL CUSHMAN

"It's the most wonderful thing in the world—I can't describe the joy of putting a piece of paper on the machine and hearing what is there!" The speaker is Linda Skroski, a music graduate from the University of Colorado who has been blind since birth. Linda can do almost anything: she skis, she sings, she can play a tune on a cash register or on a piano. And now for the first time, she can read a book without using braille, without asking someone else to read it to her, and without waiting for a prerecorded tape.

Homer Page, head of the program for disabled students at the University of Colorado, is also blind. He ran for the state legislature in 1978 in spite of what some people might consider a handicap, and during the campaign he read "hundreds of things from letters to summaries of legislative documents." Although he narrowly lost the election, he did prove that blindness need not be an obstacle to holding a government office.

Mike Smith is a blind taxpayer service representative for the Internal Revenue Service in Des Moines, Iowa. "In the four years since I have been on this job, tax rules and regulations have changed substantially, and they continue to change. I am required to do a tremendous amount of reading just to keep current." He does that reading on his own.

The Kurzweil Reading Machine makes all this possible. Physicist Mike Hingson, also blind, travels around the country for the National Federation of the Blind demonstrating the machine and teaching people how to use it. "It's the greatest thing since Braille," he said on a visit to Norlin Library at the University of Colorado, where the first machine to be installed in a university library has been in heavy use since the beginning of 1978.

A New Era of Independence

Designed by Ray Kurzweil, an engineering graduate from M.I.T. who started pro-

---

"The Kurzweil Reading Machine," by Ruth-Carol Cushman. Reprinted by permission from the January 1980 issue of *Wilson Library Bulletin*. Copyright © 1980 by the H. W. Wilson Company.

gramming computers when he was twelve, the machine uses an electronic scanner with a speech synthesizer to read printed material aloud. It is programmed for one thousand linguistic rules plus two thousand exceptions, and it can read 200 different type faces at up to 225 words-per-minute. A new era of independence has opened for the blind who can now—on their own—read a wide variety of materials: books, magazines, newspapers, business memos, job training manuals, or typed correspondence.

No longer must a blind person wait for a reader in order to dive into the latest best-seller or today's newspaper. As one user pointed out, "It's sort of embarrassing to have to ask someone you don't know to read a risqué novel out loud!" A blind University of Colorado journalism student was thrilled to discover that she could use the machine to read her own articles back to her, and other students have used it to read back their term papers and creative writing assignments.

Out of about 40,000 books published each year, only about 350 are available in braille. "The Kurzweil machine means blind persons can select from the whole range of written materials," says Julia Brody, chief of a Manhattan branch of New York Public Library where several machines are in heavy use.

At the Library for the Blind and Physically Handicapped in Virginia Beach, Linda Midgett and Barbara Style (two blind staff members) can now work directly with print for the first time. Linda has the Kurzweil machine read a text aloud, while she proofreads the braille transcription. The machine can also be used to help people suffering from dyslexia, a reading disability, by allowing them to hear the words at the same time they see them on a page. Marilyn Mortensen, special services coordinator at the Virginia Beach Library, says the machine is used by a wide variety of people, including lawyers, authors, physicians, opthalmologists, psychiatrists, an architect, an electrical engineer, a navigation specialist, blind teachers, and teachers of blind students.

The Voice inside a Box

Even children as young as first-graders learn to use the machine quickly and love it. At the Beethoven School for the Blind in Boston, the children have nicknamed the machine "Kurzie" and regard it as almost human. One happy child summed it up:

"What it does, it takes a picture and comes out in a voice. It's like a radio: You're like the radio announcer—you decide what you want to hear."

Originally this voice had a "heavy foreign accent," but a newly developed synthesizer has a deep, resonant "baritone" voice that produces a more natural sound. Like most standard synthesizers, the Kurzweil reproduces the sixty or so phonemes (basic units of sound) that make up English speech. But in addition, the machine has a system that analyzes the syntax of each sentence. It duplicates nuances in pronunciation by differentiating sounds according to their relationship to other elements in the sentence.

"Sometimes you feel as though there's really a tiny, little person sitting inside the box, and maybe you should invite him out for coffee," says Nancy Cateora, a volunteer who works with the machine at the University of Colorado Libraries.

Nancy sees the Kurzweil as one way of helping end prejudice against the blind. Although few people would admit to such prejudice, there is no doubt that it is harder for a blind person to get a job than it is for the sighted. "This machine should bring about a lessening of preconceived notions of what the blind are capable of doing," says Nancy. "In the four years I have worked with the blind, I have found their limitations are ones *I* set for them. It's *my* hangup, not theirs. . . . These minds shouldn't be wasted by being shunted into niches *we* think are appropriate." Nancy is especially enthusiastic because of the independence the Kurzweil machine gives to the blind. Within eight to ten hours of training most people can operate the machine without assistance.

It took only one hour for Linda Skroski to become adept at the keyboard, and now she trains all users as part of her job as coordinator in the Office for Disabled Students at Colorado University. "In an average week the machine is in use about forty hours, but sometimes I can't get everybody in, it's so busy," she says. Approximately 45 people have been trained to use the machine, which is usually available from seven in the morning till eleven at night at the library.

Financing the Machine

By the beginning of 1980, more than a hundred reading machines had been placed in schools, libraries, rehabilitation centers, and work settings around the country. During 1979 approximately 250 orders were filled, 64 of them through the Bureau of Education for the Handicapped, a division of the Department of Health, Education, and Welfare.

Because of the cost of the machine, many libraries have obtained financial aid for their purchase. Two private foundations, for example—the Swan Foundation and the Hill Foundation—purchased the reading machines for the University of Colorado.

In Massachusetts, $110,000 was funded as part of the Blind and Physically Handicapped area of the Library Services and Construction Act (Title 1) that enabled five public libraries (Lawrence, Newton, Peabody, Weymouth and Worcester) to purchase machines and train staff in their use. Thomas A. Ploeg, consultant for the physically handicapped at the Massachusetts Board of Library Commissioners, listed the project objectives:

- to provide blind and physically handicapped persons with access to their community's information resources;
- to provide a reading machine which will provide one method of access to information resources;
- to provide trained staff that can effectively deal with client group and reading machine;
- to provide "model situations" that can be observed by other libraries; and
- to provide information on the feasibility of using a reading machine in a variety of public library settings.

In New York the machines were considered so vital that Assemblyman Edward Sullivan and Senator Hugh Farley introduced a bill to the state legislature that would put a reading machine in each of the twenty-two public library systems. The bill was passed in July.

Improvements and Operation

One reason the Kurzweil Reading Machine suits blind people so well is that it was field-tested by blind users through the National Federation of the Blind. This testing resulted in many improvements in early models: for example, the machine was modified to read photocopies, to handle italics and columns, and to respond to additional user commands. A new compressed speech feature enabled the blind to read print at a rate fifty percent faster than normal human speech. As improvements continue to be made, older models are quickly updated by insertion of a reprogrammed cassette; it is not necessary to purchase a new machine to benefit from new developments.

To operate the machine, a user places readable material on the glass surface, and then commands the machine by striking control keys on a small computer terminal. Under the glass a camera moves back and forth across the page; it can be stopped at any time by the user and commanded to spell a word, to give punctuation, or to back up and repeat. The user can also speed up or slow down the voice and adjust its tone.

The original 1974 prototype, which could read only print typed on Ray Kurzweil's personal typewriter, occupied half a room and cost a fortune to build. The machine at the University of Colorado, manufactured about two years ago, is about the size of a photocopier and was originally priced at $50,000. Although this model seems a miracle to those who use it, current models have superseded it.

New models have been reduced to less than one-third the size of the University of Colorado model. They weigh only 90 pounds (light enough for one person to lift), and the cost has been reduced to $23,800. This new desk-top machine has a hand-scanning option that enables users to "browse" a page, explore its format, and then read material selectively. It also has a compressed speech device. At the beginning of the fall semester, the University of Colorado Libraries added a desk top model. "Since this model is portable," says Linda Skroski, "a student can check it out the night before a final exam or for a special project."

The corporation is still working on improvements. Eventually the machine will be the size of a briefcase at a cost of about $5,000. Kurzweil has also developed new products: the Kurzweil Talking Terminal, that will enable voice-impaired people to communicate orally when it is attached to any computer terminal, and a print-to-braille machine, developed for the Library of Congress.

Blind user Gayle Dougherty, who formerly directed the Kurzweil project at the University of Colorado Libraries, looks forward to the day when blind people can buy their own Kurzweil: "When we can read our own office memos, instructional materials, and letters," she says, "we can become truly independent and can end job discrimination against the blind."

4
Software

Departures from traditional pedagogical practices have precipitated changes in teaching strategies, rendering learning less laborious, less protracted, more efficient and often more enjoyable. Recent innovations in instructional hardware have dramatically altered the speed and forms of information transference. Technological breakthroughs have resulted in rendering equipment, once costly and exotic, now routinely and readily available. Improvements in many areas, but most notably in miniaturization, have made feasible lightweight, portable, complex instructional and communication devices. The resultant proliferation of hardware in many libraries generates an aura of authoritativeness, an impression of keeping abreast of the technological demands of the day.

Yet equipment by itself is only enabling; it is the accompanying software which delivers the instructional message. Decisions as to which resources to use with special needs patrons are dependent on three separate but interrelated considerations:

1. The inherent qualities of the software and how these interact dynamically with the user;
2. The limitations that disability imposes on the person utilizing software; and
3. The individuals' preferences, styles, and information-processing strategies.

An analysis of the reports of both researchers and practitioners raises the following questions which must be addressed as determinations are made about the most desirable formats for exceptional populations:

1. Outcomes: What levels of cognitive behavior will ensue as the result of the interaction with the material, i.e., does the user intend to employ the medium to accumulate data or for more complex objectives in which the content will be transformed, analyzed, synthesized, or evaluated in some manner?

2. Format: When dealing with different kinds of content, e.g., factual, psychomotor, conceptual, affective, is there a preferred mode?
3. Interaction level: What role can or should the patron employ as the software is utilized, i.e., does the material require active or relatively passive responses?
4. Rate: What pacing demands are necessitated by the materials and do these impose unreasonable pressures on the user?
5. Redundancy: What is the extent of review or "overlearning" built into the medium?
6. Motivation: Is the matter absorbing, engaging, and involving enough for learners who have often had frustrating experiences in processing information?
7. Monitoring capability: Do the components permit self-checking so that errors can be identified and correct responses confirmed?
8. Prosocial capability: Does the format allow for or require activities or responses wherein disabled users will be obliged to work jointly with peers?
9. Status-enhancing capability: Is the format basically neutral or does it add prestige rather than stigmatize the user (e.g., computer-assisted instruction is generally a highly regarded mode of learning behavior)?
10. Remediation capability: Does the medium, or any elements within it, have the potential for encapsulating, articulating, or explaining information in ways that are more efficient than alternative choices?

In employing a particular piece of software, it is vital to assess how it may be utilized to bypass disability-related limitations rather than exacerbate them. The librarian-media specialist cannot then be a mere dispenser of software, but must assess the salient learning problems of users in order to design strategies in which utilization applications are structured. In certain instances, media center personnel, because of their special talents may be called upon to assist in the design, production, or modification of software which more closely addresses the needs of clientele with impairments.

Key considerations include:

1. Kind of impairment: Does the nature of the disability restrict or restructure the use of certain categories of materials?
2. Degree of impairment: Do the complexity and severity of the disorder or dysfunction superimpose constraints on employing particular types of software?

The last, and obviously most variable factor, is the individual library user. The patron's needs and interests should be factored into the equation so that personal requirements are congruent with both software potential and disability implications.

Aspects to be weighed are:

1. Age and development: How do structure, content, and complexity of the material correlate with the maturation level of the patron?
2. Personality and character: In what ways do an individual's traits affect learning behavior, e.g., is the user tenacious, easily discouraged, flexible, a risk taker?
3. Styles and tactics: In what manner does the person's preferred learning strategies guide the media specialist in deciding upon appropriate resources?
4. Sophistication: To what extent does the user's familiarity with different modes extend options?
5. Personal goals: How do academic and career objectives affect the decision to employ particular approaches to materials?

Each individual's needs and aspirations will vary over the course of time. Media specialists must periodically test the waters to ascertain which combinations of elements should influence their decisions. Some commercial products may be usable as they are; some may need to be adapted or modified; others might be utilized effectively in nontraditional ways or with audiences for which they were not originally intended. Librarians cannot afford to be rigid in their perceptions of the usefulness of materials or overlook old standbys. Increased attention to electronic gadgets should not be allowed to obscure the potency, utility, and unequaled satisfactions inherent in the printed word. Books have unique and indispensable qualities which still make them the medium of choice in innumerable situations.

Although the need for language development in blind toddlers is especially critical, their impairment militates against expected rates of achievement in this area. These preschoolers have difficulties in comprehending the relationship between an object and its name. If books are going to provide such connections, then titles independent of illustrations and referents within the experience of the child must be employed. Blos suggests that nursery rhymes, since they emerged from the oral tradition, are especially productive in promoting language growth, learning about the world, and systematizing knowledge. Nursery rhyme collections that meet her proposed standards are suggested and supportive activities are explored.

The National Library Service for the Blind and Physically Handicapped (NLS) has developed an extensive array of services for those who have problems in processing information visually, but Bush contends that many would-be borrowers have yet to take advantage of this excellent resource. She explains the scope of this collection and the center's criteria for selection of titles. In addition to giving the librarian a comprehensive picture of the agency as well as procedures for access to their collected works, less well-known collateral activities of other agencies that complement those available through the NLS are cited. Although access to these resources was once restricted to those with visual or physical impairments, anyone who cannot manage standard print is eligible provided some substantiation of need can be made.

One of the most maligned products of common culture is the lowly comic book. Hallenbeck asserts that this disparaged artifact can be a potent motivating and remediating tool for children with learning disabilities. It can provide practice in developing such mechanical skills as left-to-right orientation and visual discrimination as well as such substantive ones as interpreting symbolism, noting connotative meanings, and identifying absurdities. When traditional materials have provided an uninterrupted stream of failures, any objects which have the potential for remedying deficits through an enjoyable format should not be lightly dismissed.

Since facility in moving freely in any given environment is essential for independence, maps are an essential tool in both orientation and mobility. Standard maps, restricted to those with vision, are worthless to blind travelers. Bentzen reports on tactile maps that can be consulted by those with sight as well as those lacking it. Informational attributes and design considerations are shared with readers.

In a complementary essay, Gill and Clark deal with the crucial issue of accuracy in the rendering of maps and other graphic displays for visually impaired people. After examining such presentations, the authors argue that computers unquestionably offer the greatest capability and reliability for generating correct models. Instructions for the development of such media are provided and the necessity for training readers in the interpretation of the symbols required to comprehend this mode of learning is underscored.

Traditional textbook-based instruction often causes insurmountable problems for adolescents with specific learning disabilities. To assist those secondary students deficient in language arts skills and reading proficiency, Deshler and Graham propose using audiotapes to negate the impact of some of the related deficits and simultaneously improve study skills. Observing that preparation of software to confront this requires more than a simple translation from print to audio format, the authors delineate guidelines and standards for the development and assessment of these tape recordings.

The recommendation that a patron without vision disorders use microfiche is often greeted without enthusiasm because of anticipated eyestrain when using that medium. Andersson's report from the National Center for the Education of the Blind in Sweden is all the more startling since it was noted that, ironically, microfiche facilitated speed and reduced fatigue in visually impaired users. Although the study was done using a small population and certain deficiencies were found in the hardware used, this unusual and unexpected application of this software reinforces the importance of a flexible, receptive attitude when exploring possible productive alternatives for serving library users with nonstandard needs.

Unquestionably, the presence of computers in media centers, schools, libraries and even a growing number of private homes has revolutionized the means by which information is stored, used, and retrieved. Dugdale and Vogel summarize several fruitful examples of its utility with students who are hearing impaired. Special attributes of this technique, e.g., the interactive aspects of some programs, the compelling appeal of the graphics, etc., have demonstrated effectiveness for those persons with auditory disabilities. The writers include pertinent samples from the instructional program that illustrate its obvious attraction. Also included is one example of the kind of modest additional adaptations necessitated by a youngster coping with a physical as well as an auditory impairment.

Although television has primarily been thought of as a channel for recreational purposes, and only secondarily for informational ones, two authors emphasize that television can be utilized as an agent of social learning. Baran reports on an experiment to determine if the self-esteem of viewers who are classified as mentally retarded could be elevated as a result of viewing a series of television programs. His finding of positive results, given the active intervention of an interpreter, suggests an important lesson for professionals that exposure to even so powerful an agent as television benefits from the presence of a mediator.

Elias has employed videotapes with another group who display exceptional needs: those classified as emotionally handicapped. He contends television and films have attributes especially potent in promoting social and affective skills and, when these are combined with other activities such as puppetry, role playing, and the like, are reinforced and subsequently generalized into the individual's repetoire of behaviors. His discussion is amplified by recommended resources for those professionals ready to employ this suggested approach.

Since knowledge is power, access to information is essential to individual capacity to seek out what is needed with precision and speed, and apply it to problems at hand. If software is adapted so that it facilitates such entry to the world of knowledge, it becomes the key to integrating the disabled user into a position of competitive status.

Traditional Nursery Rhymes and Games: Language Learning Experiences for Preschool Blind Children

JOAN W. BLOS

Language and the Blind Child

The question at first seemed simple: what stories could I recommend for reading aloud to young blind children, four years old and younger? As a specialist in language arts and children's literature, I had recently become associated with the University of Michigan's Child Development Project. There, under the direction and leadership of Selma Fraiberg, a longitudinal study of a small group of children, blind at birth but with no other discernible handicaps, was being conducted by a staff representing the fields of psychology, social work, and special education. Simultaneous with their investigation of the ego development of the preschool blind child was their commitment to provide educational, home-based guidance to these very young handicapped children and their families.[1] It was in connection with this part of the work that my colleagues came back from their work in the field to ask me, as they had been asked by parents, "What stories can you recommend for reading aloud to young blind children four years old and younger?"

I knew, of course, that accurate and versatile language would be especially important for these children and that even more than their sighted peers they would depend on such listening skills as finding the key idea, remembering sequences, paying attention to details, drawing inferences. Yet I was also aware that blindness severely limits opportunities for direct experience of the correspondence between the statements made and the thing referred to, interferes with the development of concepts of objects (as well as the concept of object constancy as a phenomenon to be explored), and confounds the establishment of body and self-image as reflected by the postponed stabilization of the personal pronoun.[2] In other words, the very disability that creates the need for superior language skills interferes with their acquisition in specific, predictable ways.

For example, in the area of language development and language play, nearly all of the children studied by the project had been successfully introduced to games such as "Patty Cake," "How Big Is Baby," and "Show Me Your Nose" before they were one year old. Yet at two years of age, and even three, they still played the same games and even the most articulate of them were not interested in stories that were read aloud. We were also puzzled because even such elemental recitals as develop from the familiar opening line "When you were very little . . ." failed to interest these youngsters. Eventually Fraiberg and Adelson were able to discover how this was related to other aspects of cognitive development.[3] For the purposes of the present discussion it will be sufficient to note that in this area of development, as in others, the problem is not that the children fail to achieve, but rather that the *rate of achievement* shows marked alteration when compared with sighted norms. With regard to word games and body-part naming we find explicit data in the files of the project.

> Carol 1:10. L. W., the case worker, played "Banberry Cross" with Carol. After L. W. touched Carol's body parts during the song, on the next time through Carol touched her own hand at "rings on her fingers" and lifted her foot at "bells on her toes." At "music wherever she goes" Carol lightly tapped the tambourine that L. W. held.
>
> Joan 1:11. She stood in the toy chest and held the doll while Mrs. C., the worker, talked to her. She asked her to say "doll" and point to the doll's hair, but she would not. Mrs. C. said "nose" and Joan touched her

---

"Traditional Nursery Rhymes and Games: Language Learning Experiences for Preschool Blind Children," by Joan W. Blos, *New Outlook*, June 1974, pp. 268–74. Reprinted by permission of the American Foundation for the Blind.

nose; she said "mouth" and Joan put her finger in her mouth. Mrs. C. then asked "Where's my nose?" but Joan was occupied with the toys and paid no attention. . . .

Elizabeth 2:1. She (Elizabeth) touched my nose and then she touches her own nose and she says "nose" to each one. Then she also touches her chin and says, "My chin." And then when she touches my chin, she also says, "My chin." She then went back to touching my nose and she said "More nose."[4]

But it is not until Elizabeth is four years and four months old that we find definite interest in recorded stories—at which time Elizabeth prefers them to TV. (When, at five, she liked a Walt Disney record of Kipling stories, her mother felt it was the rhythm of the words that attracted her most.)

Books for Preschool Children

Perhaps we can gain some understanding of the severely visually handicapped or blind child's dilemma by thinking about the kinds of books that are most often enjoyed today by their fully sighted age-mates. "Flats" are what the publishers call them, but to the reading public they are known as picture books. In the best of these large, bright volumes, the words and pictures function together, they work synergistically. Even where this degree of integration has not been attained, the illustrations are very important—at times prevailing over the words, but more often offering visual supplement to what has been said in the text. Certainly this is the case in the following excerpt from a popular picture book which may, with pictures intact, be expected to be understood by most three-year-olds:

"Trees are very nice. They fill up the sky." (p. 1 of text of unpaged book. Double spread. Art shows a leafy green forest. Boy lies on his back, looking up into trees.) "They go beside the rivers and down the valleys. They live up in the hills." (Double spread. Black-and-white drawing. Boy is fishing from tree-lined river bank. More trees in background.) "Trees make the woods. They make everything beautiful."[5] (Full color. Double spread. Sun in blue sky blazes down over tops of tall trees—some of these are evergreens, firs; there is one stand of birches. In the distance is a mountain ridge. No human figures.)

For the very young and visually handicapped child, the message may well be: "Blanks are very nice. They fill up the blank." (Sound of page turning.) "They go beside the blanks, and down the blanks. They live up in the blanks." (Sound of page turning.) "They make the blanks. They make everything beautiful." (Or is this a blank, too, being a visual term?) No wonder the parents of children studied by the project had been unable to interest their children in listening to the stories read aloud from these books!

Of course, as soon as this was clear to us, it also became clear that our task was not so much to find books that could be read aloud to these children as to locate suitable material that was not, and never had been, dependent on illustration—a prime example of which is Mother Goose. The first published editions of these traditional rhymes did not appear until the eighteenth century, but people had heard them for years before that—passing them on across the generations, relying only on oral transmission to keep them alive and fresh. With such a history it is no wonder that the rhymes, chants, songs, and games which make up the traditional nursery literature had long since been adapted to the purposes of the teller and the needs of the listener. The rhythms are clear, the rhymes give pleasure; simple actions (and tunes) often underscore the texts. When, in a later, forthcoming article, we come to consider some of the identifying characteristics of fairy, folk, and nursery tales, we shall discover extensions of many of these same qualities; we shall find that this built-in suitability for oral transmission commands special attention from those who work with young blind children.

A Language-Incentive Program

The following suggestions outline a home-based language-incentive program of activities using traditional nursery rhyme material aimed at the preschool blind child. The goals and functions of these activities are to offer functionally valid alternatives to the picture book literature of the preschool years, and to supplement the more usual and task-oriented means for the gradual induction of the child into language as a symbol system for gaining knowledge of the world, organizing its phenomena, and taking and giving pleasure with the written and spoken word.

As in so many other aspects of the education of the very young and specifically handicapped, much depends on the parents. In this context it is crucial that parents be willing, as well as able, to acquaint themselves with enough material to be able to sustain a high, varied, and spontaneous level of language stimulation through word-play games. Of course it is important that all parents do this for all of their children. Most of them do. But when we are considering the special needs of blind and visually handicapped children, we are speaking of a population for whom the period of early language acquisition is not only very important, but invariably extended. In such circumstances, the usual parental repertoire of half a dozen rhymes or so may simply not be sufficient. For this reason, the following specific recommendations are made concerning rhymes that may be used. These suggestions are supplemented by the titles of some of the better anthologies and collections of such material. They are more likely—because of their publication dates—to be found in libraries than book stores, but both sources should be consulted. Of course, asking teachers, librarians, and local book suppliers may turn up other titles of equal or greater merit.

One further comment. It is our opinion that there is, especially with regard to language, a difference between thinking about a four-year-old child who is just like any other except that he cannot see, and trying to understand what it means to be a child, four years old, who is blind. In the former construction it is imagined that vision is a separate (and separable) phenomenon; the latter has a holistic base, implying that the lack of vision affects the system totally by making a major difference in subjective levels of experience, in the world as it is perceived. This point of view will be implicit here.

Because we are thinking now of the preschool child, we have in mind the home setting and assume that parents will be its main initiators. Yet, many of the ideas offered here apply as well to small group settings and teachers may, therefore, wish to adapt them.

Early Experiments

Being aware that much of the language activity in which the young blind child engages is not strictly practical, members of the project staff sought diverse substitutes for picture books that would foster familiarity with books and spark an interest in language. At first they were very optimistic about specially made book-like toys in which pocket-like pages held various objects for the child to handle. Although some of these attracted interest and may have encouraged some naming of textures or recognition of disparate objects by their feel alone, their value proved limited. (It should be noted that we take full responsibility for the failure of the books. We are, however, grateful to Mrs. Sharon Shaffii and the members of her committee for the skillful and imaginative construction of the items used and gladly thank them for their efforts at this time.)

Other early attempts to find good material focused on commercially available books with textured pages. For instance, *Pat the Bunny*, by Dorothy Kunhardt (1962), is the prototype of this preschool genre in which swatches of varied materials are combined with conventional pictures to represent an object.[6] Therefore, when the text invites reader-listeners to "Touch Daddy's scratchy face," the illustration on the facing page offers a father in an undershirt to whose about-to-be-shaved face a bit of fine grade sandpaper has been neatly affixed. That the blind child would be deprived of all the corollary information contained in the pictures—the washbasin, the poised razor, the tiled floor (just like mine!)—is unfortunate but not irredeemable. What rules the book out is the page on which we find a tiny oval of silvery paper framed as part of a boudoir set including brush and comb. "Look in the mirror and who do you see?" the printed text gaily asks. For the blind child there is no looking. Is there no me? (Lately, we have had positive reports from parents on books of the Touch Me! series, published by Golden Press; Scratch-a-Smell books from Mulberry Books, Inc.; Golden Fragrance books, also from Golden Press; and Touch and Tell stories from Hubbard Press. All of these are priced at under three dollars.)

Finger Plays

In the final months of the project, we began to speculate that finger plays, which combine kinesthetic with auditory cues, might more accurately substitute for the early bi-sensory experience of picture books than textured books can do. We recalled that nearly all of the children observed by the project had been introduced to "Patty Cake," and that they had enjoyed it. Would other games have been equally successful if they had been offered? We believed that this was so even though the termination of funding cut short the study under whose auspices this work was being conducted and aborted the opportunity to test this hypothesis with the study's sample. We have, however, received confirmatory reports from others; Mrs. Sherry Raynor, director, Preschool Program for the Visually Impaired, Intermediate School District, Mason, Michigan, says also that she has found finger plays to be useful and successful with blind and visually handicapped children during the preschool years.

From the point of view of what to recommend to parents—and why—we believe that a significant characteristic of the games is that although some accommodation must be made for a learning process deprived of the opportunity for learning by imitation (the monkey-see-monkey-do method), the pleasure of the games themselves is *independent of vision*; the blind child and the sighted child can enjoy them similarly. Further, and finally, the games provide a natural and enjoyable basis for social interaction between child and parents or within the family group.

Because familiarity with the activity favors a relaxed mood, we suggest that the finger plays and their accompanying rhymes be introduced to the children in the context (setting) of a daily routine. Too, embedding the games in a recurrent scene makes them predictable and produces a sense of awaited pleasure: every day they put on my shoe, and now—one, two, button my shoe! we tell the funny words.

Head and Shoulders

A simple game which provides a pleasurable introduction (or review) of the names of body parts is one in which the players touch both hands to head and shoulders and clap on "one, two, three." The words are repetitive and strongly rhythmic and many actions may be improvised beyond those suggested here: "Head and shoulders, Baby—one, two, three./ Head and shoulders, Baby—one, two, three./ Head and shoulders, Head and shoulders,/ Head and shoulders, Baby—one, two, three. . . . / Knee and ankle, Baby—etc. . . . Touch the ground, Baby—etc. . . . Stand up, sit down, Baby—etc."[7]

Later, when the child has acquired more verbal facility, the following variation, "Hands on Shoulders"—from the same source—offers challenge through pacing and quick changes of action. "Hands on shoulders, hands on knees,/ Hands behind you, if you please;/ Touch your shoulders, now your nose,/ Now your hair and now your toes./ Hands up high in the air;/ Down at your sides and touch your hair;/ Hands up high as before,/ Now clap your hands, one, two, three, four." (In this example the rhythm is a straight-forward two beats for the first four lines. The second four—commencing with "hands up high"—require a little more insight to sustain the pattern and rapid tempo. They go: "*Hands* up high, *in* the air;/ *Down* at your side [and] *touch* your hair;/ *Hands* up high, *as* before,/ Now *clap* your *hands*, one *two* three *four*!")

Whatever their other virtues, rhythmic sophistication is not among those claimed by the nursery games. So, once the main beat is set, it is only a matter of adjusting stresses to keep the pattern going, the hands clapping, or the ball bouncing nicely.

From Elizabeth Matterson's well-organized collection come selections which range from the entirely simple: "Round and round the garden (Run your index finger round the baby's palm)/ Went the Teddy Bear./ One step,/ Two steps, (Jump your finger up his arm)/ Tickly under there! (Tickle him under his arm)" to the more intricate: "Five little peas in a pea-pod pressed, (Clench fingers on one hand)/ One grew, two grew, and so did all the rest. (Raise two fingers slowly)/ They grew and grew and did not stop. (Stretch fingers wide)/ Until one day the pod went *Pop*! (Clap loudly on pop)."[8] Here it would be necessary to instruct the child quite specifically concerning the gestures required by the rhyme. In both of these examples, relating the rhymes to the child's experience is rather simply accomplished. In the first case, one can have the teddy bear go round and round the table (or the counter or the living room or the bed) and demonstrate this to the child. If the second rhyme is saved for the right season, it can be introduced along with an actual pea pod—thereby extending the child's awareness of natural objects and confirming the words of the rhyme. . . .

Selection of Plays

As a final comment, we note that the person who is going to do the teaching ought to be honest about selecting plays which appeal to him as well as to the child. Since there are more than enough possibilities to choose from, no one need feel obliged to transmit something he dislikes. The child will detect fun that is phony, and then the pleasure is all spoiled and a wrong message conveyed. The same point might be generalized to all stories, tales, and poems chosen for sharing with children. It is not to be expected that adults and children will enjoy things in the same way. Still, one knows that some things please both, and we suspect that the reason these games have endured is precisely because they give mutual pleasure to adults and to children.

Summary

The young blind child tends to be conspicuously and unfortunately limited in his experience with books, stories, and rhymes. We have considered the likelihood that this reflects the combined influence of his own inability to signal his appetite for new and ongoing language play (an initial enthusiasm for finger plays and other ritualized word games is often present, but wanes) and the parents' incapacity to identify, locate, and present to him new and suitable language material.

In response to the need that is thereby created, we have made suggestions for a definite but informal sequence of language-related activities using songs, rhymes, records, stories, and some of Mother Goose. Throughout, the underlying concept has been that what the preschool blind population requires is not picture books without pictures, but intact literary material which is nevertheless accessible to the blind child's learning condition.

Notes

1. S. Fraiberg, M. Smith, and E. Adelson, "An Educational Program for Blind Infants," *Journal of Special Education* 3 (1969):121–39.
2. S. Fraiberg and E. Adelson, "Self-Representation in Language and Play: Observations of Blind Children," *Psychoanalytic Quarterly* 42 (1973):539–62.
3. Ibid.
4. See also S. Ulrich, *Elizabeth* (Ann Arbor: Univ. of Michigan Pr., 1972).
5. J. M. Udry, *A Tree Is Nice* (New York: Harper, 1956).
6. D. Kunhardt, *Pat the Bunny* (Racine, Wis.: Western, Golden Pr., 1962).
7. V. A. Tashjian, *Juba This and Juba That* (Boston: Little, 1969).
8. E. Matterson, *Games for the Very Young* (New York: American Heritage, 1969).

Books for Children Who Cannot See the Printed Page

MARGARET BUSH

Talking Books is a term that's been around long enough to have seeped into general usage, and yet it seems that many librarians still have only a vague notion of what they really are, where they come from, and who qualifies to use them. The rapidly growing efforts to help children and young people with special needs make it imperative that librarians and teachers understand that talking or recorded books symbolize a wealth of materials and services available to children who are visually or physically handicapped.

The National Library Service for the Blind and Physically Handicapped (NLS) is the arm of the Library of Congress that is charged with the production and distribution of recorded and braille books. In addition to providing books and magazines in special formats, NLS offers a wide range of support services through a network of more than 160 cooperating libraries in the United States, Puerto Rico, the Virgin Islands, and Guam. Each state, municipality, or agency in the network funds basic library services for the blind and physically handicapped. Each year, funds appropriated by Congress to regional and local libraries provide books, playback equipment, reference services, development of new technology, and bibliographic information. These funds also go toward the training of volunteers who assist with machine repairs, braille transcriptions, and narration.

Parents, teachers, and librarians serving children in public libraries and public or private schools can secure braille or talking-book services for eligible children by requesting application materials from the appropriate regional library. NLS publishes a free directory of the cooperating libraries, *Library Resources for the Blind and Physically Handicapped*, which is available on request.

All reading materials, playback equipment, and library services are provided free of charge to children who cannot read standard print because of limited vision or who have physical limitations which prevent the necessary manipulation of books.

Braille and Talking-Book Production

Although NLS began producing braille and recorded books for adults in 1931, it was not until 1952 that congressional legislation enabled it to produce materials for children. Since that time hundreds of children's books have been made available in braille, print/braille, cassette, and disc formats. There are also available children's magazines and a wide range of music instruction materials. The basic selection philosophy is that handicapped children are entitled to the same range of reading materials enjoyed by nonhandicapped friends and classmates, so book titles selected for production each year include picture books and all genres of fiction and nonfiction at varying levels of interest and difficulty for children from preschool through junior high-school ages.

Transforming the print versions of such childhood favorites as H. A. Rey's *Curious George* (Houghton, 1941) and E. B. White's *Charlotte's Web* (Harper, 1952) into braille and recorded editions is a costly, complex process. Although these forms have very different characteristics from traditional books, the policy of NLS in producing materials is to provide the most faithful rendering possible of the original work. The books are not abridged, nor are they dramatized or set against musical backgrounds. The goal is to give readers the same books that are available to fully sighted readers. There are, of course, some problems in trying to accomplish this.

Pictures are an important feature of many children's books. However, a book will succeed in braille or on a disc or cassette only if the story or text makes sense without the pictures. For readers who cannot see very

---

"Books for Children Who Cannot See the Printed Page," by Margaret Bush. Reprinted with permission from *School Library Journal*, April 1980. R. R. Bowker Company/A Xerox Corporation.

well—or perhaps not at all—the important pictures are those conveyed just by words. Some illustrations, such as maps and charts, can be produced in braille books as raised line drawings. Important pictures can be mentioned or described in a recording, but this procedure confuses children, and most of the time the decision is made to eliminate pictures.

There are special considerations in producing picture books for younger children. Each year several books are done in a print/braille format—printed text and pictures with brailled text accompanying the print on each page. These books may be read together by blind children and sighted adults or blind adults and sighted children. Special effort is made to provide picture books that stimulate other senses than vision. These include the popular "scratch and sniff" books containing fragrance strips and a few titles that have special inserts to touch such as Dorothy Kunhardt's beloved *Pat the Bunny* (Western, 1962). The picture books selected for production include a wide range of stories, songs and rhymes, and alphabet, counting, and simple information books.

Older children require a larger and more diverse collection of books to fit their wide range of interests and abilities. Catherine King, the children's literature specialist who constantly reads new books and selects the children's books and magazines to be brailled and recorded, also considers older books which have remained popular with children and are especially well written. Twice a year she meets with an Advisory Committee on Selection of Children's Books. Members of this committee are selected for their expertise in children's literature, public library service to children, or service to blind and handicapped children in one of the libraries of the network. A second advisory committee, composed of readers and librarians, meets annually to discuss readers' needs and preferences in all areas of the NLS collections.

Once selections have been made, the materials are sent to contracting agencies which have professional recording studios or braille presses. All master copies, braille and recorded, are sent back to NLS where they are carefully examined by proofreaders for accuracy before making quantities of copies for distribution to the cooperating libraries.

The braille and talking-book collections for children are similar in scope but not identical in the titles they contain—though occasionally the same book may be done in both formats. Currently, for instance, special efforts are being made to produce the most recent editions of the *Boy Scout Handbook* (Simon & Schuster, 1979) and cub scout handbooks. The recorded versions will include verbal descriptions of many diagrams which are carefully developed by NLS staff in the Washington, D.C. sound studio, while raised line drawings are constructed for the braille editions by American Printing House for the Blind in Lexington, Kentucky. A smaller number of books are brailled than are recorded since fewer people are able to use them. Recorded books most appropriate for children in preschool through third grades are usually produced on discs since the necessary playback equipment is easiest for this age group to use. Books for older children are now most frequently recorded on four-track cassettes. All recordings are done at special slow speeds so that a maximum amount of listening can be offered on each record or cassette (and copyright holders can be assured that only eligible readers will use the materials).

Eligible Borrowers

Several categories of visual or physical handicaps qualify children to receive talking-book services. Any child who lacks the necessary vision to read standard print is eligible. So is a child who has any one of numerous physical limitations which might prevent holding a print book or turning its pages. The application form for the material must be signed by a professional in the fields of medicine, social work, or education—which includes librarians. A physical handicap may also be a learning disability which has physical causes; a physician must certify an application in this latter category. An eligible borrower need not have a permanent disability. NLS service may be used temporarily or for a lifetime, depending on need.

All children registered for NLS library services are entitled to receive both a disc player and a cassette player since all talking books are recorded at very slow speeds and cannot be played on standard commercial players. New readers receive appropriate catalogs of braille or recorded children's books; catalogs are issued every two years and are usually available in large print, disc, and braille formats. There are also two NLS magazines,

Braille Book Review and *Talking Book Topics*, issued bimonthly to announce all currently produced books. Readers may use the order forms included in these magazines to request books from their library. They may also have the library select books for them at regular intervals. The books are mailed to the reader and are returned to the library by mail without a postage charge.

Braille and recorded books and playback equipment are provided primarily for the personal home use of qualified children; however, a teacher may register an eligible child for equipment and materials to use at school. These requests are granted whenever equipment is available. The teacher has a responsibility to ensure that only eligible students are permitted to use the materials. As more children with special needs are being taught in regular classrooms, teachers often find that the wide selection of books provides handicapped children with opportunities to read the same books as sighted classmates. Nonfiction titles can also be used to augment classroom teaching on many subjects.

NLS Services

In addition to the braille and talking books and playback equipment provided without charge by NLS, libraries in the network use state or local funds to purchase other materials such as large-print books and commercial recordings. Also, many libraries work closely with volunteer organizations to produce braille and recorded materials requested by individual readers and are otherwise unavailable to them. Volunteers may also narrate books by local authors or magazines which are regional or local in character or enjoyed by special interest groups. Since the libraries are part of a well-organized national network, the locally produced materials are often available through interlibrary loan to readers in other states.

Other NLS services are deposit collections (varying numbers of titles with a scheduled rotation) and the necessary equipment are loaned to any institution that serves 10 or more eligible users such as a school for the handicapped, hospital, nursing home, or public library. Libraries that do not have the requisite number of readers may request a smaller set of demonstration materials to use in explaining the service to potential borrowers.

Other Material Sources

Although the collections and services of NLS and the network libraries are quite comprehensive, there are many things which cannot be provided either because of legal restrictions or budgetary constraints. Inevitably, librarians and teachers who become first-time users of the service are somewhat frustrated to find that this is not a one-stop source for all the materials they may need. In many cases, staff members in the network libraries or at NLS can help locate needed items through the NLS union catalog and producers' and library catalogs.

Because an extended production schedule is necessary for braille and recorded editions of books, there is a time lag between the publication of a print book and its availability in special formats from NLS. It must be remembered that no book can be produced without permission from the copyright holder. Because the Library of Congress prepares these books for nonprofit purposes and for users who might otherwise never be able to read them, most publishers and authors usually grant permission without charge. Today, publishers of children's books often sell prepublication rights to other companies that will film their books or record or publish paperback editions. Sometimes the companies holding these subsidiary rights feel that Library of Congress recorded editions infringe upon their marketing rights and deny permission or stringently limit production.

Production costs for each title are very high, so the general policy is to select only those books which will be popular with most readers. It is impossible for NLS to produce every title readers might wish to use but there are other ways of supplying requests. As mentioned earlier, many organizations and individuals throughout the country will braille or record books for particular needs, and network libraries can provide specific information about this kind of service. Teachers and librarians wanting to utilize NLS materials in classroom work are urged to plan ahead. Time is a problem—such materials simply cannot be supplied for immediate use.

Textbooks and curriculum materials are the largest category of items which are not produced or distributed by NLS. While the Library of Congress is charged by its legislation to provide recreational reading and trade books to the blind and physically handicapped, Congress has provided other funding for textbooks for this audience. Each year, money is appropriated to an HEW account from which states may purchase braille and recorded textbooks from the American Printing House for the Blind. Textbooks are also recorded upon request and free of charge for individual needs by Recording for the Blind, a volunteer organization based in New York.

Librarians Can Help

For many reasons—including ignorance and embarrassment—families often fail to find help for a child with special needs. The NLS staff works continually to expand public and professional awareness of its program. Free information packets including application materials are available on request from the National Library Service for the Blind and Physically Handicapped, Library of Congress, Washington, D.C. 20542. Librarians are encouraged to order these packets and become familiar with them so they can share the information with parents of children who are having difficulty seeing print or have other problems limiting their use of books.

Librarians and teachers should assume a vital role in helping visually and physically handicapped children receive the benefits of the reading material available to them through the NLS braille and Talking Book Program.

Remediating with Comic Strips

PHYLLIS N. HALLENBECK

The use of comic strips for teaching children sequencing (similar to the Picture Arrangement subtest of the WISC)[1] and a number of other necessary skills is a relatively simple and valuable technique. Suitable comic strips can be clipped from local newspapers—with or without dialogue, depending on the reading ability of the child. As an example, the teacher can divide the strip into its panels, shuffling them well, and then direct the child: "Put the pictures in order to tell a story." This method is so effective that commercially prepared sequential pictures are available for this type of training.

As another example, many learning-disabled first- and second-grade pupils are not able to deal successfully with the Picture Absurdities items of the Binet. Comic strips may be used to remediate this deficiency also. Rather than cutting the strips into panels, the teacher can present the comic strip intact and ask the child to tell what is funny or foolish about it. It is immediately evident that these children have difficulty in grasping abstract situations, although they tend to do much better with perceptual slapstick humor. Thus, there is little difficulty in appreciating a comic strip that shows children christening a homemade raft named *Indestructible* by breaking a catsup bottle on it and then watching the raft break up and sink, the bottle remaining intact. Another readily enjoyed strip shows a man getting a parking ticket because the parking meter was hidden by a snowman which melts before the police officer appears. In another, two boys have a tug-of-war with an umbrella in the rain until it breaks and they both get wet. The child who looks at such a perceptually based humorous strip and says he doesn't see anything funny about it does not understand what he is seeing.

"Remediating with Comic Strips," by Phyllis N. Hallenbeck. Reprinted from *Journal of Learning Disabilities*, vol. 9, no. 1, 1976. The Professional Press, Inc., 101 E. Ontario St., Chicago, IL 60611.

This paper will discuss the relationship between the child's ability to understand what he sees and his ability to see humor in order to learn important skills. Guidance to help educators select and use cartoons appropriately is given. I shall give examples of types of comic strips for remediating various deficiencies, along with specific suggestions for their use.

Theoretical Background

There are several theories explaining humor which have relevance to remediation work with learning-disabled children. Wolfenstein and Kris have emphasized the role of mastery in children's humor.[2] The child must have enough understanding of his environment for him to appreciate the humorous aspect of a particular joke situation. Wolfenstein in particular warned that humor proposed by an adult may not seem funny to children because of the mastery element.

Helmers has suggested that the purpose of children's humor is to reconfirm the "unshakeable orderliness" of the world about them.[3] Especially in aggressive humor it is necessary for the child to distinguish the fantasy situation clearly so that he is not dismayed or made uncomfortable by it. In speaking of humor, McGhee stated:

> A reality-fantasy dimension becomes important here, in that the child perceives expectancy violations as being funny only when he has acquired a stable enough conceptual grasp of the real world that he can assimilate the disconfirmed expectancy as being only a play on reality. [p. 333][4]

Speaking of older children, McGhee agrees with Piaget that in the course of development the child attempts to accommodate all new stimuli into his existing schemes in a process of "reality assimilation." He further theorized that the older children are capable of "fantasy assimilation," but since accommodation does not occur with humor stimuli, the recognition of the violation of expectancy causes the humor response. "Pleasure derives from the child's certainty that the stimulus depicted does not really exist."[5] Reality assimilation of humorous situations, he added, may result in interest, confusion, or fear—but not humor.

Maier advanced a gestalt theory of humor as a sudden change and restructuring of the whole configuration, the unexpectedness of which is responsible for the humor.[6] He stressed the importance of objectivity, believing that humor does not result if the individual identifies too closely with the situation. Bateson and Fry have suggested that reversal of figure and ground is involved in joking, as the punch line requires a sudden attention to material that has previously been in the background.[7]

In relating these theoretical observations to the realm of learning disabilities, it becomes clear that mastery of the environment, distinguishing between reality and fantasy, objectivity (rather than egocentrism), restructuring a gestalt pattern, and shifting readily from figure to ground and back again are all areas which may be extremely difficult for learning disabled children. This may be the explanation for their late development of a sense of humor, and/or their proneness toward the silly or perceptual types of humor past the age when nondisabled children have shifted to more cognitive humorous situations. It is obvious, then, that successful training of learning-disabled children to appreciate comic strip humor may strengthen any or all of the above weaknesses. Some examples of the use of cartoons follow.

Encouraging Cognitive Development

As has been mentioned, slapstick or perceptual humor is most easily understood by very young or conceptually handicapped children (those who are preoperational in logic as defined by Piaget). Humor can be based on variables such as a play on words or ideas, exaggeration of the known situation, or violation of acquired expectancies (the surprise or absurd element). The last is perhaps the most frequently used by most comic strip authors. Examples are the strip in which the little girl complains she has gained six pounds in three days, causing the little boy to do some figuring, at the end of which he announces that if she keeps it up she will weigh 750 pounds in a year; or one in which a character moves a chess piece on a board and the mailman carries it off carefully while he explains that he plays chess by mail; or the professor who is explaining how flea collars work, but then comments that the trick is to get the collar on the flea.

When the cartoon is based on situations other than slapstick, much more comprehension is demanded from the reader. It has been found by researchers that there is a positive relationship between cognitive level or chronological age and complexity of cartoon situation understanding.[8] It is also known that many learning disabled and most retarded children are late in reaching levels of logical development in keeping with their chronological age.

A first area of concern with young learning-disabled children may be to distinguish clearly between fact and fantasy. Such children characteristically do not have creative imaginations, but rather tend to be very literal-minded. It may be their rootedness in the concrete which interferes with their appreciating fantasy, and the tutor or teacher may have to point out the fictional quality of the situation. "Could that really happen?"; "Could a horse really hang from a tree by its tail?"; "Could a dog really make himself look like a bird?" are questions which can be used to stimulate the perception of fantastic elements in comic strips.

Young children also tend to be egocentric in the Piagetian sense—i.e., capable of judging situations only from their own points of view. Many older learning-disabled children are still captive to egocentrism, to their great social disadvantage. The quality of objectivity may be fostered by discussion of comic situations which are not enjoyed by the child because he identifies too closely. Such situations may be either aggressive or deal with supposed stupidity or constant blundering of a strip character. Aggressive themes may stir up the insecurity of the child in managing his own aggression or dealing with it from others. Stupidity themes may be too reminiscent of errors and everyday mishaps the child himself has. When these themes appear too threatening to the child, it is best to select other themes until he feels more secure.

Learning-disabled children frequently have difficulty combining parts in different ways to make up whole patterns. Piaget's famous experiment with the wooden beads is often failed by older children who are not mentally flexible enough to unstring and restring the beads in their thoughts.[9] Guiding such children to understanding cartoons that require recombining the original elements in a new way may foster this type of flexibility. For example, a strip in which the characters are involved in announcing the rules for a rope-climbing contest in which the rope is hung from the neck of a giraffe, who is concerned about the weight of the climbers; or one in which there is talk of using the sun as a source of energy, with the comment that it would take an awfully long extension cord.

Figure-ground relationships are most readily associated with the visual sense, but exist in all other modalities as well because of the attention factor. It is *what we attend to* that determines what is figure and what is background. Deliberately shifting attention from figure to ground may be quite difficult for the learning disabled because of the mental flexibility required. Working with humorous situations requiring such shifts is often helpful in developing this ability.

Some strips require an educational background that many learning-disabled children (being nonreaders, etc.) do not have. This type of strip gives the opportunity to broaden the child's knowledge in a pleasant way. For example, the cartoon in which two little girls are telling the boy that the Andes Mountains are in South America and the Alps in Europe, and laughing because he wrote on his test paper that Andy's drugstore sells a sundae called Alps; or when the point of humor in the strip depends on understanding the word "topographical"; or when a penguin asks for some kind of food from his homeland and is offered an Arctic Delight (a bowl of ice cubes). Enrichment and education may thus be provided for children who, because of their difficulties, have a view of the world more limited than that of their nondisabled peers. Such children are not, by definition, retarded and therefore should be expected to acquire a normal background of knowledge. Learning from such strips is likely to be quite scattered, but can be important in the larger scheme of the child's development, in expanding his horizons and motivating him to learn more about his environment.

No matter what aspect of thinking is being tapped, comic strips are intrinsically motivating to most children. They will tolerate being taught, being explained to, being questioned, with considerable patience because they want to enjoy the humor, and because they want to be like other children. It is important for the teacher or tutor not to overdo, or require too much at a time. Difficult strips may be mixed with easier (perceptual) ones to set a comfortable pace for the pupil.

Advantages for Reading and Verbal Expression

In addition to the left-to-right sequencing the child must learn, strip dialogue itself is good practice in reading for learning-disabled children. Many strips are printed in all capital letters, which younger children and those with reversal problems find easier to read. For children who characteristically pay little attention to detail (and consequently read *"house"* for *"horse,"* *"will"* for *"well,"* etc.) there are comic strips that require noticing detail to make sense. The expression on a character's face, darkening of the sky to indicate passing time, the print on a small sign, are examples of some of the details essential to understanding certain situations. By using such cartoons the teacher or tutor is training the child to attend to small details, and should make the importance of this clear to the child. One can say, for example, "You have to notice little things like that or you miss the fun."

The symbolism of comic strips provides, in effect, a new code for dyslexic children to learn. Light bulbs over characters' heads indicating sudden ideas or understanding; very large letters in the dialogue or wide-open mouths indicating yelling or shouting; use of isolated exclamation points or question marks around a character's head indicating surprise or curiosity; swirls of dust or horizontal lines demonstrating speed or movement; stars floating around for injury or pain; the conglomeration of punctuation and other marks standing for profanity are all examples of this code. It is interesting that many children must be taught what the symbols mean; they are unable to derive the meaning from the context. All of the symbols are readily learned by even the most dyslexic children, however, if the meanings are consistently pointed out. Once a child has learned comic symbolism, he can use it to entertain himself in leisure time.

When a child is asked to explain why a strip is funny, he is then exercising his "verbal expression" ability to comply. The alert teacher or tutor can help him increase his vocabulary, use good syntax, and correct pronunciation in the expression of his ideas. Just as important as good language usage is the child's ability to explain or describe something *completely*. This underlies his ability to narrate an understandable story, write a composition which hangs together, and answer future essay questions acceptably. The teacher must be unwilling to settle for a partial explanation of the situation, but must insist on a complete one, even if it is necessary to supply the missing parts for the child until he can do so himself. For instance, it is not enough for the child to say, "His father is smoking a pipe and he is getting sick." Who is getting sick and why? "The little boy is getting sick *because it smells so bad*." It is also not enough for a child to say, "The goat ate the sign and got sick," when the point of the humor is that the sign said "Slow" and the goat is saying (in the midst of his illness), "But I did eat it slow."

Paine has presented the possibility of using comic strips to teach children the use of quotation marks, among other things.[10] Children can rewrite the dialogue, putting the speech of each character inside the quotation marks with appropriate punctuation, and adding "he said." Since the speech balloon is always a direct quotation, reading comics and using them in this way can help children sort out what is direct from what is indirect quotation.

Conclusions

Some ideas have been presented here for the use of comic strips in remediation work with learning-disabled children. This material is economical and almost universally available. It may be used one-to-one or made into transparencies for work with groups. A collection of strips offers opportunity for short lessons with young children who lack attention span, or longer lessons for an older, more patient child. Comics are intrinsically motivating as children want to understand the humor in order to laugh.

For remediation purposes, comic strips can be used for enrichment and incidental education in presenting facets of the world. They may be used for sequencing and better understanding of social situations. Proper choice and use can foster abstract thinking, including objectivity, reversibility of figure and ground, and restructuring whole patterns. Differentiation of fantasy and reality is implicit in comprehension of comic situations. Having the child explain completely why the strip is funny encourages good verbal expression. There are strips with dialogue printed in capitals for beginning readers, and strips without any dialogue for nonreaders. All strips require the left-to-right orientation, and many strips also require the noticing of small details for comprehension of the humor. Dialog may be used to teach the difference between direct and indirect quotations. Although this is not an exhaustive list of the possibilities, it suggests a new tool, or new uses for an old tool, to those working to remediate difficulties of learning-disabled children.

Notes

1. Wechsler Intelligence Scale for Children.—Ed.
2. M. Wolfenstein, *Children's Humor* (Glencoe, Ill.: Free Press, 1954); E. Kris, "Ego Development and the Comic," *International Journal of Psychoanalysis* 19 (1938): 77–90.
3. H. Helmers, *Sprache und Humor des Kindes* (Stuttgart, Germany: Ernest K. Verlag, 1965).
4. P. E. McGhee, "Development of the Humor Response: A Review of the Literature," *Psychology Bulletin* 76 (1971): 328–48.
5. McGhee, "Development of the Humor Response," p. 334.
6. N. R. F. Maier, "A Gestalt Theory of Humor," *British Journal of Psychology* 23 (1932): 69–74.
7. G. Bateson, "The Position of Humor in Human Communication," in J. Levine, ed., *Motivation in Humor* (New York: Atherton, 1969); W. F. Fry, *Sweet Madness: A Study of Humor* (Palo Alto, Calif.: Pacific Bks., 1963).
8. L. F. Schaffer, *Children's Interpretations of Cartoons*, Contributions to Education, no. 429 (New York: Teachers College Pr., 1930); E. Zigler, J. Levine, and L. Gould, "Cognitive Processes in the Development of Children's Appreciation of Humor," *Child Development* 37 (1966): 507–18; McGhee, "Development of the Humor Response."
9. J. Piaget, *The Child's Conception of Number* (New York: Norton, 1965).
10. C. A. Paine, "Comics for Fun and Profit," *Learning* 3 (1974): 86–89.

Orientation Maps for Visually Impaired Persons

BILLIE LOUISE BENTZEN

Commercial production of orientation maps for visually impaired persons is becoming a reality in the United States. Although much basic research remains to be done, two pioneering teams each have designed and commercially produced a map to facilitate the orientation and independent travel of visually impaired persons in the Boston, Massachusetts area.

"Orientation Maps for Visually Impaired Persons," by Billie Louise Bentzen, *Visual Impairment and Blindness*, May 1977, pp. 193–96. Reprinted by permission of the American Foundation for the Blind.

The Division of Special Education and Rehabilitation of Boston College conducted a series of dialogues in spring 1975, between visually impaired travelers, peripatologists, and the producers of these maps, in order to:

1. Make peripatologists and visually impaired travelers aware of the existence of the maps and of their possible uses
2. Acquaint peripatologists with techniques for using highly complex maps with their students
3. Learn for what purposes such maps would actually be used by visually impaired travelers
4. Provide feedback to map producers and peripatologists, from a variety of visually impaired travelers, indicating

criteria for production of future orientation maps.

The two maps were designed and produced by entirely independent teams, and the content and reproduction techniques differ greatly. Visually impaired travelers and peripatologists were asked to actually use each of the maps to plan and to travel (or have a student plan and travel) to a destination in an unfamiliar area. This was a prerequisite for participation in the dialogue and ensured feedback based on actual use, not just perusal.

Two Maps

The simplest of the two maps, the MBTA System Tactile Route Map, portrays the complete rapid transit system for the Metropolitan Boston Transportation Authority. Tactile information is presented on transparent plastic and this is backed with a corresponding four color print map of the system. The same tactile linear symbol is used to represent all four transit routes in the system; this is a furrow, 1/5 inch wide and .01 inch (5.1 mm by .25 mm) deep. Brief "Instructions for Using the MBTA System Map" are provided in braille and large type.

The highly complex Boston-Cambridge Tactual Map portrays an approximately ten-square-mile area, including all of Boston and Cambridge, and adjoining areas of Brookline and Somerville. This map consists of one visual and three tactile-visual layers, each giving different information about the same area, at the same scale. Information portrayed includes: all streets; residential areas; shopping areas, green spaces; water bodies; landmarks such as public buildings, universities and museums, with the locations of their main entrances; names of major streets; names of parts of the cities; all the rapid transit routes which serve the geographic area included in the map; and the 17 most traveled bus routes in this area. A total of 19 tactually and visually different point, linear, and areal symbols are used to represent the various kinds of information. This map is accompanied by an "Introductory Tape to the Boston-Cambridge Tactual Map," which describes the map and gives techniques for reading it. It is also accompanied by a large directory containing additional information about the rapid transit system, and an alphabetical listing of all streets and landmarks shown, with their grid reference locations.

The Dialogues

Peripatologists and agencies serving visually impaired persons provided names of visually impaired individuals in greater Boston who were known to be independent travelers. (No attempt was made to obtain a complete list of independent travelers.) Eighteen persons were selected, who were willing to plan and travel a route to a destination in an unfamiliar area, using the maps, and to share their experiences in a dialogue with peripatologists and map makers. For the convenience of participants, two dialogues were scheduled, each including visually impaired travelers, peripatologists and map makers.

The 18 visually impaired travelers received copies of both maps, and were offered instruction in their use. However, none needed assistance to enable them to read and utilize the MBTA System Tactile Route Map. Four participants currently receiving instruction in orientation and mobility were taught by their instructors to use the Boston-Cambridge Tactual Map. The remaining 14 taught themselves to read and utilized the Boston-Cambridge Tactual Map, using the introductory tape and the directory as guides.

Seventeen peripatologists in the greater Boston area were interested and willing to utilize the maps with one or more visually impaired students, to plan and travel routes to destinations in unfamiliar areas based on information provided in the maps, and to share their experiences in a dialogue. (Several who wished to participate did not have students at an appropriate level, during the time period allowed, to fulfill this requirement. They participated in the dialogue, nevertheless.) Ten peripatologists attended a training workshop to learn techniques for utilizing these maps with visually impaired students.

Visually impaired participants were asked to complete questionnaires regarding the routes they planned and traveled using the maps, the difficulties they had with the maps, what they liked best about the maps, and suggestions for improvement in orientation maps. (Data were also gathered concerning such dependent variables as extent of visual impairment, characteristics of near and distant visual functioning, extent of independent travel, and previous experiences using maps. The small size of the sample makes such data statistically irrelevant, but nonetheless informative as part of individual case studies.)

148 Software

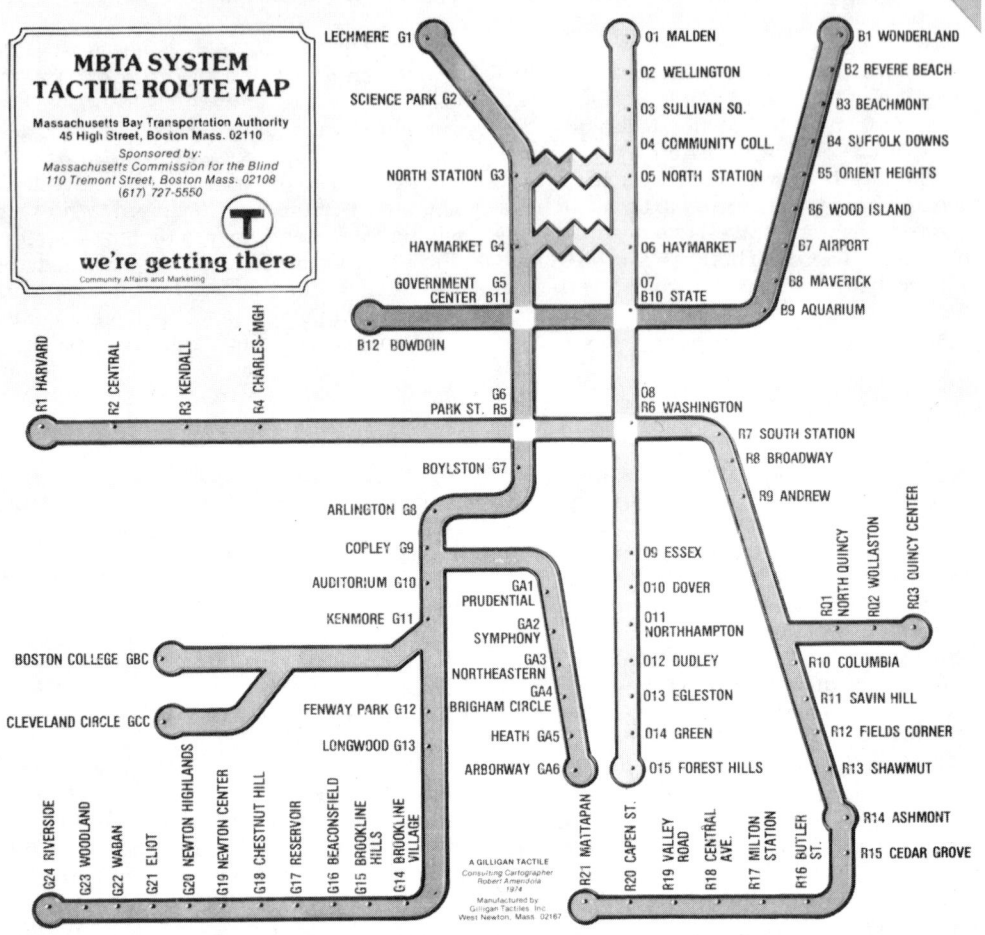

MBTA System Tactile Route Map

The information content of this map [MBTA System Tactile Route Map],[1] designed by Robert Amendola and produced by Gilligan Tactiles, Inc., consists of the complete rapid transit system (underground and above-ground) of the Metropolitan Boston Transportation Authority. All regular stops and transfer stations in the system are labeled with the initial letter of the color code for the route (i.e., R for red route) and a number. Stops are numbered consecutively from either the northern or western terminus of each route. Transfer stations are given a letter and number for each route using the station. For example, Park Station is designated G6 and R5 because it serves both the green and the red routes. All letters and numbers are either horizontal or vertical on the page. An index is provided which lists all stops on each line, in their numbered order; the index is available in braille and print.

The map is 11.0 x 11.5 inches (27.9 cm by 29.2 cm) in overall size. It is embossed in a transparent plastic, which is backed with and adhered to a registered four-color print map, containing the same information as the embossed map, but in a form intended for the use of sighted or partially sighted persons. It is believed to be the first orientation map commercially produced in the United States for both totally blind and partially sighted users. The map is flexible, but folding creates permanent creases.

Symbols used on the embossed map are a furrow, 1/5 inch wide and .01 inch deep (5.1 mm x .25 mm), representing the routes themselves, and containing dots, 1/16 inch (1.6 mm) in diameter and .016 inch (0.4 mm) high, representing the stops. A furrow in a zigzag pattern connects stops on parallel routes that are connected underground by pedestrian tunnels. The letter and number designations of stops are written in standard braille near the dot for each stop.

The print map utilizes a different color, red, green, blue, or orange, for each route. Length and directionality of the routes are schematized. Names of stops are printed in black 11-point type, under or close to the braille label for each stop.

Boston-Cambridge Tactual Map

This map [Boston-Cambridge Tactual Map][2] was designed by Knut Lieneman (Massachusetts Institute of Technology, Planning Office), and produced by Plastic Lace Corp. and Howe Press of Perkins School for the Blind. It covers a rectangular area of approximately 10 square miles [25 km], including all of Boston and Cambridge, and adjoining areas of Brookline and Somerville. The map is 23.5 x 17.5 inches (59.7 cm by 44.5 cm) in overall size, and the scale is approximately 1" = 1000' (1 cm = 0.12 km). This map is very flexible and can be folded repeatedly without producing permanent creases.

The map consists of one visual and three tactile-visual layers, each giving different information about the same area, at the same scale. These layers are registered, and bound together along the north edge. They will be described separately, from the first, or top layer, to the last, or bottom layer.

Layer 1. This layer, intended for the use of sighted persons who were assisting blind persons in the use of the map, was not specifically designed for the use of partially sighted persons. It is a transparent vinyl overlay, with black printing, showing all streets, industrial areas, shopping areas, green spaces, water bodies, and numerous landmarks such as public buildings, universities and museums. The locations of the main entrances to these buildings are also shown.

Major streets and landmarks are labeled in 8- to 12-point type. A key to the symbols for all layers is given at the bottom of this layer. Grid lines, with letters and numbers, are given along both sides and the bottom of this layer.

Layer 2. This is a tactile-visual layer, produced in polyvinyl chloride. All information that is tactually perceptible is printed, and no additional print information is given. However, it was not the specific intent of the designer and producers of this map that the visual properties would be used by partially sighted persons; visual properties were an incidental factor of the production process. Symbol choice and density were based solely on tactual discriminability and recognizability.

With the exception of print names and explanations in the key, all of the information contained on Layer 1 is reproduced on Layer 2, with the visual symbols of Layer 1 produced at varying elevations (.006 inch to .03 inch) (0.2 mm to .8 mm). The key explanations are produced in braille.

Layer 3. This is another tactile-visual layer, produced on polyvinyl chloride. It is adhered to the back of Layer 2, producing an underlay.

This layer contains, in regular braille, the names of major streets, and, in jumbo braille, the names of parts of the cities. The braille is oriented to correspond as nearly as possible to the linear direction of the street being labeled.

The reader places the fingers of one hand, palm upwards, on Layer 3 to locate the name of a street that is tactually available to the other hand on Layer 2.

Layer 4. This is another tactile-visual layer produced on polyvinyl chloride. It contains all of the rapid transit (MBTA) routes that serve the geographic area included in the map, and routes of 17 of the most traveled buses in this area.

Each rapid transit route is represented by a tactually and visually distinct linear symbol, while the bus routes are all represented by one additional tactually and visually distinct linear symbol. All stops of rapid transit routes are represented by a circle, 19/64 inch (7.5 mm) in diameter, which interrupts the line. Circles that are solidly raised represent underground stops, and circles with raised outlines represent above-ground stops. The name of each stop is written out in braille.

A key at the bottom identifies all symbols.

The map is accompanied by a large directory which, in print and braille, contains an alphabetical listing of all streets and landmarks shown, with their grid reference locations. It also lists all rapid transit stops, indicating: on what level the trains run (elevated, ground level, below ground, or on a lower level beneath another train); whether entrances lead to inbound, outbound, or all trains; whether a footbridge leads to the station; and where the platform is located in relation to the direction of the trains.

An "Introductory Tape to the Boston-Cambridge Tactual Map" accompanies each map and directory. The tape cassette describes the map and gives techniques for reading it to enable the visually impaired person to independently familiarize himself with the map.

Conclusions of the Dialogues

The MBTA System Tactile Route Map gave information sufficient only for travel from one stop to another, not to aboveground destinations near those stops. Many participants were already very familiar with all lines of the MBTA, and did not travel new routes using this map. Some, nevertheless, found that the graphic portrayal of the relationship of MBTA routes to each other clarified for them the parts of the city served by each route. As a travel aid, most participants found the index of stops to be just as informative as the map itself. This was particularly true since the labeling system for stops required reference to the index to identify particular stops.

The Boston-Cambridge Tactual Map has much greater information content, but covers a smaller geographic area. Although it is theoretically possible to plan almost door-to-door routes to destinations within the area of the map, some omissions and inaccuracies made this difficult to carry out without some need for assistance when the traveler knew he was close to his destination. Specifically, the grid reference system was not exact enough to pinpoint the location of minor streets; the building numbering system of each street was not given in the directory; and some streets were omitted. Most participants did travel one or more door-to-door routes to destinations in an unfamiliar area using this map, supplemented by soliciting aid when they were near their destinations.

The greatest benefits participants derived from the Boston-Cambridge map were not in specific route planning but in:
1. Knowledge of the spatial relationships of parts of the cities to each other
2. Understanding the relationship of major transportation links to the cities they serve
3. Knowledge of land use patterns within the cities.

Two participants found the map extremely helpful in enabling them to search intelligently for housing in the Boston-Cambridge area. They could be independent in deciding whether a possible residence was sufficiently accessible to public transportation and in close enough proximity to parts of the cities they used most frequently.

Several participants found the map most useful for helping sighted friends navigate unfamiliar auto routes in the cities.

Every item of information contained in both maps was usable by all participants. There were numerous suggestions for changes or additions, but no clear agreement on the desirability of any particular changes except for the correction of errors.

Although symbol choice and standards for symbol density for both maps were based on opinions of individual visually impaired consultants and on personal experience of the designers, rather than on results of controlled research on symbol discriminability and recognizability, no symbol was found totally illegible by any participant. Opinions varied concerning which symbols were the most difficult to locate, trace, or recognize.

There was no consensus to support the hypothesis (Amendola 1976) that the furrow as used in the MBTA System Tactile Route Map was, for these subjects, superior in tracing qualities to the varied linear symbols used in the Boston-Cambridge Tactual Map. A majority of participants favored the representation of different MBTA routes with tactually distinct linear symbols, as done in the Boston-Cambridge Tactual Map, because it facilitated following routes across intersections.

Although information density was far greater on the Boston-Cambridge Tactual Map than on the MBTA System Tactile Route Map, no participant found the information density unmanageable. Most suggestions for changes in the Boston-Cambridge map itself would, in fact, result in increasing the information content and density in some areas.

Of the 18 visually impaired participants, five had usable residual vision for some near tasks. All of these participants used both the tactile and visual features of both maps, although scanning and tracing techniques differed greatly. Layer 1 (print only) of the Boston-Cambridge Tactual Map was used by these five participants, who enhanced its visual contrast by inserting a sheet of white or yellow paper between Layer 1 and Layer 2.

Conclusions

Capable and motivated visually impaired travelers can employ both simple and highly complex maps to assist them in travel planning and also to increase their knowledge and understanding of a city. Not all visually impaired travelers will need instruction in the use of such maps if they are accompanied by effective verbal instructions.

Linear symbols consisting of both single and double lines were effective in communicating directionality and could be tactually traced by all participants.

Participants having some usable near point vision utilized both the tactile and visual coding systems of both maps.

Implications for Future Research and Development

The search should be continued for inexpensive means to commercially produce and reproduce maps of metropolitan areas for visually impaired persons. Where economically feasible, maps of metropolitan areas should include both street patterns and public transportation systems, as one of the greatest benefits derived by the visually impaired persons in this study was the opportunity to discover the relationships of parts of the cities and of specific landmarks in the cities, to transportation services.

Maps should be accompanied by instructions for their use. The instructions should be sufficiently clear and complete to enable visually impaired travelers to use the maps without the need for personal instruction in the use of each map.

Future maps for visually impaired persons should include both tactual and visual coding systems to enhance their usefulness for partially sighted persons.

Notes

1. The MBTA System Tactile Route Map, in revised form (1976), is available free of charge through the Massachusetts Commission for the Blind, 110 Tremont St., Boston, Mass.
2. The Boston-Cambridge Tactual Map is available on loan from the Research Library, Perkins School for the Blind, 175 N. Beacon St., Watertown, Mass.

Additional Reading

Amendola, R. "Practical Considerations in Tactile Map Design." *Long Cane Newsletter* 9 (1976): 22–24.

Resources for Creating Tactual Graphics

J. M. GILL and L. L. CLARK

When the visual channel of communication has been compromised by sensory impairment, the other senses assume much greater importance. Because maps and graphical representations of three-dimensional reality are significant modes of information display to sighted persons, many efforts have been devoted to imitating effectively this mode for the visually impaired and blind person. Additional impetus has been given by affirmative action programs resulting from legislation such as Section 504 of the 1973 Rehabilitation Act. This act, prohibiting discrimination against handicapped persons, requires the provision of equal access to information.

Among the attempts at tactual graphics are embossed maps created by using sewing machines or by manually embossing dots on paper. These attempts have been less than wholly satisfactory for a number of reasons, among which are: 1. the range of symbols available is very limited, 2. quality control is hard to achieve, 3. these modes are labor intensive, 4. symbols are limited to strictly single elevation form.

In the work of Schiff, Kaufer, and Mosak, it became apparent that a directional line to represent direction had clear advantages (see fig. 1).[1] Unfortunately, it was not possible at the time their work was published to reproduce this symbol precisely. Nor was it possible to describe precisely a set of symbols that were clearly and unambiguously discriminable from one another by touch. As a result of a formidably lengthy set of experiments undertaken by Gill and James, such a set of symbols was, however, identified.[2] Results of this research have been used in a kit of parts for manual production of maps.[3] The problem was then to reproduce these symbols, quickly and inexpensively in three dimensions, while maintaining consistently high quality.

"Resources for Creating Tactual Graphics," by J. M. Gill and L. L. Clark, *Visual Impairment and Blindness*, January 1978, pp. 32–33. Reprinted with permission of the Journal of Visual Impairment and Blindness, published by the American Foundation for the Blind.

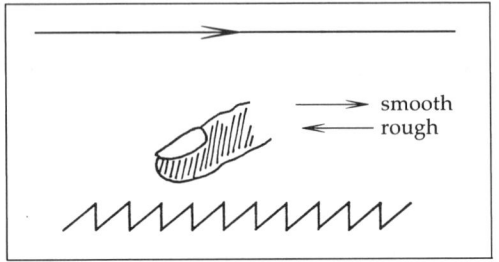

Fig. 1. Directional line

Production Methods

A survey of possible production methods was undertaken in 1973. Of the 17 systems examined, only one—a computer-assisted program—was capable of meeting the requirements. In this system, a large scale map or other graphic display is marked up with the additional information useful to a blind user, for example, gradients, bus stops, destination names, and directions. The operator of the system traces this map with a stylus connected to the computer. What is traced is then displayed on the screen of a visual display unit (VDU) or cathode-ray-terminal (CRT) tube. The map or graphic display can be modified by inserting or deleting individual lines, by moving end points of lines, and by changing the scale. (Ability to change scale is an important aid to the organization of information: Parts of a map, such as areas around an intersection, may be enlarged to include features of particular significance to a pedestrian.) Lines can be made to show different elevations or heights, and also to assume different forms: solid, dotted, or dashed. Standard symbols can be added, such as those for pedestrian crossings or steps. Moreover, text can be typed in from a keyboard and automatically transcribed into braille notations on the map or graphic display. When the operator is satisfied with the visual display, a single key is pressed and the digital equivalent of the information displayed on the VDU screen is punched on paper tape. This permits compact storage and easy modification at a later date, if required.

Engraving and Reproduction

The punched paper tape is used to control a separate unit, an engraving machine, which cuts a mirror image copy of the map or graphic display into a paper-epoxy material similar to that used for printed circuit boards. This "mother" is then used to create a copy by pouring liquid epoxy resin over the female die. Overnight, the liquid sets, yielding a master copy virtually identical to the final copies desired, and it is then used as a mold in a vacuum-forming machine (Thermoform). Although the system was designed to produce about 10 copies of the master, experience has shown that up to 15,000 copies can be produced without any noticeable deterioration in the embossing. The reaction of those to whom such maps have been shown has been uniformly favorable. Users report that the durability and clarity of the display is preserved after long use. If a genuine criterion for a sensory aid's effectiveness is its continued use after initial enthusiasm has worn off and preliminary instruction is over, then it is significant that two-year-old maps produced by this system are still in daily use.

With such advantages, it may be of more than cursory interest to replicate the system. How may it be duplicated, where, at what cost, and by whom? It can be duplicated by many organizations or groups—some may now have the capability, but not realize it. The components include:

1. A standard graphics terminal suitable for connection to a small computer
2. A numerically controlled machine tool, such as those used for engraving
3. Standard vacuum-forming machine, for example, the Thermoform Braille Duplicator
4. A small computer, or access to time-sharing on a medium or large computer

Materials required in the operation include:

1. Any material which can be readily cut by an engraving tool. Paper-epoxy laminate was named as a material of choice above, but many other materials can be used; wood is attractive, but it is expensive
2. Liquid epoxy: a one pound can will cover two map masters
3. Final copy material: rigid plastic sheet such as polyvinyl chloride; flexible polyethylene sheet for flexible maps that can be folded and put in a pocket or handbag

The computer system required is of the minimal variety which can support a graphics terminal. Note that the major work is done by the human operator tracing data for the display; the actual computing time needed is negligible. Depending on the particular system configuration, the storage of graphic data may be on punched paper tape, on magnetic tape, or on floppy discs.

The engraving machine needs a working area of perhaps 10 inches square, with a maximum depth of cut of 0.060 inch. Such machines are available both new and used. New machines cost tens of thousands of dollars, but it is often possible to acquire a used machine at little or no cost from research organizations, aircraft industries, engineering laboratories, or government surplus. In the latter case, some minor modifications may be required for this engraving purpose. It is certainly even practical to consider building one's own: there are commercially available x-y tables fitted with stepping motors that can precisely control the position of the table. The most attractive possibility, however, is the used engraving machine, since when a worn machine does not meet high precision commercial, scientific, or industrial standards, its accuracy is probably still ten times greater than that required in creating tactual graphics.

Setting Up the System

Assuming the availability of a computer system with graphic display, the availability of a vacuum-forming machine, and the acquisition of a worn engraving machine as a gift, what effort would be required to get such a system up and running? We estimate that a comfortable period would be one man-month for a qualified engineer. Thus, the least possible cost would be his time. Naturally, this is best case. What should be avoided is engineering overkill, in which far greater computer capacity than required, multiple displays, a high speed braille embosser, and so on, push costs up into the hundred-thousand-dollar range and beyond.

It should be remembered that in designing a system of graphic representation, we have concentrated on only one of the required steps. In such a system, we must:

1. Identify useful features to be represented
2. Devise a suitable code for these features
3. Manufacture the graphic display
4. Train the user in reading and interpreting the display

In the problem of identifying useful features, some studies have concentrated on the problems of maps,[4] and others on concept attainment and the immediate environment.[5] We do not expand on the technical problems involved here, beyond noting that it is necessary to have a clear idea of the symbols to be used to represent reality, and to achieve unambiguous coding of these symbols for a tactual graphic equivalent. No greater precision is possible than that achieved in the input to any computer-assisted system!

Reading and Interpreting Displays

What remains is to touch on the reading and interpretation of tactual displays produced by the system. There has actually been very little work done on interpreting these kinds of mapping and graphic techniques, save for the significant work of Berla on pseudomaps.[6] Yet we know that sighted persons must be instructed in the interpretation of two-dimensional displays that reflect the real world. It has been recognized that the ability to interpret tactual input for the visually impaired is crucial not only for the interpretation of tactual graphics, but indeed for the elementary understanding direction, shape, size, speed, and other characteristics that identify objects and their relationship in reality. A forthcoming study report of work done in Poland may, in fact, enhance our understanding of these matters: Sylwia Pyra has been studying ". . . the effectiveness of embossed drawings on the teaching of biology in schools for the blind."[7] Although these are theoretical statements from many sources, inside and outside the USA, there are few instances in which deductions have been applied to practice, and the effectiveness of the practice evaluated.

It may well be that with the availability of a computer assisted system to create complex and sophisticated representations, along with the crucial ability to create these interactively on a visual screen, and to vary symbols in three dimensions (i.e., including height of symbols), a means will be provided to create materials that can be assessed for usefulness in enhancing the development of spatiality. This may be, in fact, the most important consequence of this technological development.[8]

Notes

1. W. Schiff, L. Kaufer, and S. Mosak, "Informative Tactile Stimuli in the Perception of Direction," Monograph Suppl. 7, *Perceptual and Motor Skills* 23 (1966).
2. J. M. Gill and G. A. James, "A Study on the Discriminability of Tactual Point Symbols," *AFB Research Bulletin* 26 (1973): 19–34.
3. G. A. James and J. D. Armstrong, *Handbook on Mobility Maps*, Mobility Monograph No. 2 (Nottingham, Eng.: Blind Mobility Research Unit, 1976).
4. F. L. Franks and C. Y. Nolan, "Development of Geographical Concepts in Blind Children," *Education of the Visually Handicapped* 2 (1970): 1–8; idem, "Measuring Geographical Concept Attainment in Visually Handicapped Students," *Education of the Visually Handicapped* 3 (1971): 11–17.
5. E. P. Berla and C. Y. Nolan, "Tactual Maps: A Problem Analysis," Proceedings of the ICEBY, Madrid 1972; E. P. Berla, "Behavioral Strategies and Problems in Scanning and Interpreting Tactual Displays," *New Outlook for the Blind* 66 (1972): 277–86.
6. E. P. Berla and L. H. Butterfield, "Tactile Political Maps: Two Experimental Designs," *Journal of Visual Impairment and Blindness* 71 (1977): 262–64.
7. S. Pyra, "Effectiveness of Embossed Drawings in Teaching Biology," Dept. of Special Education, Univ. of Warsaw, 1977.
8. J. M. Gill, "Design, Production and Evaluation of Tactual Maps for the Blind" (Ph. D. diss., Univ. of Warwick, 1973). [Gives additional technical information, and listings of the FORTRAN IV software used in the prototype system.] This is available from the AFB Library, New York.

Tape Recording Educational Materials for Secondary Handicapped Students

DONALD D. DESHLER and STEVEN GRAHAM

In recent years there has been a concerted effort on the part of advocacy groups, legislators, and the courts to demand that, to the maximum extent appropriate, handicapped learners be educated with students who are not handicapped. This concept, commonly referred to as the least restrictive alternative, has been embodied in Public Law 94-142, the Education for All Handicapped Children Act.

Although the humanistic goals of the act are admirable, the regulations of the law present special education and regular classroom teachers with an educational dilemma. In order to appropriately integrate secondary level mild and moderately handicapped learners into the mainstream of regular education, teachers need the availability of techniques that:

1. Are appropriate for the cognitive, physical, and sensory characteristics of handicapped learners
2. Effectively present the curriculum
3. Maximize learning experiences for the students

While the availability of such techniques is limited, the tape recording of text material is a widely used procedure that meets the above requirements. Tape recorded reading assignments minimize students' reading deficits and thereby allow them to stay current with class assignments and to supplement the information presented in classroom lectures. Nonetheless, to ensure that students receive maximum benefits from taped materials, tapes must be prepared so that they maximize student learning through effective organization and presentation.

"Tape Recording Educational Materials for Secondary Handicapped Students," by Donald D. Deshler and Steven Graham, *Teaching Exceptional Children* 1980, 12: 52–54. Copyright 1980 by The Council for Exceptional Children. Reprinted with permission.

The purpose of this article is to describe six principles that underlie the effective use of tapes in delivering content material to handicapped learners in secondary schools.

Why Tape Text Materials?

The development and use of tapes to deliver content materials provide teachers with a technique that compensates for the specific disabilities of a handicapped learner and the curriculum demands of the school. Many handicapped learners evidence skill deficits in the basic subject matter areas of reading, spelling, and writing. A handicapped youngster at the high-school level may read in a word-by-word manner with a minimum of text organization. Although the student may approximate functional reading competency, these skills are seldom adequate for meeting the curriculum demands of secondary schools where, for the most part, content is presented in a lecture format and through reading assignments. The handicapped youngster who evidences minimum note-taking and reading skills will have great difficulty in using these skills to comprehend, learn, and master new content material. These students require techniques that can circumvent or lessen the effect of their skill deficits.

The level of cognitive development of many secondary handicapped learners is often greater than suggested by their skill development level. A 10th grade student who cannot read *A Tale of Two Cities*, for example, may be able to comprehend the delicate interaction of characters and events if he or she sees the movie. This situation implies that for many mainstreamed handicapped learners at the secondary level, teachers may emphasize the acquisition of content which is more appropriate to their cognitive development level than their level of skill development. Clearly, many handicapped learners can comprehend and learn complex information if their skill deficits are avoided or their effects lessened. The development and use of taped materials provide teachers with a technique by which appropriate content material can be acquired while the youngsters' weaknesses are circumvented or minimized.

The effective use of tapes to deliver content materials to handicapped youngsters, however, requires much more than merely taping verbatim from a book or a lecture.* Effective use of taped content material includes:

1. Decisions concerning what is to be taped
2. Use of taped materials to teach text usage and study skills
3. Effective application of principles of learning
4. Use of a marking system to aid students with coordinating tape recordings with text materials
5. Careful consideration of the mechanics of recording
6. Evaluation of the effectiveness of taped products and the learning that results from using them

Deciding What Should Be Taped

For practical reasons, an entire textbook or chapter should *not* be taped, in most instances. First, it requires too much time to tape an entire text. Second, it is difficult to maintain the student's attention and motivation on texts that have been taped verbatim. Third, listening to a long text may require more time than students have available to them. Major instructional goals and objectives should be identified and key sections of the reading assignment should be designated for taping. Material not taped may be paraphrased or briefly outlined to aid students in seeing the context within which the taped section is presented.

The decision concerning which content to tape should be made by the regular classroom teacher, who is the content expert. The regular classroom teacher is in the best position to specify which content is most critical as it relates to the major instructional objectives of a given unit of instruction.

Some exceptions apply to the guidelines of not taping everything. For example, short stories, poetry, or short literature selections must usually be taped in their entirety to maintain their effectiveness. Nevertheless, for most reading assignments in subjects such as science, social studies, health, etc., judicious decisions can be made regarding critical content to be presented on tape. Students can then be required to listen to the tape several times. Such review and concentrated exposure to key content usually promote retention and application of the material and are, therefore, more helpful than providing the student with a superficial and equal exposure to an entire reading assignment.

Teaching Text Usage and Study Skills

A major reason for taping reading assignments is to give students an alternative means of acquiring the content. However, taped reading assignments can also be used advantageously to teach test usage and study skills. While taping a reading assignment, a teacher has an excellent opportunity to demonstrate how to differentiate between main and supportive material within a chapter; how to use illustrations, graphs, charts, etc., to aid comprehension; how to use questions at the end of a section or chapter to determine major points; and how to use chapter titles, section headings, etc., to skim a reading section for main ideas. Therefore, whenever students are listening to a tape recording of reading materials, they should always have the textbook in front of them.

Using another method to teach text usage and study skills, the teacher may say on the tape, "Before reading chapter 3 let's preview the chapter to get an overview of what it will be about." At this point the teacher can take the student through an overview of the chapter by requiring the student to follow along. Similar instruction can be provided at different points throughout the tape. For example, when discussing the content in a certain graph or table, the teacher may point out parenthetically to the student how effective a particular table is in presenting the ideas contained in three pages of text. While not lengthy in nature, such hints can be highly effective in improving text usage and study

---

*Before preparing or using recorded material with a particular student, an analysis of the student's listening capabilities should be conducted.

skills that will aid the student in becoming a more effective and independent learner.

Using Principles of Learning

The preparation of effective taped materials requires the inclusion of activities and techniques that foster motivation, comprehension, and learning. Similar to the development of a reading series or a set of programmed materials, the development of taped materials requires the careful selection and judicious use of instructional techniques that follow principles of learning. In preparing tapes, it is important that teachers select materials that are interesting and motivating to students. The content selected should be moderately familiar to the student and also novel enough to be stimulating. Curiosity and motivation can be enhanced if an initial survey of the content material, along with preparatory questions designed to stimulate inquisitiveness, are provided at the beginning of the tape. Furthermore, interest can be sustained by involving the learner in a variety of activities.

Comprehension of the tape content can be facilitated by the expeditious use of summaries, paraphrases, analogies, explanations, and examples dispersed strategically throughout the tape. An initial survey of the content material will provide the learner with a structure to which specific facts or ideas can be related. Also, it is often helpful to provide concrete explanations of abstract terms. The appropriate use of these techniques will aid students in relating the content of the tape to what they already know and thus facilitate comprehension.

However, comprehension is only one aspect of instruction. In addition to understanding what is on the tape, the learner will be expected to remember important facts and relationships. In order to foster this type of learning, the tape should be prepared so that it:

1. Is well organized
2. Provides a variety of activities
3. Highlights or cues important points
4. Contains a variety of questions designed to facilitate recall and critical analyses
5. Repeats key concepts or ideas
6. Accommodates the assimilation and/or practice of new concepts or ideas

7. Provides immediate and delayed feedback

Using A Marking System

Given that a reading assignment is not taped in its entirety and that several planned activities are dispersed throughout the tape, it is necessary to develop a system for marking the textbook used by the student while listening to the recording [fig. 1]. Without such a marking system it is very easy for the student to get confused and lost. While the marking system need not be elaborate, it must be consistent so the student will know what to expect and do each time a certain mark appears in the text. As the tape is prepared the teacher should mark the written material that will correspond with it. The following represents an example of a simple marking system: (∼) A wavy line denotes material that will be paraphrased. Thus, a wavy line can be drawn in the margin beside material that will be paraphrased on the tape. The student will then know when to listen and will not try to follow all of the prescribed text. (⋯) A dotted line indicates material that will be omitted altogether on the tape. (☆) A star indicates that the tape must be stopped and that the student is to complete an activity or sample problem related to the taped material. (—) A solid line drawn next to text selections designates material that will be read verbatim on the tape. Depending on the nature of the reading assignment and related activities, marking systems can be expanded or modified to meet the prescribed needs of the student. The sole purpose of a marking system is to assist the student in coordinating the selected information presented on tape with the material appearing in the text and accompanying exercises.

Good Recording Mechanics

Once the content material is organized and ready to be recorded, it is important that the tape be prepared in a setting that is relatively free of distraction. The quality of the tape can be seriously impaired by frequent disruptions and excessive background noises. It is important that the recorded voice be fluent and audible and that appropriate pauses are made at punctuation marks, etc. Speaking rate should be between 120 and 175

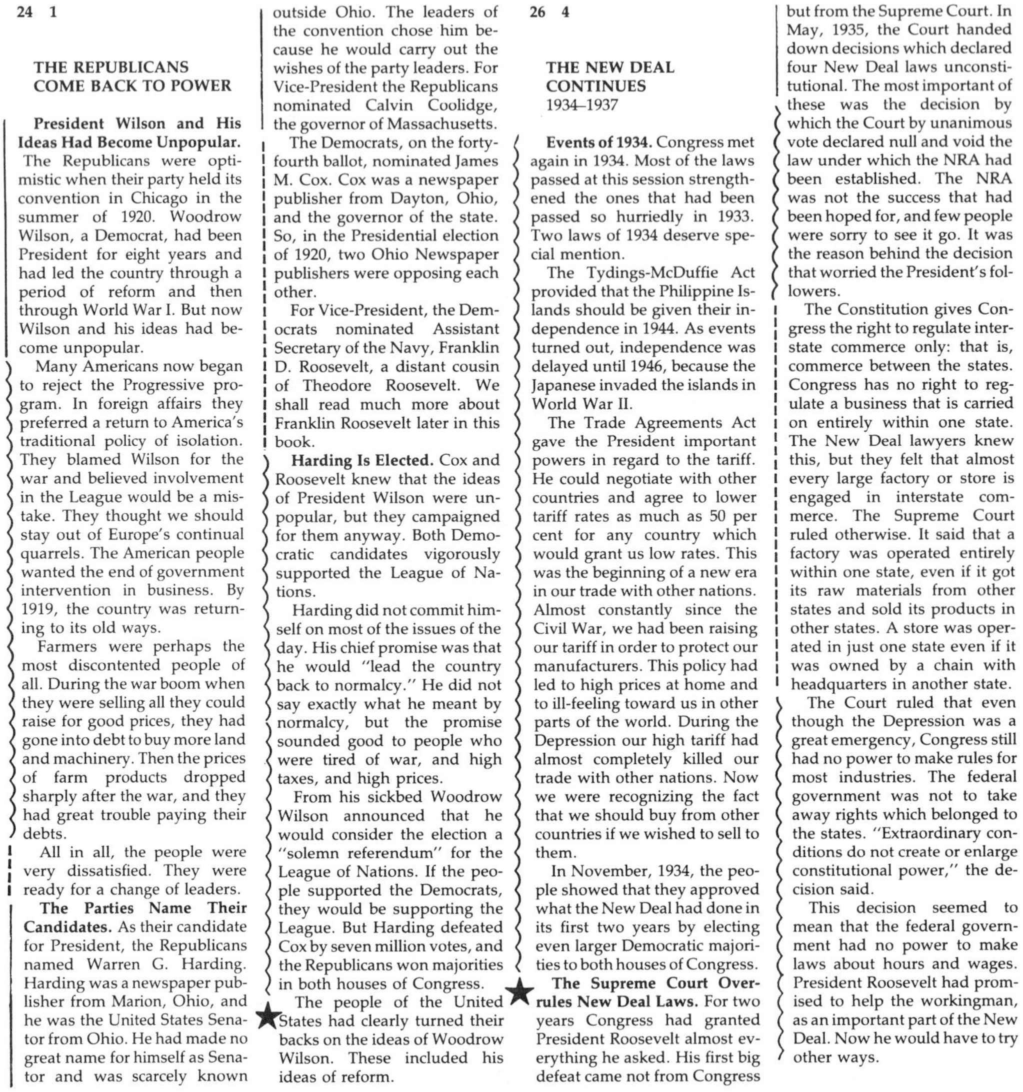

24 1

THE REPUBLICANS
COME BACK TO POWER

President Wilson and His Ideas Had Become Unpopular. The Republicans were optimistic when their party held its convention in Chicago in the summer of 1920. Woodrow Wilson, a Democrat, had been President for eight years and had led the country through a period of reform and then through World War I. But now Wilson and his ideas had become unpopular.

Many Americans now began to reject the Progressive program. In foreign affairs they preferred a return to America's traditional policy of isolation. They blamed Wilson for the war and believed involvement in the League would be a mistake. They thought we should stay out of Europe's continual quarrels. The American people wanted the end of government intervention in business. By 1919, the country was returning to its old ways.

Farmers were perhaps the most discontented people of all. During the war boom when they were selling all they could raise for good prices, they had gone into debt to buy more land and machinery. Then the prices of farm products dropped sharply after the war, and they had great trouble paying their debts.

All in all, the people were very dissatisfied. They were ready for a change of leaders.

The Parties Name Their Candidates. As their candidate for President, the Republicans named Warren G. Harding. Harding was a newspaper publisher from Marion, Ohio, and he was the United States Senator from Ohio. He had made no great name for himself as Senator and was scarcely known outside Ohio. The leaders of the convention chose him because he would carry out the wishes of the party leaders. For Vice-President the Republicans nominated Calvin Coolidge, the governor of Massachusetts.

The Democrats, on the forty-fourth ballot, nominated James M. Cox. Cox was a newspaper publisher from Dayton, Ohio, and the governor of the state. So, in the Presidential election of 1920, two Ohio Newspaper publishers were opposing each other.

For Vice-President, the Democrats nominated Assistant Secretary of the Navy, Franklin D. Roosevelt, a distant cousin of Theodore Roosevelt. We shall read much more about Franklin Roosevelt later in this book.

Harding Is Elected. Cox and Roosevelt knew that the ideas of President Wilson were unpopular, but they campaigned for them anyway. Both Democratic candidates vigorously supported the League of Nations.

Harding did not commit himself on most of the issues of the day. His chief promise was that he would "lead the country back to normalcy." He did not say exactly what he meant by normalcy, but the promise sounded good to people who were tired of war, and high taxes, and high prices.

From his sickbed Woodrow Wilson announced that he would consider the election a "solemn referendum" for the League of Nations. If the people supported the Democrats, they would be supporting the League. But Harding defeated Cox by seven million votes, and the Republicans won majorities in both houses of Congress.

★The people of the United States had clearly turned their backs on the ideas of Woodrow Wilson. These included his ideas of reform.

26 4

THE NEW DEAL
CONTINUES
1934–1937

Events of 1934. Congress met again in 1934. Most of the laws passed at this session strengthened the ones that had been passed so hurriedly in 1933. Two laws of 1934 deserve special mention.

The Tydings-McDuffie Act provided that the Philippine Islands should be given their independence in 1944. As events turned out, independence was delayed until 1946, because the Japanese invaded the islands in World War II.

The Trade Agreements Act gave the President important powers in regard to the tariff. He could negotiate with other countries and agree to lower tariff rates as much as 50 per cent for any country which would grant us low rates. This was the beginning of a new era in our trade with other nations. Almost constantly since the Civil War, we had been raising our tariff in order to protect our manufacturers. This policy had led to high prices at home and to ill-feeling toward us in other parts of the world. During the Depression our high tariff had almost completely killed our trade with other nations. Now we were recognizing the fact that we should buy from other countries if we wished to sell to them.

In November, 1934, the people showed that they approved what the New Deal had done in its first two years by electing even larger Democratic majorities to both houses of Congress.

★**The Supreme Court Overrules New Deal Laws.** For two years Congress had granted President Roosevelt almost everything he asked. His first big defeat came not from Congress but from the Supreme Court. In May, 1935, the Court handed down decisions which declared four New Deal laws unconstitutional. The most important of these was the decision by which the Court by unanimous vote declared null and void the law under which the NRA had been established. The NRA was not the success that had been hoped for, and few people were sorry to see it go. It was the reason behind the decision that worried the President's followers.

The Constitution gives Congress the right to regulate interstate commerce only: that is, commerce between the states. Congress has no right to regulate a business that is carried on entirely within one state. The New Deal lawyers knew this, but they felt that almost every large factory or store is engaged in interstate commerce. The Supreme Court ruled otherwise. It said that a factory was operated entirely within one state, even if it got its raw materials from other states and sold its products in other states. A store was operated in just one state even if it was owned by a chain with headquarters in another state.

The Court ruled that even though the Depression was a great emergency, Congress still had no power to make rules for most industries. The federal government was not to take away rights which belonged to the states. "Extraordinary conditions do not create or enlarge constitutional power," the decision said.

This decision seemed to mean that the federal government had no power to make laws about hours and wages. President Roosevelt had promised to help the workingman, as an important part of the New Deal. Now he would have to try other ways.

Fig. 1. A system of marking the reading material must be developed to help the student follow the tape recording. The samples are from L. Bernard; R. Brande; and O. Sharkey, *America and Its People* (New York: Sadlier, 1968).

words per minute. Upon completion of a recording, the teacher must listen carefully to the tape to ensure that it is understandable and that the content is correct.

Similarly, when using a tape, the student should be familiar with the mechanics of operating the tape recorder (to prevent tapes from being erased) and with the specific directions for the use of a particular tape. The setting in which the tape is used should be well ventilated, properly lighted, and free from excessive distractions and noises. The teacher should provide appropriate reinforcement and feedback.

Once a tape is prepared, proper care is essential. Tapes and tape recorders should be stored in a suitable place in an organized manner. Occasionally, each tape should be monitored by the teacher. If a tape becomes defective or difficult to understand, it should be replaced.

Evaluation

To prepare and use tape recordings of reading assignments is time consuming for both teachers and students. Consequently, if it is found that valuable preparation and instructional time is not being effectively used, changes must be made. The quality of the prepared tape recordings and the performance of the students using the recordings should be constantly monitored and evaluated. As with any teaching material or technique, tape recordings of reading assignments are *not* appropriate or effective with all students. Therefore, they should only be used with those students who show gains and benefits through their application. For those students who do benefit from their use, recorded tapes should be prepared and evaluated in such a manner as to promote the acquisition of key content materials from classes into which they have been mainstreamed and to aid them in improving their study and text usage skills. The six steps outlined in this article have been designed with those considerations in mind.

Microfiche as a Reading Aid for Partially Sighted Students

TORSTEN ANDERSSON

Before making specific aids for handicapped persons, one should investigate what the open market has to offer, to see if it is possible to use a technique which has already been developed, with or without adaptations. With this in mind, the National Center for Educational Aids for the Blind is working with the microfiche technique, and after two years of experiments has found that the system can work very well for partially sighted students. We report here on this investigation, supported by the scientific study, Project PUSS XIX of the Uppsala School of Education, Department of Education, Report No. 53, 1975.

Report of the Investigation

The purpose of the present study is to determine whether microfiche might be considered as a practicable reading aid for partially sighted persons with a visual acuity between 20/500 and 20/70 and, as such, a supplement to the reading aids presently available for those individuals. In Sweden about 170,000 persons are partially sighted. These individuals could have functioning reading vision if they were given suitable aids. Presently, in most cases one of two types of aids is used: optical aids and closed circuit television (CCTV). Common to these aids is that they give an enlarged picture, which makes fewer demands on the capacity of the retina for reading.

Nine partially sighted persons took part in the study, four male and five female. Aged between 20 and 50, their visual acuities ranged between 20/2000 and 20/100. Each participant had been provided with adequate optical equipment and had received reading training from a teacher before the tests were carried out. Four of the subjects had been recommended by an expert in the use of CCTV, and had also received training in the use of this aid.

The results were the following: Six of nine persons read faster with the microfiche system than with other optical aids. Three of

---

"Microfiche as a Reading Aid for Partially Sighted Students," by Torsten Andersson, *Visual Impairment and Blindness*, May 1980, pp. 193–96. Reprinted with permission of the Journal of Visual Impairment and Blindness, published by the American Foundation for the Blind.

four "CCTV persons" read faster with microfiche. Four of nine persons felt more strain reading with optical aids than with microfiche. Five of nine felt no difference.

The result of the luminance measurement done on several microfiche readers showed that none of them reached the minimum level claimed—the light source was too weak (see fig. 1). There are in this case, however, several possible ways to improve the equipment, and a few manufacturers have already begun to equip their microfiche readers with stronger lamps.

Microfiche Compared with Optical Aids and CCTV

The most serious disadvantage of microfiche in comparison with optical aids and CCTV lies in the direct availability of printed material for the latter. For microfiche, the photographing phase takes a few days. Furthermore, the apparatus does not allow note taking or any underlining during reading.

The optical aid is very often compact, easy to handle, and comfortable to carry. The CCTV allows note taking and is superior in terms of amount of enlargement it can produce—up to 50 times. Thus, the CCTV is probably best for those with extreme visual handicaps, and for reading newspapers, letters, etc.

Fig. 1. Luminance was measured by placing a gauge 200 mm (7 7/8") from the screen and measuring the light intensity at nine spots. The short distance was used because partially sighted persons usually have to read close to the text.

On the other hand, with microfiche it would be possible to have fewer pages included on each fiche, perhaps 24 rather than 60, making them easier to read. The largest practical enlargement that can be obtained is 3–4 times.

For reading running text, the microfiche system was shown to be superior to both CCTV and optical aids, and furthermore it seems to be specially suited for reading educational materials.

These three reading aids have to some extent different fields of application and therefore *complement rather than replace each other.*

National Center's Microfiche Service

There is now a small central library of educational books on microfiche, containing about 150 titles for students from the lower level of the comprehensive school up to high-school level. Twenty pupils with visual acuity between 20/200 and 20/70 have a comprehensive service and the activity is very effectively supervised. The routine used in supplying students with microfiche is very simple:

1. The school sends the printed books together with an order by mail to the center.
2. After registration they are forwarded to the laboratory.
3. Five copies of each fiche, ready for use, are mailed back to the center; one is passed on to the pupil and the remaining sets are available for loan.
4. A register of microfiche books is included in a catalogue of books for the blind and partially sighted students that is distributed by the center.
5. Production expenses are generally covered by the center and consequently the loan of copies is free of charge.
6. The microfiche readers are bought by the school (or sometimes rented) directly from a manufacturer. It is also possible to borrow the equipment from the center.
7. The center conducts, in collaboration with the School for the Blind, regional activities, carried out by 13 traveling special teachers. They are responsible for about 1,300 integrated partially sighted pupils and are organized in five

districts, each with one or two sets of equipment for demonstrations and tests.

So far the center has not prepared the books in any special way before making fiches, but in cooperation with the laboratory we have now started to solve certain editorial problems. For example, we have asked the laboratory to adapt the fiche specially to the partially sighted—they prefer a negative fiche, thus permitting the light from the apparatus to be concentrated only on the text (see fig. 2).

We must look more closely at the market in order to find the right microfiche reader and a manufacturer who will make a few small modifications to the equipment if necessary. A microfiche reader suitable for use by a visually handicapped pupil must have the following characteristics:

1. It must be easy to move around and should, for that reason, be equipped with a handle, and even be foldable in some way; size and weight should be similar to an ordinary tape recorder. Such a design is necessary because the pupils in the upper grade change classrooms for almost every lesson.
2. It must have an external screen to prevent reflection. The ground glass screen should have a dull finish for the same reason.
3. The lighting device should be more powerful than those presently supplied.

Many pupils meet technical aids with very strong resistance. They are afraid of exposing their handicaps, especially by use of an aid that is difficult to use or infrequently encountered. For that reason it is very important that the apparatus is easy to use and meets the above requirements. It is in this connection that a ground glass screen is to be recommended. This would make it possible to project a large-size picture on a wall, and enable a teacher, by use of the microfiche technique, to comment on a diagram or text to the entire class, and the partially sighted child need not feel isolated by the use of the aid.

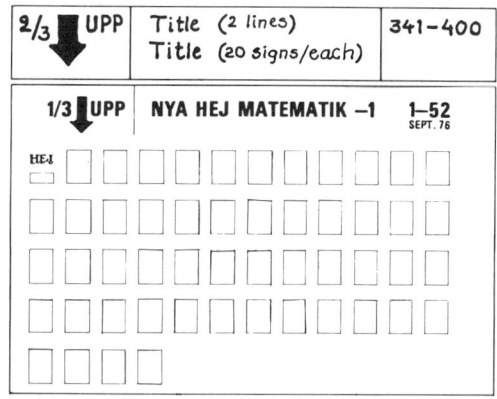

Fig. 2. Microfiche of a book on mathematics. The last line contains only four pages because it is the end of a chapter; the following chapter begins on the next fiche. The enlargement of the top of a fiche shows how certain information is given to the student: 2/3 means that this is the second of a set of three fiches. The arrow and UPP show which way to insert the fiche in the reader. Two lines of 20 characters each are allowed for the title. At right the page numbers are given.

We know that there are many individuals who might benefit by using the microfiche system. As was mentioned earlier, there are 170,000 partially sighted individuals in Sweden, but there are others who might be helped although they are not visually handicapped.

It is difficult for our center to reach groups who may be interested in receiving further information, or who would help in the development and marketing of a suitable reader. A condition for success is cooperation among educational institutions, associations for the handicapped, and government authorities.

Finally—some hard facts to consider: In West Germany there are 1.5 million partially sighted persons; in Great Britain, 1 million; and, in the United States, 2 million. I think it would be a very good idea to introduce the microfiche system to these people and to many other interested groups.

Computer-Based Instruction for Hearing-Impaired Children in the Classroom

SHARON DUGDALE and PATTY VOGEL

The Educational Setting

Carrie Busey School is an Individual Guide Education School with 22 classes of students in grades K–5, including three classes of hearing-impaired students, two of educably mentally handicapped, three of orthopedically handicapped, and one of multiply handicapped. The school is organized into units consisting of four to eight teachers working together. Each unit includes both handicapped children and nonhandicapped children. The children within a unit are grouped for math, reading, and Wisconsin Design Comprehension Skills. Mainstreaming and reverse mainstreaming take place in these groupings.

The three classes of hearing-impaired students are assigned to one large classroom which has been modified to an adaptive environment for sound. The students, whose ages range from 6 to 12 years, are grouped into two primary classes and one intermediate class. Several of these children are mainstreamed into other classrooms for some of the day. Most of them are reverse mainstreamed with approximately 60 hearing children who come to the hearing-impaired classroom for some of their work.

The hearing-impaired classroom is staffed by three teachers, one responsible for each class, and a teacher's aide, who is herself hearing impaired. Student teachers and peer teaching are also an important part of the individualized education program.

In February 1977, two PLATO [Programed Logic for Automatic Teaching Operations] terminals were added to the teaching resources in the hearing-impaired classroom. Since that time, computer-based instruction has been a regular part of the mathematics program for about 75 children. These students include the hearing-impaired children and several children with other handicaps, as well as some nonhandicapped fourth and fifth grade children. Each child receives from 1 to 2.5 hours of PLATO instruction per week, depending on his or her individual schedule and needs. The math instruction ranges from simple addition for some students to fractions and functions for others. Some children also work on phonetics and other topics on PLATO.

The Computer-Based Instruction System

The PLATO system is a computer-based education system developed at the Computer-based Education Research Laboratory (CERL) at the University of Illinois. The University of Illinois PLATO system has about 1,000 terminals connected by telephone line or microwave to a large central computer. Instructional materials are available in over 100 subject areas, ranging from lower elementary grades to university graduate course level. Terminals are located in public schools, community colleges, universities, correctional institutions, military training schools, and other institutions throughout Illinois and many other states. Each terminal consists of a screen on which the computer displays text and graphics to the student and a keyset for the student to interact with the computer. PLATO responds instantly to the student's input. Many PLATO terminals, including those used in the elementary school classrooms, are equipped also with a touch-sensitive device which allows students to communicate with the computer by touching the screen.

The Instructional Materials and Implementation

The Mathematics Curriculum

The major part of the instructional materials used with the hearing-impaired

---

"Computer-Based Instruction for Hearing-Impaired Children in the Classroom," by Sharon Dugdale and Patty Vogel, *American Annals of the Deaf* 1978, 123: 730–43. Reprinted with permission.

students has been the intermediate-level mathematics curriculum developed at the Computer-based Education Research Laboratory (CERL) at the University of Illinois.[1] This curriculum includes about 250 PLATO lessons and covers a large part of the mathematics normally taught in the intermediate grades. The PLATO curriculum provides about 100 hours of instruction for a typical intermediate grade student. Much of the curriculum has companion booklets and worksheets to help the teacher correlate the PLATO lessons with classroom activities.

The classroom teacher assigns topics for each student, or group of students, to study on PLATO. Different students studying the same topic may be assigned different sets of lessons, or different versions of the same lessons, depending on the individual needs of the students.

The teacher also sets the length of the student's session and several parameters about each student's previous experience. In generating exercises for the student, the PLATO lesson takes these parameters into account. For example, a numberline lesson in mixed numbers may include negative numbers for one student, but avoid them for another, depending on how the teacher has set each student's personal parameters. This flexibility is provided by the curriculum management system created by David Kibbey at CERL.

An instructional module can be constructed to include any combination of lessons the teacher wants. Most instructional modules have a topic of major emphasis, but also include lessons which provide readiness for later material, review of previous material, and general experience and enrichment. During a typical session on PLATO, the student works on several different lessons, some of them new and some of them continued from previous sessions.

An on-line grade book which keeps track of student assignments, progress, and performance is available to the teacher at all times. Hard copy of this information is delivered to the teacher periodically.

The individual lessons that comprise the mathematics curriculum are of several different types. Besides some lessons which are presented as straight instruction or practice, there are many lessons presented in game format or in a format intended for exploration and experience. Nearly all lessons require a high rate of interaction between the student and the terminal.

Figure 1 shows a sequence from "High Wire," a lesson on addition of fractions. In the first frame Kimberly has chosen to "hide" the monkey at $\frac{2}{3} + \frac{1}{4}$. The monkey has jumped off the platform and, starting at 0, has swung across the number line to illustrate the given problem: 2 swings of $\frac{1}{3}$ each, then 1 swing of $\frac{1}{4}$. Thomas is asked to write a fraction to "find" the monkey.

In the second frame (fig. 2) Thomas has entered 11/12, causing the feather to make 11 jumps of 1/12 each. Thomas's response is correct. The feather has stopped where it can tickle the monkey's tail, causing the monkey to drop to the ground laughing all the way. The monkey's swings and the feather's jumps match up to show that 4/12 make 1/3 and 3/12 make 1/4, thus illustrating the concept of equivalent fractions and the common denominator.

Kimberly and Thomas take turns hiding the monkey. There is also an option for PLATO to hide the monkey so that the lesson can be used for individual practice with problems chosen to suit the student's achievement level.

Figures 3–6 show examples of various other types of lessons in the math curriculum.

Many of the math lessons show the student a "level." For example, figure 3 shows "level 1 of 6" at the bottom of the screen. This means that the difficulty and complexity of the task adjust to a level at which the student can function successfully and increase as the student shows mastery. The message on the screen informs the student of his progress through the lesson.

This curriculum has been used with many hundreds of students since 1974. Results indicate that it can have a strong positive effect on student achievement in mathematics.[2]

Communication and Sharing among Students

As is the case in other elementary school classrooms, the two PLATO terminals in the hearing-impaired classroom are placed side by side. This arrangement lets the students communicate with each other while they do their PLATO work. When a student needs help understanding what PLATO is asking, the student sitting beside him at the other terminal can often be most helpful. Because the children find the PLATO curriculum so motivating, their interaction with each other at the terminals is centered around their work and does not usually take them "off task." A

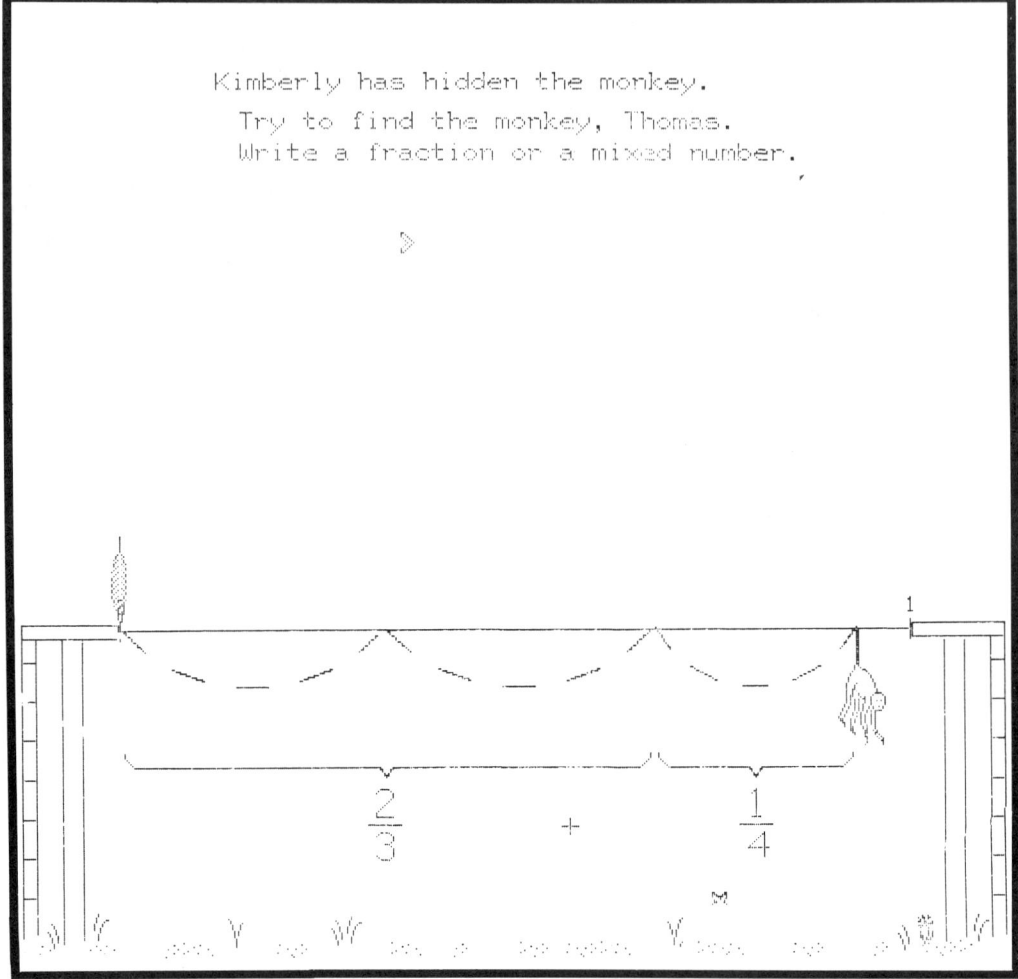

Fig. 1. Frame from lesson "High Wire." Kimberly and Thomas are practicing addition of fractions with visual feedback about common denominators.

student who needs help is rarely willing to let another child take over and do the work. More likely the student will accept only the assistance he or she needs in order to become self-sufficient again.

Of course, not all interaction between students at the terminals is initiated by a need for help. Often a student will be proud of something he or she has done and will want to show it or explain it to someone else. The students are learning to talk about their mathematics. PLATO is encouraging healthy interaction among all types and ages of children. This has assisted in the learning of social skills and the development of positive attitudes toward mainstreaming situations.

The interaction among students is not limited to children who happen to sit side by side at the terminals. Some lessons exploit the computer's capabilities for communication and sharing of ideas among students—even among students in different classes or different schools. One example of such a lesson is the paintings library.[3] In this lesson the student is asked to "paint" a particular fraction of a box. By touching the screen, he can draw lines on the box and paint areas of the box. When he has finished painting the correct

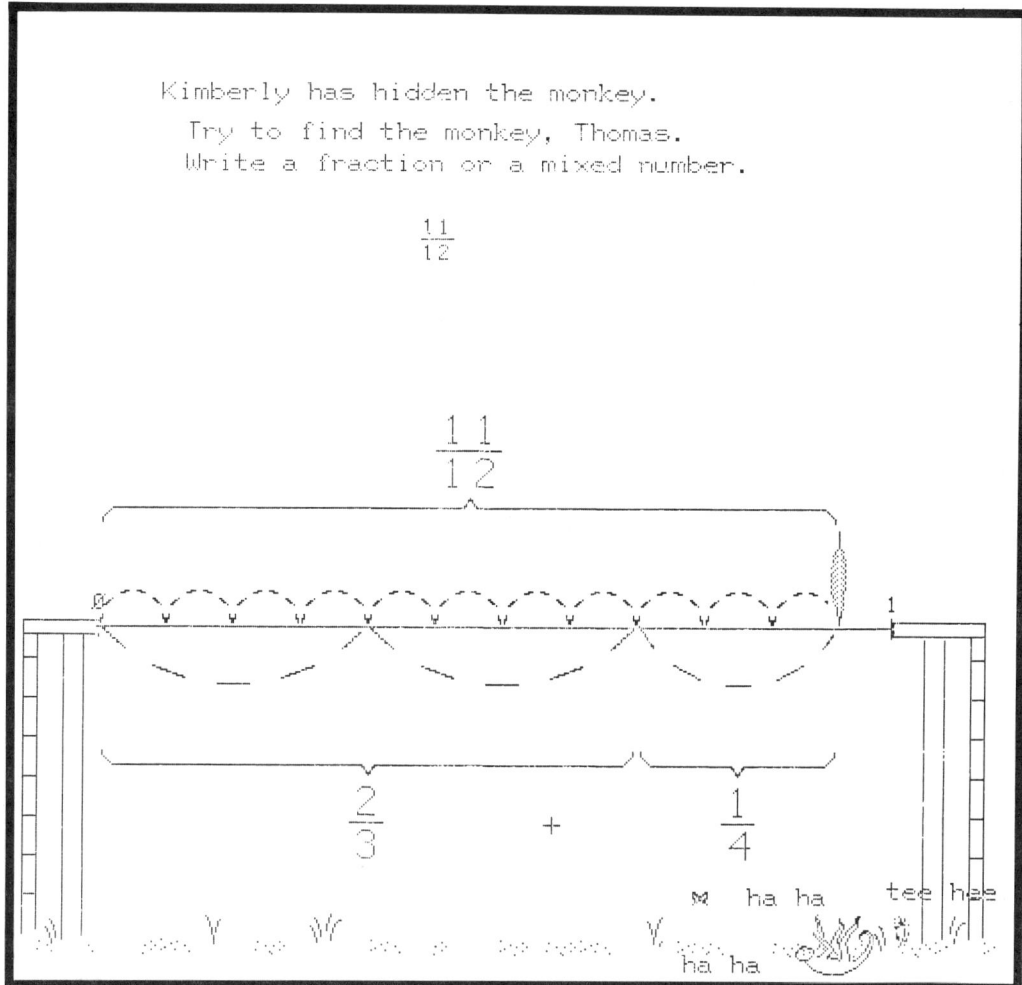

Fig. 2. Frame from lesson "High Wire." Kimberly and Thomas are practicing addition of fractions with visual feedback about common denominators.

fraction of the box, the student can choose to save his painting in the library where others may see his work.

A student's first paintings are usually quite simple. Looking at the library, the student is encouraged to try more imaginative ways of illustrating various fractions. The children show little interest in doing a painting just like another child has already done. Instead, they tend to look at other students' work to get ideas, then use those ideas to create something of their own. Figure 7 shows a few of the paintings that students have chosen to share through the library.

Social interaction is quite apparent when fads spread through class libraries. For example, one student might paint a fraction of the box to show his initials. Within a few days, there will be many paintings showing other students' names and initials. Besides encouraging communication and sharing of ideas, this lesson and others like it provide strong motivation for students to engage in tasks which require them to relate mathematical concepts to concrete models. Examples of lessons involving other kinds of social interaction include "High Wire" (fig. 2), which two students can play together at one termi-

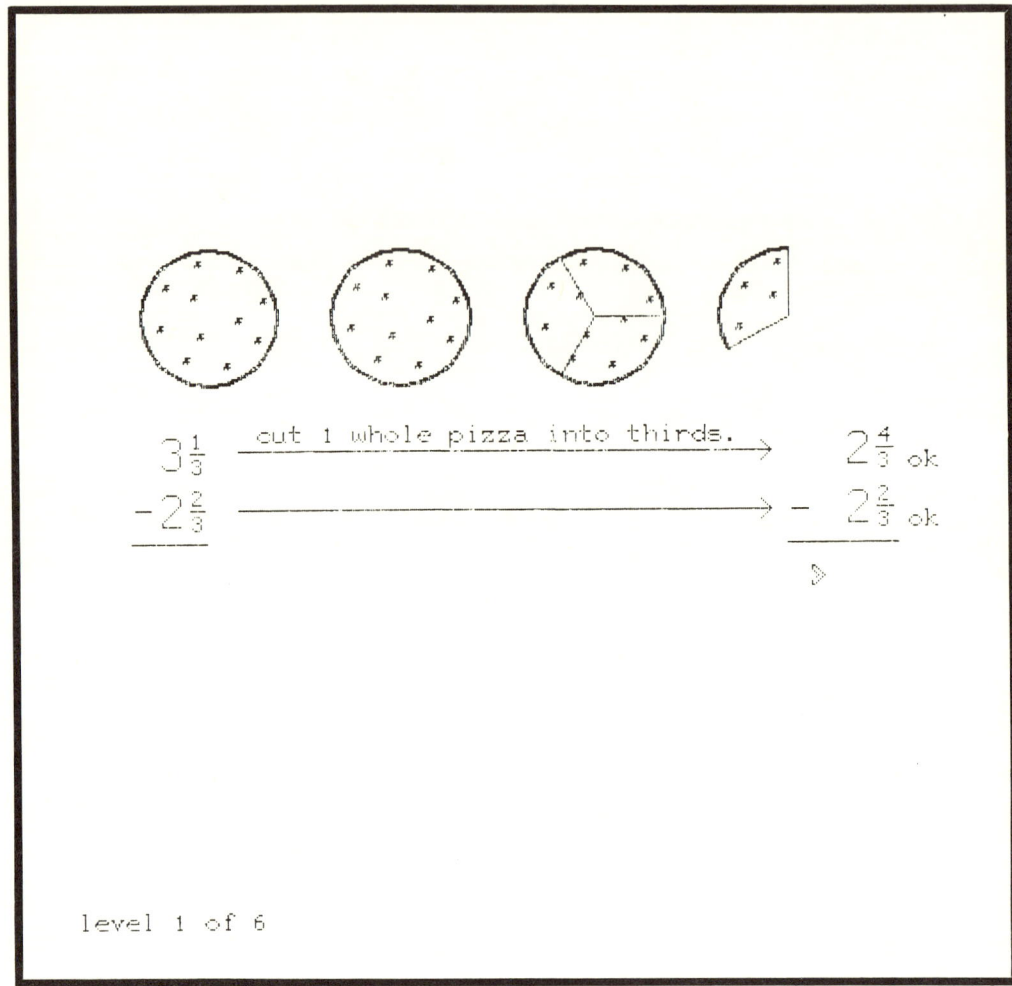

Fig. 3. Display from a lesson about subtraction of mixed numbers. The student has 3 1/3 pizzas. In order to take away 2 2/3 pizzas, he must first cut one of the whole pizzas into thirds.

nal, and "Pinball" (fig. 4), where students with high scores are listed in an interschool hall of fame. See also the descriptions of "Torpedo," a game played by students at separate terminals, and "Fractions Basketball."[4] Still other lessons designed to encourage social interaction among students are described in Weaver and Seiler.[5]

Teacher-Guided Activities

Although for most of the PLATO instruction the students work independently at the terminals, some of the lessons are used as interactive visual aids in teacher-directed activities.

One such lesson is "The Talking Robot," designed and programmed by James Wilson with the advice of Elaine Paden. This lesson provides a simulation of the production of the sounds of English speech. Although the lesson is intended for adult audience, it has been useful in helping the hearing-impaired students learn to articulate speech sounds. The robot is a rough drawing of the upper portion of the vocal tract. The student can command the robot to change the placement of the lips, the tongue, and the soft palate, thus determining the sound to be produced. The student can also type a phonetic symbol and PLATO will instruct the robot, step by

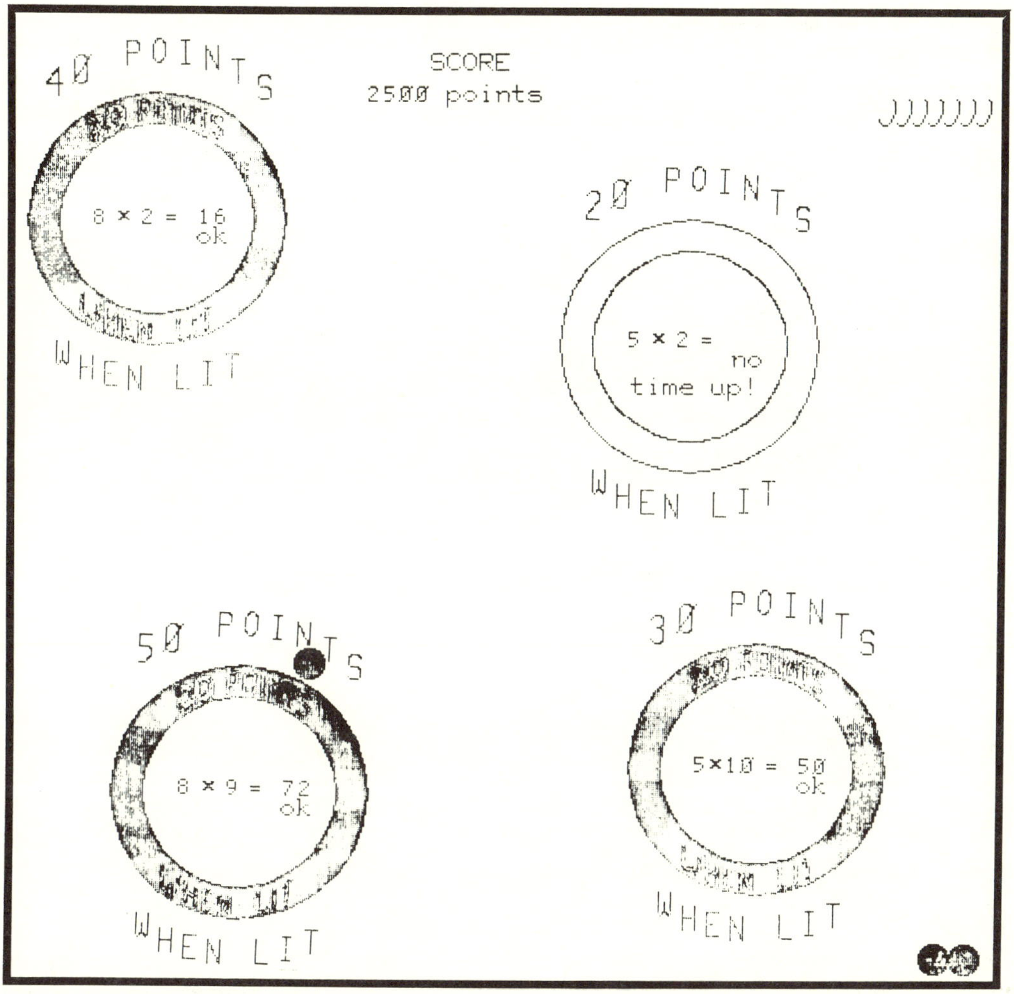

Fig. 4. Display from lesson "Pinball." The student practices number facts in the format of a pinball game. The ball bounces from problem to problem. Points are earned by answering correctly within the time limit.

step, how to form the requested sound. Figure 8 shows a display from this lesson.

Other lessons that were written for adult students have been used, with teacher guidance, to supplement and reinforce the classroom music and social studies programs.

Adaptations for Handicapped Students

As we anticipated, implementing a computer-based curriculum in the classroom for the hearing impaired was different in many ways from the work we had done previously in other classes. However, the differences were not always those we had expected. We were encouraged to find that the hearing-impaired children were very understanding and helpful in their dealings with the PLATO staff, who were just beginning to learn a few signs. At times the communication effort was frustrating for both the student and the PLATO person, and occasionally the classroom teacher would have to interpret. More often, however, the communication challenge could be met without outside help. In learning to use the computer, the hearing-impaired students actually showed less frustration than hearing students sometimes

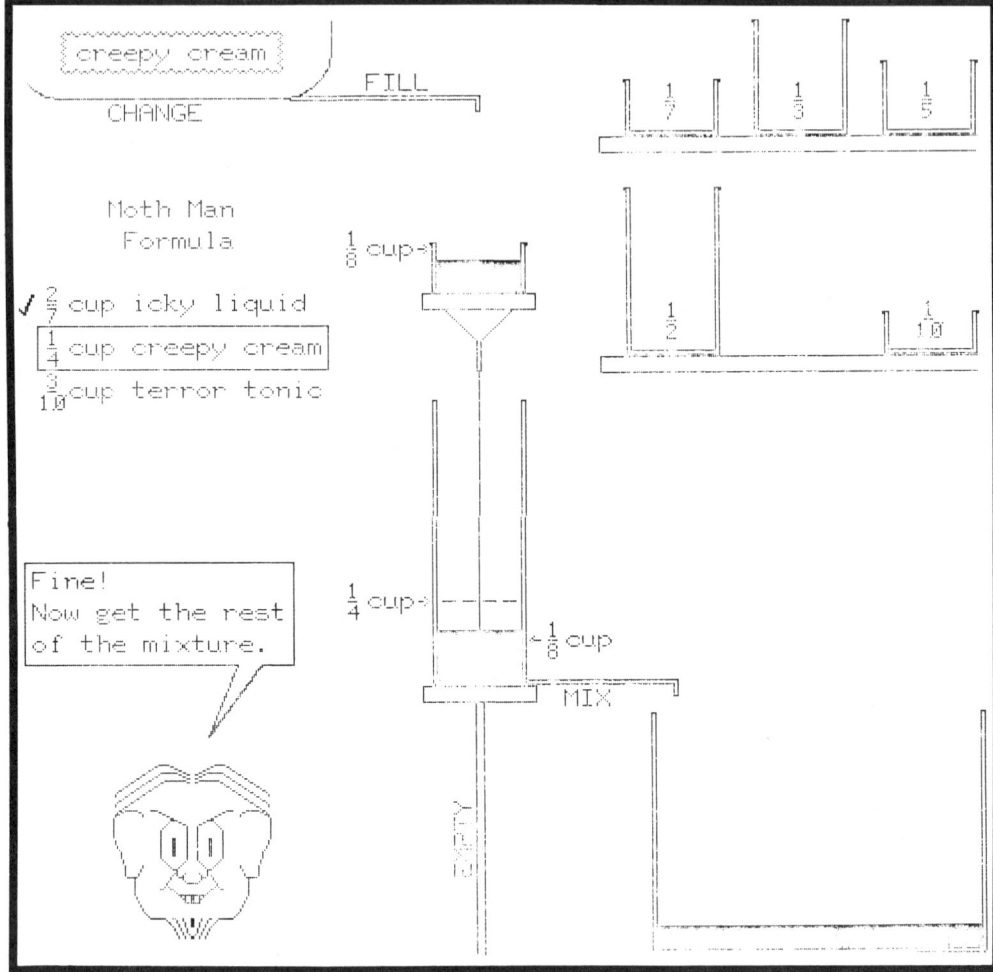

Fig. 5. Display from lesson "Make-a-Monster." The student is using measuring cups to mix up a monster formula in an eccentric scientist's laboratory. He has finished measuring out 2/7 cup of icky liquid, and is now getting 1/4 cup of creepy cream. Since there is no 1/4 cup available to measure with, the student has chosen to use the 1/8 cup and fill it twice. When the student has finished mixing the formula, he is rewarded by appearance of a suitably outlandish "monster" on the screen.

do. They seemed more ready to face small difficulties and work them out.

Within the first few days of PLATO use, it became apparent that the hearing-impaired students were having some difficulty with the lessons that require touch input. When a student touches the screen, the terminal responds with a beep. This beep assures the student that the touch has been noticed. Of course, the hearing-impaired students could not hear the beep, and therefore, sometimes could not tell whether the computer had felt their touch. This problem was easily remedied by installing a small red light beside the screen to flash along with the beep when the student touched the screen.

Some of the children use the PLATO beginning reading lessons, which require an audio device that plays recorded messages to the students. Using a special cord made by an audiologist, we connected the PLATO audio device to the teacher's microphone of the

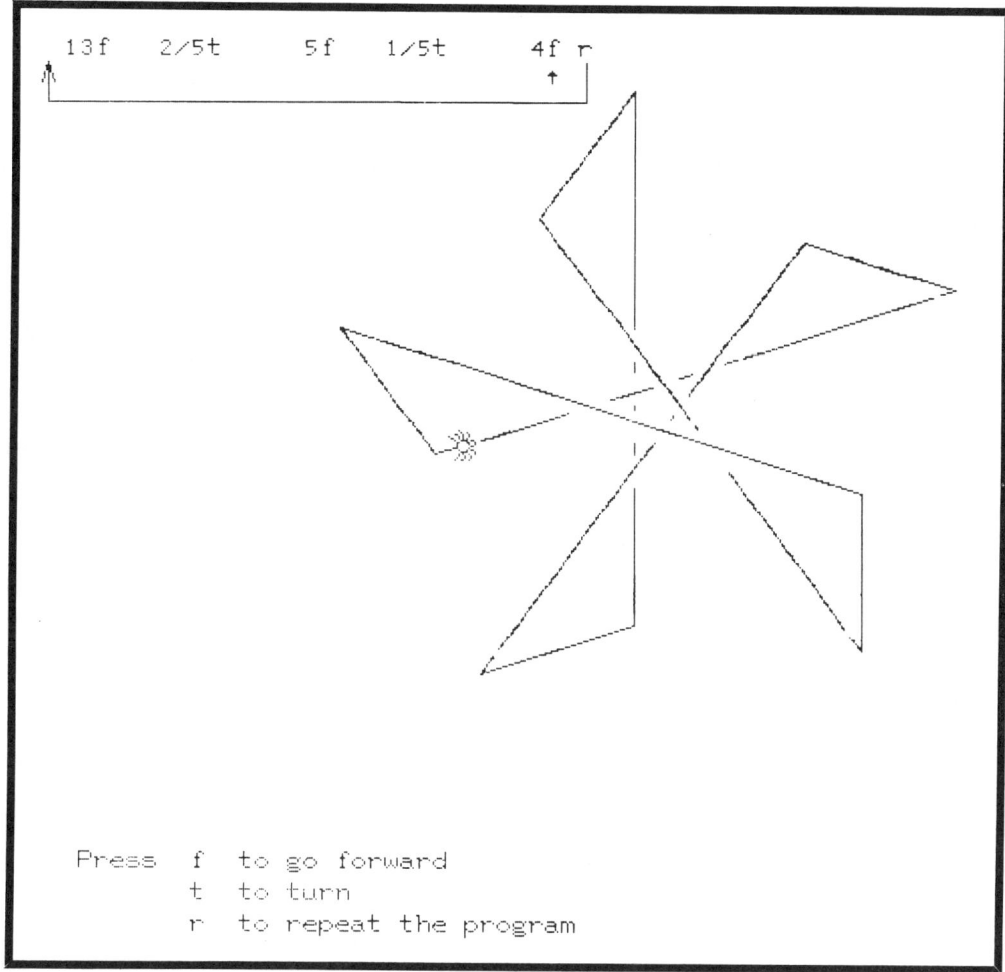

Fig. 6. Display from lesson "Skywriting and Spider Web." The student has written a program to move a spider around the screen and leave a web pattern. The key to simple programming language is shown at the bottom of the screen. The student's program is at the top of the screen.

Phonic Ear. This adaptation has enabled the hearing-impaired students to use some of the beginning reading lessons for auditory training.

Adaptations have also been necessary for one of the orthopedically handicapped children. A tray had to be built for the child's wheelchair in order to place the keyset in a position that he could reach. A sling was devised and attached to his wheelchair to support his arm above the keyset. This child is now able to use PLATO independently, as the other children do. He enjoys PLATO very much.

In general, there have been no insurmountable difficulties in implementing the PLATO curriculum in the classroom for the hearing impaired. The hearing-impaired students now use the computer just as confidently and eagerly as the hearing students at their school and other schools.

Some Initial Results

As has been the case with other schools, the response to computer-based instruction at Carrie Busey has been very encouraging.

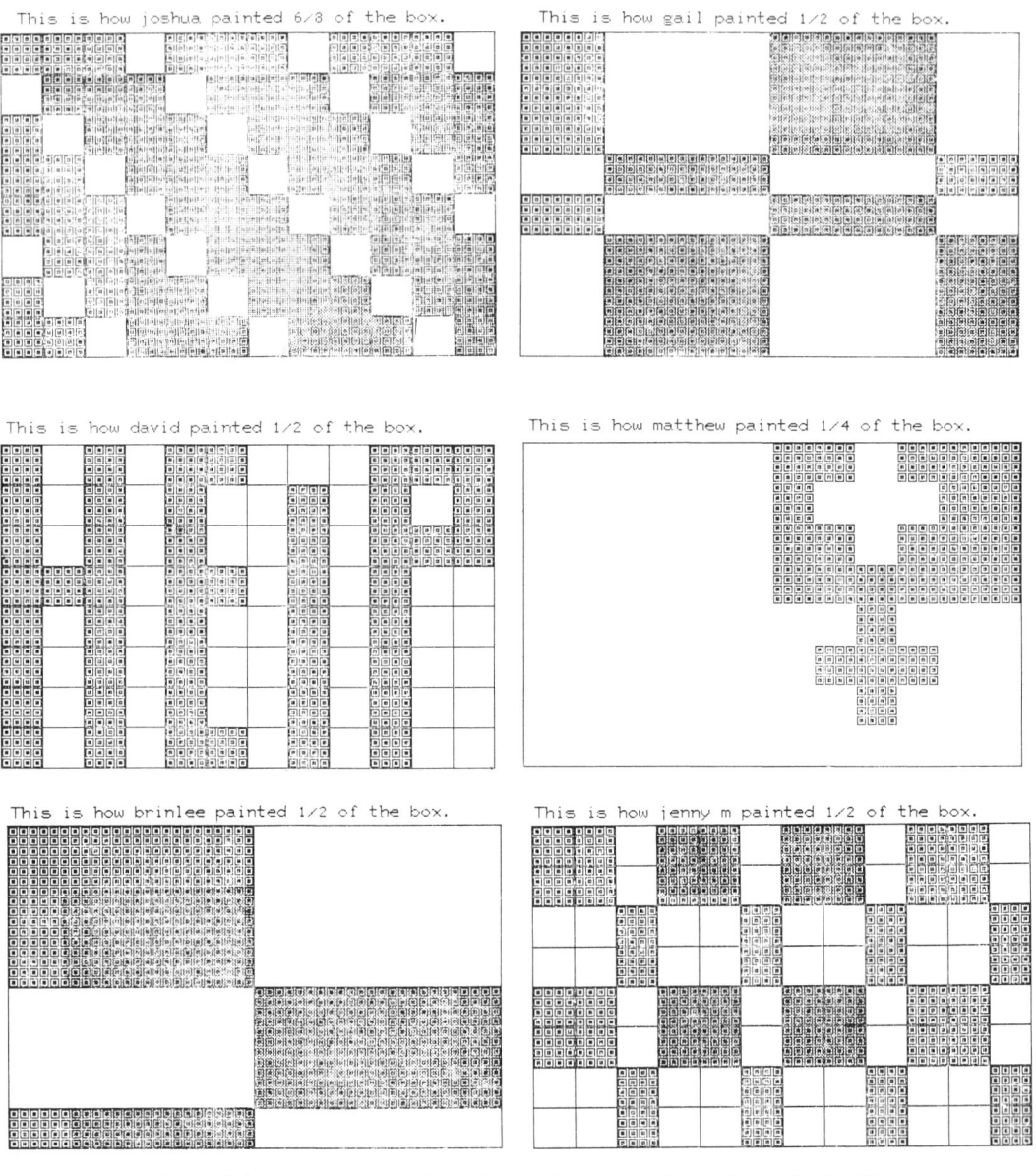

Fig. 7. A few of the paintings students have chosen to share through the library.

Attitudes toward PLATO have been very positive for both the hearing and hearing-impaired students. Students work at the terminals from 8:00 in the morning, when the buses first arrive at school, until at least 3:00 every day. Children voluntarily stay 30 to 60 minutes after school instead of going home to play. They are always eager to work on PLATO, and they often work together, helping each other understand the material being presented.

The children relate to PLATO as more than a machine. It is a friend and a teacher. For example, Bryan, who is a nine-year-old child in an EMH [educably mentally handicapped] classroom, has been using the computer as a reward in a behavior modification program. A day does not pass that Bryan does not come

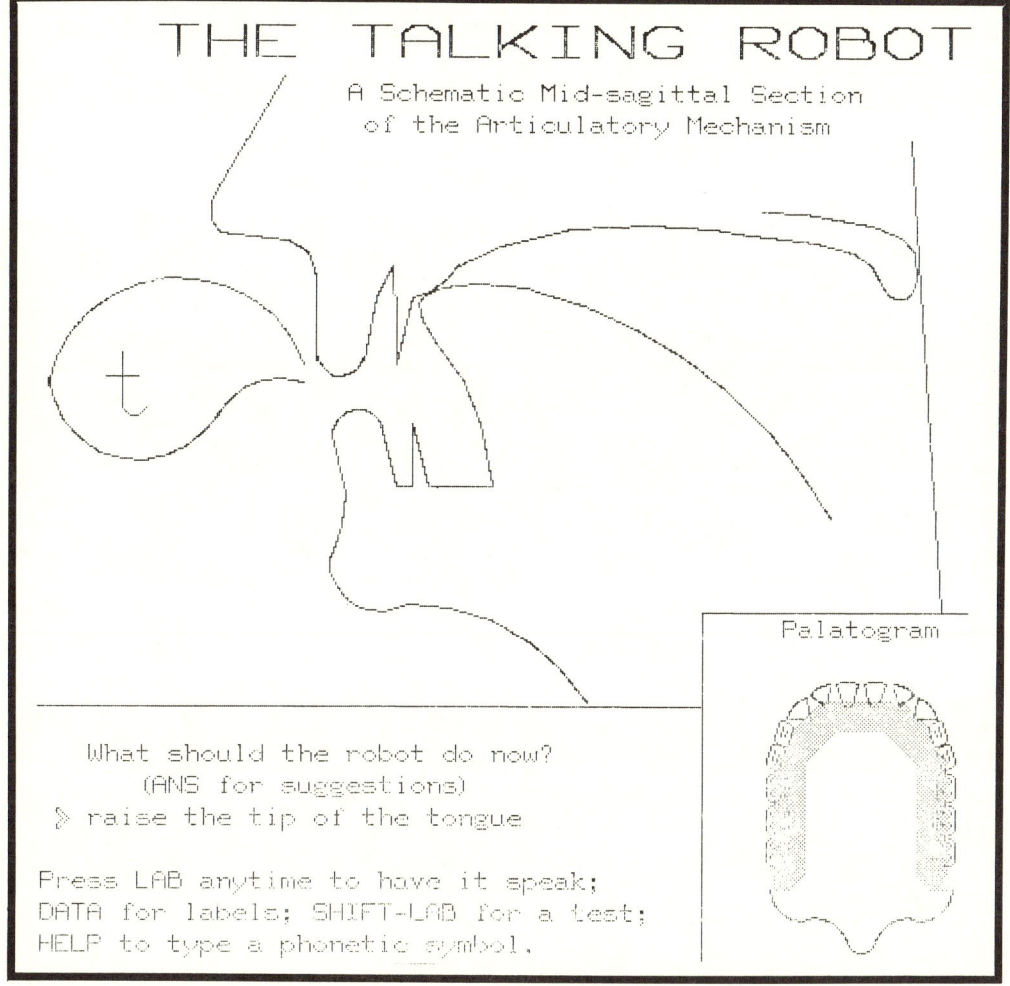

Fig. 8. "The Talking Robot." The student has commanded the robot to raise the tip of the tongue, then "speak." The sound produced is "t." Because this lesson is not designed for use by children, it is used with the teacher's guidance.

into the hearing-impaired classroom to say something nice to PLATO. This year the computer received two Valentine cards. Both were addressed "To PLATO and Miss Vogel."

The children's experience with computer-based instruction has been advantageous in many areas besides learning mathematics. It has helped them assume responsibility. During each session on PLATO the student makes many decisions about what to do next, but he knows that certain lessons must be completed before new material can be made available. In addition, the hearing-impaired children are developing a language of direction, not only for following directions, but also for giving directions to the computer.

PLATO mathematics instruction has given the students a very motivating context for improving not only their mathematics skills, but their reading skills as well. The children are learning to skim read for quick response, and are also learning to read for detail in instructions and game rules. The vocabulary expansion among the hearing-impaired children has been marked. The PLATO lessons use a vocabulary that is both practical and expressive. In all, the experiences of the children and teachers have been positive and rewarding. PLATO has proved a very useful tool for individual instruction for both the hearing-impaired students and their classmates.

Notes

1. Support for this curriculum development was provided by the National Science Foundation (US NSF C-723) and by the State of Illinois. A brief overview of this work is available in Dugdale and Kibbey (1977). More detailed descriptions of the lessons are given in the lesson catalogs (Cohen and Glynn 1974; Dugdale and Kibbey 1975; Seiler and Weaver 1976).
2. S. Dugdale and P. Vogel, "PLATO Instruction for the Hearing Impaired," Proceedings of the Second International Learning Technology Congress and Exposition of the Society for Applied Learning Technology, Orlando, Fla., Feb. 15, 1978.
3. The idea of library lessons was originated by David Kibbey. The work was begun in 1973–74 and first reported by Robert B. Davis, then Director of the PLATO Mathematics Project, at the NATO Advanced Study Institute on Machine Representations of Knowledge Conference, Univ. of California, Santa Cruz, Cal., July 1975. The resulting paper was published in *Machine Representations of Knowledge* (Davis, Dugdale, Kibbey, and Weaver 1977).
4. Dugdale and Vogel, "PLATO Instruction for the Hearing Impaired."
5. C. S. Weaver and B. A. Seiler, "Computer Assistance in the Social Processes of Learning," Proceedings of the Association for the Development of Computer-Based Instruction Systems, Wilmington, Del., Feb. 1977.

Bibliography

Cohen, D., and G. Glynn. *Description of Graphing Strand Lessons*. Urbana, Ill.: CERL Publications, 1974.

Davis, R. B.; S. Dugdale; D. Kibbey; and C. Weaver. "Representing Knowledge about Mathematics for Computer-Aided Teaching: Part II—The Diversity of Roles That a Computer Can Play in Assisting Learning." In *Machine Representations of Knowledge*, edited by E. W. Elcock and D. Michie. Dordrecht, Netherlands: D. Reidel, 1977.

Dugdale, S., and D. Kibbey. *Elementary Mathematics with PLATO*. 2nd ed. Urbana, Ill.: CERL Publications, 1977.

Dugdale, S., and D. Kibbey. *The Fractions Curriculum of the PLATO Elementary Mathematics Project*. Urbana, Ill.: CERL Publications, 1975.

Seiler, B. A., and C. S. Weaver. *Description of PLATO Whole Number Arithmetic Lessons*. Urbana, Ill.: CERL Publications, 1976.

Smith, S. G., and B. A. Sherwood. "Educational Uses of the PLATO Computer System." *Science*, Apr. 23, 1976, pp. 344–52.

Television Programs as Socializing Agents for Mentally Retarded Children

STANLEY J. BARAN

Nearly three out of every 1000 school children are classified as trainably mentally retarded. Their IQs range from 30 to 50. That these children have retarded learning abilities is obvious. What is not so obvious are the other equally debilitating characteristics of mental retardation: poor personal and social adjustment,[1] impaired parental and family adjustment,[2] poor self-concept,[3] increased dependence.[4] The President's Committee on Mental Retardation (1973) put these problems into perspective: "In many cases, retarded mental development is not the major problem. The main factors blocking individual progress may be uncontrolled emotions, or negative self-image, or entrenched negative habits that are reinforced with repetition, or physical handicaps. These 'side effects' are often more inhibiting to development than mental retardation itself."[5]

Much recent special education research focuses on the use of television as a teaching tool for retarded children. Striefel noted that "the greatest potential of TV may be in programming the stimulus side of language or other training procedures."[6] Yoder used videotaped reinforcements to increase the rate of verbalization in retarded adolescent males.[7] Ross demonstrated "the efficacy of an audiovisual presentation for transmitting academic behaviors" to retarded children.[8] Others, such as Burkland and Spradlin, have added to this body of research.[9]

Television as an Agent of Social Learning

Research on the mentally retarded and television has dealt with television primarily as an instructional medium: television can be used to facilitate language acquisition, to teach motor skills, and so on. At the same time, though, research with nonretarded children has moved into the area of television as an agent of social learning. If instructional television programs can teach the retarded, what of television's more significant potential as a socializer?

Current research indicates that television can be successfully used to transmit various socialization information and attitudes to nonretarded individuals. Indeed, Bronfenbrenner has argued that children are ever-increasingly turning to their peers and television as their prime sources of such socializing information.[10] Little has been done, however, to apply what we know about television's impact to the socialization and adjustment of retarded children. There is some support for the deliberate use of television as a social learning medium for these special children.

Although retarded children have retarded learning capacities, the learning process and abilities available to a retarded child are the same as those of a nonretarded child of the same mental age. In Johnson's words:

> Most of the evidence . . . indicates that the mentally retarded learn in the same way as normal children, youth, and adults. The laws of learning that hold true for the normal also hold true for the mentally retarded. They are not slow learners in the sense that they comprehend slowly or grasp new concepts slowly or learn a skill slowly. The slowness is related to their rate of intellectual development. That is one of the prime determiners of when they will be able to comprehend, grasp a concept, or learn a skill.[11]

The large body of evidence concerning the ability of nonretarded children to learn from television, then, can logically be applied to the retarded population, allowing for equivalent mental ages in the two groups. The same processes of learning from television that

---

"Television Programs as Socializing Agents for Mentally Retarded Children," by Stanley J. Baran, *AV Communication Review* 1977, 25: 281–89. Reprinted by permission of the Association for Educational Communications & Technology.

have been so extensively demonstrated for nonretarded individuals would operate for retarded individuals.

Television and the Retarded

Baran argued that retarded children, because of their usual isolation from the every-day environment, "will learn the social behaviors of the televised models who may represent one of the very few sources from which to acquire social skills."[12] Baran and Meyer demonstrated that retarded children do indeed learn from the characters they see on TV shows.[13] What, then, might retarded youngsters learn from a specially designed series of programs, a series of programs created for and about retarded children?

The teaching potential of television and the learning abilities of special audiences, in this case retarded people, should be of great concern to special educators, parents, educational media people, audiovisual practitioners, television programmers, and others involved with learning through television programs. The acquisition of appropriate societal norms, the development of healthy self-concept, and so on are essential for individual development. If, as Baran and Meyer (1974) contend, television can effectively serve this end, efforts should be made to provide appropriate programming for retarded people and other special minorities who seem most in need of this service.[14]

Role of Parents in Effective Use of Television

Of additional importance to parents, educators, and media practitioners is the contention, often offered by commercial television programmers, that the burden of what and how a child learns from television should fall on the parents. Putting aside the merits or faults of such an argument, what is obvious is that the parent can indeed facilitate learning from television, particularly in the case of home viewing.

Reviewing the available pertinent literature, Baran demonstrated that parent intervention in the viewing situation could serve to augment television's ability to transmit prosocial behaviors and attitudes to the child viewer.[15] The works of Poulos and Liebert and Elliott and Vasta showed that the explanation and verbalization of another person concerning the reinforcement contingencies present in the demonstration of altruistic behaviors facilitated the modeling of those behaviors.[16] Would the presence of participating and commenting parents in the viewing situation increase the amount of learning and understanding of the retarded viewer? It would seem that this would be the case.

The Demonstration Project

The project reported here used specially prepared television dramas broadcast into the home in an attempt to demonstrate the medium's ability to transmit behaviors or skills and its ability to aid in the socialization of the child. For this examination, self-esteem was used to assess the socialization function. Rosenberg argued that an individual's self-concept is the major single "anchorage point" of a person's frames of reference into which new experiences or stimuli are assimilated.[17] As such, self-concept is a prime factor in the individual's socialization and development. And self-esteem is particularly appropriate in this case because of the well documented self-esteem problems of the mentally retarded.[18]

Procedure

While the development and the subsequent evaluation of this project's television programs were based on an examination of the existing literature, the effort to use broadcast television dramas in this manner was precedent setting. As such, no formal research hypotheses will be offered. What is presented are two general assertions:

1. A specially prepared series of television dramas can effect positive socialization changes in mentally handicapped children. (A standardized self-esteem measure and the children's perceptions of their abilities in a number of different skills was used to measure this effect.)
2. A program's prosocial potential can be maximized through the use of an adult interpreter. (The evaluation of the project allowed for a comparison of children who received different levels of parental intervention in the viewing situation.)

Four half-hour television dramas were written and produced.[19] These programs employed mentally retarded people as talent and depicted them in everyday, actual situations. One program dealt with these people at a dance and at a sheltered workshop; the second depicted two retarded children preparing for the Special Olympics; the third dealt with a trip downtown by a class of young retarded people; and the fourth presented a day at a typical school for the retarded. The programs were not documentaries. They were dramas in the sense that they presented plot, conflict, and resolution. The programs were then aired on a commercial television station on four successive weekday mornings.

Prior to the airings, 160 parent-child sets were enlisted from the ranks of the parents and children of the Cuyahoga County Board of Mental Retardation in Ohio. These parent-child sets were randomly assigned to one of four conditions: In the first, the parents were instructed to view with their children and to use the specially prepared workbook that was provided to generate discussion and interaction; in the second, the parents were instructed to watch the show with their children, but only to talk about the shows when asked by the child; in the third, parents were instructed to allow their children to watch alone; and, the fourth served as the control, with neither parent nor child viewing. The workbook consisted of specific discussion questions and topics for each program.

Just prior to the actual air dates, subjects received their specific instructions and, where applicable, their workbooks. During the airings, trained interviewers contacted the subjects' parents and arranged interview sessions for the 5-day period immediately following the last telecast. At these in-home interview sessions the children were presented with a series of standardized and specifically prepared questions.

After the data were collected, chi-square analyses were conducted to test for significant differences between children who viewed and those who did not and among children assigned to the four different parental-contact conditions.

Results

One hundred and forty-four completed interviews were collected, 72 from boys and 72 from girls. Of the four conditions, 29 children were in the first, 38 in the second, 37 in the third, and 40 in the control group. All subjects were classified as trainably mentally retarded. Sixteen children from the different conditions were excluded from the analysis because interviewer "probes" and requestioning demonstrated that these subjects did not really understand the questions and, therefore, were unable to provide useful or valid responses.

There was little evidence that viewing the programs resulted in higher self-esteem levels and heightened perceptions of abilities. Each subject was administered 20 items from Gordon's (1968) "How I See Myself" self-rating scales. Each child was interviewed in a face-to-face manner, with the interviewer reading each statement and recording the subject's yes or no response. The items chosen represented the Interpersonal Adequacy and Physical Appearance factors of Gordon's scale. The author stated that the results obtained from these 20 items provided a general assessment of the child's level of self-esteem.[20] In addition, 17 specific skills highlighted in the programs were offered one at a time to the children. The subjects were asked to rate their own abilities as either none at all, some, a little, or a lot.

Viewing or not viewing made no difference in any of the Gordon items (table 1) and in only one item on the skills list (table 2). More support was offered for the second argument, that parental involvement in the viewing situation would result in better self-esteem and skill responses. Three of the Gordon items showed significant differences (table 1) as did three of the skills items (table 2). Interestingly, going to the store (skill item 9), playing sports (skill item 16), and student-teacher interaction (Gordon item 10, "get along with teachers") were each the focal points of one of the programs.

Discussion

The data suggest the potential of a series of programs designed especially for mentally retarded persons to effect social learning. Most importantly, however, is the fact that the programs themselves seem to be insufficient agents in this process. The programs *plus* parent participation produced the changes that were evident in the two tables. Given the low intelligence and low attention span of the mentally retarded viewers, it is easy to understand that it is possible for the parent to play a significant role as "interpreter."

In the present examination, television was used as it has never before been used with this special audience. Virtually all of the pre-

TABLE 1
Chi-Square Analysis of Children's Responses on Gordon Items by Condition and Viewing

Item	What Condition (1, 2, 3 or 4)	View (yes or no)
1. I stay with something till I finish.	.25	.00
2. I like to work with others.	3.47	.00
3. I'm just the right height.	5.52	.71
4. I don't worry much.	.62	.00
5. My hair is nice looking.	2.76	.03
6. I play games very well.	5.60	.06
7. I'm just the right weight.	1.33	.28
8. The girls/boys like me a lot.	3.44	.04
9. My face is pretty/good looking.	5.29	.19
10. I get along well with teachers.	11.39*	.06
11. I feel very at ease, comfortable inside.	11.63*	1.37
12. I like to try new things.	2.01	.07
13. I can handle my feelings.	1.17	.24
14. I like the way I look.	3.76	.82
15. I'm very healthy.	2.28	.13
16. I'm very good at making things with my hands.	2.22	.10
17. I'm smarter than most of the others.	4.13	.07
18. My clothes are nice.	2.93	.22
19. I'm happy with the way I am.	8.33*	.94
20. I learn new things easily.	1.94	.00

*Significant chi-square values at at least the .05 level of confidence; $df = 3$ for the "what condition" analysis, and $df = 1$ for the "view" analysis.

vious research with retarded individuals employed instructional video materials; that is, specifically prepared, task-oriented software designed for presentation to one or a few children in an educational setting. The programs discussed here were actual television dramas presented to a large audience via home receivers. This afforded the programs the status of being "television," and it allowed for parental cooperation.

In both Gordon and the skills lists, parental help in the viewing situation resulted in significant differences on three items. While it might be argued that *only* three items in each list showed significant differences, two important facts must be remembered. First, as mentioned in the results section, several of those demonstrated differences dealt with items that specifically related to individual programs. That is, the programs seemed to work. Second, the series constituted only two hours out of a week, and for that matter, a lifetime of viewing for these children. That it effected the change that has been demonstrated is testimony to the efficacy of television programming as an agent of social learning in special audiences.

More dramatic effects might have been realized had the modeling of specific behavior by the children been measured. Past research, such as that mentioned in the exposition section of this report, however, has amply demonstrated television's ability to facilitate the acquisition of specific behaviors. What is of greater import to this examination and to the children themselves is television's impact on the socialization process. What do the retarded children come to see of themselves, of their environment, of their place in that environment? To measure such an effect is admittedly more difficult, but we should be encouraged that the series discussed did have some impact in the desired direction.

It should be emphasized that this study's

TABLE 2
Chi-Square Analysis of Children's Perceptions of Their Own Capabilities by Condition and Viewing

Skill	What Condition (1,2,3 or 4)	View (yes or no)
1. hobbies and crafts	11.65	3.92
2. dancing	8.60	4.54
3. telephoning	11.88	5.32
4. dressing self	5.26	1.02
5. feeding self	5.57	1.18
6. eating out	14.79	1.23
7. taking the bus	10.51	1.62
8. telling jokes	9.71	3.04
9. going to store by self	18.14*	1.06
10. swimming	13.83	4.03
11. using money	9.53	2.72
12. telling time	14.76	3.66
13. reading	13.78	5.15
14. writing	17.08*	9.51*
15. using a calendar	7.65	.53
16. playing sports	15.92*	3.13
17. getting along with others	6.23	.43

*Significant chi-square values at at least the .05 level of confidence. 9 degrees of freedom were recorded for the "what condition" analysis, 3 for the "view" analysis.

findings should not be viewed as limited. In light of the retarded child's typical life experiences of failure, rejection, and isolation and television's history of ignoring the retarded population, the results of this effort should be viewed as most encouraging.

Notes

1. G. M. Guthrie et al., "Non-Verbal Expressions of Self-Attitudes of Retardates," *American Journal of Mental Deficiency* 69 (1964): 42–49.
2. L. A. Fliegler and J. Hebeler, *A Study of the Structure of Attitudes of Parents of Educable Mentally Retarded Children and a Study of a Change in Attitude Structure* (Syracuse: Univ. Research Institute, 1960).
3. E. A. Lawrence and J. F. Winschel, "Self-Concept and the Retarded: Research and Issues," *Exceptional Children* 39 (1973): 310–19.
4. D. Ross, "Relationship between Dependency, Intentional Learning, and Incidental Learning in Preschool Children," *Journal of Personality and Social Psychology* 4 (1966): 374–81.
5. President's Committee on Mental Retardation, *MR 73/The Goal Is Freedom* (Washington: Govt. Print. Off., 1973), p. 3.
6. S. Striefel, "Television as a Language Training Medium with Retarded Children," *Mental Retardation* 10 (1972): 27–29.
7. D. E. Yoder, "Audience Control of Children's Vocal Behavior" (Ph.D. diss., Univ. of Kansas, 1965).
8. D. Ross, "Effect on Learning of Psychological Attachment to a Film Model," *American Journal of Mental Deficiency* 74 (1970): 701–7.
9. M. Burkland, "Use of Television to Study Articulatory Problems," *Journal of Speech and Hearing Disorders* 32 (1967): 80–81; J. E. Spradlin, "Environmental Factors and the Language Development of Retarded Children," in S. Rosenberg, ed., *Developments in Applied Psycholinguistic Research* (Riverside, N.J.: Macmillan, 1966).
10. U. Bronfenbrenner, *Two Worlds of Childhood* (New York: Russell Sage, 1970).
11. G. O. Johnson, "Psychological Characteristics of the Mentally Retarded," in W. Cruickshank, ed., *Psychology of Exceptional Children and Youth* (Englewood Cliffs, N.J.: Prentice-Hall, 1971), p. 505.
12. S. J. Baran, "TV and Social Learning in the Institutionalized MR," *Mental Retardation* 11 (1973): 36–38.
13. S. J. Baran and T. P. Meyer, "Retarded Children's Perceptions of Favorite Television Characters as Behavioral Models," *Mental Retardation* 13 (1975): 28–31.
14. S. J. Baran and T. P. Meyer, "Imitation and Identification: Two Compatible Approaches to Social Learning from the Electronic Media," *AV Communication Review* 22 (1974): 167–79.
15. S. J. Baran, "Television as Teacher of Prosocial Behavior: What the Research Says," *Public Telecommunications Reveiw* 2 (1974): 46–51.

16. R. W. Poulos and R. M. Liebert, "Influence of Modeling, Exhortive Verbalization and Surveillance on Children's Sharing," *Developmental Psychology* 6 (1972): 402–8; R. Elliott and R. Vasta, "The Modeling of Sharing: Effects Associated with Vicarious Reinforcement, Symbolization, Age, and Generalization," *Journal of Experimental Child Psychology* 10 (1970): 8–15.

17. M. Rosenberg, *Society and the Adolescent Self-Image* (Princeton: Princeton Univ. Pr., 1965).

18. Lawrence and Winschel, "Self-Concept and the Retarded."

19. Appreciation is expressed to the Cleveland Foundation for funding the programs and the subsequent research and to WEWS-TV, Scripps-Howard Broadcasting in Cleveland, for producing and airing the series.

20. I. J. Gordon, *How I See Myself, a Self-Rating Scale for Students* (Gainesville: Institute for Development of Human Resources, College of Education, Univ. of Florida, 1968).

Using Programs for Emotionally Disturbed Children in Mainstreamed or Special Class Settings

MAURICE J. ELIAS

The linkage between children's social and emotional functioning and their educational attainments is becoming increasingly apparent.[1] The implementation of P.L.94-142 has created a complex situation, in which the following events have occurred:

1. Mainstreamed children are being placed in classroom settings in which their differentness is accentuated and forms a potential barrier to adequate social adjustment.
2. Schools are mandated to provide more individualized and carefully documented programs for children, emphasizing a diverse array of academic skills.
3. Only the most severe forms of emotional disturbance seem to fall under the rubric of P.L.94-142, and the contingencies appear to be structured to discourage classification of children as emotionally handicapped.[2]

This situation results, as any sensitive educator realizes, in too little attention being directed toward the social and emotional needs of special education students and other students who must coexist in the same classrooms.[3] Teachers are caught in a difficult bind. Highly structured requirements for building academic skills often come at the expense of time, materials, and training to weaken the emotional barriers that are formidable obstacles to students' using their academic skills.

But the plight of our teachers reflects an overall reluctance within our educational systems to acknowledge the profound, formative, and lasting impact of school experiences on the lives of children and families.[4] While the 3 R's are, of course, important, an overemphasis on basic academic skills has resulted in educators not being adequately sensitized to critical aspects of the social and emotional growth of children. Interpersonal problems are frequently reasons for referral, without a full consideration of the message this conveys to the child and his or her family and of the coping model it provides for other

"Using Programs for Emotionally Disturbed Children in Mainstreamed or Special Class Settings." Permission to reprint this article has been granted by Maurice J. Elias, Ph.D., Dept. of Psychology, Rutgers University, New Brunswick, NJ 08903. The author should be contacted for additional information.

students in the class. This situation should not be surprising, since affective education and behavioral programs are numerous but rarely used and prospective teachers receive virtually no formal preparation in this area.[5]

Thus, the question is how to incorporate into our schools a greater emphasis on social and affective areas that will respect existing constraints while being flexible enough to be of value for diverse groups of children and adolescents. While this may seem like an insurmountable challenge, the following section contains ideas that can give direction to such efforts.

Promising Instructional Elements for Social-Emotional Programming

Six elements that characterize an educationally sound format for enhancing children's social and emotional development are described below.

1. Interpersonal interaction: Across the entire domain of approaches to working with children, a common theme is that direct interaction with children is the key to understanding them.[6] This applies not only to teachers learning about children, but children learning to care for, respect, and become sensitive to *each other*.
2. Television and other audiovisual media: Well-prepared television material is a uniquely effective instructional tool. It can motivate children, direct their attention, provide relevant sample material, and is easily recalled.[7] It meets nearly all of Gagné's criteria for essential features of instructional design.[8] Although parents and teachers have often lamented the things children "pick up" from television and films these media can be particularly effective with behaviorally and emotionally disturbed children.[9] The principal advantages of television are that the quality of material tends to be higher (thus providing fewer distractions); it is a more public medium than film, as it can be viewed with the lights on and others clearly present; and television materials will become increasingly accessible in years to come.
3. TVDRP: TVDRP is an abbreviation for television, discussion, and role playing (or other experiential activity). The research of Salomon and others has made the exciting finding that a combination of television and discussion of the televised material produces a synergistic effect that results in greater learning than one would expect from either medium alone or from an additive combination of the two.[10] Additional evidence suggests that moving further into the experiential realm, through puppet play, role play, drawing, writing, storytelling, or other activities, consolidates gains from "TV" and "D" and increases the likelihood of generalizability and transfer.[11]
4. Gradual exposure: One cannot obtain access to the genuine feelings and beliefs of a child or adolescent instantly; nor will a youngster usually make these personal disclosures in a direct and immediate way. TVDRP allows children and adolescents to become exposed to (a) televised (or film) versions of life situations that are relevant to them or (b) televised expressions of their beliefs, feelings, or concerns. There is a progression from seeing and hearing televised material, to talking about the televised events (with veiled references to personal concerns), to indirect expression of children's feelings through activities. Discussion leaders often find that, by carefully observing and listening to children during television viewing and discussion, much can be learned that few other outlets provide access to.
5. Continuity: A successful program is likely to be one that consistently reinforces and expands the skills it seeks to impart. Programs concerning social and emotional functioning often do not follow this educational principle. Rather, one presentation might be scheduled, with little follow up. TVDRP materials exist in abundance, and activities can be planned around them at all grade levels.

One particularly important example is that of mainstreamed children. At the beginning of each school year, these youngsters face the formidable task of gaining the acceptance of their peers. All too often, what these children in fact experience is rejection.[12] Table 1 presents selected materials around which programs could be developed at the start of each year to help classrooms function in a more cohesive and supportive manner from the outset. Anticipating difficulties and working to prevent

their developing, rather than waiting until problems become severe before acting, is clearly the better course.
6. Stimulate problem solving thinking: Whether one works with adults or children, an important goal is that participants learn process skills that can be applied across a variety of current and future situations. One important set of such skills is cognitive problem solving.[13] These skills include (a) understanding all participants' feelings and viewpoints in social situations, (b) determining one's goal in a particular situation, (c) considering a variety of alternative actions one can take, a variety of consequences to any action, and linking potential actions to consequences, (d) thinking through the steps one intends to take, including potential obstacles, (e) monitoring the outcome of one's actions for future reference, and (f) renewing one's problem-solving efforts in response to obstacles.[14] Techniques for eliciting participants' cognitive problem-solving skills primarily involve guiding through questions, prompting exchanges of ideas, and structuring discussions to gradually build the various skills; specific guidelines can be found in Elardo and Cooper; Elias, Bensky and Larcen (in preparation); Elias and Salvador (1980); and Spivack et al.[15] Practical and useful guidelines for the overall leading of various types of discussion groups are provided by Rose.[16]

Suggested Steps for TVDRP Development

The instructional elements described in the previous section and video materials such as those presented in table 1 are not particularly complex; however, they require the creativity and resourcefulness of program coordinators to bring out their considerable potential value. To help orient possible program coordinators such as special education teachers, media specialists, and school librarians, several steps that can lead to successful program development are outlined in table 2. Each step will be briefly discussed.

Defining the problem. A program might be requested in response to a variety of issues, including how to help mainstreamed children become more integrated into classroom routines, how to cope with predelinquent

TABLE 1
Materials to Promote Effective Mainstreaming

Age Level:	Primary	Intermediate	Junior High	Senior High
Format: Television[a] Series Titles:[b]	All About You Ripples*	Inside/Out* Tradeoffs*	Self Incorporated* Bread and Butterflies*	Watch Your Mouth (entire) On the Level*
	Under the Blue Umbrella Vegetable Soup II (entire)	Bread and Butterflies* Vegetable Soup II (entire)		
Format: Film[c] Film Titles:	Ugly Duckling	That's My Name— Don't Wear It Out!	That's My Name . . . Skating Rink	That's My Name . . . They Call Me Names Like Other People Skating Rink

NOTE: Materials available in a variety of formats are marked with an asterisk.
  [a] Compiled by examining the 1979–1980 Teachers' Manuals of the Educational Services Division of New Jersey Public Television.
  [b] Selected programs within each series are most appropriate and can be provided upon request.
  [c] Compiled by examining *Human Relationship and Values: A Guide to Films*. From the University of Michigan Audio-Visual Education Center.

behaviors in the classroom, or how to keep emotionally disturbed children from disrupting classroom routines.

TABLE 2
Process of Developing TVDRP-Based Programs[a]

1. What problem is being addressed?
2. What are the goals of the program?
   a. skills to be developed
   b. problem behaviors to be reduced
3. Who will receive the program?
   a. direct or indirect approach
   b. regular education class, special education class, selected groups
4. What video materials are available?[b]
   a. Instructional or educational television divisions of state public television system
   b. Materials centers of state departments of education or children and adolescent services
   c. Local university or community college instructional television department
   d. Agency for instructional television audiovisual materials catalogue
   e. National Center for Educational Materials and Media for the Handicapped (NCEMMH)
   f. Psychological Cinema Register
   g. University of Michigan Audio-Visual Education Center
5. What support materials are available, and what will be needed?
   a. program guides
   b. discussion guides
   c. availability of programs for preview
   d. discussion questions
   e. materials for role play or other activities
   f. training of discussion leaders
6. What structure and format can the program take?
   a. when will it begin
   b. what time will it occur
   c. how long per session
   d. how frequent will sessions be
   e. over what period of time
   f. will it be repeated and if so, when
7. What other resources are available?
   a. space
   b. equipment
   c. money
   d. discussion leaders
8. How will the usefulness of the program and follow-through with the program be monitored?
   a. attainment of goals (short- and long-term)
   b. satisfaction of program recipients
   c. informal communications

[a] Television, discussion, and role playing and other activities.
[b] Addresses provided in Appendix.

Goals. Goals should be as specific as possible, and tied to the behaviors that prompted the request for a program. Both strengths to be built and deficits to be reduced should be considered, as well as whether the goals of the program are concerned with specific children or behavior in larger units, such as classrooms, lunchrooms, and school yards.

Recipients. A key programming decision involves the approach to meeting program goals. Which children are the ultimate focus of the program, and where will they be reached: in a regular or special classroom, or will they be removed from class to form special groups? Examples of such groups include children who are (a) severely emotionally disturbed, (b) mainstreamed, (c) pregnant and unmarried, (d) in families undergoing separation or divorce, or (e) at risk for vocational difficulty due to academic and/or social handicaps. Will these children directly receive the TVDRP program, or will TVDRP be used indirectly, to train teachers, aides, bus drivers, parents, or administrators to work more effectively with such children?

Also important is the developmental status of program recipients to allow a proper matching of materials to capabilities. Common groupings in resource lists include preschool, primary (grades K to 2), intermediate (3 to 5), junior high (6 to 8), senior high, college, adult, paraprofessional, and professional.

Video materials. The general strategy is to survey available materials with the goal of securing relevant items that afford greatest flexibility of usage for the lowest cost. Public television stations broadcast a wealth of useful materials, but there is low flexibility. However, many programs can be videotaped off the air or, in some cases, dubbed onto blank videotapes or cassettes for a nominal fee. Contact your local station for guidelines and assistance. This public education clearinghouse role is also undertaken by local, regional, or state materials centers associated with state education and children and youth-serving agencies and by many universities and community colleges. Materials can also be identified, purchased, or rented from sources listed in table 2. The most specific advice one can give is to monitor the availability of a variety of video materials and then, depending on program needs and resources, make the most feasible arrangements. Keeping an ongoing file of video materials cross-indexed by, for example, developmental status, target group, and type of social or emotional issue addressed is an important step in program development.

Support materials. For many video series, program synopses, scripts, or discussions and activity guides are available. Often, examination copies can be obtained on an approval basis, thus aiding in the selection of materials. Public television stations and universities and colleges can be of particular help in obtaining copies or addresses for making inquiries. Other support materials may be required for experiential activities or for training purposes, especially for indirect program approaches. These materials must of course be readied before a particular TVDRP program commences.

Structure and format. The considerations listed in table 2 unfortunately most often take the form of constraints. Thus, the program will likely have to fit some limited slot and format, and timing considerations may make obtaining the most desirable materials impossible. Programmers will have to be flexible and also a bit political and assertive, to ensure they are not taken advantage of and thrust into impossible situations. The optimal solution is for schools to develop prepared programs for (a) situations that commonly recur, such as helping teachers cope with behavioral difficulties, or (b) social and emotional skill-building that will occur every year, such as programs to help junior-high and high-school children clarify their vocational choices or learn to cope with peer pressure. These programs can perhaps find fixed places in the school schedule. Gradually, there can be sharing across schools and across school systems, and perhaps state and federal-level administrators within departments of education will support the formation of clearinghouses, or at least the sharing of materials. In most states, educational policy toward media usage has been woefully neglectful. However, that can change as the number of local media users grows.

Other resources. The type of TVDRP program that can be developed also depends in part on the availability of space, equipment and discussion leaders. But the critical point is that there is a TVDRP program than *can* be implemented to fit almost any set of circumstances. Special education teachers, media specialists, and school librarians can take a leadership role in ensuring that needed programs are available, and that the powerful instructional tool of TVDRP is employed. Where TVDRP advocates have persisted, school systems have often come to highly value, if not rely on, the programs they have provided.

Monitoring. Especially in the early stages of TVDRP use, it will be important to monitor user reactions and make necessary program modifications. Perhaps the video materials were inappropriate; perhaps discussions should have been more structured; perhaps puppet play should have been used instead of role play; perhaps the simulation exercises were not realistic enough. Each program is a step on the road toward a more effective program, and monitoring provides the information that allows careful refinement and improvement.

A Sample Compilation of Television and Film Resources

The task of developing an inventory of video resources may seem prohibitive at first. However, if one has in mind the topic or issue around which materials are needed, the format(s) one has access to, and the recipients of the program, the task can be quite manageable. Consider first the specific topic of facilitating group cooperation and understanding within mainstreamed classrooms. As indicated in table 1, the resources listed therein were compiled after consulting only two possible sources (see table 2). Next, consider the wider topic of family life education and coping with common life crises. Programs on some or all aspects of this topic are relevant for regular and special education settings at various grade levels, teachers and other professionals and paraprofessionals in training, and parent groups. A sample of relevant materials, drawn from the same sources as table 1, can be found in table 3.

The actual mechanics of compiling such lists are no more difficult than writing or calling to obtain the relevant catalogs and, armed with pencils, pads, and index cards, reading the summaries of the materials and noting the topic, recipient age, formats, and sources for obtaining them. In many cases, video as well as written support materials are available for preview, and one can begin to develop preferred materials for particular purposes.

A Sample TVDRP Program

Adding the discussion and activities components to video materials may be more

TABLE 3
Materials for Selected Topics in Family Life Education and Coping with Life Crises

Topic	Title	Series[a] Code	Format[b]	Recipients[c]
Parenthood	Two to Get Ready	Fs	v	s
	What's Cookin'?	Fs	v	s
	Adapting to Parenthood	na	f	s
	Growing Up Together: Four Teen Mothers and Babies	na	f	s
	Everybody Rides the Carousel	na	f	s
Child Management and Development	Home Sweet Home	I/O	v,f	i
	Spare the Rod	Fs	v	s
	I Love You When You're Good	Fs	v	s
	No Comparison	Fs	v	s
	True Blue	Fs	v	s
	Hairy Scary	Fs	v	s
	Everybody Rides the Carousel	na	f	s
	Parents and Children: A Positive Approach to Child Management	Rp	v,f	s
	Behavioral Principles for Parents	Rp	v,f	s
Caring for a Handicapped Child	It Feels Like You're Left Out of the World	na	f	s
	I'll Dance at Your Wedding	Fs	v	s
Relocation	Lost Is a Feeling	I/O	v,f	p,i
	Travelin Shoes	I/O	v,f	i
	New Kid on the Block	Fs	v	s
Adolescence				
a. General	Self Incorporated	All	v,f	j
	Then One Year	na	f	i,j
	Rookie of the Year	na	f	i,j,s
	Everybody Rides the Carousel	na	f	s
	On the Level	All	v,f	s
b. Career Choice	When I Grow Up	All	v,f	p
	It's Time to Go to Work	Ubu	v,f	p
	It's Payday	Ubu	v,f	p
	Freestyle	All	v	i
	Bread and Butterflies	All	v,f	i,j
	On the Level	Sel	v,f	s
c. Alcohol and Drugs	Jackson Junior High	All	v	i,j
	Dial A-L-C-O-H-O-L	All	v	s
	Alcohol, Drugs, or Alternatives	na	f	s
Separation and Divorce	Breakup	I/O	v,f	i
	Me and Dad's New Wife	na	f	i,j,s
	Love Me and Leave Me	Fs	v	s
	First Signs of April	Fs	v	s
	Tightrope	Fs	v	s
	There Comes a Time	Fs	v	s
	Children of Our Time	na	f	s
Death and Dying	And We Were Sad, Remember?	Fs	v	p,i,j,s
	In My Memory	I/O	v,f	i
	The Day Grandpa Died	na	f	i,j
	Where Is Dead?	na	f	i,j,s
	You See, I've Had a Life	na	f	j,s

NOTE: All materials are appropriate for in-service training of professionals and paraprofessionals, for use with college students, and for workshops with parent groups.

[a] Fs = Footsteps; I/O = Inside/Out; na = not part of a series; Rp = Research Press; All = title refers to an entire series; Ubu = Under the Blue Umbrella; Sel = selected programs.
[b] v = video; f = film.
[c] p = primary; i = intermediate or older elementary; j = junior high school; s = senior high school.

or less arduous, depending on the written support resources and group leader skills available to program coordinators. In many settings, persons can be found with the skills to aid program development. Other times, consultants from local community mental health centers, universities and colleges, or public television stations can assist in the development of program structure and support materials.

I had the opportunity to work in a consultative way with a special education setting for emotionally and academically handicapped boys. The general purposes of the program I was to develop were to increase prosocial behaviors and reduce emotional blockages to learning. I surveyed available video materials and found the "Inside/Out" series to be most appropriate and accessible.[17] The series was videotaped off the air by school personnel so it could be shown at times convenient to particular teachers. Program constraints called for a five-week program with two sessions per week. Thus, ten videotapes were selected, depicting children between the ages of 8 and 12 coping with a variety of relevant problem situations. Table 4 contains summaries of the videotapes used. One videotape was presented per session and was followed by discussions led by the boys' classroom teachers, using materials developed for them.

Following the intervention, it was found that boys undergoing training showed more statistically reliable improvement in social approach behavior, emotional control and personality functioning, and self-reliant learning behaviors than an equivalent group of boys not undergoing training. Two months after training, these gains were maintained and in fact generalized to behavior in residential settings. A full description of the project and the training materials used by teachers are available.[18] Also noteworthy is that a similar program carried out in a regular education setting led to meaningful improvements in trained children's cognitive problem solving skills.[19]

Programs such as the "Inside/Out" project can be of considerable value to both children and staff. The task of taking the lead in developing such programs for persons who are too beleaguered to begin the work themselves is very rewarding, and soon becomes a cooperative venture once the potential benefits are realized.

TABLE 4
Videotapes from the "Inside/Out" Project

Lesson #1: How Do You Show?
   This is a program about three boys and how they feel about what happens to them one day.
Lesson #2: Lost Is a Feeling
   This is a program about a boy who leaves his home and goes to a new place.
Lesson #3: Just Joking
   This program is about a boy who likes to play tricks on other people.
Lesson #4: But They Might Laugh
   This program is about how children deal with being embarrassed and with failing in things.
Lesson #5: Home Sweet Home
   This program is about two boys who feel their parents are not treating them well.
Lesson #6: Must I/May I
   This is a program about children who do not want to be told what to do, but also have to learn responsibility.
Lesson #7: I Dare You
   This is a program about what can happen, and how one feels, when peers pressure a child to do something dangerous.
Lesson #8: Getting Even
   This is a program about how children feel and what they do when other children do not want them in a group.
Lesson #9: Bully
   This is a program about a boy who bullies other boys.
Lesson #10: Yes I Can
   This is a program about how children can help themselves be happy and how good things can happen if they keep trying and work toward them.

Summary

The guidelines provided here are intended to bring to the reader's attention a powerful instructional tool, TVDRP, whose capabilities can be harnessed with only modest effort. Because of the uniqueness of educational settings and the complexity of social and emotional processes in regular and special education children, few set "packages" are broadly applicable. However, dedicated persons can use the TVDRP approach to develop programs that are appropriate for their particular settings. Once in operation, these programs can meaningfully improve the outlook for children who are difficult to reach through traditional educational techniques.

Appendix

Listing of Nationally Available Video Resources
1. *Agency for Instructional Television (AIT)*
   a. Headquarters and Midwest Office: (for AIT *Catalogue* and *Newsletter*)
      Box A
      Bloomington, IN 47402
      812-339-2203
   b. Eastern Office:
      Suite 421
      Reston International Center
      11800 Sunrise Valley Drive
      Reston, VA 22091
      703-860-4445
   c. Southern Office:
      Suite 110
      333 Sandy Springs Circle, N.E.
      Atlanta, GA 30328
      404-252-6525
   d. Western Office:
      Suite 108
      1660 S. Amphlett Blvd.
      San Mateo, CA 94402
      415-574-3437

2. *National Center for Educational Media and Materials for the Handicapped (NCEMMH)*
   Ohio State University
   Columbus, OH 43210
   614-422-7596

3. *Psychological Cinema Register (PCR): Films in the Behavioral Sciences (1978 Catalogue and 1980 Supplement)*
   Audio Visual Services
   Pennsylvania State University
   University Park, PA 16802
   814-865-6314

4. *Human Relationships and Values: A Guide to Films (1978)*
   Audio-Visual Education Center
   University of Michigan
   416 Fourth Street
   Ann Arbor, MI 48109
   313-764-5360

5. *Research Press Films*
   Box 317740
   Champaign, IL 61820
   217-352-3273

Notes

1. J. C. Abrams and F. Kaslow, "Family Systems and the Learning Disabled Child: Intervention and Treatment," *Journal of Learning Disabilities* 10 (1977): 86–90.
2. J. M. Kauffman, "Where Special Education for Disturbed Children Is Going: A Personal View," *Exceptional Children* 46 (1980): 522–29.
3. Y. Leyser and J. Gottlieb, "Improving the Social Status of Rejected Pupils," *Exceptional Children* 46 (1980): 459–61.
4. E. M. Bower, "Education as a Humanizing Process and Its Relationship to Other Humanizing Processes," in S. E. Golann and C. Eisdorfer, eds., *Handbook of Community Mental Health* (New York: Appleton, 1972); U. Bronfenbrenner, "Contexts of Child Rearing: Problems and Prospects," *American Psychologist* 34 (1979): 844–50.
5. M. M. Ravlin and W. G. Morse, *A Resource Guide to Affective/Behavioral Science Education* (Ann Arbor, Mich.: Washtenaw County Community Mental Health Center, 1977).
6. C. Schaefer, *How to Influence Children* (New York: Van Nostrand Reinhold, 1978).
7. H. Lesser, *Television and the Preschool Child: A Psychological Theory of Instruction and Curriculum Development* (New York: Academic Pr., 1977).
8. R. M. Gagné, *The Conditions of Learning*, 2nd ed. (New York: Holt, 1975).
9. M. J. Elias, *Affective Television in the Special Education Environment: The Use of "Inside/Out" with Learning Disabled and Emotionally Handicapped Boys* (Bloomington, Ind.: Agency for Instructional Television, 1978).
10. G. Salomon, *Interaction of Media, Cognition, and Learning* (San Francisco: Jossey-Bass, 1979).
11. A. Goldstein, K. Heller, and L. Sechrest, *Psychotherapy and the Psychology of Behavior Change* (New York: Wiley, 1966); D. Meichenbaum, *Cognitive-Behavior Modification: An Integrative Approach* (New York: Plenum, 1977).
12. Leyser and Gottlieb, "Improving the Social Status of Rejected Pupils."
13. G. Spivack, J. J. Platt, and M. B. Shure, *The Problem Solving Approach to Adjustment* (San Francisco: Jossey-Bass, 1976).
14. M. J. Elias, "Promising Strategies for Enhancing Children's Social-Cognitive and Emotional Development" (Paper presented at the annual meeting of the American Psychological Assn., New York City, Sept. 1979).
15. P. Elardo and M. Cooper, *AWARE: Activities for Social Development* (Reading, Mass.: Addison-Wesley, 1977); M. J. Elias, J. M. Bensky, and S. W. Larcen, *Problem Solve It! A Training Manual for Educators, Parents, and Other Persons Working with Children* (in preparation); M. J. Elias and C. A. Salvador, *Using "Inside/Out" as an Affective Education and Social Problem Solving Thinking Program*, rev. ed. (New Brunswick, N.J.: Rutgers

Univ., 1980); Spivack, Platt, and Shure, *Problem Solving Approach*.

16. R. W. Poulos and R. M. Liebert, "Influence of Modeling, Exhortive Verbalization and Surveillance on Children's Sharing," *Developmental Psychology* 6 (1972): 402–8; R. Elliott and R. Vasta, "The Modeling of Sharing: Effects Associated with Vicarious Reinforcement, Symbolization, Age, and Generalization," *Journal of Experimental Child Psychology* 10 (1970): 8–15.

17. *Inside/Out: A Guide for Teachers* (Bloomington, Ind.: Agency for Instructional Television, 1973).

18. Elias, *Affective Television in the Special Education Environment*; Elias and Salvador, *Using "Inside/Out."*

19. Elias, "Promising Strategies."

5
Program

The library is not a warehouse, nor a storehouse, nor even a treasure house of information—at least not exclusively. The resources it contains are only one component in the equation that defines its function. The patron, or potential patron, is the other key element and the program the means by which the two are profitably and pleasurably united.

To bring about this union, libraries must initiate and maintain several kinds of activities and advertise these to the community. It is essential that all those people who seek knowledge or diversion be informed of the scope of the holdings, of the breadth and depth of the collection as well as those specific components within it. Professional staff will need to prepare and circulate bibliographies, thereby responding to anticipated as well as declared information needs—in the process even creating a consciousness about the library's potential to answer inquiries.

The reference function is not restricted to directing readers to likely sources of information, but includes helping them frame appropriate questions, select potentially fruitful resources, make more efficient use of the materials chosen, and even interpret and suggest ways to effectively report their findings.

Librarians, particularly those in a school or public setting, also acknowledge their responsibility to help youngsters achieve literacy, learn to know and enjoy literature, and become judicious and informed selectors of their own reading matter. Introduction to the various genres and to individual titles is often achieved through storytelling sessions, poetry readings, puppet shows and the like. Libraries also may react to individuals with a planned agenda for reading guidance as well as by making spontaneous suggestions.

The library media center is frequently the site of bibliophilic activities. Authors, illustrators, and poets may be invited to meet directly with readers to amplify or interpret their vision. Conference calls can be arranged or correspondence between writers and their readers encouraged and the results displayed for the enjoyment of a wider audience. Some media centers even assist youngsters in making their own books which are subsequently added to the general collection. Student reviews can be made available featuring analytical reading and reporting by in-house juvenile critics, fostering emulation in others.

Student assistants, in addition to providing needed services for the professional staff, may derive many benefits from their experiences. There are numerous opportunities to develop academic, organizational, and interpersonal skills. Even more important are the encounters with literary, reference, and recreational materials that can be structured into the work routines of library club members.

Institutional and school libraries have objectives consistent with those of the parent agency. Cooperative planning with faculty and staff can ensure that materials will be made available and experiences planned to achieve mutual goals. Public libraries often seek a similar relationship with the communities they serve so that concerns of the citizens can be researched and expressed in a nonpartisan, open forum.

Much of the librarians' energy is directed toward increasing usage by patrons who are underutilizing resources and extending service to those who are unaware of the library's potential for enriching their lives. All people seek information or recreation but some never consider tapping the library's capability for addressing these problems. Others have unacknowledged needs, in which event the library's awareness programs must start on an even more basic level. Implicit in the realization of a democratic society is an enlightened citizenry. Once formal schooling is finished, the library becomes the premier agency through which education can most readily continue.

The question facing the mainstreamed library is how can its present programs be extended to include exceptional patrons. Those users who have been excluded in the past may be unaware of the ways in which the library can affect so many facets of their lives. Many disabled individuals may have valid concerns about their ability to function in this new environment. The mainstreamed library's mandates must be to aggressively seek out this new clientele, describe the scope of the holdings, specify the kinds of services available, articulate the nature of the support activities that facilitate utilization, detail procedures for securing services, and explain the channels through which assistance or guidance can be arranged.

Librarians will have to adapt certain components of regular programs to include this new population. They may have to alter the composition of the collection, adapt procedures, modify the environment, arrange new communication modes or even rethink their goals. The professional staff may begin by analyzing activities to see which have impediments in their present form. They need to then identify exclusionary factors which can be redesigned so as to maximize participation. Special bibliographies may have to be prepared that indicate formats on which data can be made available, e.g., large print, Talking Books, etc. Special acoustically controlled areas may have to be provided for notetaking or recording information so that neither the exceptional patron nor other users are inconvenienced. Storytellers will discover that signing as well as reciting stories can extend the rich literary experience to children with hearing impairments. Reference activities should be redesigned to include users with blocked communication and those physically unable to either come to the library or manage the resources within it. Those aspects of a data search usually carried out by the individual patron then become, in some few instances, part of the responsibility of the staff.

In addition, librarians should deliberately and specifically design activities to include integrated groups of disabled and nonimpaired users. The professional staff may determine to take an active, assertive role in the mainstreaming process. That is, compliance with the social goal of mainstreaming is seen by the concerned and activist librarian as implementation of the spirit as well as the letter of the law.

In any setting, it is easy to confuse process with purpose, focusing on how things have traditionally been done rather than on ultimate goals. Authors in this section have looked at the functions libraries must serve and suggested alternative routes to achieve their objectives. They have examined the various elements of standard library programming, analyzed the ability of institutions to respond to the specialized requirements of exceptional patrons and suggested areas where adaptations could profitably be made. We not only offer their specific suggestions for emulation or adaptation, but endorse the models of imaginative, flexible, enthusiastic response they reflect.

In a wide ranging report, Kramer demonstrates that poetry is a therapeutic, restorative, exciting medium of communication for people with the severest kinds of impairments. He notes that disability isolates individuals, allowing competencies to atrophy, thereby reducing opportunities for self-expression and interpersonal exchange. He has discovered that poetry offers a means whereby all persons from the very young to the elderly, institutionalized or those living independent, sometimes solitary lives, can identify, articulate, and release their feelings. Kramer discusses specific poems, how they were used, what responses they elicited and which elements in poetry precipitated particular reactions. No formula is offered here, but rather a brief glimpse into the limitless potential of the genre. The crucial role of the library is stressed: its atmosphere, ambience, and symbolic meaning adding dignity and importance to the sessions. The library, the site of choice, supported a relationship among the participants that strongly contrasted with the conditions of control, confinement, restriction, and dependence that characterized their former environments.

Major zeroes in on the particular needs of blind and partially sighted college students for library services. She reports on a survey of visually impaired students at Ohio State University that solicited responses about the quality of services and equipment available to them. As a result, a five-point list on recommendations to guide academic libraries in serving this population is offered which addresses such issues as defining the needs of this group, selecting equipment, providing access to information in a variety of formats, obtaining essential services from outside the university, and special allocation of space and staff assignment for this work.

Selvin, a professor who is blind, speaks from the perspective of a heavy and sophisticated user of library services. He points out components of the system that he has found deficient and proposes changes which would extend the usefulness of present practices. He identifies some areas in which he feels poor decisions have been made, criticizes delays in provisions of material, suggests adaptations in technology that would upgrade services and proposes changes in the policies and procedures of agencies to make them more sensitive to the needs of blind patrons.

In the education of the gifted, books take on added importance because they serve a variety of purposes in a learning project. Tennant's model, for example, shows what the purposes might be and Smith proposes that Tennant's model be used as the basis for programming for gifted youngsters. Smith examines Tennant's areas of content, process, output, and evaluation and suggests ways in which library media specialists can adapt their materials for each area so that the gifted youngster is fittingly challenged. Further, Smith outlines the knowledge and skills that professionals must acquire if such a program is to flourish.

In a thoughtful and provocative article, Matthews offers some proposals for restructuring programming for children in institutional libraries. She analyzes the effects illness and institutionalization have on the development of children and proposes that library programs can respond to the resultant problems while at the same time supporting each individual's unique habilitation goals. Activities must be individually designed to correlate with the student's present level of functioning and propel him or her to the next stage. To achieve that objective, Matthews counsels that a reorganization may be unavoidable. The library is classically considered a useful but complementary part of the educational program of the institution which houses it but its active potential is often unrealized. This perception may be too confining, since, in devising creative ways to respond to this expanded audience, professionals using the collection have given ample proof that conventional beliefs about library programs unduly limit and underestimate library potential.

Adults who are dependent because of disability or institutionalization have a wide array of information needs but are restricted in their ability to satisfy them. Lucas laments the generally inadequate response to this group, noting particularly the problems of inattention, tight-fisted funding, and censorship. She points out that there are types of problems common to this diverse population that must be addressed and focuses on the necessity for defining standards, identifying library responsibility and interlibrary cooperation, and exploring the implications of mainstreaming a population with highly restricted direct access to information sources.

The child with a severe hearing impairment has communication difficulties that often include a restricted vocabulary, a fuzzy grasp of syntactical rules, and confusion about idiomatic expressions. These factors must be taken into account when planning library programs for them. Metcalf suggests specific ways to adapt storytelling experiences, and instruction in library skills and reading guidance to maximize learning and pleasure for individuals with auditory deficits.

Gerber and Harris report that developmentally disabled children frequently have inadequate social skills. They see this lack as a serious impediment to successful mainstreaming and propose that books may be a prime remediative tool. Criteria for selecting titles useful in improving socialization and techniques for using both pictures and text to help children identify and interpret facial expressions, body language, social dynamics, and social response are detailed.

Assumptions that learning disabilities will automatically be remediated before youngsters reach high school age are unwarranted since many problems persist or are insufficiently controlled. Secondary school students are highly sensitive to any designated status that separates them from their peers and hence more apt to disguise their special needs. Becker reviews the areas in which problems are most apt to emerge and proposes policies and procedures for materials centers which can help in the academic growth, skills development and socialization of children with specific learning disabilities. She also gives suggestions for facilitating the functioning of those adolescents in the library setting.

Dain briefly looks at the particular needs of emotionally dysfunctional youngsters for a supportive library program. For these behaviorally disordered and academically deficient children, story hours offer a unique opportunity for socialization, language development, and learning. This brief report from a British librarian mirrors the experiences of her American counterparts who are working to provide support for youngsters with similar problems.

Wallick and Carter address the problems of youngsters whose impairments are of such a nature that they are often automatically assumed to be outside the responsibility of library service. Carter describes an innovative, highly successful program she developed for adolescent trainable retarded students. She defines how traditional components of library service must be adapted to the particular needs of this population and shows how behaviors in the library correlate with and reinforce specific academic goals. Of particular interest is her inclusion of these youngsters as library assistants in an "integrated" staff. She demonstrates how flexibility and ingenuity can be combined to engender opportunities for those once routinely excluded from certain experiences.

Wallick describes how stories were used in the treatment of an autistic child. Through the medium of a case study, she details how books and ultimately other media were instrumental in the therapy, socialization, and cognitive and affective development of a youngster with severe and extensive behavior problems. Although certainly a nonstandard approach, such intervention is illustrative of how titles can be used in new and imaginative ways to improve the lives of exceptional persons.

These contributors, who deal with a variety of age groups, impairments, and objectives, all share at least one common perspective: they envision the library as playing an active role in serving the individual with special needs and have proposed administrative or programmatic strategies to implement such a philosophy. Their enthusiasm and successes should provide not only viable models but the inspiration to extend such programs to other unserved or underserved individuals with exceptional library needs.

The Banquet Is Ours

AARON KRAMER

For poetry programs involving the handicapped, libraries can be a powerful ally. The greatest element of that power is the aura of the library itself, an aura that sets off unmistakable vibrations. For several years the New York Guild for the Jewish Blind hosted a poetry discussion group. As members left the noises and smells of the cafeteria or the bustle of the workroom and made their way upstairs to the place of books, an anticipatory calm seemed to envelop them. Taking their accustomed seats around the long table, they exchanged muted greetings. For an hour and a half, with total concentration and mutual acceptance, discussions ranged over world history, geography, and culture. Perhaps over the years these people might have developed sufficient inner discipline to interact even in a boiler room; but what had initiated and reinforced their learning spirit was a new factor.

Two very different situations have provided dramatic proof of this aura. Hillside Hospital, a voluntary psychiatric facility in Glen Oaks, N.Y., was experimental enough in its orientation to encourage a pioneering poetry program. Each month a new aspect of poetry received focus. In the third year, however, a change of hospital leadership took place; the monthly sessions were treated cavalierly by the new officials. Meeting times were not properly fixed and publicized; meeting rooms were not always assigned. The group was forced to become flexible, inventive, and tolerant of the intolerable—meeting wherever possible: the gym, the lawn, the cafeteria, the library. After a struggle each session succeeded; but the few *library* meetings automatically raised the level of comment and receptivity. Participants seemed to take themselves more seriously—as poets and listeners—in the room of Shakespeare, Homer, and Dante. Whenever they occupied that room, there was a sense of belonging there, of a hospitality toward their love for the well-chosen word.

For eight years a poetry program thrived at Central Islip State Hospital, a Long Island psychiatric center. Under the stimulus of weekly sessions, involving college students and predominantly adolescent patients, the participants produced a volume of original poems, *Long Night's Journey Back to Light*. Its publication, widely noted, was celebrated first at the college, then at the hospital, where a regular weekly session was followed by festivities upstairs in the library. The librarian had rearranged the room so that forty people could sit comfortably in a circle. Heightening the sense of self and occasion, the hospital director joined in welcoming and congratulating them. That quiet, familiar setting made it comfortable for even the shyest poets to read their work aloud—not as discussion entries before a private group but as published literature in a public forum. On behalf of the hospital (as on behalf of the college a week earlier) the librarian thankfully accepted three copies of their copyrighted volume to be processed and placed on the shelves of the very room which had for years been their withdrawal nook, their safety valve.

A second vital ingredient is the librarian. Often it has been the librarian who arranged for the poet-therapist's visit and coordinated the day's activities. When the Hawthorne School for Emotionally Disturbed Children opened its new library, the significance of that event was emphasized by bringing three authors to the Westchester County facility: a husband-wife team (writers of science juveniles) and a published poet. The librarian not only created a mood of anticipation by acquiring and exhibiting their books, but goaded the English department into offering a two-week poetry unit that culminated in the writing of original poems.

The major event of the day was held in the auditorium. After the science-writers lectured, the poet read—first his own work, then the three prizewinners, explaining his choices and calling forward the authors to accept ovations from their classmates. The explosive potential of the spoken word overwhelmed these supposedly "cool," "tough" children—especially when they realized that the expressive gift is universal, finding a source even in their own underestimated peers.

Attendance at the dedication ceremonies

that followed was voluntary, since the regular school day had ended. The staff was amazed by the huge number of students who stayed. The library was jammed; fervor filled the air. After the speeches, many lingered to ask about the authors' subject areas as well as the technical intricacies of writing and of achieving publication. Clearly, they had familiarized themselves with the books displayed during the past two weeks. Several whose poems had not been singled out asked for comments; in that intimate setting one could comfortably point out their strengths and weaknesses. Thanks to an imaginative librarian, the students of Hawthorne felt from its inaugural day that this was *their* wing of the institution, that a library can be more than some rows of assigned books and a No Smoking or Be Quiet sign.

In a Brooklyn secondary school, many of whose students were several years below grade level and (according to a guidance counselor) plagued by severe emotional, psychological, and drug-related problems, the librarian played an equally dynamic role. Desperate over the disuse of her facility (other than for an occasional term paper or required book report), she sought ways of bringing the written word dramatically into her students' lives. Through her initiative and with her support, a Poetry Day was organized. First, coordinated with the announcement of the poet's visit, every English teacher agreed to introduce poetry—a hitherto ignored genre—into the classroom. This meant a scurrying to the library by the teachers themselves for whatever source materials might help introduce them to poetry and to the methods of presenting it. Some encouraged their students to sample not only the few volumes of poetry on the shelves, but also those in the severely underutilized neighborhood library, and to bring their discoveries into the classroom for general discussion. Ultimately every child produced one or more poems.

The best of these became the highlight of the auditorium program. After reading them, the guest poet explained his admiration for each and called the poets forward to be honored. What happened next was an innovation made possible by the flexibility of the school authorities. Two groups of about eighty each, who had been especially enthusiastic during the previous weeks, were excused from their schedules in order to attend double-period poetry workshops. The library was the inevitable and ideal location. Here the groups had an extended opportunity to go over their own mimeographed poems, exploring what did or didn't work and why. Examples from the great poets were brought in from time to time; what stirred them most was the poet's recitation from memory of several Langston Hughes poems with whose music, language, and social commentary they could immediately identify.

Quite a few English teachers attended, and stayed on to discuss what they had witnessed. Each of the 160 students left the library with a large cluster of poems which could, in a sense, be considered a book manufactured on the spot by them. But this did not satisfy the librarian and her new allies among the teaching staff and children. At year's end they published a huge collection of student verse, dedicated to the guest poet and brought by thousands of children into homes which—in many cases—contained no other book. The graduating class included several pages of Poetry Day photos in their yearbook. Why? Because these disadvantaged and troubled youngsters had made a momentous discovery: that poetry is not an exotic realm, or one more exclusive resort for the privileged, but speaks for and belongs to the downtrodden, the ignored, the emotionally scarred, the hitherto acquiescent and silent. Simultaneously they learned that the librarian and the library also belong to them and are primary instruments toward establishing a foothold on the planet; "that a vast body of relevant and moving work had long been awaiting them in books—their proper inheritance—capable of intensifying, clarifying, criticizing, and corroborating the reality of their daily existence."[1]

The most remarkable of many such instances occurred—and continued for some years—at the rehabilitation building of Central Islip State Hospital. Its new librarian, impressed by the visible impact of the seven-week poetry program on schizophrenic adolescents using his room, proposed that the patients not be left high and dry at the end of the visiting students' fieldwork, just when creative juices were beginning to flow. Since it was essential that the library maintain its hours, he found someone to take charge for an hour each week so that he could preside over the poetry sessions. Further, he recruited typists and illustrators from among the patients, and invited the submission of new poems. For the first time under his aegis each group-member received, upon entering, a neatly bound booklet of from four to eight pages, including as many as twenty new poems, with date, issue number, and full-page drawing on the cover. He had, in effect, founded a periodical; the participants added these weekly booklets to their ever-growing poetry collections, and copies were added to the library's collection.

For someone who is handicapped, the contents of a library can be of overriding importance, dependent largely on how well the librarian knows what materials to acquire and how involved she or he is in bringing them to the handicapped person's attention. At a progressive experimental school for deaf children, splendid poetry collections literally gathered dust on the shelves. Someone had had the courage to order them; they had been duly cataloged and shelved; but no one had integrated them into the lives of the children for whom they were intended.

Two basic factors seem to have been at work here. First, neither administrators, teachers, nor parents had had enough positive contact with poetry to feel comfortable about it or to recognize its educational and liberating potentials for special children. Second, despite their openness in areas such as sports, speech, and the sciences, these people apparently felt that a deaf child could not cope with or care about poetry. Under the circumstances, the librarian might at least have put up poster-poems or exhibited groups of poems about American history, sports, animals, foreign countries on appropriate occasions. That child's particular enthusiasm might have been reinforced by a poem expressing the same enthusiasm in more vivid images and compelling rhythms.

In other words, the librarian should conceive what the community considers inconceivable. If a brain-injured child cannot read at all, and has never been introduced to either the world or the *word* of poetry, the librarian should assume that every child without exception contains a world of poetry to begin with, and that there are materials to awaken the lyricism within him or her.

> On his way to the school, the poet feels unusual trepidation . . . he is wondering what brain-injured children are like and whether thirty minutes will turn out to be far too much or too little time. . . . A mighty hailstorm has just struck Long Island. Heading toward Ronkonkoma he realizes that the magically transformed trees must also have entranced the children in their school buses. He will do what Pestalozzi and others long ago urged: begin with what the children know. Asked what the trees look like and remind them of, they immediately seem to forget that the camera eye is on them. Invited to imitate one such ice-laden tree, enjoying each other's and the poet's grotesquery, they seem to forget that he is 45 years older, a stranger, and that their teachers stand watch in the back. A severely disturbed girl sizes up the atmosphere correctly: she leaves her seat and expands her tree-imitation into a pirouette. An autistic boy, with helmet protection, pauses briefly in his perpetual raising and lowering of the desk-top. Simile has been taught without being named: What do the trees resemble today?
>
> This is now reinforced: Have you ever seen a cloud that reminds you of something else? Much response, from the girl as well, while she repeats her delicate dance motion. Someone volunteers the right word for all this: imagination. The helmeted boy pauses longer before raising the desk-top and hiding behind it. The cloud-talk leads to mention of thunder and lightning. "God makes it," a lively black girl explains. "Maybe so," adds the poet, "with a great big piece of chalk on that great big blackboard in the sky." The children laugh. She asks permission to draw lightning on the board. A classmate ridicules her effort, and does a zigzaggier one of his own. The poet points out that everybody is entitled to his particular lightning. For several minutes all are at the board simultaneously. The helmeted boy is suddenly there, asking first to add his zigzag, then to help erase the whole chalk storm.
>
> The guest had hoped to get to the first poem well before this for the minutes are ticking off fast; but obviously what is happening means more. Now everyone is seated and amenable to whatever comes next. A question: When you hear the wind at night, does it ever seem to be telling you something? . . . A few guesses are praised . . . one comes close: Hooo! The correct answer, much appreciated, is "You!!!"
>
> The class is split in two. One half is coached in saying "you!" softly; the other half says it spookily; then all together roar: "You!!!". . . the poem's refrain is performed, with increasing expertise and expectancy, by the whole class: "You! You . . . You!!!" After the first stanza, however, the girl is unable to remain seated. She begins an elaborate choreography, true to the rhythm and mood of the poem, freeing herself and giving the whole event an unexpected dimension, luckily captured on videotape, subsequently seen by large numbers of teachers and education students.[2]

The lesson is universally valid. Although a deaf child may have been categorized by the institutional staff, by his parents, and by society, as literal-minded—the librarian should assume a precious and unique imagination to be each child's birthright, perhaps withering with disuse, but still able to be stirred and released if only the right key and the right occasion are found. At the Cleary School for the Deaf, children were introduced to examples of a now dormant form of Anglo-Saxon poetry which had great popularity in ancient times. It was this game-like genre that finally unlocked K's imagination, as she spoke on behalf of the grass:

> I can't wait for spring
>   to come here
> My hair will grow more
>   but in winter, my
> hair always gets short
>   I really detest it.
> Help! in the summer time,
>   someone cuts my hair off.
> I'm going to cry.
> Kind people put some water
>   on my hair.
> My hair is getting a lovely color.
> I had marvelous time
>   with my hair,
> but I don't have a body.
> I'm happy all my life.[3]

A deaf child may have been dismissed as linguistically limited; but librarians should assume that the reference tools the rest of us use when struggling for a synonym belong equally to such a child:

> The ability to draw good revisions from her own word-store was more difficult for 16-year-old Marsha, since her language deficiency was far greater, and her patterns of language remained insistently literal after four years of work with poetry. Here, for instance, is one of her failed efforts to create a riddle poem:
>
>   I am a ball.
>   The ball bounces.
>   The ball is shot through basket.
>
> . . . One day Marsha's partner brought her a paperback of Roget's *Thesaurus*. In the past she had never agreed to go over anything she wrote, but insisted on moving to something else. This time she wrote a first draft, then turned to the book for alternate words wherever she felt dissatisfied with the original:
>
>   Wednesday is joyous
>   It is arrival of friends
>   Our friends assist us with poetry.
>   They communicate with me.
>   We discuss many things
>   So, we may comprehend.
>   There's a professor I admire.
>   He tries to be a comic.
>   He makes me chuckle.
>
> True, there is not a line of poetry in this poem, except perhaps "It is arrival of friends." But this piece was an exciting demonstration of how ready she was, more ready than we had hoped, to leap ahead in vocabulary richness if only there were a usable tool. Marsha's verbal progress strengthens our belief that it has been a mistake to characterize her as literal-minded. Higher expectations and a creative atmosphere may lead to the further emancipation of her imagination.[4]

If an emotionally disturbed child is rejected by parents and hospital or school personnel as hopelessly antisocial, the librarian should nevertheless assume that there are secret wells of positive feeling accessible to those who patiently build a trusting relationship:

> It was not easy, for me or the dozen ten-year-olds I met with [at the elementary school of a psychiatric center], to lose ourselves in the poetry and each other while surrounded by what seemed like hawk-faced staffers. The ambience was not improved when several children who had broken some rule were forced to attend in their pajamas. One such boy, characterized as "an incorrigible troublemaker," asked if I knew a poem about bugles and castles. What he had in mind was Tennyson's great song, "The splendor falls on castle walls." As I read it aloud, he flamed with pleasure, joining the refrain, which he knew by heart. He explained that he'd discovered it in the book-corner of a drug store and bought the book with his last money because he "loved the music of it and the bugles in it." Forgetting his pajamas and the faces of adult adversaries, he explained that jazz was his favorite music. I then read Sandburg's "Jazz Fantasia" [exactly the kind of poem a knowing librarian might have shown him], which he rightly interpreted to his classmates as the power of music to open our minds. The same can be said of poetry, I added. His doctor confessed later that he would never have guessed such depths and constructive passions in the boy.[5]

Conversely, the librarian should not assume—as one can discover when working with groups of brain-injured children—that the nursery rhymes we all knew thirty years ago are still being universally transmitted. When parents of such children rob them of Humpty Dumpty and Old King Cole, these figures, these rhymes, these tunes should become a joyous heritage guarded by the library serving as surrogate parent, to be transmitted in an infinite variety of audiovisual ways.

Preparing for poetry sessions with handicapped youngsters, college students have benefited immensely from library materials. They have scoured the shelves in search of the right poem to illustrate an untried approach or dramatize last week's discussion. Some of their discoveries have borne exciting, startlingly unpredictable fruit:

> . . . our stated aim . . . was to try out all sorts of things; why then not "Prufrock" . . . After hearing [this difficult and emotionally painful Eliot poem] and the discussion that ensued, a father of an emotionally disturbed boy declared: "Poets seem to be centuries ahead of the medical profession in their knowledge of the psyche."
> . . . And when questions were raised about the advisability of reading a suicide poem like "Richard Cory," the results proved that a truthful poem which may shock a bit is a better choice than an innocuous piece of garbage unrelated to life. As Ginny put it . . . "It was our poetry which started the challenge . . . and at last everyone had something very important to themselves to say to the group."[6]

The incidents related above took place at a halfway house for adolescents recently discharged from a psychiatric center; equally intense discussions were provoked at hospital sessions by poems found in library anthologies and duplicated for the whole group:

> DK's introduction of Dylan Thomas' "Do Not Go Gently into That Good Night" . . . revealed her impatience with the hospital people for apparently acquiescing to their situation, rather than "raging. " . . . As has occurred in many mid-semester confrontations, the poem provoked a clash of attitudes, with the students ranged on one side, and a strongly resisting hospital member on the other. One year the dispute had been waged on the subject of how much harsh reality children should be taught; another year the topic was what kind of poetry should be written—those who fought against teaching "too much reality," who insisted that poetry should be happy, were hospital people. In this particular discussion a hospital member disputed Dylan Thomas and the students on grounds that we must accept our fate and not "rage, rage." Such discussions arising in the early weeks involve the students passionately for the first time. At the moment the comments seem to re-label and divide us, but in fact they lead to greater unity: We/They are turning into a group of activated minds.[7]

Prior to visiting the Cleary School for the Deaf, another body of literature was tapped, with a variety of fine results. First came Emily Dickinson's "I'm Nobody! Who are you?" whose theme instantly drew together the poet, the college student, and the deaf child in a circle of happy nobodies. An untitled Halloween poem by e. e. cummings was read aloud, its music tapped out on the desks, and eventually costumed and danced by the children at a Halloween party the students attended as guests:

> hist whist
> little ghostthings
> tip-toe
> twinkle-toe
>
> little twitchy
> witches and tingling
> goblins
> hob-a-nob hob-a-nob
>
> little hoppy happy
> toads in tweeds
> tweeds
> little itchy mousies
>
> with scuttling
> eyes rustle and run and
> hidehidehide
> whisk . . . (etc.)

Poems created by children were eventually introduced:

> Stimulation can be provided from the awareness that other children have written poetry, and therefore source material from children's writing can be provided, e.g., volumes such as *Miracles, The Me Nobody Knows* or *Wishes Lies and Dreams*. . . . A fine illustration of beginning at the child's own level is evident in Dale's use of drawings with Bobbie, a young deaf girl with indications of aphasic limitations. Using . . . *Miracles*, Dale invited Bobbie to pick out lines

that she liked and draw "what they said." In response to the line "The sun is like a yellow balloon," Bobbie drew a small child holding a balloon-like sun on a string, and the sun is complete with blue eyes and a smiling face. To the line "I wish I had 100 dollars," a drawing was created showing a girl sitting on a giant dollar bill tossing money in the air. Pictorial poetry, therefore, became a nonverbal transition or parallel to the linguistic level.[8]

The introduction of such material encouraged the deaf children to reciprocate. Some, for the first time ever, with or without reference assistance, combed their neighborhood library and brought as their contributions to the new relationship pertinent poems from anthologies, magazines, and freshly discovered volumes by individual authors who were henceforth their "favorite." Nor were these shared findings limited to poems.

An identical situation can occur at the opposite end of the age spectrum. Joining a newly organized senior citizens' poetry group, a deeply depressed woman, totally drained of self-pride and purpose, announced that poetry meant nothing to her, that she had signed up for this activity rather than "rot alone at home" while her husband went "gallivanting with his cronies." Her discovery that poems can deal with deep issues in moving words galvanized her personality. For the second meeting she wrote:

> I want so much to live,
> To find what life can give,
> To cast aside past fears
> To begin my life's new year,
> In my hands to hold
> My new life's purest gold.

But a week later she arrived frantic. "I'll have to miss the next two meetings. We're going to visit my husband's family in Sicily." It was suggested that she bring back her impressions of Mt. Etna in poetry or any other form. She returned triumphant, having copied from a reference work in her local library two pages of data. It was easy, without adding or changing a single word, to shape excerpts into the following lines under her title and over her signature:

> Mt. Etna Volcano, The Highest In Europe
>
> Etna!
> We remember 475, 396, and 36 B.C.,
> 1183, 1329, 1381, 1669
> and many others.
> 1971 was the shortest . . . three months . . . from April to June . . . the Astronomic Observatory was destroyed too.
>
> Etna!
> The lava remains in fluid state for several months;
> when this inside "river" wears out,
> the melted paste
> leaves its place,
> astonishing caves and galleries.
> The magma consolidates, taking the form
> of ropes, cakes, scorise.
>
> Most of this I copied from a book.
> I didn't know anything about you, Etna! but from now on . . .

In a number of other group settings, handicapped people who brought a library "nugget" in lieu of an original piece obviously felt possessive toward their find; it was always duplicated for distribution and discussion, and was sincerely received as that person's communication. The stimulus that sparked the search for Mt. Etna happened to be a conversation with the group leader. Having succeeded once, the participant is likely to approach the library's holdings again—perhaps habitually—to satisfy her newly recognized appetite for knowledge. For the next meeting she wrote:

> I want so much to live and learn.
> I was bored, not anymore
> Though much I want
> Which I must have,
> I fear no more
> For I have found what life can give[9]

At the New York Guild for the Jewish Blind, no suggestion from an outsider was necessary. These people had apparently been availing themselves of the guild's library resources for years. The hunger for all kinds of information was exceptionally strong in every member of the group. Wide-ranging discussions kept probing new areas. Every allusion to an unfamiliar name or event served as an appetizer. They often wanted to go beyond a brief explanation to the feast itself. It became typical for someone to announce that he or she had found in the library a braille volume or periodical article on the subject introduced last week, or that the librarian had ordered it, perhaps as a Talking Book.

It took a while for students working with deaf children to consider using the school's facility, though they had used the college library intensively to learn about deafness and special education methods or to discover usable poems. When introducing verses to a deaf child, they first had to find out that smiles and nods do not necessarily mean the concept has been grasped and the words understood. Once this became clear, it was necessary to define by acting out, with the help of props. This, however, placed the college people precisely in the teaching role they needed to avoid if an atmosphere of mutuality was to be achieved. The problem was identified quickly for the student who had introduced the Halloween poem—with its "hist . . . whist . . . tweeds . . . scuttling . . . whisk" vocabulary, and for the one who had confidently brought in "I'm Nobody!"—with such words she'd previously taken for granted as "banish . . . dreary . . . public . . . live-long" and the final "admiring bog"—all within eight short childlike lines!

What made the situation even shakier was the fact that some staff personnel did not share the college group's "nebulous," untestable goals. They resented having the children wrenched away an hour each week for anything other than learning in a traditional sense; they wanted the visiting students to teach. Only after the success of the thesaurus did one begin to see students leading deaf children, then children pulling students, toward the library, so that both could refer to the dictionary or encyclopedia for a word or an allusion that had stumped them while reading a poem together. Once the field of their hour's work had widened to include the library, it became a matter of pertinent fun to look up other subjects of enthusiasm. A student and a deaf child could often be found going through a book or magazine about racing cars or baseball or insects, stopping to admire the photos, some of which became the springboards of original poems:

> Alan dreams himself an ace pitcher: "The Score was Ten to Zero." Who bats against him in the final inning? "Willie" (Mays) and "Tommy" (Agee), no less, and these two are dispatched in ten offhand syllables! Now for the ballad-like icing on the cake done in half rhyme:
>
>> Pointing to the right field
>> Babe Ruth came up to bat
>> He went to hit the ball
>> But I just struck him out[10]

At the campus reading, their momentous annual event, one of the children performed his butterfly poem:

> The Dowling student who had worked with the particular deaf child held up a poster on which the poem had been written in large letters, and the deaf child read the poem, speaking with the measured difficulty that is the mark of many deaf people, while also performing in sign language . . .
>
>> I wish I was a butterfly
>> I wish I could fly anywhere I want to.
>> I wish I could fly to France to meet a French butterfly.
>> I wish I wasn't caught by enemies.
>> If I was a butterfly, I'll enjoy myself all the time.
>> I wish I won't be stuck in a jar.
>> I wish I could fly around the garden and smell the smelly flowers.
>
> There was laughter when the youngster finished. He beamed . . . So did they all beam and applaud and bask in the warmth of the occasion, the students and the teachers and the parents and some visitors.[11]

There is one more major library resource for a handicapped person. This category includes all the non-traditional materials that readers without communicative disabilities might never consider using (though they do unconsciously all the time). Here, more than in any other situation, the degree of a librarian's flexibility and openness is crucial. Mention was made earlier of a hospital librarian who turned weekly poetry submissions into mimeographed, neatly stapled booklets which became an expanding collection for each recipient. The concept of a personal library, including publication of one's own work, did much to strengthen the egos of these hospitalized schizophrenics. In some cases that collection grew to encompass magazines and paperbacks which, in earlier years, would have floated haphazardly into and out of their lives but now became a stable, individualized center beside their otherwise characterless bed in a monolithically arranged ward on a dehumanizing institutional floor.

A similar experience developed in the work with deaf children. Each year the conclusion of the program had been marked by the students' playing host to the children, whose visit to the college had been climaxed by a public reading of their poems in the campus theatre. Because previous audiences had failed to understand the speech of the children, a student committee provided the third year's listeners with a dittoed, stapled booklet containing the text of the entire program. An attractively illustrated, dated title page, and a table of contents, helped the audience (including parents) feel they were taking home an anthology. Asking the children to autograph their work contributed to a sense of authorship and personal worth. The collections became a potentially valuable holding in the school library, since they could be used to gauge a child's development from year to year. At the college there were other values, since a new group of students could become better prepared for their forthcoming experience by examining what had been accomplished in other years. Occasionally a specialist in the field would visit the library to consult these collections for research purposes.

After several such program books annually prepared by students, an even more meaningful level of publication was achieved. In the sixth year the duplicating machinery of the school was made available. This meant that ditto stencils were placed at the disposal of each creative pairing (child and college student), and that a new poem could be instantly run off in a number of colors—lettered and illustrated by its creator—and distributed to the entire group for prompt interaction. Each new page was inserted in the ever-burgeoning folders the children took home—with copies enough left over for inclusion in the stapled program book that the audience would receive at the final session. Clearly, even greater motivation than a juvenile collection like *Miracles* can provide, was "supplied by the children viewing their own (or their classmates') poetry in print."[12]

These were, indeed, books by the deaf children—with their own idiosyncratic calligraphy, color preferences, uncorrected spelling and grammar, and—most exciting—drawings which often came closer to the imaginative and emotional dimensions of poetry than did the text. (When mainstreaming occurs, and there is a daily teacher-child relationship under way rather than the fragile mutuality and spontaneity aimed for in seven one-hour sessions per year, there is plenty of time to concentrate on correcting the grammar and spelling—but the creative moment itself should never be undermined to satisfy the zeal of pedants.)

The visual triumph merits emphasis because this new dimension of lyric expression solved what had seemed insoluble. Some youngsters had simply not been able—or ready—to produce poetry and had therefore felt excluded from the general bursts of creative activity. Now each could shine. At the theatre, drawings could now be acted out, danced, lugged in on a series of vivid posters, accompanied by ingeniously chosen and often startlingly effective props—all as part of the reading.

The hospital librarian mentioned above had similarly encouraged the patients' graphic skills, to be featured on the cover of each week's booklet. These drawings were sometimes provocative enough to serve as the basis of memorable discussions. Earlier, in preparing *Long Night's Journey* for publication, it appalled the editors that, after two years' involvement, one of the group's most sensitive, devoted members had simply not been able to shape his thoughts and feelings into poetry. He offered to attempt a drawing. The result was artistically awkward in the extreme, but what the drawing said made it worthy of prefacing the volume: it depicted a group seated in a circle, hospitably hearing each other out.

For deaf children especially, a library's visual holdings should be among its chief assets. Library walls should swarm with displays. Hundreds of marvelous professional posters are readily available, for example, and original oak-tag work produced by the children themselves can present a fine mating of poem and picture. There should also be a year-round series of well-advertised slide shows (with captions for the deaf) and regularly scheduled movies—carefully prepared for in the classroom prior to their showing. A scene-by-scene synopsis of a Shakespeare play or a Dickens novel should be in the hands of each child in advance. Videotapes related to curriculum should be part of the collection. The positive impact of such visual materials, energetically prepared for and comfortably presented, can be tremendous—unlike the crushing effect on a deaf child of a movie house experience when everybody else is entranced:

> . . . The people
> sit in the chairs. They
> feel comfortable.
> But, deaf people
> attempt to
> understand about the
> movie. It was
> hard for deaf people . . .[13]

Blind students can achieve similar successes with audio materials. When discs, for example, are transferred onto cassettes, they can easily be played in private carrels or borrowed overnight. Teachers should be encouraged to record all their poetry assignments in advance of a new semester. Beneficial to all new readers who don't yet know how to make words leap from the page, this arrangement is of particular value to the blind, since volunteer readers are not readily available and are seldom gifted in interpreting literature forcefully. The librarian's function should not be limited to providing a blind patron with the requested material and with relaxed, quiet quarters in which to hear it. The blind should be kept familiar with the complete list of audio holdings, so that their range of requests can widen far beyond a class assignment. To all who are handicapped, in fact, the library should represent a permanent treasure trove of nourishing materials, and those whose disabilities have kept them starved (often because society and family excluded them from the banquet) need more, and more kinds of, nourishment than anyone on the outside can imagine, but which we must begin to imagine. For those who are in wheelchairs, a shattering message is delivered by libraries in which turnstiles have been installed to prevent book theft, with no provision made for special patrons.

For emotionally disturbed children, a library visit can have many rewards; here the most hyperactive can glide into tranquility. But the rules of proper behavior should be established before setting out, so that these children need not feel they are (again) about to be pounced on for still one more infraction. They should be allowed to experience the richness of the feast that surrounds them, the freedom of choice, the accessibility of materials within their special spheres of curiosity.

For some troubled children, a truly private place can be magical. In the Suffolk School for the Emotionally Disturbed, a Bay Shore, Long Island facility, one innovative young teacher has experimented with works by DeFalla, Stravinsky, and Debussy. He invited the creation of free association poetry as the children listened to these highly evocative scores. Since the institution's library lacked such music, he tapped his own collection and that of the local public library. Unfortunately, the children had no choice but to work side by side in the classroom. Their awareness of one another and of adult observers made them self-conscious, somewhat inhibited at first, and perhaps less "flowing" than they might have been in separate carrels, each with a cassette that could be stopped, played over, and individually controlled for volume at the listener's whim. The effectiveness of such a library feature has been demonstrated with children who tend to lose control within a group setting and endanger the group's equilibrium:

> The "terror of the school," a long-hospitalized 13-year-old, had never before allowed himself to join the poetry partnership or even speak in more than a neutral monosyllable. Confined to a cubicle one Wednesday, he appeared accessible for the first time. Softly answering questions about a particular verse, he mentioned trips to the country. Asked what kinds of animals he'd seen there, this well-policed child at once responded: "Free."

One final instance should underscore the need to keep expanding our definition of what a library is, and what it contains. Anticipating further advances in communication with a new cluster of deaf children, a contingent of college students arrived one year to discover among the group a boy of eleven who could neither read nor write and was just beginning to identify objects by name. In infancy, not recognized as hearing impaired, he had been catastrophically misdiagnosed as mentally retarded and banished to the then infamous Willowbrook State Hospital on Staten Island. During a decade of total cultural deprivation, and utterly abandoned by his parents, he had survived by adaptation and imitation, following the behavior patterns of his fellow inmates. Recently a doctor had discovered that aside from deafness he had normal potential, and returned him to parents who did not know or welcome him and were unequipped to deal with the gigantic task of reshaping him. The school for the deaf then became his true home.

Clearly, a few weeks of one-hour meetings were not going to result in poetry. Fortunately, one particularly sensitive and persistent member of the group chose him as her partner. Her task was to identify his level of knowledge and his areas of excitement. (Very likely, when such a child is finally mainstreamed, the ideal arrangement would be a partnership with a caring, ingenious classmate rather than an occasionally visiting adult.) While other students combed library shelves all week for poems that might generate discussion or, better yet, new poems, she spent hours in search of objects that would capture him through his senses. The "books" she brought, on which the pair of them based each private hour, were vari-shaped, vari-hued, vari-voiced, vari-textured objects: a block, a ball, a paper, a cloth, a drum, a vegetable, a petal. The duo made strange combinations and constructs; he drew pictures of them and copied her lettering for their names.

Out of the corner of one's eye, one saw them gesticulating, hugging, guffawing. He often pulled her away to share his "books"—favorite objects he'd been discovering throughout the school: a fire extinguisher, a face on the bulletin board, a rotating world globe, a basketball hoop. Of course, what they learned in those seven weekly sessions went far beyond the triumph of mastering a noun and its modifier. He learned, for the first time, the quality of a developing love. At the college theater, after the others had stepped forward to read their best poems, this boy and his friend marched to the stage hand in hand with bags full of favorite objects, and proceeded—with speed and cunning—to combine them into imaginative creations: a bird, a tree, a professor that were immediately recognized and cheered.

This is not to suggest that for one such unique child the school librarian should fill an already overcrowded room with arresting assortments of objects, although colorful displays certainly belong there too. The point is that the whole universe has become a library for this child now that he is no longer limited to the horrors of one Willowbrook ward. For the librarian, as for the classroom teacher, the challenge is to bring as much of the universe as possible onto his or her walls, shelves, and display tables, and make this child—make us all—feel that the banquet is ours.

Notes

1. Aaron Kramer, "The Poet as Guest: The School as Host," in *Honeycomb* (Oakdale, N.Y.: Dowling College Pr., 1976), p. 36.
2. Ibid., p. 38.
3. Aaron Kramer and Lucien A. Buck, "Poetic Creativity in Deaf Children," *American Annals of the Deaf* 121 (1976): 33. This poem has been turned into an experimental short film by Dr. Arthur Layzer, Dept. of Physics, Stevens Institute, Hoboken, N.J., for deaf children. It is widely shown and available by arrangement with Dr. Layzer.
4. Ibid., pp. 33–34.
5. Kramer, "The Poet as Guest," p. 36.
6. Lucien A. Buck and Aaron Kramer, "Opening New Worlds to the Deaf and the Disturbed," in *Poetry the Healer* (Philadelphia: Lippincott, 1973), pp. 155–56, 159.
7. Aaron Kramer and Lucien A. Buck, "The Labeling and Delabeling of People Called 'Schizophrenic'" (Paper presented at the Sixth World Poetry Therapy Conference, Hunter College, New York City, 1978).
8. Lucien A. Buck, "A Human Context for the Cultivation of Poetic Creativity," in *Honeycomb*, p. 25.
9. The exact context out of which this episode emerged is described in Aaron Kramer's paper, "The Best Is Yet to Be" (Paper presented at the Seventh World Poetry Therapy Conference, New School for Social Research, New York City, 1979).
10. Kramer, "Poetic Creativity," pp. 34–35.
11. Stan Isaacs, "Poetry Breaks the Silence," *Newsday*, Dec. 22, 1977, p. 3A.
12. Buck "A Human Context," p. 25.
13. Kramer, "Poetic Creativity," p. 32.

The Visually Impaired Reader in the Academic Library

JEAN A. MAJOR

A visually impaired reader is one who cannot use conventional print material without adaptation. Within the population of visually impaired readers, there are two groups—those who are totally blind and those who are partially sighted. Blind readers must use media involving audio or tactile perceptions for reading. Examples of these media are tape recordings or braille literature. Partially sighted readers frequently can use printed reading material with the help of optical aids, such as magnifiers.[1]

Although the size of the visually impaired population in the United States is not known, the Division for the Blind and Physically Handicapped at the Library of Congress estimates that there are two blind persons and three partially sighted per thousand total population.[2] A disproportionate number of the partially sighted are elderly and, thus, outside the college age population. However, in view of the ratios stated by the Library of Congress, there must be a substantial number of college students in the United States who are visually impaired.

Despite the apparent large numbers of visually impaired college students, the literature of academic librarianship contains little previous research on the topic of service to those patrons. The academic librarian who wishes to initiate such a program must rely on the somewhat larger body of literature from public librarianship for information on possible programs. The present study analyzes the components of one program—that of the Ohio State University Libraries—in order to reach conclusions concerning the types of services that are most effective in serving the visually impaired student at an academic library.

"The Visually Impaired Reader in the Academic Library," by Jean A. Major, *College & Research Libraries* 1978, 39: 191–96.

Previous Research

The official position of the American Library Association has been stated in *Standards for Library Service for the Blind and Visually Handicapped*.[3] In this document, the local unit of service was defined as the "community library" and included "academic libraries which receive subsidy for provision of community library service."[4] The emphasis was on public, rather than academic, libraries. Nonetheless, the *Standards* do provide some guides to academic library service.

Basic services include: files of information concerning library services that are available to visually impaired readers from state and federal agencies; catalogs of books in alternative media available from the Library of Congress; and register of local persons available for reading and transcribing. It was also suggested that larger libraries offer the following additional services: reference materials in braille or other media that can be used by the visually impaired; a browsing collection; a study area to use with a reader; optical aids; and equipment for tape recording.[5]

Prentiss, in his 1973 report to the New York State Education Department, discussed the local library's role in providing service to the visually impaired.[6] Again, the academic library was considered only incidentally. Activities or services prescribed by Prentiss include: acquainting visually impaired readers with the services available to them; maintaining a rotating collection of materials and equipment borrowed from state or regional agencies; acquiring minimal collections of reference materials; keeping extensive collections of bibliographic tools to be used to locate materials that are already available in selective media format; and arranging for access to transcribing services for materials not already available. In addition, listening rooms and special reading aids should be "given consideration."[7]

Parkin, in his 1974 study, alluded to the "scarcity of published material specifically discussing the academic library serving the blind."[8] In an attempt to alleviate this situation, Parkin polled academic libraries in the seven-state intermountain West to learn what types of programs these libraries had instituted. He also surveyed the visually impaired students at Brigham Young University to determine their personal assessments of the adequacy of the BYU program as it was then constituted.

Parkin based his survey of academic libraries on the recommended services and equipment that are outlined in the ALA *Standards*. In reference to the *Standards*, the most commonly offered services and equipment and the percent of libraries offering them were as follows:[9]

Listening rooms	66%
Tape recorders	50%
Private study areas	47%

The second phase of the Parkin study dealt with a survey of the attitudes and assessments of the visually impaired students at Brigham Young University regarding the quality and usefulness of the program offered by their library. The visually impaired student population at BYU at the time of the study numbered thirty, but only eleven of the students could be reached. Although the response rate (37 percent) was low and students at only one school were polled, the study deserves notice because it represents an attempt to get feedback from the actual user population.

The Parkin poll of BYU students yielded quite scattered results. However, Parkin gleaned several recommendations from the students:[10]

1. Develop a catalog file of services and books available.
2. Offer orientation sessions to new blind students.
3. Provide more listening rooms.
4. Furnish a braille map of the library.

Services and Equipment

Vision impairment among college students precludes their use of the conventional reading materials found in most academic libraries. Specialized services and adaptive equipment have been developed to aid impaired students in making use of written material. The most common services and equipment will be described below.

1. Catalogs of material available in braille, recorded, or large-print form. Visually impaired students rely heavily on several national agencies for copies of required reading, particularly textbooks. This category includes catalogs listing materials available from the Library of Congress Division for the Blind and Physically Handicapped. Catalogs are produced in print and in nonprint formats that are suitable for use by visually impaired patrons.

2. Information concerning services made available to the visually impaired by local and state agencies.

3. Reading and listening rooms. Students need areas where they can meet readers or listen to materials previously recorded for their use.

4. Recreational reading. Popular books and magazines are available in braille, recorded, or large-print form, often as a rotating collection on loan from a state agency or a regional center of the Library of Congress Division for the Blind and Physically Handicapped.

5. Reference materials. Minimums usually stated are a braille encyclopedia, a dictionary, and an atlas. Occasionally, a large-print dictionary is also mentioned. Note: the most recent braille encyclopedia is a 1959 edition of *World Book*.

6. Register of local readers and transcribers. The visually impaired make extensive use of volunteer readers and braille transcribers.

7. Optical or reading aids. The category refers to any adaptive devices used by either the blind or partially sighted to aid in reading and studying. The following reading aids are of potential use in libraries.

   a) Braillewriter. A portable keyboard instrument that people use to produce braille copy. Students use braillers for taking notes while studying.

   b) Magnifiers. Several forms are available, including hand-held, illuminated, and a magnifier that uses a television screen and offers variable size and contrast. Used by partially sighted patrons.

   c) Optacon. Device that converts print into tactile impressions. Used by blind readers.

   d) Talking book machine. Machine on which to play books and magazines recorded on unbreakable long-playing records. The program that supplies talking book machines is administered by the Library of Congress in cooperation with regional libraries. Machines and recordings customarily are lent to visually impaired persons by the regional centers of the Library of Congress Division for the Blind and Physically Handicapped.

e) Tape recorders. Cassette and open reel players are used by students for note-taking, preserving lectures, and in using readers. Also, much reading material is available in taped form. A variable speed player is an adapted tape recorder, which allows readers to listen to material read faster than normal speed without distortion (compressed speech).

f) Typewriters. Braille and large-type machines are available, as well as standard type.

Study of the OSU Library for the Blind

Background

In July 1975, the Ohio State University Libraries opened a library for the blind located within an undergraduate library. The establishment of this reading room was promoted by the university's Office of Disability Services. Funding for the library was supplied by a gift from the senior class of 1973 at OSU and from a grant from the Ohio Rehabilitation Commission.

At the time of the present study (spring quarter 1976), the library for the blind had been staffed and was in operation. The staffing consisted of one full-time clerical employee and two student assistants who worked a total of thirty-four hours per week. The hours of operation for the library were as follows:

Monday–Thursday	8 A.M.–11 P.M.
Friday	8 A.M.– 5 P.M.
Saturday	10 A.M.– 4 P.M.
Sunday	2 P.M.–10 P.M.

The library for the blind housed a large collection of reading aids and some reference materials, which had been funded by the above-mentioned grant. The following list represents the equipment that was available for public service:

Equipment	Quantity
Braille writers	5
Magnifiers	
hand	1
television-type	2
Optacons	5
Reference materials	
braille dictionary	1
braille encyclopedia	1
Tape recorders	
cassette	5
compressed speech	3
reel-to-reel	5
Typewriters	
braille	1
large type	1
standard type	2

There were thirty-eight students to be served by this library during the spring of 1976.

Purposes of Study

The author was head of undergraduate libraries at OSU at the time of the study and was responsible for the operation of the library for the blind. Therefore, she was interested in learning how well the library was meeting the needs of the students it had been established to serve. With that in mind, she undertook to interview as many of the visually impaired students enrolled at OSU as possible to learn their opinions of the usefulness of the services offered and to determine which types of equipment were being used and how often. It was also hoped that useful information would be obtained that would assist other academic librarians.

Methodology

Information was gathered by administering a ten-item questionnaire to each student in a telephone interview. Often the questions merely acted as an initial point of inquiry, and students freely digressed to amplify their responses. Although there were thirty-eight visually impaired students on campus during spring quarter 1976, it was possible to reach only twenty-six of them, but all who were contacted cooperated with the study.

The twenty-six students included six totally blind and twenty partially sighted individuals. There were five freshmen, four sophomores, seven juniors, eight seniors, and two graduate students. They were enrolled in fourteen major areas of study in nine colleges of the university, with fourteen in social and behavioral science.

Interview Results

Since the degree of need for library services is a function of type of class assignment, students were asked about their reading requirements. Twenty-five answered that they had assignments in textbooks, and fourteen also stated they had reserve reading assignments, optional readings, and reading related to research papers.

Asked about their interest in various services and equipment available to them, described above in the section on services and equipment, at least half the students, both blind and partially sighted, stated they were interested in each of the items.

Responses did vary between the blind and partially sighted students. Blind students were more receptive to such services as catalogs of available material, recreational reading material, reference material, and register of local readers and transcribers. Partially sighted students were more responsive to optical aids designed to assist them in reading. Both blind and partially sighted students were interested in information on local and state services and in special reading and listening rooms in the library.

Next the students were asked what kinds of equipment would be useful to them and to which they would need access. Four of the six blind students stated their need for a braille writer. One blind student expressed a need for the Optacon. (During the year of the study, 1975–76, one student only had been trained in the use of this specialized piece of equipment. Subsequently, a training program was instituted to introduce other blind students to the Optacon.)

Four of the partially sighted students stated their need for the television type magnifier, and three expressed a need for hand magnifiers. The piece of equipment most heavily requested both by blind and partially sighted students was the tape recorder—by four of the blind students and twelve of the partially sighted. Seven of the partially sighted students stated they needed none of the equipment.

Finally, the students were requested to list the equipment in the library for the blind they had actually used. Nine of the partially sighted students and one of the blind students reported having used none of the equipment, and no piece of equipment was used by a majority of either group. Again the pieces of equipment receiving the most use were tape recorders, braille writers, and television type magnifiers.

The preceding summary suggests a certain indifference on the part of the visually impaired students toward the optical aids available. This apparent lack of interest was further borne out in the use statistics kept in the library for the blind for nine months at the time of the study.

Implications for the OSU Library for the Blind

Shortly after the opening of the library for the blind at Ohio State, an advisory committee was formed. Membership included visually impaired students, faculty, and staff, as well as persons involved professionally in work with the visually impaired. The OSU libraries staff responsible for the library for the blind and the advisory committee for the library for the blind together evaluated the results of the study and the use pattern of the library's first year of existence. In view of the strong potential support that specialized library services elicited, the advisory committee stated the service policy for the library for the blind as follows:

> The Library for the Blind assembles and maintains files of catalogs to be used by students to obtain reading materials in braille, taped, or large print form.
> The Library for the Blind actively collects, assembles, and updates information concerning the services which are available to visually impaired citizens from local, state, and federal agencies.
> The Library for the Blind maintains a collection of recreational reading material, both books and recently published popular magazines, on loan from the regional center of the Library of Congress Division for the Blind and Physically Handicapped.
> The Library for the Blind maintains a current file of names of people available locally as readers or braille transcribers.
> At the outset of each quarter, the Library for the Blind will send every new visually impaired student a copy of "Introduction to OSU Libraries for Visually Impaired Students" and "Library for the Blind." At that time, also, a session for students will be offered for the purpose of explaining individual pieces of equipment and their uses.[11]

Of the services described above, the first and second services receive the first priority attention. A collection of braille and large-print reference materials will not be considered at this time. However, the braille reference tools already owned will be kept. Because support for an extensive collection of equipment was not demonstrated in the study nor by use statistics, the advisory committee stated

No additional optical or reading aids will be acquired in the near future. Purchases may be considered at some future time if patrons express considerable need and if existing equipment enjoys substantial use.[12]

Several items of equipment had duplicates in the library for the blind, and usage did not warrant duplicates in a single location. Thus, the advisory committee recommended that

> Consideration should be given, either immediately or in the future, to dispersing throughout OSU Libraries some of the equipment owned. Space should be found in the Main Library and in the West Campus Learning Resources Center for:
> a braille writer
> a compressed speech tape player
> a reel-to-reel tape recorder and earphones
> a television type magnifier[13]

As of February 1978 the recommendation to disperse the equipment throughout the libraries was being implemented.

Although evaluation of the physical facilities was not an objective of the study, two needs became known through the interviews. Soundproof booths are needed for recording and for students to meet readers. The room occupied by the library for the blind has windows on two sides and, thus, has too much glare for some patrons to use it comfortably. The recommendation of the advisory committee follows:

> Funding is needed immediately to install blinds for the windows of the Library for the Blind. This is a critical need and should receive high priority attention. Also, funding should be sought to acquire soundproof booths for recording and for patrons to meet readers.[14]

Recommendations

The following recommendations are intended to guide academic libraries in establishing specialized library service to visually impaired students. They reflect initial steps only and are offered on the basis of the survey reported above, guidance from an advisory committee, and one and one-half years' experience with an established facility.

1. Blind readers and partially sighted readers as groups have different needs for both services and equipment. Composition of the visually impaired patron group must be known and understood at the outset.

2. Basic or most useful equipment may be a braille writer, a tape recorder, and a television type magnifier. However, knowledge of the patron group to be served may suggest alternatives to this basic list. A large collection of reading aids with duplicates of many pieces is questionable without demonstrated need.

3. Primary services are: (a) Assembling and maintaining files of catalogs to be used by students to obtain reading materials in braille, taped, or large-print form. (b) Actively collecting, assembling, and updating information concerning the services available to visually impaired citizens from local, state, and federal agencies. Other previously mentioned services may be established in time.

4. Allocated spaces should include reading rooms for patrons and their readers.

5. A program of service to visually impaired students requires a work assignment to a full-time staff member. However, the program outlined above does not constitute a full-time job in itself.

Notes

1. Sam Prentiss, *Improving Library Services to the Blind, Partially Sighted, and Physically Handicapped in New York State: A Report Prepared for the Assistant Commissioner of Libraries* (Albany: Univ. of the State of New York, State Education Dept., Division of Library Development, 1973), p. 4.
2. Ibid., p. 2.
3. Commission on Standards and Accreditation of Services for the Blind, Committee on Standards for Library Services, *Standards for Library Services for the Blind and Visually Handicapped*, Adopted July 14, 1966, by the Library Administration Division, American Library Association (Chicago: American Library Assn., 1967).
4. Ibid., p. 13.
5. Ibid., pp. 36–39.
6. Prentiss, *Improving Library Services to the Blind*, pp. 31–33.
7. Ibid., pp. 32–33.
8. Derral Parkin, "The University Library: A Study of Services Offered the Blind" (ERIC document ED 102 972), p. 3.
9. Ibid., pp. 34–48.
10. Ibid., p. 54.
11. The Ohio State University Libraries, Advisory Committee for the Library for the Blind, "Statement of Policy," adopted December 8, 1976.
12. Ibid.
13. Ibid.
14. Ibid.

Some Immodest Proposals for Improving Library Services to the Blind: Reflections of a Handicapped Library User

HANAN C. SELVIN

Borrowing a familiar phrase from another context, I should perhaps warn you that what I have to say today may be dangerous to your equanimity. I hope, in short, to prod each of you into doing what you can to improve your own library's services to the handicapped and especially to the blind. It is not that I think the blind deserve preference over other handicapped people but, rather, that I know the situation of the blind far better, being a blind person myself, so I will have to leave the details of the changes that need to be made for the physically handicapped, the deaf, and other groups to representatives of those groups.

A few words about my own history may make my ideas more meaningful. Before I lost the ability to read print entirely, some six or seven years ago, as the culmination of a decades-long process, I might have described myself, adapting the title of a French movie, as *The Man Who Loved Books and Libraries*. In this respect, of course, I was no different from thousands of professors across the country. I spent many hours in libraries and in reading my own books; I bought books compulsively; and I am surely one of the few people who own two unabridged dictionaries.

It would be impossible even to list the many new skills, gadgets, and attitudes with which I have had to become familiar in making the transition from a sighted professor to a blind one; instead, I want to focus on those aspects of my life that have to do with my professional roles of teaching, writing, and service.

There are several dozen organizations, public and private, that prepare braille or recorded books for the blind, but only two need concern us here: The Division for the Blind and Physically Handicapped of the Library of Congress [DBPH], which prepares both braille and recorded books (generally known as Talking Books, as well as the machines needed to play the latter), and Recording for the Blind, Inc. [RFB], a nationwide, nonprofit organization with headquarters in New York and twenty-eight other recording studios across the country, mostly at or near universities. Similar as the goals of DBPH and RFB may appear, their operations and products differ greatly.

The mandate of DBPH is to prepare and distribute recreational reading for the blind and those physically handicapped unable to read ordinary books. This means that the DBPH chooses which books it will have recorded, contracts with other organizations to hire a professionally trained reader for each book, and distributes the recorded books to its regional and subregional libraries across the country. At its best, the system is glorious. Indeed, it is one of the genuinely good things about being blind that one can get Talking Books, for the good ones add a wholly new aesthetic dimension to the author's words. Next time you are in the vicinity of a regional or subregional library for the blind, ask the librarian to play a little bit of any recording by Alexander Scourby, who is the king of recording artists in this field, having recorded over three hundred books. You will see what I mean by saying that such recordings transcend the printed text.

To say that I am enormously grateful to the DBPH is not to say that I am blind to its shortcomings. Indeed, some of these remediable shortcomings have vexed me so much that I have attacked them in print, both individually and collectively, as a member of the Committee on Library Services of the National Federation of the Blind. I shall cite just two shortcomings here. One is its unbelievably rigid insistence on recording whatever *it thinks* the blind want and in having this done at the same standards of quality and quantity

---

"Some Immodest Proposals for Improving Library Services to the Blind: Reflections of a Handicapped Library User," by Hanan C. Selvin, *Information Reports and Bibliographies* 1978, vol. 7, no. 2, pp. 22–26. Reprinted with permission.

as books of far greater importance. A couple of years ago the DBPH sent the subregional library in my county, twelve copies of *How to Run a Garage Sale*! Again, the cassette player that the DBPH supplies free does not contain a recording head; it plays cassettes but cannot be used to record one. My expert on such matters tells me that, in the quantity ordered by DBPH, equipping its cassette machines with recording heads and associated circuitry would have cost less than $5.00 additional! My plea that making the machine capable of recording as well as playing cassettes would multiply its usefulness to academics and other professionals was airily dismissed as "not being part of our Congressional mandate"—to produce recreational material!

Recording for the Blind follows an entirely different logic. It records *only* those books that a client requests. When a client wants a recorded copy of some book, he has someone look for it in RFB's printed catalog of the 40,000 books in its master tape library. If the book is already there, he sends his request to RFB in New York. The master tape is then inserted in a high speed tape duplicator, which prepares either open-reel or cassette tapes, depending on the user's preference. These tapes are then sent postage-free (like the recordings and machines of the DBPH) and, when the user has finished with them, are returned postage-free to RFB. At that point, the tapes are erased, checked for quality, and used to record a new book. When RFB has successfully computerized its ordering procedures, it hopes to be able to determine which books are sufficiently in demand that it would be worthwhile to keep a stock of them on hand, but this is a refinement of the procedure, not a basic change.

If the user wants a book that is not already in the master tape library or in process of being recorded at one of the studios, he sends two copies to RFB, one from which the readers make the recording and the other for the "monitor," who, in principle at least, checks the reading for accuracy. When the recording is finished, RFB will return one or both copies and, if one, pay the user for the other, again according to his wishes.

This system in its various forms works very well. The principal difficulty lies in the necessity for a sighted reader to record a book and for the book to be ordered from a central library (RFB is in fact, if not in name, a library). This means that access to books is a slow procedure, and it becomes even slower if RFB must record a book that it has not already put into its master tape library. Moreover, there is more to the reading needs of students and professionals alike than books. Academic journals, university memoranda, correspondence, student drafts of term papers, and dissertations—these are only the first nonbook needs that come to mind. I am fortunate in having found a volunteer reader who is confined to his home by a long-term illness and who, provided with an extra cassette recorder and a supply of cassettes, is delighted to enliven his days by recording this "fugitive" material for me. When I am really pressed for books that are not yet available through RFB or DBPH, he also does them, most notably when I have to review a book for an academic journal.

This arrangement takes some luck and some special efforts. For example, it would not work nearly so well if we did not have daily back-and-forth communication resulting from the fortunate coincidence that my secretary lives near him. As you can well imagine, this arrangement has required good fortune, thoughtfulness on everyone's part, and a sizeable investment in the extra machine, a second bulk eraser, and the several hundred cassettes that formed the most recent part of my personal library. Students and professionals who are not so lucky or so well off will need to use other arrangements.

The central problem in the recorded-book system is the necessity for a sighted reader. There are now under development several reading machines, which, either automatically or with the blind reader's assistance in manually tracking a small camera along each line of type, will use a small, specially programmed computer to turn the printed word into "synthetic speech"—a speech that to me sounds like a slightly drunken, Swedish Henry Kissinger (no derogation of the former Secretary of State is intended!). The most advanced of these machines is the Kurzweil Reading Machine. It not only reads the book allowed, but also, at the user's press of a button, will spell the last word, letter-by-letter and repeat all or part of a page.

In addition to the Kurzweil Reading Machine, the producers of the Optacon and the Stereo-Toner expect to develop accessory units for their machines that will enable them to do essentially the same job, except for the substitution of manually tracking each line of print with a hand-held electronic camera instead of the automatic camera of the Kurzweil machine. The Optacon now produces a tactual representation of each letter through a grid of tiny vibrators under the user's forefinger as he moves the electronic camera along the line of type. The Stereo-Toner operates similarly, except that its output is a set of musical tones instead of the vibrating letters of the Optacon.

The producers of the Optacon and the Stereo-Toner are reported to be working on attachments to their machines, which will accomplish the same purpose except for the ability of the camera in the Kurzweil machine to find and track the text by itself. Think what such a machine would mean in your library; a blind user could take any book, place it in the machine and have the book read aloud to him in fully comprehensible speech without the mediation of a sighted reader. Think of this for a moment; it means that the library of the future will have *all* of its books fully accessible to blind persons; let us hope that this future is not too far off!

One last word on these reading machines. The Library of Congreee has successfully coupled the Kurzweil machine to a mechanical Braillewriter, thus making possible the direct translation of print into braille, again without the mediation of a sighted person.

How far these machines are from being available to every library or to established blind professionals may be inferred from the current price of the Kurzweil machine. Mr. Kurzweil himself believes that the decline in price of the pocket calculator is a harbinger of what will happen with his reading machines, since many of the components are similar. It is instructive to note, however, that, although most of the development cost of the Kurzweil machine was funded by the government, the amount involved was minuscule, especially as compared to such worthy projects as the B-1 bomber or the neutron bomb.

New Direction: Technology

At this point I want to ask you to take a look into the future with me. No, not science fiction, but only those devices and techniques that are now available or are clearly visible in the near future. What these improvements require is not scientific breakthrough but relatively small changes in the laws and in the funding of applied research and development.

Improving Braille

The chief defects of present-day braille are its slowness and its bulk. Even experienced braille readers seldom attain speeds of more than 100 words per minute, which is extremely slow, compared to the speed with which sighted people read print. As to bulk, the *World Book Encyclopedia*, which takes twenty volumes in print, requires 125 in braille! Moreover, what with the necessity for a sighted braille transcriber, a proofreader, and special expensive presses, braille books cost much more than printed ones.

A new device, about the size of a standard DBPH cassette player, has recently been developed in France and is now being tested by DBPH. It replaces the braille book by a cassette of magnetized tape, from which the machine produces a moving ribbon of braille characters that pass under the user's stationary finger, much like the stream of Optacon letter-images. The user can control the speed of the ribbon, and, since the braille characters last only for the time it takes the ribbon to pass across the top of the machine, there is no problem with mashed letters, as there is in ordinary braille books. Nor are reduction of space and quality of braille characters the only virtues of this machine. It is far cheaper to duplicate magnetic tape than to reproduce braille, so that the cost of providing braille books should drop appreciably, once this system is in wide use. Moreover, one can even foresee the day when interlibrary loan of braille books will take place from a braille transmitter in the Library of Congress and a high-speed tape duplicator located in the appropriate regional or subregional library. There are technical problems here, especially that of obtaining a satellite or microwave channel of sufficient width to make possible the high-speed duplication. This one problem may require doing this duplicating at night, when the imperious demands of network television have subsided; one can only hope that such financial arrangements as will be necessary can be made. Note that this might result in interlibrary loan for braille readers being faster than for readers of printed books; so be it!

Improving the Talking Book Program

The preceding discussion on long distance braille duplication via magnetic tape leaves me to wonder whether or not the time is right for the DBPH to contemplate a similar system for its recorded books. Instead of sending out twelve copies of *How to Run a Garage Sale*, the DBPH would send out *no* copies and would wait for its readers to find this book in the bimonthly newsletter of new releases, *Talking Book Topics*. When a reader requests a book from his regional or subregional library, the library teletypes the request to DBPH, which plays its master tape over satellite or microwave lines the following night. This would save DBPH money, in not having to produce unneeded copies of some books and would save the readers frustration in having to wait for a book since each library would have a high speed duplicator and could thus "print" as many copies of the recorded book as its readers might demand. Note that this system resembles the one now used by RFB, except that the postal link between RFB and user would be replaced by the electronic link between DBPH and regional or subregional libraries. As with RFB, cassettes returned by users would be erased and checked for quality before being used to record another book.

The Telephone

One need not look to such exotic and expensive devices as the communications satellite to see how, with some imagination, existing technology could be harnessed to improve the life of the blind. Here are two ideas that have occurred to me: (1) why not provide the entire DBPH system with "800 numbers" so that users could make toll-free calls to order books from regional and subregional libraries or to use their reference services? Indeed, it ought to be possible for blind professionals, who have demonstratable need for a larger reference library, to query the reference section of DBPH or even the Library of Congress itself. This seems to me an entirely reasonable extension of the present free postage for the blind; (2) it ought to be possible to link *all* reference libraries by teletype to a computerized union catalog of recorded books, much as is now done with ERIC, MEDLARS, and other computerized search services. Moreover, such a computerized system might make possible aggregate demands for such material as academic journals, which are now routinely recorded; obviously, I am speaking here of the network's being used by RFB as well as by DBPH, since the latter would probably decline due to academic journals not being "recreational."

Looking Ahead: Human Services

As you have probably recognized, these last few ideas involve more than technology. They also involve new kinds of human services on the part of librarians and their staffs. We need not restrict ourselves, however, to those innovations that involve new technologies. Imaginative use of existing human resources can also improve library services to the handicapped.

As a beginning, it seems to me that any library, even the smallest town library, must set aside some meaningful space for the special needs of the handicapped. At a minimum, this would be a special table equipped with a Library of Congress record player, a Library of Congress cassette player, and several pairs of headphones. If more space and funds were available, the library might contemplate one or more of the following: (1) A TV magnifier for the partially sighted; this machine, of which there are several commercial versions, transforms the printed page into TV images with larger type, brighter letters, more contrast, and, if desired, white on black instead of black on white. Many people with declining vision, unable to read ordinary print for some years, have suddenly found themselves able to read almost as rapidly and easily as they once did with print. (2) The library should have at least one soundproof room in which blind readers could operate Braillewriters, which make about as much noise as a keypunch; could listen to recorded material without the need of headphones; could listen to recorded forms and examinations and record their answers on a second machine; and could work with volunteer readers for tasks in which such face-to-face interaction is necessary.

These thoughts lead me to suggest other ways in which libraries with special interest in helping the handicapped might provide useful services for them: (1) Committees of and for the handicapped. Such a committee can be remarkably effective in bringing the special needs of the handicapped to the attention of those in a position to do something about them. At Stony Brook, we have had such a committee for several years; originally started by handicapped students and faculty as an ad hoc committee, it has since been designated a presidential committee and wields considerable influence on the actions of the local administration.

(2) Volunteer readers. Every campus and every community needs a pool of volunteer readers who are available on short notice to meet unexpected needs. Sometimes, as in the case of filling out complicated forms, it will be necessary for the blind person and the volunteer reader to be in each other's presence, but in other cases it may be sufficient to have volunteer readers prepare a cassette, which the blind person can read later—another use for the soundproof rooms. Alternatively, a library for the handicapped ought to have a number of lightweight, portable cassette machines that it could lend to volunteer readers for such short-run purposes. Naturally, the library could also lend such machines to blind students who have forgotten their machines or who are having their machine repaired. In this context it seems altogether reasonable for a library for the handicapped to take the lead in recruiting a pool of volunteer readers, especially for those periods, such as final examinations, when the blind student is unable to rely on other students for significant amounts of reading or recording. Does the foregoing strike you as outrageous? If so, let me try to persuade you otherwise. A library feels no sense of outrage at being asked to provide a sufficiently high level of illumination for sighted readers, so why should it feel a sense of outrage at being asked to provide the necessities that enable a blind reader to use the library effectively? Indeed, it is part of our continuing reorientation of thinking about minorities, women, and the handicapped that ought to lead all of us, whether in these groups or serving them, to regard their specialties as equally entitled to service as are the ordinary needs of the majority.

(3) A clearinghouse for the handicapped. The library that serves the handicapped ought to keep a special collection of information about products, services, and events of special interest to the handicapped. This collection should preferably be in triplicate—braille, large type, and recorded version—and should include such material as magazines addressed to the handicapped, magazines addressed to others when they have material of interest to the handicapped (for example, a recent issue of *Consumer Reports* with an article on small cassette recorders), and copies of announcements of new products and services that will surely flood the mail of such a library.

(4) Where to locate a library for the handicapped. If all of this has led you for the first time to think of having a special facility for the handicapped in your library and if your mind has turned to that unused storeroom in the basement or some other equally remote location, forget it! You will have to locate your facility where it is easily accessible to the handicapped—not only the blind, who, sooner or later, will find their way through the maze of structures, but also the physically handicapped, who will need level entrances, ramps or elevators in place of stairs, doors, and aisles that will accommodate a wheelchair, and so on. Since every renovation of an existing library is a special case, I shall confine myself here to that happy situation in which you are contemplating an entirely new library structure. In this case, you might want to consider locating the library for the handicapped next to your audiovisual installation. Such installations provide a stock of projectors, film, TV cameras, and videotape records and, most important to use here, various recording and playback devices. It is usual for all but the smallest to employ a technician to keep the machinery in order and to make minor repairs. It should be relatively easy for such a technician to provide additional services to the handicapped, ranging from new crutch tips to charging the battery of an electric wheelchair and from repairing a damaged cassette to lending a cassette recorder to a blind student whose own recorder has become inoperative.

(5) "Missionary work." The staff of a library for the handicapped ought not only to provide the highest possible level of services to users of that library but ought also to use their special knowledge as ambassadors to the university or local community. Stony Brook, for example, has enlisted the help of the faculty of the College of Engineering and Applied Sciences, whose senior students use their design seminar to design and construct prototypes of new devices for the handicapped. As only a sample of ideas of this type, I can envision linguists becoming interested in the communications problems of the handicapped, lawyers codifying the federal and state laws applicable to the handicapped so that a blind student contemplating a professional career in a distant state would know what kinds of facilities and services might be available to him there, and physical education majors teaching the handicapped how to swim.

(6) Calendar of events. The blind students

at Stony Brook have complained to me that they are unable to keep up with current events on campus. Such events are announced entirely in print media. Although they seem to have no trouble in learning when the next rock concert is to take place, they do have trouble in keeping up with serious concerts, plays, lectures, and other cultural events. Moreover, like all students, handicapped or not, they have trouble in keeping up with academic announcements, such as new courses or new procedures, and with academic deadlines, such as the last day for dropping a course without penalty. An information system for the handicapped, as well as for the normal, ought to have two components. First, there should be an automatic telephone-answering machine, whose recorded message would include a brief summary of the day's events, academic announcements, and relevant deadlines. Second, there should be a live back-up person reachable by telephone who could supply such additional details as the program of a concert, or the name of a person with further information on some announcements. This might well be an additional task for the reference librarian manning the telephone, as described above.

(7) Recording for the Blind, Inc. [RFB] I remind you that it is the leading supplier of recorded textbooks and technical books for the blind and physically handicapped. *Textbooks* is an elastic term here, covering any book that a teacher may assign at any level, from elementary school to postgraduate training. This means that RFB often supplies recreational reading for its clients too; thus I am now reading George Eliot's *Middlemarch* and have recently finished Dickens's *Little Dorrit*. These are not the beautiful, professional readings provided by the Talking Book Program, but the Talking Book Program has not managed to include these two novels in its all-too-meager effort to record the classics. If clients of RFB needed only fiction or ordinary prose, such as is found in most textbooks in the humanities or the wordier social sciences, you would have few problems. Blind students, however, are found in all fields of learning, even including medicine; the first blind doctor graduated from Temple University's School of Medicine last year. This means that RFB is called on to provide recordings of books in fields that range from analytic geometry (in which raised line drawings supplement the verbal text) to zoology, and from foreign languages to computer programming. To prepare useful recordings of such technical books obviously requires technically trained recorders. RFB has always had a shortage of such recorders, and this is why we at Stony Brook, with our juxtaposition of the university and the Brookhaven National Laboratory, are planning to start a recording studio for RFB. However, many more will be necessary, especially as the number of handicapped students in our colleges and universities continues to increase.

Librarians and the "Blindness System"

In closing, let me introduce you to the concept of the "blindness system." This is the complex of persons, organizations, and norms that include optometrists, ophthalmologists, residential schools for the blind, rehabilitation centers, state commissions for the blind, organizations that produce recordings and braille books, manufacturers of cassette machines, national organizations of blind people, and the customs and laws that affect the blind. As librarians for the handicapped, you will want to enter the blindness system at several points and to become acquainted with its workings. As one example of the working of the blindness system, consider the situation of those who are in transition from normal sight to limited sight. For most people this transition is in the hands of optometrists and ophthalmologists. Strangely enough, these worthies know almost nothing about the rest of the blindness system; indeed, they are likely to pat their patients reassuringly on the back and say: "I'm sorry, but there is nothing more that I can do for you. . . ." As a minimum, librarians concerned with the handicapped will know successful handicapped people in the local area, people who are willing to be informal counselors to these newcomers and to show them the ways in which the newly blind can learn to cope with their handicap and to lead happy and successful lives. In the past year or two, such people have been coming to me at the rate of one every six weeks or so and, if their statements on leaving my office are to be believed, they have found my advice reassuring, as I have found the advice of my predecessors reassuring too.

Moving farther out into the blindness system, I believe that all of us should join in urging the federal government to take over the design, manufacture, distribution, and servicing of equipment for the handicapped.

This has already happened significantly in Great Britain, where, for example, the National Health Service provides an electric wheelchair free of charge to any person needing one. If you think I am being too much of a socialist here, ask anyone who has worn a hearing aid for some years to tell you of his or her encounters with hearing-aid salesmen. One such salesman, who called on my mother for many years, used to speak much more softly when she was wearing his competitor's aid than when she was wearing his!

Were our government to take over this function, we might envision many desirable changes. One would certainly be a marked decline in the cost of the special cassette machines that the blind need and in the cost of cassettes used by the blind for everything from recording lectures to personal correspondence. Again, as you may have noticed, both the DBPH cassette player and its close cousin, the modified General Electric cassette machine sold by the federally financed American Printing House for the Blind are both large and heavy. They measure approximately 8 x 10 x 2 inches and weigh approximately 5 pounds. Now contrast this with the machine that I hold in my hand, which is basically a Panasonic Model RQ314S. This measures about 5 x 7 x 2 inches and weighs something less than 2 pounds. The only significant differences between the machines are that the two large ones have a long-life rechargeable battery and variable speed controls. I should add that I have had this machine custom modified to play four track and half speed so that it will take RFB and DBPH cassettes.

If such machines were produced in large quantities and perhaps even subsidized somewhat, their price might fall to a level low enough that libraries for the handicapped might stock enough of them to lend them to blind students whose own machines are temporarily inoperative or to volunteer recorders doing special jobs for blind students. These suggestions are only those that have come to mind in the past few months, as I have contemplated my six years in the blindness system and my conversations with other members of it. As you become familiar with the blindness system, you will surely have many more ideas to add to these.

The cynics among you may reply that many of the ideas will be extremely costly, and they would be right. It is surely far more costly, however, to our society to have large numbers of handicapped people—estimates range up to several million—living and working at less than their potential. I can perhaps best summarize my feelings about this situation by urging your acceptance of the motto of the State University of New York: Let each become all he is capable of becoming.

Media Services for Gifted Students: An Overview

JANICE SMITH

In the past few years, there has been a reawakening of the need for challenging gifted students, not only for the betterment of society, but for their own self-actualization as well. Gifted programs, by their very nature, depend upon the use of extensive resource materials and media equipment with and by these students. Thus, the library media specialist, working cooperatively with the teacher, has a distinct role as a practicing professional in gifted education: that of active participation beginning with the process of instructional development and design of curriculum for the gifted, moving through the entire teaching/learning cycle, and ending with the final evaluation phase of the complete educational process. This article will examine the role of the library media specialist in detail as it pertains to one specific curriculum model, the Tennant Gifted Extension Model, developed by Carolyn Tennant, former program coordinator for gifted education in School District No. 12, Adams County, Denver, Colorado, and used as the basis of gifted program planning in Adams County.[1] The formulation of this model was based on readings from recognized authorities in gifted education such as Sandra Kaplan, Abraham Tannenbaum, Paul Torrance, Joseph Renzulli, and James Gallagher. A further discussion of Bloom's taxonomy and a staff development program designed to implement this extended role of the library media specialist will be examined in this article.

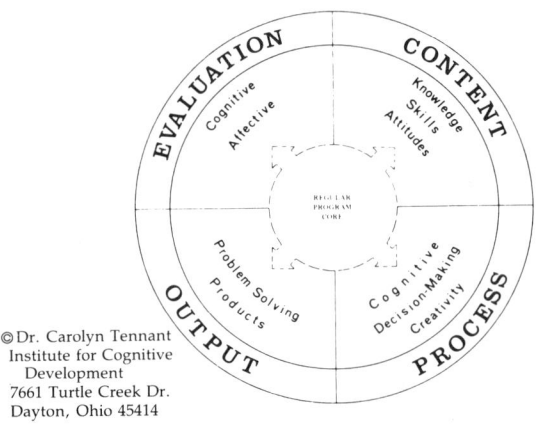

© Dr. Carolyn Tennant
Institute for Cognitive Development
7661 Turtle Creek Dr.
Dayton, Ohio 45414

Fig. 1. Gifted Extension Model

What Is the Role of the Library Media Specialist in Regard to the Gifted Extension Model?

Tennant's Model. In examining this gifted extension model (fig. 1) one notices that it describes how the regular program core can be extended for gifted and talented students. The term *qualitatively differentiated* is often used to describe an appropriate program for the gifted, which is significantly different from the regular curriculum.[2] What does that realistically mean? There are four specific areas of concern in Tennant's model that constitute a complete, balanced, "qualitatively differentiated" program for the gifted. These include (1) content, (2) process, (3) output, and (4) evaluation. The sections are not separate and isolated but are integrated into the total learning process of gifted students. It is important to emphasize that the regular program core must be a part of the education for gifted students, as it is essential for them to master all basic school learning in order to have the needed knowledge and skills to extend to other areas. Due to the characteristics of giftedness (i.e., the person learns easily and possesses a high retention rate) this task is usually accomplished with ease. This, then, leaves educators with the pressing question: "What, ideally, should gifted students be doing with their time?"

The outer portion of the circle on the model indicates the extension for gifted students which combines to form an educational program that is not only qualitatively differenti-

"Media Services for Gifted Students: An Overview," by Janice Smith, *School Media Quarterly* 1980, 8: 161–78.

ated but also complete and balanced. It is with this extended concept in mind that School District No. 12, Adams County, began to examine how to similarly extend and to qualitatively differentiate the more commonly held and traditionally accepted role of the library media specialist to meet the unique needs of the gifted and talented.

Teacher/Library Media Specialist Role Definitions. The role of the library media specialist in gifted education must be clearly defined, as must be the role of the teacher. These roles, although very different in function, must be closely aligned in terms of goals and responsibilities and must be compatible and supportive of gifted students.

The thrust of the role of the library media specialist is basically one of extension in a twofold manner: extending skills that the library media specialist already possesses as a result of his/her formalized training and experience in the field to meet the special needs and interests of the gifted and facilitating the extension of gifted students' knowledge, skills, and attitudes. In developing this extended role, the cognitive process needs to be analyzed in terms of how to provide more challenging learning experiences, not only to identified gifted students, but to *all* students as well, through appropriate media, materials and services, which will be further explored.

The Library Media Specialist's Extended Role and Tennant's Model. To see how this extended role fits into each of the four sections of Tennant's model, it is necessary to examine each in detail:

1. *Content*. In the initial phase of instructional development and design, the library media specialist, as part of the educational planning team, must (a) assess the current availability of instructional materials to achieve the stated gifted program content objectives; (b) determine the need for adapting, modifying, or purchasing media to meet curricular objectives; (c) provide for a wide range of print and audiovisual materials to allow for varying learning styles; (d) produce the necessary original media to accomplish objectives of the gifted curriculum; (e) consider the variation, not only in reading and interest levels, but also in the *cognitive* level as well; (f) initiate necessary planning strategies with the classroom teacher for the integration of media skill development, which may include the use of advanced reference materials and systems within the content of the gifted curriculum; and (g) provide for a wide range of curricular interests as well as being able to stimulate new interests through a variety of resources.

2. *Process*. In the Tennant model, process includes the areas of decision making, creativity, and cognition. The gifted student must be trained to examine various alternatives before making a final decision; be encouraged to utilize the expansion of creativity in the degree of use and type of creative expression shown in relation to his/her output; and not only be taught to think on "higher levels" and improve his/her thinking skills, demonstrated by his/her creative product, but also be taught to become an independent thinker who is able to utilize all of the thinking processes in order to reach his/her desired outcome. To relate process directly to the extended role of the library media specialist means, in one aspect, that materials must be selected with yet another criterion in mind—that of selecting materials that employ the heuristic, "discovery," and inductive strategies so strongly advocated by Renzulli.[3] These strategies are based on problem-solving methodologies of an open-ended nature that rely heavily upon appropriate support media, each of which stimulates the student to go on to further inquiry. For example, through the use of what Renzulli calls how-to-do-it books, the student is encouraged to become a firsthand investigator, which is a necessary skill for research. *The Book of Think: Or How to Solve a Problem Twice Your Size* by Marilyn Burns is an excellent example.[4]

Another aspect of process, as it appears in the Gifted Extension Model, in which the library media specialist has a definite responsibility, is that of encouraging creative and divergent reading and the use of audiovisual media through the utilization of effective questioning techniques. It is essential that the library media specialist have skills comparable to those of the classroom teacher in utilizing questioning techniques that will bring about thinking as well as the expression of it. These techniques involve, among many others, open questions and follow-through procedures that encourage the student really to think, interact, and become involved. How different is this skill from those in which the library media specialist has traditionally been trained to conduct a reference interview properly. It seems to be, again, only an extended use of skills.

A third area of process as it relates to the responsibility of the library media specialist in working with the gifted deals with the whole realm of research skills. As stated previously, library media skills, if they are to be taught in a meaningful way in context, must be planned in the initial or instructional design phase. The library media specialist must be aware of the content focus for the program and the major concepts and skills to be stressed within the program. Renzulli strongly believes that research skills are processes that a student must learn. It is vital to a gifted student's continued intellectual growth that he/she, perhaps more than other students, becomes an extremely effective and independent user of media and that the gifted student possesses a further knowledge about the existence, nature, and function of advanced reference materials and systems.

3. *Output*. As previously outlined, the gifted student utilizes his/her knowledge, skills, and attitudes to develop a product or a solution to a problem in the output section of Tennant's Gifted Extension Model. The products should reflect application of the content and process areas of learning in order to be a viable product for a gifted program. Renzulli strongly advocates that the gifted student should not simply be a consumer of knowledge but should also be a producer of knowledge.[5] With something of a dichotomy existing between two major educational issues—that of a current national concern surrounding strengthening obviously declining written language expression as observed in college freshmen, while still allowing for a variety of learning styles, in both the output as well as the input mode—what, then, are the implications for media services in the area of production? We must provide materials and facilities for the development of student products, not only in the written format, but also in a variety of media formats as well. Thomas Walker, in his article entitled "Media Services for Gifted Learners" (*School Media Quarterly*, Summer 1978), states that "the multiple talents, interests, and abilities of gifted students as well as the heuristic teaching methods often suggested in gifted curricula are especially conducive to the use of media production activities, and that these activities may be far more challenging and rewarding to the gifted child than the writing of 'summary reports' so criticized by Renzulli."[6]

Again, what specific implications does gifted student output in the media format have on the total area of library media services? First it is essential that the library media specialist possess a strong degree of technical expertise in various types of equipment operation and production techniques. Second, it may create additional and specific space and facility requirements. Next, an increase of student product development by the gifted in the media format will certainly place new and increasing demands upon the supply budget. The fact must be faced that a written research paper is much cheaper to produce than a slide-tape presentation. Last, increased student production activities may create a need for differentiated staffing to assist students in product development, to repair and properly maintain equipment, to control equipment circulation, and to maintain an adequate supply of appropriate production materials.

Table 1 briefly shows the format developed by Project THINK personnel in School District No. 12, Adams County, to assist teachers, library media specialists, and students in the necessary preplanning steps for producing a successful student product in a variety of formats. The intent of this product development chart is to identify what the specific product will be, what additional human resources, if any, will be needed, and what the equipment and facility requirements for successful completion of the product will be as well as to provide a task analysis of the skills involved in producing the desired product. This form is meant to be used as a work sheet based on the unique needs of the students as they relate to the development of specific products.

4. *Evaluation*. The final section of Tennant's model is evaluation, which, in the regular core program, is a phase most often performed by the teacher. Gifted students have the ability to perform self-evaluation after they are taught evaluative skills. Evaluation raises the following questions: How is it possible to challenge all students to their own limits so the very best products and solutions result, and how can educators help to build the kind of task commitment that has been the trait of almost all famous people? These are the people who try many alternatives and rework their products over and over until they are satisfied.

It is the library media specialist's responsibility to work cooperatively with teachers to establish stringent criteria for effective evaluation of student products. Only through high expectations and subsequent criteria will educators be able to demand the excellence of which these students are capable. Most teachers have long ago developed well-

TABLE 1
Product Development Chart

	Products			
	Specific Student Products	Human Resources	Skills Involved in Producing the Product	Equipment and Facility Requirements

I. Written Format
  A. Creative Writing
  B. Expository Writing
  C. Research Writing
  D. Persuasive Writing				

II. Media Format
  A. Audio Tapes *(Sample of how this product development chart may be utilized)*
  B. Film Productions
    16mm
    8mm
  C. Filmstrips
  D. Transparencies
  E. Slides/Slide-Tape Combination
  F. Photographics
  G. Videotapes
  H. Bookbinding
	Development of an audio tape for the purpose of recording oral history		1. Interview techniques
			2. Locate human resources relevant to the topic
			3. Operate audio tape recorder accurately
			4. Investigate production variables, i.e., background music, sound effects, narration, and editing
			5. Locate interested audiences
				1. Cassette recorder or reel-to-reel recorder with microphone
				2. Possible mixing equipment
				3. Soundproof recording booth

III. Product Sharing (Involving aspects of I and II)
  A. Interest-Sharing Centers
  B. "Brimful" Boxes (boxes of materials that focus on a specific topic)
  C. "Make-Your-Own-Book" Project (factual or creative writing with binding)
  D. Performances
  E. Make a Model Related to Your Specific Topic
  F. Chart, Graph, or Diagram Information
  G. Visual Arts				

honed skills for determining the quality of a written research paper, but these same teachers will need much more training in order to similarly evaluate media products. Moreover, the library media specialist must then work with the students to assist them in developing their own standards for self-evaluation whereby they can continually evaluate and improve their own products to the best of their ability.

How Much Background Does the Library Media Specialist Need Regarding Various Learning Taxonomies?

A fairly easily understood taxonomy often utilized in gifted programming was developed by Benjamin Bloom.[7] In this cognitive hierarchy of learning, there are six different categories, with each category dependent upon skills acquired through previous categories. These six categories are (1) knowledge, (2) comprehension, (3) application, (4) analysis, (5) synthesis, and (6) evaluation (fig. 2).

After some experience with Bloom's taxonomy, it becomes evident that the verb in any instructional objective is the key that states what behavior the student will be exhibiting. It is the verb that gives one the first clue as to the category of the hierarchy to which the instructional objective is most appropriate. It is necessary for the educator to analyze what is really expected. A task analysis of previous learning required will be most revealing in the final determination of the complexity of thinking required within each objective.

In an adaptation of a matrix developed by Sandra Kaplan, it is possible to graphically illustrate how the scope and sequence of instructional objectives in difficulty can be meshed with complexity of thinking.[8] This matrix of learning (fig. 3) charts the difficulty of the task vertically and arranges complexity of thinking according to the six categories of Bloom's hierarchy horizontally. An arc

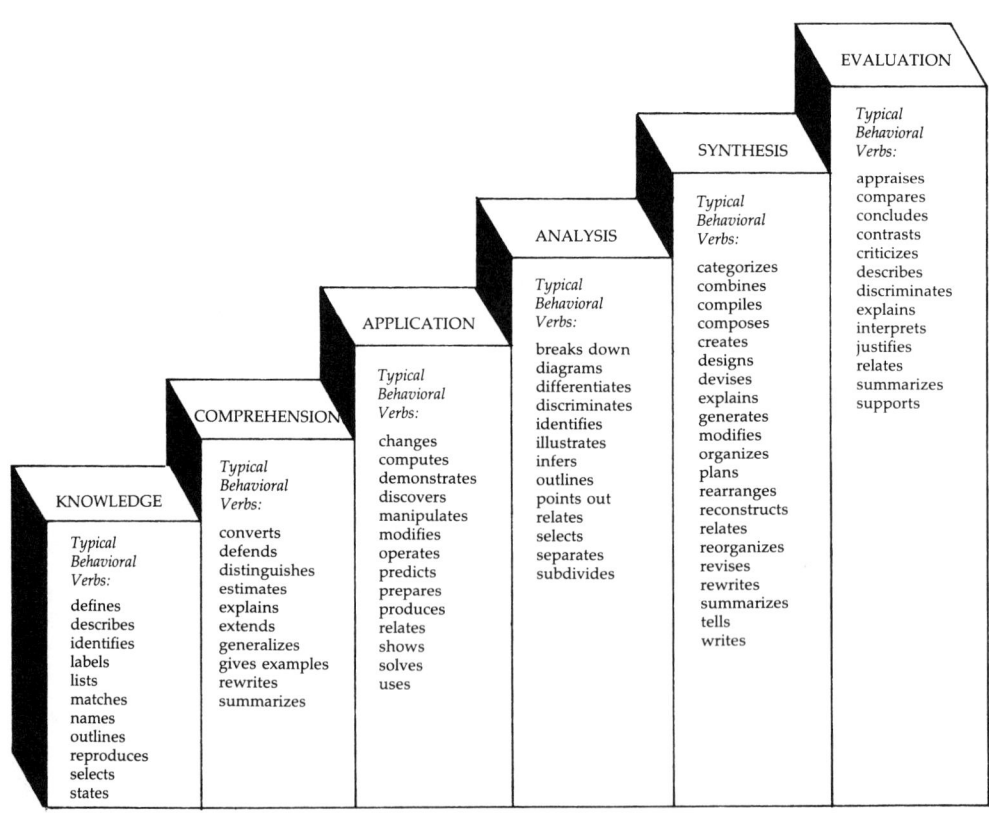

Fig. 2. Bloom's Taxonomy

drawn connecting the two points depicts the real dimension of the task; the larger arc depicts more extended learning taking place.

After working with this matrix, the library media specialists in School District No. 12, Adams County, had experience in rewriting the *K-12 Media Instructional Objectives* to extend these objectives further, not in difficulty, but in complexity of thinking.[9] A sample of one of these rewritten objectives follows:

Comprehension: Given a fable, the student will *identify* the main idea by accurately giving the fable an appropriate title.

Application: Given a fable, the student will be able to *write* a sentence that reflects that given main idea.

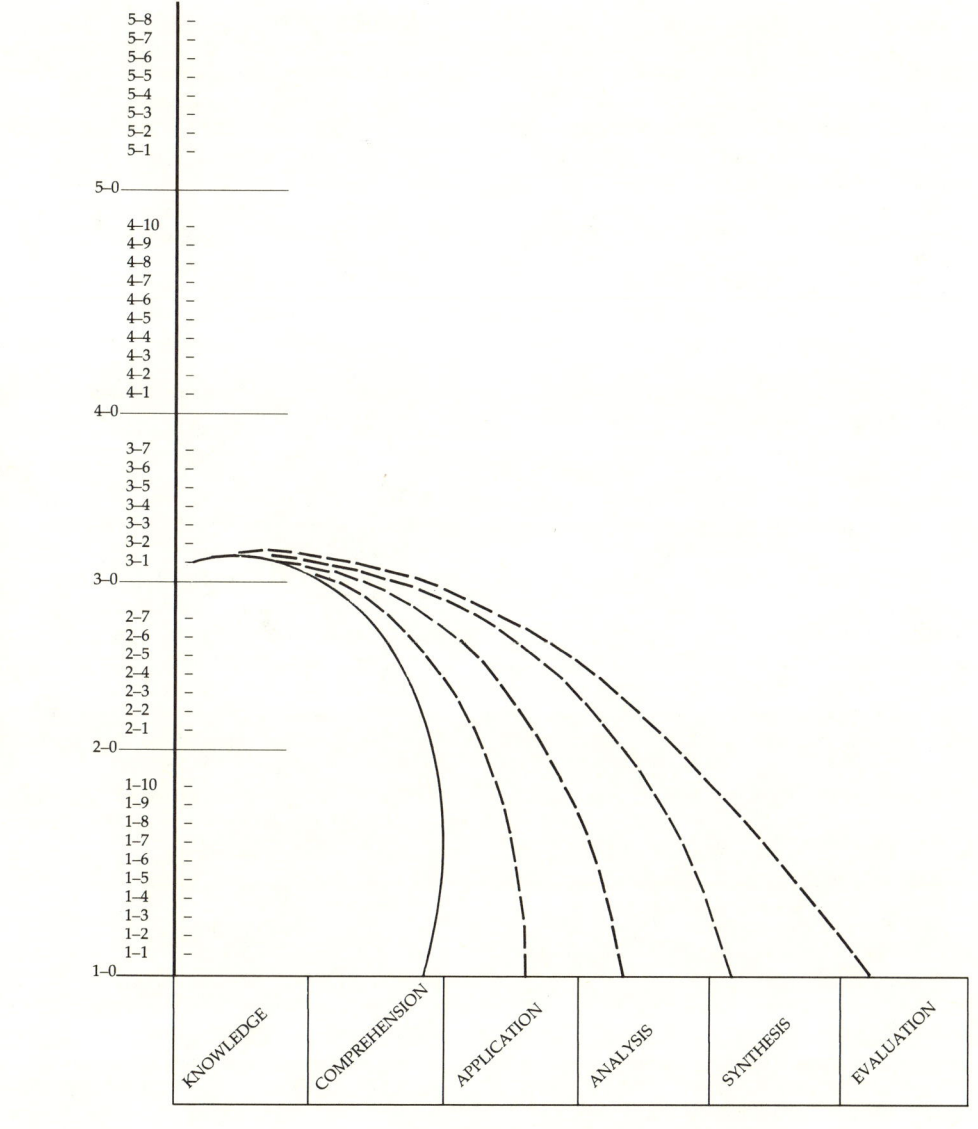

Fig. 3. Matrix of Learning

Analysis: Given two fables, the student will be able to identify the main idea of each and verbally *differentiate* between the two with accuracy.

Synthesis: After reading a collection of fables, the student will be able to *create* an original fable that clearly demonstrates a moral read in the given collection.

Evaluation: The student will be able to *defend* and *justify* the main idea used in his or her own original fable.

The practical question is, How can this knowledge and application of Bloom's taxonomy be used by the library media specialist to provide a media program with "qualitatively differentiated" services for gifted students? First, this understanding is essential in the extended responsibility that the library media specialist has in selection, that of assessing the cognitive level of materials. Through the understanding gained by experience in this process, the library media specialist will now examine the materials with complexity of the thought process in mind.

A second practical application of extending instructional objectives to provide increased opportunity for complexity of thinking is in the development of challenge centers. Educators have a clear understanding of what interest and learning centers are and what the difference is between them. But now, we are faced with a third term and an extended concept—the challenge center. Challenge centers provide learning experiences, utilizing the same content, appropriate for all students through the design of instructional tasks at various levels of complexity. Kaplan has created one standard model for developing a media challenge center that outlines the following four steps:

Determine the topic as it relates to the curriculum.
Collect appropriate media.
Identify complexity of thinking skills.
Develop a product based on the learning experience.

What Are the Implications of an Extended Role on Staff Development for the Media Specialist?

First, it is essential that the library media specialist acquire a basic understanding of the cognitive process, specifically in terms of the gifted. He/she should become aware of the historical development of gifted education, the characteristics of giftedness, and curriculum design for the gifted. School District No. 12, Adams County, has been very fortunate in having a federally funded grant from the United States Office of Education (USOE), *Project THINK*, to assist in providing a pilot project for gifted students coupled with a district staff development program to provide cognitive in-service training.

Second, the library media specialist must be thoroughly acquainted with the school district's philosophy and approach to gifted education.[10] In School District No. 12, Adams County, cognitive in-service training has been developed in part from the BASICS program, built on the work of Hilda Taba. Taba's research was the foundation upon which Lyle and Sydelle Ehrenberg based the program *Building and Applying Strategies for Intellectual Competencies in Students* (BASICS), which emphasizes the development of cognitively based teaching strategies.[11]

Third, an awareness of Bloom's taxonomy and how it applies to gifted education is, as previously discussed, a necessary prerequisite to effectively extending the role as described in this article. To reiterate, this knowledge is essential in analyzing and extending instructional objectives to higher levels of complexity and also in the development of challenge centers providing activities requiring increased complexity of thinking.

Fourth, in regard to selection, the library media specialist must be given specific training in assessing materials that promote a heuristic or discovery approach.

Fifth, the library media specialist must become very knowledgeable about advanced reference materials and systems and must become more adept at locating nearby resources to help the gifted student extend his/her knowledge and skills, especially in research areas. Fair and equitable policies and procedures for the interlibrary loan of materials from school to school, especially feeder schools from one level to another, are an essential element not only in information retrieval but also in budget considerations as well.

Last, it is imperative that the library media specialist possess a great deal of expertise in the technical areas of equipment operation and production activities. These skills must not only be present but must also continue to grow and develop as technology continues to change and to expand.

The emphasis for the library media specialist to become involved in gifted education seems to some educators to be redundant and unnecessary; in many cases, the library and its services have been the main provision for meeting some of the gifted students' needs for many years in educational history. Throughout the years, the librarian has had more contact with gifted students than any other professional in the school. Conceding the fact that such a generalization might indeed be true, educators must realize that at that point library services are, simply stated, a provision and not a program. Through such a program as the one outlined in this article, library media specialists and teachers go much further by working together as a team, by actively integrating appropriate services, materials, and the utilization of higher-level thinking skills into a complete, balanced, and well-articulated program designed to meet the unique needs of the gifted student.

Through such a media program as the one described, all students will be taught how to process information effectively in a variety of ways most appropriate to their abilities and needs. It is through a media program offering differentiated services that all students become self-actualized learners and participants in the lifelong process of learning.

Notes

1. Carolyn Tennant, "Identification of Thinking Skills by Students Participating in an Academically Gifted Program" (Univ. of Colorado, 1979), pp. 9–21.
2. School District No. 12, Adams County (Colorado), "Gifted and Talented Project THINK. Tapping Heuristic Intelligence for New Knowledge" (Northglenn, Colo., 1979).
3. Joseph S. Renzulli, *The Enrichment Triad Model. A Guide for Developing Defensible Programs for the Gifted and Talented* (Wethersfield, Conn.: Creative Learning Pr., 1977), pp. 29–40.
4. Marilyn Burns, *The Book of Think: Or How to Solve a Problem Twice Your Size* (Boston: Little, 1976).
5. Renzulli, *Enrichment Triad Model*, pp. 29–40.
6. H. Thomas Walker, "Media Services for Gifted Learners," *School Media Quarterly* 6 (1978): 253–54, 259–63.
7. Benjamin Bloom, *Taxonomy of Educational Objectives. Handbook 1: Cognitive Domain of the Taxonomy of Educational Objectives* (New York: Longmans, 1956).
8. Sandra Kaplan, National State Leadership Training Institute, Los Angeles, Calif.
9. School District No. 12, Adams County (Colorado), *Library Media Instructional Objectives; Curriculum Guide* (Northglenn, Colo., 1978).
10. School District No. 12, Adams County (Colorado), *District Guidebook for Gifted Program Development* (Northglenn, Colo., 1977).
11. Lyle Ehrenberg and Sydelle Ehrenburg, *BASICS: Building and Applying Strategies for Intellectual Competencies in Students* (Miami, Fla.: Institute for Curriculum and Instruction, 1978).

The Institutionalized Child's Need for Library Service

GERALDINE M. MATTHEWS

To develop appropriate library services for the child in an institutional setting, the librarian needs a thorough understanding of normal child development, as well as insight into the special problems facing the child who is receiving treatment for one or another handicapping condition. Knowledge of how a child learns about himself and his/her environment will provide orientation and guidelines for library program planning. Insight into some of the ways in which institutionalization affects the child's developmental stages will assist the librarian in individualizing library activities to help reduce the traumas and difficulties each child experiences as he/she tries to adjust to a handicapping condition, whether temporary or life-long. The effectiveness of the services of any library program designed to contribute to the normalization process of the child will depend on the degree to which the librarian understands the basic needs of all children and is consequently able to find ways of designing individualized programs that can address the specific needs of any particular child at crucial points in the treatment or therapeutic process. To be able to mesh the contribution of the library with the goals of the institution's treatment efforts, as well as with the highly individual and changing needs of the child, is the test and the challenge of therapeutic librarianship.

This paper will attempt: (1) to examine one of a number of systems designed to give a theoretical (or conceptual) framework for understanding the psychological needs of human beings, and to relate these principles to the basic needs of children in institutional settings; (2) to look at some of the specific effects which illness and institutionalization have on the present and future psychological development of the child; and (3) to suggest ways in which knowledge in these two areas can be used to develop a library program that is sufficiently perceptive and flexible to meet the child's expression (via words or interpretable behavior/actions) of his or her unfulfilled psychological and physical needs.

The Child as a Child

Child development has been one of the fastest-growing specialities of the last thirty years. While the field labeled "child development" has conventionally been viewed and/or dismissed (depending on attitude and orientation) as being primarily the concern of the psychologists, psychological principles and results of psychological investigations are basic to every profession concerned with child welfare and growth. As a result, new psychological knowledge is quickly assimilated into the professional literature as well as into the therapeutic activities of education, medicine, social work, parenting, communication development and other therapeutic professions. Curiously enough, there is little formal study of the subject in the ordinary library curriculum. While most of these applied areas of treatment or training have incorporated into the professional training curricula the principles of one or another system of child study in order to understand the child as he/she relates to their own particular discipline, librarians typically do not have this kind of formal requirement built into the coursework sequence. One of many organizational structures that may be useful for the librarian in orienting himself/herself to an appreciation of the child's psychological needs is the theoretical model proposed by the psychologist Abraham Maslow.[1] Although usually associated with theories of motivation, Maslow's observations have a wider application, in that they can be used to delineate individual needs and to clarify the several developmental stages through which all humans pass if not thwarted or handi-

"The Institutionalized Child's Need for Library Service," by Geraldine M. Matthews. Reprinted with permission from *Library Trends*, vol. 26, no. 3, Winter 1978, pp. 371–87, © 1978 The Board of Trustees of the University of Illinois.

capped. Even if, by training or inclination, one follows the principles of another psychological theorist such as Piaget, an understanding of this approach to child development would still serve to give librarians a structure and a model for understanding the basis and the "rationale" for the relationship the child might develop with library personnel, as well as a rationale for the therapeutic interventions and psychological needs fulfillment that the library program can supply.

Maslow's observations are based on a hierarchical system of needs which he believes is present within each individual. Maslow's needs system has been slightly adapted here to emphasize those conditions which must be present in order to contribute to the welfare and emotional/psychological growth of an institutionalized child.[2]

Physical Needs

This refers to physiological needs related to basic life maintenance. Included in this category would be carefully prepared, nutritionally adequate food, clean and healthful air, wide-ranging health care including protection from disease, complete basic program of daily hygiene, planned physical activity to meet exercise needs compatible with the handicapping condition, and a program of medical and therapeutically oriented treatment directed toward removing or ameliorating the handicapping condition.

Love Needs

The major components of love include: (1) acceptance by others with whom the child may come in contact regardless of severity or type of handicapping condition; (2) a stable, accepting relationship with adult authority figures; (3) the opportunity to develop peer group relationships; and (4) the opportunity to express love to other family, peer group, or individual friends and to feel loved in return.

Self-Actualization

Maslow summarizes this need by saying: "What man can be, he must be," while Allport refers to the same phenomenon as "becoming."[3] The motivational force related to self-actualization is considered to be a basic one by a number of different theorists operating within a variety of psychological orientations. However, to translate basic human needs into a child's terms and perceptions, one would very likely discover that the institutionalized child, like other children, seeks growth and self-actualization in the following areas:

1. *Physical development* refers to ambulation and mobility, coordination of perceptual-motor skills, self-confidence in the use of the body, and freedom of movement. Activity may range from physical stimulation for the multihandicapped, to organized sport activities for the more mobile adolescent.
2. *Interaction with environment* refers to the child's awareness of and active engagement with his/her surroundings, including human relationships. Awareness of an interaction with one's environment constitutes the first major step to self-actualization.
3. *Curiosity, play and creative expression* are considered of great significance to the individual's development. Every effort must be made to assure opportunities for the individual to satisfy his/her curiosity, to interact with his environment in a variety of play experiences (structured and unstructured), and to express himself/herself creatively to the extent permitted by individual ability.
4. *Family life* involves a wide range of experiences which should be available to each individual. This includes a family-like setting within the institution (e.g., a stable mother and father figure, small group living, and living within a family or home-type atmosphere). It also includes extended contact with families through frequent vacations, visitations, and home holidays if at all possible. Also, efforts must be made to provide for family weekends, outings with volunteers and other staff members, and visits with adoptive parents.
5. *Communication skills* must be developed as soon and as extensively as possible. It is desirable that each child acquire some form of communication (verbal or nonverbal) to the extent that he/she may establish contact with others and make known personal needs.
6. *Social skills*, which include simple manners and respect for others and their property, are essential to each individual's adjustment within or outside of an institution setting.
7. *Self-care skills* include various activities of daily living, e.g., eating, dressing,

toileting, personal hygiene, and grooming. The acquisition of these skills is an important avenue to increasing the individual's degree of independence and positive self-regard.

8. *Independence* is considered to be one of the most important of all self-actualization needs. All programs should aim at increasing independence by enabling the individual to conduct his/her own affairs to the fullest possible degree, and by recognizing personal needs and right to privacy with regard to possession of property, living area, and freedom of choice (e.g., friends, clothes, and leisure activities). Each individual has the right to tend to daily needs with the minimum degree of supervision compatible with adequate care. In addition, opportunities should be made available for the individual to increase his/her mobility in and around the facility.

9. *Interests, hobbies, and self activities* should be an integral part of the individual's daily life, and specialized programs should be developed for each resident to permit active pursuit of individual interests.

10. *Occupational adequacy* should be encouraged whenever possible. It is desirable that each individual in the quest for self-esteem and productivity have an opportunity to participate in some form of meaningful occupational activity.

11. *Formal training and educational needs*, which refer to school activities, prevocational and vocational training and counseling, and physical education, should be provided for all individuals capable of any level of participation.

12. *Recreational needs* should be met through structured and/or unstructured individual and group activities. Such experiences should be included both in the basic living unit and in specialized programs such as those that can be provided by the library and by other professional resources.

13. *Sexual development and feelings* in residents should be taken into consideration when planning programs. Each individual should be helped to identify with a proper sexual role, engaging whenever possible in coeducational activities, and receiving training in sexual development and in socially appropriate modes of expressing or acknowledging sexually motivated behavior.

14. *Religion*, or the satisfaction of spiritual needs, is an area in which individuals should be able to find fulfillment and expression. Whenever possible, children in the institution should be encouraged to participate in the religious programs offered by the facility.

Since Maslow's ideas are based on a hierarchical model, as was previously noted, it is necessary to have attained the first, most basic objectives and needs before success in other areas can be anticipated. With respect to these more elementary needs, namely adequate food and shelter and medical care, most facilities are required by a variety of federal and state laws to meet at least minimal standards of providing these basic survival-type needs. It is more difficult, obviously, to legislate love or adequately to determine whether a child feels that his or her full potential is being realized. These less tangible facets of Maslow's needs system, therefore, have become the areas which: (1) are most easily neglected; (2) are more difficult to plan and design, due to the variety of different institutional circumstances and individual lifestyles; and (3) frequently cannot be assessed precisely as they relate to each specific individual, because adequate communication with the child is often lacking. Even those self-actualization aspirations and achievements which are particularly meaningful to the individual may, from time to time, go unnoticed or unrecognized. Such areas of need are undoubtedly the most difficult to perceive and to satisfy in the developmentally disabled individual.

The Child as a Patient

Meaningful human existence depends on the acquisition and retention of a complex matrix of interpersonal experiences and positive social valences. The alternative—withdrawal into an environment of one's own making—is a choice which signifies that coping is too complicated an enterprise to undertake, much less endure. The child in a residential or long-term treatment center usually manages to adapt in some fashion, and does so by working through (and, on occasion, repeating) the various psychological stages and reactions all children go through when faced with trauma or stress. In this instance, the stress is associated with hospital treatment and the separation anxiety that is an inevitable part of the institutional experience. The child in long-term care, however, must also have the inner resources to accept institutional life as a way of living or must be helped to acquire these resources in order to accept and adapt to the environment as best as possible, if both physiological and psychological needs are to be met. The extent to which the child is able to do so is the criterion for a judgment regarding his/her degree of life satisfaction and state of inner peace.

For any child entering a treatment setting from a home-based life, predictable stages of accommodation can be observed as the child attempts to understand and then to adjust to the new environment. For very young children (under four years of age), the typical transition from the home to the hospital situation may be characterized by reactions related to protest, despair, denial, and, if the child anticipates separation for an extended period of time, by emotional flattening. This protest stage is usually characterized by outward signs of distress, such as crying, noncompliance with hospital schedules and care routines, and by persistent calling for the mother.

The next stage of adaptation typically involves less overt expressions of unhappiness, such as clutching a toy or blanket with whimpering and occasional crying. If the hospitalization continues for a week or longer, the child frequently tries to deny the entire experience (the pain and discomfort, the comings and goings of the mother) and begins to partake in institutional routines albeit in a perfunctory and dispirited manner. A long period of separation, as in a long-term illness, frequently results in the child developing the highly self-protective device of not permitting himself/herself to become excessively attached to hospital personnel, and he/she may even display a lack of openness and trust toward parents when they visit.

Older children, who have had an opportunity to be away from home from time to time and who are better able to understand the reason why hospitalization is necessary, often appear to suffer much less personal trauma from either short- or long-term treatment programs. In addition, since children between the ages of five or six and twelve are involved in the process of identifying and competing with peers, these children may well have had some opportunity to gain personal experience in coping with anxiety and stress, as well as in adjusting or adapting to changing social and physical environments. During this period in a child's life, an illness (especially a chronic one) becomes a critical formative factor in personality development and demands enormous expenditures of the child's inner psychological resources. In some cases the personality may be distorted in deeply pathological directions by chronic illness; in others, a strong premorbid ego structure may permit maintenance of the personality organization; while in still others, the illness may provide an occasion to develop defenses and coping mechanisms that may not have been acquired as young children.

In addition to the generalized reactions which children may display toward illness and handicapping conditions, certain kinds of illness seem to elicit quite divergent reactions from children. Orthopedic patients, for example, often appear to accept their situation with a positive outlook, at least initially. There may be surprisingly little overt depression and, as a rule, the children cooperate with the staff and focus on the future rather than on their present discomfort. Not only do body casts and other orthopedic devices provide visible signs of treatment, but these children often share rooms with peers who are having similar problems. Furthermore, the treatment period is usually fixed, with a definite anticipated ending date that can be shared with the child. The difficult period of treatment for orthopedic patients comes when casts or traction are removed, and when retraining the muscles or learning to walk becomes the primary focus of treatment. All of the hopes and expectations that were developed during the period of immobilization are now clearly unfulfilled, and the child may react with frustration, complaints, irritability, and loss of patience and resolve.

In contrast to orthopedic conditions, which seem to elicit active participation by the child in his own rehabilitation program, other illnesses may elicit a different response in the young patient. Children with cardiac disease, for example, often become preoccupied with monitoring their heartbeats and may adopt a passive-dependent, hypochondriacal stance; asthmatic children, on the contrary, are strikingly affected by the degree and affective direction of parental support and expression of parental concern. Amputation usually creates extreme anxiety due to the double burden of pain and the major assault on body image integrity. Blindness and deafness, if present since birth or early childhood, seem to be accepted by such children as a given condition of life. These children's affective and self-actualizing needs are often successfully worked out within the context of a social-vocational environment and training program optimally altered to circumvent or minimize the disability and to develop attitudes and self-perceptions of satisfaction and worth. Children with mental retardation will be especially affected by the kind of environment which their parents choose for them—home or institution—and by the affective/intellectual milieu provided in either setting. Mentally retarded individuals may have an especially difficult time in fulfilling needs beyond those at the basic safety level of food and bodily care. By the very nature of their handicapping condition, the mentally retarded require sustained encouragement and training to develop a realistic basis for appropriate fulfillment of independence and occupation adequacy needs.

Given this brief survey of some of the basic needs of handicapped individuals in an institutional setting, several questions may now be raised regarding the implications of these special needs for the institutional library. The answer may be that appreciation of these needs could well be the key to help the librarian determine professional expectancies, and also to delineate the library's role in the habilitation process and the relationship of the library to the multidisciplinary team typically involved in rehabilitation settings. Finally, and perhaps most importantly, the librarian's view of the library's relationship to the child and his/her treatment needs should become at once sharper and broader in focus.

The Librarian's Role in Habilitative Environments

In 1974, Lawrence Allen, a librarian and adult educator, looked at the field of special libraries[4] and concluded that while special libraries (within the context of his particular study) were indeed concerned with various issues relating to professionalism, one of the major concerns dealt with questions of the identity of librarianship, the role of the library, and how to mesh the library's functions with the total goals of the parent institution.

It is distressing to read the cries from librarians lamenting that they appear not to have valid reasons for their existence. . . . Who am I? Where do I belong? Where am I going? Akin to this is that special librarians have a particular need for an understanding of the role of the library and librarian within an institution that is different from a library . . . and a clearer picture of the forces that condition the special librarian in this work environment.[5]

While Allen did not answer these questions specifically, they are certainly valid exercises in introspection which librarians in most work situations frequently should ask themselves. The solution, at least in theory, might be a fairly simple one if librarians would define *education* and *information* as synonymous terms and view library activities as a broad range of teaching/learning interactions and experiences requiring mutual professional/client investment. This attitude and position in no way is meant to diminish the traditional information-provision role of the library, but it does perhaps provide an approach and reperception which might give greater depth and a follow-through dimension to library services in institutional settings. This professional stance might also give other disciplines increased appreciation and insight into what should be expected of any library program which purports to contribute unique services to the overall habilitative process.

Thus, the relationship of the library to the child in habilitation settings should be viewed for purposes of this discussion as one of a mutual learning process. The implicit and overriding goal of any direct or indirect contact with the library staff or library program would be to assist the child in the continuing process of Allport's "becoming." This process might consist of objective teaching or learning in the conventional and traditional sense, or it might be expressed via more dynamically oriented internalized activities which will help the child to understand himself/herself and others better and help the child in the development of feelings of self-acceptance, worth and personal competence.

The importance of the role of the library in helping the child learn to know himself in relation to his/her current life situation, and perhaps to give him/her grounds for anticipating a meaningful future, cannot be dismissed lightly. Insight, after all, is an important attribute of learning and it may be, in the end, the most valuable gift we can impart to the people we serve. For the librarian's part, he/she must plan and provide services with this learning goal in mind. It is no longer sufficient to provide little "typical" library activities (i.e., book-cart and story times) to captive groups of children nor to select an activity which superficially appears to be appropriate, but may have little to do with the child's state of need at that particular moment in his/her developmental process and coping struggles. While outward physical habilitation goals are being met and physical necessities provided for by other members of the therapeutic team, there must be some unit within the total treatment program that consciously understands the nature and importance of the higher-need levels and incorporates them as formal objectives for programming.

This is not to say that the library cannot also have improvement of physical functioning as a worthwhile goal. It can—and usually should. If, for example, the goal of the physical therapy plan is to encourage a child to reach to his/her own body midline, the library should be completely aware of the goal, offer a sensible plan and/or procedure as to how this can be facilitated in the child's contacts with library-based programs, and proceed to identify and incorporate an activity that leads to that end during the time spent with the librarian. For example, an interesting toy appropriate for the child's interest level should always be presented to encourage the desired reaching motion. However, the librarian must also be able, through personal knowledge of the child's psychological, social, and educational records, to plan activities which: (1) are appropriate for the present functioning of the child, (2) anticipate the next developmental stage, and (3) are chosen to meet the life-functioning need level the child is or should be experiencing. It should also be noted that this approach to planning library services—i.e., programs based on principles of normal child development adjusted as required by the characteristics of each person's illness and unique complex of physical and psychological needs—might very well include such traditional activities as story hours. However, librarians should not feel that a story hour is the only tool available to them or, conversely, that storytelling is the exclusive province of the library. It is entirely justifiable for the librarian to use techniques frequently associated with other treatment professionals. After all, books are not disregarded by the teacher just because they are viewed as the sine qua non of the properly furnished library. By the same token, the occupational therapist frequently relies heavily on toys (which might also be classified as instructional materials) in order to elicit certain responses from children. The librarian, therefore, while not engaging in physical or occupational therapy, should find ways to develop programs using the ideas, activities and utensils that are appropriate to the children's needs, rather than attempting to build a program that slavishly conforms to constricted current norms of what libraries are supposed and not supposed to do. In most situations this less traditional professional stance will be accepted easily by all concerned with the child, and should under normal circumstances lead to a closer, more responsible, and mutually supportive relationship with other disciplines.

Library Programming

The preceding comments on the psychology of the handicapped child are meant to highlight how important it is for librarians to understand the individuals with whom they are working. It is unfortunate that librarianship has somehow worked itself into the position of trying to impose the materials of its trade on people and situations without establishing a logical basis for the activity. Perhaps this problem arises from the fact that librarians typically are taught to deal with masses of people and to find the common thread from a much larger data base rather than to work with single individuals and approach the issues from a developmental model such as Maslow's.

The first skill which must be emphasized, therefore, is that which is concerned with developing expertise in assessing the child's present motor, social, or psychological status. Second (and building upon this assessment), the librarian should learn to be able to make a judgment about the next psychological or physical level to be encouraged and achieved. From these inferences—and the conclusions should eventually be accurate enough to qualify as clinical insights rather than mere inferences—the librarian should be sufficiently knowledgeable about the materials at his/her command to be able to prescribe (select) the right activity or item for each child and his/her idiosyncratic needs at the moment. While admittedly this process has not yet become refined or even fully understood, it certainly has reached a level that is competitive with other disciplines, such as education, activity therapy or psychology. While the librarian is not going to administer a Wechsler intelligence test before allowing a child to see a film, the data amassed in the child's chart have the potential to help the librarian (as well as other disciplines) understand the child's needs, need level, and any abnormal psychological reactions, such as withdrawal or denial, that might be contributing to the diminished receptive state of the child at the period of time available for interaction and skillful programming. The process of using this information for program planning should not be significantly different from the process used by other disciplines. The psychologist, for example, will observe a self-destructive child, ascertain when and under what conditions the undesirable activity takes place, and from a collage including his/her background of knowledge in the field, application of current research literature and practice, plus considerable ingenuity and common sense, will develop a program for the child which is designed to stop the head-banging or other self-destructive behavior. Depending on the situation and the inter- or intrapersonal variables operating, the program may involve principles of behavior modification, change of environment, change of personnel, and/or addition of any of the above plus new stimuli. The librarian, if following the same approach and presented with the same symptom complex, might find that thorough study of the child would indicate that certain library activities would have high interest value, low distractibility, could be carried on in an appropriate area, would require use of hands and feet (many manipulative and tension-reducing skills), yield an immediate reward, and would be similar enough to an activity or item adaptable to ward use that the two therapeutic program activities could act as mutual reinforcers.

Parallels to this approach can also be shown in relation to several other activity areas. For example, many children in a variety of institutional settings have problems with the development of clear or extensive speech patterns and vocabulary. Since it is obviously impractical for the speech therapist to be constantly at the side of the child, much of the progress (or lack of it) that is made in speech development or correction must occur as a result of interaction outside of the therapeutic setting as it relates specifically to communication disorders. If the librarian can acquire enough information to understand the child's problem and his/her stage of speech habilitation, and is knowledgeable enough to make (or become informed about—in this instance, sound and speech progression are well-known phenomena) an accurate assessment of the next developmental step in the corrective process, then activities designed by the library for the child should identify the short- and long-term goals, clarify ways in which the library intends to contribute to goal attainment, and document the progress toward that end. The program results, the observations made during the process, and the interfacing activities that could be presented in tandem with other disciplines will clearly indicate that library programs need not be places for mere leisure-time activities.[6] An even more specific example of what could happen in such a program might be illustrated by a child who has a speech handicap resulting from cerebral palsy. While intelligence may or may not be a complicating factor, the physical limitations may be such that speech is difficult or not understandable, and the child consequently needs to use a language board. If the language board is, for example, the one used in Bliss symbol programs, then the goal for the child will be the acquisition of vocabulary and learning how to combine symbols for the communication of ideas. In some instances, the goal might even be the further control of an arm movement so that pointing to the symbol can be carried out. Since communication is an important element in the child's life (speech or a speech substitute is vital to each person's well-being and constitutes a basic priority on which other life-enhancing conditions are built), the library, as well as all other disciplines, must devote considerable effort to establishing and/or developing this skill. However, for severely handicapped children, the mastery of language boards does not come easily. It is a progressive undertaking accomplished at great effort and only in infinitesimal increments. To assist in the process, the librarian must: (1) know the Bliss symbol structure and philosophy; (2) know the specific goals for the child; (3) understand the child's capabilities, strengths and weaknesses, and understand how to use the most intact physical and cognitive structures available in working toward mastering the symbolic language; and (4) devise a program that will help the child to reach these ends, using the library as a therapeutic setting. In related communication development areas, the same organization and procedure would be used if the goal were, for example, to become skilled in manual communication. While it would be assumed that the librarian in an educational center for the deaf would have full mastery of this technique, and that the areas that the library could work in would be related to the normalization questions common to children of potentially average capability overlaid with this particular handicap, it should be noted that manual communication may be useful for a number of other user-related disabilities that affect speech and oral communication. In these instances, new learning in communication is coordinated with the training necessary for compensating for these other deficits, and the techniques the librarian devises for meeting the coordinated goals of the child will determine how he/she designs the particular library activities for any one individual. Other problems relating to speech acquisition that the child may have could include such basic issues as need for infant auditory stimulation, prespeech training, beginning language or presyntax stimulation, and (certainly in advanced language programs where the goal is to enable the child to use language spontaneously and creatively) making needs, desires, emotions, and ideas known and, having developed this interactive mode, beginning to participate more fully in his/her own normalization process.

For reasons known only to conceptually fuzzy tradition, many institutional library programs find themselves part of the education unit. This is an unfortunate arrangement and tends to place the residents' library in the position of having to devote considerable resources to education as a department rather than to the needs of the children as a whole. A much-preferred solution is more typically found in smaller residential facilities, where the library, while perhaps not physically as large as the materials centers in major state institutions, may have more individualized and specialized input as a discipline into the total therapeutic program. Thus, the optimal relationship of the library with the education unit or department of a residential facility should be the same as its relationship with any other unit. The educational activities and obligations of the library in this association should be viewed on a par with those in others.

Viewing the relationship objectively, it is easy to see that some basis exists for the traditional close association between libraries and education units. The most obvious basis, of course, is that the relationship was borrowed from the "normal" school pattern—an organizational situation about which many school libraries frequently express unhappiness—at least in its hierarchical implications. More to the point is the fact that it is traditional to think of libraries as an ancillary service to education, although having certain commonalities in activities. This parallel, at least for libraries working in residential facilities, may tend to break down under close scrutiny. Let us look first at the education program.

Long-term facilities for the mentally retarded probably encompass the largest number of children living in institutional settings today. Because the zeitgeist has placed such great emphasis on normalization and on the development of community alternative care settings during the last few years, the children found in these institutions are usually both severely retarded and extremely physically disabled. The typical teacher or education activities, therefore, are not related to the acquisition of reading, writing or mathematical skills. Rather, the typical classroom teacher (if he/she is still found in the classroom) is involved in trying to establish or reinforce such basic functions as stimulation activities, gross and fine motor skills, self-care training, preschool readiness (such as attending and/or visual-auditory matching), and discrimination learning. If the child is functioning at a trainable retarded level, the teacher's efforts may be directed toward skills related to reading readiness, very simple number concepts, or leisure-time games and skills. For children who have perceptual problems in addition to mental deficiency, programs place great emphasis (depending on the handicap) on areas such as auditory, tactile, taste or smell stimulation, mobility in independent daily living needs, signing, and improved social interaction with others. None of these activities by law, or even by tradition, is the exclusive property of an education department. Many of the programs have, in fact, been borrowed and adapted from other disciplines such as occupational therapy and psychology, and incorporated into programs labeled education, because they are the learning experiences currently held as meaningful for children not able to manage what has been traditionally considered the proper content of an educational program. There is no reason why most of these functions cannot or should not be incorporated into formal and informal library activities. Certainly, such an approach seems logical, natural and reasonable. Since in many situations this has not been the case, a reexamination of library programming and its origins is clearly in order. In determining what this programming should be, the librarian may find it useful to rethink the traditional relationship of libraries to the education structure, as discussed earlier. He/she may also obtain some insights from the development of the education field (and others) as such disciplines have tried to cope with inherent inadequacies of approach when faced with children for whom traditional forms or programs of education have no relevance. As has been noted, a certain amount of adaptation has been necessary and, as a result, a teacher specializing in education of the handicapped child with a bachelor's or master's degree may find himself/herself engaged in teaching, eating or dressing skills—a very relevant activity for the needs of the child.

Another area of program similarity that should be examined by librarians in order to determine which library activities are being used by another group of professionals claiming identity as a discipline is the field of recreation or activity therapy. Frequently found under the heading of activity therapy are arts and crafts programs. As library programmers know, arts and crafts can include activities ranging from work with crayons and paint, to water colors, paper construction, collages, potato painting, paste and glue constructions, drawing, woodworking, ceramics, clay, or even sewing. All have been and can be used in many areas in conjunction with various programs. However, it should be noted that these kinds of planned activity are not simply designed to fill time. As in all other programs, they are planned to develop or rehabilitate certain physical or mental deficits. The objectives can range from striving to improve gross and fine movement, to a development of manipulative skills, and then to cognitive development, self-expression, and an appreciation of the general field of arts. On another level, arts and crafts are used to train and/or establish manipulative functions of the hands and arms; to encourage attending behaviors to specific tasks; to enhance dexterity; to establish a sense of size, color, shape relationships; or simply to learn a new skill or enlarge on older latent ones that bring a sense of pleasure and accomplishment to the child. For the librarian programmer, all of the above activities, goals and motivations are valid reasons for incorporating such activities into present library programs or for introducing such objectives into new programs. As the librarian examines the needs of each child, it should be part of the program-planning philosophy to determine how each of these activities can be beneficial to the child who may need to develop attention span, learn to interact with peers, learn to relate to adults, develop working habits either alone or in cooperation with others, strengthen receptive or expressive language, learn to be less destructive, and control impulses and develop self-control related to hyperactivity. The important point is not the particular activity used in a particular setting, but rather that the child's needs are assessed properly and that both activity and setting are selected with therapeutic goals for the child in mind, rather than simple attendance at some diffuse, library-sponsored activity.

Activities related to music, whether they be listening, singing, rhythm or playing an instrument, form another extraodinarily successful program element that can be used with considerable specificity by the librarian. There is considerable literature in the music field that can be extremely valuable to the library program-planner. It is easy to obtain and should be studied as an example of a rationale that has been developed by a "soft" therapy. The general goals of most music programs include providing sensory stimulation, the development of communication skills, improvement of eye-hand as well as total body coordination, and the encouragement of self-esteem and self-expression. Even more specifically, the incorporation of music into a library program can, either alone or in conjunction with another activity, be used to encourage in the individual child any of the following skills: eye contact, physical response such as clapping hands together, improving attention span, awareness of expected response to a stimulus, vocalization, finger or hand dexterity, learning the concept of taking turns and sharing, practice in the technique of relaxation, sound discrimination, development of the component parts of music, and musical composition. Again, it is necessary that the programs be tailored for the child's needs and that the librarian maintain individualized records, in a format meaningful to others, which document the claims the librarian may or may not be making for the efficacy of this or any program being offered. It is to be hoped that in all library program efforts, the librarian working with handicapped children can be adaptive in philosophy, imaginative in program construction, and educationally and psychologically equipped to enter into the therapeutic relationship as an equal and contributing professional: a feat that in many situations may require rethinking by all disciplines concerned.

Notes

1. Abraham Maslow, "A Theory of Human Motivation," *Psychological Review* 50 (1943): 370–96.
2. *Program Review Project* (Madison, Wis.: Central Wisconsin Center for the Developmentally Disabled, 1970).
3. Gordon W. Allport, *Becoming; Basic Considerations for a Psychology of Personality* (New Haven: Yale Univ. Pr., 1955).
4. Lawrence A. Allen, *Continuing Education Needs of Special Librarians*, SLA State-of-the-Art Review no. 3 (New York: Special Library Assn., 1974).
5. Ibid., p. 22.
6. Leisure-time activities do take place in the library, but in most instances where the child is in a rehabilitation facility, leisure time is also part of the therapeutic plan and should not be expected to be a time that will "just work out" without direction or that should have no direction. Almost all activities in a facility need to be planned with some therapeutic or needs fulfillment goal in mind.

Additional Reading

Bergmann, Thesi. *Children in the Hospital.* New York: International Universities Pr., 1965.
Etzioni, Amitai. *Modern Organizations.* Englewood Cliffs, N.J.: Prentice-Hall, 1964.
Gouldner, Alvin W. "Organizational Analysis." In *Sociology Today: Problems and Prospects*, edited by Robert K. Merton et al. New York: Basic Books, 1959, pp. 400–48.
Robertson, James. *Young Children in Hospitals.* 2nd ed. London: Tavistock, 1970.
Weber, George H., and Bernard J. Haberlein, eds. *Residential Treatment of Emotionally Disturbed Children.* New York: Behavioral Publications, 1972.
Whittaker, James K., and Albert E. Treischman. *Children Away from Home: A Sourcebook of Residential Treatment.* New York: Aldine, 1972.

Library Service to Institutionalized and Disabled Adults

LINDA LUCAS

A few dedicated individuals in the past have served as advocates for the institutionalized and disabled in our society, but for the most part such adults have been ignored and left to live out their lives with little hope of personal fulfillment. Since the 1960s, however, there has been a societal trend toward bringing such individuals to satisfying and productive lives.

The importance of library services in accomplishing this goal was recognized in the Library Services and Construction Act, Titles 4A and 4B, 1966, which extended state library service to state institutions and to the blind and physically handicapped. Although early library literature reflects some provision of services to the blind, the imprisoned, and the hospitalized, it is only since the 1960s that library services to other specialized groups have been mentioned to any extent. Identification of needs, development of appropriate materials, requirements for facilities and staff, sources for funding, and the development of standards are some of the topics covered.

"Library Service to Institutionalized and Disabled Adults," by Linda Lucas, *RQ* 1979, 18: 251–56.

Institutionalized and handicapped adults vary in their freedom and ability to live independently, but many of them find themselves dependent on others to satisfy their information needs. One aspect of preparing such adults for the "mainstream" of life is increasing their ability to obtain information for themselves. The term *dependent adult* will be used to refer to disabled and institutionalized adults when the common information problems of both groups are discussed.

Most adults can freely satisfy a need for information at the time it is recognized using whatever means seems appropriate. Dependent adults, however, must rely on the ability and willingness of others to meet their needs. Their dependency may result because they are legally restricted to certain areas or because they are physically, mentally, or emotionally disabled. Dependent adults may live in institutions, in halfway houses, or in private homes. They may have been born disabled or they may have become dependent as adults. Some will be dependent indefinitely; others will be dependent only during a brief period of hospitalization or incarceration.

These people have specific information needs as diverse as the individuals themselves, but they are united in their limited freedom to satisfy those needs for themselves. Librarians in all types of libraries are beginning to recognize their responsibility to actively seek to aid such adults in overcoming the barriers they face. Meeting that responsibility will be no small task since, according to the U.S. Census, 1970, more than 9 percent of working-age Americans had a health or physical condition that affected their ability to work; nevertheless, assuming responsibility is imperative.[1] Jahoda points out that, whereas for most library users the library is only one of many information sources available, for many handicapped individuals, the library may be the only information source.[2]

As mentioned earlier, examination of the literature relating to library service to dependent adults reveals uneven development. Certain groups (e.g., the blind) have been comparatively well served, whereas other groups (e.g., the adult retarded) have been poorly served. The quality and extent of service varies with the institution and the community in which the individual finds himself. Library service to dependent adults is still in a stage of experimentation and exploration.

It is discouraging to note that much writing regarding services to dependent adults still reflects a patronizing, protective attitude on the part of librarians. Only rarely is there indication that the consumers of the services should be included in planning and evaluation. Successful programs require that representatives of target groups participate at these levels.

The blind as a group are easily recognized as in need of special help in obtaining information, since they cannot use the print materials libraries traditionally house. The blind also have a long tradition of serving as their own advocates. It is not surprising then that they were the first group to receive special attention from librarians. The comparatively high quality of service to them has been due in large part to the long-term support of the Library of Congress and to state and regional library programs. Through a decentralized network approach, personalized service can be provided at the local level. Informational materials in a wide variety of formats, as well as any equipment required for their use, are available free of charge to those who are eligible. Eligibility for these services has been expanded to include individuals who are not blind but who, because of other physical limitations, cannot read standard printed material.[3]

Service to prisoners likewise has a long history, but its quality has frequently been poor. It seems likely that the same allegiance to the positive power of "uplifting reading" which led champions to the cause of public library service, also led to the establishment of prison libraries in the belief that reading would help to reform criminals.

Unfortunately, however, prison libraries often became repositories for old books donated by individuals and libraries. Such collections were often housed in an inaccessible closet, uncirculated, and unsupervised by a qualified librarian. In prison libraries both overt and covert censorship have existed. Not only had access to detective stories or books on locksmithing been restricted, but access to legal information also has been limited. Inmates literate only in a language other than English often have been unable to obtain appropriate reading material. The supply of materials for poor readers is often limited.

Such situations still exist in many institutions, but important changes are taking place. Many libraries in correctional facilities are now staffed by qualified librarians who attempt to serve their residents' needs for recreational, informational, and legal information through carefully planned collections and programs of activities as well as through cooperative programs with other libraries.[4] Such improvements in service should not be seen as a consistent trend, however. Deteriorating service is also reported.[5]

Patient libraries in hospitals, too, have a long history. Like prison libraries, they were often established as acts of charity rather than from real understanding of the needs of patients. Nevertheless, the quality of many of these libraries has improved to the extent that patients' needs for recreational reading are well met. The quality of information service provided is less consistent. Many librarians serving patients as a matter of course provide patients with general reading materials and reading guidance.[6] Yet censorship of medical and health information remains an issue.[7]

In patient libraries the censorship issue revolves around the question: Who should provide information concerning specific medical and/or health conditions? Should only the doctor provide such information, or does the patient have the right to turn to the patients' library for answers? The problem may be partially resolved as patient librarians in general hospitals become more involved in planning and implementing programs of patient education designed to aid the patient in being better informed.[8] It is unclear whether such participation of patient librarians would also extend to the answering of patients' questions that are raised or left unanswered by the patient education programs.

Beyond the blind, the imprisoned, and the hospitalized, library services to the dependent have until recently been minimal if they existed at all. The most easily identified group that has been effectively barred from service is the broad category of the physically handicapped, especially those individuals who cannot negotiate stairs because they are limited by wheelchairs and crutches or because they have disabilities such as heart conditions or arthritis that limit their activities. Legally, these individuals now have access to libraries under Section 504 of the Rehabilitation Act of 1973.[9]

Many individuals who need service, however, are not easily identified because their disability is invisible or because they are unable to move outside their place of residence. Identifying such individuals is a major problem for librarians. Successful outreach programs, as a result, must include mechanisms for identifying those who need service and for publicizing that service. There must be careful attention to the provision of access to service so that individuals are not inadvertently excluded. For example, libraries in institutions must be open during hours when individuals are not required to be participating in other activities. New federal regulations that facilities be barrier-free will make libraries more accessible for many people, but there will still be people to whom service must be taken; consequently, provision must be made for taking service to individuals who cannot come to the library.[10]

Librarians acknowledge that in order to meet information needs, those needs must first be identified. Unfortunately, at present there is only limited understanding of the information needs of people in the society at large, and there is even less knowledge of the information needs of dependent adults.[11] Moya Duplica, in focusing on the psychological and social problems of users of institution libraries, emphasizes that such people face the same life problems as other adults, but those problems are compounded by the limitations imposed by the specific disability.[12]

Sensitivity on the part of the librarian is required in order to individualize dependent patrons and to recognize that it is not the disability that is being served but rather traditional human needs as they are encountered by a disabled person. Certain experiences are common to people in dependency situations. Regardless of where they live or how long they have been dependent, they generally experience negative self-image, loneliness, depression, and invasion of privacy. The importance of such psychological problems may override the physical causes of dependency in the perception of the individual.[13] Successful library services to dependent adults, consequently, are supportive of the individual's need to deal with such problems and encourage feelings of self-worth and self-direction to as great an extent as possible.

The movement to bring the dependent into a life of independence and productivity reflects a new awareness in society of the humane and economic advantages of such a policy. Attention has focused primarily on the elimination of physical and legal barriers, but the barriers of indifference and hostility may actually be more difficult to eliminate. Librarians who are indifferent to the needs of dependent adults or who are openly hostile (as in the case of a librarian who objects to the distracting noise of an electric wheelchair as it moves through the building) can serve as effective barriers to improved library service unless others (including the disabled themselves) are alert and willing to serve as advocates.

Mainstreaming will mean that people who in the past were served in institutions—if they were served at all—will in the future be served in libraries of all types. Provision of services to these people will require careful planning. Many of the needed materials and the equipment to use them are expensive or nonexistent. Furthermore, because many libraries will find only a few people in their communities who need specific specialized services, it may seem uneconomical to establish extensive local collections. It is important to recognize, however, that the proportion of potential beneficiaries of such services will increase in the future.

A growing proportion of our population is elderly, and—with age—limiting disabilities often occur. For example, approximately thirty-three million people in the United States are over sixty, and projections show that within the next few decades there will be more than fifty million people in that age group.[14] Presently, about 65 percent of those with visual handicaps are sixty-five or older.[15] Furthermore, medical advances have resulted in the survival of a higher proportion of the disabled.

It is important to recognize also that changes in programming, collection development, and physical facilities that are aimed at the dependent can have spin-off benefits for other users. Mothers pushing strollers, librarians pushing book trucks, and library users who are just tired after a long day seem to prefer using a ramp to climbing stairs; unimpaired elderly and busy housewives looking for books to read for relaxation may enjoy high-interest/low-vocabulary books added for the reading disabled;[16] and many adults who need a simple introduction to an unfamiliar topic could benefit from the removal of the stigma of using the children's room when the adult and children's collections are combined.[17]

It is important also to recognize that specialized services need not be provided by local libraries unassisted. With its program of service to the blind and physically handicapped, the Library of Congress has pioneered the area of cooperative provision of service, materials, and equipment—a method that can be extended to serve other groups.

Because societal concern with provision of services to the broad range of disabled and institutionalized adults is relatively new, there are disagreement and misunderstanding as to where responsibility lies—especially for the funding of services. Although public libraries often have taken the responsibility for serving the homebound in their communities, they have been less inclined to see service to residents of institutions in their communities as their responsibility. Even though the individuals living in the institutions are residents of the community, they often are there not by choice but at the direction of a governmental agency. Furthermore, state and federal institutions are often located in areas where community resources are inadequate to support the additional demand for such services. One workable solution to the problem would seem to be an agreement in which library service is provided locally, supported by active cooperation with other libraries and governmental funds to aid the local library in staffing and collection development. Such programs have been proposed and developed through cooperation.[18]

Another area where cooperation must exist is in the development of standards. Divisions of the American Library Association, the Medical Library Association, and the American Correctional Association are concerned with standards for services to the disabled and institutionalized. Standards are in various stages of development.

The development of standards for service to the institutionalized that will be workable as well as meaningful, requires an awareness on the part of librarians that the institutions (both private and public) in which such services will be provided are heavily regulated by various governmental agencies. Requirements these agencies make of the institutions must be considered. Furthermore, it is important to recognize that the institutional library exists as only one element of the larger institution and that those who will implement the standards may have little understanding of their importance. Some administrator education may be required.[19]

As standards are revised for all types of libraries and for all library services, statements should be included relating to the needs of the disabled. The recent merger of the Health and Rehabilitative Library Services' Division and the Association of State Library Agencies of ALA to form the Association of Specialized and Cooperative Library Agencies reflects an awareness of the interrelationships of institutions.

The development of standards for service

raises a whole series of issues critical to the quality of that service, including collection development (the kinds of materials and their quality), staffing, funding, and responsibility for provision of service. The issue of access to service touches closely on the library's place in the institution. For the dependent the term *access* relates both to physical access and to the need to receive permission to go to the library.

Duplica has noted that the library may be one of the few places where an institutionalized person can make free choices.[20] It is unfortunate, therefore, that in many institutions library use is still regarded as a pleasant frill rather than an important part of the individual's experience. Library hours are often arranged for the convenience of the staff rather than for the convenience of the residents. There may be no special provision for delivery of service to individuals who are unable to visit the library. If a regularly scheduled activity must be cancelled to allow for a special activity such as a test, it is often the library period that is seen as expendable. Withdrawal of library privileges is sometimes used as a form of punishment for misbehavior in other areas of the institution.

Those preparing standards for service to the dependent adult have an opportunity to alter such negative attitudes by focusing on the needs of the individual resident, rather than on those of the institution, stressing the possibilities for individual development that exist in a positive relationship between the librarian and the resident in a carefully selected and maintained collection with a good program of service. Ideally, the librarian should be involved in the planning of the overall program for the individual resident.

The concept of mainstreaming means that librarians in all types of libraries must be aware of the special needs of dependent adults. Librarians who in the past have been concerned only with more traditional services must become informed on the effects of specific disabilities and on the potentially dehumanizing effects of the dependency situation. Uninformed librarians may assume incorrectly, for example, that the deaf require no specialized services, since their disability permits them to see to read a book;[21] and mainstreaming retarded adults may cause librarians some uneasiness if they assume, again incorrectly, that the retarded display the same behaviors commonly associated with psychosis.[22]

Some library school programs now include courses or certificate programs on services to the disabled and/or institutionalized, but such courses are taken by only a few students. Foundation courses that are required of all students in library school programs must include an introduction to the needs of dependent adults.[23] In order to bring such information to librarians already in the field, workshops and programs of continuing education must be conducted.

Service to the disabled and the institutionalized is in a stage of dynamic development. There is a great need for librarians who are sensitive to people and who are able to see beyond the disability to the individual. Such sensitivity must be realistic and not sentimental in order to be of value.

With more formerly dependent adults in the "mainstream" of life—earning a living, raising families, and generally participating in satisfying self-directed lives—it should become apparent to librarians that the concept underlying the provision of special materials, facilities, and programs in service to the disabled and institutionalized is not essentially different from that which underlies service to other adults—the librarian's function is to serve as an intermediary between the patron and the information he or she needs—to be a guide who negotiates a maze to achieve the desired result.

In this sense, then, all adults can be seen as "dependent" to the extent that they lack necessary skills and knowledge to locate information for themselves. Accepting such a view will help librarians adopt an attitude of sensitive service to the individual needs of all users—an attitude librarians now support in words if not always in practice.

Notes

1. "Disabled People in the U.S.: Facts and Figures," *Interracial Books for Children Bulletin* 8 (1977): 20–21.
2. Gerald Jahoda, "Librarians and the Handicapped," *Florida State University Bulletin* 4 (Aug. 1978): 5.
3. Hilda Kamisar and Dorothy Pollet, "Those Missing Readers: The Visually and Physically Handicapped," *Catholic Library World* 46 (1975):426–31.
4. "Library Services to Correctional Facilities," *Library Trends* 26 (Summer 1977); William R. Coons, "A Recent Inmate Recalls: Books and People Behind Bars at Attica," *Wilson Library Bulletin* 46 (1972):614–19; "Breaking In: Library Service to Prisoners," *Wilson Library Bulletin* 51 (1977):496–533.

5. Daniel Suvak, "Federal Prison Libraries: The Quiet Collapse," *Library Journal* 102 (1977):1341–44.

6. Eleanor Phinney, ed., *The Librarian and the Patient* (Chicago: American Library Assn., 1976).

7. "Medical Information Taboos," *Library Journal* 103 (1978):7; "Letters," *Library Journal* 103 (1978):909–10.

8. Cheryl Lynn Harris, "Hospital-based Patient Education Programs and the Role of the Hospital Librarian," *Bulletin of the Medical Library Association* 66 (Apr. 1978):210–15.

9. Access requirements are as specified in *American National Standard Specifications for Making Buildings and Facilities Accessible to, and Usable by, the Physically Handicapped* (New York: ANSI, 1961, 1971).

10. Johanna G. Sutton, "Consider the Confined: Methods of Reaching In," *Wilson Library Bulletin* 45 (1971):485–89.

11. F. Vintor Smith et al., "Library and Information Needs of the Mentally and Physically Handicapped," in *Library and Information Service Needs of the Nation* (Washington, D.C.: Govt. Print. Off., 1973), pp. 209–22; Harrison C. McClaskey, "Library and Information Needs of the Institutionalized Person," in *Library and Information Needs of the Nation*, pp. 198–204; and Genevieve Casey, "Library and Information Needs of Aging Americans," in *Library and Information Needs of the Nation*, pp. 162–70.

12. Moya M. Duplica. "The Users of Institution Libraries," *Library Trends* 26 (1978):307–15.

13. Margaret M. Kinney, "The Institutionalized Adult's Needs for Library Service," *Library Trends* 26 (1978):361–67.

14. Donald Smith in *Programs and Services for Older Americans* (Washington, D.C.: Govt. Print. Off., 1978).

15. Frances Benham, Judith Davie, and Gerald Jahoda, *Instructional Material on Library Service to the Handicapped* (Tallahassee: Florida State Univ., School of Library Science, 1978), A–26.

16. Patricia Lawson, "In Search of HILRL." *Wilson Library Bulletin* 47 (1973):691–95; Laura Arksey, "Junior Books for Senior People," *Wilson Library Bulletin* 49 (1975):512–15.

17. Arksey, "Junior Books for Senior People," p. 513; Jacqueline M. Wakefield and Catherine N. Hofmann, "Combining Your Adult and Juvenile Collections: Certifiable Lunacy or Common Sense?" *Wilson Library Bulletin* 46 (1972):513–17.

18. David C. Rittenhouse, "Prisoners, Patients, and Public Libraries." *Wilson Library Bulletin* 45 (1971):490–93; "Illinois State Library and Illinois Department of Corrections Joint Statement of Library Service," *Illinois Libraries* 59 (1977):285–87.

19. William P. Koughan, "Hospital Library Standards," *Special Libraries* 66 (1975):588–91.

20. Duplica, "The Users of Institution Libraries," p. 313.

21. Elsa Z. Posell, "Libraries and the Deaf Patron," *Wilson Library Bulletin* 51 (1977):402–3.

22. See the brochure "The Retarded Citizen and the Public Library," prepared by the State Library of Florida.

23. Some suggestions for such an introduction may be found in Frances Benham, Judith Davie, and Gerald Jahoda, *Instructional Material on Library Service to the Handicapped* (Tallahassee: Florida State Univ. School of Library Science, 1978). This is a preliminary copy for use in discussion at the Institute on Library Service to the Handicapped: Instructional Material for Inclusion in the Core Curriculum of Library Schools, held August 27 to September 1, 1978, at Florida State University.

Helping Hearing-Impaired Students

MARY JANE METCALF

Because of the nature of deafness, hearing-impaired children do not have access to the same sources of information as their hearing counterparts. Many messages from radio, television, and other forms of mass media are inaccessible to the deaf. Therefore, it is essential that libraries help disseminate the world's fund of information to the hearing impaired. Librarians can and should provide the means for children with this handicap to independently study and learn. Hearing-impaired children can and must be taught how to use a library to its fullest extent.

In many instances hearing-impaired children are retarded in the language arts, specifically reading. This retardation varies according to the degree of hearing loss. Students with moderate hearing losses typically use run-on sentences and omit prepositions, plural suffixes, and tense suffixes. The language of profoundly deaf students is typified by the omission of conjunctions, articles of speech, and prepositions, or an incorrect choice of prepositions or articles.

Reading problems quite naturally follow language retardation. These problems are not just due to a limited vocabulary. Hearing-impaired children have difficulty with syntactical structure, idiomatic expressions, and multiple meanings—things which are not always controlled in so-called high interest/low vocabulary books. For example, when one of our high-school teachers showed a filmstrip to her literature class, one frame included a caption that read, "She made a mad dash down the stairs." When the teacher asked the students what "mad dash" meant, they said that it meant "angry soap."

Avenues of Learning

Children with significant hearing losses learn primarily by sight. For this reason ideas and concepts must be presented in a visual format in order for the children to understand them. An illustration showing a person writing at a desk aids in making the word "author" much clearer than just a written, spoken, or signed definition.

Conversely, instructing with pictures alone may not suffice because hearing-impaired childen have some difficulty interpreting illustrations. Their language handicaps make it difficult for them to infer reactions, conversations, or events which are not specifically depicted in the illustrations. In order for hearing-impaired children with significant hearing losses to understand a concept or story, librarians should use both pictures and total communication (using spoken and manual communication) simultaneously.

Hearing-impaired children often have different interests than those of their learning counterparts. The extent of this difference is open to argument, but there is no question that differences do exist. There are children whose interest and maturity levels are practically the same as those of their hearing peers and there are hearing-impaired children whose interests and maturity levels are much lower than what is considered the norm for their age levels.

Storytelling

Storytelling is an experience of which no child should be deprived. It gives childen important cultural knowledge, expands their experience, and stimulates their interest in books. For this reason, storytelling is a major part of my program for kindergarten through junior high.

Hearing-impaired children can derive almost as many benefits from a storytelling session as hearing children. However, a lot depends upon which method of storytelling is used. Every method I use is visual in nature. The reason is that hearing-impaired children miss the pleasurable sounds, such as jingles, the cadence of rhymes, and vocal

---

"Helping Hearing-Impaired Students," by Mary Jane Metcalf. Reprinted with permission from *School Library Journal*, January 1979, pp. 27–29. R. R. Bowker Company/A Xerox Corporation.

TABLE 1
Comparisons of Visual Mediums

Qualities	Films	Filmstrips	Slides	Flannel Board
Shows motion	yes	—	—	yes*
Allows ample time for explanation	—	yes	yes	yes
Script can be adapted to different abilities and ages	—	—	yes	yes
Shows actual pictures from the book	yes**	yes**	yes	—

*dependent on teacher manipulation
**dependent on the film or filmstrip used

inflections which are a part of storytelling sessions for hearing children. During early childhood and the lower grades, hearing-impaired children are dependent upon the adults around them for the presentation and interpretation of all types of literature. They *need* to have the visual experience in order to enjoy and understand the story. Parents of the hearing impaired should be encouraged to tell stories at home and read and talk about the library books that their children bring home.

Visual mediums for storytelling include films, filmstrips, slides, and the flannel board. I have found that some of these methods are more effective than others. (See table 1.)

Because slide stories and flannel board stories meet more of the necessary requirements for hearing-impaired children, they understand stories in these media better than those told on film or filmstrips (and they can be more actively involved in the story as it is being told). Slide and flannel board stories can be locally produced. This gives the storyteller control over what content is included.

I have used each of the four methods singly and in combination to increase the children's understanding and enjoyment of a story. For example, "The Brave Little Indian," a participation story, is presented in a slide format and is a very simple story about an Indian boy who goes hunting for a bear. After I have twice presented the slide story, I run the film *Little Hiawatha* showing Hiawatha, as a boy, looking for a bear. This is a perfect combination because the children are treated to a repetition of the story and the story is told through the use of two media.

For another storytelling unit based on Aileen Brothers's *Sad Mrs. Sam Sack* (Follett), I use slides and a flannel board. Because the slides do not fully show the effects of the actions of this woman who fills her house with animals, flannel board figures are used to enhance the visualization of the story which increases understanding.

Library Instruction

The library skills K–8 curriculum that I created is designed to prepare students to use the library with a minimum of assistance once they reach high school. Every lesson is planned to teach one library skill or concept at a time followed by review exercises. The number of review exercises depends upon the complexity of the concept or skill and the capabilities of the children. For example, in discussing the meaning of book titles, I show the students some books, point out the titles, and then have them find and tell me the titles of other books. This lesson is reviewed before going on to the next step. However, teaching other areas in a library skills curriculum (e.g., use of the card catalog) is much more difficult and will take much longer to get across to students.

Because hearing-impaired children learn visually, I use visual material with every lesson. Overhead transparencies are used extensively because they are easily made, easily stored, and can be easily viewed by the entire class. I don't find that commercially produced audio materials such as cassette tapes are useful with the hearing impaired or deaf students.

In teaching library skills to hearing impaired children I find these points are helpful to remember:

Get teachers involved in what you are doing since they can reinforce the skills you are teaching.
Teach one skill at a time.

Repeat a statement two or three different ways if students do not understand it the first time and review lessons.

Always use visuals and total communication.

Provide individualized instruction.

Be sure to repeat or review lessons and to teach the most basic library skills.

Using the Catalog

Even though hearing-impaired students are taught to use the card catalog, their language retardation makes it difficult for them to find materials. The card catalog should contain many "see" references from simple terms to the more difficult subject headings. For example, a hearing-impaired child might not think to look under the heading *Automobiles* if he or she is looking for a book about cars. Frequently, the children cannot spell a subject they are interested in. If this is the case, they will probably approach the librarian and start describing the subject and the librarian will often have to determine what they want and spell the word for them.

At the Illinois School for the Deaf, we devised our own simplified subject heading listing based on *Sears List of Subject Headings*, 11th ed., by Barbara M. Westby (Wilson, 1977). Instead of using *Automobiles*, we use *Cars and trucks*. We use very few of the standard subdivisions because our students simply do not know what the terms mean. The standard subdivisions just make a complicated tool even more complicated to use.

If your card catalog cannot be tailored to meet the needs of a few hearing-impaired children, remember that these children need much more assistance in using card catalogs than other students.

Reading Programs

It is very important to constantly encourage hearing-impaired students to read. Because of their language handicap, they frequently become reluctant readers. Many just look at pictures but do not try to read the text. How do I persuade these children to actually read their books? One approach is to institute some kind of reward program whereby the students receive recognition for every book read. In checking on whether or not the books have actually been read, we consider the ability of each child. The amount of cooperation received from their teachers is also important. If you chose to require book reports as a method of checking, then leniency is required! From my experience, most hearing-impaired children have great difficulty writing coherent book reports. If you insist on grammatically correct book reports, writing assignments will be very tedious for the children and will take all of the enjoyment out of the incentive program. It's better to have students give oral book reports.

Teachers are an invaluable source of assistance in a reading incentive program. They know the abilities of their students: they can assist in deciding what evaluation method to use, and some teachers might even be willing to use class time to help in determining suitable books for students and followup reading evaluations.

Materials and Aids

Because hearing-impaired children can be easily discouraged, they should be provided with books that are readable for them, meet their interest/maturity level, and contain visuals that reinforce the text. Although there are numerous so-called high interest/low vocabulary books on the market, many of them contain too many difficult language patterns and sentence structures. They do not have sufficient illustrations. I have found that books with a wide disparity between interest levels and reading levels (e.g., 8th grade interest/3rd grade reading), usually are illustrated and are easier for the students to read.

One particular type of high interest/low vocabulary reading material (that has long been an anathema to librarians, educators, and parents) is comic books. Although they were once condemned, comics are used as valuable tools in the constant struggle to attract reluctant readers. Comics have such a universal appeal that now some textbooks are published in comic book formats. Two such educational series are *Awareness Pictorial Books* (Davco Publishers) and *Career Awareness Program* (King Features). Our library has educational comics, Classic Comics, and popular comic books (Donald Duck, Batman, etc.) that are sold at newstands. All of them are useful in encouraging students to read.

I use four book selection aids in finding appropriate materials. They are: Spache's *Good Reading for Poor Readers*, Strang's *Gateways to Readable Books*, McCarr's *Materials Use-*

ful for Deaf/Hearing Impaired, and the teachers suggestions. Some excellent high interest/low vocabulary books are listed in these sources. Two reading series that I purchased upon the recommendation of a teacher were the Scholastic's *Spirit Books* and *Action Books*. Not only do these have grade levels ranging from 2.0 to 3.9, and an interest range of grades 7 to 12, and a mature format, but they are well illustrated.

Periodical collections and reference collections do not need to be altered for hearing-impaired students. However, librarians should remember that these children will seek help in understanding the language in the periodicals and reference books.

Audiovisual collections should be supplemented with films which have been captioned for the hearing impaired. To date, approximately 900 educational and 700 general interest and theatrical 16mm films have been captioned and are available on a free loan basis to any agency serving the hearing impaired. For information on the captioned films program write to: Captioned Films and Telecommunications Branch, Bureau of Education for the Handicapped, United States Office of Education, Washington, DC 20202.

Librarians, who have not already done so, may want to purchase professional books on deafness. There are numerous books which overview the pathology of deafness, the methods of instruction and communication, and relevant topics to inform parents, teachers, and others working with the hearing impaired. The chief sources of professional books (and books in sign language) are:

Alexander Graham Bell
Association for the Deaf, Inc.
3417 Volta Place, N.W.
Washington, DC 20007

Gallaudet College Bookstore
Gallaudet College
Washington, DC 20002

National Association of the Deaf
814 Thayer Avenue
Silver Spring, MD 20910

Discipline

A common misconception is our library is quieter than other school libraries because hearing-impaired children supposedly cannot talk. It seems that hearing people equate deafness with an absence of vocal chords. Actually, the library is noisier than many other libraries. The reasons are that hearing-impaired children can talk or make vocal sounds because they have the same anatomical apparatus as hearing people: hearing-impaired children have difficulty controlling the loudness of their voices because they cannot hear themselves; staff talk loudly to children with residual hearing as a part of total communication, and in order to get the attention of another student at the same table, a student will often rap on the table and the vibrations attract the other student's attention.

The handicap of deafness demands *awareness, understanding, patience* and *tolerance* in a library setting. It is crucial that hearing-impaired children *use* their library resources. A librarian's attitude toward them and skill in developing and implementing library programs to meet their needs, can drastically affect a child's future use of libraries.

Selection Aids

Spache, George D. *Good Reading for Poor Readers.* New Canaan, Conn.: Garrard, 1974.
Strang, Ruth. *Gateway to Readable Books.* New York: Wilson, 1975.
McCarr, Dorothy. *Materials Useful for Deaf/Hearing Impaired: An Annotated Bibliography,* 1976. (Available from Dormac, Inc., Box 1622, Lake Oswego, Oregon 97034.)

Publishers' Addresses

Davco Publishers, 5425 Fargo Ave., Skokie, IL 60076.
Follett Publishing Co., 1010 W. Washington Blvd., Chicago, IL 60607.
King Features, Educational Division, Dept. 1254, 235 East 45th St., New York, NY 10017.
Scholastic Book Services, 904 Sylvan Ave., Englewood Cliffs, NJ 17632.

Into the Mainstream: Using Books to Develop Social Skills in Perceptually Impaired Children

PAUL J. GERBER and KAREN HARRIS

Introduction

As a result of the Education for All Handicapped Children Act, P.L. 94-142, many exceptional children are now being educated with their nonhandicapped peers in regular schools. The practice of making flexible the delivery of services for exceptional children has enabled them to be educated in the "least restrictive environment" as mandated by law. The advent of this mandate clearly affects many regular education personnel who are now challenged by the presence of perceptually handicapped children in their classrooms. Typically, these newly integrated children bear such labels as learning disabled, educable mentally retarded, or mildly emotionally disturbed.

Despite the need of educators to classify perceptually handicapped children in disability categories, there is a significant commonality in such children's psychological characteristics and learning behavior. The perceptually handicapped child may evidence many problems in diverse areas of functioning: there may be problems in the basic skills areas, in attention, memory, coordination, and controlling behavior, as well as problems in conceptualization and in perceptual processing. Not surprisingly, problems in social adjustment lead to another large area of concern for the perceptually handicapped child, especially in view of the effort to mainstream these children.

The Perceptually Handicapped Child and Social Adjustment

The perceptually handicapped child has been described as having problems in social functioning by many investigators. Kahn has written that perceptual inadequacies of perceptually handicapped children when applied to social and interpersonal relationships involve inaccurate perception and conceptualization of social and personal matters.[1] Kronick stressed that perceptual distortions and inconsistencies cause impaired feedback from the environment, resulting in confusion, inaccuracy, and disorganization in the perceptually handicapped child's life space.[2] Lewis, Strauss, and Lehtinen stated that the mechanism that organizes behavior and enables the child to perceive social situations and develop awareness of social attitudes often fails to operate properly.[3]

Not surprisingly, many perceptually handicapped children have difficulty in relating to their nonhandicapped peers. Studies by Johnson, Baldwin, and Jones have found perceptually impaired children to be lower in social acceptance than their nonhandicapped peers.[4] In mainstreamed classrooms, Goodman and Iano and others found perceptually handicapped children less accepted and more rejected.[5] Moreover, Bryan studied mainstreaming learning-disabled students and also found that they were perceived as less attractive and consequently were more often rejected than childen compared with them. Many of these children remain segregated socially despite physical inclusion.[6]

Social Perceptual Functioning

Many of the investigators into peer status of perceptually handicapped children have called for exploration into the underlying reasons for peer rejection. One such reason has been identified as a lag in sensitivity to social structures, roles, and nuances of behavior among perceptually handicapped children. In fact, it has been demonstrated that social development in such children

---

"Into the Mainstream: Using Books to Develop Social Skills in Perceptually Impaired Children," by Paul J. Gerber and Karen Harris, *Top of the News* 1979, 35: 379–84.

lags several years behind nonhandicapped children at the elementary school level. For example, research has indicated that an eleven-year-old learning-disabled child may function as low as an average seven-year-old child in social perceptual ability.[7]

The thrust of research on peer status and socioadaptive abilities in perceptually handicapped children has raised the question of how remedial practices could effectively intervene in this deficit area. Investigators have shown that these skills can be enhanced by remediative intervention in lower-functioning mentally retarded populations.[8] The prognosis then becomes more favorable for the perceptually handicapped child whose capacities and abilities exceed those of mentally retarded populations who have responded favorably to such ameliorative practices.

There are, however, two problems that impede the remedial process in the area of social perceptual functioning. First, the major emphasis in the education of perceptually handicapped children in the public schools is on academic skills; development of social adjustment training through formalized procedures has been of lesser concern. Second, there has been a lack of curricular initiative in the area of socialization training for the perceptually handicapped child. Although components of several curricular programs stress the urgency of this problem, there has been no attempt to address the issue at this crucial time when the concept of the least restrictive environment has affected the total educational scene.

Children's Literature and the Librarian

One area of promise in the regular education arena is the use of children's literature to train perceptually handicapped children in social perceptual skill building. Libraries have a particular role in implementing mainstreaming goals, since they combine recreational and academic behavior in a social setting. In bringing together children of varying abilities, strengths, and needs in a nonjudgmental environment, librarians are able to offer models and protocols for improved functioning.

Frequently literature has been used to serve a variety of nonliterary purposes. Books introduce children to worlds they've never seen; they provide children with insights into themselves, make articulate their unformed perceptions and ideas, foster language growth, and help readers understand themselves and their society. Which aspects of these common tasks of literature will be performed depends on the selection of materials. How well they will be performed depends on the guidance provided by the librarian.

Such deliberate use of literature does not distort the functions of story hour. Literature need not be overly didactic, and yet it must be at least peripherally so if it is not to be trivial. Librarians are accustomed to selecting and using books to provide a forum for the examination of social or personal problems. The plethora of books on integration, ethnic identity, such familial problems as broken homes, sibling rivalry, divorce, etc., have filled publishers' catalogs and subsequently library shelves. Through these works, many children have been helped to articulate and examine comparable crises in their own lives.

Use of Books in Concert with Psychological Characteristics

The use of children's literature for the purpose of developing social perceptual skills needs to be structured to allow for the specific psychological characteristics of perceptually handicapped children. The major social deficiency of these children is their inability to reach the central inference or main concept of a social situation. They tend to focus on details and build their social interactions accordingly. They exhibit a simple inability to piece together the perceptual cues of expression, body language, actions, and action sequence to formulate the social situation in toto. This in turn has a disastrous impact on their ability to fully recognize all of the consequential components of a specific social situation and act or react appropriately.

Using books to help remedy some of the problems common to perceptually handicapped youngsters is similar to standard library behavior but requires assessing titles by factors generally overlooked. In such instances, the specific content may be less important than the mode of presentation; the quality of illustration may be less significant than the presence (or absence) of certain features.

Books used to promote social skills should provide opportunities for frequent librarian-student commentary during the course of the reading without destroying continuity or the progression of the narrative; that is, questions should be able to be asked and answered, comments made and solicited that interrupt the continuous reading of the book. If it is necessary for the children to wait until the story is over, their ability to retain attention, respond to questions, and keep involvement high may be lost.

If children are to be helped to read such social cues as body language, facial expressions, and proximity messages, then such features must be prominent, obvious, even exaggerated in the illustrations. While subtlety, ambiguity, and complexity might be desirable in terms of aesthetics, they are counterproductive for these particular purposes.

Illustrations should be clear and uncluttered. Visual clichés, usually anathema, are highly desirable under these circumstances. Postures and expressions should be exaggerated. Style should be naturalistic, color realistic, and extraneous elements minimized or eliminated. Photographs are acceptable if expressions are clear; cartoons are likewise acceptable if salient elements are emphasized.

While some books are intended to provide an opportunity for examination of feelings and social situations, others, intended to serve very different purposes, may also be used to advantage. *The Shy Little Girl* and *How Do I Feel?* were written for the purpose of examining emotions. They present social and familial situations of happiness, tension, and resolution and so are readily usable for helping children identify responses and propose alternative methods for coping.

Norman Rockwell's Americana A B C is, in typical Rockwell fashion, a nostalgic tribute to an America that was—at least in fond memory. Its intent is a celebration of traditional perceptions and values, but the quality of its illustrations, their exaggeration, their blunt and unabashed depiction of uncomplicated feelings and situations, makes them easy to interpret for mildly dysfunctional children.

Picture Interpretation Procedure

A central inference questioning procedure is suggested to guide perceptually handicapped children in picture interpretation, leading to enhanced social perceptual functioning. The procedure is a threefold process including questioning to ascertain social perceptual cues, fostering awareness of situation-specific behavior, and articulating the emotional components. The process involves the hierarchical sequencing of the following questions, rephrased to respond to the language proficiency of the children and the particulars of the books.

Social Perceptual Cues

1. Who is involved in the sequence?
2. What is the most important thing happening?
3. What do the characters' facial expressions mean (say)?
4. What does the body language mean (say)?

Situation-Specific Behavior

1. What is the appropriate way to behave here?
   or
   Why is the character behaving this way?
2. What clues do you get (i.e., how do you know)?

Emergence of Effect

1. What kind of feeling do you get from this picture?
2. Why does this particular feeling emerge?

It must be pointed out that this procedure is viewed as being effective with the books suggested. However, some individual pictures within each book lend themselves to this technique more than others. As the social perceptual ability of the children increases, so too the stimulus value of the material may be increased.

Suggested Books

The following books are useful in developing social skills among perceptually handicapped youngsters.

Krasilovsky, Phyllis. *The Shy Little Girl.* Illus. by Trina Schart Hyman. Boston: Houghton, 1970.
Anne is painfully shy and consequently very lonely. She undervalues herself and tries to avoid rejection by becoming as invisible as possible. When a new girl enters her class and

seeks Anne out as her special friend, Anne becomes more outgoing. Color is used to good advantage, highlighting key elements within the illustrations.

Mendoza, George. *Norman Rockwell's Americana A B C*. Illus. by Norman Rockwell. New York: Dell, 1975.

Each letter of the alphabet is represented through a typically American scene. Most of the paintings are nostalgic, sentimental, and idealized. Although not all are useful for interpretation of emotions, those that are are especially rich in possibilities. There is little subtlety in the situations depicted, and all attitudes are part of the popular American ethos. The illustrations for the letter *v*, a family leaving for and returning from a vacation, are particularly useful since the same cast of characters are represented in diametrically opposed moods and attitudes.

Scott, Ann Herbert. *Sam*. Illus. by Symeon Shimin. New York: McGraw-Hill, 1967.

Sam's attempts to join family members in their activities are spurned successively by his mother, brother, sister, and father. The youngster's feelings of rejection spill forth in tears at his father's verbal reprimand and dismissal. His mother, realizing the boy just needs to belong, devises a task for him at her side. This exploration of a young child's need for attention from busy members of his family will strike a responsive note in many youngsters. The handsome, highly naturalistic drawings reveal attitudes and emotions at work in each situation.

Simon, Norma. *How Do I Feel?* Illus. by Joe Lasker. Racine, Wis.: Whitman, 1970.

Twins with different personalities and abilities live with their grandparents and older brother. One narrates the events of their days, commenting on what happens and how the boys feel about each event. Crises are minor but common, familiar to all school-age children. Expressions and body language are easily read.

Stanton, Elizabeth, and Henry Stanton. *Sometimes I Like to Cry*. Illus. by Richard Leyden. Milwaukee: MacDonald-Raintree, 1970.

Joey describes events in his young life that have made him happy, sad, angry, or hurt. He describes how he felt at the time and what he did. Tears are shown to be a normal response to various stimuli: what they mean depends on what caused them. Illustrations are very expressive and readily interpreted.

Viorst, Judith. *Alexander, Who Used to Be Rich Last Sunday*. Illus. by Ray Cruz. New York: Atheneum, 1978.

Alexander was given a dollar by his grandparents last Sunday but has managed to squander it all, ending up with a motley assortment of useless objects. Being innocent and gullible, he is easily tricked by his older brothers and led into some questionable purchases by friends.

The range of emotions displayed is broad, and facial and postural responses are exaggerated. Situations involving a naive younger child being mocked and tricked by older siblings and responding to various minor familial conflicts are sufficiently ubiquitous to offer opportunities for identification and discussion.

Wolf, Bernard. *Adam Smith Goes to School*. Photographs by author. Philadelphia: Lippincott, 1978.

Adam Smith approaches first grade with a mixture of anticipation and trepidation. There he meets his teacher, who explains the rules and procedures and her expectations. He learns the routines and is introduced to the various learning activities and to his peers. Attitudes are clearly readable in the body posture and facial expressions of Adam, his schoolmates, and his teachers. Competition, conflict, cooperation, enthusiasm, and exhaustion are all easily interpreted. This book is particularly useful since common schoolroom situations are exhibited. Its only flaw is that excessive contrast was used in printing and some salient details are consequently obscured, but this is a minor flaw in an otherwise extremely valuable book.

Notes

1. J. P. Kahn, "Emotional Concomitants of the Brain-damaged Child," *Journal of Learning Disabilities* 2 (1969):644-51.

2. D. Kronick, *What about Me? The LD Adolescent* (San Rafael: Acad. Therapy, 1975).

3. R. S. Lewis, A. A. Strauss, and L. E. Lehtinen, *The Other Child* (New York: Grune, 1960).

4. G. O. Johnson, "A Study of the Social Position of Mentally Retarded Children in the Regular Grades," *American Journal of Mental Deficiency* 55 (1950):60–89; W. Baldwin, "The Social Position of the Educable Mentally Retarded Child in the Regular Grades in the Public Schools," *Exceptional Children* 25 (1958):106–8, 112; R. L. Jones, "Early Perceptions of Orthopaedic Disability, *Exceptional Children* 38 (1972):353–54.

5. H. Goodman, J. Gottlieb, and R. Harrison, "Social Acceptance of Educable Mentally Retarded Children Integrated into a Non-graded Elementary School," *American Journal of Mental Deficiency* 76 (1972):412–17; R. P. Iano, "Sociometric Study of Retarded Children in an Integrative Program," *Exceptional Children* 40 (1974):267–71.

6. Tanis Schwartz Bryan, "Peer Popularity of Learning Disabled Children," *Journal of Learning Disabilities* 7 (1974):621–25.

7. P. Gerber, "A Comparative Study of Social Perceptual Ability of Learning Disabled and Nonhandicapped Children" (Ph.D. diss., Univ. of Michigan, 1978).

8. B. Edmonson, H. Leland, and F. M. Leach, "Social Inference Training and Retarded Adolescents," *Education and Training of the Mentally Retarded* 5 (1970):1969–76.

The Library/Media Center for the Secondary Student with Specific Learning Disabilities—Hazard or Haven?

SIDNEY G. BECKER

Teachers may send secondary age learning-disabled students to the media center for legitimate reasons or to provide relief for themselves or the student from the pressures of the classroom. Considering the large numbers of these students who have either decoding or comprehension difficulties, the center, or at least the book collection, may not be a highly popular attraction. Yet the library/media center is a mine of exciting, useful information: filmstrips, high interest/low reading level books, and other materials that will help the pupil with a learning disability perform better in the regular classroom.

However, it is probable that the professionals and paraprofessionals who work in the media center have had little or no training in recognizing the characteristics and problems of the learning-disabled child. In order to develop an appropriate, comprehensive plan, such specialists should be aware of the behavioral characteristics of the adolescent with specific learning disabilities (SLD). Accompanying the descriptions will be a series of suggestions to help the media specialist in providing for some of the educational and social needs of these youngsters in the media center.

According to National Advisory Committee on Handicapped Children,

> Children with specific learning disabilities exhibit a disorder in one or more of the basic psychological processes involved in understanding or using spoken or written language. These may be manifested in disorders of listening, thinking, reading, writing, spelling, or arithmetic. They include conditions which have been referred to as perceptual handicaps, brain injury, minimal brain dysfunction, dyslexia, developmental aphasia, etc. They do not include learning problems which are due primarily to mental retardation, emotional disturbance, or to environmental disadvantage.[1]

This official definition may facilitate the diagnosis of a child with a specific learning disability for the evaluation and placement committee, but, in planning for instructional strategies, media specialists and other school personnel need to be aware of specific behavioral characteristics that these students demonstrate that may interfere with or minimize successful utilization of media center materials.

Unfortunately, until the early 1970s there was little professional recognition of the continued impact of a specific learning disability upon a child past elementary school. As Goodman and Mann point out, there were several reasons for the neglect of the secondary student with learning problems.[2] The field itself is relatively new, and virtually all the original identification and intervention research centered on early years of the child's life. Further, there was an assumption that the maturational changes of adolescence combined with earlier invention strategies would undoubtedly alleviate the child's difficulties. Finally, problems of secondary students often went unnoticed because these students became quite adept at managing or masking their problems. They learned to compensate—borrowing friends' notes, carefully choosing classes that required few written or reading assignments. At the same time, secondary schools provided more "tracks" or ability levels of classes and offered some alternative educational opportunities other than straight academic courses. Thus, many students with learning disabilities were programmed into or chose less academically demanding course work. Others became early school dropouts or were perceived as emotionally disturbed and subsequently sometimes misplaced in special classes or in psychotheraputic situations where their particular intellectual needs were not addressed.

As the field of learning disabilities has developed and matured, professionals have come to realize that as vital as early intervention is, it often does not entirely ameliorate all learning disabilities. Educators have also come to realize that many bright disabled children have been unfairly and arbitrarily assigned to lower ability groupings in the secondary school because they must have special assistance, mostly unavailable until recently, in order to function in those higher level tracks that are more congruent with their actual ability. As educators and parents have become more cognizant of the lost potential and damaging psychological effects of the lack of ongoing intervention for learning-disabled adolescents, successful programs have been newly designed for those students who have, as their goal, normal functioning in a regular academic environment.[3] Usually these programs involve a continuum of services from self-contained classrooms to total integration in the mainstream curriculum with some resource room support provided by a special education teacher. Thus, the expansion of services for those with learning disabilities at the secondary level offers hope that the needs of each student will be better identified and differentiated, and that subsequently the entire school staff will actively participate in providing an appropriate educational program for such youth.

If school media personnel are to be successfully involved in such programs, they must first have a basic working knowledge of the kind of problems these students may have. This is not an easy task since the learners who are categorized as specific learning disabled are quite a heterogenous group. They share a common problem: they are typically bright adolescents yet have serious difficulties with one or more specific learning tasks. Further, they look and act normal. In fact, specific learning disability is frequently referred to as the hidden handicap for just this reason. As a result, these adolescents are often "unmotivated" or "lazy"; the kids who could succeed in school if they would just "try a little harder." Unfortunately, such recommendations are off the mark; their lack of school achievement is generally the result of basic central nervous system dysfunction which interferes in varying degrees with successful learning in the standard manner.

Academically, the most common problem associated with specific learning disability is serious trouble with reading, a problem as pervasive as it is difficult to remediate. Thus, such a student with average or above average intelligence may arrive at junior or senior high school after several years of intensive remedial reading intervention and still be reading 2 to 4 years below grade level. Significant disability in reading at this age tends to fall into two categories: (1) decoding problems in which the student struggles to figure out words he or she has seen many times before; and (2) even more perplexing to the teacher, comprehension problems in which the adolescent can read the words but does not remember or understand the material just examined. It is apparent that learners with such reading problems face monumental tasks when they must deal with the reading assignments of required subjects such as English, history, and science.

Not all adolescents with learning disabilities have difficulty with reading. In fact, some may decode and comprehend exceptionally well but have a particular problem with mathematics, referred to as dyscalculia, or writing, referred to as dysgraphia. A youngster who has dyscalculia may not be able to remember addition, subtraction, multiplication and division facts, yet be able to solve complex theoretical problems with the aid of a calculator. A youngster who is dysgraphic may have an inability to remember the correct formation of letters in manuscript or cursive, may have perceptual and fine motor inabilities which interfere with proper formation and spacing of letters and words, or may have serious disabilities in planning and organizing a written form of expression such as an essay or composition.

Combined with or separate from specific academic deficits, the student may experience general processing dysfunctions that will also affect his or her performance in school. For example, many learning-disabled youth have an inadequate attention span which sabotages study patterns when dealing with the lengthy and complex curriculum at the secondary level. These students frequently appear to have unexpected lacunae in their learning achievements. Further, they may experience debilitating memory problems; that is, they may not be able to remember a series of verbal directions, e.g., how to use the card catalog. Or they may be able to follow directions when first given but unable to retrieve and apply the directions a day or two later, even though they had been attentive to such instructions when originally given. Others may remember the verbal directions but be unable to recall the actual layout of the library even though they have been walked through several times: their visual memory may be impaired. According to parents, teachers, and learning-disabled adolescents themselves, a major obstacle in their daily school and social life is their lack of organizational skills. In part related to their inadequate understanding of time, these students overplan or underplan their time, such as scheduling huge blocks of time for an activity that typically only takes a few minutes. This causes obvious problems in completing school assignments, particularly long-term projects. There are, for example, the students who will rush into the library the day before a ten-page term paper is due, requesting five sources of information immediately so that they might complete the report that night.

Although a learning disability is most frequently defined in terms of its impact on the student's educational achievement, it generally has a major negative influence on the child's social acceptance by his or her peers and teachers.[4] Moreover these students, as previously stated, are sometimes misunderstood and berated by their teachers and parents for not applying themselves to school work and for not establishing friendships. These factors usually combine to reinforce a low self-concept in the child. By the time this student reaches the secondary school he or she may be defeated by school work, "act out" to draw attention away from inadequate school work or become excessively dependent upon adults for help in surviving the academic world.

Hyperactivity is among the more commonly associated behaviors when one thinks of learning disabilities. Many students with learning disabilities are not hyperactive and even most that were as young children do not appear so in the secondary school although vestiges of this behavior may be observed at this level in actions such as pencil tapping, finger drumming, and other manifestations of general restlessness. Some students with poor attention may even appear hyperactive and lethargic because they have learned that such school behavior is more acceptable or at least less likely to get one in trouble with the teacher.

In the preceding paragraphs, a rather distressing picture has been painted of the adolescent with specific learning disabilities. It is imperative to remember that a given individual may have only a few of these problems and that with appropriate educational help these youngsters learn to cope with and compensate for these problems. An appropriate education means that all who encounter the student, not just the special educator assigned to give direct intervention, must be involved in designing a suitable learning environment and specific strategies to enhance the student's success during the crucial adolescent years.

Since the media center is a setting that may be anticipated with some trepidation, it is important the staff be aware of the potential problems that the student may encounter there and plan to take some specific steps to address them. If the media center is perceived unidimensionally as a world of books, it is unlikely to be a place to elicit interest in the poor reader with a history of failure in mastering print formats. If, however, there are exciting displays and exhibits in the center, they become an enticement for the reluctant reader. SLD students not only share their peers' interest in rock groups, cars, motorcycles, sports, etc., but may have specific interests in science, music, art, that cannot be satisfied by the low-reading level books available on the subject that they can handle. Exhibits and displays, especially the type that allow for hands-on exploration of the objects, may not only bring the student to the center but provide for an advancement of knowledge. Equally helpful would be prerecorded cassettes that students could listen to in order to learn more about the content of the exhibit. Additionally, the media specialist could have a special guest knowledgeable about the contents of the display visit for a day to talk directly to students about it.

Since many of these students have difficulty remembering such things as rules and regulations, it is important that these (1) be kept clear and brief in number and content; (2) be printed on oaktag, preferably with simple (but not babyish) pictures that illustrate do's and don'ts of the media center; and (3) be displayed in a prominent place so that students who may have forgotten what they were told before can retrieve the information without embarrassment.

Considering the restlessness of some learning-disabled students, it is also beneficial to provide for a series of a variety of activities within a short period of time that will allow the student to better conform with rules of behavior. For example, a media center, in addition to the traditional books and media equipment, may have an area where quiet conversation is permitted, another area where listening to music using headphones is permissible, and another area where puzzles and quiet games are available, all labeled in a clearly legible manner. It is equally important that students who are distractible know about and use study carrels. These should be located away from noise and movement in the center. It has also been proven helpful to place a sheet of colored paper on each side of the carrel as peripheral visual stimulation may decrease on task behavior of distractible children.[5]

A common assumption seems to be that if a child has difficulty reading, the educator can just assign that pupil to alternative methods of information gathering, such as cassettes or filmstrips and everything will be fine. That may be true if the child can easily read or follow the directions on how to operate the equipment. Given a decoding problem, a memory problem or a visual motor integration problem, the situation may be disastrous. Here the media specialist can be especially helpful by making sure that the child has supervised practice in operating equipment and by being available for reinstruction without remonstrating if the student forgets or has difficulty with a particular procedure. Since overlearning is so essential to the learning disabled, it is often beneficial to have these students teach others how to operate media equipment.

Equally important for those with reading deficits is the contribution that the librarians can make to students in selecting high interest/low reading level books. They are also in an excellent position to advise various academic departments of lowered reading level textbooks and related materials that are available for students to use in their courses. The same holds true for informing teachers of films and filmstrips that can improve poor readers' understanding of textbook material. When the remedial specialist and the librarian share information about particular students, the latter can provide an array of books on a given topic with various levels of difficulty, then work individually with the learning-disabled student to select materials that match his or her reading level. Many students are embarrassed to select easier-to-read-books when preparing reports or doing research. They often feel they are the only learners with such problems and try to cover up by saying there are no good books available on the topic or alternately by choosing books that are extremely difficult.

One of the major problems that confronts the learning disabled in the media center, even those who are good readers, is the actual use of the available printed materials. Given the complexity of the organizational system and the variety of materials, it is essential that the staff develop specific lessons to help students become efficient users of the system. In most instances, a general tour and an introductory lecture will not be sufficient. For example, the card catalog often remains a real mystery for these people. Sections need to be clearly marked as to listings by author, title, or subject or the student may spend much time looking under one for another. Since all sections require the ability to alphabetize, it would also be helpful to have an alphabet clearly, but discretely, on display. Given the fact that items are filed in the card catalog in drawers that operate sequentially down and up rather than from left to right, arrows should indicate this. A model of the card catalog for students to study before attempting to use it would be of great help. Accompanying the model could be a clear, brief pamphlet containing directions, pictures, and examples of how to use the card catalog.

An equally useful pamphlet would be one showing subject divisions and their numbering within the Dewey Decimal system. Such a pamphlet could also contain a list of types of general reference materials, what they can be used for, and how information is found in them. Many librarians and media specialists have developed small group lessons to teach learning-disabled students how to locate and use these references and then actually provide practice in using these materials. Given the tendency of the adolescent to think that such lessons are not immediately useful, such efforts will meet with far greater success and are more apt to be generalized by students if they are directly connected to a specific assignment in one of their courses. Even with several supervised lessons in the use of reference material, it may be necessary to provide mnemonic devices, such as printed directional information on how a reference is organized and used, again using clear lettering and pictures. These could also be done on posterboard, laminated, and attached to a reference area with a cord or chain or posted in a prominent place near each reference type.

Equally beneficial for many learning-disabled youngsters are carefully structured and sequenced lessons in using materials such as globes and atlases. For instance, consider using large globes as they may have clearer print and thus be less visually confusing. Continents could have glued to them a small white card with clear black lettered names so that the student who has difficulty distinguishing visual configurations can readily identify the general area she or he is expected to study. Try to help the student find and use maps and globes that are not visually crowded, that is, if he or she has to locate countries, find a source that contains no extraneous information. Since some SLD adolescents have difficulty perceiving how parts relate to a whole and vice versa, the librarian could suggest to the student or have available references that show states in isolation and then clearly outlined within the country. Here it may be beneficial to help the student use transparencies to outline individual geographic regions and features as they are located in a country or continent. Using transparencies not only facilitates cognitive understanding but also provides training for a student who cannot draw a free-hand map.

With a solid grounding in the use of the library, the time will still come when the student has a research report to do and will enter the room in a state of panic. Here it is crucial that the staff reinforce that the student knows how to use the center and make help available if problems arise; that the staff will be pleased to help locate both printed and nonprinted materials pertinent to the topic being investigated. The staff can also reinforce the classroom teacher's attempts to facilitate the student's need to be better organized and make wise use of time in completing such a project by scheduling regular appointments for the students to use the center. The student may also require monitoring and some feedback in appraising his or her efficiency in the use of that time, and in locating appropriate materials.

In addition to specific supports to the academic progress of the learning-disabled adolescent, the library and media staff can also facilitate the development and maintenance of appropriate behavior standards by the learning disabled. These can best be nurtured when the adults are aware of the learning styles and behavioral difficulties of the individual student. For instance, a strong visual learner with weak language processing abilities, will respond best to a few brief sentences spoken in clear simple terms when an adult is explaining rules, praising, or correcting behavior. If the professional staff can demonstrate expected behaviors, improvement may occur more rapidly. Subtle changes in voice tone that denote anger or praise may not be noticed by this student, thus making it vital that the adult visually or tactually cue the child when behavior is unacceptable or appreciated. On the other hand, a strong auditory learner with weak visual processing abilities will benefit from explicit verbal cues as to expected behavior. Such adolescents have varying degrees of difficulty understanding visual cues such as body language that provides the typical child feedback as to the desirability of his or her behavior. This youth requires more auditory feedback in order to better monitor behavior. In addition to understandable and reliable feedback in regard to behavior, the learning-disabled student with difficulties in memory and generalization ability functions best in settings in which standards of behavior and expectations are fair and consistent although what is fair may be perceived differently by the teacher and the student. For example, if the rule is that the media center does not provide pens and pencils, the student (with memory and organizational problems) may claim that it is the specialist's fault that required work in the center was not completed. One clever media specialist surmounted this problem by having each student bring a supply of pencils to the center to be used by the student only in the center. Thus the student's responsibility was to return the pencil at the end of the period and replace the supply when depleted. Strategies such as these can often make the difference between a cooperative working environment and a hostile, nonproductive one. When the librarian/media specialist provides an environment in which the student can understand what is expected of him or her, there is a far greater possibility that the student will meet behavioral expectations and feel comfortable in that particular environment.

Recent research indicates that peer social acceptance of children with various learning problems is significantly greater when typical and atypical children are placed in cooperative learning groups.[6] The resource center is certainly an ideal setting for such positive interactions. If typical adolescents and adolescents with learning disabilities are placed in small groups with assigned, specific tasks to complete, it appears likely that both groups will help each other more and typical children will tend to choose learning disabled students as friends more frequently than when individual assignments are given and little constructive contact is provided.[7]

Many learning-disabled adolescents have become quite sensitive about their learning problems. Therefore it is essential to respect these children as intelligent young people who respond to specific remedial and compensatory strategies employed by the media specialist if they are provided in ways that do not ridicule or single out the individual student from his or her peers. The strategies suggested here comply with this need of the pupil because they can be used by both typical and atypical students.

By employing such strategies, the media specialist becomes an integral part of a school team that can help many underachieving youngsters better attain school success and thereby realize to a far greater degree their actual potential. As more colleges develop special programs for young men and women with specific learning disabilities, the role of the secondary-school media specialist becomes even more crucial to the development of research skills by the student. When a youngster has developed a solid ability in library and media usage in the secondary school, he or she will be much better prepared to function efficiently in this crucial area, essential to success in their college life.

Notes

1. *National Advisory Committee on Handicapped Children, First Annual Report* (Washington, D.C.: U.S. Dept. of Health, Education, and Welfare, 1968).
2. L. Goodman and L. Mann, *Learning Disabilities in the Secondary School* (New York: Grune, 1976).
3. M. Birely and E. Manley, "The Learning Disabled Student in a College Environment: A Report of Wright State University's Program," *Journal of Learning Disabilities* 13 (1980): 7–10.
4. M. K. Garrett and D. W. Crump, "Peer Acceptance, Teacher Preference, and Self-Appraisal of Social Status of Learning Disabled Students," *Learning Disability Quarterly* 3 (1980): 42–48; S. S. Siegel, R. Siegel, and P. Siegel, *Help for the Lonely Child* (New York: Dutton, 1978).
5. S. S. Zentall, T. R. Zentall, and R. C. Barack, "Distraction as a Function of Within-Task Stimulation for Hyperactive and Normal Children," *Journal of Learning Disabilities* 11 (1978): 540–48.
6. D. W. Johnson and R. T. Johnson, "Integrating Handicapped Students into the Mainstream," *Exceptional Children* 47 (1980): 90–98; L. Cooper, "Effects of Cooperative, Competitive, and Individualistic Experiences on Interpersonal Attraction among Heterogeneous Peers," *Journal of Social Psychology* 111 (1980): 243–52.
7. Johnson and Johnson, "Integrating Handicapped Students into the Mainstream."

Coping with the Disruptive

PAT DAIN

Between 4:30 and 5:30 P.M. on a Wednesday is fairly sacrosanct at Key Centre. It is story time. As many as 12 children have crowded into my room to listen to the stories that I read or tell.

The children who come to Key Centre are emotionally disturbed, some of them severely. All of them are so disruptive that ordinary schools cannot cope with them, and they are sent to us for a period of reeducation in relationships. They are children who are rude, aggressive, violent and anti-authority. All are behind in basic subjects—reading being very important.

They are children who would never pick up a book for pleasure, who would not join the public libraries and would probably not have access to books at home. From the point of view of the child, if you cannot read there is not much point in having books in the home. Comics appear to be the staple diet for most.

There are particular reasons for having the children in my room for this reading session. In the first place it takes away the big formality of the classroom. We are not having a lesson, we are having a get together where "mum" is going to tell us a story.

Secondly, these children are happier in a group. Isolation frightens them and the fact that they are sitting informally and close together is comforting.

Perhaps the most important fact is that telling them stories frequently leads them to talk to me. The stories they like are those whereby good triumphs over evil and everybody lives happily ever after in the end.

Many of them are of West Indian origin and they appreciate African folk and fairy tales, although they display little interest in information books on their Caribbean background. We have used several of the books by Philip Sherlock, Everard C. Palmer, and Andrew Salkey. We anticipated that they would love these stories, but they really sat forward when I started reading the "Trend" Books to them.

The Trend Books have texts that are very relevant to them so it does not really matter to these children if they are culture-based. Most of these books are about big city children and all the things that happen to them. They feel that this sort of thing could, by an easy stretch of the imagination, happen to *them*, so they listen attentively and make all sorts of comments like "If he went the other way, he wouldn't meet that thug—I know what I should do. I should . . .", and then we are away. They talk and argue, discuss, and criticize. Sometimes the story is quite forgotten when someone begins to tell a story from life, it is sometimes total fantasy, but, at least, it *is* story time and the whole thing is very therapeutic.

Books for this type of child have to be eye-catching and immediately appealing. Rarely do they browse and riffle through the pages of a book. Either the covers or the first pages they look at must arouse their interest, even a short page of prose is not likely to hold their attention.

Key Centre children lack the ability to express themselves adequately and reading aloud to them is one way of increasing their vocabulary. These words must be self-explanatory in context so that it is not necessary to stop every few minutes to say "What does 'disintegrate' mean?"

It is difficult to know how to get these children interested in the written word. Books are not a feature of their families as a rule and TV effectively kills off any opportunities to read. Therefore, the responsibilities of schools like Key Centre are very pressing. They are probably the only places where the children are exposed to books and where reading lessons come very near the top of their curricula.

There is a strange innocence about these brash and psuedo-sophisticated children. They appear to be so worldly wise about everything and yet their everyday general knowledge is pathetic. This is when one realizes that they do not read, and so they do not

---

"Coping with the Disruptive," by Pat Dain, *Library Association Record* 1979, 81: 237–38. Reprinted by permission of the Library Association.

know about the seasons, how many weeks there are in a year and other mundane facts that we always assume children have picked up from reading magazines and the daily paper.

These reading periods have a great deal to do with their social training. Learning to sit still and listen is probably the most difficult thing they have to do. They are restless, talkative and totally visually orientated so that listening instead of just gazing is a test of endurance. This, of course, is part of their failure to achieve at school so it is an area we have to emphasize. It makes this part of their socialization programme easier for us if we can interest as well as educate.

Key Centre children are very weekly-comic or magazine minded. Ones that I see fairly regularly brought in to the Centre are *Whoopee* that boasts Sweeny Toddler, Wonder Car and Frankie Stein. *Spellbound* is directed to the female of the species with such stories as "Her Heart's Desire," "Marina," and "Village of Fear." Others I could mention are *Blue Jeans, Krazy, Cheeky, Fab 208* and *Jackie*.

These papers play an important part in the lives of these children because they say all the things that they want to hear. They talk of teenage brides; stories where the young, under-functioning spotty adolescent blossoms out to be a successful model, and really all things end happily.

In the classrooms we have a very comprehensive selection of reference books on wild life, interesting places, war, cars, environment, prehistoric monsters and a host of others available for the children all the time, and they have ample opportunity to use them. They rarely do so, unless it is for some teacher-directed project. Added to this we have bought many books for use with our Black Studies and we anticipated that this would arouse discussion and argument. This was not so, the children had to be directed towards them. They showed interest for a little while, but did not pursue this when left to their own devices.

To ensure that a child reads as much as possible, questions are put that require that the pupil goes to the books to provide the answers. In fact all our teaching know-how is directed to making these children want to read, but, powerful motivation is required and the combination of inability, lack of opportunity at home, and the box in the corner may well defeat all our endeavours.

Serving the Unserved

BETTY CARTER

Libraries are typically viewed as warehouses of information and dispensers of literature. Within their confines are the answers to multitudes of questions, the great and not-so-great books individuals may read, and the necessary materials that either help a fourth grader complete a report on poisonous snakes or a philosopher contemplate a metaphysical problem. There are, however, potential library patrons who will never need to research an existential question, know the source of the Amazon River, or discuss this month's best seller. These individuals will borrow materials they may never read and browse through books they may never fully understand, but meeting their needs and providing them with instruction in library use is as crucial as it is for any other identifiable segment or member of the community. These users are often found in the classes for the trainable mentally retarded, and their education in library skills and literary appreciation is best developed in school libraries, the same setting most appropriate for all other children.

Since the adoption of P.L. 94-142, many school populations have been expanded to include students who had been previously housed in separate facilities for retarded individuals. While the "least restrictive environment" for these youngsters may well be a self-contained classroom, or set of classrooms or workshops, this accommodation does not preclude extended contact with the rest of the student body. Unfortunately, there are few places or occasions in a school setting where special needs students can interact with other children and feel a real part of everyday society. The cafeteria is one, school assemblies and pep rallies another, and the library a third. To deny them access to the school library is as inappropriate as refusing first graders the pleasures of library experience because they cannot read or properly use the card catalog.

All school librarians will not have the opportunity to serve youngsters functioning at the trainable level. Their percentage within the population is small, and strained district budgets usually dictate that specialized schooling be centralized on a few campuses. In addition, extended library use is best begun during the middle school years, for only by then is there an expectation that these students will have developed a level of behavior and a long enough attention span to allow library instruction to be both meaningful and valuable.

Library service for such exceptional youngsters must not be contrived. It is important that the library not be restructured as an area intended for token contact with their non-impaired peers, but rather be an integral part of the total educational program of the school. In order to ensure this goal, the school library must not alter either its function or purpose. Since the assigned task of all school libraries is to supplement the curriculum with print and nonprint material, provide developmental and recreational reading matter for students, and foster those behaviors necessary for independent learning, it is precisely in these three areas that instruction must be enlarged to include the trainable mentally retarded child.

Librarians should not feel reluctant to offer their traditional services just because they lack experience in working with retarded youngsters. Although special education teachers are certainly best able to define the overall goals for these students, librarians are the most qualified to translate their needs into appropriate library instruction. They are well-practiced experts who daily take an educational plan, then select materials, define appropriate behaviors or skills and develop programming which complements it, while keeping the expected audience clearly in mind.

Selecting the materials necessary to support the specialized curriculum and to provide recreational and developmental reading opportunities need not involve a major capital outlay, but rather a utilization of available resources. Magazines, particularly picture magazines like *Action Now, People, Cycle, Dynamite, Bananas* and *National Geographic World*, not only reinforce visual discrimination skills, sequencing skills and listening skills, but also provide a variety of subjects to help these students begin to define their interests.

While very few children identified as trainable will be reading in middle school, the easy-to-read Scholastic Scope series is often successful with the ones who are.[1] Intended for students in grades four to six, the books contain stories which are nonetheless still interesting to the slightly older reader, and are packaged to more closely resemble popular paperbacks than the elementary I Can Read books. Concept books with realistic photographs like Tana Hoban's *Dig, Drill, Dump, Fill* also respond to the intellectual limitations of the students without insulting their chronological ages.

Books suitable for reading aloud may include more sophisticated language, but they should still contain simple plots and concern everyday activities. No author offers a better selection of such stories than Beverly Cleary. Henry Huggins and Ramona Quimby are obviously younger than this audience, but their ages are seldom stressed and their crises of coping with a stray dog or coming home to an unplugged crock pot are universal.

Books circulated for pleasure reading will usually be heavily illustrated nonfiction volumes. The most popular in a suburban junior high school in Houston, Texas are *The Undersea World of Jacques Cousteau, The Illustrated Encyclopedia of the Animal Kingdom, Motorcycle Mutt, Great Monsters of the Movies, Peanuts Treasury, The Muppett Movie, From Cannon to Campbell: An Illustrated History of the Houston Oilers*, and *Stan Lee Presents the Full Color Comics Version of the Empire Strikes Back*. Far from being the exclusive domain of special education youngsters, these titles could easily comprise the world's best browsing list for any junior high-school library, and need not be shelved apart from the rest of the collection. Easy access can be provided by the librarian and the classroom teacher without isolating either the special patrons or their preferred reading choices.

For intellectual as well as social reasons, these students should not be limited in any way to a particular set of books or magazines. A few individuals will be quite knowledgeable in specific subject areas and their demands will be surprisingly advanced and sophisticated. Once Lisa, an older nonreader, was using a large illustrated book on birds to complete a classroom assignment. While turning the pages, she started identifying for an astonished audience species after species of the bird family—most of which were totally unfamiliar to any other students or faculty members in the school. To restrict Lisa to elementary science magazines like *Ranger Rick* or *National Geographic World* would not only be an insult, but also a disservice.

Media, other than sound recordings, can be useful. Learning is often facilitated for such exceptional students when they are able to use several senses in the process, and audiovisual materials give them this opportunity.[2] There are few prepackaged programs aimed directly at retarded adolescents functioning at this level, and most of these, like the *Work Attitudes* series from Occupational Awareness, deal exclusively with job training. However, with minor modifications in presentation like expanding introductions and breaking up timed programs, multimedia kits which have adapted favorite adolescent novels, contain simple science concepts or condensed educational movies are very successful. Resources similar to Walt Disney's *Afterschool Specials*, National Geographic's *Sharks* and Media Basics' *The Great Brain* are highly recommended. Video cassettes and 16mm films which provide a story line have also proved to be both popular and instructional.

Preparation for library skill instruction will initially involve a task analysis of established procedures. Each component of expected library behavior must be identified and then learned in small sequential steps. Retarded students are secure when operating within a detailed routine providing an ordered structure for behavior, and may be overwhelmed if told only that they will be going to the library to check out a book. Their first visit will be more relaxed if the students know beforehand that they are expected to enter the library, sit quietly at a table, listen to a lesson or set of instructions, push in their chairs, find a book, sign a circulation card, go to the desk, have the book stamped, and then sit down to wait for the others. An in-house videotape that shows other youngsters using this routine in the library is ideal for orientation, and should be followed by several short rehearsals during which the students can practice the outlined procedure. Although far removed from *Reader's Guide* and card catalog lessons, such activities develop the skills and behaviors these adolescents need in order to function in a library.

Some library skills will be more academic and closely related to instructional goals. For example, writing is usually a common component in the educational plans of these special students. The necessity of writing one's name in the small space allowed on circulation cards is good preparation for developing a legible signature. Some youngsters may not yet be able to write their names, and it will be necessary to either guide their pencils or write for them. For many, filling out a circulation card is a realistic and transferable task.

It will probably be natural for the librarian to reinforce social skills and appropriate behaviors developed in the classroom. While Kirk defines socially appropriate behaviors as "an intangible type of behavior which comes through . . . working and living with others," teachers will certainly have a well-defined list of skills they are emphasizing.[3] Since these students are as individually different as are all youngsters, they will display different levels of achievement for each skill. For example, Litton lists the uses of appropriate polite greeting and parting words as one of the social amenities to be developed.[4] For Mike, this meant not to parrot the words and phrases he heard. When the librarian would say "Good morning, Mike," he would respond "Good morning, Mike." This was as inappropriate as Tim's first greeting when he bounced into the library and asked the librarian, "Hey, girl! You want to go down to the beach and have some fun with me this weekend?"

Special education students are certainly not the only ones who need to develop their social skills. Junior high-school children are so strongly conformist that they tend to reject anyone who does not look, act, dress, or speak like everyone else in their group. However, they should not be freed from the responsibility of accepting people who are obviously different. They will never accept that responsibility or develop a social conscience if they are forever quarantined from anyone who is not like them. For them to see special students naturally operating in a regular setting is as important as it is for such students to be there.

Teachers and the library staff provide role

models for those junior-high youngsters who have never had any contact with a retarded child. Teenagers see these adults as accepting, neither patronizing nor condescending. These models do not have to speak in "baby talk," they need not shout or make facial contortions in order to be understood, and they are certainly not afraid, cruel, repulsed, or infected. Junior-high students will not lose all their prejudices solely through these contacts in the school library, but several of their misconceptions and fears concerning the retarded may well be lessened or even eliminated.

While library programming is certainly not standard for these pupils, librarians may initially feel more comfortable adapting traditional lessons. Reading aloud is enjoyable, and it develops listening skills while providing opportunities for eliciting oral language. Since many trainable children are not very verbal, it is pointless to ask nonspecific questions such as "How did you like the book?", for answers will vary from blank stares to all-purpose grunts. Questions like "Just what was that sticky stuff that Ramona had in her hair?" are far more appropriate and more likely to be answered correctly than those that demand evaluative responses.

Abbreviated book talks will give the children a preview of the resources and also direct them to various topics that might be interesting to a few individuals. These youngsters are just learning to recognize and define their own interests and such lessons will further this development. It is possible that some of these special patrons may not know there are books and magazines about high demand subjects such as motorcycles, animals, and television and movie stars, so a similar activity should be incorporated into each visit. This preselection of materials will initially help narrow the book choices for a few pupils who might be bewildered by the vastness of the school library and haphazardly check out any book rather than choose an appropriate one. Although there is a certain amount of satisfaction for retarded adolescents to simply engage in the same circulation procedures as do other students, a far greater thrill will come from enjoying a good book.

While films, video cassettes and audiovisual kits may be popular with the children, there are several problems in using these media. Learners are typically put in passive roles, and the librarian must intrude with deliberate questions and activities in order to promote their participation.[5] The students will become involved in a film if they know beforehand who the main characters are, what they will be doing, and why their actions are important. Occasionally this involvement may be unpredictable. Once when a group of trainable youth were watching *It's a Mile from Here to Glory*, four youngsters stood up during the final scenes and began running in place while the rest of the group quietly applauded the winner of the race. The other students who were in the library at the time did not laugh at their uninhibited classmates, but rather gathered around the television set to see what that exciting program was all about.

Timed audiovisual materials must also be used carefully. Multimedia packages, offering sound/filmstrip combinations, are best shown in several short intervals rather than one long one. Librarians or teachers will have to stop the programs in order to allow the students opportunities for summarizing and reviewing, as well as time to prepare for material they will be encountering in the next segment.

The most vital service that school libraries can perform is to equip all their students with the necessary tools for independent learning. This obligation is most dramatically fulfilled by allowing retarded children to work as student library assistants. Behaviors emphasized in their classrooms, such as attending to tasks, working independently, responding to suggestions, following a specific set of instructions, adjusting to different assignments, and completing jobs with accuracy and within given time limits are strengthened when applied to the less sheltered library environment. Transferable skills, such as following sequences, patterning, developing visual discrimination, and coordinating fine motor skills can be effectively reinforced in a student assistant program.

Work does not have to be created. The myriad of repetitive jobs so necessary in the daily library routine are tailor-made for these students. Each of the complex skills which must be mastered by library assistants can be subdivided into their simplest components and taught one sub-skill at a time. For example, these youngsters can not be expected to learn to shelve books by initially working in the stacks, but they can begin by separating fiction and nonfiction volumes. They can next learn to group by major Dewey classification numbers and order those books on a cart for other shelvers. Similar task analyses will allow students functioning at the trainable level to accurately alphabetize, file, operate machinery, and process books. Although each student will not be able to perform every activity, these assistants should become proficient in at least one area.

Vicki, a library aide who has worked for two years in such a program, pre-alphabetizes all but the United States—History catalog cards before they are filed in the card catelog. Her visual discrimination skills have been so finely developed that she can correctly order cards of several books by the same author and even those of subjects found in different books by identical authors. She is admittedly slower than either the other student aides or the librarian, but since she is able to do this task, and it is a real and useful one for her, it is justifiable. Moreover, the librarian is freed to perform more intellectually demanding services.

Other assistants provide different services which are related to their individual strengths and weaknesses. Co, a non-English-speaking boy, stamps books at the circulation desk, empties the book return drop, and shelves the paperbacks on revolving racks, because he can learn and perform these actions by imitation rather than through verbal instruction. Maryanne, a willing but inflexible child, had to be forced to recognize the need for assistance and ask for help when it was necessary. Consequently, her job in the library was to operate the automatic lettering machine and punch out the letters teachers requested for signs and bulletin boards. This machine cuts off when jammed, and in order to avoid being fired for not finishing her job, Maryanne had to seek help. Thus this task had the ideal components necessary to address her particular instructional goal.

Curricular development must not be the only concern in planning a special student assistant program. The interactions between these aides and their non-impaired peers need to be considered. Setting a positive tone in order to foster new relationships is important, and the best place to start is with the other assistants. These latter students must be as secure as is possible in junior high about themselves, so they will not feel the need to shun or ridicule their new working partners. They must know about the program before it is started and understand that the special helpers will be able to do their assigned tasks and are solely responsible for them. If the established workers will respect the abilities of the new aides, then so will many of their classmates.

Respect can be furthered by deliberately assigning tasks which are admired by junior-high patrons. Stamping books at the circulation desk is one and assignments that involve operating audiovisual equipment are another. One special education assistant was taught to run the video tape machine for an in-building television channel. Although the VCR is technologically complex, its operation is simple. Color coding the play, stop and rewind buttons enabled her to learn to broadcast designated videotapes. She was able to fulfill this job more efficiently than the librarian who was often distracted by other duties and would forget to start the requested programs. The subtle message that this assistant is invaluable in helping the library run more efficiently is delivered every time she performs this service.

Retarded youngsters must be offered a place in school libraries. They will benefit from the resources, activities, and social interaction incorporated into the program. If encouraged, they will also contribute their skills and talents to provide real services for librarians, faculty members, and other students. This opportunity must not be wasted.

Notes

1. Freddie W. Litton, *Education of the Trainable Mentally Retarded* (St. Louis: Mosby, 1978), p. 189.
2. Ibid., p. 59
3. Samuel A. Kirk, *Educating Exceptional Children*, 2nd ed. (Boston: Houghton, 1972), p. 231.
4. Litton, *Education of the Trainable Mentally Retarded*, p. 37.
5. Anne-Marie Forer and Mary Zojac, "Library Services to the Mentally Retarded" (Altoona, Penn.: Altoona Public Library, 1978), ED 165 728.

Bibliography

Action Now. Dana Point, Calif.: Surfer Pub. Group. Monthly.
Afterschool Specials. Burbank, Calif.: Walt Disney Educational Media, 1977.
Crist, Steven. *The Muppet Movie.* New York: Abrams, 1979.
Cycle. New York: Ziff Davis. Monthly.
Dynamite. New York: Scholastic. Monthly.

Edelson, Edward. *Great Monsters of the Movies*. Garden City, N.Y: Doubleday, 1973.

Forer, Anne-Marie, and Mary Zojac. *Library Services for the Mentally Retarded*. Altoona, Penn.: Altoona Public Library, 1978. ED 165 728.

Fron Cannon to Campbell. Houston: Gulf Coast Graphics, 1979.

The Great Brain. Larchmont, N.Y.: Media Basics with Osmond International Pictures, 1980.

Hoban, Tana. *Dig, Drill, Dump, Fill*. New York: Greenwillow, 1975.

The Illustrated Encyclopedia of the Animal Kingdom. Danbury, Conn.: Grollier, 1968.

It's a Mile from Here to Glory. New York: Time-Life Multimedia, 1978.

Kirk, Samuel A. *Educating Exceptional Children*. 2nd ed. Boston: Houghton, 1972.

Litton, Freddie W. *Education of the Trainable Mentally Retarded*. St. Louis: Mosby, 1978.

National Geographic World. Washington, D. C.: National Geographic Soc. Monthly.

People Weekly. Los Angeles: Time, Inc.

Radlauer, Edward, and R. S. Radlauer. *Motorcycle Mutt*. New York: Watts, 1973.

Schulz, Charles M. *Peanuts Treasury*. New York: Holt, 1968.

Sharks. Washington, D.C.: National Geographic Soc., 1977.

Stan Lee Presents the Full Color Comics Version of The Empire Strikes Back. New York: Pocket Bks., 1980.

The Undersea World of Jacques Cousteau. New York: World, 1973.

Work Attitudes. Los Alamos, Calif.: Occupational Awareness, 1979.

An Autistic Child and Books

MOLLIE MARCUS WALLICK

The Cognitive-Affective Framework

Children's books are useful in a multitude of ways. While providing aesthetic pleasure, books stimulate language, develop in the child a sense of self, illuminate and expand the child's own world, facilitate concept formation, transmit the culture, and expose the child to beginning literary experiences.[1] The function of books in the cognitive domain is well established. However, since books can alter perceptions and, in turn, attitudes and even behavior, their role in the affective domain becomes apparent as well.

Within this cognitive-affective framework, much concerning the literary experience is still unexplained. We know that books enhance cognition by providing additional information with which to understand the real world. We know that literature allows the reader to examine vicariously problems that may be too painful to confront directly. But just as much of the actual reading process on the basic word-recognition level remains obscure, even more tenuous is our understanding of the more complex comprehension level.

Reading is obviously a symbiotic process: the author provides printed symbols that the reader must transform into meaningful communication. Any written code potentially contains a variety of messages. Depending on his or her ability, experimental base, and need, the reader selectively perceives and selectively interprets the raw material presented by the author. This process is exaggerated in the case of the disturbed reader, who views the world through a distorted prism of his or her own faulty perception. Control over this confusing and often threatening world may be offered through the medium of books.

This report will demonstrate the way in which books were used in the treatment of an autistic child in an outpatient therapeutic preschool associated with a department of psychiatry at a large urban medical center. Since a gap exists between the anecdotal rec-

---

"An Autistic Child and Books," by Mollie Marcus Wallick, *Top of the News* 1980, 37: 69–77.

ord of his progress and a precise understanding of the process of improvement, the account is necessarily more descriptive than explanatory. Before introducing the subject of the report, it may be informative first to explore the autistic child's specific learning problems related to language acquisition.

Autism

When Leo Kanner identified early infantile autism,[2] he noted among specific impairments abnormal language development. Many recent researchers consider profound language deficit the primary disorder of Kanner's behavioral syndrome.[3] In their definition of autism, the National Society for Autistic Children included among essential features manifested prior to thirty months of age disturbances of speech, language, and cognitive capacities. In this area:

> symptoms may include (a) speech: for example, mutism, delayed onset, immature syntax and articulation, modulated but immature inflections; (b) language-cognition: for example, absent or limited symbolic capacity; specific cognitive capacities such as rote memory and visual-spatial relations intact with failure to develop the use of abstract terms, concepts, and reasoning; immediate or delayed, negative echolalia with or without communicative intent; nonlogical use of concepts; neologisms; (c) nonverbal communication: for example, absence or delayed development of appropriate gestures, dissociation of gestures from language, and failure to assign symbolic meaning to gestures.[4]

Much effort has been expended to ameliorate the autistic child's impaired language skills. Initially, most intervention efforts involved the exclusive use of operant conditioning techniques. In contrast to reflex conditioning, in which intended change is *within* the subject, the purpose of operant conditioning is to increase the frequency of the subject's *performance* through reinforcement. Among clinician-researchers using operant techniques with severely language-impaired autistic children, the best known by far is Ivar Lovaas. In general, operant conditioners have reported limited success in evoking speech in previously mute autistic children,[5] even with the exertion of extensive control over the child's environment.[6] Also significant is the fact that little successful transfer of training has been noted following operant language conditioning.

In contrast, recent reports have documented good results following simultaneous communication training.[7] The technique is called "simultaneous" because verbal language is paired with manual signs customarily reserved for the deaf; the term is also appropriate in that the method engages simultaneously the client's auditory, oral, tactile, and visual modalities. Psychologist Margaret Creedon is generally credited with the development of the innovative approach, though other practitioners in other parts of the United States told of their use of the technique at approximately the same time. Dr. Creedon used sign language because she thought a youngster with whom she was working was deaf; some months later when he started to talk, she adjusted her diagnosis and recognized the applicability of the simultaneous language method to intervention with other autistic children. Subsequent reported results after use of the approach are that some formerly mute children have learned to sign and some children from whom words had never been evoked have become communicatively responsive, while echolalia in other children has been significantly reduced.

Bernie, an Autistic Child

A child with whom simultaneous communication was used successfully in our setting was Bernie, who was four years, five months old when the new technique was introduced into the school curriculum and into his program, one year after his entrance into the school. Bernie lived at home with his father (a professional with two graduate degrees), his mother (a college graduate/homemaker), and a 1½-year-old sister.

There were no early indicators of Bernie's serious dysfunction. His parents first became concerned when their son had no speech at twenty-seven months, and when—at that time—he was uncooperative in a "normal" preschool setting. Following an extended evaluation by various specialists, none of whom found any irregularities, Bernie was seen by three independent child psychiatrists. Each of the latter physicians considered the handsome three-year-old a classic case of early infantile autism. He was referred to our setting for psychoeducational intervention.

Bernie's entering behavior at the therapeutic preschool was generally disorganized and disoriented and was characterized by considerable running around the playroom—some productive, to explore equipment, but more aimless and almost animal-like in its intensity and noise quality. Bernie manifested bizarre stereotypic gestures and self-stimulating behaviors, fleeting eye contact, frequent teeth grinding, alternating limp posturing and hyperactivity, a profound disturbance of relatedness, and complete absence of speech.

Before simultaneous communication was introduced into Bernie's program, intrusive therapy was used to interrupt Bernie's preoccupation with his own world; to make and maintain contact, to facilitate his body and affective awareness, and to enhance our social interaction. Whatever will make the therapist's presence felt by the child is used in intrusion. In Bernie's case, for example, I introduced "baby games" involving our close contact. He learned—ever so gradually—to tolerate my rubbing his tummy, fingering his face, and lowering his head to the ground. After several months, he seemed to enjoy gentle blowing on his neck and face and moved his head differentially to receive the contact. The tactile-vestibular stimulation afforded by these maneuvers not only eased my entrance into Bernie's social isolation but also served to increase his behavioral organization: it helped him process sensory input, made him more aware of his body, and brought his central nervous system to a more alert stage.

Concomitant with the high levels of affective and physical contact characteristic of intrusion, a limited behavior modification program was implemented with Bernie. The focus of the operant techniques, was on the development of eye contact and compliance—both prerequisites for training in simultaneous communication. A detailed account of the successful use of the language method with the subject of this report is available elsewhere.[8]

Suffice it to say that after nine months of simultaneous communication training. Bernie was verbalizing two- and occasionally three-word combinations (signs dropped out as he learned verbal speech), and his parents estimated his spontaneously spoken repertoire at home in excess of 150 words. Especially significant is the fact that Bernie used language with communicative intent. The following account of the function of books in Bernie's treatment will be, for the most part, of the year the preceded simultaneous communication training.

Bernie and Books

When Bernie was separated briefly from his mother for his first forty-five-minute session at the therapeutic preschool, he placed his fingers in his ears and made soft unhappy noises. (I observed over time that this hand posturing was an apparent attempt to shut out that which was threatening or overstimulating and, on occasion, even that which was too pleasant.) When his mother joined us in the playroom, Bernie immediately removed his fingers from his ears. Initially, he actively resisted any interaction with me, and, in fact, did not in any way acknowledge my presence.

Although Bernie's mother remained in the playroom throughout his second session, he made contact with her only once, pulling her to join him in looking out the window. When his eyes lit upon the water fountain, he seemed to remember his pleasurable introduction to it two days earlier; he drank briefly and skillfully from it throughout the session. Bernie no longer appeared incessantly driven to circle the periphery of the room. At times, instead, he walked freely around the playroom and picked up the color paddles, a shape sorter, and a beginner's puzzle, which were available to him on open shelves; he used all the materials appropriately. Bernie watched from a distance while I poured soapy water into containers at a water table, but chose not to join in the activity. (I discovered later that superneat Bernie avoided anything he considered messy.) On two occasions, he accepted my assistance in mounting a rocking horse and stayed on the horse briefly each time.

It was during his second appointment that Bernie demonstrated his attraction to the beginner books displayed on a slanted bookshelf. Those available were small (for child portability), colorful, of glossy paper-on-board construction (for manageability by children who lack dexterity to handle more commonly used thin pages), and were selected purposefully for their potential to stimulate language, to develop a sense of self, and to expand the child's world. Bernie chose three books in succession, examining each deliberately—and, it appeared, thoughtfully—while standing at a nearby table. He attended longer to the books than to any other available material.

On his third visit, Bernie separated easily from his mother, who monitored the session from an observation booth. By his fourth appointment, his mother reported his eagerness to come to school and his disappointment at getting into the car and finding, on occasion, that he was going elsewhere. Bernie actively resisted going home after his fifth session. Following our sixth meeting, I recorded his obvious expression of great pleasure when I entered the playroom: he covered his ears with excitement and made a loud, deep sound that sounded like "hi."

The timing seemed right for introducing intrusive therapy. Since Bernie still resisted my close proximity and since he still appeared strongly attracted to books, I adapted as my modus operandi the technique of using books to distract him while we sat together "sardine-like" in a large, comfortable chair. As might have been predicted, Bernie's initial preference for physical distance was overridden by his fascination for the tempting books which only our closeness afforded. From the beginning, Bernie positioned each book correctly for viewing and turned its pages skillfully, one by one, though with a speed that precluded my reading aloud. The proximity afforded by this book-sharing posture led naturally to the baby games described earlier. We alternately viewed a book of Bernie's choice (among those made available to him), then assumed a position for "Pat-a-cake" or for "Ride a little horsey." An invitation for book time dramatically, though sometimes temporarily, extinguished Bernie's occasional, residual driven movement around the room.

After a month, Bernie responded to Cheerios as a reinforcer and seemed to make the connection between what I required of him and his receipt of a Cheerio. The cereal bits were useful in reducing the tempo of Bernie's page-turning behavior to a pace that allowed me to read to him. He especially enjoyed such books as *Sleepy Time* (Fujikawa), *My Best Friends* (Weigle), *Fire Engines* (Izawa), *A Child's Garden of Verses* (Stevenson), *Babies* (Fujikawa), *Me* (Clure and Ramsey), *Let's Play!* (Fujikawa), and the "changing picture book," *Growing Up in Nature* (Burton). As the end of the second month of therapy approached, Bernie was turning pages skillfully, even in such thin-paged books as *Benji's Blanket* (Brown), *The Carrot Seed* (Kraus), *The Little Book* (de Regniers), *The Little Fire Engine* (Lenski), *Push, Pull, Empty, Full: A Book of Opposites* (Hoban), *We Help Daddy* (Stein), *First ABC* (Larrick), and *Machines* (Dugan). It never failed to amaze me that Bernie *always* turned the page at the appropriate time, even when it appeared that he was not giving his direct visual attention to the book. Of course, it may be that he was exercising the autistic child's unique facility for peripheral vision!

After three months of treatment, Bernie began to reciprocate during the intrusive activities that were interspersed with our book time. When I blew on him gently, he responded by blowing on me in an equally gentle fashion. When I made "fat cheeks" for him to "pop," he, in turn, invited my reciprocal action. In order to maintain our closeness in other positions and in other areas of the playroom, I deliberately moved book time from the big chair to the floor. Sitting close together on an exercise mat with our backs propped against a wall facilitated by moving Bernie later into position on the mat for location play and for such activities as "This little piggy" and "Row the boat." Bernie became progressively more responsive during the months of intrusion and much more interested in exploring me as a person: he touched my face gently several times and played with my mouth. Meanwhile, Bernie became a person in his own right, and a delightfully mischievous one at that! He especially enjoyed dashing from the playroom through the building whenever the Dutch door was left unlocked; he giggled in obvious glee when able to pulloff this caper.

Bernie's sustained interest in books carried over into his home, where both parents reported his pleasure in being read to. His dedication to books was matched qualitatively by his sophisticated use of other educational materials in the therapeutic setting, such as advanced puzzles, cylinder form boards, sequencing beads, color/shape/size lotto games, design cards for large parquetry blocks, and flannel board with accompanying teaching aids. Bernie especially sought out alphabet and number learning materials, such as a numbered jigsaw puzzle, a kinesthetic-tactile number game, number and alphabet bingo, multisensory numerals, and kinesthetic alphabet cards. In working with numbers and letters on a magnetic board, Bernie consistently placed the plastic numbers and letters in accurate spatial orientation, except for the letter *m*, which Bernie insisted should be positioned ƎǃWhen I arranged alphabet picture flash cards in sequence around a long table, I was amazed to discover that Bernie could place corresponding plastic letters effortlessly and flawlessly on the flash cards.

After two years' intervention, psychological evaluation resulted in an IQ of seventy-five, within the slow-learner range of intellectual ability. Both the psychologist and I felt that Bernie's intelligence as demonstrated in formal testing was but a conservative estimate of his potential. I also had an early gut feeling that Bernie could "read," though of course that was difficult to prove in the absence of verbal speech. (Precocious reading, untaught, has been observed in autistic children; e.g., see DeMyer.[9]) This suspicion was borne out somewhat on a home visit when Bernie was five years old: his verbal repertoire had expanded sufficiently by then to allow him to read aloud all the programs from a TV guide.

Bernie's Progress after Therapy

When Bernie left the therapeutic preschool setting after two years' attendance, he was ready for kindergarten work, and, fortunately for him, was placed in a nearby public school classroom for autistic children, taught by a skilled and sensitive teacher. For a detailed account of Bernie's two years in the special class, see Wallick and Boudreaux.[10] The brief review that follows is from that report.

An initial task included in Bernie's educational program at the public school was alphabet sequencing, using self-correcting materials. By the end of the second week, Rebus reading, beginning writing skills, and the use of the Language Master were added. Bernie preferred being busy and was self-motivated to learn. He was intrigued by teaching machines and after two or three instructional sessions could operate them unassisted.

After approximately six weeks, word recognition of names of days, months, and of the students (four children constituted the class membership, with the teacher and a well-trained assistant) was introduced, along with beginning sight words via picture/word cards. Bernie was using the Language Master independently; card were made to reinforce teaching activities, and task time increased to fifteen to twenty minutes. Speech continued to improve, and Bernie's vocabulary increased.

"Listen and Do," a recorded phonics program with accompanying worksheets, was begun in Bernie's third month of attendance. He could follow directions and point, but a prompt was required for him to underline, mark an X, or circle an object. When Bernie resisted coming in from outdoor play period, the teachers wisely rescheduled one of his favorite activities: stories on tape, or a record with filmstrip. The audiovisual materials were shown to Bernie on the playground and a fair warning given. After three days of not returning to the classroom on his own and his therefore being deprived of the activity, the problem was solved.

By midyear, Bernie was using simple sentences spontaneously, had a sight vocabulary of approximately forty words, could sequence one through twenty-five, knew the basic colors, and could identify several beginning consonant sounds. At the end of the school year, he had acquired most kindergarten skills, with his greatest lag in the area of comprehension—attributable, of course, to his language delay.

Preprimer reading and first-grade math were introduced at the beginning of Bernie's second public school year, along with a review of all previously mastered skills. Bernie continued to be self-motivated in reading and math and was especially excited about reading words in a book format. He enjoyed taking home small stories cut from old readers and read to his mother and father, who, incidentally, were always very supportive of their son and of each other. Bernie's pace was slowed only by his need to increase language comprehension skills. Within six weeks of first-grade instruction, he was reading independently and following simple instructions; however, complex directions such as "Color the dog brown *and* black" produced confusion. Bernie was intrigued by a newly acquired teaching device, "Spellbinder," and as he did with other machines, operated it unassisted within a few days; programs included prereading, reading, phonics, spelling, and math skills. Bernie's slow progress in reading during his second year was not due to an inability to read (he always learned sight words quickly), but rather to his language handicap. More advanced comprehension skills were emerging, however, albeit delayed. Most significantly, Bernie's gains were not restricted to the area of cognition, but were noteworthy in the affective domain as well.

Summary

The preceding overview documents the significant role books played in an autistic child's development—in *both* domains. It seems likely that, in Bernie's case, gains in the cognitive area would not have been as dramatic in the absence of the normalization achieved through simultaneous communication, intrusive therapy, and books. It was through our initial reading experience that intrusion into Bernie's early aloofness and social withdrawal was made possible. It was through the medium of books that Bernie gained some control over his confusing world: books assisted him in labeling familiar objects; helped him organize and see relationships among his observations; and facilitated his understanding of himself in relation to body image, growing up, and his role in the family.

It has been reported that books are the chief interest of approximately 15 percent of autistic children.[11] Far from being an isolating experience, this preference for books can be channeled creatively to the child's great advantage. Because Bernie's story is a case study, reported results are descriptive only, and not predictive for other autistic children. However, his experience suggests a challenge to clinicians and librarians to get more autistic children "hooked on books," in an attempt to facilitate their affective and cognitive growth.

Notes

1. Karen H. Harris and Mollie M. Wallick, "Books to Begin On," *Dimensions* 5 (Oct. 1976): 4–9, 26.
2. Leo Kanner, "Autistic Disturbances of Affective Contact," *Nervous Child* 2(1943): 217–50.
3. Don W. Churchill, "The Relation of Infantile Autism and Early Childhood Schizophrenia to Developmental Language Disorders of Childhood," *Journal of Autism and Childhood Schizophrenia* 2 (Apr.–June 1972): 182–97; Beate Hermelin and Neil O'Connor, *Psychological Experiments with Autistic Children* (Oxford: Pergamon, 1970); Michael Rutter, "The Influence of Organic and Emotional Factors on the Origins, Nature and Outcome of Childhood Psychosis," *Developmental Medicine and Child Neurology* 7 (1965): 518–28; Michael Rutter, "Concepts of Autism: A Review of Research," *Journal of Child Psychology and Psychiatry* 9 (Oct. 1968): 1–25; Michael Rutter and Lawrence Bartak, "Causes of Infantile Autism: Some Considerations from Recent Research," *Journal of Autism and Childhood Schizophrenia* 1 (Mar. 1971): 20–32; Lorna Wing, "The Handicaps of Autistic Children—A Comparative Study," *Journal of Child Psychology and Psychiatry* 10 (Sept. 1969): 1–40.
4. "National Society for Autistic Children Definition of the Syndrome of Autism," *Journal of Autism and Childhood Schizophrenia* 8 (June 1978):162–69.
5. O. Ivar Lovaas et al., "Acquisition of Imitative Speech by Schizophrenic Children," *Science* 151 (1966):705–7.
6. O. Ivar Lovaas et al., "Some Generalization Follow-up Measures on Autistic Children in Behavior Therapy," *Journal of Applied Behavior Analysis* 6 (Spring 1973): 131–66.
7. Margaret P. Creedon, "Language Development in Nonverbal Autistic Children Using a Simultaneous Communication System" (Paper presented at the Meeting of the Society for Research in Child Development, Philadelphia, Mar. 1973); idem, "The David School—Simultaneous Communication Using Signed English and Speaking" (Paper presented at the Annual Meeting of the National Society for Autistic Children, San Diego, June 1975); idem, "The David School: A Simultaneous Communication Model" (Paper presented at the Annual Meeting of the National Society for Autistic Children, Oak Brook, Ill., June 1976); Robert L. Fulsiler and Roger S. Fouts, "Acquisition of American Sign Language by a Noncommunicating Autistic Child," *Journal of Autism and Childhood Schizophrenia* 6 (Mar. 1976): 43–51; Bernard Schaeffer et al., "Spontaneous Verbal Language for Autistic Children through Signed Speech" (Paper presented at the Annual Meeting of the National Society for Autistic Children, Oak Brook, Ill., June 1976); Mollie M. Wallick, "The Lagniappe Effect of Teaching Sign Language to Autistic Children" (Paper presented at a symposium, "The Dysphasic Child," sponsored by Vanderbilt University School of Medicine, Nashville, May 1977).
8. Mollie M. Wallick and Mary V. Boudreaux, "Bernie: A Four-Year Psychoeducational Intervention in a Therapeutic Preschool and a Public School Class for Autistic Children," ERIC Clearing House ED 17 020 (Apr. 1979).
9. Marian K. DeMyer, *Parents and Children in Autism* (New York: Wiley, 1979).
10. Wallick and Boudreaux, "Bernie."
11. DeMyer, *Parents and Children in Autism.*

Bibliography of Children's Books

Brown, Myra Berry. *Benji's Blanket*. New York: Watts, 1962.

Burton, Leslie. *Growing Up in Nature*. New York: Child Guidance, n.d.

Clure, Beth, and Helen Ramsey. *Me*. Glendale, Calif.: Bowman, 1968.

de Regniers, Beatrice Schenk. *The Little Book*. New York: Walck, 1961.

Dugan, William. *Machines*. Racine, Wis.: Golden Pr., 1961.

Fujikawa, Gyo. *Babies*. New York: Grosset, 1963.

———. *Let's Play!* New York: Grosset, 1975.

———. *Sleepy Time*. New York: Grosset, 1975.

Hoban, Tana. *Push, Pull, Empty, Full: A Book of Opposites*. New York: Macmillan, 1972.

Izawa, Tadasu. *Fire Engines*. New York: Grosset, 1971.

Kraus, Ruth. *The Carrot Seed*. New York: Harper, 1948.

Larrick, Nancy. *First ABC*. New York: Platt & Munk, 1965.

Lenski, Lois. *The Little Fire Engine*. New York: Walck, 1946.

Stein, Mimi. *We Help Daddy*. New York: Golden Pr., 1962.

Stevenson, Robert Louis. *A Child's Garden of Verses*. New York: Grosset, 1969.

Weigle, Oscar. *My Best Friends*. New York: Grosset, 1972.

6

Outreach

Profound changes in society are affecting the lives of the disabled in significant ways. Advances in medicine have dramatically improved the functioning of individuals who only recently were considered beyond such help. Bioengineering has modified orthotics and prosthetics to help impaired people more nearly simulate standard behaviors. Architects are becoming increasingly cognizant of those subtle as well as the more obvious elements in the environment which can be altered to maximize efficient and comfortable utilization by disabled persons. Technology has drastically altered the style, format, and construction of both hardware and software used for information transmission. The field of special education is in continual flux as changes in theory and practice directly affect the lives of millions of children. Psychologists argue over such fundamental questions as definitions of exceptionalities, validity of identification and measurement devices and procedures, proper pedogogical responses, counselling practices, administrative structures, and the like.

It is quite clear that the interested public—disabled persons, scholars, professionals, advocates, and others—require access to information about this complex and rapidly growing field. With the relevant data base increasing at an astounding rate, the problems of access and retrieval have become exceedingly complicated. Libraries must guide patrons to sources of information about exceptionality and assist in framing appropriate questions in order for them to obtain usable responses.

Exceptional persons, especially those just beginning to enter the mainstream of community life, may experience a host of problems in identifying agencies, organizations, and commercial enterprises that supply needed services. Such persons require guidance in familiarizing themselves with the current accessibility status, adaptations, and accommodations of the institutions and sites they wish to use. On the other hand, churches, temples, museums, recreation centers, businesses and other entities interested in encouraging utilization of their structures must have assistance in obtaining standards and guidelines in order to modify their facilities and programs and to disseminate news of their commitment and progress to all segments of the interested audience. In this regard, the library can serve as a channel of information, a liaison and a mediator.

With any disability, there are far more people who have mild to moderate disablement than there are who are severely impaired. However, those who have the most extreme form of a handicapping condition may need the most intensive and costly efforts and equipment to remediate or compensate for their deficiencies. What this means to librarians is that those individuals comprising a low incidence population usually have, in addition to their ordinary requests, very specialized, complex needs. For example, a reader with mild visual impairment may be adequately served by large print books—a fairly simple, relatively inexpensive accommodation. But a blind person may require an Optacon, a Kurzweil machine, a Braillewriter and other specialized equipment. However, blind persons are estimated as comprising only a minute percentage of the population so that any one library can expect to count only a small number of such users among its clientele. Several accommodations can be made: librarians could define their user population by larger geographical units, they could institute or expand interlibrary cooperation, or they could act as a clearinghouse between users and other agencies which manufacture or distribute materials. Access to information about how libraries have solved such problems is essential to institutions about to undertake similar ventures.

Full service to patrons with exceptionalities implies answering the needs of others directly involved with their lives as well. This pool may include parents, siblings, teachers, therapists, and advocates. For example, before their own direct involvement, few individuals undoubtedly gave much thought to the ramifications of exceptionality. At this juncture, parents may need information about the nature of the disability, what the prognosis might be for their child, how to balance responsibilities between the exceptional child and other members of the family, what they might expect in the immediate future and over the long run, where they can go for assistance, when they should seek it, the implications of education, socialization, recreation, travel, employment and other everyday areas of functioning. In this regard too, the library has a crucial role to play in assembling, delivering, and interpreting information.

This last chapter contains not only innovative ideas for the mainstreamed library, its several contributions exemplify the cooperative spirit that is the backbone of librarianship. These final words deal with the procedures for gathering, organizing, and disseminating information as practiced by gigantic, comprehensive clearinghouses as well as by individual librarians or activists working on a local level. This variability is apt since it symbolizes the wide range of information needs required to satisfy users with impairments as well as those individuals and groups involved with their welfare and advancement.

The articles in this section describe resources deriving their content from national and even international sources. Equally important is the organization of data for neighborhood usage and how such information serves small, geographically delimited areas. What is suggested is that complete outreach cover information seekers like scholars who may wish the widest possible information pool from which to draw as well as individual library and media center users who wish practical counsel regarding what is available around the corner.

Dodson recounts the Brooklyn Public Library's pioneering efforts to expand its services to community members who need practical, up-to-date information about disability and its implications. After exploring various possibilities, it was determined that the assembling of circulating kits addressed to parents and other caregivers would serve a vital function. These kits evolved into increasingly useful resources and were supplemented by a continuously revised referral directory that identified local agencies providing specialized services. The practices herein described could readily be used as a model for other communities.

Reporting on a grass roots community movement, Baskin and Cosel recount how activists with a vision of the role librarians and libraries play in the mainstreaming process bring about change in a particular locality. Development of a coherent humanistic philosophy, organization of a coalition of individuals committed to community growth, implementation of mainstreaming plans into realities in the libraries, schools and other agencies are all described in this article. The authors show how the unique characteristics of a locality structure both the problems and the means whereby the solutions to those difficulties may be found.

Based on the requirement that individual education plans be developed for all children who fall under the aegis of P.L. 94-142, the Education for All Handicapped Children Act, and that parents be included in the formulation of those plans, Kroth and Brown explicate the role of the media specialist in that context. The authors suggest a fourfold role for personnel in the media center: providing information to teachers to share with parents; upgrading in-house skills and identifying practical procedures for integrating exceptional students; working with parents by suggesting resources which answer questions on parenting, on community agencies and organizations, and on their newly established legal rights; and functioning as a bridge between school and community in the common goal of making mainstreaming a success.

Chesley concisely and comprehensively details the structure, purpose, function, and procedures for utilizing the Educational Resources Information Center (ERIC) data base. He highlights the clearinghouse that focuses on material relevant to handicapped and gifted persons, detailing how and from which sources documents are selected and incorporated into the collection, and how information is disseminated. Implemented and proposed changes in the ERIC system are enumerated, and a list of the specialized clearinghouses is appended.

As the information available on disability and rehabilitation multiplies with astonishing rapidity, the librarian is frequently at a loss trying to monitor the direction, extent, and particulars of the growth. In this area, as in others, consultation with the appropriate data base is often the most efficient means to locate information. Erickson, contrasting ERIC and Exceptional Child Education Resources (ECER), reveals the special scope and depth of the latter resource. As patrons develop more complex and sophisticated needs, as fugitive material expands exponentially, and as more detailed and contemporary requests are made, awareness of this rich resource containing a specialized body of information on disability becomes even more crucial.

These articles reflect ways in which libraries may prepare for the mainstreaming movement. We trust that this will be neither the last chapter nor the last word on the subject. There are many more issues to be dealt with, ideas to explore, and innovations to implement before the library can be described as totally accessible to all citizens. We hope that the authors have contributed to the realization of that elusive but eminently desirable goal.

ctical advice to parents. We finally decided to put everything together under one cover in a large envelope and let the borrower take as much or as little of the information they needed. That is how the kit that later became known as "Practical Guide for Parents of Children with Special Needs" came into being.

This first kit left a great deal to be desired! There was too much and, at the same time, too little. There was not enough information covering any one exceptionality to divide by subject; but too much for a borrower to wade through if that person's interests were limited. The committee that had been set up to assist in the review of kit materials then went to work to devise a more efficient way of handling this data. After several false starts, we were finally able to make suitable subdivisions, index our holdings, and facilitate use by borrowers. The first broad subject headings were: Referral and Advocacy Materials and Bibliographies; Special Needs/Handicapping Conditions/Home Care; and Travel Suggestions (later expanded to Travel, Recreation and Accessibility). We have since added a fourth category—Gifted Children.

The materials pertaining to the broad headings are kept in brightly colored Princeton files and are relatively easy to find. Almost everything is available for circulation, but some fragile items are marked for reference use only. The material is available in Brooklyn's 57 branches as well as the central library and is kept in the area considered most visible and accessible to our borrowers. Although the material contained in the kits is not cataloged, the kits themselves are listed under the following subject headings: Handicapped; Handicapped Children; Handicapped Children, Education; Exceptional Children; Mentally Handicapped Children; Mentally Handicapped Children, Education.

As we developed our kits, we discovered that listings of the agencies set up to work with exceptional children were found in a number of reference sources, but no one source covered them all. We next went to work developing a referral directory that would include under one cover all the institutions and associations in the greater New York area designed to provide therapy and assistance for any kind of permanent disability. This work resulted in a 51-page document that is continually updated.

All of the aforementioned took time to develop, for there were no additional hands to assist with this project. During this time, a committee of adult services staff members was asked to make recommendations for achieving barrier-free accessibility in some buildings. Eventually, there was enough overlap in our concerns to set up a joint committee of children's services and adult services staff to work on all aspects of service to the exceptional. We have had many inquiries as to whether we received a special grant to subsidize this project. We did not, for we considered it our responsibility to improve on the resources our library system provides during the normal course of any working day. The use of the kits by the public has encouraged us to continue to develop and expand this community service.

Bridging an Information Gap: A Brooklyn Public Library Kit for Parents of Children with Special

MARGUER

Working with exceptional children and their parents or parent surrogates has long been an important part of Brooklyn Public Library programming. However, some years ago, we began to recognize that we needed to do more for this special group. To fulfill our responsibility, we developed "special needs kits" to satisfy the demands for concise and compact information dealing with the requirements of exceptional children and youth.

The needs of the exceptional child were highlighted five years ago for the Brooklyn Public Library when the public schools increased the number of class visits and special programs for this population. We also received a request from one of the nearby hospitals to set up a special collection of books to be used by children with learning disabilities and their parents. It was thought that, through books, parents might better be able to understand and accept their children's limitations. Next, a staff member attended an American Library Association (ALA) conference and returned determined to raise the consciousness of the children's services staff to the needs of exceptional children and their parents. She and several others were convinced that a system the size of the Brooklyn Public Library could certainly do more for these patrons. What? We did not know. We then decided to seek more information about exceptional children in order to refine what additional services the library might possibly offer that would be effective. For that purpose, we invited a panel of specialists to discuss with the staff some of the specifics regarding the wide range of disabilities affecting children and to inform us of some of the special services being offered in New York to these children and their parents. The broad perspective and dimensions of the task were overwhelming and there was a strong temptation to bury our heads in the sand.

Budgetary restrictions severely limited our ability to provide specialized materials for these children. W
choosing that which
truly wide range of l
both physical and
able one. However,
sion, one theme w
the need for inform
to the caregivers c
needs, the need to
Brooklyn there were
to assist both child a
adults were ignora
fact, the panel mem
of special services p
tions which they r
experts serving chil
trum of disabilities,
what their opposite
they normally did
other! This insight h
of action. Perhaps
the library could pla
local information as
form that parents
might at least be abl
start seeking aid.

Our next step wa
able and how best t
accessible in printed
few known resourc
away for materials o
source led to anothe
material began to gro
we would never com
For the better part
coordinator of child
material and reviewe
appreciable amount
spent researching, a
materials. We finally
what to do with, and
did not fit neatly intc
With the aid of a c
librarians, we sifted
had collected during
those items which w

The Librarian as an Advocate for the Patron with Special Needs

BARBARA H. BASKIN and RONNE COSEL

The success of mainstreaming is dependent on the responses of all agencies in the community to the legal mandates that require the provision of services to exceptional citizens. Following the passage of the Rehabilitation Act and the Education for all Handicapped Children Act, as well as state legislation, the immediate response of many communities was to determine the most expeditious means of complying with minimum requirements. Although some districts stood aloof, hoping they could slip by with token gestures, others sought to enforce not only the letter but the intent of the laws. This account is the chronicle of how one such community seized this opportunity to enrich the lives of all its citizens. The library participated in a leadership role from the inception of the grass roots movement. It provided information to its own patrons and the public at large, making its facilities an arena for integration and serving as a liaison between various agencies cooperating in this task.

The setting for this change can be characterized as a community reflecting a generally socially responsible attitude, but one that had been adversely affected by certain local conflicts. A cohort of highly vocal residents expressed their antipathy toward the establishment in their neighborhood of hostels for newly de-institutionalized mentally retarded adults in local meetings and in the press.

The community was conscious of and proud of its heritage. Providing physical access to local buildings generally involved additions which were not aesthetically pleasing and which destroyed efforts to maintain the appearance of a previous historical period: the goals of preservationists seemed in irreconcilable conflict with the mobility needs of the disabled. Fiscal problems, high taxes, and a generally depressed economy intensified the widespread feeling that frills must be cut from all budgets. Included in that category were innovative educational programs for gifted and talented children, adaptations in facilities that would make them accessible to persons with impairments, special education classes in neighborhood schools, adapted transportation services, and programs designed to find employment for disabled adults.

There were, however, countervailing forces. The local museum had initiated and was in the early stages of implementing a plan for serving individuals with special needs. The public library, while expanding its quarters, deliberately took advantage of the renovation to eliminate architectural barriers. The county library network had, for some time, been developing an extensive specialized collection of resources and reference materials for blind and physically handicapped patrons. Responding to a federal mandate, the state had funded a regional Special Education Training and Resource Center that had assembled a professional collection featuring materials of particular value to parents, special educators, and administrators, and available to others with interests or responsibilities in the area. A nearby university had instituted annual awareness programs on disability that had impacted on community attitudes. One of the local newspapers frequently featured stories that presented the notable achievements of exceptional local residents. In sum, the public reflected a wide spectrum of attitudes about roles that special needs individuals could and should play in local affairs.

A group of concerned citizens felt the time was appropriate for galvanizing the positive, supportive forces within the community to work cooperatively toward implementing mainstreaming goals. They organized the Awareness Coalition for the Exceptional (ACE), an advocacy group for citizens with special needs. Precedent for a community-based advocacy group had been set by two previously established, successful school-related organizations: the Special Education Parent-Teacher Association (SEPTA), and the Parents and Teachers of Gifted and Talented (PTGT).

However, the success of ACE was contingent on a broader participating base than had been embraced by other advocacy groups. Included could be representatives from business, cultural, recreational, and religious as well as educational institutions. Intent on working with agencies and individuals who had experience and expertise in the needs of disabled individuals while expanding their base to previously uninvolved persons, ACE defined itself from the outset as a coalition.

Mainstreaming has often been defined as the integration of exceptional children, insofar as possible, into regular schools and classrooms. ACE was committed to the belief that school was only a part of the life of any person and that the mainstream included the nonschool aspects of community life as well. In addition, members determined not to accept mere physical accessibility as a goal but conceptualized a local environment that would be hospitable, accommodating, and inclusive.

One of the first acts of the coalition was to obtain a mandate from the school board that would serve as a statement of goals, would commit the educational establishment to a major role, would give credibility and visibility to the organization and would allow access to essential administrative, secretarial, and logistical services. The mandate directed ACE to:

1. Create an awareness in the community of the needs of exceptional children and adults;
2. Arrange for the easy availability of resources to provide information to the community on the ramifications of exceptionality;
3. Encourage the dissemination of information about exceptionality;
4. Sponsor and propose in-service programs for teachers and librarians;
5. Act as a liaison and coordinator of efforts of various agencies to achieve mainstreaming goals;
6. Serve as a resource to the school board;
7. Work actively to foster attitudes of acceptance toward disabled citizens.

Once concensus had been reached regarding the goals of the Awareness Coalition for the Exceptional, the group began to define long-term as well as immediate objectives, explore sources for the funding necessary to implement their aims and seek means to advertise their purpose and solicit support from local residents.

ACE wanted to gain immediate visibility and simultaneously galvanize community spirit so an activity of great interest to launch their campaign was essential. Since sports played a potent role in the lives of local residents, enthusiasm over their local headline-grabbing hockey team pervaded the community. Plans were formulated to sponsor a competition featuring the champion hockey players against disabled athletes in a wheelchair basketball game. Underwritten by a local bank, the evening attracted more than 2,000 fans of all ages. The event was of particular importance because it focused attention on ability rather than disability, engendered considerable excitement and resulted in significant commitments of funding, time, and resources by formerly uninvolved citizens.

Although this initial event was very successful, ACE had to turn its attention to less visible, less dramatic, but equally essential, issues. The director of the library was a key member of the coalition. She was involved in redesigning the physical environment of the library in order to eliminate barriers so as to include patrons with impairments. The chairperson of ACE, a professional architectural designer and contractor, reviewed the blueprints for the renovation for adherence with established guidelines. For the opening of the remodeled facility, the library planned on scheduling "The Kids on the Block," a puppet show involving youthful characters with a variety of disabilities. The program would serve the dual function of providing first class entertainment and informing the public that the library was responsive to the needs of exceptional patrons.

The library also turned its attention to an examination of its own resources. Policies were formulated that set criteria for selection of books and journals useful to people seeking information on disability. As a symbol of its commitment to the concept of mainstreaming and as an indication of its perception of the role of the library in the process, ACE set aside almost three quarters of its profits from the sports night for the purchase of needed materials. A continuing problem of libraries is keeping its vertical files current. The Brooklyn Public Library procedure was tapped as a possible model for updating ephemeral material on disability. In a rapidly changing field, this inclusion was acknowledged to be a major resource for the community.

Concurrently, proposals for a cooperative role were shared with public school library personnel. In a meeting with the library/media director, representatives from ACE presented her with a host of references—bibliographies evaluating print and media resources, publications of advocacy groups, materials from the collection of the Special Education Training and Resource Center as well as resources available through the International Year of the Disabled Persons committee. An in-service workshop was designed for librarians working with youngsters in kindergarten through twelfth grade which dealt with analysis and use of juvenile and young adult fiction featuring characters who were disabled. The public television presentation, "People You'd Like to Know," was promoted as an additional medium for instructional materials personnel as well as for special education and regular classroom teachers.

ACE was also responsible for instituting a school-wide awareness week. During that period, teacher training sessions took place, instructional media were introduced and demonstrated, and a film, *The Invisible Children*, was shown to staff and later to children with extremely positive results. Faculty were encouraged to find the means for integrating this product on exceptionality into their classrooms. Although intended as a district-wide effort, awareness week was piloted in one school, offering an opportunity to evaluate its effectiveness and make whatever changes were necessary before full implementation for the following year.

The Awareness Coalition for the Exceptional urged inclusion of topics relating to impairment on Superintendent's Day. This annual program would include three relevant sessions: a workshop on attitudes toward disabled persons, a disability simulation activity, and *Reel to Reel*, a media center experience offering opportunities to view available resources on film or tape. One major and immediate result was staff awareness of locally available but underutilized resources.

The founders of ACE perceived community antipathy as the result of a lack of accurate information about disability and few opportunities for direct interaction with people sustaining impairments. The combined effect of no information, misinformation, few role models, and no first-hand experience served to enforce rejection and avoidance reactions. Certain factors must coexist if positive interaction between disabled and able-bodied persons is to take place: access to an adapted arena; programs that support cooperative activities; and information leading to understanding. The library has a key role to play in each of these crucial areas.

Welcome in the Parent

ROGER KROTH and GWENETH BLACKLOCK BROWN

A majority of the public school systems in the United States have policies that require from one to two parent-teacher conferences a year. In addition, the new Education for All Handicapped Children Act, Public Law 94-142, requires parental participation in placement decisions and in the development of individual educational plans (IEP) for each handicapped child. In general, parents and teachers have not been well prepared for this increased interaction. School media specialists can play a major role for the significant adults in a child's life by providing information and techniques for improved cooperative efforts.

Initially, the sweeping new civil rights law for the handicapped may create tension and upheaval in schools as parents and school personnel find themselves unprepared for their responsibilities. As the law is implemented, the school media program can profoundly effect the quality of the interactions among parents, children, and school personnel. To develop a media program that fosters successful interactions, media specialists need a firm understanding of Public Law 94-142 and its implications for all involved individuals.

The most striking change ushered in by the new law is that unprecedented numbers of handicapped children will be provided a free appropriate public school education. In 1975, when framing the new law, Congress pointed out that more than half of the nation's eight million handicapped children do not receive appropriate educational services and one million are excluded entirely from the public schools. Today, education is recognized as the handicapped person's right, and Congress seeks by law to guarantee a quality education for all children. By September 1, 1978, all children between ages three and eighteen must be served, and by September 1, 1980, all children between ages three and twenty-one must be served. While the requirement for the ages three to five and eighteen to twenty-one will not be applied where inconsistent with state law, by 1980 many states will attempt to educate children ages three through twenty-one. The increase in numbers of handicapped children served will result in a vastly different teaching and learning atmosphere than has ever existed in the nation's public schools.

A second avenue of change for the schools involves the law's requirement that children must be placed in the least restrictive educational environment. To the maximum extent possible, handicapped children will be mainstreamed, that is, educated with children who are not handicapped. One outcome of the least restrictive environmental requirement is that in most schools both regular and special education teachers will confront a new population of students. Mild to moderately handicapped children will be placed in regular classes with teachers who may never have received the educational experiences necessary for successfully carrying out their new tasks. Similarly, most special class teachers, experienced in providing quality education environments for mild to moderately handicapped students, will for the first time teach the severely handicapped children, who previously were placed in residential facilities or left at home. One needs little imagination to sense the frustration, anger, and feelings of inadequacy likely to surface in regular and special teachers unless media program services, in-service education, and experience provide the needed support.

Perhaps the greatest challenge faced by teachers will be that of working closely with parents, particularly in the development of individualized educational plans. Recognizing that it is impossible to provide appropriate educational services without focusing on the needs of the individual children, Congress requires that each child enrolled in a program have a written statement outlining his or her individualized educational plan. The plan must be jointly developed by a qual-

"Welcome in the Parent," by Roger Kroth and Gweneth Blacklock Brown, *School Media Quarterly* 1978, 6: 246–52.

ified school official, the child's teacher, and the child's parents or guardian. If possible, the child should participate in the planning. To a greater extent than ever before, teachers will be expected to develop a sharing, working relationship with parents and children. Since few teachers were provided preservice educational experiences related to parent-teacher interaction, most teachers find the prospect of parent conferences and joint educational planning a frightening one. The media specialist can expect concerned teachers to seek out the media program for information relating to parent education and conference skills as well as practical advice for teaching handicapped children.

Parents, too, will need information relating to their roles as educational planners. Welcoming individual parents as well as parent groups to the media center services can facilitate the development of positive parent attitudes toward the school and aid in the successful implementation of the law. Most parents of handicapped children will be interested in information relating to community resources and services, educational programming, and their rights under the law. The media specialist will need to understand parent rights and should make available to parents copies of the law and summary pamphlets, which are distributed at no cost from the Bureau of Education for the Handicapped.

The media specialist will be in a unique position to help bridge the communication gap between school and home as changing conditions, brought about by the law, create a need for information. The quality school media program will be one in which the media specialist takes an active role in seeking out the needed information and provides educational leadership for both parents and teachers. Consider for a moment the following conditions:

- Parents are not a homogenous body. As Bridge points out, in addition to the variables of ethnicity, religion, education, and income, a wide variety of attitudes, values, and child-rearing practices must be taken into consideration.[1] These variables exist in parents of exceptional children regardless of the exceptionality, and they influence all parent-school interactions.
- Parents have different needs and interests at different times. The age of the child and the length of time since parental awareness of the learning problem greatly influence the parents' informational needs.
- While parents are a diverse group with distinct learning needs, most share fear, frustration, and disappointment in child rearing beyond that typically experienced by parents of nonhandicapped children. Many parents, in their struggle to find help for their child, too often have found ignorance, fear, or indifference among the medical and educational establishments. After going through the typical stages of denial, guilt, and a search for services, many parents finally turn their frustrations into militance and a demand for social action. Thus, school personnel may find their interactions with parents colored by a wide range of parental responses to an extremely difficult situation.
- Parents are becoming more knowledgeable about exceptional children. One can scarcely pick up a popular magazine without being exposed to articles about learning problems in children. Segments of TV programs have been devoted to topics such as learning disabilities, autism, hyperactivity, etc. Through every kind of media, a wide range of advice is offered to parents regarding educational procedures, the use of medication, behavior management techniques, and other intervention strategies.
- Parents are becoming more a part of the educational team. On their own initiative, parents have become more involved in school programs than in past years;[2] they are expected to be an active participant in planning for the education of their own children according to P.L. 94-142; they are becoming a factor in providing counsel to school personnel through parent advisory groups;[3] and they are serving schools in a volunteer fashion.[4] In fact, many school media specialists have appreciated the help of parent volunteers in the media centers.
- Almost all parents and teachers of both regular and special education pupils will engage in at least one educational conference a year. According to the May 1976 issue of *Phi Delta Kappan*, "There is a trend toward parent con-

ferences which is sufficient that by 1980, 90% of all U.S. districts will be using them." This could affect between thirty and fifty million students and their parents and two to three million teachers, depending upon the extent to which secondary pupils are included. In addition, parents and teachers of the eight to nine million exceptional children are expected to meet periodically to work on education plans for the children. It would seem that most teachers have learned conference skills by doing. There has been little attention paid to this activity in pre-service or in-service training programs; yet, in addition to holding the normal educational conferences, the regular teacher is often the first person to raise the question of exceptionality with parents of mildly handicapped children and, thus, begin the referral process.

Clearly, the above conditions result in the need for information by the participants (parents and educators), with the most natural source of information being the media center. The media specialist will be the key person in the development of a program that fosters positive outcomes from the above conditions. The types and quantities of materials to be available will depend on the degree to which an individual school has become involved with handicapped children and, of course, the age levels of children within the facility. It would be impossible within the limits of this article to cover all the books, films, filmstrips, directories, etc., that would be helpful to parents or those working with parents. Some materials will be included as examples, but the reader must realize that a careful analysis of the population to be served is an important step in the information selection process.

Information for Parents

All parents experience a wide range of oftentimes confusing emotion during the child-rearing years. Parents of exceptional children, however, often feel alone in their struggle to find services or to personally adjust to the family changes brought about by the presence of an exceptional child. There is no doubt that books, films, and television programs influence their attitudes, feelings, and behavior. Media can make an individual laugh or cry, discourage or inspire, and provide information critical to the solution of life problems. The media specialist can help parents of handicapped children face reality and cope with their adjustment problems through the effective selection and use of media.

There are a number of books written by parents describing family adjustment to the handicapped child. Some of these are quite good, making it easy for the reader to emphathize and learn from the way the authors handled their own difficulties. Many of those books would be helpful, not only to parents, but also to siblings of the handicapped child. Depending on the age and exceptionality of the child, some of the books may be helpful to his or her own adjustment.

Since many communities have local chapters of national associations of people interested in a particular type of handicapping condition, these organizations are a logical place to start to obtain a reading list. The associations usually have an active group of parents who are well read and who can help recommend appropriate books or pamphlets. Also available from most local chapters are reading and film lists on the various handicapping conditions developed by the national organization. Another source of good reading material for parents is *Selected Reading Suggestions for Parents of Mentally Retarded Children* issued by the U.S. Government Printing Office. Many of the readings on the list are broad in scope and would be helpful to parents of children with handicapping conditions different from mental retardation.

Some parents have not faced the fact that their child is handicapped. This is particularly true of parents of children with learning disabilities or mild to moderate behavior disorders. Many counselors, media specialists, and directors of special education report an influx of telephone calls after a television program such as "Puzzle Children" or after parents have seen the filmstrip *A Walk in Another Pair of Shoes*. The school media specialist can be helpful to these parents by having materials available for study. Lists of these materials also are available from the local chapters of national associations.

Conference Skills

Since the vast majority of public school-teachers will be involved in parent-teacher conferences in the coming years, both teachers and parents will be interested in improving their conference skills. The basic motivation behind parent conferences is the belief that children will grow academically, socially, emotionally, or physically because of the interaction. Teachers seek to provide parents with information regarding the child in the classroom and to elicit information from the parents that will enhance the teacher's understanding of the child. There has also been an increase in parents and teachers cooperatively engaging in problem-solving activities. Unfortunately, in a small percentage of the interactions, the child suffers rather than improves. This may be due to hostility between the participants or to a lack of understanding of what is expected. The problem, of course, is that with *mandated* conferences, even a small percentage of failures can affect millions of children. For example, if 10 percent of the conferences lead to deterioration rather than improvement of a child's performance and thirty million conferences are held a year, then three million children could be adversely affected.

The regular classroom teacher is often the first line referral for special education services. The teacher observes the child in the classroom and detects deviant learning patterns. Since these patterns are usually discussed with parents prior to formal referral for evaluation, it is crucial that this conference is handled skillfully. Insensitivity on the part of the teacher can set up barriers to appropriate service. Some books that may be helpful to both regular and special education teachers include:

Barsch, Ray J. *The Parent Teacher Partnership*. Reston, Va.: Council for Exceptional Children, 1969.

D'Evelyn, Katherine E. *Individual Parent Teacher Conference*. New York: Bureau of Publishers, Teachers College, Columbia Univ., 1963.

Garrett, Annette. *Interviewing: Its Principles and Methods*. New York: Family Service Assn. of America, 1942.

Kelly, E. J. *Parent-Teacher Interaction—A Special Education Perspective*. Seattle: Spec. Child, 1974.

Kroth, Roger. *Communicating with Parents of Exceptional Children*. Denver: Love, 1975.

Kroth, R. L., and R. Simpson. *Parent Conferences as a Teaching Strategy*. Denver: Love, 1977.

Parents' conference skills are a dimension that often is not covered but is very important. Parents often come to conferences without any idea of what to expect and enter the session in a passive posture, rather than as an active participant. The National Education Association has a filmstrip and record entitled *Conference Time for Teachers and Parents: A Filmstrip for Teachers* (1972), which would be helpful for in-service training. The kit includes a filmstrip for parents, which is geared toward helping parents learn conference skills.

Parenting Skills

Most parents become parents with little or no formal training for the job. This is most assuredly true for parents of exceptional children.

There are two approaches to providing parent education; one can be likened to preservice training of teachers (i.e., parent education for high-school students) and the other can be likened to in-service training of teachers (i.e., parent education for parents who have children in preschool programs). Both approaches seem necessary if educators are serious about helping individuals become better parents.

Exploring Childhood (1975) is a federally funded program developed for junior and senior high schools in which students learn about child development and themselves while working closely and regularly with young children. The program includes a wide range of materials for teachers, administrators, parents, and students and could easily be presented in most schools. Modules relating to helping children with special needs are an integral part of the educational package.

Two bibliographies that media specialists should have available to help parents and to aid teachers interested in developing parent programs are:

Help for Parents of Handicapped Children—An Annotated Bibliography, compiled by Eastern Pennsylvania Regional Resource Center and Pennsylvania Resources and Information Center for Special Education, King of Prussia, PA 19406.

Parenting in 1976: A Listing from PMIC, compiled by Parenting Materials Information Center, Early Childhood Division, Southwest Educational Development Laboratory, Austin, TX 78701.

Journal articles related to special education, which may be useful to both parents and teachers, are abstracted in *Exceptional Child Education Resources* published by the Council for Exceptional Children, 1920 Association Dr., Reston, VA 22091. The journal, *Exceptional Parent*, should be of particular interest to parents and to those educators involved in the development of parent education programs.

Media specialists and educators will be taking leadership roles in providing education for prospective parents at the secondary school level and for parents with children already in the public schools. Parents need information, and it is usually desirable for educators to provide it in settings that consider the parents and their individual needs, rather than to rely upon a "grab bag" of information provided by the popular media. Determining the needs of a particular group of parents is a prerequisite to providing a successful parent program.

Parent Education Kits

Many educators are interested in providing parents and staff members with parent education training but do not have the time to develop parent education programs. There are a number of commercial materials that require a minimum amount of background to use. Usually the materials have guides and manuals for leaders and participants and worksheets. These materials require the user to have a tape recorder, phonograph, slide or filmstrip projector.

The following kits address various phases of parenting, parent education, or working with parents.

> *Systematic Training for Effective Parenting* by Don Dinkmeyer and Gary D. McKay. American Guidance Service, Inc., Circle Pines, MN 55014, 1976.
>
> *Managing Behavior: A Parent Involvement Program* by Richard L. McDowell. B. L. Winch and Associates, P.O. Box 1185, Torrance, CA 90505, 1974. Also distributed by Research Press, Champaign, Illinois.
>
> *Even Love Is Not Enough: Children with Handicaps*. Parent Magazine Films, Inc., 52 Vanderbilt Ave., New York, NY 10017, 1975.
>
> *The Art of Parenting* by Bill R. Wagonseller, Mary Burnett, Bernard Salzburg, and Joe Burnett. Research Press, Champaign, IL, 1977.
>
> *Keeping in Touch with Parents: The Teacher's Best Friends* by Leatha Mae Bennett and Ferris O. Henson. Learning Concepts, 2501 N. Lamar, Austin, TX 78705, 1977.

Parent Organizations

Since the media specialist cannot have all the materials available that teachers and parents find useful, it will be helpful to become acquainted with those organizations to which one can refer people or from which one can get additional information.

There are national associations for most of the handicapping conditions, and some of the traditional categories are served by more than one organization. These organizations usually have a strong parent component. They have quantities of materials explaining the purpose of the association, reading lists, films, etc. Often they are able to refer the person who wants a more direct contact to local or state organizations. Since one of their major functions is to educate the public about a particular handicapping condition, a significant part of their budgets is for the dissemination of materials. Following is a list of national associations with addresses that should be helpful:

> Alexander Graham Bell Association for the Deaf, 3417 Volta Place, N.W., Washington, DC 20007.
> American Coalition of Citizens with Disabilities, 1346 Connecticut Ave., N.W., #817, Washington, DC 20036.
> American Council for the Blind, 1211 Connecticut Ave., N.W., #506, Washington, DC 20036.
> Association for Children with Learning Disabilities, 5225 Grace St., Pittsburgh, PA 15236.
> Epilepsy Foundation of America, 1828 L. Street, N.W., Washington, DC 20036.
> International Association of Parents of the Deaf, 814 Thayer Ave., Silver Spring, MD 20910.
> National Association for Mental Health, 1800 N. Kent St., Rosslyn, VA 22209.
> National Association for Retarded Citizens, P.O. Box 6109, 2709 Avenue E. East, Arlington, TX 76011.
> National Association of Parents of the

Blind-Deaf, 525 Opus Ave., Capitol Heights, MD 20027.
National Association of the Physically Handicapped, 6423 Grandville Ave., Detroit, MI 48228.
National Easter Seal Society for Crippled Children and Adults, 2023 W. Ogden Ave., Chicago, IL 60623.
United Cerebral Palsy Association, 66 E. 34th St., New York, NY 10016.

The media specialist should become familiar with the local organizations. These can be found in the Yellow Pages in the telephone directory. The local associations can be particularly helpful since they analyze and respond to local needs and often have information regarding questions most commonly asked. For instance, the Association for Children with Learning Disabilities (ACLD) disseminates a publication entitled *A Directory of Summer Camps for Children with Learning Disabilities*. Most local associations will have this directory on file. All organizations requesting a copy of the directory will be sent a publication entitled *The 1976 Directory of Education Facilities for the Learning Disabled*. These directories list facilities by state. Local associations often have films or books that they are willing to loan or rent for a small fee. Often members are willing to speak to small groups or lead discussions. Some organizations have a speakers bureau.

Another organization toward which many parents should be directed is Closer Look, National Information Center for the Handicapped, P.O. Box 1492, Washington, DC 20013. This federally funded center provides a national parent information retrieval service available to parents who are unable to find the help they need locally.

Looking Ahead

The involvement of parents of handicapped children in the schools is the start of a new era. While many educators have a long history of close working relationships with parents, for the most part parents have not been actively involved in the education of their children. As parents become better informed of their rights and about special education procedures, and as school personnel become more skilled and secure in working with parents, the parent-school interactions should become increasingly positive and fruitful.

The school media specialist faces an exciting challenge as parents enter the public education foreground. Designing a media program that fosters positive and successful home-school relationships, relationships that continue to develop throughout the child's school years, will create a greatly improved living and learning atmosphere for adults and children alike.

Notes

1. R. G. Bridge, "Parent Participation in School Innovations," *Teachers College Record* 77 (1976):366–84.
2. Ibid.
3. G. E. Greenwood, W. F. Breivogel, and R. E. Jester, "Citizen Advisory Committees," *Theory into Practice* 16 (1977):12–16.
4. G. Scholes and R. Kroth, *Getting Schools Involved with Parents* (Reston, Va.: Council for Exceptional Children, 1978).

The Educational Resources Information Center

ROBERT E. CHESLEY

The Educational Resources Information Center (ERIC) was established as a national educational data base in 1966. In the past years it has become widely recognized as the preeminent source for locating and acquiring a wide variety of educational documents.

The mission of this information network, sponsored by the National Institute of Education (NIE), the primary educational agency for research and development, is to acquire bibliographic control over documents and journal articles in the field of education, to announce their availability, and to make the documents widely accessible to researchers, teachers, administrators, policy makers, librarians, students, and the lay public. The ERIC system consists of several collaborative components:

1. A network of 16 subject area clearinghouses, which acquire and catalog documents for announcement in the abstract journal *Resources in Education* (RIE) and provide other user services.
2. A central processing facility, where documents are received and system support is provided.
3. An ERIC Document Reproduction Service (EDRS), which films documents and produces microfiche for sale.
4. A contractor, which publishes *Current Index to Journals in Education* (CIJE).
5. The US Government Printing Office, which produces RIE.
6. A central ERIC management team within NIE, which manages the contracts and sets policy for the system.

ERIC Clearinghouses

The 16 ERIC clearinghouses span the broad field of education. Their scope covers educational subject areas, levels of education, or significant educational problems or activities. The ERIC Clearinghouse on Handicapped and Gifted Children, operated by the Council for Exceptional Children, is one of the 16. Its operation is typical of the activities of the other ERIC clearinghouses. The primary objective of this clearinghouse is to acquire documents in special education and to select, catalog, and process the documents for entry into the ERIC system. The scope of the Clearinghouse on Handicapped and Gifted Children includes:

> The education of children and youth deemed exceptional: the gifted, the talented, the aurally handicapped, visually handicapped, mentally handicapped (retarded), developmentally disabled, physically handicapped, socially maladjusted, emotionally disturbed, abused/neglected, speech impaired, learning disabled neurologically handicapped, autistic, culturally different handicapped or gifted, multiply handicapped, and severely handicapped.
>
> Major areas include behavioral, psychomotor and communication disorders; cognitive functioning and learning problems of exceptional children; administration of special education programs and services; preparation and continuing education of professional and paraprofessional personnel in special education (including competency based teacher education); preschool learning and development of the exceptional child; general studies on creativity; statistics and incidence data relating to exceptional children, more specifically, mainstreaming of exceptional children; education in the least restrictive environment; and theory, treatment, and prevention of child abuse and neglect. (ERIC, 1979, p. 21)

In addition to processing documents to be announced in *Resources in Education* (RIE) and making microfiche available through subscribing libraries, the clearinghouses catalog and annotate approximately 20,000 journal

---

"The Educational Resources Information Center," by Robert E. Chesley, *Exceptional Children* 1979, 46: 194–99. Copyright 1979 by The Council for Exceptional Children. Reprinted with permission.

articles each year that are announced in the monthly publication, *Current Index to Journals in Education* (CIJE). Clearinghouses also develop publications that synthesize and summarize knowledge and research about significant problems in their respective fields. They also produce and distribute other products such as bibliographies, fact sheets, and search reprints to serve the information needs of ERIC users.

Clearinghouses conduct computer searches of the ERIC data base, usually on a cost recovery basis; prepare columns for professional journals; conduct workshops at education conventions; and prepare information bulletins.

Subscribers to ERIC Microfiche

The subscribers to the monthly collection of ERIC microfiche can be categorized as follows:

University libraries	77%
State education agencies	6%
Intermediate and local agencies	10%
Federal government	4%
Other	3%

Although the ERIC Document Reproduction Service fills orders each year for an additional 70,000 individual titles of ERIC documents in microfiche (37 percent) and paper copy (63 percent), it is through these subscribing customers at libraries and other agencies that the public has by far the greatest access to the information contained in the ERIC system. One subscriber alone (San Mateo Educational Reference Center) duplicated over 160,000 ERIC microfiche for its clients during 1978.

Acquisition and Selection

Documents considered for ERIC are acquired in a number of different ways:

1. Clearinghouses have established linkages with over 123 professional education associations that help identify appropriate documents.
2. General solicitation for documents is made through newsletters and other outreach activities.
3. Specific solicitation for individual titles that come to the attention of clearinghouse personnel is made through professional contacts with the field.
4. Standing arrangements are made by clearinghouses with over 479 institutions, organizations, and associations for documents they produce.
5. The ERIC Processing and Reference Facility solicits and has ongoing arrangements with 161 government and international organizations for the regular acquisition of documents.
6. Unsolicited documents are forwarded to the system by individual authors.

Through these avenues the ERIC system acquires over 30,000 educational documents a year, of which approximately 16,000 are selected for input and announcement in RIE. Responsibility for selection rests with the individual ERIC clearinghouses. General system criteria specified in the *ERIC Processing Manual* (ED 092 164) are overlaid with clearinghouse criteria pertinent to their subject area.

Documents are announced monthly in RIE in one of three categories: (1) both in microfiche and in paper copy format (72 percent); (2) solely in microfiche format, due to copyright restrictions or reproducibility problems (22 percent); and (3) neither microfiche nor paper copy but considered to be of such significance that they should be announced to the educational community (6 percent). Availability and cost information are cited for documents in category 3.

Resources in Education (RIE)

Approximately 4,500 institutions or individuals receive RIE. Subscribers are predominantly college and university libraries, although many are professional associations, public libraries, and/or individuals. Over 60 countries are represented on the subscription list.

Current Index to Journals in Education (CIJE)

Approximately 2,000 libraries, agencies, and individuals subscribe to CIJE, which, as a monthly publication, announces and catalogs articles that have recently appeared in over 750 educational journals and periodicals. Approximately 20,000 journal articles are indexed each year and announced in CIJE.

Information Analysis Products

ERIC was established as a decentralized system to capitalize on the subject matter expertise existing in different locations around the country. Clearinghouse management and personnel reflect this expertise. Through contacts with their respective fields, with the user community in these fields, and with the help of advisory groups, clearinghouses identify important educational topics in their areas. Each year they commission authors to write information analysis products on these topics. These products consolidate information on research and practice in pertinent areas. Over 1,500 information analysis products have been produced during the past 10 years. They represent a consolidation of knowledge in priority areas of education and are an important resource to the field.

Clearinghouses disseminate these products to key associations and educators in their subject field, and publicize and market them through appropriate professional journals and newsletters. The products are also announced in RIE and are available through the ERIC Document Reproduction Service. A special collection of 600 information analysis products for 1975–77 has recently been put on sale in microfiche format. During the past year over 150,000 copies of information analysis products were purchased by individuals in the field of education. Over 300,000 free copies of other materials were disseminated by the system.

Activities with Professional Associations

Within the past year ERIC was represented at 118 meetings of professional associations. This representation is important to the continued flow of documents into the system. Papers are collected and contacts made that allow for acquisition of documents. Clearinghouse personnel were invited to make presentations at 80 of these meetings and operated booths at 71 of the meetings in order to create further awareness of ERIC and its utility to educators. Cooperative arrangements with many of these associations provide opportunities for publication and further availability of special products.

Workshops

Clearinghouses conduct workshops at meetings of many professional associations and for special groups of educators, schools of education, librarians, and subscribers to the ERIC microfiche collections. In 1979, over 250 ERIC workshops were attended by over 8,000 participants, primarily teachers and administrators. In addition, a recent survey of libraries that house ERIC microfiche collections indicated that a typical library trains over 800 individuals per year in the use of its ERIC collection.

User Services

Although building the data base is the primary mission of clearinghouses, their facilities are available to the public who may seek assistance in solving educational problems through the use of ERIC materials and search tools. Across the clearinghouses during the past year, there were over 19,000 visitors who used these services. More than 4,600 computer searches were conducted.

Many requests for assistance or information do not require the use of computer searches. Some of the requests for information can be answered by information analysis products or other off-the-shelf publications; some require manual searches for specific documents; and others are referred to more appropriate sources for responses. In 1978 the ERIC system answered over 85,000 individual inquiries from the education community.

Journal Articles

A large number of professional associations, both national and local, serve educators across the country. These associations range from broad interest groups such as the American Educational Research Association and the American Association of School Administrators to the more specialized interest groups such as the Council for Exceptional Children, the American Association of Physics Teachers, or the National Council of

Teachers of English. Many of these associations publish journals through which they communicate with their membership, most of whom are practitioners in the nation's schools. ERIC clearinghouses have arrangements with approximately 110 of these journals to carry articles, information for regular columns, and announcements of ERIC products and services. These journals combined reach over 175,000 educators.

Information Bulletins

Because the mailing lists consist of special interest groups, they represent an efficient form of targeted communication. During 1978 the 16 clearinghouses distributed 36 information bulletins to over 170,000 individual educators. This method of supplying targeted communications was expanded so that in 1979 approximately twice as many information bulletins were distributed to educators.

Computer Searching

ERIC was originally designed as a data base that could be searched by computer. With over 350,000 citations currently in RIE and CIJE, the computer is essential in conducting comprehensive searches for specific subject matter. Over the years, computer searching has progressed from independent centers housed (mostly in universities) that use batch-process searching on their own computers to on-line interactive search services with sophisticated programs that permit searching of the entire resume, including abstracts, descriptors, and identifiers. Although the major on-line search services provide access to many more files than ERIC, it is one of the most heavily used files in all subject areas.

The Directory of ERIC Computer Search Services, published by the ERIC facility, lists 341 locations where educators can have computer searches run. The directory lists only those willing to provide services to outsiders, usually on a cost-recovery basis. The actual number of locations that conduct ERIC searches is significantly greater (numbering in the thousands). It is estimated that the number of on-line computer searches of the ERIC file done by the four major vendors is now over 150,000 per year. This does not include the number of searches conducted at more than 50 other institutions that also subscribe to the ERIC computer tapes and have their own computer search capabilities.

Information Centers

Among the 675 subscribers to ERIC microfiche are a number of centers which specialize in providing teachers and administrators with comprehensive information in response to requests. Thirty-four of these centers are state education agencies that have received NIE grants to develop dissemination systems to provide information to educators. Although ERIC is not the only source of information used by these centers it is the primary source. ERIC has worked closely with state education agencies for over 10 years by providing information for their users.

In addition to information centers operated by state education agencies, numerous intermediate agencies also provide such services. Examples of these include the San Mateo Educational Reference Center (SMERC), San Mateo, California; Resource Services in Education Center, Merrimac, Massachusetts; and the Area Cooperative Educational Services (ACES), New Haven, Connecticut. These centers provide high quality comprehensive information services in education and have amassed a great deal of experience over the years in serving the needs of educational practitioners. SMERC, one of the largest, last year conducted over 25,000 computer searches of the ERIC files, primarily for classroom teachers.

System Improvement

From its inception, the ERIC system has used technology and made improvements without disrupting the basic nature and purpose of the system. Some of these changes were designed to bring about more effective operation of the system; others were in response to user needs. Briefly, changes and new services within the past two years include the following:

1. Workshops for microfiche subscribers.
2. List of documents unavailable on microfiche provided to microfiche subscribers.

3. All pages filmed in right-reading orientation on microfiche.
4. Increased quality control measures that have reduced problem documents by a factor of three.
5. On-line computer ordering of documents from ERIC Document Reproduction Service.
6. Computer searching capability in all ERIC clearinghouses.
7. "Identifier clean-up" to reduce scattering of uncontrolled identifiers.
8. Arrangements with professional associations for greater printing and distribution of information analysis products.
9. Courtesy microfiche copy to contributing authors.
10. Review and improvement of the RIE format.
11. Increased solicitation of significant foreign documents.
12. Formal arrangements with major education groups and organizations for automatic acquisition of documents.
13. Use of optical character recognition for input of data.
14. New data fields: geographic origin, language of document, and governmental level from which document originates.
15. New Directory of ERIC Microfiche Collections.
16. New Directory of ERIC Search Services.

In addition to the changes that have already been made, a number of studies or activities for system improvement are scheduled for implementation in the near future, including:

1. Vocabulary Improvement Project to review and revise descriptors used to access the ERIC system.
2. Annotated bibliography of articles and studies about ERIC.
3. Directory of RIE subscribers.
4. New microfiche products:
Monthly RIE in standing order collection. Annual cumulations of RIE with annual indexes.
Cumulative Title Index and Author Index.
Cumulative Descriptor and Identifier Usage Report.
5. Revised publication type codes allowing users to search by the type of document.
6. Publication type index for RIE.
7. Price codes in RIE to prevent retention of out of date prices.
8. Slide-tape orientation to ERIC with visuals on color microfiche.
9. Videotape production of ERIC training material.
10. Assembly of ERIC system materials for new microfiche subscribers.
11. Brochure containing cost and source information for ordering ERIC materials.
12. Studies and projects with implications for ERIC:
Technology study to investigate how technology can be used to improve input and access to the system.
Acquisition and selection study to improve acquisition techniques and selection criteria.
Seminars on information needs and technology of information systems.

Available Publications

The following publications on the ERIC system are available free as long as the supply lasts:
How to Use ERIC
Directory of ERIC Search Services
Directory of ERIC Microfiche Collections
ERIC Information Analysis Products, 1975–77

To obtain these publications contact: ERIC Processing and Reference Facility, 4833 Rugby Avenue, Suite 303, Bethesda, Maryland 20014.

Summary

Documentary evidence shows that ERIC is indeed used by the education community. Activities are planned to increase this use through better awareness of and access to both ERIC and its information analysis products. Through ERIC, knowledge, experience, and information produced by researchers and practitioners can be made available to teachers, administrators, and other professionals involved in improving education in the nation's schools.

Following is a list of the 16 ERIC clearinghouses:

Adult, Career, and Vocational Education
  Ohio State University
  1960 Kenny Road
  Columbus, Ohio 43210

Counseling and Personnel Services
  University of Michigan
  2108 School of Education Building
  Ann Arbor, Michigan 48109

Educational Management
  University of Oregon
  Eugene, Oregon 97403

Elementary and Early Childhood Education
  University of Illinois
  College of Education
  Urbana, Illinois 61801

Handicapped and Gifted Children
  Council for Exceptional Children
  1920 Association Drive
  Reston, Virginia 22091

Higher Education
  George Washington University
  One Dupont Circle, Suite 630
  Washington, D.C. 20036

Information Resources
  Syracuse University
  School of Education
  130 Huntington Hall
  Syracuse, New York 13210

Junior Colleges
  University of California
  96 Powell Library Building
  Los Angeles, California 90024

Languages and Linguistics
  Center for Applied Linguistics
  1611 North Kent Street
  Arlington, Virginia 22209

Reading and Communication Skills
  National Council of Teachers of English
  1111 Kenyon Road
  Urbana, Illinois 61801

Rural Education and Small Schools
  New Mexico State University
  Box 3AP
  Las Cruces, New Mexico 88003

Science, Mathematics, and Environmental Education
  Ohio State University
  1200 Chambers Road, Third Floor
  Columbus, Ohio 43212

Social Studies/Social Science Education
  855 Broadway
  Boulder, Colorado 80302

Teacher Education
  American Association of Colleges for Teacher Education
  One Dupont Circle, N.W., Suite 616
  Washington, D.C. 20036

Tests, Measurement and Evaluation
  Educational Testing Service
  Rosedale Road
  Princeton, New Jersey 08540

Urban Education
  Teachers College, Columbia University
  Box 40
  525 West 120th Street
  New York, New York 10027

Additional Reading

Educational Resources Information Center, *ERIC Clearinghouse Scope of Interest Guide.* Unpublished manuscript, June 1979.

Exceptional Child Education Resources: A One-of-a-Kind Data Base

DONALD K. ERICKSON

Exceptional Child Education Resources (ECER) is a privately owned, special interest, 25,000 record data base developed and maintained by the Council for Exceptional Children of Reston, Virginia. It is the only data base whose content focuses exclusively and comprehensively on the professional literature related to the education of all exceptional children—gifted and handicapped. But before I proceed with more detail on the data base itself, let me provide some historical and comparative information on the development of this specialized information resource.

Background of CEC Information Services

It is a well-documented fact that the 1960s was the decade for the beginning of many education-related data bases in the United States. Perhaps the most widely known and used of these is the Educational Resources Information Center (ERIC) program, which marks its inception in 1965 and the establishment of the first ten ERIC Clearinghouses in June 1966. Concurrent with the appearance of the ERIC system and, to a large degree as a direct outgrowth of that event, the Council for Exceptional Children (CEC) planted the CEC Information Center in the education landscape in June of 1966. Since then the CEC Information Center has played at least two major roles.

First, although the CEC Information Center was not initially funded by the ERIC program, it has served as the ERIC Clearinghouse on Handicapped and Gifted Children since 1966.[1] In this role it has performed all the normal functions of an ERIC Clearinghouse including the input of exceptional child education literature citations to the ERIC publications, *Resources in Education* (RIE) and *Current Index to Journals in Education* (CIJE). These citations are naturally a part of the total ERIC data base and will be retrieved when searching that data base.

Second, under the terms and conditions of its initial grant from BEH [Bureau of Education for the Handicapped], the CEC Information Center was to be far more encompassing than other ERIC Clearinghouses were then permitted to be. BEH with strong philosophical support from CEC, wanted to establish a "comprehensive" information program.[2] From the beginning the CEC Information Center was committed to:

1. View as its audience any person who might have an interest in the education of handicapped and gifted children, including teachers, administrators, researchers, psychologists, students, parents, legislators, and other related professional and paraprofessional personnel.[3]
2. Document the entire range of professional literature in the subject area whether it was published or unpublished, copyrighted or uncopyrighted, fugitive or accessible. This included all relevant periodical literature, curriculum guides, program reports, guidelines and descriptions, textbooks, books by and for parents, course manuals, research and statistical reports, and many others.
3. Develop an array of information products and services that would do justice to the comprehensive coverage of the subject area and also address the information needs of the diverse audiences.

To summarize this section permit me to make the following observations:

"Exceptional Child Education Resources: A One-of-a-Kind Data Base," by Donald K. Erickson. Reprinted with permission from *Illinois Libraries*, vol. 59, 1977.

1. CEC, with USOE [United States Office of Education] and NIE [National Institute of Education] grants and contracts, has been the sole operator of the ERIC Clearinghouse on Handicapped and Gifted Children since 1966. In carrying out the functions of that project, CEC has been the primary contributor to the ERIC literature data base in the area of educating handicapped and gifted children.
2. CEC, during the same period of time that it was operating the ERIC project developed the CEC Information Center, which has now been incorporated into the CEC Information Services and Publications Unit. This is a major organizational component at CEC which performs the functions of data base development; information services; training in the use of information services; and information products, publications, and periodicals. The ERIC Clearinghouse is a project within the Information Services and Publications Unit.

In terms of data base content, ECER includes all citations submitted to the ERIC system on educating handicapped and gifted children plus items that go beyond the ERIC scope. At the present time this includes copyrighted documents, dissertations, and non-print media whose focus is the education of exceptional children. These additional features are what make ECER different from ERIC. The comprehensive coverage of this specific special interest area sets it apart from all other data bases. It is important to keep these distinctions in mind when selecting a data base for searching on computerized retrieval systems. If you are looking for information on any aspect of the education of handicapped and/or gifted children, you will always get more comprehensive coverage if you use the ECER data base.

ECER Acquisitions Policy and Procedures

It is the policy of CEC Information Services *to acquire selected professional materials that relate to or are concerned with the education and training of handicapped and gifted children and youth.* The terms in this policy statement are explained in the following paragraphs:

acquire selected . . .
The CEC Information Center locates, obtains, and examines literature on the education of handicapped and gifted children and youth. All documents received are reviewed and screened before their selection for entry in the CEC data base. Data base entries must satisfy the requirements specified in this acquisitions policy statement.

professional materials . . .
Documents may be of a print or nonprint nature including books, monographs, research reports, literature guides, curriculum guides, program descriptions, journal articles, pamphlets, newsletters, films, cassettes, film loops, filmstrips, videotapes, and other related materials. Instructional materials for use by children are not included.

that relate to or are concerned with . . .
Documents are considered for review if their content has implications for the education of handicapped and gifted children and youth. The document may be pertinent to: (a) other professions such as medicine, law, architecture, psychology, and social work; (b) other educational mission areas such as early childhood, disadvantaged children, vocational and career education, physical education, and recreation; and (c) other curricular areas such as reading, mathematics, social studies, and science.

education and training . . .
Activities in the Information Center focus on the education of handicapped and gifted children. Acquisitions sought concern theory, research, programs, practice, and teacher education related to this focus. Acquisitions should deal with topics such as instruction, counseling and guidance, administration of programs and services, preparation of professional and paraprofessional personnel (pre-service and in-service), support services, institutional placement and de-institutionalization, federal and state law, policy and the legislative process, litigation, incidence and statistical information, professional organizations, and information for parents which will be beneficial in the educational planning for and placement of their handicapped and gifted children and youth. The acquisitions program also covers the literature on child abuse and neglect.

handicapped and gifted children and youth . . .
Handicapped and gifted (exceptional) children and youth are those individuals (a) who deviate from the normal in cognitive, sensory, affective, physical, and behavioral domains, or (b) who require a program of special education services including instructional materials, special teaching methodology, specially trained personnel in a day school program (special class, resource room, consulting teacher program, regular class placement, diagnosis and treatment center), special school, residential or private school, hospital, or home instruction setting.

Eleven years of operation have helped CEC to establish a fairly fixed set of procedures for carrying out the acquisitions policy. Yet we are constantly seeking to identify either overlooked or new resources that will contribute to the comprehensiveness of our acquisitions program. Major sources that are regularly examined and/or contacted for both published and unpublished documents include: *Publishers Trade List Annual; Books in Print*; publishers' announcements and product lists; published bibliographies; and publication lists from various sources—state departments of education (divisions of special education); rehabilitation and mental health agencies; local education agencies; agency, project, and organizational newsletters; subscription agencies; university presses; special education R & D centers; federally sponsored programs, projects, and networks; professional organizations; and selected conferences and conventions.

Other procedures are also employed in an attempt to find the hard to locate or fugitive type literature. These include targeted direct mail solicitation; direct personal contact with specific organizations, agencies, projects, or individuals; "Call for Documents" in selected journals; and open invitations at special meetings and workshops. We also attempt to capitalize on the good will of "informants" who are members of the many informal communication networks that exist in the various areas of our total scope.

The building of a comprehensive data base is a complex, continuing, and never completed task. We have given this function a high priority and believe that ECER is not only a unique data base but one of high quality which cannot be overlooked or ignored when resources on the education of handicapped and gifted children are being sought.

ECER Products and Services

Exceptional Child Education Resources

Exceptional Child Education Resources (formerly known as *Exceptional Child Education Abstracts*, ECEA) is the print presentation of the ECER data base. ECER, a quarterly publication in its ninth volume year, contains all citations entered in the data base. Every citation, including journal articles, give author, title, source, publication date, availability and/or ordering data, descriptors, and an abstract or descriptive summary of the document or article. Each issue of ECER has a subject, author, and title index for that issue. The fourth issue of each volume year contains a cumulative index for the entire volume year. Beginning with volume 9, no. 1 (Spring 1977), two new sections were added to ECER. One section lists recently completed doctoral dissertations in special education. The second section contains a listing of nonprint resources that are directly applicable to the training of special education personnel.

Custom Computer Searches

CEC maintains the capability to do on-line interactive computer searching of the entire ECER data base. Of all the data base access tools employed, the computer search permits the quickest, most accurate and up-to-date location of data. The searching package used allows full text searching of all relevant fields including the abstract. The computer file is updated with new citations eight times a year and consequently is always more current than any other resource. To ensure the most efficient use of this powerful tool, CEC may be reached by telephone (703-620-3660) and strongly suggests that any person who wants a computer search done call and negotiate the search with one of CEC's information specialists. These specialists have a comprehensive knowledge of the data base and are aware of the best searching strategies for locating the information you want.

In addition to the ECER data base, CEC can conduct searches of all other on-line educational data bases.

Topical Bibliographies

There are times when the most up-to-the-minute information is not essential but a good overview of a subject area is important. In these cases a topical bibliography will often meet the need quite nicely. To meet this need CEC has developed a series of 66 different bibliography titles, each one of which addresses a specific area of concern. Each bibliography contains the most relevant citations on the topic area. They are drawn directly from the ECER data base. The printed bibliography citations include author, title, publication date, source, availability, descriptors, and an abstract or descriptive summary. Most bibliographies are updated on an annual basis. New titles are added to the series as needed and unused ones are dropped. Sample titles include:

Attitudes toward the Handicapped
Child Abuse
Mainstreaming—General
Early Childhood Identification
Learning Disabilities—Secondary Level
Gifted—Teaching Methods/Curriculum/Teacher Training

Selective Dissemination of Information (SDI)

The SDI is an addition to the information services provided by CEC. Its purpose is to automatically and regularly provide current awareness of all literature acquired in specific topic areas on a subscription basis. An SDI subscriber receives eight computer printouts a year. Each printout contains citations (title, author, publication date and source, availability data, descriptors, and a 200-word abstract) of every item acquired in the subject area since the last printout. Twenty-one different topic areas have been selected by CEC and are available on an SDI basis.

Use of Resource Library

CEC maintains a noncirculating resource library at its headquarters in Reston, Virginia. This library contains the "hard copy" of every document entered in the ECER data base as well as current issues of periodicals that are scanned for appropriate articles to be included in the data base. All journal articles cited in the ECER data base and the entire ERIC data base are available in microfiche. All standard library reference tools are also available. The public is encouraged to use this resource.

A Final Comment

As an organization, the Council for Exceptional Children has been very much a part of the rapid growth and development of the information industry which has occurred during the past 10 to 15 years. The ECER data base and related services described in this article are evidence of that involvement. But long before computers, data bases, on-line searching systems, batch modes, and inverted files were a part of our vocabulary, CEC had made a firm commitment to the discovery, transmission, and dissemination of information that would lead to more effective educational programs for handicapped and gifted children. Founded in 1922, CEC has a long history of seeking and discovering new and creative ways of advancing the education of all exceptional children. The ECER data base services are only a part of the total information services of CEC. And the extensive information services provided by the organization are only a portion of the total program of the organization.

Notes

1. From 1966 until 1976 the CEC Information Center received funding from USOE's Bureau of Education for the Handicapped (BEH). From 1974 to 1976 this funding was gradually reduced to zero since CEC has assumed most of the support that had been provided by BEH. It should also be pointed out that since 1974 CEC has had an NIE contract for continued operation of the ERIC Clearinghouse component of the Information Center program.

2. The CEC Information Center was established and funded approximately six months before the Bureau of Education for the Handicapped was created. Thus, to be absolutely accurate, the early funding for the center came from the Handicapped Children and Youth branch which was housed in USOE's Bureau of Research.

3. By legislative mandate, BEH could not provide funding for activities in the area of the gifted. CEC itself supplemented the early federal grant in order to assure that the gifted would be included. In recent years NIE has contributed to the support of this content area.

Index

advocacy groups, 258
American National Standards Institute (ANSI) standards, 5, 13
American Printing House for the Blind, 142
autism, 258

basal readers, 50–51
bibliotherapy, 77–78
blind. *See* Visually impaired
book selection
    for the emotionally disturbed, 43, 242–244, 251–252, 259–260, 262
    for the gifted, 37, 80–86
    for the hearing impaired, 42, 50–54, 239–240
    for the learning disabled, 42, 70–72, 73, 242–244, 248
    for the mentally retarded, 41, 61–62, 242–244, 253
    for the physically handicapped, 40–41
    for the visually impaired, 42, 135–138, 139–142, 207–208
book stacks, 15–16
books, high interest/low ability, 50–54, 61–62, 64–68, 248
braille, 139–140, 209–210

Captioned Films and Telecommunications (CF&T), 95–96
Captioned Films for the Deaf (CFD), 91–93, 240
censorship, 232–233
child development, 222–223
color usage, 7, 26–27, 30
comics, 142–146, 239, 251, 252
communication, 228–229, 258, 259
computers
    adaptations to, 168–169
    instructional uses, 162–172
    searches, 281, 282, 283, 288, 289
Council for Exceptional Children (CEC), 286–289
Current Index to Journals in Education (CIJE), 280, 281–282, 286

deaf. *See* Hearing impaired
directories, 270
disabled
    attitudes toward, xii–xiii, 18–19, 43
    definition, 12
    employees, xii, 12, 127
    images of, xii–xiii
Division for the Blind and Physically Handicapped of the Library of Congress. *See* National Library Service for the Blind and Physically Handicapped

Education for All Handicapped Children Act of 1975 (PL 94-142), xii, 4, 178, 274
Educational Resources Information Center (ERIC), 280–285, 286
Elementary and Secondary Education Act (ESEA), 95
emotionally disturbed
    book selection for, 43, 242–244, 251–252, 259–260, 262
    materials selection for, 43, 260–261
    poetry programs for, 43, 260–261
    social problems of, 178–180, 241–244
    television for, 178–184
ERIC Clearinghouse on Handicapped and Gifted Children, 280–281, 287
ERIC Clearinghouses, 284–285, 286
Exceptional Child Education Resources (ECER), 286–289

films, 59, 91–93, 240, 254
furnishings, 6–7, 15–16, 25, 33, 248

games, 46, 63, 134–138, 259
gifted
    book selection for, 37, 80–86
    programming for, 214–221
graphics, 152–154

hearing impaired
  book selection for, 42, 50–54, 239–240
  communication devices for, 98–99, 100, 101
  computer usage with, 162–172
  language disorders of, 53, 237
  library instruction for, 238–239
  materials selection for, 42, 54, 237–239
  mathematics curriculum for, 163–164
  poetry for, 194–201
  reading problems of, 50, 53, 100, 237
  social skills development of, 163–166
  storytelling for, 237–238
humor, 143–146

Individualized Education Program (IEP), 4, 35, 44, 46, 274
information centers, 283
institutionalization, 224–226

kits, 62, 63, 254, 269–270
Kurzweil Reading Machine, 36, 42, 89, 126–128, 208–209

labeling, 6, 9
language, 101–105, 134–136
learning disabled
  book selection for, 42, 70–72, 73, 242–244, 248
  characteristics of, 42, 143–145, 246, 247
  definition of, 69, 245
  library service for, 37, 72, 247–250
  materials selection for, 42
  reading guidance for, 72–78, 143
  sense of humor in, 143
  social adjustment of, 42, 241–244, 250
  visual perceptual disorders of, 69–70
Learning Is For Everyone (LIFE), 55–64, 94
libraries
  academic, 202–206, 207–213
  hospital, 233
  institutional, 222–235
  prison, 232
library
  assistants, 255–256
  Bill of Rights, 13
  programs. See Programs
  staff. See Staff

magazines, 41, 62, 253, 254
mainstreaming, xi, xii, xiii, xvii, 4, 5, 9, 19, 43, 56, 155, 162, 178, 179–180, 232, 234–235, 241, 271, 272, 274
maps, 14–15, 17, 18, 146–151, 152–154
materials, 16, 129–131, 254, 255
  selection for emotionally disturbed, 43, 260–261
  selection for hearing impaired, 42, 54, 237–239
  selection for learning disabled, 42
  selection for mentally retarded, 41, 61, 253
  selection for physically handicapped, 40
  selection for visually impaired, 42
  selection principles, 35–37, 40, 44–49, 65–66, 129–131, 228–229
media. See Materials
Media Development Project for Hearing Impaired (MDPHI), 96

Media Services and Captioned Films (MSCF), 93
mentally retarded
  book selection for, 41, 61–62, 242–244, 253
  library service for, 55–64, 252–256
  materials selection for, 41, 61, 253
  programs for, 57–61, 229–230, 255
  sensory learning by, 23–24
  socialization of, 173–177, 241–244, 254–255, 256
  storytelling for, 59, 60
  television for, 173–177
microforms, 16, 159–161, 281, 283–284

National Advisory Council on the Education of the Deaf (NACED), 93
National Center for Educational Media and Materials for the Handicapped (NCEMMH), 93
National Information Center on Educational Materials (NICEM), 95
National Instructional Materials Information System (NIMIS), 95
National Library Service for the Blind and Physically Handicapped, xv, 41, 139–142, 207–208, 210

Optacon, 42, 89, 106–118, 208–209
outreach, 56, 265–266, 269–289

parents, 56, 157, 174–176, 267–270, 274–279, 287
periodicals. See Magazines
physical plant
  accessibility, xvi, 1, 2, 5, 8, 11–12, 13, 14–16, 19, 31, 271
  acoustics, 10, 28–29, 33–34
  ambiance, 2, 29–30, 31–34
  ceilings, 10, 29
  construction, 9–11, 13, 14, 15, 17, 23–24, 29, 211
  costs, 17–18
  design criteria, 5–7, 16, 25, 29, 31–34
  lighting, 25–27
  parking, 8, 14
  renovation, 13, 17, 272
  safety, 7, 8, 16, 17
  space utilization, 5, 6, 210, 211
  support facilities, 2, 16
  surfaces, 9–10, 15, 23–24, 25, 29
  temperature, 27
physically handicapped
  book selection for, 40–41
  materials selection for, 40
pictures, 63, 237
poetry, 192–201
Programed Logic for Automatic Teaching Operations (PLATO), 162–176
programs, 187–189, 226–231
  accessibility, 12, 13, 17, 188, 233, 235, 266, 269–284
puzzles, 63, 259

reading
  problems, 50, 53, 100, 155, 237
  recreational, 53
recordings, 62, 155–159
Recordings for the Blind (RFB), 207–208, 212

Regional Media Centers for the Deaf (RMCD), 93–95
Resources in Education (RIE), 280–281, 286

software. *See* Materials
staff, 5, 6, 8, 19, 211, 233–235, 269, 273
    competencies, xiii, xv–xvi, 235
storytelling, 59, 60, 237–238

Talking Books, 139–140, 203–204, 209
technology, 87–90, 91–96, 100–101, 104–105
television, 122–126, 179–184, 256
    captioned, 95–96
    closed circuit (CCTV), 119–121, 159–160, 256
    in socialization, 173–177
Telephone Teletype for the Deaf (TTY), 97–99
toys, 62–63

visually impaired
    book selection for, 42, 135–138, 139–142, 207–208
    language development in, 134–138
    library services for, 202–206, 207–213, 232
    materials selection for, 42
    optical aids for, 159–160, 203–205, 210
    poetry programs for, 192, 197, 200
    volunteer readers for, 211
Vocational Rehabilitation Act of 1973, xii, 4, 11, 12

Text designed by Muriel Underwood
Cover designed by Ellen Pettengell
Composed by Modern Typographers, Inc.,
 in Linotron 202 Palatino
Printed on 50-pound Glatfelter,
 a pH-neutral stock, by Malloy
 Lithographing, Inc.
Bound in B-grade Holliston cloth
 by Decker Bindery